Prehistory of the Southwest

A School of American Research Book

NEW WORLD ARCHAEOLOGICAL RECORD

Under the Editorship of
James Bennett Griffin

Museum of Anthropology
University of Michigan
Ann Arbor, Michigan

In preparation:

Jerald T. Milanich, Ann S. Cordell, Vernon J. Knight, Jr., Timothy A. Kohler, and Brenda J. Sigler-Lavelle, McKeithen Weeden Island: The Culture of Northern Florida, A.D. 200–900
Moreau Maxwell, Prehistory of the Eastern Arctic

Published:

Linda S. Cordell, Prehistory of the Southwest
Michael J. Moratto, with contributions by David A. Fredrickson, Christopher Raven, and Claude N. Warren, California Archaeology
Robert E. Bell (Ed.), Prehistory of Oklahoma
James L. Phillips and James A. Brown (Eds.), Archaic Hunters and Gatherers in the American Midwest
Dan F. Morse and Phyllis A. Morse, Archaeology of the Central Mississippi Valley
Lawrence E. Aten, Indians of the Upper Texas Coast
Ronald J. Mason, Great Lakes Archaeology
Dean R. Snow, The Archaeology of New England
Jerald T. Milanich and Charles H. Fairbanks, Florida Archaeology
George C. Frison, Prehistoric Hunters of the High Plains

Prehistory
of the
Southwest

Linda S. Cordell

Department of Anthropology
University of New Mexico
Albuquerque, New Mexico

1984

ACADEMIC PRESS, INC.

(Harcourt Brace Jovanovich, Publishers)

Orlando   San Diego   New York   London
Toronto   Montreal   Sydney   Tokyo

Cover design by Vincent J. Yannie

ACADEMIC PRESS, INC.
Orlando, Florida 32887

United Kingdom Edition published by
ACADEMIC PRESS, INC. (LONDON) LTD.
24/28 Oval Road, London NW1 7DX

Library of Congress Cataloging in Publication Data

Cordell, Linda S.
    Prehistory of the Southwest.

    (New World archaeological record)
    Includes index.
    1. Indians of North America--Southwest, New--
Antiquities. 2. Pueblo Indians--Antiquities. 3. South-
west, New--Antiquities. 4. Indians of North America--
Southwest, New--History. 5. Pueblo Indians--History.
I. Title. II. Series.
E78.S7C67 1984   979.01   84-6387
ISBN 0-12-188220-9 (alk. paper)
ISBN 0-12-188222-5 (pbk. : alk. paper)

PRINTED IN THE UNITED STATES OF AMERICA

84 85 86 87   9 8 7 6 5 4 3 2 1

Contents

3

Intellectual Frameworks for Southwestern Prehistory   49

4

The Paleo-Indian Period   121

5

The Archaic Period   153

6

The Adoption of Agricultural Strategies   181

7

Early Southwestern Villages to A.D. 900   213

8

Systems of Regional Integration, A.D. 900–1150   245

9

Abandonments   303

10

The Late Prehistoric Aggregated Villages   327

List of Figures

List of Tables

Preface

The purpose of this book is to provide an up-to-date synthesis of southwestern prehistory for students, scholars, and other interested readers. The literature of southwestern prehistoric archaeology is vast and is being augmented at an accelerating pace. This book is not a catalog of that literature or of known southwestern archaeological sites. Rather, it should serve as an introduction to primary sources and to the intellectual context of contemporary research issues.

The organization of the book reflects three concerns: (1) that sufficient background and vocabulary for discussion of prehistory is provided; (2) that chronological sequence is followed and topical issues addressed where chronologically appropriate, and (3) that adequate emphasis is given to the diversity of the prehistoric remains.

The first chapter introduces the cultural heterogeneity of modern native southwestern peoples and, briefly, the prehistoric cultures. Diversity in the natural environment and methods used to reconstruct prehistoric environments are the subjects of the second chapter. The third chapter discusses the classificatory frameworks and vocabulary traditionally used by southwestern culture historians. The development of these schemes of time and space systematics is described within the context of general intellectual trends in American anthropology and the history of southwestern archaeology. Together, the first three chapters provide essential background for the chronologically organized chapters that follow.

Chapters 4 and 5 consider Paleo-Indian and Archaic period prehistory, respectively. Together the chapters review southwestern prehistory from the oldest archaeological complexes to materials dating to about A.D. 1, after domestic crops had been accepted from Mesoamerica.

The spread of agricultural technology in the relatively inhospitable southwestern environments is a topic of active research in the 1980s. Issues involved in attempting to explain the adoption of agriculture and examples of the diverse kinds of behavioral strategies used prehistorically to ensure agricultural success are considered in Chapter 6. Increased sedentism and the appearance of villages together are one consequence of dependence on domestic crops. Early southwestern villages, and other changes related to sedentism are discussed in Chapter 7.

Chapter 8 is concerned with the first large-scale, regional, southwestern cultural systems: those of Chaco Canyon in New Mexico, the Casas Grandes area of Chihuahua, and the Gila and Salt drainages of Arizona. The chapter also describes some of the diverse and less-complex systems that were characteristic of most of the Southwest while the regional systems were at their height. Chapter 9 focuses on the well-documented systemic collapses and abandonments during the period from A.D. 1150 to 1300. Traditional explanations and new approaches to the problem of abandonments are presented.

Chapter 10 explores the character of the prehistoric record from about A.D. 1300 to 1540 and reviews contrasting interpretations of the kinds of social and economic organizations thought to be prevalent in Pueblo sites of this time period. Chapter 10 also briefly considers the beginnings of the Historic period in the Southwest and discusses some of the issues relating to Spanish disruption of the native traditions and to the archaeology of southern Athapaskan peoples.

The professional literature of southwestern archaeology of the 1980s reflects a healthy diversity of opinion in interpretation, and heated arguments about the nature of past cultures abound. I have attempted to treat the major issues fairly, and to provide the reader with sufficient background so that he or she may pursue the primary literature and follow the arguments as they develop.

I am indebted to my colleague Jeremy Sabloff for encouraging me to undertake the task of writing this book. The writing was facilitated by the award of a National Endowment for the Humanities resident scholarship at the School of American Research, Sante Fe. I thank Dr. Douglas W. Schwartz and the staff of the School for the opportunity they gave me. Materials for this book and assistance were graciously provided by Tom Windes, Steve Lekson, Jerry Livingstone, and Catherine Ross of the Chaco Center; Dwight Drager and James Ebert of Remote Sensing, Southwest Cultural Research Center; Arthur Olivas, Nancy Fox, Rosemary Talley, Marsha Jackson, and Stewart Peckham of the Museum of New Mexico; Lewis R. Binford, James Chisholm, Matthew Schmader, Eric Ingbar, Marian Rodee, June-El Piper, Christina G. Allen, and Charles M. Carrillo of the University of New Mexico; Ellen Horn of the Arizona State Museum; Michael B. Schiffer and J. Jefferson Reid of the University of Arizona; Steven LeBlanc of the Los Angeles County Museum; George J. Gumerman and Shirley L. Powell of Southern Illinois University, Carbondale; Cynthia Irwin-Williams of the Desert Research Institute, University of Nevada, Reno; Larry Agenbroad, of the University of Northern Arizona; and Fred Plog of New Mexico State University. I am equally indebted to my colleagues and to my students for the challenges of their ideas.

Prehistory of the Southwest

1

Introduction

The North American Southwest is a culture area encompassing diversity in landforms, contemporary Native American societies, and prehistoric traditions. This chapter provides a brief introduction to the land and to its modern and prehistoric inhabitants.

Introduction

The North American Southwest is a land of contrasts and diversity. The physical landscape includes extensive mesas (tablelands), rugged mountains, and low-lying deserts. The mesa country is generally high (above 1524 m) and is bisected by steep-walled, narrow canyons. Much of the mesa country is sparsely covered with vegetation, and there are extensive areas of bare rock. Piñon and juniper woodland occur on mesa tops where soils have developed and not eroded away. Many of the mesas are composed of layers of sandstones and shales. Weathering of the softer sandstones creates caves and rockshelters in which some prehistoric inhabitants built their homes, as did, for example, the cliff dwellers of Mesa Verde in Colorado. At the contact zone, where sandstones overlie impermeable shales, springs that provide important water sources may be found. The mountain areas of central Arizona, northern New Mexico, and southern Colorado rise majestically from the mesa country. A few peaks are snowcapped year-round, but most contain areas of either alpine meadow or ponderosa pine and Douglas fir at their highest elevations and stands of piñon and juniper below these. Winter snows in the mountains provide water that feeds the great Southwestern rivers: The Rio Grande, San Juan, and Colorado. Although vegetation along the banks of rivers is lush, it is sparse elsewhere and consists of stands of yucca or strangely shaped cactus such as ocotillo and saguaro. Except for a few weeks of the year, when golden aspen light the mountainsides in fall or when desert cacti bloom in spring, the landscapes of the Southwest, though not colorful, are impressive landscapes of shape, mass and form.

Temperatures are commonly in the 90s during hot summer days in the Southwest. In winter, the high mesas and mountains are bitterly cold and often snowcapped. In spring, strong winds carry sand and dust that often obscure the landscape. Most of the time, though, the air is remarkably clear and the vistas are grand; for example, the residents of Albuquerque can usually see the peak of Mount Taylor on the western horizon, at a distance of about 97 km.

Despite the variety of landforms and vegetation, the entire Southwest is united by its dry climate. Everywhere, water is the most critical resource for people. Yet despite the harsh climate, the temperature extremes, and the aridity, the prehistoric peoples of the Southwest developed a way of life dependent on farming native American crops: corn, beans, and squash. They used a variety of ingenious techniques to cultivate the soil and conserve moisture (Figure 1.1) and are responsible for some of the most spectacular native architecture in the Americas north of Mesoamerica—for example, the cliff dwellings of Canyon de Chelly, Arizona (Figure 1.2); the stone towers of Hovenweep, Utah; the multistory stone structures of Chaco Canyon, New Mexico; and the multistory abode buildings of Casa Grande, Arizona, and Paquimé, Chihuahua.

It is the agricultural adaptation that most clearly defines the Southwest as a culture area. Precise boundaries for any culture area are often difficult to specify. In a brief and useful way, the Southwest is often described as extending from Durango, Mexico, to Durango, Colorado, and from Las Vegas, New Mexico, to Las Vegas, Nevada (Figure 1.3). The native peoples within this area are heterogeneous in language and culture, but the cultivation of corn, beans, and squash sets this region apart from both the

Figure 1.1 Waffle Garden, Zuni Pueblo, New Mexico. Gardens such as these are among the many ingenious techniques Southwestern peoples use to conserve moisture for agriculture. (Photograph by Jesse Nusbaum, ca. 1910. Courtesy of the Museum of New Mexico.)

Figure 1.2 White House, Canyon de Chelly, Arizona. The cliff dwellings of the Southwest have long excited the imaginations of tourists and professional archaeologists. (Photograph from The Collection of Fay-Cooper Cole. Courtesy of Lewis R. Binford.)

Figure 1.3 The Southwest culture area, which includes portions of the United States and Mexico. (Illustrated by Charles M. Carrillo.)

hunting-and-gathering areas of California and the Great Basin and the bison-hunting lands of the western Great Plains. The southern boundary of the Southwest is perhaps the most difficult to define, for the prehistoric peoples of Mesoamerica also depended on farming the same crops. However, whereas Mesoamerica was one of the centers of American civilization, with complex prehistoric states and empires such as Teotihuacán, the Toltec state, and the Aztec empire, achievements of this scale did not occur in the Southwest. Culturally, then, the Southwest is defined in two parts: (1) by what was present prehistorically—agriculture, the use of digging sticks, flat grinding stones (metates) and handstones (manos), the manufacture and use of ceramics, the construction of aggregated multiroom villages as well as dispersed settlements, and the occasional development of more complex towns with some unique forms of public architecture; and (2) by what was absent—the achievement of state-level societies with well-developed systems of writing and notation, large urban centers, and public architecture on the scale of the pyramids of Teotihuacán.

The prehistoric peoples of the Southwest acquired their basic cultural patterns by accepting aspects of Mesoamerican culture (especially the basic crops, possibly pottery and some irrigation techniques, and perhaps some religious beliefs) and adapting these to the environmentally diverse and high-risk agricultural settings of the Southwest. Throughout their prehistory the people moved between periods of sedentism and mobility. At times they depended more on hunting and gathering and were therefore relatively mobile. Periods of regional integration occurred, when large areas of the Southwest seem to have been incorporated into one economic or social system, but these always had a tenuous hold, and eventually large centers were abandoned as their populace returned to village life.

Contemporary Peoples

The descendants of the prehistoric inhabitants of the Southwest live among the ethnically and linguistically heterogeneous Native American groups of the area. It is a tribute to these people that, despite incursions of Western Europeans, religious persecution, cultural prejudice, and periods of forced acculturation, much of their native culture has remained intact. Native languages are still spoken, religious customs observed, and value systems maintained. The ethnographic literature on Southwestern peoples in voluminous (bibliographies may be found in Ortiz 1979; Spicer 1962; Vogt 1969), but only the most cursory overview can be given here to serve as an introduction for the prehistory.

The major native cultural traditions of the Southwest are those of the Pima and Papago of southern Arizona and Sonora and the related peoples of northern Mexico; the Yuman-speaking peoples of the Colorado River Valley and Baja California; the Pueblo Indians of Arizona and New Mexico; and the Athapaskan-speaking peoples—the Apache and Navajo (Figure 1.4). Three of these four traditions (Pima–Papago, Yuma, and Pueblo) developed within the Southwest over the course of millennia. The Apache and Navajo are relative newcomers. Their ancestral homeland is far north, in interior Canada and Alaska, where their linguistic relatives still live. The ancestors of the Navajo and Apache probably entered the Southwest in the early sixteenth century.

Southern Peoples

Most of the vast land area of northwestern Mexico and adjacent southern Arizona is the traditional homeland of agricultural peoples who speak languages of the Uto-Aztecan family. These peoples include the Upper Pima and Papago of Arizona, the Papago and Lower Pima of Sonora, the Tarahumara, the Yaqui, the Mayo, and the northern Tepehuan. Their enormous indigenous territory includes relatively lush river valleys, such as the Yaqui, Mayo, Salt, and Gila, as well as inhospitable deserts and mountainous upland regions. Some of the major differences among the native peoples relate to their particular environments; other differences are ascribable to variations in their interaction with Western European cultures.

All of these people lived in rancherias, that is, settlements composed of spatially separated dwellings of nuclear- or extended-family units. Among those groups inhabiting river valleys (e.g., Upper Pima, Yaqui, and Mayo), individual houses were closer together and communities were larger than among either mountain or desert settlements (e.g., Tarahumara, northern Tepehuan, Papago). Floodplain irrigation was prac-

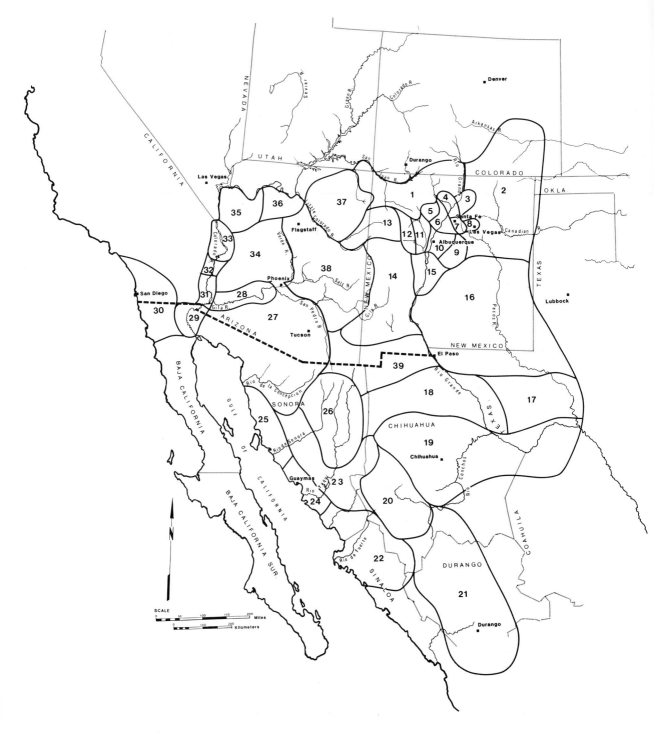

ticed by riverine communities and could be very productive. The Yaqui, for example, obtained two crops a year; they also had access to abundant wild plant foods. Mountain-dwelling groups generally relied on rainfall for farming and supplemented their crops with substantial amounts of wild plant foods and game. Desert groups, such as the Papago, generally planted *akchin* fields, which are fields located on the outwash fans of arroyos (ephemeral drainages), and gathered substantial amounts of wild plant foods. Where water sources and agricultural production were relatively secure, residential groups were sedentary throughout the year; however, various patterns of residential movement characterized other groups. For example, the Tarahumara families maintained fields in several different locations and, since contact with the Europeans, have kept herds of goats. During the agricultural season, families may have to move from one agricultural plot to another; and in winter, families move their goats to sheltered canyon locations. Many groups of the Papago engaged in biannual residential moves, living in greatly dispersed farmsteads near washes during the summer rainy season and moving to foothill villages in fall, when water was available only at the village reservoir.

House types and other structures within the rancherias varied considerably. For example, Tarahumara rancherias might consist of five or six one-room log houses with adjacent stone or log grain-storage cabins and a flat, open patio for outside work space. Papago settlements consisted of several dome-shaped brush structures with slightly excavated floors, and separate ramadas (sunshades), outdoor cooking areas, and a small house used as a menstrual seclusion hut. Traditional Yaqui rancherias are composed of several flat-roofed, rectangular, wattle-and-daub houses with separate ramadas and outdoor cooking areas all enclosed by a high cane fence. Families living in the same rancheria are often relatives. Among the Yaqui and Mayo, residence patterns are bilateral, as they tend to be among the Tarahumara. The northern Tepehuan, Pima, and Papago residence patterns are generally patrilocal. Extended families are not usually economically self-sufficient, and communal work parties are a common feature of most of these groups. Craft production of domestic items such as pottery varied in organization as well as technology. For example, although all Tarahumara women learn to make pottery, in practice some villages are known to produce especially good ceramics and these are exchanged through barter. Throughout the Southwest, pottery is made without the wheel by building vessel walls with coils of

---

Figure 1.4 Historic tribal territories of Southwestern peoples. The Upper Pima, Papago, Lower Pima, Tarahumara, Yaqui, Mayo, and northern Tepehuan constitute the traditional southern, Uto-Aztecan–speaking peoples. The Maricopa, Cocopa, Quechan, Halchidoma, Mohave, Yavapai, Walapi, and Havasupai speak Yuman languages of the Hokan language family and are tribes of the western tradition. The Rio Grande Pueblos and the Laguna, Acoma, Zuni, and Hopi are the traditional northern peoples; they speak diverse languages. The Apache and Navajo entered the Southwest late in prehistoric times and speak Athapaskan languages related to those of interior Canada. 1, Navajo; 2, Jicarilla Apache; 3, Northern Tiwa; 4, Tewa; 5, Jemez; 6, Rio Grande Keresan; 7, Tano; 8, Pecos; 9, Tompiro; 10, Southern Tiwa; 11, Laguna; 12, Acoma; 13, Zuni; 14, Chiricahua Apache; 15, Piro; 16, Mescalero Apache; 17, Jumano; 18, Suma; 19, Concho; 20, Tarahumara; 21, Tepehuan; 22, Mayo; 23, Lower Pima; 24, Yaqui; 25, Seri; 26, Opata; 27, Upper Pima and Papago; 28, Maricopa; 29, Cocopa; 30, Diegueño; 31, Quechan; 32, Halchidhoma; 33, Mohave; 34, Yavapai; 35, Walapi; 36, Havasupai; 37, Hopi; 38, Western Apache; 39, Jano–Jocome.

clay. The Papago, Tarahumara, and Yaqui use a paddle (flat object held outside the vessel) and anvil (stone held inside the vessel) to shape and finish pottery, whereas the Pima and formerly the Opata (who are now ethnically extinct) produce pottery by the coil-and-scrape technique (shaping and finishing the vessel by smoothing the coils and scraping inside and out with a gourd or sherd).

Political organization beyond the level of the individual rancheria is highly variable and reflects interactions with Europeans. Most groups seem not to have had aboriginal patterns of supravillage organization, except in times of war, when villages would unite under the leadership of the hierarchy of war sodalities. As a result of contact with the Spaniards, and especially of the efforts of the Jesuit missionaries, a structured organization of officials served to unite several rancherias and provide an interface between them and the Spanish colonial government. This village organization typically comprises a *gobernador,* with *capitanes,* *'tenientes* (Lieutenants), and subsidiary officials. As described by Spicer (1969), the contrasting histories of the Mayo and Yaqui are illustrative of the effects of European contact. The two Indian groups, speaking dialects of the same language and living much the same way, were at war with one another at the time of initial Spanish contact. The Mayo allied themselves with the Spaniards, whereas the Yaqui fought and defeated the Europeans. The Yaqui requested Jesuit missionaries, and both groups had peaceful relations with the missionaries for more than 100 years. From 1740 until 1887 both Mayo and Yaqui (often in combination) staged a series of revolts. The fighting escalated after Mexican independence (1821). After severe Indian defeats in 1886 and 1887, the Mexican government attempted to pacify the Mayo by offering them work on the Mexican haciendas and to pacify the Yaqui by giving them plots of land along the Yaqui River. The Mayo resistance was broken. Mexican residents moved into Mayo villages and took political power from them. Although the Mayo participated in a messianic religious movement, much of their ethnic distinctiveness has been lost. After 1886 the Yaqui were forcibly dispersed throughout Sonora, and to Oaxaca and Yucatán; many fled to the United States, where their descendants still reside. Those Yaqui remaining in their homeland continued to fight intermittent guerrilla warfare against the Mexican government. Many Yaqui were again forcibly deported under the Diaz regime, which ended in 1910. Those Yaqui remaining in Sonora retain a tremendous cultural pride and Yaqui nationalism, as do those in Arizona. Their allegiance is to Yaqui religion and also to the "traditional" eight Yaqui peublos, which were in fact established by the Jesuits. In contrast, few Mayo retain an ethnic identity that is very different from their Mestizo neighbors.

Religion among these groups is a combination of syncretisms, blendings, of Native Yaqui and Catholic beliefs and some compartmentalization, where borrowed and native elements are conceptualized as belonging to different realms. There is also considerable variation among the groups, although all but the most isolated are nominally Catholic. Holy Week ritual, summer Saints' Day celebration, and *Matachine* (an all-male dance group dedicated to the Virgin Mary) performances are virtually universal. At the local level, rainmaking rituals and dances are held among the Tarahumara and the Papago, and deer dances are features of Yaqui ritual. Shamanism and witchcraft are widespread, and beliefs often include the association of serpents with springs and water sources, sun and moon deities, and the ritual importance of deer and flowers.

Western Peoples

In historic times, various tribes speaking Yuman languages occupied the lower Colorado River Valley, the lower Gila River Valley, and adjacent uplands in Baja California, California and Arizona. The Yuman languages belong to the Hokan language family. Within Baja California, the Cocopa occupied the delta of the Colorado River and the Tipai, Kiliwa, and Paipai lived in the neighboring highlands. (*Pai* means "people" in Yuman. Here it refers to all Yuman-speaking peoples.) Northwest of the Cocopa, in modern California, the tribal groups were the Diegueño, Kamia, and Paipai. North of the Cocopa, along the Colorado, the tribes were the Kalyikam, Kohuana, and Quechan (Yuma) at the confluence of the Gila and Colorado rivers, then the Halchidhoma, Mojave, and Havasupai of the Grand Canyon. The Walapai and Yavapai occupied the uplands in the vicinity of the Grand Canyon. The Cocomaricopa and the Opa lived along the lower Gila. During the historic period, the Halyikam, Kohuana, Halchidhoma, Opa, and Cocomaricopa merged to form the Maricopa tribe, and the Chemehuevi moved to the Colorado River from California. Despite brief contacts with Spanish explorers and with the famous Jesuit missionary, Father Eusebio Kino, the Pai were not missionized or conquered by the Spaniards. The presence of Europeans had major effects on the Yuma through the introduction of horses and wheat and through slaving activities; however, it was not until the California gold rush of the 1850s that Euro-Americans regularly entered Pai territory and not until the 1880s that the Pai accepted various reservations.

During the historic period, and possibly prehistorically as well, the Pai area was one in which numerous population movements, migrations, and alliances of tribal groups took place. The Maricopa, for example, allied themselves in warfare with the Pima, and their culture reflects considerable blending of Yuma and Pima traits.

The tribes living along the Colorado River practiced agriculture on the river's floodplain. In spring, the Colorado River overflowed its channel, inundating an area that could be as much as $\frac{1}{2}$ mile wide. When the flood subsided, in summer, this area was planted. However, the Colorado has always been rather unpredictable; in some years the spring flood could be a month late, and in some years no flood occurred. In addition, the river frequently changed course along its lower reaches, sometimes creating lakes in the Mojave Desert. The riverine Pai made biannual residential moves, living in temporary shelters or ramadas on the floodplain during the summer and moving to the foothills of neighboring mountains at the end of the harvest. In addition to domestic crops, the Yuma practiced semicultivation of six species of native wild grasses, and all groups depended to a great extent on hunting, gathering, and fishing. Mesquite may have been about 50% of the Pai diet. Because of variations in the floodplain, fields were rarely located in the same place each year, and structures on the floodplain were ephemeral. The Maricopa, in part due to their extensive contact with the Pima, eventually used canal irrigation to divert water from the Gila.

Winter villages in the mountain foothills were composed of a loosely arranged series of rectangular pithouses. They were very large and accommodated several nuclear families. During the nonagricultural season, these houses served as bases for hunting and gathering activities.

Upland groups generally practiced some rainfall farming and a great deal of hunting and gathering. House forms were variable for these groups. In Baja California, wattle-and-daub structures were built; elsewhere, combinations of stone and wattle and daub were used in house construction. The use life of even the more permanent Yuma houses was not very long, because at the death of an individual, the house, as well as all possessions, was burned as part of an elaborate death and mourning ritual.

The Yuma generally expressed a preference for patrilocality, and villages were inhabited by members of named, totemic patrilineages. Village leadership was frequently in the hands of a particularly charismatic and spiritually powerful male, and some villages had additional councils of elders. Shamans had considerable religious power but were not village headmen. Among some groups, such as the Quechan (Yuma), village leadership may have been hereditary, but leaders ruled through their authority as respected persons rather than through their inherited right to exercise power.

Tribal leadership became important in times of warfare, and Yuman war organization was similar to that of the Yaqui. In historic times, warfare seems to have been extremely prevalent in the Yuman area. Tribes could mobilize hundreds of warriors and move them over great distances. In addition, the Yuma formed alliances among themselves during periods of warfare, and these actually spread to incorporate some of the Pima. A major alliance was formed that included the Mojave, Quechan, Yavapai, Kamia, and Chemehuevi. Allied against this group were the Cocopa, Halchidhoma, Paipai, Diegueño, Cocomaricopa, Opa, and the Gila Pima and Papago.

Yuman peoples produced a number of craft items, including mats, baskets, blankets, and pottery. The latter was finished by the paddle-and-anvil technique and was generally a plain brownware. The Maricopa, however, traded with the Pima for the red slips and clay used by the latter to produce their own ceramics. In addition to being recognized as exceptional in warfare, the Yuma were also active traders. They maintained an elaborate network of trails throughout their territory, with many crossing the Mojave Desert.

All men were endowed with sacred religious power, and individual dreams were improtant in attaining it. Public religious ceremonies involving sponsorship included curing rituals and initiation rites for both males and females. The death ritual was particularly elaborate. Individuals were cremated and, as noted, personal property and houses were burned during the death ceremonies.

Northern Peoples

Although the Pueblo Indians of Arizona and New Mexico share many aspects of their culture, the languages they speak are diverse. The Hopi live in several communities clustered on and around three small mesas that form the southern margins of the Black Mesa area of Arizona. The First (east) Mesa communities are Walpi, Sichomovi, and Tewa Village. The communities of Second (middle) Mesa are Shongopavi, Sipaulovi, and Mishongnovi. The Third (west) Mesa communities are Oraibi, Lower

Moenkopi, Hotevilla, Kyakotsmovi (New Oraibi), Upper Moenkopi, and Bacabi. With the exception of the residents of Tewa Village, which was founded in the seventeenth century by migrants from the Rio Grande Valley, the Hopi speak the Hopi language, which is within the Uto-Aztecan family of languages. The people of Tewa Village speak Tewa, which is related to other languages spoken among the Rio Grande Pueblo Indians (see following).

At the time of European contact, the Zuni occupied six villages near the Zuni River in western New Mexico. After 1692 they settled at a single village, called Halona or Zuni. The Zuni language is not closely related to other Pueblo languages but has been linked to Penutian, a language of some California peoples. East of Zuni, the Acoma live at their ancestral village on a high mesa top above the Rio San Jose and Acoma Creek, and at two villages (Acomita and McCartys) below the mesa to the north. The Acoma speak the same dialect of the Keresan language as the Laguna, their immediate neighbors to the east. Keresan is not related to any other known Native American language. The Laguna occupy six villages (Old Laguna, New Laguna, Seama, Encinal, Paguate, and Mesita) on both sides of the Rio San Jose. The Pueblo Indians of Zia, Santa Ana, San Felipe, Santo Domingo, and Cochiti also speak Keresan, but their Eastern Keresan dialect differs from the Western Keresan spoken at Acoma and Laguna. Zia and Santa Ana are located on the Jemez River west of Albuquerque. San Felipe, Santo Domingo, and Cochiti are located within the Rio Grande Valley, where they form a wedge between pueblo villages speaking Tanoan languages.

There are three related Tanoan languages spoken today. Tiwa is spoken at Isleta and Sandia, the southernmost Pueblo villages of the Rio Grande Valley, and at Taos and Picuris, the northernmost pueblo villages. There are dialect differences between the Southern and Northern Tiwa speakers. Tewa is the Tanoan language spoken at San Juan, Santa Clara, Pojaque, San Ildefonso, Nambé, and Tesuque, as well as at Tewa Village on First Mesa at Hopi. Towa is a Tanoan language that today is spoken only at the pueblo of Jemez on the Jemez River north of Zia. Towa was spoken at Pecos Pueblo, on the upper Pecos River, until that pueblo was abandoned in 1838. The Tanoan languages are similar and are part of the Kiowa–Tanoan language family, which is related to other languages spoken by some peoples of the Great Plains. In addition to these languages, Pueblo speakers of Piro and Tompiro lived along the Rio Grande south of Isleta and east of the Sandia and Manzano mountains during the early historic period. These villages were abandoned as the result of events related to the European conquest, and although descendants of these groups live among some of the contemporary Pueblo, their languages have been lost.

Of the peoples living in the northern portion of the Southwest, the Pueblo bore the brunt of early and continued contact with the Spaniards. Coronado visited Zuni and the Rio Grande pueblos in 1540, and the first Spanish Colonial capital in New Mexico was established near San Juan Pueblo in 1598. Missionization was pursued most ardently among the Rio Grande Pueblos during the seventeenth century, and the repressive activities of the friars was a major factor leading the Rio Grande Pueblos to unite and revolt against the Spaniards in 1680. Reconquest was not accomplished until 1692–1693 under Don Diego de Vargas.

The Pueblo Indians live in compact villages rather than in rancherias, and agriculture is everywhere important among them. The Hopi, lacking perennial streams, divert some water from washes but rely on rainfall for farming; they plant fields in diverse topographic settings in order to ensure that at least some of the fields obtain enough moisture to produce a crop. Other villages rely on both irrigated and rainfall-watered fields. Among all the Pueblo, hunting and gathering were historically important supplemental subsistence activities. Although villages were occupied year-round, family members might spend large parts of the agricultural season at fieldhouses near their crops, and work parties would use temporary camps, such as piñon-collecting and hunting camps, at other times.

Pueblo villages are composed of contiguous rectangular rooms of one or more stories, arranged around open plaza areas. Both stone and adobe are used in village construction. Family households use a series of interconnecting rooms for living and storage. In multistory pueblos, ground-floor rooms are most often used for storage, and in all pueblos, the flat roofs are used as additional work areas. Ritual paraphernalia may be stored in special rooms. All pueblos have special ceremonial rooms (kivas) in which some ritual activities take place. Among the Western Pueblo (Hopi, Zuni, Acoma, and Laguna), kivas are rectangular and incorporated into roomblocks. Among the Eastern Pueblo, kivas are separate, round structures.

Differences among the Pueblo besides language, relate to social organization, political organization, and religious practices. Among the Western Pueblos (Hopi, Zuni, Acoma, and Laguna), the matrilocal household is generally the basic unit of social organization. Above the level of the household, the Western Pueblo organization is dominated by named, matrilineal, exogamous clans. The clans, as corporate groups, control agricultural land and other resources, and each clan is responsible for conserving ritual knowledge and maintaining some ritual paraphernalia. Western Pueblo leadership is often described as theocratic, in that the leaders are the male ritual heads of the specific lineages responsible for the religious obligations of each clan. In addition to the clan rituals, the Kachina cult has tribewide membership among the Western Pueblo, and there are additional tribal ceremonial associations. The Kachina cult involves representation of a series of supernatural beings who are associated with bringing rain and well-being to the pueblo. The Kachinas are represented by men in dramatic, masked performances. Other important tribal associations are concerned with social control (the ritual "clowns"), game and hunting, curing, and warfare.

Some ritual performances occur at specific times during the year (e.g., at the solstice). Other ritual activities occur at an appropriate time, such as when a series of retreats, prayers, and other activities have been completed. Since any particular ceremony may require the completion of a number of preliminary activities by each of several groups (clans, societies, etc.), these activities must be accomplished before the ceremony can take place. Ceremonies are generally done for the good of all the people, and, in fact, they may initiate or conclude certain economic tasks such as the planting of the crops. The timing of these events and their orderly progression throughout the year are therefore crucial to maintaining village life. Finally, it is important to note that individuals gain positions of leadership and knowledge by assuming obligations and by being initiated into ceremonial groups. The process of education and initiation to greater responsibilities continues throughout much of a person's life. For ceremonies to be effective, there must be enough knowledgeable elders drawn from the leadership of different associations to contribute each of the necessary aspects of the ceremony.

The actual organization of clans, the Kachina cults, and ceremonial associations varies among the Western Pueblo. For example, the coordination of activities is most diffuse among the Hopi and most centralized at Zuni. Nevertheless, it is important to emphasize the degree of coordination that must be achieved.

The organization of the Tanoan Rio Grande Pueblo contrasts most markedly with that of the Western Pueblo. Among the Tanoans, the bilateral extended family is the basic household unit of organization. Above the level of the household, the Tanoan organization is dominated by nonexogamous dual divisions (moieties). It is most common for children to belong to the moiety of their father, but there are exceptions, and individuals sometimes change moiety affiliation during their lifetimes. In general, it is the moiety leadership that is responsible for the coordination of activities. For example, among the Tewa one moiety is responsible for leadership during the late fall, winter, and early spring, whereas the opposite moiety assumes leadership for the agricultural portion of the year. In addition to the moieties, there are also ceremonial associations whose membership crosscuts moiety lines. These are concerned with the same types of activity as those mentioned for the Western Pueblo; however, it has been noted that, whereas assuring rainfall is more important in the west, the concerns of curing, hunting, and warfare are more important in the east. The Kachina cult is also important among the Eastern Pueblo, except in Taos, where it is absent. In contrast to those of the Western Pueblo, however, Eastern Pueblo masked Kachina performances are not performed publicly. These and other rituals are maintained in secret among eastern groups, in part because the Eastern Pueblo were subjected to the most extreme and sustained religious persecution during Spanish Colonial times. In addition to the religious hierarchy, the Eastern Pueblo are governed by a series of "outside" leaders, that is, the *gobernador, capitanes,* and *'tenientes* established during Spanish hegemony.

The Keresan-speaking pueblos and, apparently, Jemez have been described as organizationally intermediate between the Western and Eastern patterns, for their organizational systems contain elements common to both west and east. These pueblos have named, exogamous, matrilineal clans that are characteristic of the Western Pueblo, as well as patrilineal moiety divisions associated with the kivas.

In addition to the pursuits involved in agriculture, gathering and hunting, the ceremonial concern for rainfall, curing, social control, and hunting, and to the compact nature of their settlements, the Pueblo share other aspects of culture, both symbolic and tangible. For example, among all Pueblo Indians the cardinal directions are associated with specific colors, and color and directional symbolism are important. The Pueblo origin myths are also similar, involving a female creator and the emergence of people from a dark, wet underworld. Peublo craft items include finely made ceramics, which are finished by coiling and scraping and painted with well-executed designs, well-made textiles, stone and shell jewelry, and the more prosaic items such as stone arrowheads, manos, and metates.

This book is concerned with the prehistory of the native cultural traditions of the Southwest. The southern, western, and northern peoples occupied landscapes ranging from low, hot deserts to river valleys, and cool, semiarid plateaus and mountains. Within the large area of the Southwest and its diverse environments, a variety of subsistence adaptations was practiced in historic times. Some peoples practiced only limited cultivation of crops, deriving most of their food from wild plant and animal resources. Other groups engaged in irrigation agriculture supplemented by hunting and gathering. Settlement patterns were and are equally diverse. Some people occupy small hamlets composed of only a few houses. Elsewhere, compact villages of hundreds of people are the usual settlement type. It is apparent in examining the long prehistoric trajectory of these peoples that there has also been great diversity in material culture, subsistence economy, and settlement patterns over time. For example, throughout most of the prehistoric period, the Western Pueblo area was characterized by rancherias rather than the compact villages known there today. A reversal of this pattern occurred in the lower Sonoran Desert region of Arizona and Chihuahua, for in that area in the thirteenth and fourteenth centuries, settlements consisted of large, compact, multistoried adobe "Great Houses." Yet, the inhabitants of these communities may have been among the ancestors of the modern Pima and Papago, who occupy rancherias today. Changes in economic strategies, village organization, and aspects of material culture are an important feature of the prehistoric Southwest. This book concentrates on the indigenous traditions of the Southwest (the Pima–Papago, Yuma, and Pueblo). The Athabascan speakers (Apache and Navajo) are included only in the final chapters, reflecting their late entrance into the Southwest.

Prehistoric Cultures

The living native peoples of the Southwest have been briefly described in terms of their similarities and diversity. As has been mentioned, some of the characteristics they display today are the result of a very recent phenomenon: the contact and interaction with western European culture. Over the millennia prior to this contact, events and gradual processes occurred that also greatly affected peoples' ways of life: The acceptance of the basic cultigens from Mesoamerica, trade and interaction with the state-level societies of Mesoamerica, and natural events such as shifts in rainfall patterns all had diverse effects on local populations. In the absence of written records, which might provide information about the symbolic, religious, and intellectual aspects of cultures, archaeologists generally define cultures on the basis of material remains (houses, ceremonial structures, stone and bone tools, ceramics, etc.). It is probably only rarely that any archaeological culture corresponds directly to descendant living societies.

Archaeologists working in the Southwest have defined four major archaeological cultural traditions (and a number of minor ones) that can be considered ancestral to

Figure 1.5 Prehistoric cultural traditions of the Southwest. The Patayan area includes the Colorado River and adjacent uplands, historically the home of the Yuman-speaking tribes. The Anasazi area of the Colorado Plateaus is considered the traditional homeland of the Pueblo. The Mogollon area of northern Mexico, southern New Mexico, and southeastern Arizona was inhabited by Pueblo peoples in the prehistoric period. The Hohokam area of south-central Arizona is the historic homeland of the Pima and Papago. (Map by Charles M. Carrillo.)

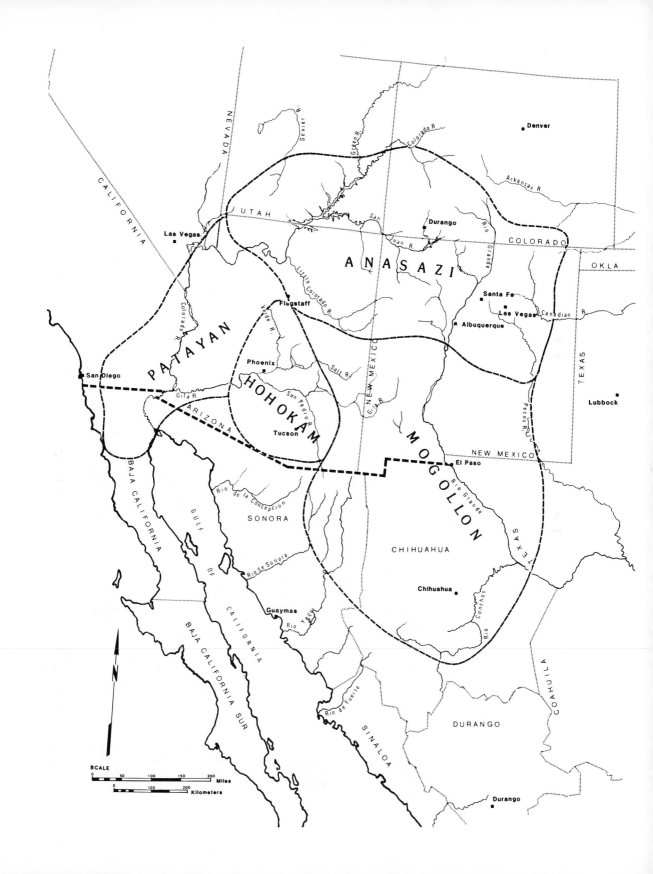

the indigenous cultures. These traditions are the Hohokam, Patayan, Mogollon, and Anasazi (Figure 1.5). Each of these is defined here and more fully described in Chapter 3. Briefly, however, the Hohokam tradition centered in the lower Sonoran Desert regions of Arizona and adjacent Chihuahua and Sonora. Throughout much of the prehistoric period, Hohokam settlements were of the rancheria type. Hohokam ceramics were finished by paddle and anvil and fired to a buff color. Decorations were made with red paint. Some archaeologists view the Hohokam tradition as ancestral to the modern Pima and Papago.

The Patayan tradition is represented by sites in the Colorado River Valley, from the Grand Canyon to the delta and adjacent uplands. Archaeologically, the Patayan area is still poorly known; however, upland settlements are generally of the rancheria type. Ceramics were finished by paddle and anvil, and most were unpainted. Patayan ceramics were apparently somewhat casually fired, and surface colors range from buff to gray. Most archaeologists agree that, in a general way, the Patayan tradition was ancestral to the modern Yuman-speaking tribes.

The Mogollon tradition occupied an extensive area in what is today southeastern

Figure 1.6 Anasazi pottery on display in the early twentieth century. Black-on-white painted ceramics (top two rows) were made for serving and storing. The cooking ware (bottom row) is corrugated. (Photograph from the collection of Fay-Cooper Cole. Courtesy of Lewis R. Binford.)

Arizona, southwestern New Mexico, and adjacent Sonora and Chihuahua. Rancheria communities composed of pithouses and coiled-and-scraped ceramics fired to a brown or red-brown color were typical of most of the Mogollon tradition. After about A.D. 1000, however, some portions of the Mogollon area saw the development of compact villages of contiguous rectangular rooms, with roomblocks massed around plazas. After A.D. 1000, painted ceramics in parts of the Mogollon region were decorated with black paint on a white slip. Much of the Mogollon area was abandoned in prehistoric times, and archaeologists believe the descendants of the Mogollon are incorporated within some of the modern Western Pueblos.

Remains of the Anasazi tradition are found within the northern portion of the Southwest, from northern Arizona and New Mexico into southwestern Colorado and southeastern Utah. Although rancherias are typical of some parts of the Anasazi area throughout the prehistoric period, the Anasazi were the first in the Southwest to adopt compact villages of contiguous rectangular rooms. Anasazi ceramics were finished by coiling and scraping and were generally fired to a gray or white core color. Painted ceramics throughout most of the area were decorated with black designs on a white slip (Figure 1.6). Much of the northern portion of the Anasazi area was also abandoned during the prehistoric period, and archaeologists agree that the modern Pueblo peoples are descended from the Anasazi tradition.

Conclusion

Knowledge of the prehistory of the Southwest derives largely from archaeology and from the contributions of other sciences, such as zoology, paleobotany, geology, and paleoclimatology. To write a prehistory (i.e., the narrative description of past lifeways and events,) depends on the integration of various scientific approaches to the material remains of the past and the evaluation of data and interpretations provided by those approaches. Most of these fields of study, especially archaeology, are in a period of both critical assessment of method and development of appropriate bodies of theory. One cannot overemphasize the dependence of prehistory on the methods and theories of the sciences devoted to interpreting the past. As these sciences develop, our confidence in narrative prehistory increases. The past is composed of a series of events and other "facts," but the scientific techniques needed to infer what these were from the remains available for study are constantly changing and being refined. This book provides an introduction to Southwest prehistory, to the narrative events and processes of the past. It is not a study of Southwestern archaeology, which would include detailed treatment of the development of method and theory within archaeology. Nevertheless, in the following pages, disagreements among scholars about the interpretation of the past are discussed. It is believed that these areas of dispute are important because they illuminate questions that require more data or new methods and theories for their resolution.

There are many reasons for scholarly interest in Southwestern prehistory. Four, in particular, have motivated my own interest and appear as recurrent themes throughout this book. First, material remains from the past are relatively well preserved in the

Southwest. Due in part to a natural aridity that favors preservation, this is also a result of the low density of modern population and the lack of industrial development. There are very real and immediate threats to the archaeological resources of the Southwest, particularly where urban populations are established and growing and where fossil fuels are being mined. Nevertheless, the abundance and variety of materials that have been preserved permit a much richer view of the past than is often possible.

Second, and probably in part because of the fine preservation conditions, the Southwest has long been an area in which students have received their first training as archaeologists. Students often bring innovative ideas to their work and explore these in the Southwest. Thus, the prehistory of the Southwest has benefited from the application of new techniques and methods.

Third, many issues of concern to anthropology in general have been and can be readily examined in the Southwest. For example, anthropologists are interested in understanding the conditions under which people adopt agriculture and a sedentary way of life; various questions pertaining to the adoption of agriculture can be examined in the Southwest. Similarly, there is a general interest in the development of regional systems of trade and exchange, which can be explored with Southwestern data. Anthropologists are also interested in the processes involved in the development of complex social systems. The Southwest offers insights into these processes because complex social systems did emerge at certain times but were not sustained. As a result, another set of inquiries focuses on the disruption of regional systems or the collapse of systems of political integration and abandonments of large areas. Many theoretically derived explanations for these phenomena can be productively examined in the Southwest, where the data from the past are well preserved and where innovative techniques have been used to address these issues.

Finally, the prehistory of the Southwest is important because it is a large part of the cultural heritage of the native peoples who live there. For all these peoples, the temporal depth of written history is relatively shallow compared to the millennia over which their cultural traditions have developed. All the native peoples, of course, have strong traditions of oral history, but archaeologists should provide their own information and promote a clear understanding of how they have developed their interpretations so that the information thereby derived may become part of the cultural history of the native peoples of the Southwest.

2

The Natural Environment

This chapter examines the natural environments within which prehistoric cultural developments took place. Modern environments are baselines from which prehistoric environmental changes are extrapolated. The geology, climate, vegetation, and fauna of the modern Southwest are discussed, followed by consideration of various methods of interpreting past environmental conditions.

Introduction

The natural environment imposes a set of conditions to which any society must adapt if it is to survive. Compared to many areas of the world, the environmental constraints of the Southwest are relatively harsh. The entire region is arid. The lack of moisture restricts the abundance of vegetation and game animals and the location and size of areas suitable for agriculture. Water sources are extremely important to the contemporary peoples of the Southwest, as they were to the prehistoric population. Additional constraints of the natural environment include short growing seasons in some areas and poorly developed soils in others. The range of behaviors that societies use to cope with environmental conditions will depend, in part, on population size and available technological knowledge. Nevertheless, an understanding of the general configuration of the natural environment, and of problems associated with it, is basic to an appreciation of the kinds of adaptations made.

Some cultural solutions to environmental problems have short- and long-term effects on the environment, and they may condition future adaptations. For example, prehistoric timber-cutting for building material, firewood, or to clear agricultural land may increase surface erosion and eventually lower the water table, rendering crop raising impossible. Prolonged irrigation of poorly drained soils may lead to irreversible damage by mineralization and salinization.

In addition to defining limiting conditions, the natural environment provides the resources that are crucial for social survival; that is, those used for food, tools, shelter, or trade items. The distribution of arable land is, of course, critical for crops, but throughout prehistoric times (and into the historic period), Southwestern peoples depended to some extent on wild plant foods and game. At certain times, the availability of wild foods may have been the key to survival. Some materials with limited natural occurrences were widely traded prehistorically, including obsidian, high-quality cherts, and petrified woods that were useful for tools, as well as luxury items such as shell and turquoise, which were important to the culturally defined network of social interactions. The distribution and relative abundance of various resources significantly affect the ways in which societies are organized.

The natural environment also determines preservation of the archaeological record of the past. Thus, specific environmental characteristics are important to the kinds of materials that are likely to be preserved and those that are not. Although the preservation of perishable items such as wood, seeds, and animal bones in many parts of the Southwest enables a richness of interpretation of prehistoric lifeways that is not possible in other parts of the world, in some places in the Southwest conditions are not favorable to the preservation of organic remains. In these areas, cultural historical and basic chronological questions are still unresolved. The use of the natural environment by our modern society is frequently critical to the recovery of archaeological remains as well as to their destruction. It is not coincidental that a great deal of information on the San Juan Basin became available in the 1970s, when uranium exploration and coal mining attained major importance in the U.S. economy. Federal law requires assessment of cultural resources prior to mining or otherwise modifying public land. Intensive archaeological surveys have been conducted in the San Juan Basin, a major producer of energy resources. In the nineteenth century, grazing activities throughout enormous areas of the Southwest had precipitated erosion conditions that exposed many archaeological sites and destroyed countless others.

Finally, interpretations of the prehistoric events in the Southwest rely on climatic and other environmental changes; for example, regional abandonments have been attributed to droughts in some areas, to destruction of trees needed for firewood in others, and to salinization of fields in still other areas. Evaluation of these interpretations requires an understanding of how past environments are reconstructed and the means by which the magnitude of change is discerned.

There are many ways of describing natural environments. Landscapes may be characterized by landform types (mountains, plateaus, etc.), weather patterns (cold deserts, hot deserts, etc.), vegetation zones (Transition, Upper Sonoran, etc.), or dominant plant and animal communities (short grass prairie, shadscale–kangaroo rat association, etc.). Because the characteristics of any natural environment are the result of interactions between the atmosphere and the lithosphere, it is reasonable to begin a discussion of the environments of the Southwest with these. The natural environment of the Southwest is perhaps best characterized by its diversity with respect to landforms, temperature regimes, precipitation patterns, vegetation, fauna, and mineral resources.

Physiographic Provinces

The culturally defined Southwest does not correspond to one physiographic province, but rather includes portions of four major provinces. These are described here and illustrated in Figure 2.1. The western and southern portions of the cultural Southwest lie within the Basin and Range physiographic province but are not coincident with it. The province extends from about Agua Caliente and San Luis Potosí in Mexico to portions of Idaho and Oregon. In general, the Basin and Range province is characterized by a series of narrow, rugged, usually north–south trending parallel ranges of mountains interspersed with structural basins. In the southern section of the Basin and Range province in the United States, which includes part of the cultural Southwest, less than half the surface area is mountainous. Although the mountains generally rise abruptly from the basin floors, the ranges are usually not so vast as to impede travel. The province is primarily dependent on winds from the Pacific to bring the essential moisture over the high mountains to the west, but the mountains trap most of this moisture, so the province itself is dry. Internal drainage, frequently resulting in ephemeral lakes or playas (*barriales* in Mexico), is characteristic of much of the province; however, the southern section is drained in part by the Rio Grande and the Gila, Colorado, Yaqui, and Conchos rivers. Land surfaces within the province consist of gravel fans rising from valleys to the base of the surrounding mountains, either dry lake beds or river floodplains in the central portions of the basins, and

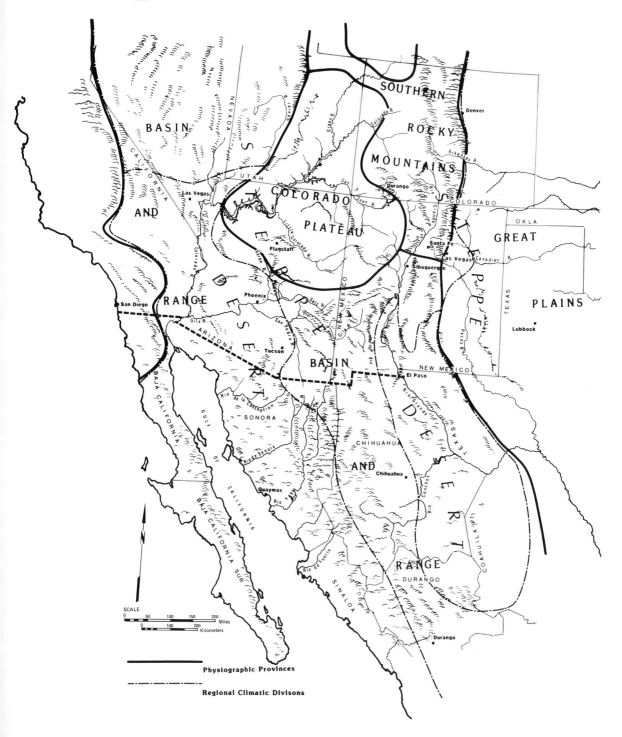

SOUTHERN

ROCKY

MOUNTAINS

BASIN

Denver

NEVADA

UTAH

COLORADO PLATEAU

Las Vegas

Durango

COLORADO

AND

San Juan R

OKLA

GREAT

Flagstaff

Santa Fe

Little Colorado R.

Las Vegas

Canadian R

Albuquerque

PLAINS

RANGE

Phoenix

San Diego

Salt R.

ARIZONA

Gila R.

San Pedro R.

Tucson

NEW MEXICO

TEXAS

Lubbock

BASIN

NEW MEXICO

BAJA CALIFORNIA

El Paso

Rio de la Concepcion

SONORA

CHIHUAHUA

AND

GULF OF CALIFORNIA

Rio de Sonora

Rio Yaqui

Chihuahua

Rio Conchos

COAHUILA

Guaymas

Rio

BAJA CALIFORNIA SUR

CALIFORNIA

RANGE

SINALOA

Rio de Fuerte

DURANGO

N

Durango

SCALE
0   50   100   150   200
                          Miles
0   100   200
                    Kilometers

—————— **Physiographic Provinces**

—·—·—·— **Regional Climatic Divisons**

rugged mountains. Deposits of salt, copper, and lead are among the resources that are commercially exploited today in the southern section of the Basin and Range province and that were important to the prehistoric population as well.

The central and north-central part of the cultural Southwest lies within the Colorado Plateaus province, although the province does extend north beyond the Southwest. This province is characterized by high elevations: most of the land surfaces are higher than 1524 m and some mountain peaks reach elevations of more than 3657 m. The plateaus manifest extensive areas of nearly horizontal sedimentary rock formations, but there are also down-warped basin structures such as the San Juan and Gallup–Zuni basins, and elevated igneous structures, particularly along the plateaus' margins. Examples of the latter are the rock formations of the Grand Canyon section (including the San Francisco Mountains of Arizona), the Datil volcanics of central Arizona and New Mexico, and the San Juan Mountains of southern Colorado and northwestern New Mexico.

Aridity is also a feature of the province. The principal drainage is through the Colorado River system, including important tributaries such as the San Juan and Little Colorado rivers. Most of the rivers within the province are deeply entrenched and have high gradients. Land surfaces may consist of nearly flat plateau segments (mesas) and tilted plateau segments (cuestas) with steep-walled canyons and escarpments. The volcanic areas contain obsidians that were important prehistoric lithic sources. Much of the spectacular stone architecture of the Anasazi is made of the local sandstones of this province. Today, coal and uranium are extensively mined in some areas of the plateaus. Although certainly not of major economic importance, coal was used prehistorically in some areas as a fuel for firing ceramics.

The cultural Southwest extends into the southernmost portion of the Southern Rocky Mountain province, which includes the San Juan Mountains on the west slope and the Sangre de Cristo Mountains on the east. Between the two groups of ranges are the San Luis Valley in the north and the Rio Grande Valley in the south. The southern Rocky Mountains are primarily composed of metamorphic rock, but there are extensive areas of igneous inclusions in the San Juan ranges. Elevations within the province range from about 1524 m in the valleys to peaks of over 4267 m. The Southern Rocky Mountains have a great effect on weather patterns (discussed in the following), but generally the mountains themselves are quite well watered. The mountains provide a significant watershed for large areas of the Southwest. The major drainage to the east is the Rio Grande and its tributaries; the Dolores and San Juan rivers and their tributaries drain the area to the west. The province is well known for its mineral resources; however, few of these were used prehistorically. The prehistorically important mineral resources include igneous rock, primarily basalts and obsidian, fine-grained chert, galena (lead ore), turquoise, and malachite.

Figure 2.1 Physiographic provinces and regional climatic divisions of the Southwest. The Southwest includes portions of the Basin and Range, Southern Rocky Mountains, Colorado Plateaus, and Great Plains physiographic provinces. Two broad climatic divisions, desert and steppe, are represented. (Map by Charles M. Carrillo.)

At times during the prehistoric period, the cultural Southwest extended short distances onto the Great Plains province; thus, portions of the Raton section, the Pecos Valley, and the Llano Estacado were inhabited or used extensively by Southwestern peoples. Elevations range from 1828 to 2133 m in the Raton section to between 609 and 1524 m in the Llano Estacado. Topographic relief is slight. Most of the rocks are flat-lying sedimentary deposits overlain by silts, sands, and gravels that were washed eastward from the Rockies. The Raton section is exceptional in having high mesas capped by lava flows. Past climatic changes enabled Southwestern argiculturalists to establish communities on the margins of the plains. The important drainages within the area are the Cimarron and the Pecos rivers. The generally arid southwestern plains contain extensive salt deposits that were used prehistorically. Other resources procured from the Great Plains prehistorically include bison and cherts from the Edwards Plateau of Texas.

In sum, the Southwest encompasses a tremendous amount of physiographic diversity. Elevations range from 30.4 m above sea level in the basins of the western Basin and Range province to peaks up to 4267 m in the southern Rocky Mountains. Rugged mountains, mesas, canyons, and broad valleys all occur within the area, as do formations of sedimentary, igneous, and metamorphic origin. The physiographic provinces of the Southwest extend far beyond the area included within the cultural boundaries. In general, the cultural boundaries in the west, north, and east are defined by the limits of agricultural production. These limits, as well as the diversity of natural vegetation, are largely conditioned by the regional climate.

Climate

At the broadest, most inclusive level, subcontinental areas of related climates are grouped in the same domain (Bailey 1980). At this very general level, the entire Southwest falls within the Dry domain. Occupying about one-fourth of the earth's land surface, dry climates are characterized by water deficits; that is, the rate at which water is lost annually through evaporation is greater than that gained through precipitation. Beyond this very general characterization, diversity is, once again, the rule.

In all dry areas, moisture is a limiting factor for vegetation. Precipitation derives from cyclonic, orographic, and convectional storms. Cyclonic rainfall patterns are the result of large air masses of low pressure moving across a path determined by the jet stream. Due to the large size of these low-pressure systems, they influence precipitation in a general way over large areas. The Southwest has cyclonic rainfall patterns of two types: a biannual pattern characteristic of the west and rainfall with a single maximum in the east. The biannual pattern centers in Arizona and extends into southern Utah, Nevada, southwestern Colorado, eastern California, and Sonora, Mexico. The primary maximum precipitation in the western area occurs in July and August and derives its moisture from the Gulf of Mexico. The secondary maximum occurs in winter, from December to March, and usually peaks in February. The moisture for the winter storms, originating from the Pacific Ocean and the Gulf of California, consists typically of soaking rains or snowfall in the higher elevations. This moisture is absorbed by the soil and encourages early greening of rangeland. The winter precipitation is followed by a very dry period from April through June. The summer maximum may account for 50% of the annual precipitation, but the storms are of a different type. Summer rainfall is produced by largely high-intensity thunderstorms of generally short duration. Partly due to the intensity of the storms, and also because the ground has dried out during the spring, the summer rains do not penetrate the soil as well as the winter precipitation, and much of the summer moisture is lost to runoff (Comeaux 1981; Trewartha 1966).

The eastern portion of the Southwest, including most of New Mexico and Colorado, westernmost Texas, and much of Chihuahua, Mexico, has a different pattern of cyclonic rainfall. In this area, there is a single maximum in the late summer months of June and July. These storms derive their moisture from the Gulf of Mexico in the same way that summer storms are produced in the west, and like the western storms they are of high intensity and short duration. Because cyclonic storms are conditioned by the jet stream, shifts in that stream will have a great effect on storm patterns in the Southwest. Such changes will affect the western and eastern parts of the Southwest differently. For example, a northward shift in the jet stream would deprive the western area of important winter precipitation but have little effect in the east. This observation is important, because paleoclimatic reconstructions (discussed in detail below) that are derived from one part of the Southwest cannot be generalized to the entire area. Convectional and orographic storms contribute to the differences in local precipitation patterns.

Convectional storms occur in the summer, when the ground surface receives maximum solar radiation. Heat from the ground is transferred to the air and rises quite suddenly and rapidly through the air above the earth's surface, cooling very rapidly. This type of air movement produces violent local thunderstorms. These high-intensity storms generally begin in the afternoons, when the ground has had sufficient time to heat. A great deal of rain is generated by these storms, but the velocity is also high and crops may be damaged, washes flooded, and soil eroded. In general, the storm tracks of convectional rainfall are not very predictable, and areas just outside the track receive no precipitation.

Orographic precipitation occurs when winds carrying some moisture are forced upward to cross a mountain barrier. The amount of precipitation depends on the moisture content of the air and the height and mass of the mountains. Generally, large mountain masses act as catchment areas for precipitation. The Southern Rocky Mountains, the Mogollon Mountains, and the central mountains of Arizona (the Bradshaws, Sierra Anchas, and Gilas) receive more orographic precipitation than do the small mountain ranges of the Basin and Range country. Orographic precipitation may occur at any time of year when there are moisture-bearing winds. At times, during the winter, winds from the Gulf of Mexico predominate over the eastern portion of the Southwest. The orographic winter storms provide the snowfall for the Southern Rockies. Also in winter, moisture-bearing winds originating in the Gulf of California occasionally enter Sonora and Arizona, causing orographic snowfall in the high mountains. Orographic precipitation, of course, occurs primarily on the windward side of mountains. The ranges themselves are barriers to precipitation on their leeward sides. Thus, the northeastern portion of Arizona receives very little winter precipitation, because it is on the leeward side of the central mountains.

It is common to discuss the distribution of precipitation in terms of average yearly amount. From this perspective, the Southwest is divided into two regional climatic divisions (Figure 2.1). The desert division is characterized by fewer than 20 cm of annual precipitation. The steppe division receives generally less than 50 cm of precipitation annually. It should be obvious, given the foregoing discussion, that average precipitation is somewhat misleading. Yearly deviations from the average may be extreme, and not all precipitation is useful for vegetative growth. For example, although the mean annual precipitation in Santa Fe, New Mexico, is 35.9 cm, recorded deviations since 1950 have ranged from 16.9 to 51.2 cm. Also, as noted, the particularly high-intensity summer thunderstorms may damage natural ground cover and crops. Given the generally dry climatic regime of the Southwest as a whole and the erratic nature of the distribution of precipitation, reliable sources of water are of critical importance to contemporary and prehistoric populations. The major rivers of the Southwest (Figure 2.1) are clearly important; however, not all of them are either completely useful or beneficial for crops. For example, most of the northern portion of the San Juan is so deeply entrenched that its waters are not useful for irrigation. Irrigation from the Rio Grande was and is extremely important to contemporary peoples of the area; however, flooding does occur and can be disastrous. In 1886, for example, floods destroyed not only the fields but also much of the village of Santo Domingo, New Mexico, and the town of San Marcial, New Mexico, was destroyed by floods in 1886 and 1929. Seeps and springs may be more important sources of water for domestic use (and for hand watering of crops) than the rivers. Over much of the Colorado Plateaus province, where drainages are entrenched, this is especially true. The presence of seeps and springs is conditioned by overlying rock of differential permeability. For example, at Mesa Verde relatively permeable sandstones overlie impervious shales. The seeps and springs that occur at the contact zone of the two formations were an important source of water for the prehistoric population.

In addition to precipitation, the length of the growing season and the temperature and humidity ranges are critical for successful agriculture. High temperatures and low humidity cause the high rate of evaporation and evapotranspiration that creates the water deficit characteristic of the Southwest. The frost-free period is that portion of the year during which vegetation will normally grow, presupposing an adequate amount of moisture. Modern hybrid corn is considered to require a 120-day frost-free period; however, when corn is grown with inadequate moisture, as it is over much of the Southwest, the crop matures more slowly and a longer growing season is necessary. In general, temperature range is determined primarily (not exclusively) by latitude and altitude. In the Southwest, temperature decreases northward from 1.5 to 2.5°F for every degree of latitude. Temperatures also generally correlate inversely with elevation, but this is conditioned by several topographical factors. The direction of exposure is important for the amount of insolation received and, therefore, for temperature. Contrasts are marked, especially in deep, narrow valleys and canyons with east–west orientations. Canyons of this sort are common on the Colorado Plateaus province and in mountainous country. For example, temperatures recorded at the same elevation on the north and south walls of Frijoles Canyon, New Mexico, differed by 13°F. Temperature differences are also noted between the east and west flanks of north–south oriented mountains, with temperatures on the west flanks generally being higher. Other well-known factors of topography that influence temperature are air drainage and wind shifts, which can cause temperature changes in narrow valleys. Especially on clear, still evenings, cool heavy air drains into canyon bottoms, so temperatures at these locations may be several degrees below those on the sides of canyons. For example, at Mesa Verde the shortest growing season is within canyon-bottom settings, at elevations of about 1920 m, and not on the 2500-m mesa top (Erdman *et al.* 1969).

Two other general observations about temperatures are important to germination and the growing season of crops. In many areas of the Southwest, daily temperature changes are greatest in spring, when the germination of seeds may be endangered. For example, in New Mexico the daily average range in temperatures in April may be as much as 39 °F (Houghton 1959:70–71). Also, variability from year to year in the length of the growing season, particularly in mountainous areas, may be extreme; although the mean length of the growing season at Taos, New Mexico, was recorded as 138 days over a 10-year period, variations of more than 30 days occurred from one year to the next during the same period (Houghton 1959; Tuan *et al.* 1973).

Over much of Southwest, particularly in the low-elevation areas of the Basin and Range province, the growing season is adequate for corn and other crops. The limiting condition for crops in these areas is moisture. In the Southwest's mountains and high-elevation mesas, the growing season is frequently not sufficient for corn, and the annual variabilities in the length of the growing season and the amount of precipitation make agriculture risky.

As noted, the combination of high temperatures and direct solar radiation, most marked in the low-elevation areas of the western and southwestern Basin and Range province, conditions evaporation and evapotranspiration rates. For example, the average evaporation and evapotranspiration rates (combined) at Phoenix, Arizona, are 381 cm, but Phoenix receives an average of only 17.8 cm of precipitation (Comeaux 1981).

The general aridity in the Southwest and the ranges in temperature are important factors affecting the natural vegetation found in the region. The varieties and distribution of natural vegetation are next considered.

Natural Vegetation

A consideration of the plant life found in the Southwest is important for two reasons. First, many of the plants were sources of food and raw materials for the prehistoric population. Second, the natural vegetation provides the habitat for animals that were equally important resources.

Most models of ecosystems describe paths of energy flow, because radiant energy from the sun is the limiting factor for life. In dry climates, however, water is the critical variable, and models that reflect this situation are more useful (Noy-Meir 1973). Vegetation in dry regions must be adapted to moisture that enters the system in the short-duration events (such as a thunderstorm) that occur unpredictably in any one area. In addition, edaphic factors—soil depth, friability, moisture-retention characteristics, and mineral composition, are important.

A number of adaptive mechanisms are found in plants that enable them to withstand arid conditions. Some plants (drought evaders) remain inactive during dry periods and photosynthesize only when moisture becomes available. These include desert annuals that produce seeds that remain viable for long periods of drought and perennial plants that store water and nutrients in bulbs and rhizomes. Drought-persistent plants (xerophytes) maintain some photosynthesis throughout dry periods. Many desert shrubs persist through drought periods by shedding most of their leaves, stems, and rootlets, which reduces their activity and water requirements. Other desert plants maintain nearly constant levels of photosynthesis but have evolved adaptive structures that minimize water loss. For example, some have waxy substances on their leaves that retard transpiration. Others, such as the succulents and cacti, store water internally. Still other plants (phreatophytes) develop specialized root systems and long tap roots that enable them to use ground water. Cottonwood is among them (Comeaux 1981; Hunt 1967; Noy-Meir 1973).

Soil types have a marked effect on vegetation. With respect to soil texture, clayey, silty, and loamy soils retain moisture only near the surface. Where these soils predominate, shallow-rooted plants are common. Sandy, gravelly, and rocky soils allow percolation of water to deeper levels. On these soils, deep-rooted perennial shrubs predominate. Plants also have different tolerances of salts and other minerals that accumulate in desert soils, particularly at playas and along their edges—characteristic features of the Basin and Range country. Salt grass, arrowweed, and pickleweed tolerate considerable salinity and are found in certain zones along the edges of saline playas according to the amount of salt present in the soil (Figure 2.2).

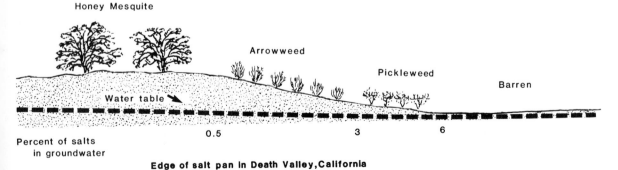

Figure 2.2 Edge of salt pan: plant distribution reflecting salt tolerance. Desert plants such as pickleweed and arrowweed tolerate higher percentages of salt in soil than does mesquite. (Adapted from Charles B. Hunt [1967] by Charles M. Carrillo.)

The direction of exposure is important for the moisture retention of soil and will, therefore, influence vegetation cover. North- and east-facing slopes are generally wetter than south- and west-facing slopes. North slopes may support stands of trees and shrubs, whereas south-facing slopes at the same elevation may support only desert annuals and cacti.

Any areas within the Dry domain that contain fresh water, such as spring-fed ponds, rivers, and streams, will support riparian plant communities, which might consist of cottonwoods, willows, reeds, and ferns.

Overviews of the Southwestern environments usually present vegetation patterns as if they were determined exclusively by latitude and elevation. Although it is certainly true that these broad vegetation zones exist and are a useful shorthand for characterizing plant communities, they do obscure some of the diversity, conditioned by exposure, soil type, and water availability, that are found at any one elevation and latitude. Throughout many parts of the Southwest, several very different plant communities may be found in close juxtaposition. Zonal characterizations also minimize some of the comparability among disparate latitudes and elevations that happen to be conditioned by the same factors.

Plant Provinces

The system of description used here follows Bailey's (1980) delineation of provinces. A province is a contiguous geographic area characterized by a broad vegetation type and a uniform regional climate. The provinces comprising major portions of the Southwest are the American Desert province, the Chihuahuan Desert province, the Mexican Highlands Shrub Steppe province, the Upper Gila Mountains Forest province, the Colorado Plateaus province, the Rocky Mountain Forest province, and the Great Plains Shortgrass Prairie province.

The most extensive section of the American Desert province within the Southwest is the creosote bush–bursage section. Creosote bush covers large areas and is the most widely distributed plant. Cholla (a cactus) is also common. The vegetation on rocky slopes consists of paloverde, agave, sotol, ocotillo, and saguaro, with bitterbrush as a common shrub. Chamiso and creosote occur below 914 m in the Mojave Desert. The Joshua tree predominates along the northwestern edge of the province, with a belt of juniper and piñon along the higher northern edge. Interior basins are generally saline and support stands of the salt-tolerant plants (mesquite, arrowweed, and pickleweed).

The Chihuahuan Desert province consists of short grasses and shrubs, with creosote again covering extensive areas of land. Mesquite dominates in places where soils are deep, and ocotillo, agave, yucca, and sotol occur on slopes. Mountains within the province may, if they are high enough, support a belt of oak and juniper woodland; on some of the highest mountains, piñon grows interspersed with oak. Along water courses, cottonwoods are common.

Between the American Desert province and the Chihuahuan Desert province is a highland area referred to as the Mexican Highlands Shrub Steppe Province. At the lowest elevations, the characteristic plants are desert varieties; for example, saguaro, paloverde, and creosote. Grasses, such as grama, cover the high plains of the province, and open stands of mesquite, yucca, cholla, and other shrubs and cacti are common. A submontane zone of vegetation on the hills and the lower slopes of the mountains is represented by several species of oak and a few juniper. On the higher mountains, pines may occur along with oak and, in the sheltered upper slopes of the highest mountains, Douglas fir and white fir are found in limited numbers.

The Upper Gila Mountains Forest province comprises more than 93,000 km² in Arizona and New Mexico. Within the province, vegetation is primarily zoned by elevation. Below 2100 m, mixed grasses, chaparral brush, oak–juniper, and piñon–juniper woodlands occur. From about 2100 to about 2400 m, the vegetation is an open forest of ponderosa pine, with piñon and juniper on the south-facing slopes. On the dry rocky ground above about 2400 m, Douglas fir and aspen occur with limber pine.

The Colorado Plateaus province consists of great areas of bare rock. At low elevations, arid grasslands are extensive, though not dense. Sagebrush is common in locations with fairly deep soils. The most extensive vegetation zone in the province, the piñon–juniper woodland, is generally quite open, with grama and other grasses, herbs, and shrubs occuring among the trees. Above the piñon–juniper woodland, there is a montane zone. In the southern part of this zone, ponderosa pine is dominant and may be associated with Douglas fir, although the latter generally occurs in more sheltered sites or at higher elevations. In the northern part of the province, lodgepole pine and aspen are the dominant trees of the montane zone, and at the highest elevations, Engelmann spruce and subalpine fir are characteristic. In the San Francisco Mountains (Arizona), bristlecone pine is associated with spruce. San Francisco Peak is the only mountain in Arizona that contains alpine meadowlands; however, a few more northern mountains in the province have small areas of alpine meadows above timberline.

The Rocky Mountain Forest province is distinctive for its well-marked altitudinal zones. The woodland zone adjacent to the Colorado Plateaus has extensive areas of piñon and juniper, which often alternate with ponderosa pine depending on the direction of the exposure. Rocky slopes may host dense stands of mountain mahogany and scrub oak; sagebrush and grasses cover large areas and may extend to the ponderosa pine and Douglas fir forest. Above this forest, a zone of subalpine vegetation is dominated by Engelmann spruce and subalpine fir and is succeeded finally at even higher elevations by the areas of treeless alpine meadows.

Only a small portion of the Great Plains Shortgrass Prairie province occurs within the Southwest. The characteristic grasses (grama and buffalo grass) are a ground cover for sunflower and locoweed, the typical plants. Scattered piñon and juniper occur over some of the area, particularly on slopes near the foothills of the southern Rockies. Riparian plants are found along the limited watercourses.

A comparison of the plants characterizing each of the provinces indicates that many are found throughout the Southwest, although they may be more abundant in one province than another. Widespread distributions of understory plants associated with the woodlands and forests are also characteristic; for example, the virtually ubiquitous cholla, bunchgrass, and chenopodium (goosefoot). The density of the understory plants and their particular configurations vary with elevation, direction of exposure, and soil condition.

Economic Uses of Plants

A great many plants of the Southwest have edible parts and were used as sources of food by both prehistoric and contemporary peoples. Some of the more important are mentioned here. (The interested reader is referred to Castetter 1935; Harrington 1967; Knight 1978.)

Agave was an important food source throughout the low desert areas. The leaves and the centers (crowns) of the plant are roasted and may be stored. Sotol hearts were used in a similar way. The young stems and hearts of saltbush and yucca were eaten, as was yucca fruit, which could also be boiled and stored. Cactus fruits from the prickly pear, cholla, hedgehog cactus, and saguaro were made into a variety of foods. In addition, cholla joints were roasted and stored. The bulbs of wild onion were eaten, and wild potato tubers were eaten fresh or stored and later made into a gruel. The fruits and pods of various plants were eaten alone or mixed with other foods. Among the more important were evening primrose, mesquite, hackberry, serviceberry, and juniper berry. In addition, the inner bark of juniper was sometimes chewed as an emergency food. The seeds and nuts of wild plants were often ground with cornmeal or parched, stored, and eaten or ground into meal alone. The more important seeds and nuts came from saguaro, goosefoot, lamb's-quarter, Rocky Mountain bee plant, bunchgrass, Indian ricegrass, sunflowers, paloverde, oak, and piñon. In addition, many varieties of plants were used as greens and, importantly, as medicinal herbs.

Other economic uses of plants included timbers from piñon and Douglas fir, fibers for baskets and sandals from yucca, paint pigments made from Rocky Mountain bee plant, roofing thatch made from riparian grasses and reeds, and firewood from the woody portions of shrubs and from woodland and forest trees. In general, Southwestern peoples possessed an intimate knowledge of the vegetable resources available in their environments, exploiting most of them for food, medicinal purposes, clothing, shelter, or fuel.

In conclusion, the characteristics of vegetation distributions in dry regions should be reemphasized. First, as noted, many species either are dormant entirely (the drought evaders) or limit the production of seeds (xerophytes and phreatophytes) until moisture conditions are adequate for successful reproduction. The most nutritious parts of plants, and the parts most often used for food, for example, the reproductive parts (fruits, seeds, and nuts), are often not available. Also, because the weather conditions that trigger plant reproduction are erratic, the ability to predict—on a long-term basis—when and where plant foods will be available is very low. For example, although piñon nuts are a highly nutritious source of food and piñon trees are widely distributed throughout the Southwest, the reliability of piñon nut crops in any one area from year to year is very low. Second, due to the fact that the distributions of plants are controlled by microenvironmental factors such as soil depth, soil salinity, direction of exposure, and soil composition, very large stands of a single plant type in one area are rare; thus, it is often difficult to gather sufficient quantities of wild plant food without moving over great distances. Both of these factors—unpredictability and small areas of pure stands—also affect the mobility of game animals. Finally, compared to other parts of North America, the overall productivity of the Southwestern environment is relatively low. The average annual net aboveground productivity in arid regions varies between 30 and 200 g/m^2. For semiarid zones, net aboveground productivity ranges between about 100 and 600 g/m^2 (Noy-Meir 1973). For human populations, dependent on plant resources, the Southwest is a high-risk environment.

Fauna

Animals not only require food and water for survival, they must maintain their body temperatures within tolerable limits. In dry climates, animals generally display considerable flexibility in behavioral patterns, which, combined with their mobility, allows them to use the temporally and spatially heterogeneous resources available. In part due to the nature of the dry-climate vegetation, most dry-land herbivores are indiscriminate feeders, subsisting on a variety of less desirable foods as preferred foods disappear (Noy-Meir 1974). This dietary flexibility allows them to colonize a wide variety of vegetation zones. It therefore is not surprising that the larger herbivores, which are particularly important game animals for humans, may be found in virtually all parts of the Southwest. For example, although mule deer are most abundant in the ponderosa pine forests, they are ubiquitous throughout the Southwest and may be encountered regularly among the paloverde and cactus shrubland of the American Desert province, the piñon–juniper woodlands and slick rock areas of the Colorado Plateaus, and the grassland communities characteristic of the lower elevations of the Southern Rocky Mountains. There are two generalizations about the differential distributions of animals within the Southwest that are useful to consider. First, there is generally more diversity in large body-size animals in the mountain and plateau areas and more diversity in small body-size animals in the lower desert areas. Second, the differences in the distributions of animals may relate more to their specific behavioral responses to predators than to their food requirements.

The three most common Southwestern game animals—with very extensive distributions—are mule deer, pronghorn antelope, and Rocky Mountain bighorn sheep. As noted, mule deer occur throughout the environments of the Southwest. They are not selective browsers, but prefer oak, piñon, juniper, Douglas fir, ponderosa pine, and the understory plants associated with these trees. They are usually found most abundantly in broken country and along the borders of dense forest areas, and less frequently in more open settings. Pronghorn antelope occur at a variety of elevations from Colorado to Mexico and from the Shortgrass Prairie to the American Desert. Despite the variety of elevations they inhabit, they prefer open plains and open valleys and avoid rough terrain. This preference relates primarily to their defensive strategy of outrunning predators. Rocky Mountain bighorn sheep, in contrast, require steep, rocky terrain for protection, and it is the terrain rather than the elevation that is critical. Bighorn sheep are relatively rare today (except where herds have been reintroduced into areas and are protected); however, their distribution in the archaeological record suggests that they occurred virtually throughout the Southwest.

Four fairly large game animals are important but have more restricted distributions in the Southwest. White-tailed deer occur in the Chihuahuan Desert, although their numbers there are not as great as those of the mule deer. Elk are today of local importance only in the Colorado Plateaus, the Southern Rocky Mountains, and the Upper Gila Mountains, although they may have had more extensive ranges in the past. Bison were, of course, very abundant on the shortgrass plains. In the very remote past (see Chapter 4), their range extended west into south-central Arizona. Bison require extensive grasslands and their distribution in the historic period was coincident with these; consequently, they were found only on the easternmost margins of the Southwest. Finally, collared peccary, occurring primarily in the desert areas of the southern Southwest, are fairly common in the paloverde communities of the southern portions of the Chihuahuan Desert province, although its range may extend farther north.

Large predators are generally not important sources of food because, although they are of large body size, they usually hunt singly or at night, which increases the difficulty involved in searching for and pursuing them. Nevertheless, large predators are more numerous, and more diverse, in the highlands and mountains that also support the more abundant herbivore populations: mountain lions and bobcats occur in the Southern Rockies and the Upper Gila Mountains, and black bears are found primarily in the Southern Rockies. The smaller carnivores are more numerous and more widely distributed throughout the Southwest: The coyote is found everywhere in the region and foxes are widely distributed.

Smaller animals generally account for the bulk of the remains found in archaeological contexts. Jackrabbits and cottontail rabbits proliferate throughout the Southwest and are frequently the major components of archaeological faunal assemblages. The ranges of these two animals are not mutually exclusive: jackrabbits prefer open terrain that allows them to escape predators by outdistancing them, whereas cottontails prefer dense vegetation in which they escape predators through concealment. In addition to rabbits, small animals such as pocket gophers, prairie dogs, kangaroo rats, woodrats, squirrels, and voles are abundant in the Southwest and are frequently encountered in archaeological sites. Some of these animals burrow into abandoned rooms and trash, but most were probably at least occasional sources of food. Within the Southwest, the low desert areas generally have the fewest large- and medium-size animals. In the American Desert province, there are few large mammals, but kangaroo rats, pocket mice, and ground squirrels are common, and there is considerable variety in reptiles such as snakes and lizards. These small animals did constitute important sources of food in the prehistoric and historic periods. Finally, along water courses, animals such as muskrats and beavers are locally important.

Various birds are important to contemporary and prehistoric peoples of the Southwest. The feathers of certain species of birds are required for various items of religious paraphernalia, such as dance costumes, prayer plumes, and kachina representations. Among the more important birds are various species of hawks, owls, and eagles. Bones of these birds occur in archaeological contexts, as do those of a variety of waterfowl and turkeys. Throughout the arid Southwest, the rivers and ponds continue to be the important habitat areas for migratory waterfowl that they were in the past. In addition, it has been suggested that prehistoric agricultural practices, such as the diversion of floodwater from streams to fields, may have created larger areas of wet habitat for these birds (Emslie 1981). Turkeys were domesticated prehistorically by some groups in the Southwest and were probably used for their feathers as well as for meat. The only other prehistoric domestic animal is the dog.

In sum, the arid and semiarid conditions of the Southwest encourage generalized animal feeding strategies. For this reason, most of the fauna are able to colonize and adapt to diverse habitats. The contemporary distribution of game animals and the archaeological record both reflect considerable homogeneity in fauna represented. Mule deer, pronghorn antelope, jackrabbits, and cottontails are the most characteristic Southwestern animals. Locally, other animals are important. In the southern desert areas, reptiles and small rodents are more abundant. In the mountains and the high plateau country, elk, mountain lions, and bears predominate. The archaeological record indicates that throughout the Southwest a diversity of animals were hunted, including birds. Largely because agriculture is a risky strategy in much of the region, gathering and hunting were always of economic importance. As noted, gathering would not consistently provide secure sources of food in sufficient quantity to feed very many people. Hunting may have been similarly risky as an economic base. In the very early periods of Southwestern prehistory, when human population density was low and groups were highly mobile, hunting and gathering were sufficient for subsistence. Later, with higher population densities, agriculture became critical, although gathering and hunting retained important subsistence roles.

Some of the practices necessary for agriculture may have had adverse effects on some game animals. For example, clearing woodlands and forests for agricultural fields and for firewood may have reduced the amount of habitat preferred by deer. Other agricultural practices, such as irrigation, would have expanded the habitats of some animals, particularly several species of birds. The diverse effects of agricultural production are discussed in Chapter 6. Here it is important to note that the general aridity of the Southwest and the erratic patterns of rainfall limit the natural productivity of the entire region. Even relatively minor changes in climate may have rather marked effects on the landscape and concomitantly on the flora and fauna. Southwestern climates have not been stable throughout either the historic or prehistoric periods. As noted, many interpretations of change in the archaeological record are attributed to environmental fluctuation. In order to evaluate these interpretations, it is necessary to understand how paleoenvironmental reconstructions are derived. This is the topic of the following section.

Paleoenvironmental Reconstruction

The intent of the following paragraphs is not to describe a series of past climatic events. Rather, it is to present the kinds of data used to infer past environments, the information that each data source provides, and particular problems associated with specific data sources. In part because past variations in climate and environmental shifts have so often been invoked as causal factors in culture change observed in the Southwest, methods of paleoenvironmental reconstruction are well developed in the area, and refinements are continuously being made. All the techniques of paleoenvironmental reconstruction ultimately depend on the principle of uniformitarianism developed by geologists of the eighteenth century. This principle states that the geological record is the result of processes that continue and may be observed today. It is for this reason that understanding the contemporary environment is crucial to reconstructions of the past.

In the Southwest there are five sources of paleoenvironmental data that are widely used by archaeologists: geomorphological, palynological, dendroclimatological, macrobotanical, and faunal studies. Each of these provides data appropriate at slightly different levels of precision and each has inherent weaknesses and strengths. Ideally, generalized schemes should include information from many sources, and attempts along these lines are the most promising (e.g., Euler *et al.* 1979; Wendorf and Hester 1975). The sources of data are discussed separately here in order to contrast their unique features.

Geomorphology

Geomorphological studies in the Southwest have been concerned primarily with documenting past episodes of arroyo cutting and filling. In the latter part of the 1800s and in the early 1900s, there was great concern among Southwestern farmers and ranchers, geologists, and government agricultural personnel, because considerable erosion was occurring, arroyos were cutting deep channels, groundwater levels were falling, and vegetation along arroyos was dying. Many people attributed these phenomena to overgrazing. In a series of articles, geologist Kirk Bryan (1925, 1929, 1941) discussed the erosional effects of vegetation changes on Southwestern landscapes. Bryan demonstrated that the soil profiles in modern arroyos revealed fossil arroyos that had been cut during erosional cycles of the past and were separated from the modern arroyo by observable disconformities that indicated periods of alluviation during which the arroyos had been filled. It was important to the arguments of the time that some of the fossil arroyos contained the bones of extinct fauna and others were associated with prehistoric pottery. These observations supported Bryan's belief that episodes of erosion and arroyo cutting could be attributed to climatic change in addition to overgrazing, because there were no domestic livestock in the prehistoric period.

The relations among arroyo cutting and filling and climatic change are not straightforward and continue to be debated (e.g., Cooke and Reeves 1976; Hall 1977; Love 1980). According to Bryan (1941) and others, erosion would occur during dry periods when vegetation is reduced and runoff is not slowed or spread by plant roots. Arroyo cutting would take place because during a dry period, although rains would be infrequent, the intensity of individual storms would not be diminished. Conversely, a wet period would encourage vegetation and periods of alluvial deposition or channel filling.

Since Bryan's work, a number of investigators (e.g., Hall 1977; Love 1980; Martin

1963) have argued that arroyo cutting is more commonly associated with periods of increased precipitation, which increases runoff and the amount and velocity of water carried in arroyos. Martin's model of the effects of precipitation on arroyo cutting is actually more complex and is based on data from hydrological studies and pollen analysis. Martin argues that a change in the seasonal distribution of rainfall is the relevant factor. In essence, Martin correlates an increase in summer rainfall with arroyo cutting and the prevalence of pollen of plants that thrive in disturbed ground. He suggests that episodes of arroyo filling correlate with winter-dominant precipitation and plant pollen from species that require high levels of ground water. Historic data and current observations, which include modern meteorological data, will eventually resolve these issues. At present, it appears that several factors are instrumental to arroyo formation, including drainage-basin size and morphology, the type and density of vegetation within the drainage system, and the characteristic intensity of rainfall events.

The precision with which past episodes of arroyo cutting and filling may be dated varies considerably, depending on local conditions. In some cases, resolution is only on the order of hundreds or thousands of years. For example, an episode of arroyo cutting may be associated with the bones of Pleistocene fauna or with a Pleistocene soil horizon. In such cases, the formation of the arroyo could probably not be dated with accuracy beyond a bracketing interval of a few thousand years. Under unusual conditions, dating may be much more precise. For example, at Black Mesa, Arizona, a number of "fossil forests" (Figure 2.3), where trees were buried in alluvium, have been exposed by recent erosion (Euler *et al.* 1979). In these instances it is possible to obtain tree-ring dates for the germination and death of the trees within an accuracy of 25 years, allowing very precise dating of the alluvial deposits by correlation with the tree-ring dates. In many cases, ancient arroyos in the Southwest are dated by reference to archaeological materials (primarily ceramics) found within them. The accuracy and precision of these dates depend on how well the archaeological materials have been dated in other contexts and on an understanding of how they were introduced into the geological record. For example, an arroyo forming in A.D. 1500 may cut through an archaeological site that was occupied between A.D. 900 and 950. Ceramics from the site that were found in the arroyo would not date its formation but would provide the earliest time after which it could have developed.

Beginning with Bryan's work and continuing to later studies, attempts have been made to correlate episodes of arroyo cutting and aggrading across the entire Southwest or large areas of it (Bryan 1925; Euler *et al.* 1979). The reasoning here is that if changes in arroyo patterns are associated with climatic change (as they appear to be), they should reflect global climatic shifts. As noted earlier, changes in the cyclonic storm pattern, influenced by the jet stream, would affect large portions of the Southwest, though the implications are different for the eastern and western zones. On the other hand, changes that are the result of convectional storms are expected to have only local effects. This situation may introduce considerable complexity; for example, one study (Love 1980) of sedimentation in Chaco Canyon showed that parts of Chaco Wash were being cut at the same time that other parts of the wash were being

Figure 2.3 Tree buried in alluvium at Black Mesa, Arizona. The alluvial deposits can be dated by determinng the germination and death dates of the tree through the tree rings. (Photograph courtesy of George J. Gumerman.)

alluviated, because streams emptying into Chaco Wash originate in areas with different rainfall regimes.

In general, it is clear that past episodes of arroyo cutting and filling must be related to climatic change, at least in part. The formation of deeply entrenched arroyos and the headward expansion of arroyos would have had considerable impact on the land available for prehistoric farming and the kinds of farming strategies that would have been effective. Careful dating of episodes of arroyo cutting provide considerable insight into local archaeological sequences. The better local patterns are understood, documented, and precisely dated (if possible), the clearer the regional interpretations should become.

On a rather different scale, a temporally broader one, geomorphological studies of a different nature are important to paleoenvironmental reconstructions. Studies of the geological deposits within which the sites of the earliest inhabitants of the Southwest (the Paleo-Indians, see Chapter 4) are found are keys to understanding the environmental contexts of the late Pleistocene. These studies are primarily concerned with describing the kinds of sediments at Paleo-Indian sites and, based on the principle of uniformitarianism, inferring the processes responsible for their deposition. For example, at Blackwater Draw (discussed in Chapter 4), the occurrence of artifacts within a layer of mudstone indicated that the implements had been deposited when there was a pond present. The presence of water-worn gravels and sands is an indication of the earlier existence of a stream where none may be present today. The different kinds of sediments deposited in one locality are good indexes of climatic change. Thus, a transition from water-abraded gravels to mudstones to wind-deposited sand would indicate a change from stream to pond to an absence of water at the site. The precision with which such sediments can be dated varies, but it is generally not great. Frequently the deposits are dated on the basis of correlations with artifactual or faunal remains, using the latter as index fossils. If faunal remains are present, these may be dated directly through the application of radiocarbon dating. Although early in the history of the investigation of late Pleistocene archaeological sites in the Southwest it was common to describe climatic changes in broad, regional terms and to infer synchroneity in change, later studies are more conservative. Again, it is important to develop an understanding of changing environmental conditions within rather limited areas and to date these as precisely as possible before generalizing.

Palynology

Palynology is the branch of science concerned with the study of fossil pollen, referred to as microbotanical remains. Plants produce pollen, some of which is buried and preserved. Pollen can be extracted from soil samples through a combination of chemical and mechanical procedures. Once extracted, individual pollen grains are visible under the microscope; because pollen of different genera and sometimes different species of plants have different morphological characteristics, it is possible to identify the plants represented in the sample. By knowing the climatic and edaphic tolerances of the plants in the pollen recovered, the environmental conditions prevailing when the pollen was deposited can be reconstructed. The pollen grains themselves cannot be dated directly, and dates are assigned on the basis of geomorphological studies, radiocarbon dates from associated materials, or dates obtained from archaeological sites. Palynology has had a long history in Europe. In the Southwest, palynological research was stimulated largely by the work of Paul S. Martin (1963) and his students (e.g., Bohrer 1962, 1970; Hevly 1964; Schoenwetter 1966).

Pollen, by reflecting vegetative communities of the past, should be a sensitive indicator of climatic change; however, there are problems in interpreting pollen profiles that cannot be ignored. For example, there is always a discrepancy between the present plant cover and the surface pollen rain; that is, the relative frequencies of pollen types found on the surface of the ground do not mirror the frequencies of the plants growing in the vicinity. One reason is that some species, such as piñon, are overproducers of pollen, whereas other species, such as gourds and cacti, produce relatively little pollen. In addition, some pollen is particularly light and can be wind-transported over considerable distances. For example, pollen samples from the surface at Mesa Verde contain small amounts of spruce pollen, although the nearest spruce trees are about 80.5 km away (Martin and Byers 1965:125). There seem also to be some soil conditions that differentially preserve pollen. For example, pine pollen is more abundant in fine-grained than in coarse-grained sediments (Euler *et al.* 1979). These conditions make it difficult to infer the past vegetative communities directly from the pollen frequencies represented; but because these sources of variation are known, they can be tested for systematic biases.

It is far more difficult to make climatic inferences from pollen that is recovered from archaeological sites, although the relative precision with which these pollen samples can be dated makes them desirable. For example, a study that compared the pollen frequencies from room floors with those from room features (such as hearths) at the same site in Chaco Canyon (Cully 1979) demonstrated completely different pollen profiles. The same study found different pollen frequencies among pollen samples recovered from various portions of the floor of the same room. Clearly, some of the differential pollen distribution is the result of human activity—from plant processing or by inadvertent introduction (it might cling to clothing and be taken from place to place). Some differential distribution undoubtedly also occurs, because some parts of a room, farther from doorways than others, do not trap wind-blown pollen. Few archaeological samples collected in the past that have been used in paleoenvironmental reconstructions were designed to minimize the effects of this sort of variation.

Changes in pollen frequencies may also be difficult to interpret. For example, one significant change in the pollen at Mesa Verde (Martin and Byers 1965:122) was an increase in tree pollen following the prehistoric abandonment of the mesa. Such a rise in tree pollen frequency could be interpreted as indicating either increased precipitation or a regeneration of the natural forest allowed by the discontinuation of land clearing and firewood cutting. In another example, modern pollen samples from stock tanks near Cienega Creek, Arizona (Martin 1963), showed that local aggrading of the creek floodplain, which provides increased suitable habitat for grasses that will then deposit proportionately more pollen, will locally mask the tree pollen blown in from higher elevations. An increase in grass pollen in relation to tree pollen is often cited as an indicator of general drying conditions. But in this case, a local development produced the same pollen profile as that produced by widespread climatic change. Similarly, increases in the percentages of plants that invade and thrive in disturbed ground and fine alkaline soils (such as goosefoot and pigweed) are difficult to interpret. Higher percentages of these plants may reflect climatic desiccation and lowering of the water table, but they may also be the result of human disturbance of the ground surface through agricultural activity or house construction.

In part because of these difficulties in interpretation, some studies of pollen that attempt to measure climatic change (rather than cultural activity) use the pollen ratios of pine to juniper or of piñon to ponderosa pine because these seem quite consistently to identify the plant community types that reflect climate (Euler *et al.* 1979). Although this approach seems promising, it should be noted that extensive prehistoric reduction in woodland cover by humans for firewood has been documented (Betan-court and Van Devender 1981) and might be expected to affect these ratios. Palynology, used in conjunction with other methods of paleoenvironmental reconstruction, is certainly an important research tool. As is the case with geomorphological studies, ongoing research will undoubtedly clarify the mechanisms responsible for changes in pollen spectra and enable a higher degree of confidence in interpretation.

Dendroclimatology

In many ways, dendroclimatology, or the study of past climate through tree rings, is the best-developed and most precise source of paleoclimatological information available in the Southwest. The astronomer Andrew E. Douglass, who established the Laboratory of Tree-Ring Research at the University of Arizona, is generally considered to be the founder of the science of dendrochronology (tree-ring dating), of which dendroclimatology is a subfield. Douglass was not the first to discover that trees could be cross-dated (Dean, in Fritts 1976); however, his work established the scientific discipline. Douglass's primary interest was sunspot activity and the influence it might have on weather patterns. Initially working at Lowell Astronomical Observatory in Flagstaff, he noted that the variations in tree-ring width in tree stumps in the area showed patterned regularity. Although he knew that ring width in trees of the eastern U.S. forests was conditioned by shading and competition for nutrients, he reasoned that the differences in ring width in Southwestern trees might reflect variation in available moisture, because moisture is the limiting condition for plant growth in arid areas. The tree rings themselves might then allow him to reconstruct past climatic conditions, which could be tied to cycles of sunspot activity (Fritts 1976).

Some trees produce annual, observable, cortical rings as the result of a growth spurt in early spring that terminates in late summer or fall. The cell structure produced at the beginning of the growth season is different from that at the end, so a sharp boundary generally separates yearly rings. Starting with living trees (from which a small core may be taken) or newly cut trees, it is possible to count back from the present and observe the variation in width of rings produced each year (Figure 2.4). Thus, one of the primary advantages of dendroclimatology for the archaeologist, as well as for the astronomer, is that precise dating to a specific year is possible. The correlation of a single ring with one year is not always possible, however. If there are limiting factors at the beginning of the growing season, no ring may be formed that year; if stress occurs within one growing season, two rings may be formed. For these reasons, it is necessary to examine and cross-date many specimens. It is also essential to examine trees that are growing under climatically stressed conditions. Trees thriving in locations where there is abundant water (for example, along a stream or where the water table is high) will not manifest variations in ring width that can be attributed to climatic change. In the Southwest, deciduous trees (e.g., cottonwood) that normally grow in riparian settings cannot be used for paleoclimatic reconstructions. Fortunately, trees that were often used in prehistoric building, such as piñon and Douglas fir, are appropriate for extrapolating past climates.

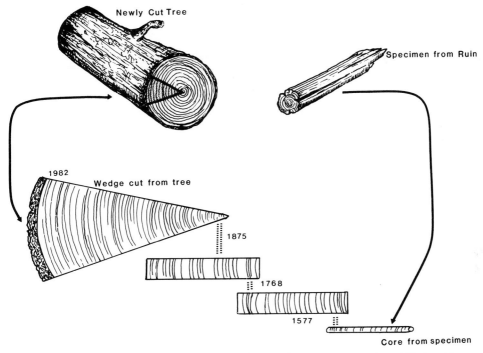

Figure 2.4   Dendrochronological reconstruction. The annual variation in tree-ring width in arid areas allows for chronological and paleoenvironmental reconstruction. (Illustrated by Charles M. Carrillo.)

The width of any tree ring depends on factors other than climate: age of the tree, height within the stem, species, and other factors. Dendroclimatologists correct for these factors by estimating their effects on ring growth and removing these from the measurements. This procedure is referred to as *standardization,* and the resulting values are *ring-width indexes*. "The standardized indices of individual trees are averaged to obtain the mean chronology . . . for a sampled site" (Fritts 1976:25). Generally, deviations from mean ring width are not plotted for every year, because ring growth is, in part, conditioned by moisture conditions over the preceding 3 years (Fritts *et al.* 1965:120; Schulman 1956:40). Usually, 5- or 10-year means are plotted as standard deviants from the mean chronology (Figure 2.5). It is important to remember that a tree-ring index chronology is derived from trees growing within the same area and therefore is influenced by the climate of that area. Each master chronology has a unique variance and cannot be directly compared to other master chronologies (Euler *et al.* 1979): The master chronology from Mesa Verde, which was derived from Mesa Verde trees, cannot be directly compared to the master chronology from Hay Hollow Valley or to any other.

As Fritts (1976) emphasizes, dendroclimatological reconstructions are based on models or hypotheses of the influence of various climatic factors (moisture, temperatures, soil conditions, etc.) on the development of tree rings. Fortunately, the

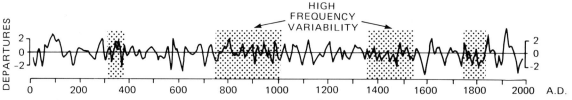

Figure 2.5 Tree-ring chart: deviation from mean ring width. Dendroclimatologists usually plot 5- or 10-year average deviation from mean ring widths to construct charts such as this composite chart of 10-year averages from the Colorado Plateaus. (Adapted from Jeffrey S. Dean [1983].)

systematic maintenance of modern meteorological records in many parts of the Southwest facilitates continual evaluation of the models and has led to exciting refinements in dendroclimatological reconstruction. Advances include the application of multivariate statistical analyses to dendroclimatological problems, which has, for the first time, enabled quantitative rather than simply qualitative paleoclimatic reconstruction. In essence, monthly records of temperature, atmospheric pressure, and precipitation of a number of locations in the Southwest have been kept for at least 50 years. These records have been compared to the growth patterns of trees in the vicinity of the recording stations. In addition, the physiological responses of trees grown under measured and partly controlled laboratory conditions have been recorded. These data have enabled the development of a new and complex model of the relation between the environment and tree growth.

Two developments are particularly interesting. First, although precipitation and temperature over the year prior to the growing season and of the growing season itself are the primary factors influencing ring development in stressed conifers, there are other relations that differ from species to species and from one setting to another.

> In effect, each species responds to conditions of different parts of the year preceding the growing season and therefore records in its growth rings climatic information slightly different from that recorded by each of the other species. Thus, in addition to the annual climatic information contained in tree-ring sequences, inter-annual (seasonal) variability in climate is preserved as well. (Rose *et al.* 1981:4)

Second, using the new models of tree growth, it is possible to extract information about environmental conditions other than temperature and precipitation. For example, one can estimate past surface runoff or atmospheric pressure anomalies (Rose *et al.* 1981). It should be noted that to apply modern meteorological data to living and archaeological tree specimens it must be demonstrated that the trees are of the same statistical population. This may be difficult in some cases, particularly those in which archaeological wood is recovered from areas where no trees (or very few trees) are currently growing—a common situation.

Certainly, paleoclimatological data from tree-ring studies are the most temporally precise and generally accurate information currently available. There are, however, some limitations that must be considered. Tree rings are better indicators of situations of low rainfall than of conditions of high rainfall, due to the fact that when trees are not under the stress of low precipitation, ring width varies with other environmental conditions such as soil nutrients. Also, no ring will be produced under the very severe or harsh conditions that may occur at the beginning of the growing season; therefore, it is difficult to extrapolate the actual extent of climatic deprivation for very bad years. Finally, tree-ring reconstructions emphasize short-term fluctuations and suppress low-frequency, long-term variations as a result of the standarization procedures that are used to compile the indexes from several individual trees. Most other sources of archaeological paleoenvironmental information are sensitive to long-term rather than short-term fluctuations, so it is sometimes difficult to correlate dendroclimatological data with these other studies. Finally, accurate dendroclimatological data are available for only the past 2000 years (Dean 1983; Euler *et al.* 1979), so they are not appropriate for the entire range of time that people have been in the Southwest. Tree-ring reconstructions are not of sufficient temporal depth to be used for the Paleo-Indian or Archaic portions (before A.D. 1) of the archaeological record.

Southwestern paleoclimatologists distinguish two kinds of environmental processes. Low frequency processes (LFP) are those with periodicities longer than a human generation (25 years). LFP underlie episodes of arroyo cutting and deposition and raising and lowering water tables. High frequency processes (HFP) are responsible for annual variations in climate. Variation in rainfall and growing season reflect HFP (Dean 1983). Although some HFP do interact with local topographic features to initiate LFP, the relations among processes are so complex that identical conditions rarely occur. Further, the different temporal natures of the processes are such that most human adaptive strategies are geared toward coping with HFP rather than LFP.

Tree-rings are the most precise indicators of HFP and can yield information about two kinds of variability. First, tree-rings indicate the amplitudes of departures or the relative amounts of precipitation. The amplitude can be seen as the distance above or below the mean plotted on tree-ring charts (Figure 2.5). Second, tree-rings provide frequency information observable in the number of oscillations from high to low values within temporal periods. Figure 2.5 is a composite chart of tree-ring values from the Colorado Plateaus, plotted at 10-year intervals. The periods A.D. 310–380, 750–1000, 1350–1560, and 1730–1800 are intervals during which there were relatively rapid oscillations from high to low values. The intervening periods were times when the prevailing patterns persisted for longer periods of time (Dean 1983). It is likely that many human strategies that were appropriate responses to conditions of low frequency changes in rainfall would not be successful under situations of high frequency changes in rainfall pattern.

Macrobotanical Studies

Studies of macrobotanical remains (seeds and plant parts) provide another source of paleoenvironmental information. The recovery of plant remains from archaeological sites in the Southwest has a long history. The remains of corn and other cultigens were often recovered in order to provide information on the history of plant domestication (see Chapter 5). In order to recover smaller plant material, one of various water-flotation techniques is generally used (Watson 1976). Water flotation depends on the principle that particles of plants, particularly if they are carbonized, are lighter than soil particles and less dense than water; consequently, when the soil matrix is submerged in water, organic materials float and can be trapped in fine mesh, sorted, and identified under 10- or 20-power magnification. This technique was reportedly used by Volney Jones in 1936 to recover plant remains from adobe bricks of the Franciscan mission at the Hopi pueblo of Awatovi, and by Hugh Cutler in the 1950s to recover charred seeds from the screened dirt from Higgens Flat Pueblo, a Mogollon site near Reserve, New Mexico (Cutler, in Watson 1976:79). Despite these early efforts, flotation was not used consistently in the Southwest until the mid-1960s (Struever 1979). Generally, macrobotanical information is relevant to interpretations of prehistoric subsistence and economic practices rather than to paleoenvironmental studies. This is because seeds and other small plant fragments that are introduced into archaeological sites by their original inhabitants may have been obtained at varying distances from the site, either directly or through exchange. These remains are therefore not necessarily informative about the vegetative composition of the environment in the immediate vicinity of a site. But one type of macrobotanical study, that of fossil packrat middens, is used for paleoenvironmental reconstruction.

Packrats gather plant materials within a restricted area of about 30–100 m from their dens. They are apparently not selective, and the plants they gather provide a representative sample of plants in the immediate vicinity (Betancourt and Van Devender 1981; Van Devender and Spaulding 1979). "In protected perch areas, crystalization of packrat urine through desiccation cements waste debris containing plant fragments, animal bones, fecal pellets, dust, and pollen" (Betancourt and Van Devender 1981:656). In the laboratory, this material is segregated in water, screened, dried, and identified by standard techniques. Only a few studies of fossil packrat middens are available for the Southwest (Betancourt and Van Devender 1981; Van Devender et al. 1978; Van Devender and Spaulding 1979). There are important advantages of these studies, for, unlike pollen, which can be transported over great distances by wind, the limited foraging radius of packrats ensures that the vegetation in their middens is local. Also, a portion of the entire midden can be dated by radiocarbon, so it is possible to date accurately the vegetation sample it contains. Finally, packrat middens are preserved remarkably well in rockshelters and other sheltered locations in the Southwest, and the time span for which they are relevant is longer than that for dendroclimatological studies. For example, two packrat middens from Chaco Canyon, dated to an age of 8600 to 7400 B.C., contained material indicating that Douglas fir, Rocky Mountain juniper, and limber pine were dominant plants in the area at that time. Middens from the same area, dated to between 3550 and 2480 B.C., show that the vegetation pattern had shifted to one in which piñon–juniper woodland was characteristic (Betancourt and Van Devender 1981).

As yet, the use of macrobotanical remains from fossil packrat middens is such a new technique that evaluative studies and comparisons with other techniques of paleoenvironmental reconstruction have not been made. On the basis of available studies, the technique seems promising.

Faunal Studies

The identification of faunal remains from archaeological contexts is sometimes used in paleoenvironmental reconstruction, especially when species are found outside their present ranges or habitat areas. Particularly with respect to the larger animal species, the paleoenvironmental inferences are not always convincing. As noted earlier, most of the medium and large body-size animals of arid and semiarid areas are not choosy feeders, and finding them outside areas in which their preferred food occurs may mean relatively little. Also, when these animals are found in archaeological sites, it cannot be inferred that they were living in the immediate vicinity. During the historic period, Southwestern peoples traveled considerable distances on hunting expeditions, and their ancestors probably did as well. For example, hunting parties from the New Mexico pueblo of Laguna are reported to have traveled up to 258 km from their village on hunting expeditions (Cordell 1979; Ellis 1974a,b). Also, in the historic period, game was frequently obtained through trade.

The recovery of very small animals, including invertebrate fauna, from archaeological contexts in which they may or may not be intrusive can provide valuable paleoenvironmental information. Some species of small rodents seem to have rather narrow environmental tolerances, and this can be informative. In one study, the remains of two species of mice (*Microtus mexicanus* and *Peromyscus leucopus*) were recovered from archaeological sites in a part of the Jemez Mountains of New Mexico which is too dry today for these animals. On this basis, it has been suggested (Holbrook 1975; Holbrook and Mackey 1976) that the climate in the vicinity of the sites was wetter in about A.D. 1200, when the sites were occupied. However, the mice may well have entered the sites after the prehistoric abandonment of the sites.

Small rodents and invertebrate fauna are useful in paleoclimatic reconstructions of quite remote time periods. Masked shrews and meadow voles that were recovered, from deposits dating to between 9500 and 9200 B.C. on the southern plains of New Mexico indicate that considerably cooler summers characterized the area at that time (Wendorf and Hester 1975; also see Chapter 4). A variety of snails retrieved from the same area supports the interpretation of relatively cooler summers, and some species indicate the presence of more moisture at that time as well (Wendorf 1961).

In sum, geomorphological, palynological, dendroclimatological, macrobotanical, and faunal studies are all used in paleoenvironmental reconstructions in the Southwest. These techniques are frequently complementary in the data they provide, but they differ in the time periods for which they are useful, the chronological precision they afford, the accuracy with which they can be used to retrodict climate and past vegetation patterns, and the interpretive issues they raise.

Discussion

The Southwest is characterized by considerable environmental diversity. A variety of resources were available for prehistoric populations to use for food, building material, firewood, tools, and other items. Nevertheless, the characteristic aridity limits the natural productivity and affects the reliability with which some resources occur. The aridity poses, and has posed, a challenge for people living in the Southwest; it has also been an important factor in the preservation of archaeological remains. Some of these remains, such as wood, plant seeds, and the bones of small rodents, are useful in helping archaeologists reconstruct the prehistoric environments of the Southwest and the economies of prehistoric peoples.

In addition to preserving archaeological remains, some characteristics of the arid Southwest promote their destruction. Desert and semidesert environments are relatively fragile in the sense that small and short-term disturbances can have disproportionately great effects. The rate at which the environment recovers from a disturbance is also rather slow. Erosion may be initiated by a short drought or overgrazing, either of which destroys plant cover, or by the wind as it carries thin layers of sand and soil from an archaeological site. Arroyo cutting, gullying, and aeolian deflation also destroy countless acres of soils and frequently the archaeological remains contained in these soils.

By far the greatest impact on the archaeological resources of the Southwest results from human activity. Prehistoric Southwesterners seem to have used archaeological sites as sources for some kinds of materials. For example, the practice of using timbers from old, abandoned sites in new construction is well documented throughout most of the prehistoric period, yet the level of disturbance to sites before the modern period was certainly minor.

Today the archaeological resources of the Southwest are most affected by resource development and by the relatively enormous population growth in the region. As noted, parts of the Southwest are mineral-rich, containing fossil fuels and other resources that are being actively mined. Very large areas of the Colorado Plateaus are being mined for coal. In addition to this strip mining, subsurface drilling is done for gas, oil, and uranium. Although drilling disturbs a smaller area of surface than does strip mining, there are associated land-modification activities, such as construction of access roads. These activities permanently alter much of the surface and subsurface. With wise and appropriate planning, archaeologists can work with resource companies and Federal agencies to see that some sites are saved and protected. Law requires that the adverse effects on cultural resources be mitigated, generally through a program of systematic recording, data recovery, and analysis conducted prior to site destruction. In practice, this legal requirement has meant that archaeologists have surveyed, tested, and excavated thousands of sites that they might not otherwise have seen. A great deal of information has accrued on the basis of this work; however, the ultimate value of much of the information, in terms of increasing our general understanding of Southwestern prehistory, archaeological method, or culture change, will probably be debated for some time to come. The ultimate result, though, is that some of the cultural resource base is destroyed. Observations cannot be reexamined or confirmed, and new information cannot be extracted at a later date. This situation puts a very great burden on the researchers conducting archaeological salvage.

In addition to mining, two other land-modifying activities in the Southwest, inundation projects (the construction of reservoirs) and timber cutting, are having a great impact on archaeological resources. Numerous reservoirs are being constructed in the Southwest for flood control, for recreation, or to provide hydroelectric power. Archaeological surveys and research programs designed to extract information from sites scheduled to be inundated are among the very large-scale projects currently being carried out in the Southwest. Although one might think that sites are destroyed when flooded, this is not necessarily the case. There have been several studies designed to document the effects that flooding has on different kinds of archaeological sites and archaeological materials (e.g., Lenihan *et al.* 1977).

Very large areas of public land in the Southwest are used for the commercial production of timber. The activities associated with timber harvesting (creating access roads, pushing trees, chaining and removing timber) disturbs the surface and immediate subsurface. There is potential destruction of archaeological materials; consequently, surveys to locate cultural resources and research programs designed to recover information from these resources prior to timber cutting are initiated. Although some aspects of timber harvesting damage archaeological materials, it is not clear that the activity completely destroys all archaeological resources. As with inundation, research is currently evaluating the long- and short-term effects of commercial lumbering on archaeological remains.

Finally, the Southwest, as part of the nationel "sun belt," is receiving an enormous influx of population. Urban areas, such as Phoenix, Tucson, Albuquerque, El Paso, and Salt Lake City, are among the fastest growing areas in the country. Projections indicate that much smaller centers, such as Farmington, Kingman, Flagstaff, and Grants, may well be major urban areas before the turn of the century. Simple increases in population and the spread of urban areas virtually ensures the destruction of cultural resources. The destruction occurs as housing is built, roads are paved, water lines are installed, and as individuals and groups become involved in "recreational" pothunting. The impact of these activities can be devastating; not only are the contents of sites removed from their context, but in some cases large sites are entirely destroyed. Although it is nearly a certainty that pothunting will have particularly devastating effects on Southwestern archaeological resources, some archaeologists are hopeful that educational programs aimed at developing public awareness and respect for cultural resources may help to reduce the anticipated damage.

This very brief discussion of current activities that are having a great impact on archaeological resources should be sobering. Southwestern archaeology has long enjoyed a distinctive role in American archaeology, in part because ruins were so abundant that the area could serve as a major training ground for generations of archaeologists. In addition, the climate and the low population density virtually ensured excellent preservation of archaeological resources that are not often preserved in other kinds of settings. Some of these materials, such as fiber baskets, netting, sandals, painted wooden slats, cotton textiles, and fur and feather blankets, allow archaeologists an unusual view of the richness of the daily life of Southwestern peoples. The preservation of building timbers and macrobotanical and microfaunal remains enables considerable detail in reconstructing the environments in which the prehistoric population lived and in documenting changes in the natural environment. The degree to which archaeologists have used these resources to provide an understanding of the cultures and culture change in the Southwest must be critically examined, because in the near future the resources that will be needed to answer fundamental questions will be much reduced in number.

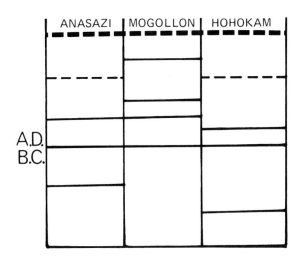

| ANASAZI | MOGOLLON | HOHOKAM |

A.D.
B.C.

3

Intellectual Frameworks for Southwestern Prehistory

The systems of classification used in archaeology describe similarities and differences in the formal properties of artifactual remains as these occur over time and through space. The units of observation considered most important for classification reflect general ideas about culture held by professional archaeologists; these ideas change as archaeology and anthropology develop as disciplines. This chapter defines the classificatory frameworks currently used in Southwestern archaeology and provides historical background to their formulation. This chapter also explores some problems inherent in the use of these systems of classification.

Introduction

Knowledge about the prehistory of any area develops within the context of the questions researchers bring with them to the field. The Southwest is no exception. The kinds of questions pursued are the result of complex interactions among the specific historical circumstances of the investigations, the prevailing paradigms or theoretical orientations of the time, and the techniques of data recovery available. Although the archaeological ruins in the Southwest were known to the Pueblo and non-Pueblo Indians and to the Spanish explorers and colonists, all of whom predated American culture in the area, the development of Southwestern prehistoric archaeology took place within the broader framework of the culture history of the United States. The first recorders of Southwestern antiquities were associated generally with the U.S. Army reconnaissance of the then newly acquired territory. The earliest descriptions were by William H. Emory (1848) and J. H. Simpson (1850), as part of the army's topographical surveys. Slightly later, a series of expeditions, both privately and publically supported, provided the opportunity for a number of men who are justifiably considered the fathers of Southwestern archaeology to enter the field. Among them were Frank H. Cushing, Adolf F. Bandelier (Figure 3.1), Jesse W. Fewkes, Walter H. Hough, James Stevenson, Cosmos and Victor Mindeleff, Byron Cummings, and Edgar L. Hewett (Figure 3.2).

These early explorers were not professional archaeologists, because archaeology, as a discipline, did not exist. Yet these men explored, often mapped, and sometimes excavated an enormous number of ruins throughout the Southwest. Many of their maps and notes are invaluable documents, not only in the historical sense, but in some instances because they have not been surpassed by more recent work. In traversing the Southwest on horseback and on foot and viewing hundreds of ruins, these men developed a holistic perspective on the Southwest that remains unmatched. The men were charged with collecting both ethnographic and archaeological material culture items for eastern museums. In the course of these activities, they often became familiar with Pueblo groups and used ethnographic information to interpret the archaeological remains they encountered. Cushing, for example, used extensive ethnographic data that he obtained from his experiences at Zuni in order to interpret prehistoric remains. Fewkes relied on a variety of Pueblo myths and legends, but mostly those of the Hopi, in order to explain the ancient ruins. The essentially atemporal aspect of this early work is understandable within the context of the time. First, the antiquity of man in the New World had not yet been demonstrated (see Chapter 4). Second, within the prevailing theoretical framework of unilineal evolution, as developed by E. B. Tylor in England and L. H. Morgan in the United States, all American Indian cultures were viewed as representing essentially the same stage of development. Third, and most important, there were no techniques available to assign calendar dates to the ruins of people who lacked written records. Finally, the most visible remains recorded by the early explorers were the ruins of large, compact villages, which are very similar to the villages occupied by the modern Pueblo Indians. In characterizing the Southwest as essentially homogeneous and Pueblo, they were emphasizing only the obvious.

Figure 3.1 Adolph F. Bandelier. (Photograph courtesy of the Museum of New Mexico.)

Background for the First Framework

The work of three men began the revolution in Southwestern archaeology that would provide data for the first systematic classification of remains with respect to the dimensions of time and space. First, Nels Nelson (1914, 1916) demonstrated the value of the use of systematic stratigraphic excavation in his work in the Galisteo Basin of New Mexico. Concerned with demonstrating the chronological order of pottery styles that occurred in the Rio Grande area, he conducted test excavations at a number of sites in the basin. At San Cristobal Pueblo, which had been abandoned early in the

Figure 3.2 Edgar L. Hewett. (Photograph courtesy of the Museum of New Mexico.)

historic period, Nelson found deep trash deposits that enabled him to show the sequential order of pottery styles. He then applied the general order to tests he had made at other sites in the basin where the sequence was incomplete. Second, A. L. Kroeber (1916) published a brief account of what, in essence, amounts to a combination of the direct historical approach, working backward from the known, and a frequency seriation of ceramics from surface collections. Kroeber was studying Zuni clans, and he would relax in the evening by walking over various abandoned sites in the vicinity of Zuni, first noting and later collecting potsherds. He observed that some ceramics (redwares) were common at Zuni itself but occurred less frequently than black-on-white sherds at other sites. Still other sites had only black-on-white sherds. He suggested that, starting with the present, as represented by the sherds at still-inhabited Zuni, one could order the sites *in time* through the decreasing frequency of red to black-on-white ceramics. It was Leslie Spier (1917) who applied and refined the approach advocated by Kroeber and combined seriation with the stratigraphic methods employed by Nelson. Spier worked in the Zuni area and used stratigraphic tests at some of Kroeber's sites to confirm Kroeber's sequence. He also examined the frequencies of the ceramic wares as these occurred on the surface of sites that appeared to have had only brief occupations, thus enabling him to avoid problems of stratigraphic mixing. Spier was able to order sites temporally from surface collections in the Zuni–White Mountain area.

These three contributions marked a turning point in Southwestern archaeology. They demonstrated that sites could be ordered relative to one another along the temporal dimension, that the principles of stratigraphy derived from geology could be applied to archaeology, and that ceramics were sensitive indicators of temporal changes. In the years between these demonstrations and 1927, a number of investigators applied the direct historical approach, stratigraphic excavation, and ceramic seriation to various areas of the Southwest.

One of the problems in developing an integrated chronological picture of Southwestern prehistory was the difficulty in correlating changes between areas. Most of the ruins in the Southwest had been abandoned prior to European contact, but in fact very few had been abandoned at the same time, so it was not possible to use the direct historical approach in most areas. Also, the pottery-making traditions seemed to differ considerably from one locality to another. Thus the sequence established for Zuni and the White Mountains would not necessarily be appropriate for the Galisteo Basin or the Pajarito Plateau. Certainly one of the most famous and ambitious projects ever launched in the Southwest was designed to firmly establish the major principles derived from the work of Kroeber, Spier, and Nelson in a complex archaeological situation and to acquire materials that would be appropriate for tying the temporal developments of one area to other areas. This project was the expedition of the R. S. Peabody Foundation for Archaeology to Pecos Pueblo headed by A. V. Kidder (Figure 3.3).

Figure 3.3   Alfred V. Kidder. At Pecos Pueblo. (Photograph courtesy of the Museum of New Mexico.)

Kidder at Pecos

Kidder began work at Pecos Pueblo in 1915 and continued through 1929, with an interruption during the First World War. Kidder (1931) was characteristically explicit in stating his reasons for selecting Pecos Pueblo for excavation: It had the longest documented history of continuous occupation of any of the Rio Grande Pueblo ruins, it had been a large town, known to the Spanish explorers of 1540, and it had been abandoned in 1838. The latter date allowed for the application of the direct historical approach. The topographic setting of the site, a low mesa, provided a situation in which deep trash deposits could be expected to yield material of considerable age. (The trash deposits were, in fact, deeper and more extensive than Kidder had initially anticipated, although they did not yield materials of great age.) Pecos was known to have been a major center of trade during the early historic period; therefore, Kidder suggested, "in its deposits are to be found bartered objects which permit accurate chronological correlation of other contemporary cultures, both Pueblo and Eastern" (Kidder 1931:589–590).

In 1924, based in part on the first six seasons of field work at Pecos and work that Kidder and others had already accomplished in the San Juan drainage (Kidder 1917) and elsewhere in the Southwest (especially Bandelier 1892; Cummings 1915; Fewkes 1911a, 1912; Hough 1914, 1920; Kidder and Guernsey 1919; Prudden 1903), Kidder published the first comprehensive synthesis of Southwestern archaeology (1924). The volume remains a classic. In it, Kidder summarized his work at Pecos, briefly described the modern Pueblo peoples of New Mexico and Arizona, and reviewed what was then known of Southwestern archaeology. He organized the data available into the first historical reconstruction of the Southwest, identifying several areas in which more chronological information was needed (Kidder 1962:351).

The Major Southwestern Traditions

At the end of August 1927, Kidder invited Southwestern archaeologists and those in related disciplines to his field camp at Pecos to discuss fundamental problems of Southwestern archaeology, develop a plan for resolving those problems, and "lay foundations for a unified system of nomenclature" (Kidder 1927:489). Those attending the first Pecos Conference included individuals whose work laid the foundations for Southwest prehistory. Among them were Neil Judd, excavator of Pueblo Bonito in Chaco Canyon, New Mexico; Jesse Nusbaum, who worked extensively at Mesa Verde, Colorado; A. E. Douglass, who developed tree-ring dating; Frank H. H. Roberts, Jr., who excavated pre-Pueblo sites in Chaco Canyon and elsewhere, as well as the Folsom site of Lindenmeier in Colorado; Earl Morris, who excavated Aztec Ruin, New Mexico, as well as early pre-Pueblo sites in Colorado; Sylvanus Morley, who excavated Cannonball Ruins and sites in McElmo Canyon, Colorado, before going on to a distinguished career in Maya archaeology; Walter Hough, who contributed greatly to the archaeology of the Hopi area; Mr. and Mrs. C. B. Cosgrove, who excavated the Swarts Ruin in the Mimbres Valley, New Mexico; Charles Amsden, who excavated at the Galaz Ruin in the Mimbres Valley; Byron Cummings, who established archaeology at the University of Arizona and who excavated Kinishba Pueblo, Arizona, and Cochise Culture sites, including Double Adobe; and Emil W. Haury, who excavated Ventana Cave and the key Hohokam site of Snaketown. The gathering at Pecos was the beginning of a tradition. Irregularly at first, but annually since the end of the Second World War, Southwestern archaeologists reconvene the Pecos Conference at the end of the summer field season. The conference meets in various locations, but returns to Pecos every 5 years. The major goal of the first Pecos Conference, that of developing a systematic nomenclature, was realized in the formulation of what is now termed the Pecos Classification. It provided the first conceptual framework for organizing the data of Southwestern prehistory.

The Pecos Classification: The First Framework

The participants at the first Pecos Conference wished to order chronologically the developments in Southwestern prehistory. At the time, chronological orderings could be based only on observations of stratigraphy supplemented by some historic records for the most recent end of the sequence. There were no techniques then available for assigning calendar dates to sites. Although tree-ring dating was being pursued, it was not until 1929 that the tree-ring sequence was firmly tied to the Christian calendar. The conference therefore defined culture stages characterized by diagnostic traits or elements. Although a particular stage might in theory be defined by any number of traits, the conference participants selected those that showed variation over time or were indexes of "growth." Not surprisingly, architecture and ceramics were key elements in the classification. The former was considered valuable in indicating cultural growth or refinement; the latter had been demonstrated to be temporally sensitive. For ceramics, it was decided that using changes in styles of cooking wares (rather than painted serving vessels) was the simplest for preliminary chronological considerations. The nomenclature adopted by the conference and the diagnostic traits for each culture stage are as follows (and see Figure 3.4):

Basketmaker I, or *Early Basketmaker:* This was a postulated preagricultural stage. The category is no longer used; rather, the developments envisioned now relate to the Archaic (Chapter 5).

Basketmaker II, or *Basketmaker:* Pottery is not present; however, agriculture is known, and the atlatl (spear thrower) is used.

Basketmaker III, or *Post-Basketmaker:* Dwellings are pithouses or slab houses. Pottery is made. The cooking ware is plain, without plastic (scoring, incising, and appliqué) decoration. The people of this and the preceding Basketmaker stages do not practice cranial deformation.

Pueblo I, or *Proto-Pueblo:* This is the first period during which cranial deformation is practiced. Culinary vessels have unobliterated coils or bands at the neck, and villages are composed of aboveground, contiguous rectangular rooms of true masonry.

Pueblo II: Corrugations extend over the exterior surfaces of cooking vessels. Small
   villages occur over a large geographic area.
Pueblo III, or *Great Pueblo:* This period is characterized by the appearance of very
   large communities and artistic elaboration and specialization in crafts.
Pueblo IV, or *Proto-Historic:* Much of the Pueblo area is abandoned, particularly the
   San Juan region. Artistic elaboration declines and corrugated wares gradually
   disappear, giving way to plainware.
Pueblo V, or *Historic:* This is the final period, including A.D. 1600 to the present.

   In addition to producing the Pecos Classification, the conference addressed other
issues. There was general agreement that, although key elements in Southwestern
cultural developments, such as maize agriculture, were derived from Mexico, most of
Southwestern culture was the product of autochthonous growth. After discussion of
the variety of shapes and internal features of kivas, the conference adopted a broad
definition of the term: "A kiva is a chamber specially constructed for ceremonial
purposes" (Kidder 1927:491). It was suggested that a binomial system of ware terminology be used in naming pottery types. The first name would refer to a place in
which the type was well developed, and the second name or term was to be technologically descriptive. An example of this is *Mimbres Black-on-white.* Finally, A. E.
Douglass gave a report on his work with tree rings and appealed to those present to
help gather specimens for his research. These subsidiary accomplishments of the
Pecos Conference were all accepted by the participants.
   Several points should be made regarding the Pecos Classification itself. First, the
scheme is developmental and not strictly chronological. In countering some objections to the use of the Pecos Classification, Roberts (1935b:21) noted that, despite the
fact that the ordering of periods has chronological implications, developments were
not expected to be synchronous throughout the Southwest, nor were all developmental stages expected to be represented in every area. In order to minimize the chronological implications of the classification, Roberts (1935b) suggested a revision in
terminology that dropped the numerical designations (i.e., Basketmaker, Modified
Basketmaker, Developmental Pueblo, Great Pueblo, Regressive Pueblo, and Historic
Pueblo). The Roberts modification is not generally used by Southwestern archaeologists, although it appears in some writings (e.g., Wormington 1961). Roberts also
noted that the scheme carried no implications with respect to the pace of change; thus,
there was no intent to presume a gradual transition from one culture stage to another.
Some changes were expected to have been rather abrupt. It should be noted that
calendar dates derived from tree-ring studies are available for most of the Pueblo area,
and consequently writers do attach dates to the various stages of the Pecos Classification. The dates vary, of course, depending on the geographic area of concern. When
generalized dates are suggested, they introduce an artifical sense of the pace of culture
change and minimize the variability that actually characterizes the archaeological
record. The Pecos Classification, as published, emphasized changes in skeletal characteristics (cranial deformation), architecture, and ceramics. At the time, the first were
considered important because it was not known if the "long-headed" Basketmaker

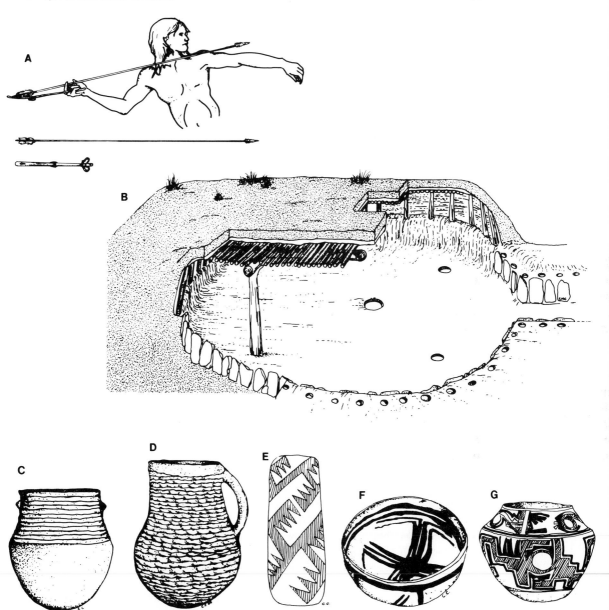

Figure 3.4 A, Basketmaker II; the atlatl (spear thrower); B, Basketmaker III; the pithouse; C, Pueblo I; neck-banded cooking vessel; D, Pueblo II, corrugated cooking vessel; E, Pueblo III; cylindrical vessel; F, Pueblo IV; Rio Grande glaze bowl; G, Pueblo V; vessel from the historic period at Zuni. (Illustrations by Charles M. Carrillo.)

peoples were of the same genetic stock as the "short-headed" Pueblo, who had posteriorly flattened skulls as the result of using hard cradle boards. The genetic continuity of Basketmaker and Pueblo populations is now generally accepted. Architecture and ceramics were used as diagnostic traits, in part because these permitted comparison among areas. Kidder (1927) indicated that village types, sandals, pictographs, and other traits could also be interpreted as having undergone developmental change. Roberts (1935b) elaborated some of these developments for basketry, textiles, weapons, houses, painted ceramics, and other items.

There eventually were some modifications in terminology and a restriction of the geographic area to which the Pecos Classification was applied. By 1936, it had become obvious that the Basketmaker–Pueblo continuum was a phenomenon of the northern Southwest. In order to separate this area from other areas and other traditions of the Southwest, Kidder (1936a) suggested that the name *Anasazi* be applied to the northern tradition. He stated that, although *Basketmaker–Pueblo* might be used to refer to the northern sequence, it was unwieldy and might cause confusion if one wanted to refer to either of the sequential elements separately. Kidder (1936a:590) suggested the adoption of the word *Anasazi* which, he stated, means "old people" in Navajo. (Actually, *Anasazi* means "enemy ancestors" in Navajo, but few archaeologists were aware of the precise translation.) This proposal, and its widespread acceptance, is somewhat unfortunate in retrospect. First, it may seem disrespectful to contemporary Pueblo peoples to use a term from the Navajo language to refer to Pueblo ancestors. In addition, Pueblo V in the Pecos Classification refers to the period from 1600 to the present. It is certainly misleading to refer to living Pueblo people as Anasazi. Nevertheless, the term *Anasazi* was quickly adopted in the literature of the Southwest.

Two additional categories were added to Southwestern chronologies. The application of tree-ring dating to archaeological sites in the Southwest revealed that great antiquity (beyond a few centuries before the Christian era) for the Basketmakers could not be demonstrated. On the other hand, acceptance of the finds of Folsom Man indicated that humans had been in the Americas since the end of the Pleistocene (see Chapter 4). As Kidder stated, "we immediately encounter a paradox, for while the upper end of our time scale is being distressingly compressed, its lower end is being vastly expanded by the recent unequivocal determination of the high antiquity of Folsom Man" (1936b:142). The lower end of the chronology has been divided into Paleo-Indian and Archaic periods. *Paleo-Indian* refers to all sites of late Pleistocene age in the Americas. The Paleo-Indian stage is characterized by hunting and gathering, and some of the hunted species are now-extinct Pleistocene forms. *Archaic* is also generally used throughout the Western Hemisphere to refer to a cultural stage in which hunting and gathering was the subsistence base. The Archaic follows the Paleo-Indian, and all species that are hunted are modern. In the Southwest, the Archaic is generally dated from about 5500 B.C. to the beginnings of sedentism at about A.D. 200.

At the Pecos Conference held in 1929, the general utility of the Pecos Classification was discussed. At that time, an entire group of archaeologists indicated that the classification did not seem to be useful for them. The members of this group were working in the Gila and Salt basins of central Arizona, where developments were

Figure 3.5 Group photograph at Gila Pueblo Foundation, Globe, Arizona. Harold S. Gladwin and Nora Gladwin are fifth and sixth from the left, respectively. Others are not identified. (Photograph taken about 1931–1933 and reproduced courtesy of the Arizona State Museum.)

dissimilar to those of the San Juan drainage. The distinctiveness of the Arizona desert area had been noted earlier (e.g., Mindeleff 1896) but had not been systematically explored. In 1931, researchers met at Gila Pueblo, the headquarters of Gila Pueblo Archaeological Foundation, a research institution established by Harold S. Gladwin in 1928 near Globe, Arizona (Figure 3.5). There, a framework for classifying materials from the Arizona desert area was worked out, and later, in 1931, it was reported at the Laboratory of Anthropology in Santa Fe.

The Hohokam Sequence: The Second Framework

Although fieldwork in the Arizona desert had been initiated by Bandelier (1890, 1892), Cushing (1890), and others, the work that provided the basis for the Hohokam sequence had been inspired by Kidder's publications (Schiffer 1982:302) and therefore depended on stratigraphic excavation and studies of ceramics. These had been conducted at sites in the Tonto Basin (Schmidt 1926, 1928) and in the Gila and Salt basins, particularly at Casa Grande, the Grewe site, Sacaton, and Adamsville (Gladwin 1928). Most of the crucial work was carried out by Gladwin and his associates at Gila Pueblo.

The Pima word *Hohokam* was applied to the remains found in these areas. Although usually translated as "those who have gone," or "those who have vanished," Haury provides a more literal Pima translation, referring to things that are "all used up":

> A characteristic of Piman languages is the manner of pluralizing the word by duplication of the first syllable. Thus, *hokam* is one thing all used up, and *hohokam* means more than one. . . . If a tire on one's automobile blows out it is *hokam;* if two go, *hohokam.* (Haury 1976:5)

Emphasizing those traits that were the bases of the Pecos Classification, Roberts (1935b) summarized the major distinguishing features of the Hohokam in contrast to the Anasazi. The Hohokam used the paddle-and-anvil technique to finish pottery, in contrast to the scrape-and-polish finishing done in the Pueblo area. Rectangular, single-unit dwellings were characteristic, as were cremations and the use of extensive systems of irrigation. Originally the Hohokam sequence was divided into six stages, although the first, the Pioneer period, was only inferred in 1931. The existence of the Pioneer period was later confirmed in excavations at Snaketown (Gladwin *et al.* 1938). The Hohokam sequence comprised the Pioneer, Colonial, Sedentary, Classic, Recent, and Modern periods in its initial formulation. Subsequently, a number of investigators have questioned whether the Pioneer remains are to be attributed to the Hohokam culture (DiPeso 1956; Schroeder 1953b), an issue that is treated below. And in a recent discussion (Gumerman and Haury 1979), the Recent and Modern periods have been

Figure 3.6   Pioneer period Hohokam bowl. Snaketown Red-on-buff bowl, geometric design, from Snaketown. (Photograph by Helen Teiwes, courtesy of the Arizona State Museum.)

Figure 3.7 Hohokam ball court. The excavated west half of ball court no. 1, Snaketown, 1935. View is to the east. (Photograph by Emil W. Haury and reproduced courtesy of the Arizona State Museum.)

dropped. This decision reflects uncertainty in attributing continuity from the Hohokam to the contemporary Pima. Brief characterizations of the Pioneer, Colonial, Sedentary, and Classic periods are given here.

During the Pioneer period, dwellings are at first quite large and square, with slightly depressed floors and walls of poles and brush. Some of these dwellings have two entryways, which may indicate that they either were residences for more than one family or served special functions. Later houses in the Pioneer period are either square with somewhat rounded corners or rectangular with right-angle corners, slightly depressed floors, and an entrance passage in the center of one wall. Domestic architecture remains the same until the Classic period; however, early Pioneer houses are generally larger in floor area than those constructed later. The cremations of the Pioneer period are secondary interments in pits or trenches accompanied by crushed, burned pottery as grave offerings. The paucity of calcined bone indicates that the actual crematory fire was not at the burial site. In addition to cremations, both flexed and extended inhumations occur at Pioneer period sites (Morris 1969). Throughout the Hohokam sequence, the majority of ceramics are nonpainted wares. During the beginnings of the Pioneer period, ceramics are well-made, undecorated, brown to gray wares, although some have a red slip. The painted ceramics, which first occur later in the Pioneer period than the plainwares, consist of vessels with red-painted geometric designs applied to a buff background (Figure 3.6). Some ceramics are decorated by incised lines or grooves. In addition to these traits, simple ceramic figurines, stone bowls, stone palettes, stone axes, and items made of shell obtained from the Gulf of California and the Pacific Ocean are known from the Pioneer period.

During the Colonial period, the Hohokam experienced considerable geographic expansion. Domestic architecture remains the same; however, new architectural forms include platform mounds and ball courts. The former are generally caliche-capped trash mounds; the latter are large elongated structures with expanded end fields (Figure 3.7) and east–west orientations. These structures have been variously interpreted as dance grounds, wells, or ball courts analogous to those of Mesoamerica. Irrigation canals, which may have been present during the Pioneer period, are well developed. Colonial period cremations include both primary and secondary burials, and these occur in both pits and trenches. In addition to ceramics, crematory offerings include projectile points, stone vessels, slate palettes, and stone axes. Ceramic vessels of the Colonial period are larger than those of the Pioneer period. Although plain-wares continue to dominate assemblages, incising and grooving are no longer practiced. Colonial period painted ceramics (Figure 3.8) show an increase in the variety of geometric forms, but bands composed of small life-form designs are characteristic (Figure 3.9). The Colonial period figurines (Figure 3.10) are realistic, with clothing

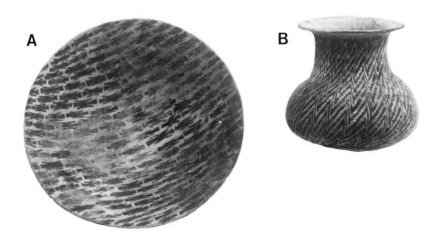

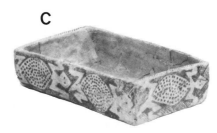

Figure 3.8 Colonial period Hohokam ceramics. A, Gila Butte Red-on-buff bowl; B, Santa Cruz Red-on-buff jar; C, Santa Cruz Red-on-buff rectangular form. Variety in vessel forms is characteristic. All items are from Snaketown. (Photograph by Helga Teiwes and reproduced courtesy of the Arizona State Museum.)

Figure 3.9 Colonial period Hohokam jar. Santa Cruz Red-on-buff jar from Snaketown. The design motif is a band of dancing figures. (Photograph is reproduced courtesy of the Arizona State Museum.)

and ornamentation being depicted. Elaborate stone palettes (Figure 3.11), stone bowls carved in animal effigy forms, and mosaic mirrors of the fitted iron pyrite plates are all products of fine craftsmanship.

Domestic architecture during the Sedentary period continues as it had before (Figure 3.12). Ball courts were constructed, but these were oval and generally smaller than those of the Colonial period. Platform mounds of the Sedentary period show evidence of repair or remodeling with several caliche cappings. Cremations are of the same forms as they were during the previous period. Some of the Sedentary period storage vessels are of very large size, and the characteristic jar form shows a pronounced angular shoulder (Gila Shoulder; Figure 3.13). Few life forms are executed on the painted ceramics; complex geometric designs predominate (Figure 3.14). The ceramic figurines consist only of heads, but inasmuch as these have hollow bases, they may have been attached to bodies made of perishable materials. There is less elaboration in the carved-stone assemblage of bowls (Figure 3.15) and palettes and less diversity in the shell species represented in jewelry (Figure 3.16). Shell of the Sedentary period was etched and painted. Another innovation of the Sedentary period is the cooper tinkler bell (Figure 3.17), which may have been imported from Mesoamerica.

Figure 3.10 Hohokam figurine head. Late Santa Cruz phase (ca. A.D. 900) from the Ring site. (Photograph reproduced courtesy of the Arizona State Museum.)

The Classic period is characterized by the aggregation of the population into fewer but larger sites. There are several rather dramatic changes that have been interpreted as evidence of an incursion of non-Hohokam people into the Hohokam area—for example, the construction of multistoried great houses, the introduction of polychrome pottery (Figure 3.18), and an increase in the number of inhumations. (Inhumations occur, although not frequently, throughout the Hohokam sequence and cremations are abundant in the Classic.) Despite these changes, much of Hohokam culture remains the same. Villages continue to consist primarily of single-unit houses, although the villages themselves are now enclosed by compound walls. The well-known sites, such as Casa Grande, contain both great houses and single-unit dwellings. Domestic architecture of the single-unit house shows a change to construction using either solid clay walls or clay walls reinforced with posts. Red-on-buff ceramics and Hohokam plainwares continue to be manufactured but, as noted, polychromes occur as well. Cremations are secondary and were placed in jars. In general, there is a decrease in luxury stone items (palettes, bowls), and shell, although abundant, is not elaborately decorated. Ball courts continue to be built, but these are fewer in number than in preceding periods, reflecting the decrease in settlements that accompanied population aggregation.

At the end of the Classic period, great houses are no longer constructed, and polychrome ceramics and inhumations are no longer characteristic. Single-unit houses of pole and brush are built and compound walls enclosing settlements continue. The ceramics are predominantly plainwares of reddish color and rather porous texture. This stage of Hohokam development was originally referred to as the Recent period (Gladwin and Gladwin 1934; Roberts 1935b) and viewed as transitional to Pima and Papago culture known from about 1600 on. In the Modern period, Pima and Papago houses remain pole and brush or clay structures; inhumation is generally practiced, and ceramics are either plainwares resembling the pottery of the Recent period or highly polished redwares.

The hallmarks of Hohokam culture, which are most apparent from the Colonial through the Sedentary periods and into the early Classic, are irrigation canals, ball courts, platform mounds, cremation, elaborate work in stone and shell, red-on-buff pottery, and ceramic figurines. Most workers emphasize the similarities among certain traits, particularly platform mounds, ball courts, ceramic figurines, iron pyrite inlay

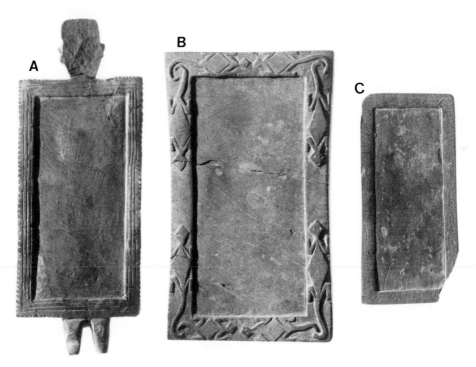

Figure 3.11 Hohokam stone palettes. A and B are from Snaketown; C is from Roosevelt 9:6. (Photographs courtesy of the Arizona State Museum.)

Figure 3.12 Hohokam domestic architecture. Hohokam pithouses are better described as houses in shallow pits. Note the short entry with the step down to the floor; post hole pattern, and central heating pit. The house is as excavated at the Second Canyon site (Helga Teiwes photographer. Photograph reproduced courtesy of the Arizona State Museum.)

Figure 3.13 Sedentary period Hohokam jars. Sacaton Red-on-buff jars with pronounced vessel shoulders. (Courtesy of the Arizona State Museum.)

Figure 3.14 Hohokam Sedentary period bowl excavated at Snaketown. (Reproduced courtesy of the Arizona State Museum.)

mirrors, canal irrigation, and copper bells, to comparable features and items from Mesoamerica. This has led to various interpretations of Hohokam origins, and to an unfortunate proliferation of referential terminology. Until the 1970s, the more elaborate Hohokam developments were known nearly exclusively from sites along the rivers, the Salt and particularly the Gila. Away from the rivers, sites lack irrigation canals, and there may be little indication of craft specialization in stone and shellwork. Inhumations are more common in sites away from the rivers, and painted ceramics are scarce. These observations led Haury (Figure 3.19) to propose a distinction be-

Figure 3.15 Three Hohokam carved stone bowls. (Courtesy of the Arizona State Museum.)

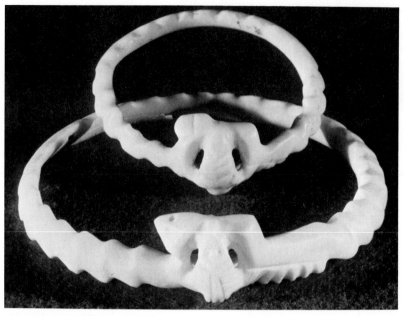

Figure 3.16 Hohokam shell bracelets. These are glycymeris shell carved with bird and snake motifs. (Photograph courtesy of the Arizona State Museum.)

tween River Branch Hohokam and Desert Branch Hohokam (Table 3.1). Both branches were to have derived from a widespread western hunting and gathering base (Desert Culture, see Chapters 4 and 5), and the differences between the two branches were viewed as primarily the result of different environmental adaptations, with canal irrigation depending on the rivers and providing a secure agricultural economy that permitted the cultural elaborations of the river branch.

Based in part on archival accounts of the Pima and in part on his excavations at San Cayetano del Tumacacori, DiPeso (1956) argued that the differences between the prehistoric manifestations along the rivers and those of the desert, especially during the Colonial and Sedentary periods, suggested more than adaptations to contrasting environments. He uses *O'otam,* a Pima term meaning "person," to refer to the initial Pioneer period inhabitants of the Arizona deserts. *Hohokam* is reserved by DiPeso for a group that he believes were later migrants from Mesoamerica. According to this view, the Hohokam are a Mesoamerican group that founded settlements mostly along the rivers, expanded into the desert during the Colonial period, then returned to the

Figure 3.17 Hohokam copper tinkler bell. Copper bells appear in the Sedentary period and may have been imported from Mexico. (Illustrated by Charles M. Carrillo.)

Figure 3.18 Tonto Polychrome jar. Polychrome pottery, such as this example, has been related to the appearance of non-Hohokam peoples in the Hohokam area during the Classic period. (Photograph courtesy of the Museum of New Mexico.)

river areas. The Hohokam eventually left southern Arizona, leaving the O'otam to be the ancestors of the modern Pima.

A different interpretation has been offered by Schroeder (1957, 1960, 1979a), who argues that the Hohokam migrated from Mesoamerica and arrived within the Gila and Salt drainages at about A.D. 500. He refers to the initial inhabitants as Hakataya (meaning "Colorado River" in the Walapai and Havasupai Indian language) and relates these people to groups from the lower Colorado River area. According to Schroeder (1979a), the Hakataya occupied a vast territory of the desert, west from Baja California and San Diego to southern Nevada and the Grand Canyon and east to the Mogollon Rim. As might be expected from the size and diversity of the Hakataya area, Schroeder has divided the Hakataya into a number of branches, some of which he suggests are ancestral to the later Yuman-speaking tribes. Finally, based on reexcavations at Snaketown, Haury (1976) has modified his view of the Hohokam. He now concurs that the Hohokam represent a migrant Mesoamerican group; however, he would date the intrusion from the beginning of the Pioneer period. He views the Colonial and Sedentary periods as indicative of more intense interaction with Mesoamerica, but without substantial additional migration. Finally, he sees a gap between the end of the Hohokam Classic and the modern Pima.

The question of Hohokam origins is by no means settled. In 1931, when a framework for Hohokam prehistory was suggested, it was most important to emphasize the differences between Hohokam and Anasazi cultures. At that time, too, the origins of the Hohokam were not known, because no remains predating the Colonial period had been explored. In order to find the origins of Hohokam culture, Gila Pueblo undertook a number of surveys. No ancestral Hohokam remains were encountered in

Figure 3.19   Emil W. Haury. Dr. Haury is a major figure in Southwestern archaeology. In addition to his extensive work with the Hohokam, he also defined the Mogollon as a separate cultural tradition. Here Dr. Haury looks over the Gila River valley from Gila Butte, Arizona. San Tan Mountains are in the background. (Photograph courtesy of the Arizona State Museum.)

northern Sonora or in the deserts west of the Hohokam heartland. North of the Hohokam area, along the Verde River valley, the remains appeared to be Anasazi and not Hohokam. Expeditions surveyed east to the upper San Francisco River area of New Mexico and then down along that river into southern New Mexico. The sites encountered in this area seemed distinct from both Anasazi and Hohokam developments (Gladwin and Gladwin 1934), and after excavation at two sites (Haury 1936), another Southwestern culture was defined.

The Mogollon Sequence: The Third Framework

By 1936 a number of investigators had explored the rugged Mogollon Mountains area of southeastern Arizona and southwestern New Mexico (e.g., Hough 1914, 1920).

Table 3.1

River Branch and Desert Branch Hohokam Traits[a]

River Branch	Desert Branch
Cremation	Earth burial
Red-on-buff pottery, not polished; redware, black interiors	Red-on-brown pottery, not polished; redware, red interiors
Full-troughed metate, well-shaped	Block metate, some shaping, not troughed as a rule
Great arrays of projectile points, delicate workmanship	Limited projectile point types, few in number, workmanship inferior
Well-developed carved stone, few chopping, scraping, or cutting tools	Carved stone weakly represented; abundant roughly chipped chopping, scraping, and cutting tools
Slate palette; stone and shell jewelry, abundant and elaborate; figurine complex strong	Slate palette little used; stone and shell jewelry, rare and simple; figurines rare
Large-scale irrigation systems, drawing water from streams	Limited irrigation canals, designed to catch surface runoff
Subsistence primarily agricultural; heavy Salado intrusion after 1300	Subsistence primarily collecting; little affected by Salado

[a]After Haury (1950:547).

At that time, the most detailed work had been carried out at Classic Mimbres sites, such as the Swarts Ruin (Cosgrove and Cosgrove 1932) and Cameron Creek Village (Bradfield 1931), which yielded the distinctive and spectacular Mimbres Black-on-white ceramics (Figure 3.20). The Classic Mimbres sites consisted of single-story masonry pueblos with central plaza areas. Pithouses had also been found to underlay the classic pueblo structures. The presence of pithouses, pueblos, and black-on-white pottery led to the interpretation that the remains in the Mogollon area were a southern manifestation of the Basketmaker–Pueblo continuum, although the inspiration for the outstanding Mimbres Classic ceramics was problematic. In 1931 the Gila Pueblo surveys examined two sites in the Mogollon area, Mogollon Village and the Harris site, which yielded ceramics that seemed to reflect Hohokam affiliation (Gladwin and Gladwin 1934; Haury 1936) and therefore warranted further investigation. These sites were excavated during 1933 and 1934 by Emil Haury. Comparing his data with both the Hohokam and Anasazi sequences, Haury found that there were enough differences among the three to support a separate cultural designation for the Mogollon Mountains sites, and he therefore proposed the Mogollon culture. The name *Mogollon* is derived from the mountains in which these sites are found, which in turn had been named after a Spanish Colonial governor of New Mexico.

The specific importance of both Mogollon Village and the Harris site is that together they provided information regarding pre-Classic Mimbres temporal developments in

Figure 3.20   Classic Mimbres bowl. Mimbres Black-on-white bowl with antelope representation. (Courtesy of the Museum of New Mexico.)

the Mogollon area. Using the principles of stratigraphy and ceramic comparisons, as advocated by Kidder, Haury was able to show that developmental trends in the Mogollon area were different from those in either the Hohokam or the Anasazi areas. In contrast to the Hohokam, who were primarily agricultural or combined agriculture with gathering, the Mogollon subsistence base appeared to have been about equally dependent on hunting and agriculture. Also in contrast to the Hohokam, the Mogollon apparently practiced inhumation—only a few cremations were found. The stratigraphic sequence of house forms indicated a change from round pithouses to rectangular ones; and also unlike the Hohokam, the Mogollon houses were entered by way of a sloping ramp rather than by a short step down from the entryway. The Mogollon also had large ceremonial structures formally similar to houses, which did not occur among the Hohokam. Finally, the Mogollon artifact inventory did not include palettes, figurines, mosaics, or carved stone vessels. Mogollon ceramics did resemble Hohokam ceramics in being red- or brownwares, but they were finished by scraping and polishing and not by paddle and anvil.

In many ways the Mogollon seem to more closely resemble the Anasazi; however Haury noted important differences. First, red-on-brown and slipped-and-polished red-ware ceramics were not an Anasazi feature. Second, the relatively deep Mogollon pithouses with ramp entryways (Figure 3.21) were unlike those to the north in the Pueblo area. The Mogollon pithouses also lacked certain floor features that were associated with pithouses in the San Juan region, especially benches, deflectors, and sipapus. (Sipapus are small holes in the floor that have been considered analogs of the *shipap,* the place of emergence from the underworld that features importantly in Pueblo religion.) On the basis of stratigraphy and some Pueblo trade ceramics, Haury was able to show that pithouses in the Mogollon region were in use until quite late and in fact were contemporaneous with Pueblo II surface structures in the San Juan region. Third, Mimbres Classic aboveground masonry pueblos were poorly constructed, which Haury interpreted as evidence that masonry construction techniques had been borrowed from the Anasazi. Finally, Haury was impressed by the analyses of the skeletal material from the Mogollon sites he excavated. These were characterized as a short-headed population, and they did not practice cranial deformation, as did the Pueblos. In general, then, there seemed to be enough information to warrant a

Figure 3.21 Mogollon pithouse as excavated. In contrast to Hohokam houses, Mogollon pithouses are relatively deep and the sides of the pit form part of the wall. The entryway on the right is long and slopes down to the floor. A small square stone-lined hearth is in front of the entryway. The holes in the floor are from the excavation of subfloor features. (Photograph courtesy of Steven A. LeBlanc.)

separate cultural designation for the Mogollon. Further, the Gila Peublo surveys indicated that Mogollon ceramics, and presumably therefore Mogollon culture, were
widely distributed geographically, extending from the Little Colorado River on the
north to well into Chihuahua (Mexico) on the south, and from Globe (Arizona) on the
west to the Rio Grande and El Paso (Texas) on the east.

The very large areal extent of Mogollon culture virtually ensures variability in the
distribution of trait complexes and the timing and sequences of various developmental changes. When Haury first defined the Mogollon, he suggested a sequence of
developmental phases appropriate to the Mimbres area in which he had worked. His
earliest phase, the Georgetown, is characterized by roundish pithouses with one flat
side and an inclined entry passage. Ceramics associated with the Georgetown phase
consist of both plainwares and polished redwares. His second phase, the San Francisco, is characterized by rectangular pithouses with lateral entryways. In addition to a
continuation of the ceramic types found in the Georgetown phase, the San Francisco
ceramic assemblage also includes red-on-brown painted types and a red-on-white
painted type. The subsequent phase is designated the Three Circle and is distinguished on the basis of rectangular pithouses with stone linings and lateral inclined
entryways and the introduction of the first black-on-white painted ceramic type in the
area (Mimbres Boldface Black-on-white). Some older ceramic types continued to be
produced. The final phase of Mogollon development in the Mimbres area is the
Classic Mimbres or Mimbres phase. The diagnostic features are one-story masonry
pueblos and Mimbres Black-on-white ceramics (Figure 3.22). Polished redware and
plainware continued to be produced. Following the Mimbres phase, the Mimbres area
was abandoned by the Mogollon and soon reinhabited by Pueblo peoples, who
produced polychrome ceramics and built pueblo dwellings. This final phase of prehistoric occupation had been termed the Animas phase by the Gladwins (1934), a
designation that was retained. Although there were local abandonments in the
Mogollon area after A.D. 1000 or 1150, there was also aggregation of population at
some very large sites, such as Kinishba, on the upper Little Colorado, and at Point of
Pines. As Reed (1948) has argued, in the fourteenth century after the Anasazi abandonment of the San Juan region, the pueblos of east-central Arizona were at their height.
Reed termed the aggregate of traits known from the area extending from the Little
Colorado south to the Gila and as far west as the Verde River Valley the *Western
Pueblo* tradition.

From the foregoing it appears that one result of the formulation of the Pecos
Classification was the fragmentation of what had been regarded as a single basic
Southwestern culture into three prehistoric cultures (Anasazi, Hohokam, and Mogollon), each characterized by slightly different constellations of material traits and developmental trends in burial practices, architecture, and ceramics. The Gila Pueblo
surveys of the Southwest did not provide the information needed to clarify the question of Hohokam origins, but they did indicate variations in architecture and ceramics
over space. Stratigraphic excavation in the Mogollon area supported the conclusion of
the existence of a separate developmental trend. Gila Pueblo surveys also extended
from the Hohokam area west to the Colorado River (Gladwin and Gladwin 1934),

Figure 3.22 Mimbres Black-on-white bowl. Classic Mimbres Black-on-white bowl with geometric design. The hole in the center was made at the time of interment. (Photograph courtesy of the Maxwell Museum of Anthropology.)

where remains were encountered that were dissimilar to those of the Hohokam, Anasazi, or Mogollon.

The Patayan: The Fourth Framework

In historic times the Colorado River area was inhabited by tribes speaking Yuman languages. The Gladwins designated the remains they encountered along the Colorado River as a separate Yuman root. This designation is no longer used, but the distinctive archaeological material from the broad area west of the Hohokam region and north to the Grand Canyon area (Figure 1.5) is treated as representing a separate cultural tradition.

Early investigations along the Colorado River were carried out by Malcolm Rogers of the Los Angeles State Museum (Rogers 1939) and by Harold S. Colton of the Museum of Northern Arizona (Colton 1939, 1945). While agreeing with the Gladwins that the Yuman-speaking tribes probably did have a long history of occupation along the Colorado River, Colton (1945) did not wish to assume that the archaeological materials encountered there were deposited by Yuman speakers. For that reason, he suggested that the term *Patayan,* meaning "old people" according to a Walapai interpreter, be applied instead of *Yuman.* The oldest artifacts found in the Colorado River area were lithics, which Rogers described (1939). The later ceramic assemblages were unlike those of the Hohokam, Anasazi, or Mogollon. The Colorado ceramics were finished by paddle and anvil, but they were rarely painted and they varied in color from buff to reddish and gray (Figure 3.23). Most of the area included within the definition of the Patayan was then known only from archaeological survey, so architectural forms and burial practices were largely conjectural (Colton 1939). Nevertheless, where data from excavation were available, architectural diversity was characteristic. Rectangular earth lodges with lateral entryways, masonry surface structures with small rectangular rooms, and deep pithouses lined with timber all were reported (Colton 1939).

One problem with Colton's formulation is that he had little information about the lower Colorado River. Consequently, he relied on ethnographic descriptions of the Yuma, a practice which he admitted was dangerous. In an explicit and careful evaluation of the northern Colorado River materials, Colton compared the traits found with those known from the Anasazi, Mogollon, Hohokam, and Patayan as postuated from

Figure 3.23 Patayan jar. Lower Colorado buffware jar with tapered chimney neck rim and rounded Colorado shoulder. (Photograph by W. W. Wasley from the collection at the San Diego Museum of Man. Photograph reproduced courtesy of the Arizona State Museum.)

Table 3.2

Colton's Comparison of Shared Traits from the
Cohonina Plateau and Flagstaff Areas with the
Anasazi, Mogollon, Hohokam, and Patayan[a]

	Cohonina Plateau area[b]	Flagstaff area[b]
Anasazi	33	47
Mogollon	31	50
Hohokam	42	23
Patayan	47	25

[a]Adapted from Colton (1939:21).
[b]Percentage of traits in common.

the ethnographic sources describing the Yuma. Table 3.2 reproduces this comparison for the Cohonina Plateau and the Sinagua area around Flagstaff. Based on this comparison, Colton classified the Cohonina remains as Patayan and the Sinagua as Mogollon (in each case because of the greatest percentage of shared traits). Some investigators, for example, Rogers, did not recognize the Patayan as a single cultural tradition, because it appeared to be a mixture of ceramic and architectural traits from a number of areas. Rogers (1945) included the Cohonina, Cerbat, and Prescott areas within the Patayan, but he retained the designation *Yuman* for remains from the lower Colorado River. The differences in terminology and classification created considerable confusion. Rogers (1945) proposed a three-stage scheme (Yuman I, II, III) for developments during the ceramic periods of the lower Colorado River.

On the basis of excavations at the Willow Beach site and examination of Rogers' ceramic collections, Schroeder (1952, 1958) completely revised the ceramic typology and questioned Rogers' suggested chronology. At the Pecos Conference of 1956, held at the Museum of Northern Arizona in Flagstaff (Schroeder 1957), a number of archaeologists met to clarify the confusing Colorado River terminological situation. The group adopted the term *Hakataya* to refer to the culture of the upper and lower Colorado river and adjacent areas. The constellation of traits characterizing this group included subsistence based on inundation (not irrigation) agriculture, hunting, and gathering; stone-lined roasting pits for food preparation; ceramics finished by paddle-and-anvil technique but of varying colors resulting from uncontrolled firing; hermetically sealed vessels for food storage; mortars and pestles; percussion-flaked choppers rather than ground stone axes; temporary circular shelters; houses of variable form but generally not compact contiguous-room settlements; and predominance of cremation (although inhumation was practiced in some areas). Rock shrines and rock-pile trail markers were also considered important. Although it was suggested that *Hakataya* be applied to both the upper and lower portions of the Colorado River, with *Patayan* reserved for the upper portion and *Laquish* used for the lower portion, the proposal was rejected by the 1957 Pecos Conference, which agreed to retain the term *Patayan* for the entire area of western Arizona below the Grand Canyon.

In 1960 and in his synthesis of 1979, Schroeder again introduced the term *Hakataya* but modified its referents. In this latter formulation, Schroeder argued that Hakataya should be used to refer to the basic brownware tradition of most of Arizona, including the Patayan, the Sinagua, and the Pioneer period Hohokam remains that predate A.D. 500. In essence, this definition reflects Schroeder's view that the Hohokam, as an ethnic group, migrated into the Gila and Salt river valleys in about A.D. 500 and that the tremendous variation included within the rest of the Hakataya area can be ascribed to varying cultural influences. As McGuire states,

> The diversity incorporated by this concept is extreme, even exceeding the material culture variability of the ethnographic Yumans. Groups such as the Cerbat, Pioneer Hohokam, and Salado share few aspects of ceramic chronology, architecture, settlement pattern, and subsistence. More importantly, each of these groups is more similar to other roots than to one another. . . . In view of these patterns, the few traits Schroeder finds in common for these groups . . . appear inadequate to support a common culture across all of western Arizona. (1982:221–222)

In view of this consideration, McGuire and Schiffer's 1982 summary of southwestern Arizona prehistory, and the precedent established by the 1957 Pecos Conference, the term *Patayan* is retained here.

Despite considerable research, the Patayan area remains poorly documented compared to other Southwestern regions. Particularly unfortunate is the lack of well-developed chronologies for the Patayan of the lower Colorado River. Nevertheless, Waters (1982) has reevaluated Rogers' original ceramic typology for this area and finds that this original chronology is supported by more recent surveys, limited stratigraphic excavation, and radiocarbon dates. Waters suggests that Rogers' terms, *Yuman I, II,* and *III,* be replaced by *Patayan I, II,* and *III,* but that the scheme otherwise be unaltered. This view is accepted here. More archaeological information is available for the northern and upland Patayan area, but there continues to be disagreement regarding interpretations of the materials encountered. Generally, three cultural manifestations are delimited in the upland Patayan region: Cohonina, Cerbat, and the Prescott.

The Cohonina tradition was originally defined on the basis of ceramics—San Francisco Gray, a paddle-and-anvil finished ware generally fired in a reducing atmosphere. The tradition is found in the area west of Flagstaff and south of the Grand Canyon. On the basis of excavations, primarily at Harbison Cave near Red Butte, Jennings (1971) described three Archaic phases that may be ancestral to the later Cohonina, although continuity is debated (Cartledge 1979). Ceramic production began in about A.D. 950. Sites of this period appear to have primarily been circular pithouses. In some areas these are distributed in clusters along ridges overlooking drainages with deposits of arable alluvial soils. This pattern and the presence of trough metates and two-hand manos suggest the importance of cultigens. The subsequent Medicine Valley focus, dated from about A.D. 950–1100, shows a shift to masonry or boulder-lined surface structures. Many sites contain only one rectangular surface room; however, larger sites of 8 and 12–15 rooms have been recorded. Schwartz (1956, 1959) argued that the Cohonina population increased between A.D. 900 and 1100 and thereafter precipitously declined. Both he and McGregor (1951) have argued that the Cohonina migrated to the Grand Canyon and were ancestral to the Havasupai. Cartledge (1979) found that in the vicinity of Sitgreaves Mountain there were a greater number of early than late sites. He suggests that, rather than reflecting population decline during the Medicine Valley focus, the preceding Cohonina focus may have been primarily season-al, with greater population movement and therefore more sites. The Medicine Valley focus would then represent a more sedentary population but not necessarily a larger one. In contrast to Schwartz, Euler (1977) and Euler and Green (1978) do not find the evidence of a Cohonina–Havasupai continuity convincing. Euler argues persuasively that the Cerbat were ancestral to both the Havasupai and the Walapai. The bulk of archaeological data seems to support Euler's view, but this makes the "disappearance" of the Cohonina problematic. Perhaps, as Cartledge (1979) suggests, the Cohonina were more closely affiliated with the western Anasazi, in which case they may have joined these people after A.D. 1200.

The Cerbat, according to Euler (1977), were probably restricted to the desert and riverine areas bordering the Colorado River in the vicinity of the Mohave valley from about A.D. 700 to about 1150. Their diagnostic artifacts are Tizon Brownware, an undecorated, oxidized, paddle-and-anvil finished pottery; flat milling stones with one-hand manos; and small, triangular, concave-based projectile points. Cremation is the mode of burial practiced, and brush wickiups and rockshelters are used as habitations. Between about A.D. 1150 and 1300, the Cerbat occupation expanded into the upland area that had been occupied by the Cohonina. Cerbat sites dating between the 1300s and the 1860s are located within the traditional area claimed by the Havasupai and Walapai, between the Black Mountains along the Colorado River in the west to the Little Colorado River in the east. Northward contraction of Havasupai and Walapai territory occurred during the 1860s as the result of warfare with the Yavapai (Euler 1977).

The Prescott branch of the Patayan cultural tradition is an upland manifestation south of the Cohonina, in the vicinity of Prescott, Arizona. The diagnostic ceramics are several types of painted and undecorated Prescott Grayware that were fired in uncon-trolled atmospheres, resulting in surface color variation from orange to brown to gray (Colton 1958; Euler and Dobyns 1962). Colton (1939) recognized two phases on the basis of intrusive Anasazi ceramics: the Prescott phase, dating from about A.D. 900 to 1100, and the Chino, dating from about 1025–1200. Shallow oval pithouses have been attributed to the Prescott phase. Architecture dating to the Chino phase includes masonry pueblos of up to 25 rooms; small, masonry hilltop "forts"; and cobble-based brush structures. Chino phase burials are extended inhumations. Trough and basin metates, three-quarter grooved axes, and stone pottery anvils are included within Prescott assemblages.

The Sinagua Problem

The name *Sinagua* was applied to archaeological remains found in the vicinity of Flagstaff, Arizona (Colton 1939, 1946). Some of the Sinagua traits, such as rock-tempered, predominantly paddle-and-anvil-finished plain brown pottery and masonry-lined pithouses, seemed distinctive from Anasazi, Hohokam, and Mogollon characteristics. On the other hand, there are significant similarities: black-on-white painted ceramics were like those of the Anasazi, Hohokam ball courts occur in the area, and much of the late prehistoric pottery and architecture is within the range of the late Mogollon.

The complex constellation of Sinagua traits has been variously interpreted. Colton (1939, 1947) considered the Sinagua a branch of the Mogollon. McGregor (1936, 1937, 1960) refers to the Sinagua as Patayan, and Schroeder (1979) includes Sinagua within the Hakataya.

Sinagua prehistory has been viewed in relation to the inferred effects of the eruption, beginning in A.D. 1064, that created Sunset Crater (Colton 1960; McGregor, 1936, 1937; Pilles 1979). Three phases of the Sinagua tradition are recognized in material dated prior to 1064: Cinder Park, Sunset, and Rio de Flag, dating from about A.D. 500 to 700, 700 to 900, and 900 to 1064, respectively. Throughout this sequence, Sinagua culture seems to have uniform ceramics, architectural styles, settlement plans, and subsistence strategies (Pilles 1979). The characteristic ceramics are types of Alameda Brown, a usually paddle-and-anvil finished ware. Trade ceramics from the Kayenta Anasazi and the Hohokam occur in the earlier phases. During the Rio de Flag phase, Cohonina trade wares are common. House types show considerable variation and include circular or subsquare pithouses with lateral entries or antechambers, tepee-like structures, masonry-lined pithouses, and small masonry surface structures. Overly large circular pithouses may have been associated with intercommunity ceremonial activities. Pithouse villages are located along the edges of large basins or parks. Both rainfall and floodwater farming could have been practiced at the park locations. Stone fieldhouses, check dams, and irrigation ditches are part of the farming technology used in areas away from the parks.

Although major eruptions associated with Sunset Crater took place in the years 1064–1065 and 1066–1067, geological investigations in the 1970s indicate continued episodes of volcanic activity for a period of about 200 years after the initial eruption (Pilles 1979). These studies, and a reevaluation of the archaeological data (Pilles 1979), suggest that previous interpretations of the post-eruptive Sinagua are inaccurate. Archaeologists (Colton 1939, 1946; McGregor 1941) had argued that the effect of the initial eruption was the deposition of substantial amounts of volcanic ash, which acted as a mulch and also added nutrients to the soil. Prehistoric farmers, according to this interpretation, immediately recognized the benefits of this soil, and a number of culturally different groups moved into the Flagstaff area to farm. According to this view, Hohokam, Mogollon, and Anasazi peoples joined the Sinagua, creating the contemporary (1070–1120) Padre, Angell, and Winona phases. Slightly later (1130–1200), these elements amalgamated in the Elden focus. This was succeeded by the Turkey Hill (1200–1300) and Clear Creek (1300–1400) foci, after which the volcanic ash was to have eroded away, causing the area to be abandoned. In questioning this view, Pilles (1979) notes that although volcanic ash does serve as an effective mulch, it does not increase the soil nutrients. Further, he finds no convincing evidence of either substantial population increase following the eruption or of substantial numbers of Hohokam, Mogollon, or Anasazi migrants. He argues that the Hohokam manifestation is limited to one or a few items at most sites, with the exception of a single pithouse and its adjacent trash mound at Winona Village (McGregor 1941). Pilles suggests that the

> Hohokam presence in the Flagstaff area may be better explained as part of the general expansion of the Hohokam out of the Gila–Salt River Valleys, possibly to facilitate the acquisition and distribution of raw materials and other trade goods. With this interpretation, the single pit house at Winona Village might represent a Hohokam trader engaged in a trading post-like situation, rather than part of a transplanted Hohokam village. (1979:472)

Aside from the pithouse at Winona, the most substantial evidence of Hohokam intrusion is the presence of 13 ball courts in the Sinagua area. Pilles interprets these ball courts as an acceptance of Mesoamerican ceremonial complexes, without the Hohokam as agents in this introduction. The Hohokam evidence is the most substantial of any of the proposed migrant groups. The Kayenta Anasazi are credited with introducing masonry construction to the Sinagua, but Cartledge (1979) and Pilles (1979) both indicate that such construction was present prior to the eruption. The evidence for other colonies of migrants is far more tenuous. In this revised view, the later portions of Sinagua prehistory are better understood in terms of local developments allied with general trends among the Western Anasazi.

The Sinagua case is particularly interesting, because rather than representing a new inventory of cultural traits or a new sequence of the appearance of features (as was true for the definition of the Hohokam and Mogollon), the Sinagua area revealed a complex blending of elements. At times, the area was distinctive. At other times, it incorporated elements of other defined cultural traditions. Initially, the assortment of external elements was interpreted as indicating migrations of various groups of people attracted by a local phenomenon—the deposition of volcanic ash. Not only has the modern view of the influence of the ashfall been reevaluated, but, as archaeologists continue to explore the Southwest, it is clear that the prehistory of *many* areas produce complex combinations of local developments and mixed external traits.

Approaches to Refinement

Major changes in the intellectual perspectives in American anthropology and archaeology that began in the 1920s, are reflected in the way that Southwestern archaeologists approach their data. The grand schemes of unilineal evolution fell into obsolescence in American anthropology, to be replaced in part by a school of thought generally referred to as *historical particularism,* which was dominated by Franz Boas. Historical particularism is concerned with defining the unique qualities and attributes of specific cultures, rather than with comparing general trends of universal development. The stratigraphic revolution in the Southwest was carried out by men who were trained in the Boasian tradition, which is in part why emphasis was placed on distinguishing the Anasazi, Hohokam, Mogollon, and Patayan cultures. As stated above, in

1927 there was little temporal depth available for the development of the diversity of Native American cultures, because the antiquity of man in the New World had not been established conclusively. In fact, 1927 marked a major turning point for this latter issue, for it was in that year that the finds at Folsom, New Mexico, were accepted by at least a portion of the scientific community (see Chapter 4). These finds demonstrated the presence of man in North America during the Late Pleistocene (about 10,000 years ago), which provided enough time depth to allow for the diversity of the indigenous development of American cultures. The impact of these developments on American archaeology was to encourage investigators to define temporal and spatial diversity and to attempt to trace the roots of various Native American tribal groups.

As Southwestern archaeologists pursued these investigations, it became obvious that there were minor variations in trait complexes and in rates of change across geographic areas: Even within the Mogollon culture area, variations in house types or changes in technology were found from one river valley to another. Within the Anasazi area, it became obvious that the prehistory of the upper Pecos Valley, as reflected at Pecos Pueblo and surrounding ruins, was quite different from that already documented in the San Juan area. Archaeologists working elsewhere in the United States encountered similar diversity; for example, in the Midwest, archaeologists systematized their data according to a scheme that has come to be called the McKern taxonomic system. A very similar system was proposed for the Southwest by the Gladwins (1934).

Roots, Stems, Branches, and Phases

The Gladwins' plan organizes information within four hierarchically arranged categories. The first, broadest, and most inclusive category is the *root,* or the basic cultural source from which later peoples are believed to have developed. In their original formulation, the Gladwins related some roots to Southwestern linguistic stocks: the Yuman, Hohokam, Caddoan, and Basketmaker. The second category of the plan divides each root into *stems,* which are major geographical areas. The Basketmaker root contains both a Little Colorado and a San Juan stem. The third category, *branch,* refers to culture areas within a stem. The San Juan stem was divided into Kayenta and Mesa Verde branches. Finally, branches are divided into *phases,* which represent temporal and spatial variations within the branch and are generally named after local geographic features. Within the Mesa Verde branch, the La Plata phase is earlier than the Mancos phase. In this scheme, assemblages are organized on the basis of the number of traits they have in common; therefore, sites with the most traits in common would be grouped into the same phase. A practical problem arises at this point, because some sites may have been occupied over a long enough period for considerable cultural change to have taken place, or sites may have been occupied at one time, abandoned, and then reoccupied later by peoples with a different cultural inventory. For these reasons, the *component,* which is the manifestation of a particular phase at an archaeological site, is the basic unit of classification. Similar components are grouped within the same phase. Although not part of the Gladwins' original scheme, Colton (1939) suggested that the component be added as an important conceptual device, a suggestion that was accepted by researchers. Colton also advised that the term *focus* be substituted for the Gladwins' *phase,* because this modification would bring the Southwestern scheme closer to the McKern system of the Midwest (cf. McKern 1939). Although this would have been a useful adjustment, it has not generally been followed.

In practice, components within a relatively small geographic locale are first grouped together within the same phase on the basis of shared traits. The number of traits used in comparison, and their level of specificity, is unfortunately generally not standardized, a problem that leads to considerable confusion among professionals as well as students. For example, consider the following three hypothetical components:

Trait	Component A	Component B	Component C
House form	Round pithouse	Round pithouse	Oval pithouse
Floor features	Fire pit, bench	Fire pit, bench	Fire pit, bench
Roof	Cribbed logs	Cribbed logs	Cribbed logs
Grinding tools	Slab metate	Trough metate	Slab metate
Ceramics	Gray neck-banded	Gray neck-banded	Gray corrugated

The three hypothetical components share the same basic house type, although the shape varies from round to oval. They also share the same floor features and roof structures. All three have metates and gray pottery, but metate shape varies, as does decorative treatment of the ceramics. Are the three similar enough to be grouped into the same phase? Are commonalities in house type and floor features more or less important than commonalities in ceramic type and metate shape? Answers to these questions are not intuitively obvious, and many such enigmas plague scholarly writings in Southwestern archaeology. There are nonarbitrary methods for reaching a decision. For example, A. C. Spaulding (1953, 1960) advocates standard statistical procedures for determining which traits cluster nonrandomly. Spaulding's approach, which would resolve a great deal of ambiguity, has not been followed in the Southwest. Although scholars frequently agonize in print over the definitions of various phases, the most common solution is nearly always to consider ceramics, and secondarily architecture, to be more important than any other diagnostic element. It is likely that, for the hypothetical example, components A and B would be grouped into the same phase, and that C would be considered representative of a different phase. The emphasis on ceramics and architecture, of course, relates to the original reasons for using these traits as basic attributes of the Pecos Classification; that is, ceramics have been demonstrated to be temporally sensitive, and architecture is considered a hallmark of trends of development.

Students are undoubtedly confused when first confronted with the plethora of phase designations currently in use in the Southwest, the proposed modifications of phases, and the diversity of ceramic types used as phase markers. In order to mitigate the complexity, some authors have presented the data of Southwestern prehistory with reference to more simplified and generalized schemes. For example, McGregor (1965) divided Southwestern prehistory into 12 temporal periods, which were designed to characterize evolutionary trends throughout the Southwest.

Environmental Adaptations

A different approach was used by Martin and Plog (1973) in their more recent synthesis. These authors examine the temporal dimension in terms of four major developmental periods: Paleo-Indian, Desert Culture (Archaic), Pit House Dwellers, and Pueblo and Town Dwellers. Following this, they discuss diversity within each of these categories in terms of adaptation to major environmental zones. Thus, the Anasazi are described with reference to their adaptation to plateau settings, the Mogollon are viewed as an adaptation to the mountains, and the Hohokam are seen as a desert adaptation. There is much to recommend this treatment, because many of the characteristic traits of each major cultural tradition relate to behaviors appropriate in certain physical settings. For example, this is true of the characterization of the Hohokam as dependent on extensive irrigation agriculture or the Patayan as reliant on inundation from the Colorado River. On the other hand, as noted above, similarities and differences among ceramic assemblages are frequently used as key phase and culture markers, and these do not always correspond to environmental zones. For example, certain kinds of Mogollon ceramics (and architectural styles) occur not only at sites in the Mogollon Mountains but also within the low desert areas of northern Chihuahua and Sonora. Also, the Anasazi area is typically defined to include the Rio Grande drainage, which comprises an area of mountains and a major river valley and is not topographically similar to the Colorado Plateaus.

Provinces

In a more recent approach, Plog (1979), following Ruppé (1953), presented data on the western Anasazi in terms of *provinces*. The use of provinces is of interest because the areas involved are related to general theory and to empirical data. The theory derives from analyses of the amount of territory required to sustain population equilibrium at different population densities. Using estimates from some of the better-documented areas, Plog suggested territory sizes of 10,000 to 15,000 km^2. Using hexagons of this size centered over some of the more obvious homogeneous areas (such as Mesa Verde), Plog found that the other hexagons in the grid fell over previously defined homogeneous culture areas, and that there was a good correspondence between the boundaries of areas that were based on the hexagons and those identified by archaeologists working with empirical data. As is clear from his full discussion (Plog 1979), province boundaries, and indeed the provinces themselves, are marked only during some time periods. Because the provinces are defined largely on the basis of stylistic attributes in ceramics and architecture, the observation indicates that the organizational properties reflected in these styles were not static but changed over time, and some attempts to explain these changes have been made (Plog 1983).

As provocative as are the uses of McGregor's time periods, Martin and Plog's environmental zones, and Plog's provinces, the literature of Southwestern archaeology is written in terms of local phases. The student who wishes to pursue a particular topic or issue therefore needs a guide to terminology. For this reason, Tables 3.3–3.10 have been prepared. Three comments about the tables are in order. First, calendrical dates appear in the first column of each chart, although up to this point such dates have not been discussed in the text. Many of these dates have been derived from tree-ring chronologies. Second, space limitations make it impossible to list the criteria considered to be diagnostic of each phase. The references given should be consulted for this information. Finally, the reorganization of data is an ongoing process in Southwestern archeology, and it must be recognized that changes in and refinements of the sequences presented will continue to be made.

Some Problems with Developmental Schemes

The Pecos Classification and the other developmental schemes used in the Southwest suggest that changes in architecture and ceramics occur synchronously within the same area. Although the phase schemes recognize that such change may not occur over very broad geographic regions (such as the Mogollon Mountains), it is generally assumed that at the branch level there should be little variation. The empirical data of archaeology have long shown that homogeneity within contemporary phases of the same branch does not always exist. A classic demonstration of this point is the recognition that within the Chaco branch of the Anasazi culture, between about A.D. 1000 and 1130, two entirely different architectural styles and village plans co-occur in the same very small geographic area. One style consists of large, multistoried, planned pueblos (such as Pueblo Bonito). The other style consists of single-story, small, unplanned pueblos (such as the village identified as Casa Rinconada). Ceramics from the large pueblos and small pueblos are virtually the same. Also within the Anasazi culture, the Chaco, Mesa Verde, and Kayenta branches are distinguished on the basis of architectural styles. Yet excavations have demonstrated that within the same site all three styles of construction may be present (Martin and Rinaldo 1960; Martin *et al.* 1961). Any scheme of classification that minimizes or ignores these kinds of variation will not represent a faithful rendering of the diversity that can characterize the archaeological record.

The assumption that uniformity will characterize the material culture of closely related people rests on what has been termed the *normative* view of culture. Within the normative intellectual paradigm, it is assumed that a single culture consists of a constellation of shared ideas (or norms) held by all members of the culture and is reflected in similarities in material culture and other phenomena, such as belief systems and social organization. For our own, and other complex societies, the normative view obviously will not serve to characterize the culture as a whole. Belief systems and material culture will vary with economic status, level of educational attainment, geographic area, and other factors. Think of the differences in material culture between high-income and low-income neighborhoods within the same community. If manifest contemporary diversity within the archaeological remains of a single locale is ignored through application of a classification scheme that is not designed to reflect variation, archaeologists may not conceptualize cultural and societal complexity when it exists. There are other reasons why the normative framework may be inadequate for describing either contemporary or archaeological cultures; some variation may be functionally related to variations in activities. For example, the house plan and material inventory of a house belonging to a family in a modern American city may differ substantially from the plan and contents of a summer mountain cabin belonging to the same family. The electrical appliances, fine furniture, clothing, and other artifacts in one house will contrast markedly with kerosene lamps, rustic furniture, and other items in the cabin. Most important, the differences do not indicate that the two dwellings are used by members of two different cultures with different norms of behavior. Among societies organized very differently from our own, the patterns of behavior and their material correlates may be equally variable for functional reasons. For example, the fairly permanent winter residences of families of herders will differ substantially from the small summer camps used by the same people as they move animals to dispersed and temporary pasture areas. Differences in house size, volume of storage facilities, and the portability of items in each type of residence again do not reflect cultural differences. One of the goals of archaeology is to provide accurate descriptions of various past ways of life. If all variation is assumed to reflect diversity in cultural norms, these descriptions will be erroneous. It is an obligation of archaeology to determine which aspects of the cultural inventory of past societies are the result of functional and social differences, and which are not.

In addition to describing past lifeways, archaeology is concerned with describing the ways in which change occurs over time. The developmental schemes applied in the Southwest were prepared before methods of assigning calendar dates to prehistoric sites were available. Consequently, either stratigraphic information *or* unverified notions involving trends in "refinement" were applied to facilitate the temporal ordering of remains. It has been noted that in these schemes, architecture is considered an index of development and growth; thus it is assumed that there is a trend from simple, perhaps crude house forms, such as pithouses, to refined and perhaps complex forms, such as pueblos, For example, Haury (1936) interpreted the appearance of crudely built aboveground pueblo structures in the Mimbres area as evidence that this architectural form had been borrowed from the Anasazi. Archaeological data available demonstrate that pithouses were in use in the Pueblo area in the Rio Grande Valley, the upper Little Colorado, and Black Mesa (Cordell and Plog 1979) long after the Anasazi had "developed" the ability to build pueblos. Among the most recent pithouses built as dwellings were those constructed at the modern Hopi town of Bacabi in the twentieth century, many years after the Hopi and their ancestors had learned the technology of constructing aboveground rooms. These examples suggest that pithouses and pueblos probably serve different functional purposes within the context of the entire culture. Either form may be used as a dwelling, depending on various behavioral and demographic factors. It is incumbent on archaeologists to define the circumstances under which each would be built, rather than to assume that one form is a more advanced elaboration of technology. When Kidder suggested that developmental patterns could be discerned in classes of archaeological material, such as rock art or basketry, the tools for chronological ordering were not available. The continued use of developmental schemes is not always warranted by current information.

In addition to describing lifeways and the course of change in cultures over time, archaeologists share with their anthropological colleagues the obligation to try to explain the patterned diversity in culture. Developmental schemes describe changes without providing any explanations for the particular change involved. In some cases, the change is viewed as a natural development, which, in view of the above discussion of the use of pithouses or aboveground pueblos, cannot be accepted. Within the normative framework, as noted, material culture items are seen as reflections of ideas shared by members of a society. When a change appears in the archaeological record, a change involving material culture, it is frequently interpreted as being the result of the introduction of a new group of people with a different set of norms: The appearance of multistoried great houses in the Hohokam area, along with polychrome pottery, was interpreted as evidence of an incursion of a new group of non-Hohokam people. Again, in view of the current paradigm, which emphasizes that variation in material items may reflect differences in function or social organization, such interpretations must be questioned. As the studious reader of most Southwestern prehistories should notice, an enormous number of migrations are postulated. Certainly some of the emphasis on migration is the result of the observation that most Southwestern archaeological sites, and some entire regions, were abandoned after varying intervals of time. The inhabitants of these sites and regions must have gone somewhere, and migration into other areas is a logical supposition. Nevertheless, migration is not an easy phenomenon to demonstrate in the archaeological record (cf. Reed 1949; Rouse 1958), especially if change in the material culture inventory can be ascribed to other factors. If archaeologists are to attempt to interpret change, then various explanations for particular changes, including migrations, must be evaluated against a set of independently derived data. Archaeology must follow the basic procedures of any science. Rather than assume the operation of particular processes that are not directly observed, the processes must be formulated as propositions and tested.

Although Southwestern archaeologists work with a vocabulary and conceptual devices derived from developmental classification, these are not adequate to the tasks of accurately describing the variation in the archaeological record and the course of culture change or of evaluating various explanations offered for culture change.

Methods of Dating

Chronological control is crucial to describing and explaining culture change over time and the variability of cultural manifestations over space. The rate of change in various classes of material culture or in organization cannot be assumed; it requires an independent frame of reference. The Southwest has long been considered unique in

American archaeology because it is an area in which precise chronological control is possible in the absence of written records. A chronological framework, calibrated to calendar years, has been derived through the use of dendrochronological, radiocarbon, archaeomagnetic, and obsidian hydration dating techniques. As is discussed later, the full potential of the application of these techniques has not been realized, and numerous chronological problems remain. Nevertheless, these techniques, and some others, provide the essential frame of reference for Southwestern prehistory.

Dendrochronology

Dendrochronology in the Southwest was developed by the astonomer A. E. Douglass. The historical background of Douglass' paleoclimatic research and the basic principles involved in tree-ring dating are discussed in Chapter 2. The dating of Southwestern archaeological sites is the main concern here. During the 1920s, by working back from live and recently cut trees, Douglass was able to extend the tree-ring chronology to A.D. 1280. After soliciting the aid of archaeologists and obtaining wood from various archaeological sites, Douglass developed another sequence of rings spanning 580 years, but this floating chronology was not tied to the sequence that began in 1280. In order to bridge the gap between 1280 and the older sequence, Douglass first sampled timbers from the Hopi village of Oraibi. The results of this work pushed the chronology back to 1260 but no further. In June 1929, a partially charred timber excavated from Showlow Ruin by Lyndon Hargrave and Emil Haury provided the link necessary to tie the floating chronology to the present and therefore enabled the placement of many Southwestern ruins with reference to the Christian calendar. Among the ruins that were immediately dated by this event were Pueblo Bonito, Aztec, Cliff Palace, Betatakin, Kiet Siel, and Waputki (McGregor 1965; Wormington 1961). The benefits of tree-ring dating were, of course, immediately apparent to archaeologists, and during the 1930s, major institutions such as Gila Pueblo, the Museum of Northern Arizona, the University of Arizona, the Laboratory of Anthropology of the Museum of New Mexico, and the University of New Mexico established programs designed to secure wood specimens from archaeological sites. Many sites were dated.

As noted in Chapter 2, materials appropriate for tree-ring dating are wood specimens from drought-resistant species such as Douglas fir, piñon, and yellow pine. Trees that normally grow in well-watered settings, such as cottonwood, are not datable because their ring width does not vary as a response to climatic stress. Species such as juniper can sometimes be dated, although with difficulty, because juniper frequently produces aberrant ring patterns. Fortunately, the species that are appropriate for dating are also often found in archaeological contexts, where they were used as roof support posts, roof beams, and sometimes as interior wall supports for adobe-walled structures. It is also possible to date charcoal of sufficiently large size, so wood from prehistoric firepits can be dated.

The utility of tree-ring dating goes beyond providing calendrical dates for sites. The Laboratory of Tree Ring Research at the University of Arizona provides archaeologists with useful supplementary data. The species of tree is identified, which can be useful in studies of the use of wood resources. It is possible to discern whether wood used at a site was available locally or imported over considerable distance. Changes in the use of different species of trees in the same locality may indicate depletion of certain kinds of trees. The preferential use of different kinds of wood for fuel, as opposed to building material, may also be discerned. When dates are reported, two dates are usually given. The first date is taken from the pith of the tree, when possible, which indicates when the tree began its growth. The second is an outside date that should approximate the year in which the tree was cut. Comparisons among pith and cutting dates can suggest whether or not mature forest was being culled for building material. When outside dates are given, these are accompanied by symbols with which archaeologists should be familiar. Outside dates followed by a *B* (bark present), *G* (beetle galleries present), *c* (outermost ring continuous), and *r* (outer ring continuous around available circumference, but full section not present) all indicate cutting dates. The symbols *v* and *vv* following a date indicate that the dates are not cutting dates. The single *v* suggests that the date is close to the cutting date, whereas *vv* indicates that it is not possible to estimate how far the last ring is from the true outside of the specimen. In general, of course, cutting dates are the most reliable indicators of construction dates.

Evaluation of tree-ring dates within the archaeological context from which they come is a responsibility of the archaeologist and can be very informative. For example, if cutting dates from primary beams or roof support posts cluster tightly at 1290, this indicates that the series of rooms from which the specimens were obtained was planned or built in that year. One or very few cutting dates prior to 1290 might indicate that the people constructing the room had reused wood from a previous structure (a common phenomenon). Dates after 1290 in secondary architectural features might indicate repair to the rooms. Analyses of the clustering of tree-ring dates and architectural features have enabled archaeologists to describe, in detail, the construction and use patterns of prehistoric pueblos. For example, Jeffrey Dean (1969, 1970) was able to show that Betatakin (Figure 3.24) (Tsegi Canyon, Arizona) was founded in 1267, although the cave in which it is located was first occupied in 1250. Three room clusters were built in 1267, and a fourth cluster was added in 1268. In 1269 and 1272, a number of trees were felled, cut into appropriate lengths for use as primary and secondary beams, and stockpiled. These beams were used in the construction of more than 10 rooms and at least one kiva, which were built in 1275. After 1275, rooms were added at a slower pace, until a population peak of about 125 persons was attained in the mid-1280s. Dean's analysis strongly suggests that the immigration to the site in 1275 was anticipated and planned for, and that the subsequent growth was probably the result of internal population expansion.

Tree-ring dating is the most precise method of dating available to Southwestern archaeology, and it has been used extensively. Nevertheless, some problems exist that are worth reiterating. In some areas of the Southwest, wood preservation is poor, and for that reason tree-ring dates cannot be obtained. Some sites, particularly those along rivers, may contain structural timbers of nondatable cottonwood. In some areas of the

Figure 3.24 Betatakin Ruins, Navajo National Monument, Arizona. Dean's (1969, 1970) study of tree-ring dates from the site enabled him to reconstruct the construction and occupation history of the ruin. (Photograph courtesy of the Museum of New Mexico.)

Southwest where wood is generally scarce, wood used for fuel and some construction may consist largely of dead wood that has been scavenged from the landscape. Given the generally dry climate, scavenged wood may be considerably older than the sites in which it is used. Frequently, despite the appearance of good preservation and appropriate wood, only a small number of specimens submitted for analysis prove to be datable. At some of the very large and planned Southwestern sites, such as Casas Grandes, timbers were abraded and squared for use as beams. The dates obtained from these must be published as *vv* dates; they too may greatly precede the time at which construction took place. The published dates for these sites will reflect periods during which final construction occurred, but if the sites were occupied over a long period, or if there are several temporally distinct components, the initial occupations will not have been dated. Finally, for reasons that are not entirely clear, archaeologists have failed to collect tree-ring samples from many sites and other areas, the dates from which would be useful; for example, few of the known sites in the San Juan Basin have been dated. In part, the failure to collect samples can be ascribed to the general reliance Southwestern archaeologists have placed on ceramic cross-dating.

Ceramic Cross-Dating

Ceramic types have been used as key cultural and temporal markers in Southwestern classificatory schemes. When tree-ring dating became available, dates were assigned to ceramic types. It was assumed that an abundance of a particular type at a site indicated that that type had been manufactured there, and that it could be dated on the basis of tree-ring dates obtained from the site (Breternitz 1966; Colton 1956). When the particular type was found at other sites, these sites were dated indirectly through ceramic cross-dating. This approach provides a quick method for roughly ordering sites in time, but it has been much abused and has obscured some basic questions. First, studies of the paste composition of ceramics (Kidder and Shepard 1936; Shepard 1942) demonstrated that an abundance of a particular ceramic type at a site does not necessarily indicate that the type had been manufactured there. A number of types were assigned dates on the basis of sites into which they were traded. Because trade relations are imbedded in the general context of social relations, the date at which trade ceramics may be accepted will reflect factors other than the simple availability of the type. Suppose that an abundance of Type A is found at Site 1, which is dated to 1400. Type A may have been manufactured as early as 1350 at Site 2 but traded to Site 1 50 years later. If all sites on which Type A occurs are dated to 1400, a considerable error is introduced. In practice, too, the absence of a particular type may be taken as evidence that a site was abandoned before the type was made. Site 3, lacking Type A, may be given an abandonment date earlier than 1400. If Site 3 is outside the trade network of Type A for social and political reasons, the abandonment date is false. These problems are not minor. Ceramic cross-dating has been so widely applied in the Southwest that entire regional chronologies may be seriously in error (Cordell and Earls 1982b; Cordell and Plog 1979; Schiffer 1982).

Of equal importance is the fact that archaeologists wish to understand variation in the rate of change. Ceramic cross-dating assumes that variation is either negligible or that the rates at which pottery is traded or copied are known. Thus, archaeologists have assumed what, in fact, they wished to learn. The value of tree-ring dating is that it is culturally independent. Ceramic cross-dating, even when bolstered by the precision of tree-ring dates, depends on cultural processes that are in many cases poorly understood.

As noted, conditions of preservation or other factors may prohibit the application of dendrochronology to specific sites. Importantly, the tree-ring chronology does not extend to the early portions of the Southwestern sequence (the Paleoindian and Archaic periods). In these situations, radiocarbon dating is the most precise, culturally independent technique available.

Radiocarbon Dating

Radiocarbon dating was developed by Willard F. Libby and his associates at the University of Chicago in 1947. Libby, a physicist, was studying cosmic radiation and became interested in radioactive carbon, because it occurs naturally and could be used both as a tracer element and to date the organic materials in which it is found. Radiocarbon dating depends on the fact that cosmic rays in the earth's upper atmosphere produce neutrons that react with nitrogen, yielding ^{14}C, the unstable carbon isotope: $^{14}N + n \rightarrow {}^{14}C + p$. ^{13}C is also produced, but this isotope and normal carbon, ^{12}C, are both stable. ^{14}C is not stable but decays at an exponential rate, such that half the original material remains after 5730 years, half of that after another 5730 years, and so on. Importantly, ^{14}C enters into chemical reactions in the same way that normal ^{12}C does. Some of the carbon dioxide produced in the atmosphere contains radioactive carbon ($^{14}CO_2$), but most carbon dioxide is $^{12}CO_2$. Plants absorb carbon dioxide in photosynthesis, and animals feeding on plants (and other animals) take in carbon dioxide. Because $^{14}CO_2$ is chemically the same as normal carbon dioxide, plants and animals, while they are alive, contain the same proportion of the carbon isotopes that exist in the atmosphere. This is an extremely small amount. The equilibrium concentration is about 1.2 parts ^{14}C to 10^{12} parts ^{12}C. At death, when carbon dioxide is no longer replenished, the radiocarbon decays at the known rate, reverting to nitrogen by giving off a beta particle. In radiocarbon dating, the age (in radiocarbon years) of the sample T is determined by the formula (Ralph 1971):

$$T = 5730 \left(\log_2 \frac{^{14}C}{^{12}C} \text{ present} - \log_2 \frac{^{14}C}{^{12}C} \text{ sample} \right)$$

In conventional radiocarbon dating, the amount of radioactive carbon in the sample is measured indirectly by measuring the amount of radioactivity in the sample—or the number of disintegrations per minute per gram of carbon. Because of the low level of radioactivity, this method is somewhat inefficient and requires a fairly large amount of carbon (between about 10 and 50 gm, depending on the material) and is accurate in dating materials to an age of about 50,000 years. The actual decay of radiocarbon is a random process, so only an average of half of the ^{14}C will decay every 5730 years. For this reason laboratories report radiocarbon ages along with the standard deviation. For example, a date may be given as 12,290 ± 50 years. The date should be read, and interpreted, to mean that there are two chances out of three that the age of the sample is between 12,340 and 12,240 years. Finally, it should be noted that radiocarbon dating depends on the assumption that the amount of cosmic radiation has been constant, and this is now known to be false (Goss 1965). Rather, over the last 2000 years there has been considerable variation, so dates within this range may be as much as 250 years from their true ages. Radiocarbon laboratories correct for this error using calibrations obtained from tree-ring studies of sequoia and bristlecone pine (Ralph 1971).

Radiocarbon dates are accurate and calibrated to the Christian calendar. They may be derived from virtually any organic sample, such as charcoal, wood, bone, and shell. The technique provides accurate dates beyond the temporal range of tree rings and is therefore essential for the Archaic and Paleoindian periods, and it may be necessary for any site in which wood that is appropriate for tree-ring studies is not found. Finally, a new method of radiocarbon dating (Bennett 1979) promises to have considerable value for archaeologists, although no results of the application of this method are available for its evaluation in the Southwest. The new method uses high-speed accelerators (cyclotrons and tandem Van de Graaff generators) to measure directly the number of ^{14}C atoms in a sample. Although experimental and costly, this method requires only milligrams of carbon (as opposed to grams) and may be accurate to ages of 70,000 years. The small sample size required by the accelerator method may make it possible to date materials with extremely small carbon contents, such as the organic paint used in some ceramic decorations.

Despite the importance of radiocarbon dating, a number of problems with its use should be recognized. First, many published dates for the Southwest were obtained when radiocarbon dating was in its infancy and methods of sample processing were not refined. These dates were obtained from specimens of solid carbon, rather than carbon gas, and are not considered reliable. Second, it is difficult to interpret radiocarbon dates when excavators have employed arbitrary metric levels in excavation and grouped deposits that may span considerable time. This problem is particularly acute with respect to early excavations of rockshelters and cave sites. In these situations, deposition may be very slow, and the cultural events of interest may be reflected in very thin lenses of material. If these are dated through the use of radiocarbon dates obtained by combining charcoal flecks from a 10- or 20-cm level, the dates will not be precise for the cultural remains of interest. Finally, some Southwestern dates reflect what Michael Schiffer refers to as the "old wood" problem (Schiffer 1982:324). Desert hardwoods, such as mesquite, paloverde, and ironwood, are long lived, attaining ages of several hundred years. The outer rings of the wood of these species will yield the year in which the tree was cut or died, but the inner rings may date to several hundred years earlier. Charcoal flecks obtained for radiocarbon dating cannot be assumed to come only from the outer rings; radiocarbon dates from such flecks may be considerably older than the cultural contexts in which they are found. In addition, because Sonoran Desert wood is very hard and difficult to cut when green, dead limbs from living trees, dead trees, driftwood, and wood scavenged or reused from cultural contexts may have been used as fuel. Radiocarbon dates from charcoal will therefore consistently be too early for the hearths with which they are associated. The "old wood" problem is severe in the chronology of the Sonoran Desert, where the hardwoods are the only species available for construction and for fuel.

Archaeomagnetic Dating

Archaeomagnetic dating is now frequently used in the Southwest, both as a supplement to tree-ring dating and in situations in which tree-ring dating is not possible due to a lack of appropriate samples (Weaver 1967; Windes 1980). The technique depends on two well-documented natural phenomena. First, the earth's magnetic field is not stable but constantly shifts in intensity and direction. Second, when clay is heated beyond 200 °C, the magnetic fields of iron particles within the clay take on the magnetic orientation of the earth's magnetic field at that time and place, remaining stable unless heated beyond 700°C. In order to date a sample, it is necessary to have an accurate map of the past positions of the earth's magnetic field. In the Southwest, maps have been generated by plotting the magnetic orientations of hearth samples taken from sites that have been dated by tree-rings and radiocarbon; however, there are still some ambiguities and inconsistencies. A critical problem is that there is no agreed-upon archaeomagnetic map for the period prior to A.D. 600. Nevertheless, archae-

Figure 3.25 Taking archaeomagnetic samples. Thomas Windes prepares archaeomagnetic samples from a burned feature at Chaco Canyon, New Mexico. Note the aluminum cubes and plaster used to jacket the sample. (Photograph reproduced courtesy of the Chaco Center, National Park Service.)

omagnetic dates are very useful. Samples appropriate for the technique include hearths and burned areas on floors or walls that have been heated to 200°C. Because the analysis of samples depends on comparing the modern position of the earth's magnetic field at the location of the sample with that reflected by the minerals within the sample, it is essential that the location of the sample be precisely fixed and measured. Loose chunks of burned adobe are not suitable for dating. The collection of samples (Figure 3.25) is time consuming and requires training and specialized equipment, including aluminum cubes, which may be obtained from the laboratories processing the samples. Despite some of the difficulties in obtaining samples and dates, the technique is of great value. For example, comparisons among tree-ring dates and archaeomagnetic dates from the same site offer the potential of precisely determining the use span of the site, because tree-ring dates should reflect the year of construction and archaeomagnetic dates should be close to the final date for the use of features such as hearths. Analyses of this sort are being pursued for Pueblo Alto, a large town site in Chaco Canyon (Windes 1980).

Obsidian Hydration Dating

Obsidian hydration dating was developed by the geologists Irving Friedman and Robert L. Smith (1960) and refined primarily by the work of D. L. Clark (1961) (see Michels and Bebrich 1971 and Michaels and Tsong 1980). The basic principle involved is that obsidian, like all glass, will slowly absorb atmospheric or ground moisture. When a fresh surface is exposed (by the removal of a flake, for example), this surface will also begin to absorb moisture. Molecular water drawn into obsidian advances along a demarcated front that can be seen under a microscope as a thin, uniform rim, and the thickness of this rim, indicating the amount of molecular moisture absorbed, can be measured. The rate at which obsidian hydration rims are formed is not constant but varies primarily with the temperature. Obsidian hydrates more quickly in warm climates than in cold ones. Although temperature is the major influence on the rate of molecular absorption, there is also variation due to slightly different compositions of different obsidian sources. New techniques of analysis (Michaels and Tsong 1980) permit very accurate compositional characterizations of obsidians. Laboratory-induced hydration of specific sources, for fixed periods, at constant temperatures allows construction of source-specific and temperature-specific hydration rates. Obsidian samples are relatively easy and inexpensive to process, allowing many samples from a particular site or locality to be analyzed. Calibrations are available for many sources in the Southwest, and the technique is being used successfully (e.g., Russell 1981). In many Southwestern sites where hearths or timbers are present, obsidian hydration dating may be used in conjunction with radiocarbon and tree-ring dating. A great number of Southwestern sites, however, are lithic scatters that may not contain temporally diagnostic artifacts. If such scatters contain obsidian, obsidian hydration dating is invaluable. In a study of a series of lithic sites in the Jemez Mountains, New Mexico (Baker and Winter 1981), obsidian hydration studies indicated that most sites dated to the late Archaic. One site, however, was apparently of the later Pueblo age (Russell 1981). In this case, the site was also distinctive in the kinds of lithic artifacts represented, lending support to the hydration study.

The techniques discussed above are those that are quite frequently employed in Southwestern archaeology. In addition to these, there are several experimental techniques being pursued in the Southwest, an area that offers the precise chronology of tree-ring dates as a control. Among these are fission-track dating of mica inclusions in ceramics and thermoluminescent dating of sandstone, both of which may have broad applicability once they are sufficiently developed.

New Frameworks, Elaborations, and Current Chronologies

Since the 1930s, Southwestern archaeologists have worked on the formulation of local and regional sequences and the assignment of calendrical dates to them. In addition, there has been an effort to link various prehistoric remains to specific linguistic or ethnic groups. Not all of these efforts have been successful, and the literature reflects a considerable amount of controversy in interpretation. Chronological revisions make up a substantial portion of the literature of Southwestern archaeology and will likely continue to do so. The history of debates within various regions of the Southwest is not given here. Rather, a summary of regional frameworks and some assessment of recent chronological discussions and areas of disagreement are provided as background necessary to further treatment of the post-Archaic developments in the Southwest. This review should serve to underscore areas in which further research is necessary. Most of this discussion involves regional traditions that have been introduced above. The Fremont of central Utah is discussed for the first time here.

The Fremont

The Fremont tradition, considered by some to be Southwestern, lies north of the Anasazi and Patayan areas in Utah and westernmost Nevada (Figure 1.5). First defined by Morss (1931) on the basis of work in the Fruita area of central Utah and initially viewed as a peripheral variant of the Anasazi, subsequent investigations warrant its interpretation as a separate culture tradition with five regional variants: Great Salt Lake, Unita, San Rafael, Sevier, and Parawan (Table 3.3). Among the traits considered useful in characterizing the Fremont in general is the production of unpainted graywares using the coil-and-scrape technique. Some ceramic types have plastic decoration, and some late Fremont types are decorated with black paint. The Fremont tradition is also characterized by the use of moccasins (as opposed to the sandals of the Anasazi area) of a distinctive type, composed of three pieces of hide, with a single untanned piece with the dew claws retained, made from the hind leg of a large animal, serving as the sole. Another Fremont diagnostic is the one-rod-and-bundle basket. Fremont sites generally consist of a few pithouses with associated storerooms or granaries. The latter are either masonry or adobe. Kivas are not documented for Fremont sites. Agriculture apparently depended on the distinctive type of corn, Fremont dent, that may have been well adapted to short growing seasons. An abundance of faunal remains and wild plant foods may indicate that the Fremont were less dependent on agriculture than were the Anasazi. The abundant rock art in the Fremont area is stylistically different from that of adjacent areas (Figure 3.26). Two other Fremont traits have been seen as linked to the Mogollon area: the "Utah type" metate with a shelf in addition to the grinding surface, which is known from early Mogollon sites, and the frequent use of a fugitive red pigment on pottery, which may have been an attempt to copy Mogollon redwares. Finally, some Fremont sites and localities are known for elaborate, unfired clay figurines (Figure 3.27), which are unique among Southwestern figurines (Jennings 1978:155–234).

There is considerable controversy in the literature regarding Fremont origins, ethnic affiliation, and the eventual fate of Fremont peoples (e.g., Aikens 1966; Gunnerson 1969; Jennings 1978; Lipe 1978; Madsen and Berry 1975). Nevertheless, the five variants of Fremont culture have been defined and dated, and some have been divided into sequential phases (Table 3.4). The views regarding Fremont origins may be summarized as follows. Earlier investigators tended to regard the Fremont as derivative of the Anasazi, perhaps a regional development stemming from the expansion of Anasazi communities after about A.D. 950. This view has not fared well, largely because Fremont sites have been dated antecedent to the Anasazi expansion of this time.

Table 3.3

Fremont Geographic Variants and Phase Dates*a*

Great Salt Lake
  Levee phase, A.D. 1000–1350+
  Bear River phase, A.D. 400–1000
Unita
  Whiterocks phase, A.D. 800–950
  Cub Creek phase, pre-A.D. 800
San Rafael
  (no phases recognized) A.D. 700–1200
Sevier
  (no phases recognized) A.D. 780–1260
Parawan
  Paragonah phase, A.D. 1050–1300
  Summit phase, A.D. 900–1050

*a*After Jennings (1978).

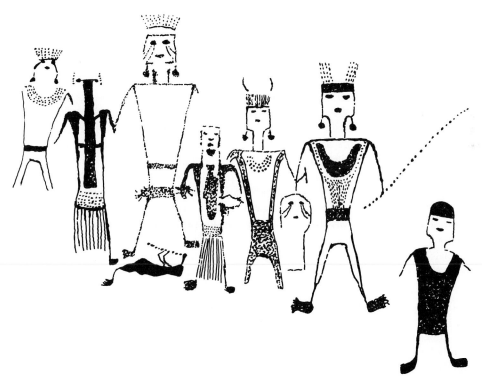

Figure 3.26 Fremont rock art. Fremont petroglyphs differ stylistically from those of the surrounding areas. (The illustration is adapted from Schaafsma (1971) by Charles M. Carrillo.)

Figure 3.27   Fremont clay figurine. (Illustrated by Charles M. Carrillo. Adapted from *The Ancient Culture of the Fremont River in Utah* [Morss 1931, Peabody Museum Papers, vol. 12, no. 3] with permission from the Peabody Museum of Archaeology and Ethnology, Harvard University.)

Another interpretation characterized the Fremont as Plains-related, emphasizing the importance of bison hunting reflected in some Fremont sites and the use of moccasins, tepees, shields, and shield pictographs. This view has also been largely abandoned, even by those who initially proposed it (Aikens 1966, 1978). Jennings considers the Fremont to be a development from a local Desert Archaic base in response to the same early Mogollon or Hohokam "pulsations from southwestern New Mexico and northern Mexico that triggered the Anasazi developments" (1978:155–156). These pulsations are to have reached the Fremont area by about A.D. 500. This interpretation of Fremont origins is probably the most widely accepted, although Madsen and Berry (1975) have argued that there is an apparent hiatus between late Archaic and Fremont assemblages that may span a period of up to 2000 years. Further dating of early Fremont sites should eventually resolve this issue.

The question of Fremont ethnic affiliation is, of course, not separate from that of Fremont origins. Thus, if the Fremont are seen as regional variants of the Anasazi, their ethnic affiliation is viewed as being Pueblo (Gunnerson 1969). In this regard, both Virgin branch Anasazi and Kayenta branch Anasazi have been associated with the Fremont. Ethnic affiliation with the northwest Plains peoples, particularly the Athapaskans, has also been suggested. Neither of these two views is currently in favor, and as noted, the Fremont are generally considered to be a separate, distinct Southwestern culture with internal regional variation. The eventual fate of the Fremont is, at present, equally poorly understood. As Table 3.4 indicates, not all areas were abandoned at the same time, and it is possible that there was considerable population redistribution within the Fremont area after A.D. 1550 or 1200 (Lipe 1978). Attempts to link the Fremont with the northern Paiute, the Shoshone–Comanche, and the southern Paiute (Gunnerson 1969) have been effectively criticised (Euler 1964; Lipe 1978), as has the attempt to link the Fremont with Athapaskan speakers of the northwest Plains. Lipe (1978:388) suggests that "the Fremont drifted south during the 1200s and 1300s, much as the Anasazi did, perhaps in response to similar pressures," although he notes that evidence of the incorporation of Fremont groups into Pueblo cultures is notably lacking. The difficulty in finding evidence of "unit intrusions" among the post-abandonment Pueblos is not unique to the Fremont, and is taken up in detail in Chapter 9.

The Lower Patayan

A number of problems beset the formulation of a chronology for the remains of the ceramic period in the lower Patayan area (Waters 1982). These include a paucity of culturally independent dates (and no tree-ring or archaeomagnetic dates), very few vertically stratified sites, and considerable confusion regarding the definitions of various ceramic types. Both the lack of chronometric dates and the absence of vertically stratified sites relate to the geographic characteristics of the lower Colorado River valley and the kind of cultural adaptation probably associated with this setting. First, before the construction of modern dams, the Colorado River was characterized by very large annual floods that deposited massive amounts of silt along its lower courses (McGuire 1982:19). During the historic period, the Yuma Indians of this area planted fields in the floodplain after the summer floods had subsided but moved to high ground, above the river, in the winter. The structures associated with the agricultural season were ephemeral and their locations changed from year to year, depending on shifts in the river channel and areas of silt deposition. Assuming that the prehistoric agriculturalists of the lower Colorado River Valley practiced a similar farming strategy, the absence of stratified remains is expected, and the annual inundations and deposition of silt would obscure even the few cultural materials left behind.

The confusion surrounding the lower Patayan ceramic typology is the result of two different investigators using the same set of names for very different types. Thus, Rogers (1945) distinguished the lower Patayan types on the basis of differences in surface treatment, rim form, vessel form, and only secondarily on variations in temper. Schroeder (1952) relied on temper as the primary criterion for the various types, but used Rogers' type names. For the various reasons discussed by Waters (1982), the type definitions applied by Rogers and as presented by Waters are accepted here. Although no adequately refined Patayan chronology exists, Waters' discussion is considered most useful in providing a baseline for the future construction of such a sequence.

As discussed by Waters, the Patayan chronology is divided into three developmental periods, with chronological implications. These are simply labeled Patayan I, II, and III. Patayan I includes five ceramic types (Colorado Beige, Colorado Red-on-beige, Colorado Red, Black Mesa Buff, and Black Mesa Red-on-buff), all of which display direct chimney-neck rims on jars, the Colorado shoulder on jars (Figure 3.22), red clay slip, burnishing, rim notching, punctate and incised decorations, lug-and-loop handles, and the manufacturing process of hemispherical casting and basket molding. The chronological position of this assemblage of types is based on its association with intrusive Hohokam sherds at two stratified sites, five radiocarbon dates, and its absence at Patayan II and Patayan III sites. The intrusive Hohokam sherds are Santa Cruz Red-on-brown of the Colonial period. The five radiocarbon dates, which were obtained from charcoal, range in age from A.D. 825 ± 80 to 1050 ± 65. Although Waters suggests dates of about A.D. 700 to 1050 for Patayan I, on the basis of the "old wood" problem and associated difficulties with the Hohokam chronology a beginning date closer to A.D. 875 or even 900 is probably more reasonable.

The ceramic types considered diagnostic of Patayan II are Tumco Buff, Parker Buff, Palomas Buff, Salton Buff, and their painted red-on-buff equivalents (e.g., Tumco Red-on-buff). Attributes of ceramics that are new in the Patayan II assemblages include recurved rims, stucco finish, new vessel forms, and an increase in fine-lined geometric designs. The chronological placement of Patayan II depends on geological interpretations and the dating of Lake Cahuilla, some intrusive sherds, radiocarbon dates, similarities in design between the Hohokam type Casa Grande Red-on-buff and the Patayan Tumco Red-on-buff, and the absence of the diagnostic types from Patayan I and Patayan III sites. Although Waters comments on the wider geographic distribution of Patayan II than Patayan I ceramics, the chronology of this period is far from precise. Waters suggests dates of between A.D. 1000 and 1500.

Some ceramics of Patayan III—Palomas Buff, Parker Buff, and their painted equivalents—continue from the previous period. Colorado Buff and Colorado Red-on-buff are new types. Waters notes that the differences between Patayan II and Patayan III ceramics are subtle. Three radiocarbon dates and the association of the Patayan III ceramic types with metal and glass items at some sites support the placement of these types within the historic period (ca. 1600 to the late 1800s and early 1900s). One of the changes associated with the Patayan III period is the desiccation of Lake Cahuilla and the subsequent redistribution of the Patayan population.

A final comment on the paucity of information regarding the Patayan ceramic period chronology is warranted. Although Patayan sites have been identified as trails, rock shrines, and habitation sites, no sites with architectural features have been excavated. Most remains appear to be of ephemeral limited-activity camps. McGuire (1982:220) cites Rogers' description of a Patayan jacal structure, uncovered from 2.5 m of Colorado River silt near Andrade, Baja California, as a clear indication of the difficulties encountered in defining the kinds of settlements associated with this group.

The Anasazi

The Pecos Classification is still applied over much of the Anasazi area; however, it has been dropped for the Rio Grande Valley and supplemented by sequences of local phases in the Mesa Verde, Kayenta, Rio Puerco, Acoma, and other areas. Some of the commonly used local Anasazi phase sequences are presented in Table 3.4. Because the most distinctive and most frequently compared Anasazi sequences are those of the Chaco Canyon, Mesa Verde, Kayenta, and Rio Grande branches, these are briefly discussed below.

Chaco Canyon   The chronology for Chaco Canyon results from intensive archaeological work begun in 1971, supplemented by previous research (Hayes *et al.* 1981; Judge *et al.* 1981; Toll *et al.,* 1980). Paleo-Indian, Archaic, and Basketmaker II sites in the canyon are not of concern here. Basketmaker III sites are roughly dated from A.D. 400–500 to about A.D. 725 or 750. Sites generally consist of 1 to 12 subcircular, semisubterranean pithouses with antechambers or large ventilator shafts and associated slab-lined cists. Locally produced ceramic types are Lino Gray and its decorated equivalent, La Plata Black-on-white. Sites occur frequently on mesa tops bordering the canyon, but many probably also are buried by alluvium in the canyon floor. Pueblo I sites, dating from about A.D. 750 to 920, witnessed a change to aboveground dwelling units, initially of jacal and adobe and later of sandstone slabs and adobe or rough-coursed masonry, with associated proto-kivas and later with kivas. In addition to Lino Gray, neck-banded Kana-a Gray culinary vessels were produced. White Mound Black-on-white and Kiatuthlanna Black-on-white are the major painted types. There was an

Table 3.4

Selected Anasazi Phase Sequences by Area

Mesa Verde[a]	Chaco Canyon[b]	Kayenta[c]	Grand Canyon[d]	Red Rock–Puerco[e]	Acoma[f]
			Jeddito, Kisyatki		
Mesa Verde	Late Pueblo III		Horsefly Hollow	Pueblo III	
	Early Pueblo III	Toreva	Klethla	Wingate	Kowina
McElmo	Late Pueblo II				
				Late Pueblo II	Pilares
Mancos	Early Pueblo II	Lamoki			Cebolleta
Ackmen		Wepo		Red Mesa	Red Mesa
Piedra	Pueblo I	Tallahogan		Kiatuthlanna	Kiatuthlanna
Lino	Basketmaker III	Dot Klish		White Mound	White Mound
	Basketmaker II	Lolomai	White Dog		
Archaic	Archaic				

[a]Hayes (1964); [b]Hayes *et al.* (1981); [c]Gumerman and Euler (1976); [d]Lipe, William D. (1970) Anasazi communities in the Red Rock Plateau, southeastern Utah. In *Reconstructing prehistoric Pueblo societies,* edited by W. A. Longacre, pp. 84–139. School of American Research and University of New Mexico Press, Albuquerque; [e]Wendorf, Fred, Nancy Fox, and Orian Lewis (editors) (1956) *Pipeline archaeology: Reports of salvage operations in the Southwest.* Laboratory of Anthropology and Museum of Northern Arizona, Santa Fe and Flagstaff; [f]Dittert, Alfred E., Jr. (1959) *Culture change in the Cebolleta Mesa region, central western New Mexico.* Unpublished Ph.D. dissertation, Department of Anthropology, University of Arizona, Tucson.

increase in the number of Pueblo I sites in the canyon, and these sites showed the beginning of a trend away from the mesa tops to bottomland locations. These developments parallel changes elsewhere in the San Juan area.

During early Pueblo II, A.D. 920–1020, there was a divergence in site types within Chaco Canyon. Although there was a slight decrease in the number of early Pueblo II sites, the number of habitation rooms per site increased, suggesting an increase in population. Most sites continued to be small, consisting of straight lines of a double tier of living and storage rooms, often built of coursed masonry, and a partially masonry-lined kiva. Diagnostic ceramics consist of the culinary type Tohatchi Banded, and the decorated type, Red Mesa Black-on-white. At the same time, construction at three sites, Una Vida, Pueblo Bonito, and Peñasco Blanco, departed from the "typical" pattern, in that each had rooms of more than one story, and wall construction at each was of a higher quality of craftsmanship than at other Chaco sites. (It should be noted that although each of these three eventually became large "town" sites, they were relatively small in the early Pueblo II period.) It has been suggested that these three sites may have served as local centers for the pooling and redistribution of agricultural resources.

The period from A.D. 1020 to 1120 has been referred to as the Classic Bonito, because it was during this time that construction at the major town sites was completed. These are the justly famous, multistoried planned sites of Peñasco Blanco, Casa Chiquita, Pueblo Alto, Kin Kletso, Pueblo del Arroyo, Pueblo Bonito, Chetro Ketl,

Hungo Pavi, Una Vida, and Kin Nahasbas within Chaco Canyon. Also at this time, soil and water control features were constructed in the canyon, and a system of roads linking Chaco with various outliers (multistoried pueblos in Chacoan style but well outside the canyon proper) were also built. In addition to these, most of the sites in Chaco Canyon and in the San Juan basin continued to be relatively small, single-story, village sites. Ceramics at both village and town sites are of the same types; corrugated utility ware is initially Coolidge Corrugated and is later replaced by Chaco Corrugated. The major black-on-white types are Escavada and Gallup. During the late Bonito phase (1120–1220), population in Chaco Canyon declined. There was some new construction at New Alto, Kin Kletso, and Casa Chiquita, and a few small pueblos were built, but generally these were not made with the elaborate Chacoan masonry characteristic of the preceding period. Ceramics were dominated by imported types: culinary wares from the Chuska area, Sosi Black-on-white from the Tusayan (Hopi) area, and types imported from the Mesa Verde area (Mancos Black-on-white)—or local imitations of the Mesa Verde type, McElmo Black-on-white. Finally, a Mesa Verde phase is distinguished within Chaco Canyon between A.D. 1220 and 1300. This period is characterized by occupational use of cave sites and the tops of buttes (in addition to more traditional locations), a change in burial patterns, and the appearance of Mesa Verde Black-on-white and St. Johns Polychrome ceramics. Although once interpreted as evidence of a migration of Mesa Verde Anasazi into the Chacoan area, later analyses (Toll *et al.* 1980) suggest a change to increased economic interactions with the Mesa Verde Anasazi rather than a migration. By 1300, however, Chaco Canyon was abandoned. Although chronological refinement is important, the major issues in Chacoan archaeology do not involve chronology. The sequence presented above has been derived from a series of tree-ring and archaeomagnetic dates. Because this scale of developments at Chaco Canyon is greater than that imagined earlier, and because it is not known among the modern Pueblo peoples, research issues involve adequately describing the nature of the Chacoan system and attempting to explain how it developed from a Basketmaker III–Pueblo I base similar to that found in the rest of the Anasazi region.

Mesa Verde   The prehistory of Mesa Verde has been described in terms of the Pecos Classification, regional phases (O'Bryan 1950), and local phase schemes that differ between Wetherill Mesa (Hayes 1964) and the adjacent Chapin Mesa (Rohn 1977). The very local phase schemes are of most interest to researchers working within the Mesa Verde area. The Pecos Classification is used to characterize developments here because it is more general and it adequately fits the developments described (Rohn 1977:233). Basketmaker II sites are known for the Durango and Animas areas (Morris and Burgh 1954) but not from the Mesa Verde proper. Basketmaker III dates from A.D. 575 or 590 to 750. Houses are shallow pithouses with antechambers oriented to the south. Banquettes, central clay-lined circular hearths, wing walls, four-post roof supports, and storage pits are typical house features. Sites are most often located on ridges on the mesa tops, although there are also indications that rockshelters were used. Stone implements include trough metates, fairly small, basal-notched projectile points (indicating the presence of the bow and arrow), and grooved stone mauls. The diagnostic ceramic type is the plain Chapin Gray. Painted Chapin Black-on-white is also diagnostic. Both corn and beans have been recovered from Basketmaker III sites at Mesa Verde. Pueblo I is dated from about A.D. 750 to 900. Very large sites consisting of several parallel rows of contiguous surface rooms of jacal or adobe and associated squarish pithouses are generally located on the mesa tops. Chapin Gray and the neck-banded Moccasin Gray are the common utility types. Chapin Black-on-white, Piedra Black-on-white, Abajo Red-on-orange, and Bluff Black-on-red are the common painted types. Squash may have been added to the crop inventory and turkeys kept or domesticated.

Rohn (1977) divided Pueblo II into early and late phases. His early phase dates from about A.D. 900 to 1000. Sites, generally smaller and more widely spaced than those of Pueblo I, occur on low ridges on mesa tops and on talus slopes (Hayes 1964). They consist of a few surface rooms, generally of jacal or unshaped stone set in abundant mud mortar, with associated circular kivas. Kiva features include low masonry pilasters, banquettes, ventilators, hearths, sipapus, and four-post roof supports. Ceramic diagnostics are the corrugated Mancos Gray and Mesa Verde Corrugated types, with the painted Cortez and Mancos Black-on-white as new types. Late Pueblo II is dated from about 1000 to 1100. Sites are similar to those of early Pueblo II, but surface rooms are more generally of sandstone masonry and kivas are partially stone lined. Wall niches and six masonry pilasters are new documented kiva features. In addition to kivas, other ceremonial structures are tower kivas and very large kivas. Artificial reservoirs (for domestic water supplies), stone check dams, shrines, and fieldhouses are also documented. Site locations expand onto portions of mesa tops where the soils are not ideal for agriculture. Sites are also located on talus slopes and some are in rockshelters. Mesa Verde Corrugated and Mancos Black-on-white are the common ceramic types; redware trade types (Wingate, Puerco, and Tusayan Black-on-red) were imported, as were Sosi, Dogoszhi, Gallup, and Escavada Black-on-white types. Burials occur in both flexed and extended positions, and skulls show cradleboard deformation.

Pueblo III has also been divided into early and late phases (Rohn 1977). Early Pueblo III is dated from A.D. 1100 to 1200. Sites are located near canyon rims, in rockshelters, on talus slopes, and in canyon bottoms. At most sites, kivas are wholly or partially enclosed by rooms and walls and display the Mesa Verde keyhole-shaped form (Figure 3.28). Habitations are often of two stories, and tower kivas are more common. Shrines, reservoirs, stone check dams, and fieldhouses are present. Ceramics include corrugated utility types (two varieties of Mesa Verde Corrugated) and Mesa Verde Black-on-white. In addition to previously mentioned trade types, Chaco Black-on-white and Tusayan Polychrome have been identified. Late Pueblo III sites date from 1200 to 1300. Nearly all habitation sites at Mesa Verde are located within rockshelters. Some sites are four stories high, but there is considerable variety in house form and size, in part due to the constraints of building in rockshelters. Specialized agricultural features and shrines continue. Mesa Verde Corrugated and Mesa Verde Black-on-white are present, and forms include canteens, mugs, dippers, and

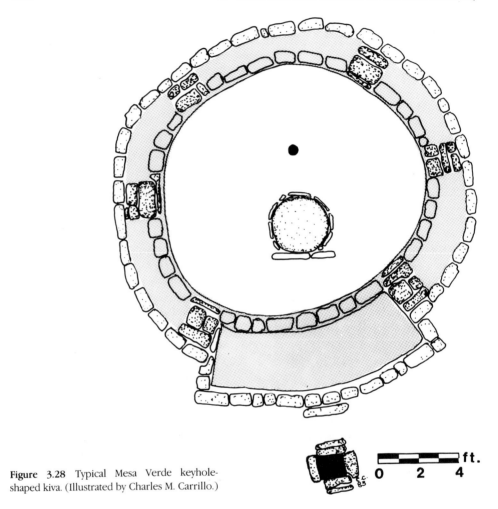

Figure 3.28 Typical Mesa Verde keyhole-shaped kiva. (Illustrated by Charles M. Carrillo.)

ollas, in addition to bowls and jars. A variety of perishable items have also been recovered, including leather moccasins, wooden fire drills, yucca-ring baskets, willow-withe mats, rush mats, and prayer sticks. By the end of this phase, Mesa Verde had been abandoned.

As was the case for Chaco Canyon, the Mesa Verde chronology is well developed. In many respects, Mesa Verde shows the gradual progression in architecture and ceramics that some adherents of the Pecos Classification expected to be characteristic of the Anasazi as a whole. This is not surprising, because the Mesa Verde area was frequently used as a standard reference for the Anasazi. Major research issues involve attempts to explain the changes in the locations of sites from mesa top to talus slopes to rockshelters, the ultimate abandonment of the area by the Anasazi, and the nature of Mesa Verde society, especially in comparison with the Anasazi of Chaco Canyon.

Kayenta   Syntheses of the Kayenta Anasazi are the result of large-scale, long-term contract programs, for example, the Glen Canyon project (Jennings 1966) and the Black Mesa project (Gumerman and Euler 1976), and surveys (Dean *et al.,* 1978; Matson and Lipe 1978). Generally these have provided abundant high-quality information, including precise chronological and paleoenvironmental data (e.g., Euler *et al.* 1979); however, results of these various projects have yet to be synthesized into a systematic whole. The need for a regional synthesis is critical because, although the broad outlines (and much detail) of the cultural history and settlement distributions are well known, one of the important observations that has emerged is that many domestic sites were inhabited very temporarily, even seasonally (e.g., Matson and Lipe 1978; Powell 1983). This makes it essential that various subareas be correlated for general characterizations of population growth, decline, and movement to be made.

In general, it can be stated that Basketmaker II and III materials, dating from around A.D. 200 to 750, are quite well represented; they include a variety of perishable items recovered from White Dog Cave in Marsh Pass (Guernsey and Kidder 1921). This early part of the Anasazi sequence is not substantially different from that documented elsewhere; for example, circular pithouses, Lino Gray and Lino Black-on-white ceramics, one-hand manos, metates, and twined woven bags, basketry, nets, and sandals are reported. Pueblo I (ca. 750–975) and Pueblo II (ca. 975–1100) also parallel developments elsewhere in the Anasazi area. Kana-a Gray ceramics and Kana-a Black-on-white give way to Tusayan Corrugated, Black Mesa Black-on-white, Sosi and Dogoszhi Black-on-white, and black-on-red types. Pithouses continue to be the most common habitations. Surface rooms, primarily for storage, are either in arcs or in L-shaped configurations and are jacal or jacal-and-masonry structures. An overall population increase throughout these periods has been noted, and sites occur in various topographic settings.

Although village aggregation occurred by 950 and 1050 in the Chaco Canyon and Mesa Verde areas, the same phenomenon did not occur until about 1150 in the Kayenta area. At this time, some areas (e.g., Black Mesa, the Virgin River) were abandoned and large pueblo sites were constructed in others (e.g., Tsegi Canyon). Pithouses continued to be constructed. Villages consisting of rectangular, masonry, surface rooms arranged in a square on the perimeter of an open courtyard formed a common pattern. Generally, villages were composed of room clusters, each consisting of living rooms, storerooms, and granaries. Kivas were generally circular and masonry-lined. Keyhole-shaped kivas are also documented. The famous Tsegi Canyon sites of Kiet Siel, Betatakin, Scaffold House, Lolomaki, Batwoman House, and Twin Caves Pueblo were built and occupied between 1250 and 1300, when Tsegi Canyon was abandoned (Dean 1970). "Kayenta style" ceramics, consisting of negative-painted designs, were produced from about 1150 to the 1300s.

In general, chronological problems have not assumed major proportions in the Kayenta area. As noted, most workers use local phase sequences, which are advantageous in terms of precision. Because various local areas were abandoned at slightly different times, and because some phases were absent in some areas, and finally because not all sites were occupied year-round, it becomes critically important to integrate the local schemes. As yet, this has not been accomplished.

Rio Grande Valley   The chronological framework used in the northern Rio Grande Valley was formulated by Wendorf and Reed (1955) and diverges most from the Pecos chronology. As with the other Anasazi areas, local phase schemes have been developed for subareas of the Rio Grande (Table 3.5). The broader framework includes a long preceramic period, lasting until about A.D. 600. The first ceramic period is termed the Rio Grande Developmental and dated from 600 to 1200. Sites dating to the beginning of this period are relatively rare. Sites dating to the later part of this period are somewhat more numerous. The earliest ceramic sites yield both Lino Gray and brownware culinary pottery and San Marcial Black-on-white decorated ware. The slightly later sites (roughly contemporaneous with Pueblo I) yield neck-banded pottery of both the Kana-a Gray and Alma types. These sites consist of rather simple circular pithouses, sometimes with associated aboveground jacal rooms. After 900, villages become larger and more numerous. Sites consisting of 10 to 20 surface structures and from 1 to 4 kivas are reported. Ceramics include Kwahe'e Black-on-white, considered a poorly made cognate of Chacoan types.

The Coalition period (1200–1325) is characterized first by a shift from mineral to carbon paint in most of the northern Rio Grande and by the retention of subterranean round kivas. Rio Grande kivas are generally simple, adobe-lined, subterranean structures with four roof-support posts. At about 1300 there was a pronounced increase in population, increased regional differentiation, the appearance of aboveground kivas incorporated into room blocks, and the production of Galisteo Black-on-white ceramics, which resemble late Mesa Verde Black-on-white. Pueblos were constructed of coursed adobe in some areas and of masonry in others.

The Rio Grande Classic (1325–1600) is characterized by red-slipped glaze-decorated ceramics in the northern Rio Grande. The glazeware was presumably made in imitation of the Zuni and Little Colorado area ceramics, where the use of glaze preceded its appearance in the Rio Grande. Population in the area reached its prehistoric maximum. Large aggregated communities were present, and there was an elaboration of material culture. Some diagnostic traits are decorated pipes, elaborate axes, carved bone tools, stone effigies, mural paintings, and variety in vessel forms. Some of the well-known large Classic period sites are Paa-ko, Tijeras Pueblo, Kuaua, Arroyo Hondo, San Marcos, San Cristobal, Giusewa, Unshagi, Otowi, Puyé, Tsankawi, Tyounyi, and Pecos Pueblo. Many of the large Classic pueblos were occupied for only relatively brief periods or were occupied, abandoned, and reoccupied.

The Historic period is dated from 1600 to the present. Excavations at Pecos Pueblo and Paa-ko provide most of the information for this period—in addition, of course, to ethnographic information from the modern Pueblo peoples and historic documents.

In the Wendorf and Reed formulation, the Rio Grande area is viewed as marginal to developments in the San Juan area. That is, stylistic developments follow those in the San Juan, kiva architecture and domestic crafts are viewed as simplified versions of those in the San Juan, and population aggregation follows the population increase that occurred after the San Juan area was abandoned. Although this characterization is certainly true, the Rio Grande Valley environment is less severe than that of the San Juan and the western Colorado Plateau—the environment of the Rio Grande is not

Table 3.5

The Anasazi Sequence in the Rio Grande Valley

Date (A.D.)	Pecos Classification	Rio Grande sequence[a]	Taos area[b]
1900			
1800	Pueblo V	Historic	
1700			
1600			
1500	Pueblo IV		
1400		Classic	Talpa
1300			
1200	Pueblo III	Coalition	Pot Creek
1100			Valdez
1000	Pueblo II		
900			
800		Developmental	
700			
600	Basketmaker III		
500			
400	Basketmaker II	Pre-Ceramic	

[a]After Wendorf and Reed (1955).
[b]After Wetherington (1968).

marginal. Research in the Rio Grande area focuses on describing changes in subsistence and environment over time.

The Hohokam

Some of the major problems besetting Hohokam chronology relate to the nature of Hohokam developments, and others relate to the character of archaeological remains in the Lower Sonoran Desert. As discussed above, in 1931 the Pioneer period of the Hohokam continuum was inferential. Remains attributable to the Colonial period are widespread, but the Gila Pueblo surveys failed to locate pre-Colonial sites. The full-blown character of the Colonial, which includes painted ceramics, irrigation canals, platform mounds, and ball courts, suggested that there were undiscovered, simpler, pre-Colonial remains, but these surveys failed to locate them.

The Hohokam sequence was established on the basis of excavations at Snaketown, where Pioneer period remains were found. In 1964 and 1965, Emil Haury returned to Snaketown in part to resolve conflicting interpretations of the chronology. His work was "intended to clarify the criteria that are recognized as phase hallmarks, the temporal order of the same, and the correlation of the sequence with the year values in the Christian calendar" (Haury 1976:39). Snaketown is a very large and complex site, encompassing 60 trash-filled mounds and an area of more than 1 km². The ordering of phases at Snaketown, which Haury reaffirmed during the 1964–1965 field seasons, was based on the development of a temporally sensitive ceramic chronology based on the stratigraphic ordering of types and the ordering of other cultural traits (e.g., houses, and stone, bone, and shell artifact types) associated with specific ceramic types. Regarding the ceramic types that are the basis of the chronology, Haury relied on "the assumption that there was a slow and continuing stylistic change" (Haury 1976:97).

The phase hallmarks of the Hohokam sequence are the ceramic types first described by Haury in 1938 (Gladwin *et al.* 1938), modified by the deletion of Santan Red ceramics and the San Tan phase. These are listed in Table 3.6. The temporal order of these types was based on stratigraphic tests that included information from the trash-filled mounds, the superimposition of room and house floors over trash deposits, and the stratigraphic relations between cremations and other features. The reexcavation of Snaketown confirmed Haury's original ceramic sequences, although there were no clear cases of Estrella on Vahki trash. Nevertheless, three cases of this particular sequence had been described by Gladwin *et al.* (1938:32).

The correlation of the sequence of phases with calendrical dates was approached using two general strategies. First, the occurrences of intrusive sherds from the Anasazi and Mogollon areas were noted and used for cross-dating. Second, a battery of culturally independent chronometric techniques was applied. These included tree-ring, radiocarbon, archaeomagnetic, obsidian hydration dating, as well as alpha recoil track dating of mica inclusions in ceramics. As might be expected, these techniques did not yield comparable or consistent results, and Haury exercised his judgment in selecting dates that he believed were most reasonable. Unfortunately, the tree-ring specimens failed to produce dependable dates. Most of the trade ceramics originated in the Mogollon area, and of the types found at Snaketown, San Francisco Red and variations thereof are the most common. San Francisco Red was a long-lived type and therefore not particularly useful for chronological distinctions. Of the Anasazi pottery, the most abundant type at Snaketown is Kana-a Black-on-white, followed by slightly less but equal amounts of Black Mesa and Deadmans Black-on-white. These occur in contexts related to the Santa Cruz and Sacaton phases at Snaketown. Later Anasazi types, such as Red Mesa Black-on-white, and Mogollon types, such as Mimbres Black-on-white, were not found at Snaketown, leading Haury to suggest dates of 700–900 for the Santa Cruz phase and 900–1100 for the Sacaton phase.

The 16 archaeomagnetic dates and 29 radiocarbon dates from Snaketown have generated the most controversy. The archaeomagnetic dates can be interpreted in two ways, depending on which curve is used for the magnetic field prior to A.D. 600. Haury accepted the DuBois curve, because it "provides a better fit for the rate of cultural change" (1976:332), agreed with the dates for the Anasazi trade ceramics, and was consistent with the older radiocarbon dates. The 29 radiocarbon dates were evaluated by Haynes and Long (1976). Their interpretation is that the Snaketown sequence extended from about the time of Christ to A.D. 1200, and that certain cultural phases were contemporaneous rather than sequential. Specifically, they note the contemporaneity of Vahki and other Pioneer period phases, the early Pioneer–Estrella transition phase through the Sweetwater–Sacaton transition, and the sequence beginning dur-

Table 3.6

Hohokam Ceramic Components[a]

Period	Phase	Pottery type
	Civano	Casa Grande Red-on-buff
		Gila Polychrome
		Tonto Polychrome
		Gila Red
Classic		Gila Plain
	Soho	Casa Grande Red-on-buff
		Gila Red
		Gila Plain
Sedentary	Sacaton	Sacaton Red-on-buff
		Sacaton Red
		Sacaton Buff
		Gila Plain
	Santa Cruz	Santa Cruz Red-on-buff
		Santa Cruz Buff
		Gila Plain
Colonial	Gila Butte	Gila Butte Red-on-buff
		Gila Plain
	Snaketown	Snaketown Red-on-buff
		Vahki Red
		Gila Plain
	Sweetwater	Sweetwater Red-on-grey
		Sweetwater Polychrome
		Vahki Red
		Gila Plain
Pioneer	Estrella	Estrella Red-on-grey
		Vahki Red
		Gila Plain
		Vahki Red
	Vahki	Vahki Plain

[a]After Gladwin *et al.* (1938:170).

ing the Snaketown–Gila Butte transition and extending through the Sacaton phase. Haury (1976:336–337) disagreed with this interpretation, accepting a date of about 300 B.C. for the beginning of the Vahki phase and discounting the possible overlapping of phases. His rationale for the first decision is based on the acceptance of the early dates from the DuBois archaeomagnetic curve and "the need to accommodate the evolving stages of the Hohokam" (Haury 1976:336). Even more strongly, he states: "I am influenced by the belief that the Hohokam cultural evolvement was slow and steady. Evidence of differing rates of maturing, such as spurts and lapses, have not been demonstrated" (1976:337). Haury's rejection of the possibility of contemporary phases rests on his belief that the pottery types used as phase markers were not produced simultaneously, which he bases on their stratigraphic order at the site.

At a symposium on issues in Hohokam prehistory held in 1978, Haury's chronology was evaluated by F. Plog (1980). F. Plog's (1980) critique of the Hohokam chronology involves four conceptual issues. First, he maintains that too little attention was given to the complex processes involved in the formation of the trash-filled mounds that are the basis of stratigraphic interpretation. Plog used cluster analysis, a statistical technique, to show that Mound 29 strata do not conform to an orderly sequence of deposition from early to late. The cluster analysis indicated that Mound 29 was built up by a complex process in which trash was dumped between two small mounds to create one large mound. Second, he argued that Haury's interpretation over-emphasizes the degree of postoccupational mixing of deposits. Third, he disagrees that the ceramic types used as phase markers did not overlap during their use at the site. Plog used data from the Hohokam site of Los Canopas to show that the temporal ordering of sherd contents from well-sealed house floors could be based on the changing percentages of Sacaton and Santa Cruz Red-on-buff. This temporal ordering was maintained even if the numbers of Gila Butte, Snaketown, and Sweetwater sherds were added together as contemporary types. Finally, Plog argued that interpretations of the Hohokam sequence were made without comparing observed distributions with expected ones: Although Haury found the association of Kana-a Black-on-white in Santa Cruz and Sacaton phase contexts significant, Plog found that: "Kana-a occurs in Sacaton, Santa Cruz, Gila Butte, Snaketown, Sweetwater and Estrella deposits in virtually direct proportion to the percentage of the total deposits that these phases represent . . . (and) is not more characteristic of any one phase than of any other" (1980:7).

In order to develop a chronology for Snaketown, Plog uses statistical techniques to evaluate the goodness of fit between the radiocarbon dates and various alternative chronological hypotheses. The two classes of hypotheses he considers relate to (1) the proposed beginning date of the sequence and (2) the possibility of temporal overlap of phases. His analyses (which result in the chronology shown in Table 3.7) allow him to reject a starting date for Snaketown before A.D. 300 or after 400, and they indicate a phase overlap for the Vahki and all other phases except Sacaton and an overlap for the Snaketown, Sweetwater, and Gila Butte phases. F. Plog considers the Vahki phase to be "a functionally specific or ethnically defined phenomenon with a long duration" (1980:10). His reanalysis puts the Hohokam chronology rather more in line with the pace of culture change manifest elsewhere in the Southwest.

Schiffer (1982) criticises Plog's treatment on three counts. First, he argues that Plog uncritically accepted Haury's phase assignments for dated contexts. More important, he notes that the use of statistics for the entire radiocarbon-date corpus assumes that the dates represent an unbiased sample. Finally, he believes that Plog minimized the processes that can produce stratigraphic mixing and therefore deemphasized stratigraphic evidence demonstrating discreteness and ordering of phases. Schiffer's chronology for the Hohokam (Table 3.7) differs from the others in several respects. First, Schiffer incorporates available chronometric data from a number of Pioneer period

Table 3.7

Hohokam Chronologies

Haury (1976)		F. Plog (1980)		Schiffer (1982)	
Classic		Classic		Classic	
Civano	1300–1450	Civano	1350–?	Civano	1300–1450
Soho	1100–1300	Soho	1100–1300	Soho	1175–1300
Sedentary		Colonial		Sedentary	
Sacaton	900–1100	Sacaton	950–1150	Sacaton	1000–1175
		Santa Cruz	750–950		
Colonial		Pioneer		Colonial	
Santa Cruz	700–900	Snaketown	550–750	Santa Cruz	875–1000
Gila Butte	550–700	Estrella	A.D. 350–550	Gila Butte	800–875
Pioneer				Pioneer	
Snaketown	350–550	?		Snaketown	750–800
Sweetwater	200–350			Sweetwater	700–750
Estrella	1–200			Estrella	650–700
Vahki	300 B.C.–A.D. 1			Vahki	A.D. 500–650

(In the F. Plog column, the vertical label "(Vahki)" spans the Sacaton through Estrella rows.)

(Vahki)

sites (and from late Archiac sites as well). Second, Schiffer evaluated the context of each date, accepting only those that are well associated with the cultural events to which they are supposed to apply. Schiffer does not assume that the radiocarbon dates represent an unbiased sample; rather, based on his observations regarding the "old wood" problem, he generally assumes that the radiocarbon dates are too old. Finally, for the time periods falling after the Pioneer, he relies on the archaeomagnetic dates.

Schiffer's chronology attempts to account for the "old wood" problem by applying a consistent strategy. He assumed that phases did not overlap. For any large series of dates for a particular phase, he assumed that the phase cannot begin before the latest date. Since radiocarbon dates are expressed as a range, and in order to offset the compression his approach to chronology involves, Schiffer takes the early end of the range expressed in the date. He notes that this procedure may make his chronology too long. Schiffer's chronology is based on more information than that derived primarily from the Snaketown excavations; however, the data base he has available is still extremely limited, and he considers his phase boundaries to be "highly provisional" (1982:335). Particularly important is his admission that the boundary between the Vahki and Estrella phases represents a compromise and, in regard to the Vahki phase, he states: "Clearly, little basis can be found at present for assigning a beginning date to Vahki. Nevertheless, my best estimate is about A.D. 500. I believe it equally likely that the true beginning lies after as before this date" (1982:335).

The controversies over the Hohokam chronologies should stimulate research to resolve them. It should be expected that additional data will be acquired from Pioneer period components at sites other than Snaketown, that radiocarbon dates will be obtained more frequently from the charred remains of annual plants, and that the archaeomagnetic curve prior to A.D. 600 will be firmly established. Until these efforts are realized, it is probably unwise to accept any of the three chronologies with confidence. Most of the discrepancy in Hohokam dating concerns the period prior to A.D. 1000. The later portion of the Hohokam sequence is here considered to be relatively accurate. The "old wood" problem, coupled with the overlapping radiocarbon dates noted by Haynes and Long (1976), argues against placing much confidence in radiocarbon-based chronologies and particularly against accepting a single radiocarbon date as accurate for the Vahki phase, as Haury has done. Whether or not the Vahki phase is contemporaneous with other Pioneer manifestations at Snaketown is not resolved, but the Vahki phase appears to be represented at other sites (Morris 1969). Haury indicates quite close parallels between early Hohokam and early Mogollon ceramics, suggesting that the types involved appear to be "cousins" (Haury 1976:330), perhaps derived from a Mesoamerican source, as suggested by Kelley (1971). If this is true, dates from the Mogollon area would indicate the production of local ceramics at about A.D. 250–300, a date that is acceptable for the beginning of the Vahki phase.

There is little good evidence for tying the rest of the Pioneer sequence to the Christian calendar; however, Haury (1976) notes the appearance of cotton during the Sweetwater phase. This plant occurs in the Kayenta area during the A.D. 700s (Ford 1981), indicating that the Sweetwater phase should date closer to the eighth century. Again based on general trends in the Southwest, the great expansion of agricultural communities occurred at about A.D. 800, and the Colonial period, which represents such an expansion, might be dated to that time. Further support for this view is presented by LeBlanc (1982) on the basis of similarities between design styles in Santa Cruz Red-on-buff and Sacaton Red-on-buff and the Mogollon type Boldface Black-on-white dating to A.D. 800–1000. A general chronology that does not contain the refinements of any of the three current calibrations may be accepted here, because the available evidence does not support the detail suggested in the literature. This chronology is not consistent with the Haury (1976:340) "long count." The Pioneer period is provisionally dated A.D. 300 to 800, and the Colonial A.D. 800 to 1000. Until further evidence is produced, the integrity of Haury's phases is accepted, but the phase duration, which presupposes a known rate of culture change, is not.

In addition to the chronological problems encountered at Snaketown, the applicability of the Hohokam core-area sequence to the Desert Hohokam has been questioned. Some investigators have proposed local phase designations to apply to the Tucson Basin and the Papagueria. These are given in Table 3.8. As the table indicates, there is a lack of consensus regarding dating of the phases. These may be resolved in the future.

The Mogollon

Assignment of calendrical dates to the various Mogollon phases has also involved considerable controversy (e.g., Bullard 1962), but the problems encountered are not as extreme as those in the Hohokam area. The Mogollon chronology has been devel-

Table 3.8

Hohokam Phase Sequences

Date (A.D.)	Period	Gila Basin[a]	Tucson Basin[b]	Papgueria[c]	
1600					
1500	Protohistoric		Tucson		
1400					
1300	Classic	Civano			Sells
1200		Soho	Tanque Verde	Sells	
1100					Retraction
1000	Sedentary	Sacaton	Rincon	. Topawa	
900		Santa Cruz			Efflorescence
800			Rillito	Vamori	
700	Colonial				Stabilization
600		Gila Butte	Canada del Oro		
500		Snaketown	Snaketown		
400					Initial colonization
300		Sweetwater	Sweetwater	Amargosa I–II	
200					
		Estrella			
100	Pioneer		?		
A.D. 1–300 B.C.					
		Vahki			

[a]After Haury (1976).
[b]After Greenleaf (1975).
[c]Right column, Rosenthal *et al.* (1978); left column, Masse (1980).

oped on the basis of excavation of many more sites and far more radiocarbon and tree-ring dates than have been obtained for the Hohokam. The excavated sites indicate there was considerable local variation; researchers have defined five separate Mogollon branches (Table 3.9). The proliferation of branches and local phase chronologies has made it difficult to correlate changes across the Mogollon area. Syntheses (Anyon *et al.* 1981; LeBlanc 1982; Rice 1980) have recognized broadly synchronous changes among the various branches (Table 3.10). This observation is also basic to Wheat's (1955) study of the Mogollon, in which he suggested a simplification by arranging various Mogollon developments into five periods (termed simply Mogollon I–V). Valuable though Wheat's synthesis is, it is based on the relatively limited amount of chronological data available to him, and the more recent syntheses (Anyon *et al.* 1981; Berman 1979; LeBlanc 1982; Rice 1980; Stuart and Gauthier 1981) do not use his categories. The awkward alternative is to point out broad similarities among the Mogollon branches but retain local phase designations.

Published dates for the beginning of ceramics in the Mogollon area, and therefore the beginning of the Mogollon sequence, vary by an order of magnitude from 600 B.C. to A.D. 200 (cf. Anyon *et al.* 1981; Martin and Plog 1973). The very early dates are based

Table 3.9

Mogollon Phase Sequences[a]

Date (A.D.)	Mimbres	Pine Lawn	Upper Little Colorado	Forestdale	Point of Pines
1500			Zuni Glazes period	Canyon Creek	Point of Pines
1400					
1300				Pinedale	
1200		Tularosa	Tularosa		Pinedale Tularosa
1100	Mimbres Mangus		B/W period	Linden	
1000		Reserve	Reserve-	Carrizo	
900	Three Circle	Three Circle	Snowflake B/W	Dry Valley Corduroy	Reserve
					Nantack
800	San Francisco	San Francisco	Early B/W	Forestdale	
					Circel
700					Prairie
600	Georgetown	Georgetown– Pine Lawn	Plainware, period	Cottonwood	
500					
400		Archaic (Cochise)	Prepottery	Hilltop	Prepottery

[a]After Stafford and Rice (1980:15).

on radiocarbon determinations of metric levels at a cave site and are not supported by other data. Quite early dates from the Hay Hallow site may not be associated with ceramics (Berry 1982). Dates of A.D. 200 are generally more acceptable. The earliest Mogollon phase has been termed the Cumbre phase in the Mimbres Valley, the Hilltop phase in the Forestdale Valley, and the Pinelawn phase in the Reserve area. The traits considered diagnostic of the Cumbre phase include circular to oval pithouses, the presence of plain pottery with a fugitive red wash, red-slipped but not highly polished ceramics, and the placement of villages on high, rather inaccessible knolls. At about A.D. 550 there are changes warranting new phase designations (Georgetown, Plainware period, Cottonwood). These are the production of San Francisco Red pottery—a highly polished, red-slipped type—construction of circular and D-shaped pithouses, and location of sites in various topographic settings. In the Mimbres Valley, sites are relocated on the first terrace above the river.

By about A.D. 650, red-on-brown pottery was being produced in the southern Mogollon area, and black-on-white ceramics appeared in the upper Little Colorado area at about the same time. This development has been termed the San Francisco

Table 3.10

Selected Mogollon Sequences

Date	Mimbres[a]	General Mogollon[b]	Mogollon[c]	Mogollon[d]	Mimbres[e]
1200				Mimbres	
1100	Mimbres Mangus	Mogollon V			Mimbres
1000					Late Pithouse
900	Three Circle	Mogollon IV	Three Circle	Three Circle	Three Circle
800					
	San Francisco	Mogollon III	San Francisco	San Francisco	San Francisco
700					Georgetown
	Georgetown		Georgetown		Early Pithouse
600				Georgetown	
500					Cumbre
400		Mogollon II (San Lorenzo)			
300					
200		Mogollon II (Georgetown)			
A.D. 1–300 B.C.		Mogollon I			

[a]Haury (1936).
[b]Wheat (1955).
[c]Bullard (1962).
[d]Graybill (1973).
[e]Anyon et al. (1981).

phase (Haury 1936), or the Early Black-on-white period in the upper Little Colorado (Longacre 1964). Aside from the change in ceramics, the Mogollon cultural inventory remains as it had been before. The end of the San Francisco phase is signaled by the production of a new ceramic type—Three Circle Red-on-white, an increase in village size at some sites, an expansion of population along secondary drainages, and a decrease in the size of individual pithouses. Dating these changes has been somewhat controversial. Most investigators have placed the beginning of the Three Circle phase at about A.D. 900 (Bullard 1962; Haury 1936; Wheat 1955); however, Graybill (1973) places the date at 850 and Anyon et al. (1981) cite a date of 750. The tree-ring dates available for the Three Circle phase in the Mimbres Valley range from 801 to 964; however, the only cutting dates cluster between 858 and 898, and the few dates after 900 are from contexts that do not securely date house construction. The phase hallmark is the first production of Three Circle Red-on-white, and the arguments about the phase dates focus on the determination of the date of the first production of this type. The position taken by Anyon and his colleagues is that the three Mogollon types—Three Circle Red-on-white, Boldface Black-on-white, and Mimbres Black-on-white (which is diagnostic of the succeeding phase)—appeared sequentially during the Three Circle phase and required a rather slow evolutionary development. They therefore prefer an early beginning date for the Three Circle phase. Others (Stuart and Gauthier 1981) are not convinced that gradual changes are characteristic of ceramic design styles and therefore favor a date of 850. There does not seem to be enough well-controlled tree-ring data to resolve this issue, and it is preferable not to make assumptions about the rate of stylistic change in ceramics or in other material culture items. But *if* population increase and expansion in the Mogollon area are synchronous with this development elsewhere in the Southwest, a date of about 800 or 850 is preferred.

In the Mimbres Valley, the final "pure" Mogollon phase is the Mimbres Classic, for which dates of 1000 to 1150 are given. Elsewhere in the Mogollon area, particularly in the Mangas Valley (Gladwin and Gladwin 1934), a phase referred to as the Mangas phase is interposed between the Three Circle and the Mimbres Classic. An interesting discussion has developed regarding the Mangas phase. As originally defined, the Mangas phase is characterized by Mangas Black-on-white pottery and *small* (between one- and four-room) surface structures. Anyon *et al.* (1981) argue that Mangas Black-on-white is identical to Three Circle Black-on-white and note that it occurs with Three Circle phase pithouses *and* Classic Mimbres aboveground pueblos in the Mimbres Valley. Most of the dated, surface pueblos in the Mimbres are quite large (60–125 rooms). Anyon and others argue that the transition from pithouse to pueblo in the Mimbres Valley was abrupt and that the Mangas phase does not exist there. Elsewhere, particularly in the Mangas Valley, Boldface Black-on-white apparently does occur on sites with 1 or 2 surface rooms. It can reasonably be argued that these small sites are either functionally different from the pithouse occupations of the Three Circle phase pithouses of the Mimbres Valley, or that they represent populations that were initially outside the network of relations that centered in the Mimbres Valley during the Classic and therefore did not obtain Mimbres Black-on-white until sometime after it was first produced (Stuart and Gauthier 1981). In order to resolve this issue, the manufacturing locations of Boldface and Mimbres Black-on-white would have to be determined (it would also be useful to know how long Boldface Black-on-white was produced). Although this has yet to be accomplished, Robinson (1980) examined the mineral constituents of painted ceramics from 16 Mogollon sites between Apache Creek and the Mimbres Valley. His analysis suggests increasing variability and decreasing uniformity in the mineral constituents of painted types through time, but the differences between Boldface and Classic Mimbres is not marked along these dimensions.

Outside of the Mimbres Valley, the period from about 1000 to 1100 is termed the Reserve phase in the Pine Lawn Valley, and the Point of Pines areas. Throughout, there appears to have been an increase in site density, an increase in sites in minor drainages, a shift to the construction of aboveground contiguous-room pueblos, and a change to black-on-white ceramics. There is considerable architectural variability, and pithouses continued to be used in some areas. Reserve Black-on-white, a type fired in a reducing atmosphere, is the phase diagnostic. Other ceramic types include Reserve Indented Corrugated and Reserve Plain (each with a smudged variant) (Berman 1979). Various textured types (incised corrugated, punched corrugated, etc.) also occur on Reserve phase sites.

Although some Reserve phase traits, such as square masonry-lined kivas and some items in the lithic assemblage, are viewed as continuations of the preceding Mogollon developments, the use of black-on-white color schemes in ceramics and the move to aboveground pueblo structures have been interpreted as the result of Anasazi influence. This interpretation suffers from two weaknesses: first, functional explanations for the use of aboveground pueblos have been advanced (and are discussed more fully in Chapter 7); second, the mechanisms for Anasazi influence have not been elaborated.

The period from A.D. 1100 or 1150 to 1300 or 1350 in the Mogollon area is one of considerable regional diversity. In the Mimbres Valley, the Animas phase follows the Classic Mimbres, and, as noted, some writers regard this development as essentially non-Mogollon. In a characterization of the Animas phase by Anyon *et al.* (1981), the building of adobe pueblos as opposed to cobble-walled structures, a shift in settlement to the southern, drier portions of the Mimbres Valley, and a ceramic assemblage that includes types relatable to Casas Grandes (Playas Red Incised, El Paso Polychrome, and Ramos Polychrome) are viewed as marked departures from the Mimbres Classic and as evidence of a close tie between the Mimbres Valley and the important Chihuahuan area of Casas Grandes.

In sum, the Mogollon chronology, at least from the Mimbres Valley, presents somewhat fewer problems than the Hohokam chronology. The first appearance of ceramics, marking the beginning of the Mogollon continuum, may be about 100 years earlier than in the Hohokam area, but it is also likely, given the "old wood" problem, that the inceptions of ceramics in both areas are more nearly contemporary. There seems to be little support for a beginning date of A.D. 900 for the Three Circle phase, but the suggested starting date of A.D. 750 is not well documented either. Until more data clarify this issue, a compromise date of about A.D. 800 is not entirely unrealistic. There is little disagreement about the first construction of aboveground rooms at A.D. 1000. These rooms are associated with both Boldface Black-on-white (Mangas Black-on-white) and Mimbres Black-on-white. More information is required in order to determine whether or not Boldface was produced later than A.D. 1000 in some parts of the Mogollon area.

Outside of the Mimbres Valley, late Mogollon developments are not so clear cut. In the large area of central Arizona above the Mogollon Rim, extending from Hay Hollow Valley to the Chevelon drainage and the Upper Little Colorado and Flagstaff areas, the period between about A.D. 1050 and 1450 is one of changing settlement patterns, possible local hiatuses, and village aggregations (Plog 1983a; Upham 1982). As noted above, much of this area has been considered Sinagua or Western Pueblo. In a review of the information from this area F. Plog (1983a) suggests that during some periods, local areas developed strong patterns that influenced the ceramic assemblages and settlement configurations in other local areas. Further, the locations of strong patterns shifted over time. Between A.D. 1050 and 1100, Winona Villages appears to have been an important center, although its influence was primarily within the Flagstaff area rather than region-wide.

Between about A.D. 1125 and 1200, the Flagstaff area extended its influence as far east as the Chevelon drainage. The major large and distinctive sites near Flagstaff include Ridge Ruin, Juniper Terrace, and Three Courts Pueblo. Ceramics produced and traded throughout the area include late Alameda brownwares and Flagstaff and Walnut Black-on-white.

After about 1270, the major center of population density and influence seems to have shifted south and east. Very large aggregated sites include Chavez Pass Pueblo, Kinnickinick, and Grapevine Pueblo. The ceramics associated with the area at this time include Jeddito Yellow and White Mountain Redwares.

The kind of organization Plog (1983a) and Upham (1982) envision over the area is not appropriately described within existing normative schemes. Their view is examined in more detail in Chapters 7 and 10.

The area below the Mogollon Rim from Canyon Creek to Eagle Creek is also generally considered Mogollon. After A.D. 1200, very large, aggregated villages were founded at Turkey Creek in the Point of Pines region, and at Kinishba, Tundastusa, in the Forestdale area, and at Grasshopper Pueblo. Graves and others (1982) interpret these large settlements as typical of Late Mogollon patterns. They argue that the organizational pattern was fundamentally different from that suggested by Plog and Upham for sites above the rim (see Chapter 10) and not unlike that known among the Western Pueblos during Historic times.

Summary and Conclusions

The literature of Southwestern prehistory is written in a vocabulary that is tied to developmental and normative views of culture, whether or not contemporary archaeologists find these views appropriate for describing the patterning of similarities and differences in material culture. Three very broad and general chronological categories may be distinguished. These are the Paleo-Indian, the Archaic, and the "later" periods. Within the third category geographic differences are quite marked, and archaeologists have distinguished four major cultural traditions in the Southwest to reflect these differences: Anasazi, Hohokam, Mogollon, and Patayan. Within each of these four cultural traditions, various temporal periods have generally been distinguished, although those of the Patayan have been the least well documented. Finally, geographic variation within each of the four general cultures has generally been described in terms of local phase chronologies.

Although archaeologists may view local phase schemes as a convenient shorthand for characterizing the assemblages of particular areas at particular times, such schemes do obscure certain characteristics of the archaeological record. There have been times and places within the Southwest when local diversity in ceramic and architectural styles is more characteristic than homogeneity. Diversity may also characterize the rates at which various attributes change. In order to better describe and explain the patterning found in material culture throughout Southwestern prehistory, it is necessary to describe change with reference to culturally independent dimensions. Several dating techniques are available for Southwestern archaeology that should enable the use of time as such a reference dimension. Unfortunately, they have not been applied with as much thoroughness as is desirable. Despite the shortcomings of the conceptual devices and chronological sequences, it is possible to use the general chronologies to describe major features of Southwestern prehistory. The following chapters make use of such contributions.

4

The Paleo-Indian Period

Paleo-Indian occupation of the Southwest dates to about 9000 B.C. The remains reflect a hunting and gathering subsistence strategy carried out during periods of marked climatic change. After an introduction to the late Pleistocene archaeology of the Southwest, this chapter discusses the distinctive Paleo-Indian tool complexes, the environmental context of Paleo-Indian adaptations, and some interpretations of Paleo-Indian economic activities.

Introduction

The term *Paleo-Indian* refers to late Pleistocene American Indians, people of Asian origin whose ancestors crossed the Bering Strait land bridge sometime during the late Wisconsin glacial period. The determination of the date of the(se) journey(s) has been a continuing problem in archaeology and geology. As only the remains of fully modern *Homo sapiens* have ever been found in the Western Hemisphere, the ancestors of American Indians could have arrived in North America at any time after fully modern *Homo sapiens* evolved. Those peoples who physically most resemble American Indians are extant populations in Asia, which indicates that Asia was the source of American Indian groups. The early American Indians could have trekked from Siberia into Alaska when the Bering land bridge (an 1800-km-wide land mass extending from St. Lawrence Island to the Diomedes) was exposed. Subsequently, people could have migrated into the southern portions of North America at any time at which a nonglaciated corridor existed between the Cordilleran and the Laurentide ice sheets (although one archaeologist [Fladmarck 1979] suggests reconsideration of a coastal route). Geological studies (Hopkins 1967) indicate that the Bering land bridge was open and passable several times between about 23,000 and 8000 B.C. There is no consensus among geologists about the precise timing of an open corridor through the interior of Canada (Rutter 1980). Recent information suggests one favorable interval between about 17,000 and 18,000 B.C. and a second after 12,000 B.C. (Stalker 1980). A suggested coastal route is less well documented. From a geological standpoint, it is therefore conceivable that Paleo-Indians could have entered North America at several times between about 23,000 and 8000 B.C.

More precise dating depends on archaeological evidence of man's presence in North America. Archaeological finds of reputedly great antiquity are subject to very careful scrutiny. Minimal criteria for their acceptance include clear evidence of the presence of man, that is, either skeletal material or undisputed artifacts or features that can be dated (such as a hearth containing charcoal). These must be in their original depositional context in undisturbed deposits, where their stratigraphic position and minimum age can be determined (Haynes 1969). The Clovis or Llano complex (discussed below), dated to about 9500 B.C., has consistently met the minimal criteria and is not disputed. Of the several finds that may be of greater antiquity, the most promising are those from Meadowcroft Rock Shelter near Pittsburgh, Pennsylvania (Adovasio *et al.* 1978). Some of the materials from Meadowcroft may date to 17,000 B.C. Undisputed finds of equal antiquity are not known from the Southwest. The artifacts from the lowest levels of Sandia Cave, New Mexico, are sometimes cited as predating Clovis; however, the evidence is ambiguous and disputed, and the Sandia materials are here treated as contemporary with Clovis.

Throughout the Americas the Paleo-Indian period is characterized by climatic fluctuations and local climates that are considerably different from those of today. Early Paleo-Indian sites are associated with mammoth, camelid, giant sloth, large extinct forms of bison, and other Pleistocene species. By about 6000 B.C. these species had become extinct, but the Paleo-Indians of much of North America continued to pursue a highly mobile hunting and gathering way of life in the context of climatic and associated vegetational shifts. The Paleo-Indian period generally ends at about 5500 B.C. with the beginning of the Archaic stage, which is characterized by hunting of medium and small game animals and intensive use of wild plant foods. In the Southwest, the Archaic was a prelude to the acceptance of cultigens from Mexico.

The archaeological remains found in the Southwest that date to the Paleo-Indian period are not unique to the Southwest. Artifacts of the Clovis complex have a nearly ubiquitous distribution throughout the areas of North America that were unglaciated during the late Wisconsin. Folsom and other Plano complexes, which succeeded Clovis in portions of the Southwest, are distributed throughout the Great Plains. Artifacts of the Cochise and San Dieguito complexes, which followed Clovis in parts of the Southwest, appear to be extensions of industries characteristic of the Great Basin and the Desert West. Although the Southwest was not a distinctive, bounded culture area during the Paleo-Indian period and is not the home of the oldest known Paleo-Indian sites, the Southwest has been a key area for researchers interested in Paleo-Indians. In part, the research focus is the result of an event that had great intellectual consequences for American archaeology: the discovery and acceptance of the Folsom site.

The Discovery of Folsom

The Folsom site holds a deservedly important place in the history of American archaeology, because it provided the first incontrovertible evidence of man in North America during the late Pleistocene (Figure 4.1). Ever since the 1860s, when Boucher de Perthes' finds of European Paleolithic tools were accepted as genuine, American scientists had been looking for equally crude and ancient remains on this continent. Such artifacts were eventually found, and some exaggerated claims for the antiquity of man in North America were made on very shaky evidence (Dall 1912; Hrdlička 1926.

Ales Hrdlička, one of the most prestigious anthropologists of the early 1900s, expressed skepticism about crude tools being ancient, realizing that they were probably unfinished items. He was also concerned by the fact that humans usually bury their dead and that skeletal remains associated with early deposits may have been introduced after deposition. Finally, as a physical anthropologist, he was aware that no evidence for premodern man, such as Neanderthals, existed in the Americas. In addition to this healthy skepticism, Hrdlička was a stubborn man, and having made up his mind that man was not in the New World during the Pleistocene, he consistently rejected finds, some of which have since proved to be quite old (Wilmsen 1965). Before the advent of radiocarbon dating or the routine use of precise stratigraphic controls, the antiquity of archaeological remains was extremely difficult to prove conclusively (and is still a problematic task). However, Hrdlička was one of a few very prestigious men in the small field of anthropologists of his day, and his attacks against those who would disagree with him were so "increasingly personal" that few men wished to risk their reputations by going against his dicta (Wilmsen 1965:179).

In the summer of 1925, after heavy rains, George McJunkin, a self-educated black

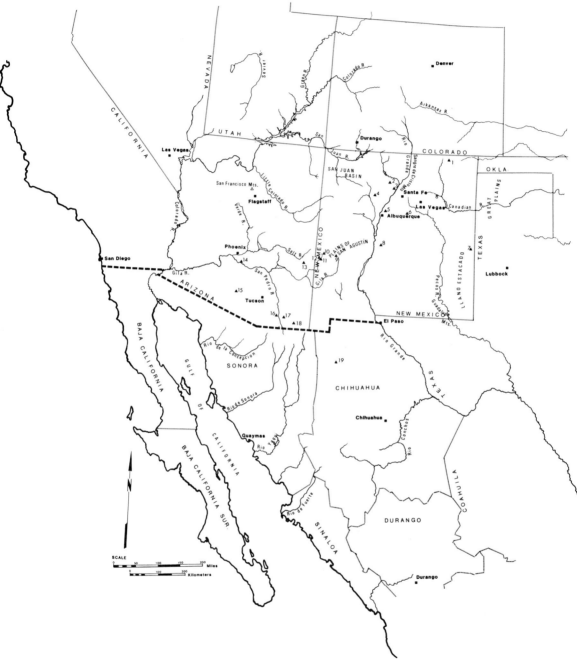

Figure 4.1 Paleo-Indian and Archaic sites of the Southwest. The sites located on this map are discussed in Chapters 4 and 5. 1, Folsom Site, N. Mex.; 2, Jemez Cave, N. Mex.; 3, Ojala Cave, N. Mex.; 4, Arroyo Cuervo, N. Mex.; 5, Sandia Cave, N. Mex.; 6, Lucy Site, N. Mex.; 7, Blackwater Draw, N. Mex.; 8, Mocking Bird Gap, N.

cowboy, noted very large animal bones protruding from an arroyo west of Folsom, New Mexico. The finds were reported to J. D. Figgens of the Colorado Museum of Natural History (now the Denver Museum of Natural History), who sent a party, under the supervision of his son, to the site in the summer of 1926. During that summer two point fragments were found in loose fill. Although a third fragment was found in matrix associated with the rib of an extinct form of bison, the find had been removed to a laboratory in Denver, so its original context could not be proved. In fact, the find was regarded with skepticism and "there was a definitely hostile attitude toward suggestions that the occurence might be of importance worthy of further investigation" (Roberts 1938:533). Nevertheless, the Colorado Museum again sent a field party to Folsom, in 1927. Fortunately, in that year, when another point was found imbedded in a matrix associated with bison ribs, all work ceased and telegrams were sent to notable archaeologists inviting them to examine the find in situ. Among those who responded were Frank H. H. Roberts, Jr., Barnum Brown, and Alfred V. Kidder. These three were convinced of the association of man-made tools and the fossil bison, and they reported to that effect at the annual meeting of the American Anthropological Association. It is indicative of the philosophical climate of the times that "in spite of the convincing nature of the evidence, most of the anthropologists continued to doubt the validity of the discovery" (Roberts 1938:533).

Finally, in 1928 a cooperative expedition to Folsom was organized by the American Museum of Natural History and the Colorado Museum. The American Museum staff included Barnum Brown and Clark Wissler, in addition to several graduate students. With the continued appearance of points associated with bison bones, various prominent specialists including archaeologists, geologists, and paleontologists became convinced of Folsom's authenticity (Roberts 1938).

The acceptance of the discoveries at Folsom was of broad significance for at least two reasons. First, as Roberts (1938:534) noted, it legitimized further research in Paleo-Indian studies. Second, the Folsom site provided the necessary evidence of a temporal framework of sufficient length to allow for indigenous development of the diverse languages, customs, and adaptations of the American Indian.

Paleo-Indian Research

Following the acceptance of the Folsom finds, the intensity of Paleo-Indian research increased, so it is not surprising that scholars were drawn to the Southwest. Although sites of late Pleistocene age are still relatively rare in the Southwest, as they are elsewhere in North America, a few areas have yielded abundant Paleo-Indian material. Blackwater Draw, on the Texas–New Mexico border, and the San Pedro River valley in southeastern Arizona have produced most of the excavated Paleo-Indian sites in the

---

Mex.; 9, Bat Cave, N. Mex.; 10, Tularosa Cave, N. Mex.; 11, Córdova Cave, N. Mex.; 12, Wet Leggett Site, N. Mex.; 13, Cienega Creek Site, Ariz.; 14, Snaketown, Ariz.; 15, Ventana Cave, Ariz.; 16, Murray Springs, Ariz.; 17, Whitewater Creek, Ariz.; 18, Double Adobe, Ariz.; 19, Casas Grandes, Chihuahua, Mexico. (Map by Charles M. Carrillo.)

Southwest. Other areas that have been closely examined by archaeologists, such as the San Juan Basin, have produced relatively little of late Pleistocene age. These variations relate both to the geological contexts of the material and to characteristics of Paleo-Indian assemblages. Given the great antiquity of Paleo-Indian remains, they will most often be covered by more recent geological deposits. Only those areas that have been subject to recent, quite severe erosion will expose late Pleistocene strata. Past intervals of erosion may well have destroyed many of these deposits; for example, the Blackwater Draw area is one of the most badly eroded areas in New Mexico, and the remains found in the San Pedro River Valley were exposed in arroyo cuts that began to form in the 1880s. Further, with the exception of cave sites, which afford special protection, all known Paleo-Indian sites, at least in New Mexico, are located within areas currently undergoing moderately severe to extreme erosion (Cordell 1979:132).

Paleo-Indians were hunters and gatherers. This economic base generally requires considerable mobility to pursue game and to acquire sufficient plant foods. Most sites left by transient hunters and gatherers are highly ephemeral and will be invisible to the archaeologist after only a few years (Deetz 1972). Only under rather unusual conditions are camps that are thousands of years old preserved, and when they are, their antiquity may not be recognized. The artifacts that survive the millenia are made of durable materials, primarily stone and sometimes bone. Most of the stone items are debitage (the products of tool manufacture) or nondistinctive items such as sharp flakes that were used for cutting or scraping. These simple, effective items continued to be used by more recent peoples until the widespread introduction of metal tools. An isolated lithic scatter of nondiagnostic debris might have been produced either by recent peoples on a foraging expedition or thousands of years ago by Paleo-Indians. Although archaeologists are developing methods that are appropriate for distinguishing between very ancient and more recent lithic scatters, presently the only unambiguously ancient tools are the very specialized, distinctive, and relatively rare projectile points. Unless one of the specific Paleo-Indian projectile point types is found at a camp site, it may not be possible to assign the site to the appropriate time period.

Until recently, most of the known Paleo-Indian sites in the Southwest were kill or processing sites—places like the Folsom site, where big game animals were killed or butchered. This situation is a consequence of the archaeological record and the state of archaeological method. Kill and processing sites are most often found and brought to the attention of archaeologists, as the Folsom site was, because bones are discovered protruding from arroyo banks. Further, because the sites represent activities of the hunt, they are most likely to contain the distinctive projectile point types that allow them to be assigned to Paleo-Indian times. However, intensive archaeological surveys, conducted for a variety of reasons, have located many Paleo-Indian camp sites at which activities other than hunting were carried out. Although a great many of these sites have not yielded projectile points and are therefore difficult to date accurately, they are beginning to provide more information about Paleo-Indian settlement and technology. The nature and distribution of Paleo-Indian materials allow interpretations about the ways in which humans first used the environments offered by the Southwest.

The Southwest was well south of the limits of the continental ice sheets of the Wisconsin, but the climates and associated vegetation patterns of the late Pleistocene were markedly different from those of today. Montane glaciers occurred as far south as the Mogollon Rim of Arizona and the Sangre de Cristo Mountains of New Mexico. Surface moisture was frequently more abundant than it is today. There was a series of Pleistocene lakes both in the Estancia Basin and in the Plains of San Agustin. Paleontological studies (Axlerod 1967; Slaughter 1967) indicate that during the late Wisconsin there was a lack of seasonal variability in temperatures, a situation referred to as *climatic equability*. Palynological data suggest that the boundaries of vegetation zones may have been considerably lower in elevation, and local vegetation patterns very different from those known at present. For example, a boreal pine forest with occasional spruce developed in the Llano Estacado at about 8400 B.C. (Wendorf 1970), and it has been suggested (Hall 1977) that a ponderosa pine forest was present in the vicinity of Chaco Canyon before 5000 B.C.

As paleoclimatological data accumulate and analytical sophistication increases, it becomes apparent that generalized models of gradual climatic change (e.g., Antevs 1955, 1962) may not be appropriate characterizations of late Pleistocene–early Holocene transitions. Rather, the available evidence suggests that quite rapid changes in climate separated a series of "quasi-stable climatic episodes" (Bryson *et al.* 1970:72). The biotic response to such episodes may be very fast, occurring in just a few decades. Finally, even gradual, global climatic changes (such as a gradual increase in solar radiation) will produce rapid and *diverse* climatic changes, depending on local and regional conditions. For example, the annual southern shift in the jet stream causes rainfall to increase in California but to decrease in eastern Colorado (Bryson *et al.* 1970:55–56).

Very few areas of the Southwest have been the subjects of detailed environmental studies of the late Pleistocene and early Holocene; however, the data that have accumulated since 1927 allow some preliminary interpretations of man's social and technological adaptations to a variety of climatic changes. These interpretations are of interest to quite general issues of cultural evolution.

The following section provides an overview of the Paleo-Indian assemblages found in the Southwest and an assessment of the chronology of these assemblages. The succeeding section gives some of the more detailed paleoenvironmental information, which provides a context for understanding Paleo-Indian adaptation, and is followed by the integration and interpretation of these data relative to Paleo-Indian economy and settlement.

Overview of Paleo-Indian Complexes

Paleo-Indian complexes of the eastern Southwest are distinguished primarily on the basis of distinctive projectile point styles (Table 4.1). Although the point forms included within a single complex may be technologically or stylistically different, they are grouped together because they are not spatially or temporally separable and

Table 4.1

A Guide to Southwestern Paleo-Indian Complexes

	Late	
Early	East	West
Sandia	Folsom	San Dieguito (?)
two point types	Folsom, Midland points;	Lake Mohave, Silver
Clovis	end scrapers, denticulates;	Lake points
two point types; bone:	bone: needles, disks, flakes	
points, batons, punches,	Plainview	
foreshafts, scrapers; stone:	Plainview, Milnesand,	
end scrapers, gravers,	Meserve, Belen points	
backed blades	Agate Basin	
Ventana Complex (?)	Agate Basin points;	
two point types; side	scrapers, notched flakes	
scrapers, gravers, choppers	Firstview	
	Firstview, San Jon points	
	Cody	
	Eden points, Scottsbluff	
	points (two types); Cody	
	knife	
	Jay	
	Jay points	

probably represent the workmanship of a single group of people. For example, Folsom points and Midland points resemble each other in outline, but Folsom points are fluted (Figure 4.2). The fluting process involved an elaborate technology not associated with the manufacture of Midland points (Judge 1970). The two point types are included in the same complex here because they have been recovered from the same components at the Scharbauer site near Midland, Texas (Wendorf and Hester 1975) and at the Hanson site in north-central Wyoming (Frison and Bradley 1980). Brief characterizations of each complex are given here with the emphasis on the Southwestern manifestations of the complexes.

Sandia   There are no known, undisputed sites in the Southwest that predate Clovis. Among those complexes that are frequently mentioned as possibly antedating Clovis are the Sandia materials from Sandia Cave (Hibben 1941, 1946, 1955) and the Lucy site (Roosa 1956a, 1956b). Sandia Cave is 15 miles northeast of Albuquerque, New Mexico. The site yielded Folsom and later artifacts in addition to those termed Sandia. Although radiocarbon dates ranging from 33,000 to 15,000 B.C. have been reported for Sandia (Crane 1955, 1956; Hibben 1955), questions have arisen with respect to the association of the cultural material and the fossil bone that was used for radiocarbon dating, the interpretation of the stratigraphic position of the Sandia artifacts within the cave, and other problems (Bryan 1965; Irwin 1971; Stevens and Agogino 1975). Al-

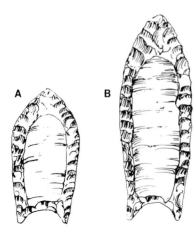

Figure 4.2 Folsom points. Distinctively fluted by the removal of a longitudinal channel flake, Folsom points provided the first solid evidence of the contemporaneity of man and Pleistocene fauna in North America. Length of A is 5 cm. (Illustrated by Charles M. Carrillo.)

though Sandia points have been reported from many areas, the only other known Sandia site is the Lucy site, in the Estancia Basin of New Mexico. Unfortunately, the Lucy site has been subject to aeolian deflation and has produced a mixed assemblage including Sandia, Clovis, and Folsom points as well as Archaic artifacts.

The diagnostic Sandia artifacts consist of two types of single-shouldered points, some of which show basal fluting and wear patterns restricted to one lateral edge (Figure 4.3) (Judge n.d.; Wormington 1957). Considering the unilateral wear observed on some of the Sandia points, Judge (n.d.:13) has suggested that the Sandia "points" may be Clovis knives.

Clovis and Sulphur Spring Cochise   The Clovis complex is characterized by two projectile point types: (1) Figure 4.4A; the point is fairly large (7 cm average length), lanceolate in shape, fluted, and concave based. Fluting generally occurs on both faces,

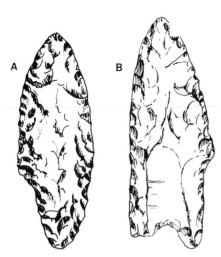

Figure 4.3   Sandia points. A, Type 1 Sandia point; length, 7.3 cm; B, Type 2 Sandia point with basal fluting. (Illustrated by Charles M. Carrillo.)

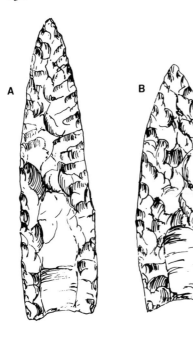

Figure 4.4 Clovis points. A, Type 1 Clovis points are large and lanceolate. Fluting extends only part of the way up from the base; length, 14.5 cm. B, Type 2 Clovis points are smaller and generally triangular in outline; length, 9.8 cm. (Illustrated by Charles M. Carrillo.)

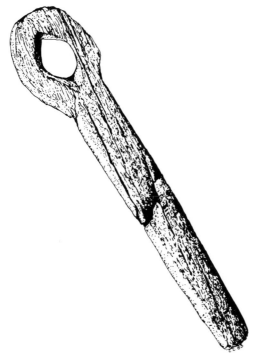

Figure 4.5 Shaft wrench or baton of mammoth bone. Tools such as these are known from European Upper Paleolithic deposits, where they are referred to as *batons de commandement*. This specimen was found at the Murray Springs, Arizona, Clovis site. It is 259 mm long and 21 mm thick, and believed to have been used to straighten wood or bone spear shafts. (Illustrated by Charles M. Carrillo from Haynes and Hemmings [1968].)

occasionally on one face, but extends for only a short distance along the length of the point. Flutes frequently terminate in hinge fractures, and multiple flutes are not uncommon. Heavy basal and lateral grinding are typical of finished points. (2) Figure 4.4B; the second type is similar to the first, but is generally smaller, with a triangular blade that is widest at the base (Hester 1972; Judge n.d.; Sellards 1940; Wormington 1957:57–58). Other Clovis artifacts include spurred end-scrapers, large unifacial side scrapers, flake knives, some backed worked blades, gravers, and perforators, and bone tools—points, foreshafts, awls or punches, scrapers, fleshers, and shaft wrenches or batons (Figure 4.5) (Haynes 1970, 1980).

Radiocarbon dates from Clovis sites cluster tightly between 9500 and 9000 B.C. (Haynes 1970). The dates are consistent with geological interpretations of stratigraphy and with the association of Clovis and Pleistocene fauna. Virtually all excavated Clovis sites have yielded the remains of mammoth. Bison, horses, camels, cervids, tapirs, canids, antelope, bears, and jackrabbits are also reported (Haynes 1980; Haynes and Hemmings 1968; Hester 1972; Judge n.d.:22–27).

Materials from Ventana Cave in the Castle Mountains near Sells, Arizona, appear to be as old as Clovis and should probably be included within the Clovis complex. Ventana Cave is deeply stratified with deposits dating to the Paleo-Indian, Archaic, Hohokam, and contemporary Papago periods. Artifacts from the layer of volcanic debris within the cave have been attributed to the Ventana complex (Haury 1950). This assemblage includes two projectile points, one leaf-shaped with two shallow basal notches, the second leaf-shaped with a basal concavity (Figure 4.6). The second point has been considered "a local imitation of a Clovis point" (Haury and Hayden 1975:v). The point is not fluted, however, and differs from both Clovis and Folsom points (C. V. Haynes, personal communication, 1981; Irwin-Williams 1979). Other artifacts included in the Ventana complex are irregular side scrapers, long side scrapers made on flakes, dischoidal and core scrapers, gravers, choppers, planes,

Figure 4.6 Ventana complex points. Points recovered from the basal levels of the deeply stratified Ventana Cave, Arizona. A, Leaf-shaped point with two shallow basal notches; B, broken leaf-shaped point with basal concavity. (Points adapted from Emil W. Haury [1950]. Illustrated by Charles M. Carrillo.)

hammerstones, and a grinding stone (Haury 1950). The associated fauna included bison, horse, sloth, and tapir (Colbert 1973; Haury 1950). A radiocarbon date of 9,350 B.C. ± 1200 has been reported from the cave layer yielding the Ventana complex artifacts (Haury and Hayden 1975).

The Sulphur Spring phase of the Cochise tradition, identified at a series of sites exposed by modern erosion along Whitewater Creek, Arizona (Sayles and Antevs 1941), remains chronologically ambiguous. The Sulphur Spring artifacts include an abundance of small milling handstones, percussion-flaked knives, axes, and hammerstones that do not closely resemble other known assemblages. No projectile points occur at Sulphur Spring components. Great antiquity for the Sulphur Spring material has been accepted by some researchers (e.g., Duncan 1971; Martin and Plog 1973) because the bones of mammoth, dire wolf, bison, antelope, and coyote were found above Sulphur Spring artifacts at the type site of Double Adobe. Paleontologists generally agree that mammoth were extinct in North America by about 6000 B.C. and that dire wolf had become extinct sometimes before then. Although the physical positions of the fauna and the artifacts are not disputed (Haury 1960), a radiocarbon date of 5806 B.C. ± 370 from Double Adobe does not support contemporaneity with Clovis. Although the artifacts and fauna appear to be in situ, they occurred in alluvial sediments, which suggests the possibility of secondary deposition.

Most of the western Clovis sites are referred to as kill sites. The exceptions are Blackwater Draw El Llano, which has been interpreted as a redeposited camp site (Hester 1975), and the incompletely reported site of Mockingbird Gap near Socorro (Weber and Agogino 1968; R. Weber, personal communication, 1981). Thus, the Clovis complex is defined largely on the basis of kill sites, and so does not manifest the range of tool types characteristic of more diverse activity settings. Both Sandia and Ventana caves appear to have been used as camping places. Both yielded Pleistocene fauna and might tentatively be included with the Clovis complex on these grounds. If the antiquity of the Sulphur Spring sites could be confirmed, they might represent special activity loci, as Whalen (1975) has suggested. In any case, although including the cave materials might be viewed as diluting the notion of the Clovis complex, such a broadening aids in interpretation of Clovis subsistence strategies, a topic to be discussed at greater length below.

Following Clovis, there is a divergence in Paleoindian traditions in the Southwest. In the eastern portion of the Southwest, Paleoindian assemblages are similar to those of the Great Plains, although they are not as diverse in point types. In the eastern Southwest, Folsom, Plainview, Agate Basin, Firstview, Cody, and Jay complexes are present. In the westernmost part of the Southwest, along the Colorado River, and in southern California, Clovis is followed by the San Dieguito tradition. There appears to be a gap in occupation between these two areas, for the next manifestations in the western area belong to the Chiricahua phase of the Cochise tradition, which must be considered Archaic.

San Dieguito   The San Dieguito complex (Warren 1967) is characterized by the stemmed and shouldered points of the Lake Mohave and Silver Lake types (Figure 4.7), small leaf-shaped points, leaf-shaped knives, ovoid large-domed scrapers, rec-

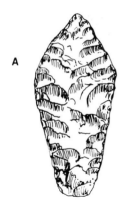
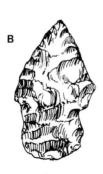

Figure 4.7   San Dieguito complex points. A, Lake Mohave point; B, Silver Lake point. (Illustrated by Charles M. Carrillo.)

tangular end and side scrapers, engraving tools, and cresents (Warren 1967:177). Unfortunately, except for the C. W. Harris site on the San Dieguito River, California, most of the San Dieguito materials are known from surface sites. The C. W. Harris site produced radiocarbon dates of 5130 b.c. ± 350 and 4590 b.c. ± 400, although Warren argues that the complex may date as early as 9000–6000 b.c. (Warren 1967:181). At Ventana Cave, artifacts of the San Dieguito complex are stratigraphically above the Ventana complex remains (Haury 1950).

Folsom   The Folsom complex, which follows Clovis in the eastern Southwest, includes the distinctively fluted Folsom point and the Midland point (Figure 4.8). Folsom points are fluted on both faces for nearly the entire length of the point. This required careful preparation of the point preform and also frequently resulted in breaking the point during manufacture. Fluting of this quality is a lost art, and archaeologists have reconstructed the process of Folsom point manufacture by piecing together fragments of points broken while they were being made. Of two recent reconstructions of the process, one is based on collections from the central Rio Grande Valley (Judge 1970), the other on collections from the Hanson site in Wyoming (Frison and Bradley 1980).

Other artifacts associated with the Folsom complex include a variety of scrapers, especially end scrapers, bifacially prepared cores, bifacial knives, denticulates, backed flake tools, composite tools, burins, and gravers (Frison and Bradley 1980; Irwin and Wormington 1970). Bone and antler items include tine flakers, needles, beads, and incised disks.

At Folsom kill and processing sites, the associated fauna include large extinct forms of bison and modern forms such as antelope, canids, and jackrabbits. One feature of Folsom kill sites is the relatively small numbers of bison represented. Folsom kill sites have an average of 15.25 bison per site, compared to an average of 98.25 per site at other late Paleo-Indian kill sites (Judge n.d.:61).

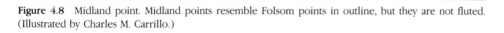

Figure 4.8   Midland point. Midland points resemble Folsom points in outline, but they are not fluted. (Illustrated by Charles M. Carrillo.)

Folsom sites are well documented in the eastern Southwest, in part because the point types are easily recognized. Sites are reported in the central Rio Grande area (Judge 1973), on the Plains of San Agustin (Beckett 1980; Berman 1979), in the San Juan Basin (Judge 1982), and near St. Johns, Arizona (Longacre and Graves 1976). Most of the sites within the area appear to be camps rather than kill sites. In part this reflects recent intensive site surveys (Judge 1970, 1982).

Plainview   The Plainview complex (Johnson and Holliday 1980; Knudson 1973; Sellards *et al.* 1947; Wheat 1972) has been defined somewhat ambiguously. Here (following Johnson and Holliday 1980; Judge n.d., 1982; Wheat 1972), the complex includes Plainview, Milnesand, Meserve, and Belen points (Figure 4.9). Plainview points are parallel-sided with slightly concave bases. Thinning was accomplished through transverse parallel bifacial flaking. Milnesand points are formally similar but have straight bases and more small, vertical, basal, thinning flake scars. Meserve points have transverse blades, and some are resharpened Plainview points. Belen points are laterally thinned with a slight basal concavity and may represent a Rio Grande variant of either Plainview or Milnesand points (Judge 1973). Plainview sites occur primarily on the Llano Estacado and adjacent areas of Texas. Belen sites, as noted, occur in the central Rio Grande Valley. The Plainview complex is considered part of a southern Plains tradition.

Agate Basin   The Agate Basin complex is characterized by a single point type. Agate Basin points (Figure 4.10) are long and slender with slightly convex sides. They are basally constricted with either straight or nearly pointed bases. Other Agate Basin stone tools include scrapers, notched flakes, perforators, and retouched flakes (Irwin-

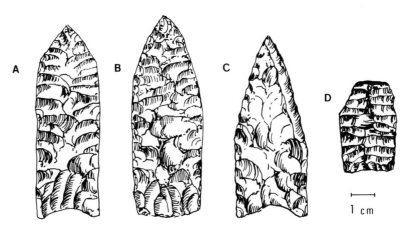

Figure 4.9 Plainview complex points. A, Plainview point; B, Milnesand point; C, Meserve point (resharpened Milnesand point); D, Belen point (broken at midsection); length, 3.2 cm. (Illustrated by Charles M. Carrillo.)

Figure 4.10   Agate Basin complex point. (Illustrated by Charles M. Carrillo.)

Williams *et al.* 1973). Agate Basin complex sites are not reported for the Southwest proper, except for their occurrence at Blackwater Draw; they seem to be concentrated on the northern Plains.

Firstview   The Firstview complex, as defined by Wheat (1972), includes points recovered from the Olsen–Chubbock site in Colorado and from those previously identified as Portales from Blackwater Draw and as San Jon from the San Jon site on the Llano Estacado. The points (Figure 4.11) resemble Milnesand in outline and are transversely flaked. Final edge grinding was done perpendicular to the long axis of the point (Judge n.d.). Firstview complex points are not well represented in the Southwest outside of the Llano Estacado. Irwin-Williams (n.d.:16) considers the Firstview complex to be a variant of the Cody complex.

Cody   The Cody complex (after Wormington 1957) includes Eden points, two types of Scottsbluff points, and the Cody knife. Scottsbluff points are shouldered points with transverse parallel flaking and broad stems. The Type II Scottsbluff point (Figure 4.12[C]) has a more triangular blade than that of Type I (Figure 4.12[B]). Eden points, long and narrow with only slightly constricted bases, are collaterally flaked with a pronounced median ridge (Figure 4.12[A]). Cody knives have transverse blades and sometimes may have been fashioned from Scottsbluff points (Figure 4.12[D]). Other Cody complex artifacts include end scrapers, raclettes, denticulates, notched flakes, and knives (Irwin-Williams 1973). Cody complex sites are quite well represented in the eastern Southwest and adjacent areas of the Plains. In addition to Cody components at Blackwater Draw, Cody sites have been found in the central Rio Grande Valley (Judge 1973; Judge and Dawson 1972), the Arroyo Cuervo area (Irwin-Williams 1979), the Plains of San Agustin (Berman 1979), and the San Juan Basin (Wait 1976), and Cody complex points, as isolated finds, have an even wider distribution throughout much of the Southwest.

Jay   Irwin-Williams (1973, 1979) defined the Jay complex as Archaic. In other discussions (Stuart and Gauthier 1981; Wait 1981), Jay is attributed to late Paleoindian times. This latter determination is based in part on the general resemblance of Jay points to late Paleoindian points of the Great Plains. The diagnostic Jay artifact (Figure 4.13) is a fairly large, shouldered point that is similar to Hell Gap points in outline. Other Jay complex artifacts include well-made leaf-shaped knives and a variety of scrapers (Irwin-Williams 1973). Jay materials are known from the central and northern Rio Grande area, the Arroyo Cuervo area, the San Juan Basin, and the Plains of San Agustin.

Figure 4.11   Firstview complex point. (Illustrated by Charles M. Carrillo.)

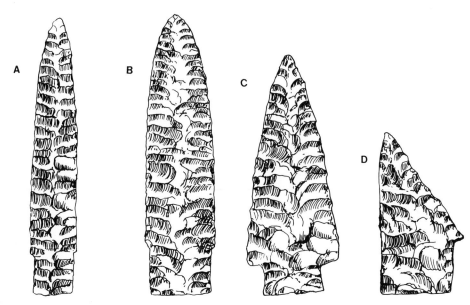

Figure 4.12   Cody complex artifacts. A, Eden point; length, 10 cm; B, Scottsbluff Type 1 point; length, 8 cm; C, Scottsbluff Type 2 point; length, 7 cm; D, Cody "knife"; length, 5.2 cm. (Illustrated by Charles M. Carrillo.)

Paleo-Indian Chronology

The complexes just discussed have been presented in their generally accepted chronological order: Folsom, Plainview, Agate Basin, Firstview, Cody, and Jay. Radiocarbon dates range from 8900 B.C. ± 550 for the Folsom site of Lindenmeier in Colorado to 5820 B.C. ± 240 for the Cody site of Lamb Springs in Wyoming. Irwin-Williams (1973:5) suggests a beginning date for the Jay complex of 5500 B.C. Thus, these late Paleo-Indian complexes span a period of about 3000 or 3400 years, depending on whether Jay is included within the sequence. If one assumes a gradual transition from one complex to the next, a general chronology for the Paleo-Indian period can be derived that approximates some published chronologies. There is not, of course, any incontrovertible reason to assume gradual change of this sort.

Another approach has been taken by Tainter and Gillio (1980). Following a procedure discussed by Long and Rippiteau (1974), they derived weighted averages of radiocarbon dates for several Paleo-Indian complexes. Their results are of interest for several reasons, although they must be taken cautiously because they were obtained from a rather small sample. One of the remarkable aspects of a sequence based on weighted radiocarbon averages is that it differs from the generally accepted order; thus, the derived sequence is Folsom, Firstview, Plainview, Agate Basin, and Cody. In

Figure 4.13   Jay point; length, 7.3 cm. (Illustrated by Charles M. Carrillo.)

addition, except for the relative recency of Cody, there appears to be a very tight cluster of dates for Firstview, Plainview, and Agate Basin. Tainter and Gillio tested the statistical significance of the differences in radiocarbon ages of the complexes and found all values to be significant at the .05 level, except for that between the age of Folsom and Firstview. This suggests that Folsom and Firstview cannot be temporally distinguished, but that the other complexes can.

Two additional sources of information might be used to clarify the temporal position of the Paleo-Indian complexes, although these are also less than satisfactory. First, one might compare the sequential order of complexes obtained in stratified archaeological deposits. Second, one might examine the types of bison associated with the complexes. There are only two multicomponent sites that provide sufficient information for the first approach: Hell Gap, Wyoming (Irwin-Williams *et al.* 1973) and Blackwater Draw, Locality 1 (Haynes and Agogino 1966; Wendorf and Hester 1975). Hell Gap is a geologically complex site, and the sequence of Paleo-Indian point types is based on material recovered from four separate localities. The sequence is as follows: Goshen (approximating Plainview), Folsom, Midland, Agate Basin, Hell Gap, Alberta, and Cody. (Hell Gap and Alberta complexes are northern Plains manifestations.) The sequence from Blackwater Draw, Locality 1, is Folsom and Agate Basin (considered contemporary), Firstview, and Cody. The sequences contradict each other and neither one supports the radiocarbon ordering.

The paleontological literature suggests that there were genetic changes in bison populations throughout the Paleo-Indian period. In a very general sense, the overall trend in bison evolution is one of decreasing size. Complexities arise because clinal gradients existed in time and space; diminution seems to have occurred earlier in the north than in the south (Guthrie 1980; Wilson 1980). Examinations of a number of bison from paleontological and archaeological sites support the overall trend in size reduction, but they also indicate a large area of overlap in the measurements and some problematic multimodal distributions (Frison 1974:242; Guthrie 1980). This has led to a suggested taxonomic revision that groups the fossil forms of *Bison antiquus* and *Bison occidentalis* as subspecies of modern *Bison bison* (Wilson 1980), and to considerable debate regarding the genetic linkages among various bison populations (cf. Guthrie 1980; Hillerud 1980). Until these problems and others concerning bison evolution are resolved, it is not possible to correlate Paleo-Indian complexes with the form of bison represented for chronological purposes. One observation of bison evolution is of interest to the temporal considerations here. Frison (1974:242–243) remarks that:

> Evidence from a large number of bison kill sites now suggests a gradual size diminution of the species and furthermore that the endpoint in this trend in size was reached somewhere between 6,500 and 3,000 years ago. Recently recovered evidence suggests an acceleration of this diminution during the Altithermal interval, and additional data are being sought.

From the studies of paleoclimatic change previously discussed, it is apparent that marked change can be rapid and can produce diverse local or regional conditions. The paleontological data for bison suggest long-term trends with accelerated rates of change that may have been triggered by abrupt climatic change. The cultural responses to changed conditions are, of course, potentially much more rapid than the genetic changes reflected in the bison populations. If Paleo-Indian populations pursued bison wherever the animals were present in sufficient numbers, it would be expected that the ranges of various Paleo-Indian groups would expand and contract as conditions on the western margins of the Plains became more or less able to support bison herds.

The rapidity with which these relatively minor fluctuations may have taken place, as well as their marked ecological and cultural effects, is suggested by a study of a well-documented, rapid, recent climatic change on the Great Plains (Bryson *et al.* 1970). A shift in the pattern of westerly winds occurred about A.D. 1160, resulting in a migration of agriculturalists to the Texas–Oklahoma Panhandle by A.D. 1220 and ending agricultural occupation of areas farther to the west at the same time; by about A.D. 1550, agriculture on the Panhandle had once again become impossible.

It seems likely that the ambiguities in the radiocarbon and stratigraphic sequences for the Paleo-Indian period reflect an inability to isolate rapid cultural changes with appropriate precision. A great many more radiocarbon determinations are necessary, as are detailed studies of the expansion and contraction of rangeland during Paleo-Indian times. Given the present state of the chronological record, it appears that Clovis and Cody are excellent horizon markers within the Paleo-Indian period, whereas the other complexes are not.

It should also be noted that Clovis, Folsom, and Cody have the widest spatial distributions in the Southwest. This may be an artifact of archaeology itself in that Clovis and Folsom are easily recognized and Cody is both easily recognized and broadly defined. On the other hand, the wide geographic distributions of Clovis, Folsom, and Cody suggest that they reflect hunting strategies that could have spread because of particularly favorable environmental circumstances. Alternatively, the distributions may indicate economic strategies that were flexible enough to have been appropriate across a range of environmental conditions. A preliminary evaluation of the alternatives may be made by examining current information pertaining to the paleoenvironmental record and studies relating to the economic bases reflected by the complexes.

Paleoenvironmental Considerations

Only a very few areas within the Southwest and adjacent portions of the Great Plains have been the subjects of the kinds of detailed paleoenvironmental studies that are useful for the Paleo-Indian period. Those locations that have been studied provide valuable baselines of information that will eventually be supplemented by studies from other areas. The most complete information comes from Blackwater Draw, New Mexico, and the San Pedro River valley, Arizona. Some supplementary data are available from Hell Gap, Wyoming.

Blackwater Draw is a broad, shallow valley in the Llano Estacado of eastern New

Mexico and western Texas. Today the only water on the Llano occurs in playas, most of which are dry except following rains, but a few of which hold highly saline water. There is no flow-through drainage in Blackwater Draw. The valley floor is marked by deflation, and there are extensive areas of sand dunes on either side of the valley (Wendorf, 1961, 1970). Grassland vegetation types dominate the Llano. Some pygmy oak and sand sage occurs in areas of deep sand. Larger shrubs and trees are quite rare, although mesquite occurs along some of the southern drainages. Juniper and piñon are present only on the escarpments of the Llano (Wendorf 1975). The most numerous animals at Blackwater Draw are kangaroo rats and grasshopper mice. Wendorf and Hester's (1975) synthesis of the late Pleistocene environments draws on geology, palynology, and vertebrate and invertebrate paleontology. The results of these studies are discussed here in somewhat simplified form.

The earliest geological deposits exposed are of Pleistocene age, but they antedate the presence of Paleo-Indians. A pine and spruce forest extended to the southern edge of the Llano at the end of this period (about 11,500 B.C.). A discontinuous layer of mudstone was formed in ponds that were present in the area. Paleo-Indian cultural materials of the Clovis, Folsom, and Agate Basin complexes were all deposited within the relatively short span of time between 9000 and 8000 B.C. The Clovis remains occur near the base of a wedge of brown sand and silt that was deposited by a spring. The change from pond-deposited to spring-deposited sediments is interpreted as indicating reduced water flow as the result of a general drying trend. The pollen recovered from the brown sand wedge, although insufficient for statistically reliable counts, showed a decrease in pine and an increase in composites and grasses consistent with the interpretation of drying conditions. The vertebrate fauna from the Clovis deposits are remarkably diverse. Some species, such as meadow voles and masked shrews, occur today in areas where it is cooler than it is on the Llano Estacado. In addition, the presence of cotton rat and armadillo negates the possibility that winters were much cooler than they are today. These fauna suggest a fairly equable climate with mild winters and cool summers. Some of the species recovered, especially muskrat, indicate more surface moisture in the past than at present. The Clovis materials have been radiocarbon dated to between 9500 and 9200 B.C.

Folsom and Midland points occur in the wedge of brown sand, although they are stratigraphically above Clovis. An erosional disconformity separates the brown sand from the layer of diatomaceous earth deposited above it. The diatomaceous deposit signals a rise in the water table and the presence of the shallow, discontinuous ponds in which the diatoms flourished. About halfway through the diatomaceous earth deposit, the pollen spectra show an increase in pine and the presence of some spruce, which indicates a reinvasion of boreal woodlands. The deposit of diatomaceous earth has been dated to 8500–8300 B.C. and termed the Lubbock Subpluvial (Wendorf 1970). Midland points were not found within the diatomaceous deposits, but Folsom and Agate Basin artifacts do occur. Folsom points do not appear above the layer of diatomaceous earth.

An erosional disconformity and a change in the pollen spectra indicate that drying conditions marked the end of both the Lubbock Subpluvial and the Folsom occupation. Deposits above the disconformity are carbonaceous silts, indicating a return to more mesic conditions. Cultural materials within the carbonaceous silts consist of Firstview complex artifacts and artifacts of the Cody complex. The latter occur on the eroded surface of the carbonaceous silt layer. A series of deep blowouts similar to those of today indicates that a very clear drop in the water table occurred after the deposition of the carbonaceous silts. Cultural materials deposited above these silts belong to the Archaic and more recent time periods.

In sum, all of the Paleo-Indian artifacts from Blackwater Draw were deposited during times when it was considerably wetter than it is today. The most mesic periods occurred prior to the deposition of the Clovis artifacts. Although it was somewhat drier than it had been before Clovis, surface water was more abundant during Clovis times than it is today. The faunal diversity present during the Clovis period includes forms indicative of an equable climate.

The climatic conditions that prevailed when the Clovis artifacts were deposited must have continued to the time when the makers of Folsom and Midland points began to use the area. No marked depositional event signals the disappearance of Clovis or the transition to Folsom. The Lubbock Subpluvial was a marked climatic change of short duration that occurred very quickly. About halfway through the subpluvial, pine and spruce, which had been locallly absent since just prior to Clovis, reappeared in the area. It has been suggested (Wendorf 1970) that Folsom points, but not Midland points, may represent a technological specialization to bison hunting in forested areas; therefore, the technology, per se, seems to have preceded the reappearance of the forest. Also, if the Folsom technology reflects specialization of this sort, then it was not an exclusive adaptation. This observation follows from the interpretation that Folsom and Agate Basin points were deposited contemporaneously during the brief Lubbock Subpluvial.

Both Firstview and Cody artifacts were deposited within the layers of carbonaceous silts. The two complexes are stratigraphically separated, with Cody being the more recent. The vegetation may have consisted of a mixture of tall and mixed grasses that changed to short grass, scattered shrubs, and desert shrubs at the end of the period (Haynes 1975). The deposits in which the Cody artifacts appear are not indicative of wetter conditions than those which prevailed while Firstview materials were deposited. Nevertheless, both Firstview and Cody complexes occur in the sequence in association with an inferred climate and vegetation that supported herds of bison. An apparently quite severe period of desiccation terminated the Paleo-Indian occupation of Blackwater Draw.

Additional contextual information about the Clovis period is provided by various studies carried out in the San Pedro River valley of southeastern Arizona. The San Pedro River valley and the tributaries lying within the Basin and Range physiographic province have yielded the greatest concentration of Clovis sites in North America: the Escapule, Lehner, Naco, Murray Springs, and Leikem sites (Haynes 1970). The upper valley, which has yielded the Clovis sites, extends roughly between the Huachuca and Mule mountains. The valley is relatively flat and broad. Several historic sources describe the valley as grass covered "with small stands of cottonwood, walnut, ash and some oak along the water course. The river supported beaver and some fish" (Haury *et al.* 1959:4). The valley has been eroding since the 1880s, resulting in the denudation of the grassland, a lowering of the water table and concomitant disappearance of beaver and fish, arroyo cutting, and the near elimination of large deciduous trees along the river (Haury *et al.* 1959:5). Grassland communities and encroaching mesquite and blackbrush are currently the dominant vegetation. Relict stands of cottonwood, willow, ash, and oak are confined to the river channel (Haury *et al.* 1959:4).

The Lehner Ranch site, which was discovered after heavy rains in 1955, has provided geological, paleontological, and palynological data relevant to the Clovis period (Antevs 1959; Haury *et al.* 1959; Haynes 1970; Lance 1959; Mehringer and Haynes 1965). The invertebrate fauna and pollen recovered from basal deposits at Lehner Ranch suggest that cooler and wetter conditions existed prior to about 9500 B.C. Paleo-Indian materials are not associated with these deposits. An erosional disconformity, indicating desiccation, separates these levels from those containing Clovis artifacts and the remains of mammoth, bison, horse, tapir, camel, rabbit, muskrat, and bear (Haynes 1970; Mehringer and Haynes 1965). The Clovis materials extend from a layer of coarse gravels, interpreted as a stream channel, through various layers of stream- or spring-deposited sediments to the base of a black organic silty clay loam soil (Antevs 1959; Haynes 1970). Pollen from these deposits shows a relatively high abundance of pine, oak, and juniper, indicating climatic conditions that are somewhat cooler and wetter than those of today (Mehringer and Haynes 1965). Pollen samples from the black organic layer above the Clovis deposits, as well as from beds lying conformably above the organic layer, show a decrease in tree pollen. Otherwise, both pollen and invertebrate fauna from the Clovis levels, as well as from the beds above them, indicate desert grassland and riparian communities. The pollen spectra can be duplicated in the vicinity of modern *cienegas* (wet meadows), except for the higher frequency of mesquite pollen in the modern examples.

The information from Lehner Ranch shows some interesting similarities to that from Blackwater Draw, but there are important differences as well. Like Blackwater Draw, the data from Lehner Ranch indicate that cooler and wetter conditions preceded Clovis. Conditions during the Clovis deposition indicate more surface moisture than is known today in the San Pedro River valley, but conditions were still less favorable than those of the pre-Clovis period. The diversity of fauna reported from Lehner Ranch is comparable to that from Blackwater Draw during Clovis times. There is similarity, too, in that no marked depositional change occurs with the end of Clovis. Unlike the situation at Blackwater Draw, however, there is no evidence of reforestation following Clovis. Rather, conditions approximate those of the historic period before its very recent erosion. A desert grassland with *cienegas* seems to have prevailed. This indicates that the Lubbock Subpluvial, as noted at Blackwater Draw, was either a local phenomenon or, more likely, a local response to a global weather change that had different consequences farther west (cf. Wendorf 1970). Importantly, there are no Folsom, Midland, Agate Basin, or later Plano artifacts at Lehner or the other San Pedro River valley sites. Subsequent manifestations in the area relate to the Chiricahua and later phases of the Cochise tradition.

The Hell Gap site consists of four Paleo-Indian localities in a wooded valley near Guernsey, Wyoming (Irwin-Williams *et al.* 1973). Only a composite chronology for the site, one that integrates information from the four localities, is available. Clovis artifacts are not present at the Hell Gap site itself. Artifacts of the Goshen (similar to Plainview), Folsom, Agate Basin, and Hell Gap complexes occur in the lower portions of a geological unit labeled E. They are separated by an apparently minor erosional episode from artifacts of the Alberta and Cody complexes, which were also deposited within Unit E. Unit E consists of a series of silts and discontinuous carbonaceous layers. Archaeological remains occur frequently in the carbonaceous layers. Although Folsom and Cody complexes are separated within Unit E, they appear to have been deposited under comparable climatic regimes. On the basis of pollen data, it has been suggested that the Cody Complex may have been associated with a period of relatively increased effective moisture (Irwin-Williams and Haynes 1970). At Hell Gap the depositional unit overlying Unit E also contains late Paleo-Indian complexes (Frederick and Lusk) that are primarily northern Plains in distribution. The data from Hell Gap, although less detailed than would be desirable, indicate a somewhat fluctuating climate throughout the Paleo-Indian period with, perhaps, the overall trend toward a decrease in effective moisture. As at Blackwater Draw, no marked depositional event marks the appearance of the Folsom complex. Unlike Blackwater Draw, however, the interpretation of the Hell Gap stratigraphy (Irwin-Williams *et al.* 1973) suggests that Midland points are slightly more recent than Folsom points. Because no mention is made of forest conditions prevailing during that deposition of either Folsom or Midland points at Hell Gap, it might be suggested that the Folsom technology was flexible enough to be effective within both forested and more open environments. The sequence at Hell Gap suggests that conditions on the more northern Plains remained conducive to bison hunting following the Cody occupation.

The paleoenvironmental data available are sufficient to indicate that the earliest specialized Paleo-Indian points (Clovis) appear slightly after a period of greatly increased effective moisture. No marked depositional changes correlate with the introduction or disappearance of the specific, specialized Paleo-Indian complexes. In all three areas discussed, a major period of desiccation does seem to coincide with the less-specialized complexes of the Archaic. Importantly, the timing of this desiccation is not synchronous, but seems to occur first in the south and west and later in the east and north. At least at present, the paleoenvironmental information does not support the notion that Clovis, Folsom, and Cody were particularly widespread because they coincided with especially favorable environmental conditions. If further research documents the extent of changes coincident with the Lubbock Subpluvial in the eastern portion of the Southwest and the later changes postulated by Irwin-Williams and Haynes (1970) in the same area, the argument will be much strengthened.

Paleo-Indian Economy and Settlement

As a general characterization, Paleo-Indians were hunters and gatherers, exercising highly mobile strategies and manufacturing sophisticated hunting tools and a diversity of items appropriate for butchering game and processing hides, wood, and bone. In this section a more detailed view of the economic activities and settlement distributions of the different Paleo-Indian groups is provided. The information presented is based on studies that have gone beyond descriptions of sites to deal with issues other than chronology. Not all Paleo-Indian complexes have been examined within this larger cultural context. There has been considerable interest in the economy and settlement patterns reflected by both Clovis and Folsom, though far less attention has been given to the Southwestern manifestations of Plainview, Firstview, and Cody, or to the economy represented by the San Dieguito tradition. The emphasis on Clovis and Folsom in this discussion is therefore an artifact of archaeological interest, reflecting the results of recent studies.

The association of Clovis artifacts with mammoth has led to popular acceptance of the idea that Clovis hunters were highly efficient hunters, perhaps relying nearly exclusively on mammoth. In some writings (e.g., Martin 1973), Clovis hunters are credited with the extinction of mammoth in North America. Although it is clear that Clovis hunters killed mammoth and used mammoth bone and ivory for tools, there are empirical and theoretical reasons for questioning the suggested dependence of Clovis on mammoth. The empirical issues relate to an apparent difference between Clovis kill sites and kill sites of later Paleo-Indian groups, analogies to elephant behavior, and the fauna represented at Clovis processing sites. The theoretical questions involve economic strategies that would have been appropriate given the distribution of surface water and the equable climate documented for the Clovis period.

In a review of Paleo-Indian literature for the *Handbook of North American Indians,* Judge (n.d.) developed a typology of Paleo-Indian sites based on frequencies of projectile points and scraping tools, the mean number of artifacts per site, completeness of projectile points recovered, and the presence of faunal remains. The typology allowed him to distinguish among camp sites, kill sites, processing sites, and quarries reported in the literature. Of interest here is the observation that most reported Clovis kill sites did not conform to kill sites of later Paleo-Indian complexes. Judge (n.d.:27) notes that except for the Miami site in Texas (Sellards 1952), reported Clovis kill sites fit his category of processing sites or what he terms unsuccessful kill sites. These latter show low frequencies of artifacts, high frequencies of complete Clovis points, and no butchering tools. The high frequencies of whole points is unusual, because it is expected that these would have been retrieved by hunters for later reuse. The absence of butchering tools at these sites suggests that the animals may not have been butchered at all, and further, that, although the mammoth were wounded by Clovis hunters, the animals may have died sometime later and not been processed. Haynes (1980) made a similar observation based on the data from the San Pedro River valley site of Murray Springs. At Murray Springs, which Judge would consider a mammoth-processing site, the carcasses of four mammoth and several bison were recovered. Haynes notes that the bison were more thoroughly dismembered than were the mammoth, perhaps suggesting more complete utilization of meat from bison than from mammoth.

Addressing this issue from a very different perspective, Saunders (1980) compared the relative age distributions of mammoth from five Clovis sites with the age structure of fourteen family units of African elephants. The African elephant family unit normally consists of an elderly female matriarch, her offspring, including males up to sexual maturity, and females and their offspring. Saunders found that the relative age distributions of mammoth from Lehner Ranch, the Dent site in Colorado, and the Miami, Texas, site approximated those of the elephant family units. The age distributions of the mammoth from Murray Springs and Blackwater Draw do not fit the elephant family model. Saunders interprets these data as indicating two different mammoth procurement patterns. In the first case, he views Clovis hunters as "catastrophically cropping" a family unit of mammoth. In the second, he infers opportunistic scavenging of carcasses or isolated individual kills.

Intriguing though Saunders' analysis is, it is not without problems. The efficiency with which family units of elephants are cropped by African game personnel depends in part on the bunching behavior of the elephants (family units bunch around the matriarch when alarmed), but success also depends on the use of rifles. Although archaeologists do not know precisely the techniques used by Clovis hunters to penetrate mammoth hide (Haynes 1980), bunching behavior would seem to be quite an effective defensive tactic against men on foot armed only with spears or lances. Additionally, it is difficult to have much confidence in Saunders' interpretation until comparative data from paleontological sites as well as from other archaeological sites are presented (Agenbroad 1980). There is, however, an interesting paradox of sorts if Saunders' interpretation of "catastrophic cropping" is accepted. If Clovis hunters had the ability to slaughter family units of up to 13 mammoth at a time, why would scavenging be necessary?

Some insight into this apparent dilemma can be gained by examining Clovis site distribution and the raw materials used to manufacture Clovis points, because these archaeological data provide information about the environment in which Clovis lived and hunted. As noted, Clovis sites are widely distributed throughout North America; however, within areas of the Southwest that have yielded Clovis and later Paleo-Indian sites, the Clovis sites and isolated Clovis points are found in very diverse topographic settings: At Blackwater Draw, Clovis materials occur within the confines of the draw but also throughout the eroded uplands away from the major drainage (Broilo 1971). The distributions of isolated points are somewhat difficult to interpret, because these may represent sites that are beginning to be uncovered by erosion, single items lost by Clovis hunters (Hester 1975), or points that were scavenged by later peoples and subsequently lost (Cordell 1979; Wendorf and Miller 1959). Nevertheless, a great amount of survey data (Stuart and Gauthier 1981), as well as data from previously reported sites (in Judge n.d.), is consistent in documenting Clovis artifacts in upland settings. Frequently, as in the Blackwater Draw area and in the central Rio Grande, Clovis sites are associated with ancient playas (Broilo 1971; Judge and Dawson 1972). In addition, Clovis artifacts, especially the points, were made of high-quality lithic source material frequently obtained from great distances. Haynes (1980) notes that although collections show that multiple local lithic sources were used, materials from up to 300 km are frequently documented. In his study of Clovis and other points from Blackwater Draw, Broilo (1971) found that many of the lithic source areas used for the Clovis artifacts could only be reached by crossing upland areas. Whether Clovis peoples traveled 300 km to obtain raw materials, or whether they acquired these materials in trade, the distributions of sites and the diversity of stone sources used indicate little restriction of movement for groups of people.

The apparent lack of constricted mobility during Clovis times and the association of Clovis sites with playas both indicate abundant surface moisture, which would have made water and forage available to the game Clovis people hunted. This is, of course, supported by the paleoclimatological reconstructions discussed above, which also indicate climatic equability or a lack of seasonality during Clovis times. Plentiful water and abundant forage for game would provide a setting in which large game animals could be widely distributed, their movements less restricted by environmental constraints than at later times (Broilo 1971; Duncan 1971). Given this set of circumstances, a hunter could spend an inordinate amount of time searching for game. One effective strategy that reduces search time is to observe the activities of carrion-feeding birds. Whether or not Clovis hunters practiced a strategy that combined cropping family units with effective scavenging, the environmental reconstructions as well as the anomalies in Clovis kill sites suggest that there would have been a very high risk in focusing on mammoth as the major game animal. In fact, the faunal assemblages from Clovis processing sites indicate a more diverse economy (Judge n.d.). The bones of rabbit, bear, and tapir recovered from the Lehner Ranch site were calcined and charred, indicating that they had been roasted (Haynes 1980). Knowledge of the degree to which the Clovis economy incorporated wild plant foods is not directly available from the archaeological record, due to the problems of preservation of the plants themselves and to the lack of specialized, diagnostic equipment used in plant processing. Nevertheless, most archaeologists (e.g., Haynes 1980; Hester 1975; Judge n.d.) consider that plant foods must have been an important part of the economy. This determination is guided by (1) the environmental reconstructions indicating a lack of seasonality and widely distributed and abundant resources, (2) the distribution of artifacts in diverse topographic settings, and (3) the analogies to modern hunters and gatherers.

In a comparative study of hunters and gatherers represented by 58 societies around the world, Lee (1968) found that only 11 societies could be considered primarily those of hunters (50% or more of their subsistence from hunting). Of these 11, only 2 live outside the arctic or subarctic regions; these 2 groups depend about evenly on hunting, fishing, and gathering. It is not surprising that hunting rather than gathering is emphasized in the far north, because the growing season is so short that plant foods are insignificant. Binford (personal communication, 1978) suggests that all hunters and gatherers outside the tropical rainforests are generalists. The term *generalist* describes a strategy in which food is taken in proportion to its abundance in a particular environment. For temperate areas, estimates indicate that about 60% of the diet is vegetable food and 40% game, which is approximately the proportions of these foods available. The use of ethnographic analogy is always somewhat dangerous for Paleo-Indian studies, because modern hunters and gatherers have been constrained to inhabit some of the least productive environments in today's world by the expansion of agriculturalists. Yet the ethnographic analogies allow the expectation that Clovis (and other Paleo-Indian) sites should reflect a broader range of activities than hunting. In this light, the materials associated with the cave sites, Sandia and Ventana, may well represent other aspects of the Clovis economic base.

By the end of the Clovis period, mammoth and other Rancholabrean fauna became extinct in North America. Later Paleo-Indian sites in the eastern Southwest are associated with now extinct, large forms of bison and with modern fauna. Paleo-Indian sites following Clovis in the chronology of the western Southwest are associated exclusively with modern fauna. The possible role that humans may have played in the extinction of mammoth is moot. Some workers, notably Martin (1973) and also Saunders (1980), implicate man directly. Their arguments depend on Clovis hunters having a very efficient mammoth-killing technology and generally minimize the difficulties involved in killing these animals (Agenbroad 1980; Frison 1978; Haynes 1980). Martin's model, particularly, contains many unfounded assumptions that are not amenable to empirical test; for example, he assumes consumption rates of 10 pounds of meat per day for individuals, exclusive reliance on meat, and extremely wasteful behavior. Others (Guilday 1967) cite habitat destruction, range restriction, and competition as more likely immediate causes of the extinction of Pleistocene megafauna, including mammoth. The decrease in climatic equability and increase in seasonal change, would also influence changes in environmental structure. Although the argument will likely continue as long as researchers have the imagination to pursue it, it seems that the paleoenvironmental data support only a limited role, if any, for humans. As has been noted several times, Clovis mammoth sites occur stratigraphically above episodes of desiccation and contain evidence of more moisture than do succeeding levels. The apparently very dry conditions preceding Clovis may have stressed populations of mammoth so severely that perhaps only with a very long interval of ameliorated conditions might their numbers have been replenished. It is worth emphasizing that the stress factor of critical importance would have been the diminution of the long grasses and browse that mammoth foraged on, rather than water per se. The paleoenvironmental data indicate that tall grasses did not reestablish themselves over extensive areas of the west following Clovis times. The extinction of mammoth seems to have been a somewhat delayed response to a dry interval and the failure of the appropriate habitat to be reestablished for a sufficient length of time to allow recovery. By the time grasslands (mixed and short) were well established on the western Plains, the animals that were in a position to benefit from this situation were bison.

It is not until after about 9000 B.C. that bison numbers greatly increase in the archaeological and paleontological record of the Plains (Guthrie 1980). This has been attributed to the expansion of the shortgrass prairies, the extinction of two potential bison predators (lions and short-faced bears), and the expansion of the bison niche to include coarse midgrass stems, a feeding strategy that became available after the extinction of mammoth, horse, and camelids (Guthrie 1980). There are no data that would indicate precisely how long it took for bison to populate the plains in the vast numbers that are known from the early historic period. The archaeological record suggests that, perhaps, during the Folsom period, bison were not as numerous as they later became.

As noted above, the number of bison represented at Folsom kill sites is considerably lower than at other late Paleo-Indian kill sites. At most Folsom kill sites, bison were apparently maneuvered into natural traps, such as steep-sided sand dunes or lava tongues, where they were dispatched. The strategy of stampeding bison into jump situations was not widely used until later. As Frison (1974) has pointed out, the successful use of the bison drive and jump depends on the size of the herd rather than the skill of the hunter. Bison are quite agile, and unless there is a mass of animals sufficient to prevent a change in direction, bison confronted with a jump situation will simply turn around. Frison suggests that the large bison associated with the Folsom complex

> may have been more of a solitary or small-herd type than the present-day, smaller, large-herd oriented form. Procurement strategies very likely changed through time also as a result. In fact, maneuvering of small groups of bison into arroyo and sand dune type of traps may have been more favorable for procurement of the early, larger forms, than was the stampeding of large herds over jump-offs which gained favor in later periods. (1980:76)

Three studies link the Folsom complex to larger forms of bison and the strategies that may have been appropriate to hunting them. Wendorf (1970, 1975) views Folsom as possibly representing a specialized adaptation to the conditions of the Lubbock Subpluvial, when there was a return of parkland and boreal forest species to the southern Plains. The suggestion is that the vegetation complex would not have been conducive to sustaining very large aggregated herds. In his study of projectile points from the Blackwater Draw area, Broilo (1971) noted that, in contrast to the generalized use of lithic raw materials for Clovis points, 78% of the Folsom points studied were made of material from a single source—Edwards Plateau chert. Although the chert outcrops some 300 km from the western end of Blackwater Draw, the Edwards Plateau is connected to Blackwater Draw on the east. Broilo further noted that Folsom sites are located primarily within the confines of the draw and not distributed along the uplands as well. From these observations he inferred that the playas in the vicinity of Blackwater Draw were probably no longer reliable, that bison and their hunters were following the major drainage, and that the hunters were procuring raw materials at one locality along the route of bison movement. If this were the case, there may have been an advantage to maximizing the use of the raw material itself.

In his study of the technique of manufacturing Folsom points, based on broken artifacts from the Rio Grande Valley, Judge (1970, 1973:170–178) found a failure rate of about 25% in attempts to flute and finish the points. Although this may seem wasteful, he argues that prior to fluting, the Folsom preforms were used as knives and that various biproducts of the fluting process were also used as tools. Thus the channel flakes and snapped tips served as cutting implements. He states that the Folsom points "can be considered part of a complex implement system in which efficiency in material utilization was maximized" (Judge 1973:178).

In essence, both Broilo's and Judge's works infer high mobility for the makers of Folsom points; quality raw material was conserved by making tools from the stages and products of the preparation of the points themselves. Elsewhere, Judge (n.d.)

relates the mobility reflected in Folsom technology to small and dispersed herds of bison. The relation is corroborated to some extent by Frison's (1974) observations of modern bison behavior. In essence, bison become quite wary and suspicious of humans in the regular course of ranching operations. During today's controlled hunting of bison, the animals become extremely wild and difficult to find. Frison (1974:15) suggests that because of these characteristics, intermittently pursuing bison would be a more rewarding strategy than doggedly following the same animals day after day. If the bison being hunted by Folsom hunters were in small dispersed groups, hunters would have needed considerable mobility to allow a herd to rest between encounters. The hunters would also have needed alternative resources to sustain themselves between successful kills. The data with which to evaluate the role of other food sources in Folsom economy must come primarily from camp sites; although many of these have been recorded (e.g., Judge 1973), few have been excavated. Unfortunately, too, at excavated camp sites, such as the Rio Rancho site near Albuquerque, faunal remains were not recovered (Dawson and Judge 1969; Judge n.d.:32). Detailed information on other resources is available only from the Lindenmeier site, near Fort Collins, Colorado (Roberts 1935a, 1936; Wilmsen 1974), and here a diversity of smaller faunal species including rabbits, cervids, canids, and pronghorn is reported.

Although it is tempting to link the highly specialized Folsom point with a high-mobility strategy of bison hunting, it must be remembered that not all aspects of the Folsom complex are equally specialized, and that Midland points accompany these assemblages. From the limited camp site data available, Folsom hunters appear to have used a diversity of resources, probably also including plant foods (Wilmsen 1974).

Other than Folsom, the late Paleo-Indian complexes of the Plains do show an emphasis on very large communal kills. For example, at the Olsen–Chubbock site in Colorado (Wheat 1972), 191 bison were driven into an arroyo in a single kill. It is difficult to determine how frequently, either within a year or over decades, such kills took place. Frison (1978, 1980) has argued persuasively, on the basis of the age distributions of the animals killed, that most drives of this magnitude took place in the late fall and winter. His examination of butchering practices from several sites also indicates that animals were cut into units and stored in frozen ground. Whether or not such practices could have been carried out year after year is not known. Grass range that is essential for bison is limited by the amount of water available. Throughout the Holocene there is evidence that long-term cycles of aridity periodically reduced bison numbers (Guthrie 1980; Reher 1977b), which would have made the mass drives impossible. The eastern Southwest in general is much drier than the Plains, and it seems that some of the lack of diversity in Paleo-Indian complexes in the Southwest may reflect conditions of local and regional aridity that were not felt further north or east. Thus, there may have been times when bison hunting was not an appropriate economic strategy in the Southwest simply because the animals were not present in sufficient numbers. When archaeologists have more precise temporal information for the late Paleo-Indian complexes, it may be possible to correlate the appearance of complexes such as Plainview and Cody with westerly shifts in rangeland. Similarly, the absence in the Southwest of Hell Gap, Alberta, and other northern Plains complexes may be correlated with regional cycles of aridity and the contraction of rangeland to the north.

Conclusion

It is tempting to view Clovis as providing the generalized hunting and gathering technology that was basic to later developments in the Southwest. The San Dieguito tradition of the west may represent a continuation and intensification of that aspect of the technology involving emphases on smaller game and plant processing. Folsom and the later Paleo-Indian complexes would involve specialization in the direction of heavy utilization of large game resources. There is, as yet, no convincing evidence for more than limited human use of the central-southern Southwest after Clovis until the much later Archaic cultures such as the Chiricahua Cochise. The apparent gap in occupation may not be real: It may reflect failure to recognize a nonspecialized technology as ancient; it may reflect an absence of exposed landforms of appropriate age. On the other hand, if the gap in occupation is real, detailed analyses of the paleoclimatic and vegetational structure of the south-central Southwest will be necessary to a preliminary understanding of its cause.

In the foregoing discussion, no mention has been made of population size or population density throughout the Paleo-Indian period. This is a reflection of the difficulties involved in trying to derive such information from the archaeological record: Very few sites are exposed for study; estimates of the numbers of people that may have been camped at a particular site or who may have participated in a bison kill are extremely difficult to derive; and establishing precise contemporaneity among sites is beyond the available dating techniques. In most instances, archaeologists rely on ethnographic analogies that may not be appropriate. Except in unusual environmental situations (such as the Aleutian Islands), population densities for modern hunters and gatherers are quite low (not more than 1 person per square mile) and band size usually does not exceed 50 persons. Because Paleo-Indian groups were hunters and gatherers, it is generally assumed that in group size and population density they paralleled their modern counterparts. It must be remembered, however, that modern hunters and gatherers have been circumscribed by the expansion of agriculture and generally occupy environments of low productivity, a situation in which population densities should be regulated at low levels. If equally low population densities are assumed for the Paleo-Indian period, two interpretive problems arise. First, the rather late Paleo-Indian kill sites that have been the subject of careful excavation indicate that a tremendous amount of meat was used. Among the best studies, both outside the Southwest, are Wheat's (1972) discussion of the Olsen–Chubbock site and Frison's (1974) analysis of the Casper site. The Olsen–Chubbock site represents a bison jump and Casper, a bison trap. Olsen–Chubbock is interpreted as a single-incident late spring kill. The Casper site represents a late fall kill that may have taken place over a period of several weeks. The amount of meat recovered in each case is, however, astounding if small group size is also assumed. The amount of meat taken, as estimated from disarticulated bone and butchering marks, is given as 69,000 pounds (31,400 Kg) of usable meat, tallow, and internal organs from Olsen–Chubbock and 42,000 pounds (19,000 Kg) of meat, exclusive of hearts, tongues, livers, and some other internal organs, for Casper. Even if it is assumed that large communal hunts were relatively infrequent, and that meat was stored in frozen ground for winter supplies in some cases, it is nearly impossible to account for the processing and consumption of the amounts of meat indicated.

The second problem in accepting small group size and low population density for the Paleo-Indian period relates specifically to discussions of the origins and spread of agriculture, topics that are presented in the next two chapters. Briefly, however, (following a line of reasoning expressed most clearly by Boserup [1965]) some archaeologists argue that economic change, particularly change involving intensification of labor, is the result of population pressure (e.g., Binford 1968; Cohen 1977; Spooner 1972). If population densities are assumed to have been low for late Paleo-Indian and early Archaic hunters and gatherers, the adoption of agriculture in the Southwest (as well as elsewhere in the world) becomes very difficult to explain. As is discussed in the succeeding chapters, the Southwest is an appropriate laboratory for consideration of this issue.

There is one aspect of the economic data of the Paleo-Indian period of the Southwest that has implications for considerations of population dynamics. Following Clovis, groups in the western Southwest seem to have been dependent on plant foods and nonmigratory, relatively small game, whereas groups in the eastern Southwest depended on bison and a supplement of plant foods and small game. Assuming that the economic mainstays have some effect on the rate of overall population growth and the levels at which semistable population equilibria are reached, conditions existed for markedly different rates of population growth and for different levels of semistable population densities of groups participating in each economic system (see Stuart and Gauthier 1981 for an extended theoretical discussion of this observation). In the west, population growth would have been dependent on the availability of diverse resources, a situation that may have been conducive to a slow but steady rate of population increase in which an equilibrium was reached at quite low population densities. In the east, population growth and expansion would have been regulated primarily by the presence of bison, which in turn was dependent on the rather abrupt expansions and contractions of rangeland. Population growth may have been slow, but movement into areas attractive to herds would have been immediate. It is important to recall that although expansion and contraction of bison range may be ultimately related to global changes in climate, these may have diverse local effects (whatever conditions caused the Lubbock Subpluvial of the Llano Estacado, the synchronous development in the San Pedro River valley seems to have been desiccation). These conditions indicate that when the Southwest is viewed as a whole, the heterogeneity in subsistence economy would be expected to produce periodic, sometimes very rapidly occurring situations in which regional population growth and density were at great variance with the available, "average" food supply. Further, the amount of territory over which a particular subsistence strategy was practiced would have fluctuated considerably as well.

Although the environment and subsistence base were markedly different from today during Paleo-Indian times, the regional interplay among different economic systems has always been a feature of the Southwest. For example, in historic times, Pueblo agriculturalists and Navajo pastoralists, each with different rates of population growth and different territorial and mobility requirements, are interdigitated within the Southwestern landscape. It is most tempting to view the heterogeneity as characteristic, with no one strategy dominating either the entire region or portions of it for a great length of time. The archaeology of the Paleo-Indian period, beset with problems of low site visibility, poor preservation, and imprecise chronology, provides a perspective for understanding the inherent diversity of the Southwest. During Paleo-Indian times this diversity was illustrated by the differences among hunting and gathering economies. There were differential emphases—on plants as opposed to game—and a variety of strategies appropriate to the behavioral characteristics of the different animals hunted. The economic strategies had consequences for group mobility and population growth that became increasingly important through time. The diverse natural environment of the Southwest and the human environment as characterized by different levels of mobility and population growth provide much of the context for understanding the significant developments of the Archaic.

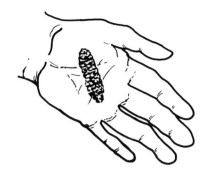

5

The Archaic Period

The Southwestern Archaic dates from about 5500 B.C. to about A.D. 100. Stone tool assemblages are less specialized and less distinctive than those of the Paleo-Indian period. Throughout most of the Archaic, economies were based on hunting and gathering with emphasis on small game and plants. This chapter first examines the way archaeologists classify and interpret Archaic assemblages.

During the Archaic, cultigens were adopted from Mesoamerica. This economic change eventually profoundly altered the course of Southwestern prehistory. Until the beginning of the 1980s, archaeologists believed corn was present in the Southwest at about 3500 B.C. but had little effect on people's lives until about A.D. 1. Many explanations were offered to explain the lag. It is becoming clear that it was not until about 1500 B.C. that corn made its first appearance in the Southwest. This chapter explores the environmental contexts for the adoption of crops and examines various explanations for the acceptance of agriculture.

Introduction

The term *Archaic* refers both to a period of time and to a way of life. The Archaic in the Southwest is generally dated from about 5500 B.C. to about A.D. 100. As a way of life, the Archaic is characterized by continued hunting and gathering. In contrast to the Paleo-Indian period, there is an increased dependence on plant foods, and the game animals hunted are all modern species. The tools used by Archaic hunters and gatherers reflect this economic base; small manos and metates (grinding stones) were used in plant processing and generally less specialized projectile points were probably used as both dart points and knives. In general, the tools from Archaic sites are made of local materials, suggesting a decrease in group mobility.

As described above, the Archaic represents a pan–North American and, in fact, a worldwide post-Pleistocene adaptation. Throughout the world, as the Pleistocene climates gave way to those of the recent period and vegetation patterns and faunal distributions came to approximate their present form, hunters and gatherers relied increasingly on locally available resources. Depending on the character of the local environment, these resources varied from one area to another. In coastal and riverine settings, the economic base included fish and shellfish in addition to plants and terrestrial game, while in the far north, hunting continued to predominate because the short growing season precluded the use of much plant food. In inland, temperate areas of the world, there seems to have been a slightly greater reliance on plant foods than on game.

As discussed in the preceding chapter, it was during the Archaic that cultigens were first adopted by Southwestern peoples. Although initially, domestic crops did not appreciably alter the Archaic way of life, they ultimately had a tremendous impact on Southwestern cultural developments. Because hunting and gathering was a stable economic base for millions of years of human evolution and because agriculture generally requires more labor than hunting and gathering and is also often more risky, there must have been important reasons for the initial cultivation of crops. Theoretical discussions purporting to explain the origins of agriculture have dominated much of the recent archaeological literature. The Southwestern data are applicable to situations in which domestic plants were accepted rather than to conditions of initial domestication; nevertheless, an understanding of the context of agricultural adoption in the Southwest facilitates evaluation of some current theoretical arguments.

Although detailed knowledge of the Archaic is critical to the culture history of the Southwest and to general issues of cultural evolution, it is important to realize that the archaeology of the Archaic suffers from many of the same problems of Paleo-Indian archaeology: The remains are ephemeral because they are those of mobile hunters and gatherers; sites are obscured by more recent geological deposition, and many undoubtedly were destroyed by ancient episodes of erosion; the artifactual remains at Archaic camps may include few, if any, temporally diagnostic tool types; and Archaic chronology and paleoenvironmental reconstructions are far less precise than is desirable. In addition, because the fauna associated with the Archaic are of modern form and because Archaic peoples emphasized plant processing, the antiquity of Archaic sites is not generally obvious to casual observers. Finally, there has been less archaeological interest in the Archaic than in either the Paleo-Indian period or later prehistoric periods. This seems to be a reflection of both the fact that Archaic sites are not important for establishing the time of man's entry into the Americas, which stimulated much of the Paleo-Indian research, and the fact that the remains are not as rich (in ornamental items or impressive architecture) as are later Pueblo sites.

Before the 1970s, archaeological interest in the Southwestern Archaic primarily focused on documenting the history of the use of corn as well as its genetic relation to corn from other parts of the Americas. For this reason the most intensively studied sites were rockshelter and cave locations at which corn and other perishable items may be preserved. These excavations yielded a range of artifactual materials unknown for the Paleo-Indian period. Cave sites sometimes preserved basketry, fiber sandals, rabbit-fur blankets, and twig figurines. Some of these objects are much like those used by later Pueblo peoples; consequently, some archaeologists attempted to link particular Archaic assemblages with later prehistoric cultures and with their ethnographically known descendants.

The archaeology of the Archaic has been pursued through two quite distinct conceptual frameworks. Some investigators have been most concerned with defining and describing the general Archaic subsistence adaptation. Others have viewed the Archaic as a starting point for tracing the ethnic culture history of Southwestern people.

The framework that emphasizes general adaptation is most clearly seen in the concept of the Desert Culture as defined by Jesse D. Jennings:

> The archaeological Desert Culture is seen as evidence of a specialized, successful way of life geared to the rigor and apparent biotic parsimony of the Desert West. The term must be understood as a *general* one, implying not an unvarying complex of archaeological traits or a period of time but a culture *stage* wherein wide exploitation of available species is a diagnostic attribute. (1964:152–153)

For Jennings (1964:153), the Cochise sequence of southern Arizona is a regional variant of the broad Desert Culture, one quite stable and successful adjustment to the moisture-deficient west.

The second, and very different, conceptual framework emphasizes historical, linguistic, and ethnic continuities from the Archaic to recent times, as exemplified in the approach of Julian D. Hayden. Writing on his work in the Sierra Pinacate of Sonora, Mexico, Hayden argues that the distribution of the Amargosa complex, a widely distributed western Archaic manifestation similar to the Pinto complex, parallels and is ancestral to the historic distribution of Piman speakers, thereby indicating that Piman speakers are the descendants of the makers of Amargosa tools. In Hayden's view, the Cochise tradition represents a local variant of the Amargosa complex with which it has ancestral ties.

In a cogent statement recognizing the disparity in conceptual frameworks, Irwin-Williams (1967) argues that analysis and synthesis must take place on two different levels. On one level, analysis is what she terms *integrative*. Integrative analysis seeks to recognize material traits that link Archaic Southwestern complexes to the Archaic way of life in general and to adaptation to the desert environment of the west. For example, the prevalence of small manos and grinding slabs relates to plant processing, an activity that was part of the basic subsistence adaptation throughout the Desert West. These tools are therefore important to understanding a general way of life and would be included in the integrative level of analysis. As Irwin-Williams states (1967:445), most of the material traits originally enumerated as characterizing the Desert Culture relate to the integrative level of analysis. The second level of analysis is termed *isolative*. Here one attempts to select those traits and patterns of distribution that set the culture history of one area apart from other areas. For example, although the presence of projectile points is indicative of hunting and is therefore important to analysis at the integrative level, a particular form or style of point may have a limited temporal or spatial distribution and so be germane to the isolative level of analysis. The artifacts of the Amargosa complex may be viewed in this manner.

The isolative level of analysis and synthesis attempts to organize data in a way that is informative about culture history. It seeks to document relations among peoples from a synchronic perspective and to trace the changes in artifact inventories of groups over time. Unfortunately, analysis and synthesis at this level suffer from empirical and theoretical problems. Among the empirical issues is the fact that Archaic assemblages generally contain few distinctive, specialized tools. Consequently, existing descriptions emphasize projectile point types, and generally assume that the point types are cultural or temporal markers. In addition, very few Archaic sites are adequately dated, so it is difficult to define precisely the temporal range of artifact types, including point types, that seem to be temporally sensitive.

Isolative analysis attempts definition of prehistoric cultural groups, and cultural continuities and discontinuities. Archaeologists have little developed theory that permits specifying the range of artifacts appropriate for defining cultural identity. It is sometimes assumed that cultural identity is reflected in artifact styles. Not only are there very few studies and virtually no theory that guides delimiting the conditions under which stylistic behavior does or does not relate to cultural identity, there is little information that is useful for defining purely stylistic attributes of stone tools (Weissner 1983 is a useful beginning in this task). For example, the width of a projectile point blade and blade serration may be seen as stylistic. However, if the points functioned as cutting and piercing tools, these attributes relate to function and may be found among very different and unrelated cultural groups.

These are the sorts of problems that make analysis and synthesis on the isolative level extremely difficult. Until appropriate theory is developed and basic empirical studies undertaken, all such cultural historical formulations are subject to criticism. Nevertheless, syntheses at the isolative level allow archaeologists to present descriptive frameworks that encapsulate their ideas about spatial and temporal relations among assemblages. One such framework has been developed by Irwin-Williams for the Southwestern Archaic. The scheme is widely used in the Southwestern literature and organizes a great deal of previously existing information.

Irwin-Williams proposes that by about 3000 B.C. four interacting traditions had crystallized within the Southwest (Irwin-Williams 1979). Collectively, these are referred to as the *Picosa* culture, an acronymn derived from the names of three well-known Archaic complexes: *Pin*to Basin, *Co*chise, and *San* Jose. A summary version of the traditions constituting the Picosa culture is presented here.

Picosa: A Synthesis on the Isolative Level

Western Tradition

The westernmost tradition of the Picosa culture is referred to as the San Dieguito–Pinto tradition. Materials relating to this tradition are distributed from southern California to southern Arizona and, within the Great Basin, north to southern Nevada. Most of the known sites are surface sites found at the ancient lake basins of southern California. The San Dieguito–Pinto tradition includes the Pinto Basin and Amargosa complexes, which seem to have been derived from the San Dieguito tradition discussed in the previous chapter. The most distinctive artifacts are Pinto Basin points and those of similar styles (Figure 5.1). These are generally straight-stemmed points with concave bases. Some points are shouldered, and serrated edges are common. Other stone tools include flake choppers, flake scrapers, and scraper planes. Ground stone items include small cobble manos and shallow-basin grinding slabs. Largely because most of the sites are surficial, there are very few dates available for the tradition.

Northern Tradition

The northern tradition of the Picosa culture has been termed the Oshara tradition (Irwin-Williams 1973), and it has been divided into a number of sequential phases, primarily on the basis of survey and excavation carried out in the Arroyo Cuervo area of north-central New Mexico. Oshara sites are also found in the San Juan Basin, the Rio Grande Valley, the Plains of San Agustin, south-central Colorado, and southeastern Utah. As noted in the preceding chapter, Irwin-Williams considers the Jay complex to be Archaic rather than Paleo-Indian, and the Jay phase is the first phase of the Oshara tradition. Diagnostic Jay phase artifacts include large, slightly shouldered projectile points, well-made leaf-shaped knives, and well-made scrapers. Other archaeologists (Judge 1982; Wait 1981) consider the Jay materials to be Paleoindian. The issues involved relate, in part, to interpretations of projectile-point morphology. Some writers (Honea 1969) consider Jay points to be quite similar to the Paleo-Indian Hell Gap points and to be a direct development from the Paleo-Indian Angostura points of the Plains. Irwin-Williams (1973) argues that the resemblance between Jay and Hell Gap is

Figure 5.1 Pinto Basin point; length, 3.7 cm. (Illustrated by Charles M. Carrillo.)

fortuitous and sees a much closer relation between Jay assemblages and Lake Mohave points of the San Dieguito–Pinto tradition.

Another aspect of the dispute involves interpretations of culture history. Irwin-Williams (1973) contends that Cody represents the last Paleo-Indian manifestation in the northern Southwest and that Paleo-Indian peoples moved north and east onto the Plains sometime around 6000 B.C. She further avers that there was a hiatus in occupation in the Oshara area, followed by a movement into the area of Archaic peoples whose closest cultural affiliation was to the west. This movement was to have occurred at about 5500 B.C. By including Jay within the Paleo-Indian tradition, other authors are suggesting a continuity between Paleo-Indian and Archaic peoples. No attempt to resolve this issue is made here. The argument itself, it may be suggested, demonstrates the difficulty of pursuing analysis at the isolative level. Essentially, until archaeologists understand what variation in projectile-point morphology means in terms of behavior, interpretations are based on as yet unsupported assumptions.

In the Oshara area, the Jay phase is followed by the Bajada phase, which Irwin-Williams suggests dates from about 4800 to 3200 B.C. The Bajada tool assemblage shows general continuity with the preceding Jay phase. Bajada points (Figure 5.2) are distinguishable from Jay points by the presence of basal indentation and basal thinning. In addition, the assemblage contains "increasing numbers of large chopping tools and poorly made side scrapers on thin irregular flakes" (Irwin-Williams 1973:7). Small cobble-filled hearths and earth ovens have been found at Bajada phase sites in the Arroyo Cuervo area. In some areas, such as the Plains of San Agustin, archaeologists have described the presence of Bajada points in assemblages characterized as Chiricahua Cochise (Whalen 1975). Chiricahua Cochise belongs to Irwin-Williams' southern tradition, so it is unlikely that Bajada points represent cultural markers.

The San Jose phase follows the Bajada phase in the scheme proposed by Irwin-Williams (1973, 1979). She would date the phase from slightly before 3000 to about 1800 B.C. The San Jose phase includes materials previously described as the San Jose complex (Bryan and Toulouse 1943) and the Apex complex (Irwin-Williams and Irwin 1966). San Jose points (Figure 5.3) are similar to Bajada points but are more frequently serrated along the edges, smaller in total length, and tend to have a shorter stem-to-

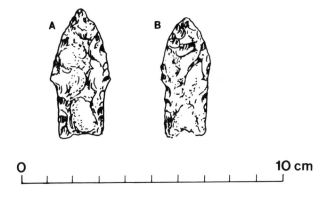

A   B

0   10 cm

Figure 5.2 Bajada points; length of A, 4.5 cm. (Illustrated by Charles M. Carrillo.)

Figure 5.3 San Jose points. A, Complete point; length, 7.5 cm; B, point broken and resharpened; length, 3.1 cm. (Illustrated by Charles M. Carrillo.)

blade ratio. The tool kit is dominated by poorly made side scrapers on thin flakes and large chopping tools. Well-made side scrapers and bifacial knives of the earlier Archaic complexes are rare or absent. Ground stone implements include pounding stones, shallow-basin grinding slabs, and manos made on small cobbles. Large, cobble-filled subsurface ovens are features that have been found at some sites.

The succeeding Armijo phase, about 1800 to about 800 B.C., includes materials that have been termed the Lobo complex (Bryan and Toulouse 1943), the Santa Ana complex (Agogino and Hester 1953), and the Atrisco complex (Campbell and Ellis 1952). Irwin-Williams (1973:11) describes the projectile points as "evolved late forms of the old serrated San Jose style with short widely expanding stems and concave or (later) straight bases" (Figure 5.4). Other artifacts that relate to the isolative level are not well defined, but small bifacial knives, flake scrapers, drills, and choppers or pounders are documented. Most of the discussion of the Armijo phase treats the appearance of maize in the Oshara tradition at this time.

The next phase in the Arroyo Cuervo area has been termed the En Medio, which is suggested to date from about 800 B.C. to A.D. 400; it is followed by the Trujillo phase, dated from about A.D. 400 to 600. The En Medio phase is characterized as showing considerable continuity with the preceding phases, although there is an increased emphasis on ground stone tools and further stylistic variability in the total assemblage. En Medio phase projectile points are described as "variations of stemmed corner notched forms which trend through time toward the use of increasingly long barbs"

Figure 5.4 Armijo points. (Illustrated by Charles M. Carrillo.)

(Irwin-Williams 1973:13). The Trujillo phase is viewed as representing a continuation of trends established in the En Medio phase with the introduction of "limited quantities of plain grey ceramics" (Irwin-Williams 1973:13).

The importance of the dating of the En Medio and Trujillo phases is that together they span the transition from late Archaic to early Anasazi. The emphasis placed on continuity in artifact inventories indicates that Irwin-Williams views the Oshara tradition as a development in place from early Archaic to the Pueblo–Anasazi sequence.

Southern Tradition

The southern tradition incorporated within the Picosa culture comprises the two later phases of the Cochise tradition that were mentioned in the preceding chapter: the Chiricahua and the San Pedro. Chiricahua phase artifacts are known from Ventana Cave, from the San Pedro River Valley, from the Cienega Creek site on the San Carlos Reservation (Haury and Sayles 1947), from the Wet Leggett site (Martin, Rinaldo, and Antevs 1949) in western New Mexico, and from Bat Cave on the Plains of San Agustin (Dick 1965a). Surface finds have been reported from north-central and northeastern Arizona, the Moquino locality of northwestern New Mexico, and the Galisteo Basin of north-central New Mexico (Irwin-Williams 1979; Irwin-Williams and Beckett 1973; Lang 1977b). Although the distribution of Chiricahua Cochise artifacts has been suggested to extend into northern Chihuahua and Sonora (Irwin-Williams 1967), some illustrated material (Rinaldo 1974) appears to resemble the succeeding San Pedro Cochise.

Chiricahua Cochise assemblages are often dominated by cobble manos and shallow metates and a large number of quite amorphous scrapers and choppers, all of which relate to plant processing and are therefore uninformative with regard to culture historical reconstructions. Projectile points are formally diverse; however, many are side-notched with concave bases. Others are diamond-shaped and may be serrated or unserrated; some have short contracting stems (Dick 1965a; Irwin-Williams 1967, 1979).

Although dated to the Archaic in general, more precise dating of the Chiricahua phase is problematic. For example, although the stratigraphy at Ventana Cave should have been enlightening, two very different interpretations of the timing of the origin of the Chiricahua materials have been provided (Figure 5.5)—each based on informed geological interpretation. In Antevs' sequence, dates of between 7000 and 3000 B.C. are suggested for the Chiricahua phase, whereas in Bryan's reconstruction the phase is dated between 2000 and 1000 B.C. The differences between these chronologies is so marked and each is so well defended that Haury (1950:539) concluded, "I see no alternative for the archaeologist but to bide his time until the picture clears." Fortunately, a series of radiocarbon dates has somewhat clarified the situation, and these support Bryan's chronology rather than Antevs'. According to the new dates, the Chiricahua phase would extend from about 3500 to 1500 B.C. (Whalen, 1971, 1975).

The San Pedro phase follows the Chiricahua in the southern portion of the Southwest. Excavated material comes from the San Pedro River valley, Cienega Creek,

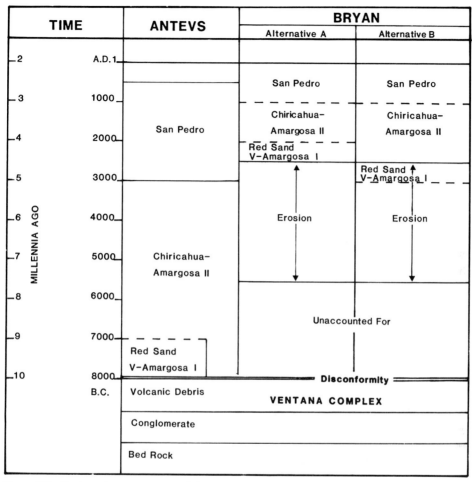

Figure 5.5 Geological interpretations of the chronology of the Chiricahua phase of the Archaic from Ventana Cave, Arizona. Antevs (1955) interpreted the stratigraphy as indicating dates of between 7000 and 3000 B.C. for the Chiricahua phase. Bryan's (1965) interpretation would date the phase to about 2500 B.C. Recent radiocarbon dates support Bryan's chronology. (Adapted by Charles M. Carrillo from Haury [1950:529, Figure 114].)

Ventana Cave, Bat Cave, Tularosa Cave, and other localities. Artifacts from the Casas Grandes area of Chihuahua (Rinaldo 1974) and from Sonora (Johnson 1966) are acknowledged as variants of the San Pedro Cochise (Di Peso 1979). Finally, surface finds from northwestern New Mexico and the Rio Grande Valley area are reported (Cordell 1979).

The typical San Pedro projectile points are large, low-corner or side-notched points with straight to convex bases. In some assemblages, points with bulbous convex bases and serrated points occur. Other chipped stone artifacts include a variety of scrapers and denticulates, bifacial knives, and choppers. Ground stone metates have a deeper basin than those of the Chiricahua phase, and mortars and pestles occur, though infrequently (Irwin-Williams 1967). Dates for the San Pedro phase are given as 1500 to 200 B.C., with the caveat that the upper date is subject to revision (Whalen 1971, 1975).

At the isolative level of analysis, there are problems in interpreting the continuity of the Cochise at both the early and late ends of the continuum. The new radiocarbon dates indicate a considerable gap between the Sulphur Springs and Chiricahua phases of the Cochise. This discrepancy again gives rise to the issue of the interpretation of the original Sulphur Springs sites (see Chapter 4). Two alternatives seem possible. First, the undoubted physical association of Sulphur Springs artifacts and Pleistocene megafauna may not be cultural, but rather the result of geological processes. Second, the gap in dates may represent a real hiatus in the occupation of portions of southern Arizona.

At the late end of the Cochise sequence, the problems relate to new interpretations of Hohokam origins. On the basis of excavations at Tularosa Cave, Cordova Cave, Bat Cave, and a number of early Mogollon sites, historic continuity between the San Pedro Cochise and the Mogollon is generally accepted (Martin 1979; Martn *et al.* 1949, 1952). The information obtained from the Cienega Creek site also suggested continuities from the San Pedro Cochise to both the Hohokam and the Mogollon (Haury 1957:25). Figure 5.6, adapted from Haury's report, illustrates this view. More recently, based on reexcavations at the important Hohokam site of Snaketown, Haury (1976) concluded that the Hohokam represent a migration of people from Mexico who were not related to the indigenous Cochise. In part, this reinterpretation reflects Haury's evaluation of the Snaketown chronology, a topic of considerable debate (Doyel and Plog 1980; Schiffer 1982). The new interpretation is partially based on the presence at Snaketown, during the earliest occupation of the site, of "a well-developed ceramic complex, clay figurines, cremations, a sophisticated and lengthy canal system, excavated wells, shaped trough metates, stone bowls with sculptured surfaces, turquoise mosaics, and a well-developed shell industry . . . [which] appear as a cluster in southern Arizona with no local indigeneous antecedents" (Gumerman and Haury 1979:77). Viewed as a cluster, these traits may well seem to be intrusive at Snaketown. On the other hand, ceramics, wells, and cremations are known from late San Pedro Cochise contexts (Haury 1957; Morris 1969), and the existence of a lengthy canal system during the initial occupation at Snaketown has been questioned (F. Plog 1980; Wilcox 1978).

Eastern Tradition

The fourth and easternmost tradition of the Picosa culture is not formally named, but it includes materials referred to as the Hueco complex in southeastern New Mexico and the Coahuila complex of Coahuila and eastern Chihuahua in Mexico and west Texas (Irwin-Williams 1979; Taylor 1966). A great many diverse wooden objects are characteristic of the Coahuila complex (Taylor 1966). The lack of similar material from the sites north of the Mexican border (which may be due to preservation conditions) makes it difficult to use these for specific comparisons. Although not

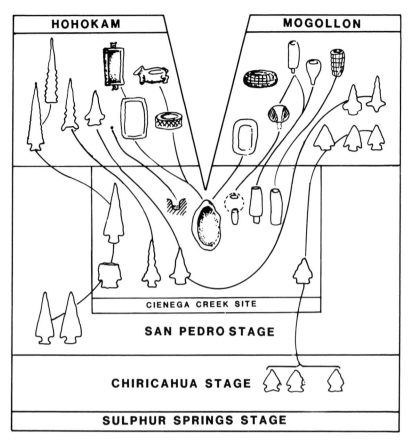

Figure 5.6 Cultural continuity from the Chiricahua Cochise to the Hohokam and Mogollon, interpreted from the Cienega Creek site. This illustration, adapted from Haury (1957), indicates the perception of gradual change from the Archaic Chiricahua Cochise phase to the Hohokam and Mogollon traditions. Haury has since reinterpreted the origins of the Hohokam. (Illustrated by Charles M. Carrillo.)

numerous in Coahuila assemblages, the projectile points include oval forms, types with contracting stems and strong barbs, and notched and stemmed points that have counterparts in sites in New Mexico and Texas (Irwin-Williams 1979; Taylor 1966). As a whole, the Archaic materials from the southeastern Southwest are considered ancestral to the Jornada Mogollon (Irwin-Williams 1979). In general, of the four traditions Irwin-Williams proposes, the Oshara is the most detailed. This situation reflects Irwin-Williams' ongoing research in the Arroyo Cuervo area (Irwin-Williams 1973). In sum, Irwin-Williams' formulation of Picosa culture reflects her view that during the Archaic the Southwest consisted of four interacting cultural traditions: the San Dieguito–Pinto, the Oshara, the Cochise, and a southeastern tradition. As a group, the four are considered to differ from Archaic traditions elsewhere in North America (e.g., the Plains Archaic, the Archaic of northern California, the Archaic of the Columbia

Plateau). Irwin-Williams also sees of the four as ancestral to later traditions in the Southwest: The San Dieguito–Pinto tradition is viewed as leading to the later Colorado River peoples (Irwin-Williams 1967, 1979). Schroeder (1979a), however, cautions that more information is needed to clarify this relation. The Oshara tradition is viewed as ancestral to the Anasazi of the Colorado Plateaus and the Rio Grande Valley. The Cochise tradition is seen as leading to the later Mogollon culture. Whether or not the Cochise also underlies the Hohokam culture is debated. Finally, the Hueco and Coahuila complexes are considered ancestral to the Jornada Mogollon.

In the preceding chapter, suggested relations between changes in hunting patterns and changes in climate and environment were discussed. Paleoclimatological data available for the Archaic indicate that, although there were periods of relatively more or less moist conditions, overall climatic perturbations were less severe than they had been during Paleo-Indian times. Yet, the onset of the Archaic marked a change from relatively large-game hunting, at least in the eastern Southwest, to small-game hunting and more use of plant food. Toward the end of the Archaic, domestic crops were accepted by Southwestern peoples. The environmental context of this economic change is of interest in order to evaluate proposed explanations for the acceptance of agriculture.

Paleoenvironmental Considerations

The Natural Environment

The same considerations that pertained to environmental reconstructions of the Paleo-Indian period also obtain for the Archaic. In essence, some climatic changes may have been quite rapid, and climatic fluctuations of global or continental scale are expected to produce diverse local effects. Unfortunately, too few areas have been subject to intensive climatological studies relevant to the Archaic, and major issues are unresolved. Although lacking ideal precision, some studies of pollen, macrobotanical remains, and faunal material have been useful for developing characterizations of the environments of the Archaic.

The beginning of the Archaic coincides with environmental changes in parts of the Southwest. Pollen data (Oldfield and Schoenwetter 1975) suggest a decrease in effective moisture and indicate the presence of an essentially treeless prairie in the Llano Estacado at about 6000 B.C. These observations are corroborated by studies of fossil packrat middens from the nearby Guadalupe Mountains (Van Devender *et al.* 1978). Packrat middens contain materials collected within a radius of about 100 m from the shelters where they are preserved. The middens from the Guadalupe Mountains show that the juniper–oak woodland that had been present until about 6000 B.C. was later replaced by desert scrub and grassland communities. Pollen analyses from the San Pedro River valley (Mehringer 1967) also indicate the presence of desert species at about 6000 B.C. Materials from packrat middens from the desert areas of Texas, Arizona, California, and Nevada indicate the replacement of woodlands by desert species at about the same time. Van Devender and Spaulding (1979:706) comment that "the end of the early Holocene woodlands in these now warm deserts appears to have been a rapid, widespread, synchronous event." The early Archaic appears to correlate with the retreat of woodlands from warm desert areas of the Southwest.

The period from about 5500 to about 2900 B.C. has been termed the *Altithermal* (Antevs 1955) and characterized as a time of relatively hot and dry conditions. The nature of the Altithermal climate continues to be debated. The issue is primarily relevant to the problem of the apparant gap in the sequence between the San Pedro and Chiricahua phases of the Cochise discussed above. A very hot and dry period might have discouraged occupation of the Sonoran Desert. However, Van Devender and Spaulding (1979) suggest that the term *Altithermal* either be discarded or restricted to the northern Mohave Desert and the Great Basin, where a warm and dry climate for this period has been documented. They interpret the packrat midden material and atmospheric wind patterns as indicating warmer global temperatures and a decrease in winter rainfall, but they suggest an increase in summer rainfall throughout the Sonoran and Chihuahuan deserts. Some support for the suggested increase in summer rainfall is available from the Llano Estacado, where lake deposits continued to form until about 2900 B.C.

Several lines of evidence indicate a trend toward increased moisture at times during the later Archaic. However, whether this increase in moisture was synchronous over the entire Southwest (as was suggested by Antevs' proposed Medithermal of 2500–3000 B.C.) is not known. Nevertheless, geological studies (Powers 1939) indicate that the San Agustin Basin reached its maximum depth of about 30.5 m of water at about 1500 B.C., followed by a lowering of the level of the lake thereafter. In the Estancia Basin, Lake Meinzer formed at about 2000 B.C. and became desiccated shortly before 100 B.C. (Bachuber 1971). Pollen from the Llano Estacado also records an increase in pine, interpreted as an increase in effective moisture, between about 2600 and 2700 B.C. (Hafsten 1961). Although inadequately dated, macrobotanical material from packrat middens and microtine rodents from Atl-Atl Cave in Chaco Canyon indicates wetter and warmer conditions at about 2200 B.C. (Judge 1982; Neller 1976). Finally, although these variations in climate should not be ignored, it is worth reiterating Haynes' observation that, for the Llano Estacado from about 2000 B.C. to the present, there were "cycles of erosion, deflation and dune activity alternating with alluvial deposition and soil development, but amplitudes of the cycles did not approach those of the previous cycles" (Haynes 1975:83). Thus, the cultural events of the late Archaic, especially the adoption of crops, took place during periods of climatic fluctuations that were less severe than those of preceding periods.

The Cultural Environment

The situations to which human societies adapt include the contexts created by other societies as well as those of the natural environment. The amount of territory through which a particular group moves in order to gather and hunt may in part be determined by the movements of neighboring groups of people. In addition, the cultural environment can provide information relevant to technological change. A cultural environment that includes agricultural communities is qualitatively different from one constituted entirely of hunters and gatherers. The former provides information about alternative sources of food, whether or not these are accepted. This section first examines the general demographic context of Southwestern Archaic adaptations, which has implications primarily for group mobility. Then it explores the qualitative content of the cultural environment.

Demography   Throughout the Southwest, population seems to have increased throughout the Archaic. There are more documented late Archaic than early Archaic sites, and although this may be a reflection of the higher probability associated with finding sites as time depth decreases, late Archaic sites are also generally larger and distributed throughout a greater range of environmental zones than are early Archaic sites. It is not likely that the increased number of sites is a result of greater group mobility, because some late Archaic sites contain the remains of houses, suggesting some residential permanence.

Shallow, oval pithouses (excavated about 0.5 m below the ground surface) are reported for the San Pedro Cochise (Martin *et al.* 1949; Sayles 1945), and structures marked by circular configurations of postholes occur at the Pinto Basin Stahl site in southern California (Harrington 1957) as well as the San Jose phase sites in the Arroyo Cuervo area (Irwin-Williams 1973). More than 23 circular houses, with slightly excavated floors and mud brush and grass walls, possibly dating to between 2500 and 1800 B.C., have been excavated near El Paso (O'Laughlin 1980:135–138). Given the imprecision in dating Archaic sites, it is not possible to determine whether population growth during the Archaic was gradual or characterized by episodic changes. It has been suggested that in the Southwest and Desert West, economic dependence on plant foods and small, nonmigratory game would be conducive to gradual population increase and the attainment of population equilibrium at quite a low population density. This trajectory would depend on relatively stable climatic conditions, without the severe sorts of stress that either would necessitate migration out of the area or produce high mortality levels. The relatively low-amplitude climatic changes of the Archaic, compared to those of the Paleo-Indian period, would have been appropriate to a gradual population increase.

Subsistence and Settlement: The Integrative Level of Analysis

Throughout at least the early half of the Archaic, Southwestern peoples were mobile hunters and gatherers. Later, by about 1000 B.C., the Archaic peoples were using a limited amount of corn in their diets. Information about the food resources of Archaic groups is available from usually perishable material preserved in rockshelter sites and, indirectly, from the locations of open sites. Neither of these two sources of data is unambiguous.

While floral and faunal remains from rockshelters are the more direct evidence of past subsistence, there are pertinent problems that should be recognized. First, cave sites may represent the loci of seasonal activities or other special uses and therefore may not contain the entire range of foods used by Archaic peoples. Second, not all of the floral and faunal materials recovered in caves are the result of human deposition. Raptorial birds and mammalian carnivores introduce animal bones as well, and special techniques should be employed to distinguish these from cultural deposits (Thomas 1971). Third, controlled experiments (Gasser and Adams 1981) indicate that differential destruction of plant remains by bacteria and rodent activity may occur. In general, plants with dense inedible parts, such as corncobs, have the highest probability of survival. Plants with dense edible parts, such as small seeds, have less chance of preservation. Plant foods that are not dense, such as greens and tubers, have the least survival potential (Munson *et al.* 1971). Techniques of processing and cooking also condition the probability of survival and identification. Plants that are boiled are less likely to be preserved than those that are charred or roasted, because boiling increases the water content and destroys cell structure (Minnis 1981:162–164). Finally, archaeological recovery of plant remains may depend on the use of special techniques, such as flotation and pollen analysis, that were not commonly practiced until fairly recently. Thus, information about the diversity of plant foods used by prehistoric peoples is incomplete.

Three very well known cave sites that have yielded quantities of perishable food items are Bat Cave (Dick 1965a), Tularosa Cave (Heller 1976; Martin *et al.,* 1952), and Cordova Cave (Martin *et al.* 1952). Bat Cave is located on the southeast side of the Plains of San Agustin and overlooks the ancient lake bed. Tularosa Cave is situated on the north side of Tularosa Creek, a tributary of the San Francisco River. Cordova Cave is on the west side of the San Francisco River below Pine Lawn. A diversity of wild plant remains is recorded for the Archaic levels of these caves, including pigweed, grasses, hackberry, goosefoot, walnut, juniper, prickly pear, Indian ricegrass, and yucca. Among the larger animals reported from Tularosa Cave and Bat Cave are bison, pronghorn antelope, mountain sheep, Sonoran deer, and mule deer. The remains of numerous rodents, which may have been introduced by nonhuman predators, were recovered from the caves. As Berman (1979) has noted, the plant resources recovered from the cave sites mature in late summer or early fall. She suggests either that the caves were occupied at that time of year or that they were used to store these foods. At least in the instance of Bat Cave, the latter seems most likely, because most of the floral remains were recovered from very small, crevice-like side chambers of the cave and from an area outside the cave that may have been used for plant processing. In any case, the floral and faunal remains suggest a highly diversified economy in which plant foods were of considerable importance. The similarity of food remains among the three caves is expected, because they are in similar environmental settings and in fairly close proximity.

The second approach to delimiting Archaic subsistence, that is, the examination of site locations and artifact inventories, is exemplified by Irwin-Williams' (1973) studies in the Arroyo Cuervo area and by survey work in the San Juan Basin (Allan *et al.* 1975;

Reher and Witter 1977). Irwin-Williams (1973) notes that most Archaic camp sites in her areas of interest are located in canyon heads where the resources of three productive microhabitats (canyon rims, canyon bottoms, and springs) are near and water is present. The resources of these habitats include wild grasses, cactus, amaranth, juniper, piñon, and rushes. She further suggests that limited activity sites in nearby upland and mountain areas were used as hunting camps. The physical association of the larger camp sites with the areas of diverse vegetable resources indicates that plant procurement was, possibly, more important than hunting.

It has long been noted that Archaic sites are frequently located in deflated sand dunes. This is to be expected, in part, because wind erosion removes the overburden from the Archaic remains. After noting that not all deflated sand dunes expose Archaic sites, Reher and Witter (1977) suggest that within dune areas, Archaic sites were associated with locations of relatively high botanical diversity, reflecting the subsistence pursuits of Archaic groups. This suggestion was tested during survey work in a portion of the San Juan Basin (Allan *et al.* 1975) by comparing the diversity of vegetation found on dunes with Archaic remains with that of comparable landforms lacking Archaic sites. Although the test confirmed the association of Archaic sites and dunes with diverse plant cover, suggested causal relations have been questioned. Soil conditions that act to retain water would also produce the observed diversity, and human populations may have been attracted by the availability of water rather than by the diversity of plants. Archaic wells excavated into dune deposits are documented for the Llano Estacado (Hester 1975), and similar wells were dug through alluvial deposits to reach groundwater at Cienega Creek (Haury 1957). It has also been suggested that a diversity of plant resources would have been attractive to a variety of animal species and that the potential for acquiring game would have been most important to Archaic peoples. Until the hydrology and geomorphology of dune sites are known through excavation as well as survey, conclusions linking areas of local botanical diversity to Archaic occupation are probably premature.

As noted above, the tool inventories of Archaic sites indicate a mixed hunting and gathering economy. The grinding stones are important for seed processing, and the numerous large scrapers, chopping tools, and scraper planes indicate reliance on plants in general. It was also suggested (following Judge 1982) that serrated projectile points may have been used in fiber processing. Other technological Archaic features related to plant processing and the storing of plant foods include roasting ovens, storage pits cut into cave floors, digging sticks, and baskets. Items related to hunting, in addition to projectile points, include various snares and atl-atl fragments recovered from cave sites (Martin *et al.* 1952).

In sum, the climatological information available for the Archaic indicates that, although moisture conditions varied, overall climatic perturbations were less severe than they had been during Paleo-Indian times. The faunal and botanical remains recovered from Archaic cave sites show that Archaic peoples had detailed knowledge of the available wild foods in the Southwest and that they had the technology to obtain the resources they needed. Nevertheless, there is evidence that corn and squash were being cultivated, at least sporadically, by about 1000 B.C. or perhaps somewhat earlier.

The presence of corn and squash is known primarily from cave sites where macrobotanical remains have been preserved. There is also some evidence of corn, in the form of pollen, from caves and open late Archaic sites. Although the dating of this early corn is not precise, its adoption into an Archaic way of life is undeniable.

Horticulture: The Qualitative Environment

The most important New World crops—corn (*Zea mays*), beans (*Phaseolus* sp.), and squash (*Cucurbita* sp.)—were domesticated in Mesoamerica between about 7000 and 3000 B.C. The relevant data are from the semiarid Tehuacán Valley in central Mexico and from dry caves in interior Tamaulipas, eastern Mexico (MacNeish 1958, 1967). The earliest known corn was recovered from Coxcatlan Cave in the Tehuacán Valley and dated to the El Riego phase, about 6500 to 4800 B.C. It seems likely that corn was derived from teosinte (*Euchleana mexicana*), a tropical grass that is corn's genetically closest extant relative (Beadle 1981) (Figure 5.7). The early Tehuacán corn is a popcorn with cobs only about 2 cm in length. It could have been used only as a supplement to other food resources. Other cultigens dating to the El Riego phase at Tehuacán include chili peppers (*Capsicum* sp.), avocados, green-striped cushaw squash (*Cucurbita mixta*), and possibly cotton (*Gossypium* sp.). MacNeish (1967) suggests that during the El Riego phase, people lived in small groups and subsisted primarily on gathering and hunting, supplementing their diets with the cultigens.

During the succeeding Coxcatlan phase at Tehuacán, dated between 4800 and 3500 B.C., bottle gourds (*Lagenaria siceraria*), warty squash (*Cucurbita moschata*), and the common bean (*Phaseolus vulgaris*) were added to the list of cultigens. By this time, groups are described as semisedentary, living in aggregated communities through much of the year but fragmenting into smaller units to forage during the dry season. During the Abejas phase at Tehuacán, dated between 3500 and 2300 B.C., new domesticates included jack beans (*Canavalia ensiformis*), tepary beans (*Phaseolus acutifolius*), pumpkins and summer squashes (both *Cucurbita pepo*). The corn associated with the Abejas phase had become considerably larger (cobs of around 10 cm) and more productive. Within the Tehuacán Valley some pithouse villages may have been occupied year-round. The Tehuacán Valley is a long way from even the southern Southwest. The Tamaulipas area of northeastern Mexico may have been the source of crops that were accepted in the Southwest.

In the Tamaulipas area, the Infernillo phase is approximately contemporaneous with the El Riego phase at Tehuacán. The earliest cultigens from the Infernillo phase are bottle gourds, chili peppers, and possibly *Cucurbita pepo*. The common bean is the next cultigen to be included, but corn does not occur until about 3000 B.C. Despite the variety of crops grown in Tamaulipas, gathering and hunting continued to be major subsistence pursuits for another 1000 years.

The presence of corn and other cultigens in Mesoamerica provided the cultural environment for technological change that would ultimately have a tremendous impact on the Southwest. Knowledge of new and potentially useful plants is not sufficient

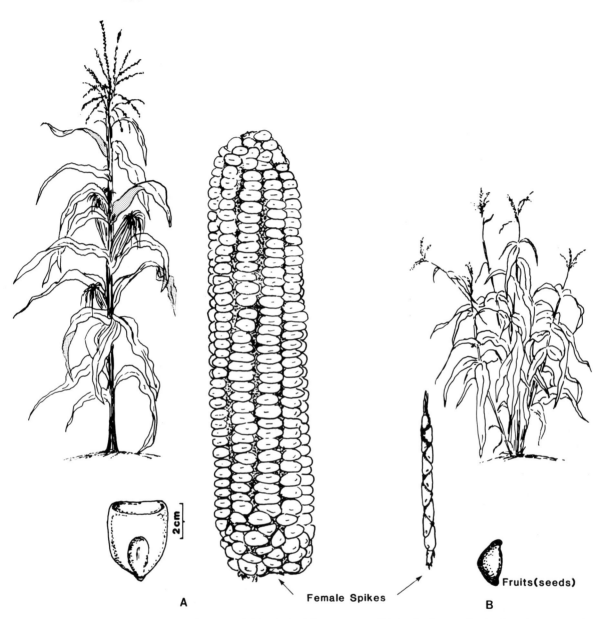

A

Female Spikes

Fruits(seeds)

B

Figure 5.7 Modern corn (A) is derived from teosinte (B), its far less productive but closest genetic relative. Plant scale: 1 cm = approximately 20 cm; female spike scale; .8 cm = 1 cm. (Illustrated by Charles M. Carrillo.)

to explain their acceptance into a peoples' economic inventory. Some of the important Mesoamerican crops, such as chili peppers and avocados, were not grown prehistorically in the Southwest. Common beans eventually became widespread Southwestern crops but were not accepted until about 350 B.C., long after they were in general use in Mesoamerica. In order to develop a perspective on the context in which cultigens were accepted in the Southwest, an examination of the basic subsistence patterns of the Archaic is necessary.

The Evidence of Early Cultigens in the Southwest

The earliest Southwestern crops—corn, bottle gourds, and beans—belong to what Ford (1981) has called the *Upper Sonoran Agricultural Complex.* The notion of a crop complex implies common geographic origin and a mutual association with particular environmental conditions. Individual species of a complex may subsequently be spread into other geographic areas. A few preliminary considerations of the Upper Sonoran complex of crops are in order prior to a consideration of their assimilation into the Southwest.

The botanical data from Tehuacán and Tamaulipas indicate that the Upper Sonoran agricultural complex had a long history of cultivation in Mexico prior to its appearance in the Southwest. The distribution of these cultigens in northern Mexico and in the Southwest corresponds to the Upper Sonoran life zone, which occurs at elevations above 2000 m, where there is sufficient precipitation to grow these crops without irrigation. All of the earliest maize in the Southwest is of an early Chapalote type: a small-cob popcorn that is phenotypically and genetically diverse. Sometime before 500 B.C. in northern Mexico, the early Chapalote corn introgressed with teosinte. The resultant corn appears in the Southwest at Bat Cave and Jemez Cave. This hybrid corn shows even more variability in row number, cob length, and cupule structure than does the earlier Chapalote. Finally, within a few centuries of the appearance of the hybrid corn, an eight-row flour corn, referred to as Harinoso de Ocho or Maiz de Ocho, was introduced into the Southwest and interbred with the teosinte-introgressed corn (Ford 1981; Galinat and Gunnerson 1963; Mangelsdorf *et al.* 1967). Although this corn was planted in a casual manner by Southwestern peoples and its potential was not recognized, all further corn types that were grown in the Southwest can be derived from the maize that was present in the area by 300 B.C. (Ford 1981).

The types of maize that were eventually derived from teosinte-introgressed Chapalote and Maiz de Ocho were adapted to a variety of environmental conditions and show a diversity of morphological characteristics. Reventador is a flint corn (the kernels are soft on the interior but hard on the exterior) that was derived from the Chapalote–teosinte hybrid and grown in the Hohokam area. Pima–Papago corn refers to two types of drought-resistant corn that were widely cultivated in the Southwest and were derived by crossing Chapalote with Maiz de Ocho. Onaveno, the flint variety of Pima–Papago corn, and Maiz Blando, the flour or soft-kerneled variety, differ by the mutation of a single gene that could have occurred anywhere (Ford 1981). It is significant that despite the development of new and more productive varieties of corn, Chapalote continues to occur throughout the later archaeological record of the Southwest.

The earliest squash in the Southwest (*Cucurbita pepo*) is a versatile plant that provides edible seeds and fruit and thick rinds that were used as tools and containers. The squash from Southwestern sites that date before about A.D. 900 are all of a single variety. After A.D. 900, several varieties of *Cucurbita pepo* were grown, but it is not known whether these reflect local development or were the result of further contact with Mexico (Ford 1981). Bottle gourds are also useful containers, and their seeds are edible. The plant does not tolerate short and cool growing seasons. Although it was eventually cultivated in many parts of the Southwest, it was apparently not grown in the more northern latitudes or at high elevations (Ford 1981).

Common beans include types we recognize as pinto beans, red kidney beans, and navy beans. The plant was eventually grown throughout the Southwest, and it may have been the only bean grown at some Pueblo sites (Ford 1981). Following Kaplan (1965), it has often been noted that corn and beans complement each other in two respects. First, beans contain a high level of the amino acid lysine, which enables efficient digestion of the protein available in corn. Second, whereas corn generally depletes nutrients from the soil, beans, as legumes, return nitrogen to the ground; consequently, when corn and beans are planted in the same field, problems of nutrient depletion are ameliorated (Castetter and Bell 1942). Because of this complementarity, it has been considered surprising that beans are later than corn in the archaeological record. However, some native Southwestern wild plants may also supply lysine and not all Southwestern people traditionally note the nitrogen–fixing properties of legumes.

To summarize, the Upper Sonoran complex had a long history of cultivation in Mexico prior to its acceptance in the Southwest. The earliest corn to be planted in the Southwest was phenotypically variable and not highly productive. On the other hand, if planted above 2000 m it required neither supplemental watering nor substantial attention. Fixing the date at which corn first appeared in the Southwest has long been a problem. Dates of at least 3500 B.C. appear in the literature, but these have been reevaluated.

Corn is known from the Archaic levels of Bat Cave (Dick 1965a; Mangelsdorf 1954, 1974; Smith 1950). The early radiocarbon dates for its occurrence have been questioned (Berry 1982; Ford 1981; Mangelsdorf *et al.* 1967) and portions of the cave are currently being reexcavated by crews from the University of Michigan. Nevertheless, based on cultural context, a date of about 1000 B.C. for the Bat Cave maize seems reasonable (Ford 1981; Minnis 1980). A similar type of corn occurs in an undated but preceramic context at Swallow Cave, Chihuahua (Mangelsdorf and Lister 1956). Tularosa Cave and Cordova Cave also yielded numerous remains of corn (Kaplan 1963; Martin *et al.* 1954); radiocarbon dates indicate an age of about 300 B.C. for these cave deposits. In the Arroyo Cuervo area, Armijo and En Medio rockshelters contained evidence of maize (Ford 1981; Irwin-Williams and Tompkins 1968). In these shelters, the evidence consists of maize pollen; although the findings from neither site have been published in detail, radiocarbon dates between 1500 and 550 B.C. are reported.

Jemez Cave, in the Jemez Mountains (Alexander and Reiter 1935; Ford 1975, 1981), produced maize in an undated deposit beneath a level radiocarbon dated to 490 B.C. Lo Daiska Rockshelter, near Denver, contained corn in the earliest occupation levels (Irwin and Irwin 1959). A single radiocarbon date for the oldest occupation suggests a period from about 1150 to 2800 B.C., but the stratigraphic association between the corn and the date is problematic (Ford 1981). O'Haco Rockshelter, in the Chevelon Creek drainage of Arizona (Briuer 1975), yielded corn remains. Although dates of 3000 B.C. are reported for this occurrence, these have been questioned (Minnis 1980). O Block Cave, in the Pine Lawn Valley (Martin *et al.* 1954), produced maize that is dated to about 850–650 B.C. on the basis of radiocarbon dates. In addition to these sites, excavations at Ojala Cave (Traylor *et al.* 1977) near Bandelier National Monument, and at Fresnel Rockshelter (Wimberly 1972), near Tularosa, New Mexico, have recovered maize in Archaic contexts, but the findings of neither project have been published in detail.

Maize pollen was recovered from the Cienega Creek site (Haury 1957; Martin and Schoenwetter 1960), but the reported radiocarbon dates obtained from two laboratories are so disparate (2250 B.C. and A.D. 250) that interpreting them is difficult. Redating of the Cienega Creek deposits produced dates averaging 500 B.C. (Berry 1982). A single grain of maize pollen was recovered from the Double Adobe site (Martin 1963) and may date to about 1900 B.C. Corn pollen was also recovered from the Matty Wash site near Tucson and may date to about 270 B.C. (Martin 1963).

In addition to corn, the remains of squash (*Cucurbita pepo*) are known from all the preceramic contexts in which maize has been found, with the possible exception of Cordova Cave (Ford 1981). Bottle gourds and the common bean occur in Southwestern contexts, but not as early as corn. Ford (1981) considers dates of about 300 B.C. for bottle gourds from Tularosa Cave and Cordova Cave to be generally applicable. The bottle gourd was not present at Bat Cave or Jemez Cave. The common bean occurs at Bat Cave, Tularosa Cave, Cordova Cave, and Fresnel Rockshelter. Dates for the introduction of the common bean are not as precise as they might be, but Ford (1981) suggests that 300–500 B.C. may be reasonable.

Explaining the Acceptance of Agriculture

Two immediate questions about the early cultivation of crops in the Southwest may be addressed: (1) What were the immediate mechanisms through which the introduction of crops took place, and (2) why were these crops accepted? There can be no very satisfactory answer to the first question, because an answer would involve reconstructing specific events that are not visible in the archaeological record. It may be noted, however, that the Upper Sonoran Agricultural Complex was grown in Mesoamerica and northern Mexico for about a thousand years by nonsedentary peoples. Within the context of mobility and periodic interaction among groups of people, it is likely that knowledge of particular plants and specimens of potentially useful plants would be readily exchanged.

An answer to the second question entails an examination of the current issues in archaeological and anthropological theory. Prior to the 1950s and 1960s, the "invention" of agriculture by man was seen as an almost natural outgrowth of an "evolutionary trend" toward more complete control over the natural environment. As such, it did not require an explanatory framework. Very important studies of modern hunters and gatherers (Lee and Devore 1968) dispelled a number of ethnocentric myths about the hunting and gathering way of life. It is now well documented that hunters and gatherers generally invest less labor in subsistence activities than do agriculturalists. Most hunters and gatherers work only about 2 days a week acquiring food. On the other hand, nonindustrial agriculturalists work, particularly seasonally, as many as 4–6 days a week. Children, even young adolescents, are not typically part of the labor force among hunters and gatherers, but they are among agriculturalists. Hunters and gatherers are just as healthy, if not healthier, than agriculturalists. Studies of skeletal remains, especially from the Southwest (El-Najjar 1974; El-Najjar *et al.* 1976), indicate that horticultural populations show more evidence of poor nutrition than do hunters and gatherers. Finally, archaeological evidence indicates that the early domestic crops were not highly productive (Flannery 1968; Harlan 1967). All of these observations lead to the conclusion that, rather than being the result of a natural trend, agriculture requires an explanation.

Currently, there are two theoretical models that attempt to explain the origins of agriculture and may be considered relevant to situations, like that of the Southwest, in which agriculture was adopted. One model relies heavily on Boserup's (1965) argument that demographic pressure is the independent variable in causing technological change. In the archaeological literature, this theoretical framework is elaborated in the seminal work of Lewis R. Binford (1968). Briefly, this model depends on documenting a situation of population disequilibrium in an area where potential domestic plants (or animals) exist. As elaborated by Binford, an area that supports low-density hunting and gathering populations is seen to receive increments of people displaced from sedentary communities outside the area. The increased numbers of people are forced to develop the more intensive strategy involved in plant domestication. In theory, population disequilibrium might also occur if depleted game resources forced hunters and gatherers to supplement their diets with cultigens.

More recently, Sanders and Webster (1978) raised serious questions about the general applicability of Boserup's thesis. Sanders and Webster argue that, although population pressure may constitute the primary factor involved in agricultural intensification in stable environments (such as the tropical forest areas that Boserup's original research concerns), in differently structured environments other factors may be equally important. Specifically, they contend that in natural environmental settings that are characteristically variable (because of marked deviations from average rainfall, for example), intensified production may be undertaken in order to reduce subsistence risk. Agriculture might therefore be initiated or adopted in order to supplement periods of poor yields of collected foods.

A discussion of subsistence strategies as practiced by the Basarwa (San, Bushmen) of the Kalahari Desert affords some perspective on conditions that seem to be important to the acceptance of agriculture by peoples who inhabit semiarid and arid environments. The example draws primarily on a study by Hitchcock and Ebert (in press).

Today, only about 5% of the Basarwa derive their entire subsistence from hunting and gathering; however, the transition to food production is not a one-way process. Groups often alternate between food production and hunting and gathering; agriculture, where practiced, is only supplemental to foraging. It has long been thought that contact with Bantu agriculturalists provided the necessary and sufficient conditions for the adoption of food production by the Basarwa. Similar arguments, involving Mesoamerican agriculturalists, have been made with respect to the prehistoric Southwest (Haury 1976; Schroeder 1965). In the Basarwa case, archaeological and historic data demonstrate that, although contact with agriculturalists and knowledge about agriculture probably dates to 1500 years ago, it has effected no appreciable changes in Basarwa hunting and gathering. In addition, as Hitchcock and Ebert note:

> if we accept the diffusionist model of the spread of agriculture, we would expect those groups in closest proximity to food-producing people . . . to be the ones who would be most involved in agriculture. The distribution of food-producing households reveals that this is just the opposite of the case. (in press:63)

In fact, those Basarwa who live closest to Bantu settlements tend to be the least involved in agriculture. For the Basarwa, cultural and environmental factors are cited to explain this unexpected distribution: (1) Basarwa cultural values do not favor food production; (2) those groups in close physical proximity to agriculturalists generally have access to agricultural produce, either through trade or employment; and (3) it is near the Bantu towns that livestock damage to crops is highest and that the Basarwa have the least success in raising food (a consideration that is not applicable to the prehistoric Southwest).

With respect to Archaic populations in the Southwest, there are, of course, no archaeological methods for determining whether cultural values favored foraging rather than agriculture. On the other hand, the fact that appropriate crops were available in Mexico long before they were used in the Southwest certainly suggests that the opportunity to acquire agricultural technology is not a sufficient cause for its adoption.

For the Basarwa, a complex set of factors leads to the incorporation of food production among some groups; however, among these, population pressure that restricts mobility and environmental degradation (caused by the expansion of cattle grazing into the Kalahari, and not by climatic change) are apparently the most critical. As described by Hitchcock and Ebert (in press), Basarwa foragers must be highly mobile in order to gather foods when and where these are available. This high-mobility requirement discourages storage. Foraging groups are generally quite selective in their food procurement, gathering the more productive resources available in their environment. In times of abundance, their foods are restricted to preferred items. In lean times, these groups forage more widely and a wider variety of foods is incorporated into the diet. There are high risks in foraging. Droughts can be devastating to a group with no stored resources. When mobility is restricted by the encroachment of cattle-grazing peoples into the Kalahari, some Basarwa adopt agriculture; thus, although agriculture is accepted to reduce risk, as Sanders and Webster suggest, the risk itself is engendered by regional conditions of overpopulation.

A similar conclusion has been reached by Winter (1976) in his analysis of the diffusion of agriculture into the Great Basin and the Southwest. Winter examines the conditions during the nineteenth century in which various southern Paiute (and perhaps some Chemeheuvi) engaged in farming. He notes that, although some groups were forced by various Euro-American agents to adopt farming, this influence was short-lived. Other groups

> appear to have adopted farming on their own after the native food gathering complex was disrupted due to the destruction of the natural plant communities by livestock. . . . Many Numa groups developed farming or raiding economies during the decade following A.D. 1850, apparently in an effort to fill an economic vacuum created by the disappearance of the native seed resources. (Winter 1976:426)

Winter also suggests that the very late (ca. A.D. 400) adoption of horticulture by the Fremont culture of central Utah occurred at a time when favorable environmental conditions had allowed the expansion of Anasazi agricultural populations into southern Utah. The Anasazi farming people might well have restricted the foraging ranges of the Great Basin groups, who would then have adopted horticultural strategies in order to counter the regional population imbalance.

The ethnographic, historic, and archaeological data presented above suggest that in environments characterized by risk due to variability in rainfall or growing season, crops may be adopted to minimize the effects of environmental degradation and reduced mobility related to conditions of regional population imbalances (also see Cordell and Plog 1979). It is worth noting here that regional overpopulation may occur despite what may appear to be quite low population densities—it is the overall productivity of a particular environment that determines the level at which it is saturated. For example, it would be expected that a relatively resource-rich setting like the Mississippi valley would support higher population densities of hunters and gatherers than would the less naturally productive semiarid Southwest.

Based on the information provided in the sections on the natural and cultural environments of the Southwestern Archaic adaptations, it is possible to explore hypotheses advanced to account for the acceptance of cultigens from Mexico. It is suggested that a situation of regional imbalance between population and resources is a precondition for the adoption of agriculture. Such a situation may result either from environmental degradation or from an increase in population. The climatic data available for the Archaic, although not abundant, tend to suggest that environmental degradation was not the key factor. Rather, these data indicate that climatic fluctuations during the Archaic were less severe than they had been in Paleo-Indian times and that generally wetter conditions prevailed from about 2500 to about 100 B.C. It was thus during a period of increased moisture, a generally favorable climatic episode, that agriculture was accepted. Population increase as a causal mechanism requires either a set of circumstances in which population growth is, for some reason, unchecked, or evidence of a population expansion from an adjacent area. At present, anthropologists have an incomplete understanding of the factors that are instrumental in causing a population growth that is sufficient to necessitate migration of some of the population. Two current ideas, which are not mutually exclusive, involve the effects of sedentism and dietary modifications.

In his original discussion of agricultural origins, Binford (1968) argued that hunters and gatherers practice various population-limiting behaviors (abortion, infanticide, increased spacing of births, etc.) so that women's mobility is not severely hindered. He suggested that post-Pleistocene hunters and gatherers exploiting riverine resources in favorable areas became sedentary and, with sedentism, the cultural practices used to regulate population were dropped. This model has been criticized (Cowgill 1975; Hassan 1981:212), and in a more recent discussion (Binford and Chasko 1976), it was suggested that sedentism and the maintenance of stored food could provide more evenly balanced caloric and nutritional requirements throughout the year, which would encourage population growth. In addition, some have argued (e.g., Frisch 1977) that an increase in carbohydrate consumption, which would have occurred as more plants were incorporated in the human diet, leads to a greater proportion of body fat and a reduction in the age of menarche. As Hassan (1981:224) cautions, however, the evidence for a link between body fat and age at menarche is not conclusive.

Despite the problems in specifying the causal mechanisms involved in population growth, models based on sedentary "donor" areas pushing excess population into the Southwest have been presented to account for the acceptance of agriculture (e.g., Glassow 1972, 1980). One source of excess population may have been Mesoamerica, where food production and sedentary horticultural villages were widespread by at least 1000 B.C. In this case, no invasion of peoples from Mexico bringing agriculture to the Southwest is envisioned. As is discussed in chapter 6, agricultural technology in the Southwest differs considerably from that practiced in Mexico. Rather, because sedentary communities existed early in Mesoamerica, the overflow population from this source could have placed pressure on the indigenous Picosa culture groups (Cordell 1979).

Although conditions of prior sedentism are considered in virtually all current models of agricultural origins (cf. Hassan 1981:213–217), there are other circumstances that could promote population–resource imbalances; these might have existed along the eastern margins of the Southwest in the area contiguous to that in which the earliest use of cultigens is currently known. For example, if the late Plains Archaic witnessed a dramatic increase in bison hunting and the establishment of large, seasonally occupied camps along the western Plains margins (Frison, 1978), mobility options for some hunters and gatherers west of the Plains may have been reduced. The result would have been a situation of regional population imbalance and restricted mobility—conditions similar to those described for the Basarwa. Perhaps, like the Basarwa, some local groups occasionally planted crops to supplement poor natural yields and returned to foraging in times of natural abundance.

In sum, current anthropological theory suggests that the origins and spread of horticulture result from stress related to an imbalance between population and available natural resources. In some kinds of environments, particularly stable ones, the stress factors may relate to a need to increase the amount of total natural productivity. In those environments that are variable, like the Southwest, the stress involved may be related to reducing the risk of occasional droughts when increased mobility is precluded. The available data do not support the notion that cultigens were accepted to offset or buffer conditions of degradation of the natural environment. Rather, paleoenvironmental reconstructions indicate that crops were first cultivated in the Southwest during a time of slightly increased moisture. The economic base to which crops were added was one of eclectic hunting and gathering. This early Archaic economy, the tool inventory of which included manos, grinding slabs, roasting pits, and heavy choppers that were appropriate for processing corn as well as wild plant foods, was to some extent preadapted to the acceptance of crops. If simple opportunity was sufficient to explain the acceptance of cultigens, then it would be expected either that some of the earliest Mesoamerican crops (e.g., chili peppers) would have been adopted in the Southwest, or that corn would have appeared in the Southwest shortly after its domestication in Mexico. In fact, the archaeological record indicates that neither of these alternatives occurred. Corn seems to have been accepted as a supplementary food by peoples living within the Upper Sonoran zone long after it was domesticated in Mexico. Southwestern peoples continued to be quite mobile for about 1000 years after the acceptance of corn. It was proposed that conditions of regional overpopulation are important to the initial use of corn. Three possible sources of excess population were suggested: sedentary communities in coastal California, sedentary communities in Mesoamerica, and the expansion of bison-hunting populations on the Plains. Although none of these may be ruled out entirely, neither does the archaeological record support one over the others.

The type of corn accepted was not highly productive and could not have provided a sufficient source of food when planted casually. As a tropical grass, corn is at considerable risk in the higher latitudes of the Southwest. On the other hand, the crops of the Upper Sonoran Agricultural Complex could be grown in these latitudes without irrigation. They might have been rather casually planted by Archaic groups for use as a supplemental resource in those areas where they did not require a great deal of care and where their cultivation did not greatly interfere with other subsistence pursuits. The cultivation of crops of the complex eventually spread throughout the Southwest, assuming primary importance as a subsistence strategy among many Southwestern peoples; however, another crop complex became important to peoples living in the low, hot Southwestern deserts. This second complex was accepted later and in a different adaptive context.

Other Southwestern Crops

Although the crops of the Upper Sonoran Agricultural Complex were the first to be cultivated everywhere in the Southwest, between about A.D. 300 and 500 a new crop complex was accepted from Mexico. Unlike the former, which was transmitted initially among mobile hunters and gatherers, the latter complex was introduced first to people who had already made some commitment to agriculture. The recipients of the new crops were the apparently sedentary Hohokam, who practiced irrigation in favorable areas of the lower Sonoran Desert. The new crops, termed the Lower Sonoran Agricultural Complex (Ford 1981), are plants that tolerate the high temperatures of the desert but also generally require irrigation. The Lower Sonoran Agricultural Complex includes cotton, tepary beans, sieva beans (*Phaseolus lunatus*), jack beans, possibly scarlet runner beans (*Phaseolus coccineus*), green-striped cushaw squash, warty squash, and pigweed (*Amaranthus hypochondriacus*). Nearly all of these crops are known from the Tehuacán Valley by the time of the Coxcatlan phase. The exceptions are sieva beans, scarlet runner beans, and pigweed.

The sieva bean has been found only rarely in prehistoric Southwestern archaeological contexts. It is known from a few Hohokam and Anasazi sites dating after A.D. 1100. The origins of the sieva bean, which resembles the South American lima bean and with which it is sometimes confused (Gasser 1976), are obscure. One variety of the sieva occurs in the Tamaulipas area and in northern Durango, Mexico, in sites that predate A.D. 1100 (Ford 1981; Gasser 1976). Scarlet runner beans are even more problematic in the Southwestern archaeological record. One such bean was identified in an unprovenienced context from Pueblo Grande. A second example, identified as a possible scarlet runner or sieva bean, was recovered from the same site in a context postdating A.D. 1100 (Gasser 1976). Ford (1981) concurs with a previous assessment (Nabhan 1977) that there are no uncontested prehistoric examples of the scarlet runner bean in the Southwest. Scarlet runner beans are cultivated by the Hopi, but they may have been introduced to them during the historic period. The pigweed (*Amaranthus hypochondriacus*) is also presently difficult to evaluate. It is known with certainty from post-A.D. 1100 context in central Arizona (Bohrer 1962). Although dates of A.D. 500 for this pigweed have been confirmed from Tehuacán, its putative ancestor (*Amaranthus powelli*) is a native plant in Arizona. It is therefore possible that domestication of the pigweed took place in Arizona (Ford 1981:19).

In contrast to the crops of the Upper Sonoran Agricultural Complex, the crops of the Lower Sonoran Complex did not spread into southern Arizona as an interrelated group. Cotton and tepary beans occur at about A.D. 500. Jack beans and green-striped cushaw squash are not well documented before A.D. 700–900. Sieva beans and warty squash are never common and appear only after A.D. 1100. Pigweed also occurs after A.D. 1100, although it may have been domesticated within the Southwest. The evidence for domesticated scarlet runner beans is not conclusive. Of all of these plants, only green-striped cushaw squash gained wide acceptance in the Southwest. Ford (1981) suggests that its spread may be related to the fact that, although the plant is not a good dry-farming crop, it is very productive when irrigated. It may therefore have been accepted by peoples who used various forms of intensive agriculture, including irrigation.

Making a commitment to agriculture—investing time and energy in crop production—drastically changed the ways of life of Southwestern peoples and conditioned many of the subsequent cultural developments that came to characterize the South-west. In order to understand these developments, it is necessary to appreciate the ecological relations among the people, their crops, and the variable Southwestern environment. These, then, are the subjects of the next chapter.

6

The Adoption of Agricultural Strategies

This chapter explores some of the factors that were important to the spread of agriculture throughout much of the Southwest. A variety of ingenious technological methods for enhancing yields were developed to ensure against the marginally favorable and often unpredictable climatic conditions. These are discussed in the context of the case studies drawn from various periods and a variety of Southwestern environments.

Introduction

By about A.D. 900, agriculture had spread throughout most of the Southwest. In some areas, domestic crops provided the majority of the people's food requirements, and a considerable amount of labor was invested in attempts to ensure agricultural success. Various devices were constructed to divert water to fields, to conserve moisture, and to slow soil erosion. In other parts of the Southwest, there are few tangible remains of this sort, and agriculture seems to have remained supplemental to hunting and gathering. In still other locations, agriculture was a short-lived experiment that failed. This chapter explores some of the conditions important to the spread of agriculture and describes some of the diverse agriculture practices used in the prehistoric Southwest. The factors that are considered especially important to the diversity of subsistence strategies include aspects of local environments, prevailing climatic conditions, and population densities.

Archaeological interest in prehistoric agriculture and the recovery of plant and animal remains has a respectably long history in the Southwest, but major efforts to reconstruct prehistoric agricultural practices are relatively recent. In part these efforts reflect the development of new recovery techniques such as flotation and pollen analysis. They are also the result of the ecological orientation in archaeology that became prominent in the 1970s. Only recently did archaeologists working in the Southwest begin systematically to record agricultural features during the course of site surveys and routinely to collect paleobotanical data in the course of excavation. This chapter includes a series of case studies to illustrate the variety in prehistoric agricultural practices, innovations in research strategy, and interpretations made by the archaeologists. The case studies are not restricted to a single prehistoric period, cultural area, or environmental zone. They are drawn from different times and places in the Southwest (Figure 6.1) and show effects of local environmental conditions, prevailing climate, and population density on the subsistence system represented.

Factors in the Spread of Agriculture in the Southwest

Interrelated factors important to the spread of agriculture include decreased population mobility, manipulation of crops, storage practices, and population expansion. As noted in the preceding chapter, one can understand the acceptance of corn and other crops of the Upper Sonoran Agricultural Complex among people who could not hunt and gather over sufficiently large territories during lean periods. Although the early corn does not seem to have been very productive, it would have required little

Figure 6.1 Sites discussed in Chapters 6 and 7. 1, Elk Ridge, Utah; 2, Cedar Mesa, Utah; 3, Longhouse Valley, Arizona; 4, Black Mesa, Ariz.; 5, Chaco Canyon, N. Mex.; 6, Taos, N. Mex.; 7, Cochiti Pueblo, N. Mex.; 8, Santo Domingo Pueblo, N. Mex.; 9, San Marcial, N. Mex.; 10, Zuni, N. Mex.; 11, Flattop Site, Ariz.; 12, St. Johns, Ariz.; 13, Chevelon, Ariz.; 14, Hay Hollow Valley, Ariz.; 15, Forestdale, Ariz.; 16, Pinelawn Valley, N. Mex.; 17, Point of Pines, Ariz.; 18, New River and Agua Drainage, Ariz.; 19, Snaketown, Ariz.; 20, Gu Achi, Ariz. (Map by Charles M. Carrillo.)

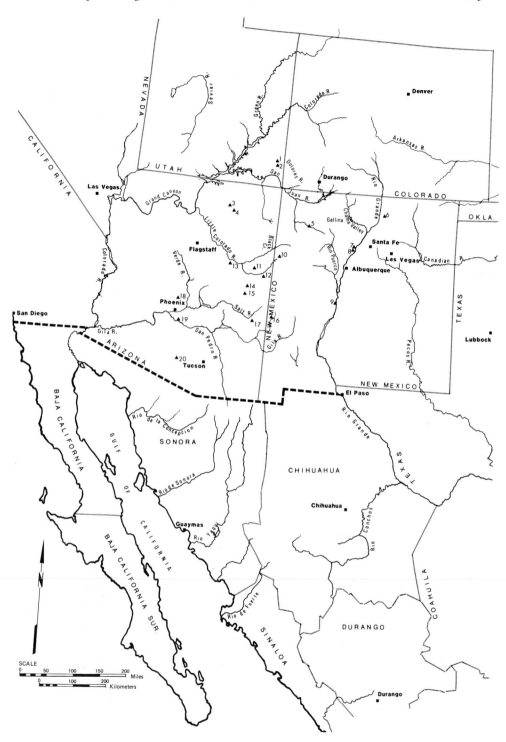

Table 6.1

Nutritional Aspects of Domesticates and Wild Plant Foods
of the Southwest[a]

	Calories (per 100g)[b]	Protein (per 100g)[b]	Carbohydrates (per 100g)[c]
Crop			
Beans, common (raw)	340	22.5	61.9
Corn	348	8.9	72.2
Squash, summer	19	1.1	4.2
Squash, winter	50	1.4	12.4
Pumpkins	26	1.0	6.5
Wild food			
Seeds			
Amaranth	36	3.5	6.5
Lamb's-quarter	43	4.2	7.3
Saguaro	609	16.3	540
Tansy mustard	554	23.4	71.0
Pigweed	360	—	—
Fruits			
Cholla	393	12.2	79.0
Prickly pear	42	0.5	10.9
Prickly pear (dry)	280	1.7	62.0
Saguaro (dry)	499	10.3	70.0
Nuts			
Black walnuts	628	20.5	14.8
Piñon	635	—	—
Other			
Cholla stems	—	1.6	—
Mesquite beans	419	14.9	73.0
Purslane	20	—	—

[a]Adapted from Ford (1972).
[b]Edible portion only.
[c]Includes fiber.

tending when grown in settings above 200 m in elevation and could have produced as much or more food per unit of land than most customarily gathered wild seeds. Table 6.1 provides a rough comparison of some of the nutritional aspects of domestic crops and wild plant foods used in the Southwest. Corn and beans compare quite favorably, in caloric content and protein, to many of the wild seeds and other foods. As discussed in Chapter 2, however, one of the characteristics of natural vegetation patterning in the Southwest is that large stands of a single plant type in one area are rare. This suggests that a great deal more energy was expended gathering wild seeds equal in caloric value to the corn grown in a small field. If people normally move over large portions of the landscape as they gather and hunt, locating and collecting enough wild plant food does not constitute a problem. When movement is restricted, however, the advantage of having pure stands of an even moderately productive crop is obvious.

Corn provides less food value than some foods, especially piñon nuts and walnuts. Although piñon is widely distributed in the Southwest, piñon nut crops are extremely unreliable from year to year. Good piñon yields occur only 1 year out of 7 to 14 in the same area. Yearly variability in production is true of other nuts as well (Wing and Brown 1979:147), including black walnut, which has a far more limited distribution in the Southwest than does piñon.

The genetically variable teosinte-introgressed corn that was present in the Southwest by 300 B.C. was amenable to the human manipulation and selection that could substantially enhance its productivity and reliability as a crop. Human selection could also have produced varieties of corn that could have been grown successfully in many settings, including those below elevations of 200 m.

Corn, as a tropical grass, grows near the limits of its tolerances in the Southwest. The critical factors important for the growth of corn are the amount of water the plant receives, the length of the growing season, soil conditions including nutrients, and safety from damage from pests, crop diseases, and strong winds early in the growing season. Of these, the amount and timing of moisture during certain portions of the growing season are the most critical.

Modern hybrid corn requires about 40–60 cm of water during the growing season (Minnis 1981:197). The distribution of moisture at key times during the growing season is equally important. Field studies and experiments indicate that mild water stress at the beginning of the growing season may not substantially damage yields, although there must be enough moisture to ensure seed germination. Similarly, moisture stress at the end of the season, when grains are mature, has little effect on the crop. However, water deprivation when the plant is at the tasseling or silking stage may decrease yields by 50 to 75% (Classen and Shaw 1970; Minnis 1981).

Through a combination of strategies involving seed selection (which would emphasize and modify the genetically controlled characteristics of maize), planting decisions, and horticultural practices the combined problems of deficient moisture and short growing seasons are much reduced. By selecting seed corn from plants showing resistance to dry conditions, structural properties of the corn planted in the Southwest were developed and maintained. The two varieties of Pima–Papago corn, which were eventually planted over much of the Southwest, differ from other varieties of corn in two respects. First, the *mescotyl* will grow to 25–30 cm in length, compared to about 10–15 cm in modern hybrid varieties of corn. The elongated *mescotyl* allows seed to be planted at considerable depth, where the seed can use ground moisture retained from winter precipitation in order to germinate. Second, the corn produces a single long radicle rather than a number of seminal roots, enabling the plant to tap and use ground water for growth (Bradfield 1971; Collins 1914).

It is impossible to know many, if not most, of the agricultural practices used prehistorically in the Southwest, but some of the techniques documented among contemporary Southwestern peoples certainly extended into prehistoric times. Careful selection of field locations helps ensure sufficient water for corn. Fields may be placed in areas of deep soils with good moisture-retaining properties; on slopes that are exposed to the north or east, which receive less direct solar radiation and therefore hold moisture; within stream floodplains or the mouths of arroyos, which are naturally irrigated; or in sand dunes, which allow the penetration of moisture from the atmosphere and retard its evaporation. When corn is planted in locations where subsurface moisture is lacking, water from precipitation runoff or from streams or springs may be diverted during the critical periods of the growing season.

Modern hybrid corn requires a growing season of about 120 days, which is available throughout much of the Southwest. When corn is grown under dry conditions it matures slowly and may need a growing season of 130 to 140 days (Hack 1942). If sufficient moisture can be made available to the crop, the length of the growing season is less critical. Some of the strategies of field selection that are appropriate for increasing the amount of water available to corn are not appropriate to ensure suffi- ciently long growing seasons. The growing season on north- or east-facing slopes is generally considerably shorter than that on south- and west-facing slopes. The dual problems of insufficient moisture and short growing seasons can be compensated for by planting fields in a variety of topographic settings, as the contemporary Hopis do today (Hack 1942; Whiting 1937). Hopi fields are planted at different elevations, at various locations along arroyos, and across arroyos and arroyo terraces. Additionally, crops may be planted at several times so that some harvest is obtained even if there is a late spring or early autumn frost. Finally, the Hopi maintain different varieties of corn, some of which are adapted to drought conditions, some to short growing seasons, and some to strong winds. As Plog (1978:358) comments, "in an area where environmental variation is so extreme, a hybrid with average tolerance would clearly be maladaptive."

The maintenance of selected varieties of maize is usually accomplished by wide spatial separation of fields. The practice of dispersing fields also lessens the chance of complete crop failure, for although some fields may be ruined by too much or too little water, other fields may not be affected. Among some of the Rio Grande Pueblos, if spatial separation of fields with different varieties of maize is not possible, squash is planted as a border crop (Ford 1981).

Although it is often difficult to classify the races of maize recovered in archae- ological collections (Anderson and Cutler 1942; Gasser 1980), it is noteworthy that all the major varieties (Chapalote, Reventador, Onaveno, Maiz de Ocho, and Maiz Blan- do) continued to be planted in various parts of the Southwest throughout the pre- historic period. It is possible that the major varieties were retained because each was adapted to slightly different environmental conditions.

The kinds of practices that ensure yields of corn in the Southwest—planting in different locations, multiple plantings during the growing season, careful selection of seed corn, maintenance of the separation of different varieties of corn, and the diver- sion of water to crops when necessary during the critical periods of the growing season—all require a substantial investment of time and energy during the agri- cultural period. This investment has consequences for group mobility, for as long as the reliability of crops is important, their tending requires that people remain near their fields during the agricultural cycle.

Some of the practices that helped ensure a reliable harvest in the higher and relatively well-watered elevations of the Southwest also permitted the expansion of farming into the lower-elevation, arid areas. The selection of drought-resistant varieties of maize was clearly important to this expansion. Providing additional moisture to fields during the tasseling and silking stage of the growth of maize, through diverting runoff or planting along water courses, enabled agriculture to expand into appropriate settings within the desert areas.

Corn requires relatively large amounts of nitrogen, phosphorus, and potassium for growth (Minnis 1981:188). Continuous planting of corn in the same field can deplete these nutrients and eventually reduce agricultural yields. Many Southwestern peoples plant corn in hills that are widely spaced within the fields. During each succeeding year, new hills are made between the hills used during the previous season. This practice effectively leaves much of the field fallow, minimizing problems of soil depletion (Castetter and Bell 1942; Hack 1942; Hill 1938; Nagata 1970). The Hopis also allow corn stalks to decay in their fields, which returns nutrients to the soil. The people of Zia Pueblo fertilize fields by spreading wood ash on them (Euler 1954). Beans are sometimes planted in the same hills with corn. The bacteria associated with the roots of these legumes enrich the soil with nitrogen. Where water is diverted to crops or when crops are grown on floodplains, the soil is naturally replenished by nutrient-rich sediments (Castetter and Bell 1942; Minnis 1981).

Damage to young plants by the strong winds common during the spring in the Southwest is offset, in part, by the practice of planting seeds in clusters within the hills. Although the seedlings on the outside of the cluster might be damaged, some protection is afforded to the inner plants. Small amounts of brush may also be placed around the hills to protect the plants. Some field locations, such as arroyo bottoms, also afford shelter against wind damage (Hack 1942; Plog 1978). The depredations of some pests, such as birds and rabbits, may be lessened by guarding fields. The practice of planting corn in widely separated hills probably limits some of the damage that may occur through attacks of diseases because there is less opportunity for crop diseases to spread throughout the entire field.

Food storage practices reinforce sedentism and may lead to population growth or geographic expansion. When crops are grown successfully, stores can be maintained to be used when necessary—throughout the winter and especially in the late winter and early spring, when the availability of wild foods is at its lowest. A supply of corn sufficient to provide seed for the next planting must be stored as well.

Corn is quite easily stored without much preparation. The kernels may be left on the cob or removed and dried, a time-consuming process but one that reduces the amount of bulk. Ease of caching is no advantage for highly mobile groups, but it is critical when people stay in the same place for any length of time. In order to effectively store corn and other crops, locations that are dry and protected from rodents and other pests are needed. Dry caves and rockshelters may be used if these can be effectively guarded. Storage facilities of various kinds may be constructed, for example, stone- or mud-lined cists or pits, granaries, or special storage rooms. Depending on the amount of produce that must be cached and the availability of suitable locations, some amount of time may be necessary in order to secure adequate facilities. As the amount of agricultural production increases, of course, the amount of time needed to prepare the crops and store them increases as well.

As cached food becomes more abundant and more important, it must be guarded effectively from possible human theft in addition to pest damage; therefore, some portion of a population might be left to protect the stores throughout much of the year. If there is an increase in the amount of stored food available, and a surplus is reliably produced each year, two consequences may follow. People may remain sedentary much of the year, living on stored food and making periodic trips to gather wild resources; and enough surplus may be produced to support an overall increase in population. These conditions can, in turn, promote population expansion into new areas. Groups that are sedentary throughout much or all of the year are likely to diminish the supply of game animals and wild plant foods in their immediate vicinity. It is therefore preferable to limit the number of people who are permanent residents in any one locality. Excess populations may be expected to found new communities, If the crops that yield a productive and reliable surplus in certain habitats can be moved successfully to new habitats, as is the case with the developed, drought-resistent varieties of corn, it can be expected that, overall, agriculture will expand.

The expansion of agriculture was, in part, a result of a successful manipulation of crops that were first adopted to provide some subsistence security during poor times. It is most unlikely that agriculture was either adopted or intensified simultaneously by all people living in the Southwest. Increased foraging on the landscape, which would have been an appropriate response to lean periods, was probably restricted by the presence of other more mobile foraging populations. Decreased mobility would increase the necessity to obtain reliable crops. Efforts that are required to produce a reliable crop in the Southwest, where environmental factors are not ideal for tropical plants, entail an investment of time and energy that positively reinforces sedentism. As people reduced the amount of territory they exploited in order to be closer to their crops, they further depleted the supply of locally available wild resources. This, in turn, encouraged the production of even more reliable crops, as well as the establishment of new communities. If new communities were founded in areas where crops could be grown successfully, the process should have been repeated.

In fact, new communities were founded in many settings where agriculture was productive, and in many areas, further population growth resulted. It should be expected, too, that some new communities were established in locations where environmental factors did not permit the reliable production of crops. These experiments would have to have been abandoned and new locations tried. If these were unavailable, efforts would have to have been made to increase production in favorable settings in order to feed more people. Consequently, appropriate mechanisms for integrating larger groups of people would also become a necessity (Plog 1974).

The course of agriculture in the Southwest from about A.D. 200 until the historic period reflects a pattern of geographic expansion and contraction, population dispersal and aggregation. Some areas were colonized successfully and, in them, agricultural communities were quite stable. In other areas there were initial attempts to support agricultural communities, but they were abandoned. In some areas agricultural production was increased substantially through the use of various technological innovations, such as water-control devices. In these situations, quite large communities developed with elaborate mechanisms of social integration. In the long run, however, not all of these were successful, and despite considerable efforts to ensure a successful crop yield and the distribution of food to consumers, abandonments were necessary. As Plog states:

> The Hopi did ultimately develop an agricultural strategy appropriate to the substantial variability in rainfall characteristic of the Colorado Plateau, yet by the time they did so, most portions of the plateau had been abandoned. We must consider the possibility that the archaeological record of the northern Southwest is not a record of success, but of failure. Local populations may never have developed a combination of social organization and subsistence strategies that were adaptive to local conditions. (1974:160)

This observation is apt. Sites and quite large regions were abandoned prehistorically, and the most persuasive arguments relating to the causes of abandonment consider a combination of failures in agricultural production and social organization (see Chapter 9). Nevertheless, once prehistoric Southwestern peoples became committed to agriculture, because a return to hunting and gathering was no longer viable, a number of very sophisticated approaches to increasing crop yields were used. In many instances, technological devices were developed that permitted reliable yields in areas that do not support agriculture today. The fact that these measures ultimately failed does not indicate a lack of ingenuity or technical skill on the part of prehistoric peoples. Rather, conditions of long-term environmental degradation in some cases, or the inability to enhance productivity to support further population increase in others, underlay the ultimate lack of success. Given the overall difficulties and risks involved in agriculture in the Southwest, it is important to explore the diversity of techniques that were used to enhance production and to make production more reliable. This is the topic next developed.

Diversity of Prehistoric Agricultural and Subsistence Strategies

The kinds and combinations of features associated with agriculture are diverse, and several archaeologists have proposed typologies to describe them (e.g., Hayes 1964; Plog and Garrett 1972; Vivian 1974; Woodbury 1961). Here, the discussion largely follows Vivian's usage (1974). Generally, the term *agricultural feature* is applied to modifications to the landscape that function to control water or soil erosion or both. *Agricultural systems* are combinations of discrete features. Fieldhouses, which are usually small structures built near fields and occupied during some or all of the agricultural season, may be part of agricultural systems, but they are not usually considered agricultural features. It is not always easy to distinguish between features constructed to conserve soil and those built to conserve water, because most of the known types of features do both. To confuse the matter even more, some soil- and water-control features, constructed to prevent damage to houses or villages, are not associated with fields or with agriculture.

The most commonly noted agricultural features include bordered gardens, check dams, contour terraces, canals, headgates, diversion dams, and ditches. Bordered gardens are generally rectangular plots enclosed by low earth or stone borders. Some bordered gardens are covered with a mulch of gravel (see below). Bordered gardens often occur in contiguous grids, covering very large areas. Check dams consist of one or several low stone walls constructed across arroyos. Soil builds up and is held behind each dam, creating small field areas. The dams also slow the flow of water in the arroyos, allowing it to soak into the ground and preventing erosion. Contour terraces are lines of stones, either one or two courses in height, built along the contours of slopes. Contour terraces help retard soil erosion and capture water washing off the slope.

Canals, ditches, headgates, and diversion dams are features that function to move water from one place to another. They are part of *irrigation systems,* as the term is generally used. Canals are wide, deep channels cut into the ground that serve to carry water. Ditches, narrower and shallower than canals, function the same way canals do and are often associated with them. Headgates are features of stone or earth that are used to control the flow of water from a canal or ditch into a sluice. Diversion dams of either earth or stone temporarily impound water, restricting its flow into a canal or ditch. Finally, reservoirs that either are entirely man-made or incorporate natural depressions are found in many parts of the Southwest. The reservoirs, however, seem to have been used to store water for domestic uses rather than for agriculture.

Agricultural features are exceptionally difficult to date, and the proximity of the features to sites that are dated is used as a rough indication of the ages of the agricultural features. As imprecise as such age determinations are, there is very little evidence for the construction of agricultural features before about A.D. 900. Sites that were occupied prior to this are rarely associated with evidence of attempts to intensify agricultural production. The Hohokam heartland may be exceptional in this regard, because given the paucity of rainfall, irrigation may have been necessary to produce any crops at all. Nevertheless, over most of the Southwest in the early centuries A.D., population densities were apparently low enough that subsistence security was assured through a combination of hunting, gathering, and agriculture.

Available information shows that the distribution of water and soil conservation features in the Southwest crosscuts both cultural and natural areas. Irrigation canals, for example, are not limited to the Hohokam area or to the Lower Sonoran Desert. However, the sale of Hohokam canals greatly exceeds those on the plateaus. Systems combining various devices are found throughout the Southwest. Some of the diversities in the agricultural systems encountered, their appropriateness with respect to the habitats in which they are found, and some insights about the degree of organization of labor and technological skill required to build and maintain them may be illustrated by the case studies discussed below.

Agriculture in the Mountains: Point of Pines

The first detailed study of prehistoric farming systems in a relatively well-watered area of the Southwest was by Woodbury (1961) in the Point of Pines area of east-central Arizona (Figure 6.1). The research was conducted in the context of the University of Arizona's Arid Land Program, which was designed as an interdisciplinary effort to conduct basic research about man's long-term use of arid lands. The Point of Pines area had been the location of the University of Arizona's field school since 1946, and field school projects provided an immediate context for Woodbury's work.

Point of Pines is in the mountainous portion of eastern Arizona on the San Carlos Indian Reservation. The archaeological sequence extends from the Archaic Cochise, dating to about 2000 B.C., to its prehistoric abandonment at about A.D. 1450. Although corn pollen from the Cienega Creek site is the first evidence for cultigens in the area (see Chapter 5), Woodbury's study concerns farming practices that probably postdate A.D. 1000, when the presence of masonry architecture and villages indicates an increased emphasis on farming. Although most of the village sites in the area are small, the population achieved its maximum size in the fourteenth century, when a number of large sites were occupied contemporaneously. The largest of these covered an area of 4 acres (about 10 ha) and consisted of about 800 ground-floor rooms. Following this peak, the population declined until the area was abandoned. The agricultural features found at Point of Pines may be dated to the period between about A.D. 1000 and 1450, but more precise dating within that span was not possible.

The prehistoric villages and farms described by Woodbury occur within a zone of low ridges separated by small valleys with intermittent streams. Much of the area is grassland interspersed with ponderosa pine and smaller stands of piñon and juniper. The nearby Nantanes Mountains would have provided a hunting area for deer, peccary, turkey, bear, and smaller game that were important food resources for the prehistoric inhabitants.

From the perspective of agriculturalists, conditions at Point of Pines are relatively more favorable than they are in many areas of the Southwest. The frost-free period is estimated to be about 165–170 days and the mean annual precipitation about 46–48 cm. About one-third of the precipitation occurs as snow between November and February. This moisture penetrates the ground and is important for the germination of seeds in the spring. The spring season, from April through June, receives the least amount of precipitation during the year. Precipitation during July and August is characterized by high-intensity thunderstorms, sometimes accompanied by hail, which can damage crops. There is high variation in precipitation from year to year, and either dry or wet years can be disastrous for crops. Early frosts are also known to occur and would have adversely affected crops.

Woodbury suggests that the occurrence of two distinct geological deposits in the area may have been important to village location and prehistoric agriculture. Some of the ridges at Point of Pines are composed of conglomerate and tuff. These have been rounded to nearly flat summits that were used as village and farm sites. Other ridges are capped with basalt, weathered into rugged malpais surfaces that offer no topsoil for farming. Agricultural land may be available below the low scarps at the edges of these formations. Another relevant observation is that soils in the area are shallow and easily eroded when the natural cover of vegetation is removed. Not surprisingly, many of the agricultural features observed in the Point of Pines area were important in retarding or preventing erosion of the soil.

Prehistoric agricultural fields at Point of Pines depended entirely on rainfall. Water was neither diverted from permanent sources nor stored. Prehistoric wells and reservoirs are located in the area but seem to have been used only for domestic purposes. The agricultural features at Point of Pines are bordered gardens, check dams, and contour terraces.

The most common type of field pattern at Point of Pines consists of series of terraces that follow the contours of slopes. Most occur on slopes with gradients of about 5%. Woodbury suggests that these features would have slowed runoff from heavy rainstorms and retarded soil erosion. The rocks and boulders of these features occur throughout the area, so construction of the linear borders would have resulted in the clearing of long strips of land for cultivation. Bordered gardens are not common at Point of Pines. They occur as contiguous grids, generally on gentle slopes and on nearly level areas. Check dams across arroyos at Point of Pines occur on slopes ranging from 5 to 21% in groups of from 10 to 50. Woodbury suggests that the primary function of the terraces was to hold soil behind them, forming a series of small fields. Additionally, they would have slowed runoff, allowing it to penetrate the field, and retarded gullying. All three of these features occur at W:9:30, the Clover Park site (Figure 6.2), where they surround a village of about six rooms.

The field systems described occur extensively throughout the Point of Pines area in a diversity of settings. Their primary functions appear to have been to conserve soil and moisture. Woodbury suggests that the overall strategy of farming was similar to that practiced at the modern Hopi villages, in that the diversity of field locations would have lessened the risk of crop failure in any one location due to either an abundance or a deficiency of rainfall. (Many of field types found at Hopi villages, however, do not occur at Point of Pines, because of differences in local topography.)

The high quality of the data Woodbury collected at Point of Pines allowed other archaeologists to evaluate their ideas about the effectiveness and efficiency of different agricultural techniques.

Plog and Garrett (1972) suggested that the particular combinations of agricultural features constructed in an area should be those that are both most appropriate to the particular land forms, soils, and water conditions found and least costly in labor to build and maintain. As an example, they used information from modern soil conservation and agricultural studies to evaluate the effectiveness of different agricultural features on land of increasingly steep slope. Although there is some overlap, they found that the effectiveness of irrigation gives way to gridding with single courses of stone and finally to terracing as the slope increases. The particular kind of analysis they used would also be appropriate for evaluating the effectiveness of different agricultural features in relation to other environmental characteristics, such as soil type. Plog and Garrett also used modern information to estimate labor costs involved in building and maintaining irrigation canals, bordered gardens or terraces made of two or more courses of stone, and contour terraces or grids made of one course of stone. As would be expected, grids and terraces of one course of stone are far less costly than irrigation canals; bordered gardens or terraces of two or more courses of stone fall between in labor cost.

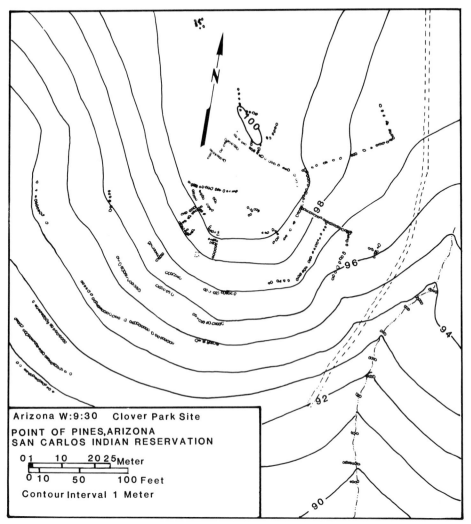

Figure 6.2 Agricultural features at the Clover Park site, Point of Pines, Arizona. Terraces follow the contours of the slopes. Bordered gardens appear as partial grids. A series of check dams was constructed along the arroyo. (Adapted from Woodbury [1961:17] by Charles M. Carrillo.)

Woodbury's data allowed Plog and Garrett to compare the distribution of agricultural features at Point of Pines with their expected distribution based on the actual areas of land of different slopes at Point of Pines. Although a complete analysis would have included other aspects of the Point of Pines environment as well as estimated labor costs for the agricultural features found there, the analysis indicated a close agreement between the expected pattern and the one actually found.

Plog and Garrett's study suggests that the diversity of agricultural features found at Point of Pines is, in part, due to the attempt to suit each feature to the characteristics of its location in the landscape. Overall, the Point of Pines example illustrates that even in places that were relatively favorable for agriculture, an investment in agricultural features were made. The construction of the features seems to occur late in the prehistoric occupation of the area, suggesting that alternative options, such as moving to another location, were not feasible. The particular features that were constructed do not seem to have required either great labor investment or the coordinated efforts of many people. Nevertheless, the features were well suited to conserving water and soil in a topographically variable setting and reflect technological expertise. Where mobility continued to be an alternative to agricultural intensification, mobility may have been preferred. This situation seems to have applied to the early Anasazi settlement of Black Mesa, Arizona.

Agricultural Risk and Seasonal Settlements at Black Mesa

Black Mesa is a large landform on the Colorado Plateau of northeastern Arizona (Figure 6.1). The modern Hopi towns are located along the mesa's southern edge. The focus of the research described here is an area of about 200 km² on northeastern Black Mesa that was leased to the Peabody Coal Company by the Navajo and Hopi tribes. Through the Black Mesa Archaeological Project, archaeological investigations in the lease area have continued since 1967. As part of this project, Powell (1983) examined the settlement strategies of the Black Mesa Anasazi. Her study combines innovative uses of ethnoarchaeological and archaeological data and has implications for reevaluating the settlement histories of other Southwestern areas.

Prehistoric occupation of the northern portion of Black Mesa spans the period from about 600 B.C. to A.D. 1150. Previous research had suggested that throughout this time there had been population growth and an increasing dependence on agriculture. Prehistoric agriculture could not have been very reliable on northern Black Mesa. The annual rainfall varies from 25 cm on the southern edge of the mesa to 50 cm on the northern edge. Today, most precipitation falls in summer, but there is marked variability in rainfall patterning from year to year. There are no permanent sources of water within the lease area. The length of the growing season is also highly variable and ranges from about 120 to 150 days. Paleoclimatic reconstructions, based on studies of sediments, pollen, and tree rings, suggest oscillating conditions of drought and more mesic intervals in the past. There was no overall trend toward lower water tables, surface erosion, or deforestation.

The structure of the environment at Black Mesa indicates that reliance on agriculture would have been very risky. Laboratory analyses of plant remains from excavated sites did not indicate any evidence of increasing dependence on corn over time. Also, compared to many parts of the Southwest, the habitation sites on Black Mesa are quite small—their modal size is about 16 m². These observations, combined with ethnographic information about Native American peoples practicing some horticulture in similarly risky environments, led Powell to consider the possibility that the habitation sites on Black Mesa were not occupied year-round.

A review of ethnographic literature of 12 societies living in semiarid areas of North America showed that they relied on a combination of horticulture and hunting and gathering. Most groups alternated between summer and winter settlements in different habitat areas. A demonstration of seasonal use of habitation sites at Black Mesa would, of course, have major implications for interpretations of the prehistoric settlement history.

To examine the possibility of seasonal use of the Black Mesa Anasazi sites, Powell analyzed the material culture correlates of 34 recently abandoned, seasonally occupied Navajo camps. She emphasized variables that would be most useful in determining the season of use, rather than variables that relate to cultural differences between Anasazi and Navajos. Her concern was also with isolating variables that could be measured in the archaeological record. Her study focused on two types of Navajo camps: summer fieldhouses and fall–winter piñon camps. The first variable she considered was the proportion of interior space to total site space, because it is likely that more activities are carried out indoors in winter than in summer. Therefore, a group of the same size would require a larger area of protected indoor space in winter habitations than in summer habitations. Statistical analyses of the Navajo data supported the proposition that there is proportionately more interior space at piñon camps than at agricultural fieldhouses. Powell also found that the fieldhouse structures were smaller than structures at piñon camps and that the amount of outside activity area was greater at the fieldhouses than at the piñon camps. Because most archaeological data gathered on site surveys includes only the total area of sites, Powell compared the total site size for summer and winter sites and found a statistically significant difference in size, with summer sites being larger.

Powell looked at differences in the distributions of hearths and artifacts at Navajo fieldhouses and piñon camps. As would be expected, she found that the winter piñon camps had interior hearths necessary for warmth and lacked outside hearths; summer fieldhouses characteristically had outside hearths as well as interior hearths. Finally, although the frequencies of artifacts found at fieldhouses and piñon camps were similar, artifact densities were higher at the latter. This relation follows from the observed differences in overall site size.

Powell applied these results to Black Mesa Anasazi sites. For each site, she recorded occupation phase, number of inside and outside hearths, location (upland or lowland) of the site, densities of ceramics and lithics, enclosed habitation area, number of habitation rooms, total site area, and exterior area. Powell found that she could divide the Anasazi sites into two groups based on the amount of interior space. Small sites had fewer than 14.8 m² of inside space; large sites had 17.2 m² of inside space or more. In accord with her expectations about possible summer use of the small sites, she found that these had proportionately more outside than inside hearths. Artifact density was not appreciably different on small and large sites. As she expected, she

found that the large sites had more interior hearths, suggesting that they were occupied in winter. Contrary to her expectations, small sites had less exterior area than
did large sites.

Powell further divided the Anasazi sites into temporal periods. She examined small
sites dating before A.D. 1050, small sites occupied after 1050, large sites occupied
before 1050, and late large sites dated post-1050. Although she found that small sites
were similar in the variables measured for the duration of the occupation of Black
Mesa, there were differences between large early sites and large late sites. She found
that (1) over time there was an increase in total site size within the large-site category;
(2) large late sites had fewer outside hearths than large early sites; and (3) only within
the category of large late sites did more than one inside hearth per habitation unit
occur. In some respects, then, the large early sites were similar to the small sites.

In order to further evaluate the possible seasonal use of the Black Mesa sites, Powell
attempted to use independent data derived from the analyses of faunal and macrobotanical remains. Although these data were less than satisfactory for a number of
reasons, she found that the large late sites had some fauna that were obtained in the
spring as well as the most diverse faunal inventories of all sites. These sites also had
more diverse floral remains than did the other categories of sites. She found that the
floral diversity at all small sites and early large sites was virtually identical. Powell
acknowledges that some of the variation could be due to differences in the length of
time that sites were used and the numbers of people using the sites. However, after
reviewing all her analytic results, she concludes that:

> Small sites were occupied during the summer, and large late sites were occupied year-round.
> Large early sites are a problem; however, I am swayed by the structure sizes and the low floral
> diversity, as well as by the midden and storage patterns, to suggest that this group of sites, too,
> was seasonally occupied, but during winter. (Powell 1983:128)

The implications of Powell's research for interpretations of northern Black Mesa
prehistory are great. She was unable to confirm either an increasing dependence on
agriculture or a trend in continuous population growth. Her research suggests that the
area was used only seasonally until A.D. 1050, when there is evidence of year-round
occupation. Thus, for the early portion of Black Mesa occupation, the summer residences of the population would be outside the study area. Given the shift to year-
round use of the region, resource depletion could have occurred rather rapidly,
nearly ensuring its abandonment within 100 years.

Very similar situations may have occurred in other areas of the Southwest. As long
as regional population densities remained low, seasonal movement may have been an
option employed by many people and may have obviated the need to invest labor in
construction of any agriculture facilities. Certainly much more attention needs to be
devoted to distinguishing seasonal from year-round use of habitation sites.

The Black Mesa case exemplifies a situation in which year-round occupation cannot
be assumed. In the next example, the archaeologist provides evidence for year-round
use of a site in an area that had been considered one of the most inhospitable in the
Southwest.

Agriculture in the Desert: Gu Achi

The Papagueria, homeland of the Papago Indians, consists of a large area of the Sonoran Desert in Arizona and Sonora, Mexico. The desert landscape is often considered resource poor and inhospitable to man. The Papagueria lacks the permanent streams of the Hohokam heartland and, in part for this reason, its prehistoric inhabitants have been referred to as Desert branch Hohokam (Haury 1950). In this formulation, the Desert branch is seen as practicing only a minimal amount of agriculture and achieving a lower level of cultural development than the River branch Hohokam, who could produce agricultural surpluses by using the Gila and Salt rivers for irrigation.

The excavation of Gu Achi, a large Hohokam settlement in the Papagueria near Santa Rosa, Arizona (Figure 6.1), provides new information relevant to Hohokam subsistence in the desert and interpretations of closer relations between the Desert and the River branches of the Hohokam. Excavations at Gu Achi were undertaken as a salvage project by archaeologists from the Western Archaeological Center of the National Park Service for the Bureau of Indian Affairs. The analysis of the Gu Achi data was conducted by Masse (1980) several years after the excavation had been completed.

According to Masse, the Papagueria offers resources that are important to human settlement. The complex geological history of the area provides a diversity of lithic source material. Two vegetative communities, an upland community dominated by paloverde and suguaro and a community characterized by creosote and bursage found primarily on the alluvial valley floors, offer a diversity of edible plants. In addition, the washes of the desert support riparian species such as mesquite, which has edible pods, and other useful plants. Faunal resources are also diverse and include bighorn sheep, deer, antelope, jackrabbits, cottontails, and other smaller animals. Although all of these resources are potentially useful, water is the limiting factor for human settlement. There are no permanent streams, and springs are few. The closest permanent spring to the site of Gu Achi is at Ventana Cave, more than 11 miles away.

The amount of precipitation received in the Papagueria follows a diminishing gradient from east to west. At the eastern edge, near Sells, rainfall is between about 23 and 30 cm. In the far western area, near Yuma, it is only 7.6 cm a year. In the vicinity of Gu Achi, rainfall averages about 25 cm a year. More than half of this moisture occurs during the summer growing season. This amount of moisture alone is not sufficient for agriculture unless local topographic features concentrate the rainfall and runoff water from a network of washes, permitting agriculture on outwash slopes. According to Hackenberg (1964), a minimum of 17.8 cm of rainfall is necessary to sustain the kind of floodwater farming pursued by the Papago. There must also be sufficient fertile alluvial soils on outwash slopes to form an apron of top soil and plant material at arroyo mouths. These aprons, or fans, are referred to as *akchin* by the Papago and are often the sites of fields. The most important topographic feature for the prehistoric settlement at Gu Achi is Gu Achi Wash, a broad wash containing about a meter of silty alluvial fill that borders the site.

Gu Achi was first occupied in about A.D. 500, and according to Masse was continuously inhabited until 1050 or 1100. Most of the excavated features, however, date to the period from A.D. 850 to 1000. These features cover an area of at least 150,000 m², making Gu Achi the most extensive Hohokam settlement in the Papagueria before A.D. 1000. The year-round occupation at Gu Achi required water for drinking as well as for crops, but there is no permanent water at the site. Masse suggests that the first occupants may have excavated shallow wells in the bottom of Gu Achi Wash, a Papago method of obtaining water known to have been used since the Late Archaic. During the later, most intensive stages of occupation, however, a reservoir with an interior diameter of 30 m was constructed at the site. A mud turtle, a reptile that requires permanent water, was among the faunal remains recovered, indicating that the reservoir held water throughout the year.

Information about the subsistence base at Gu Achi was derived from macrobotanical and pollen analyses, faunal studies, and a consideration of site survey information from the mountainous areas north of the site. Although they are diverse, faunal remains are rare at Gu Achi. Of the mammals, jackrabbits are the most abundant, followed by bighorn sheep and mule deer. Other mammals identified include cottontail rabbit, squirrel, badger, and bobcat. Despite this variety, the minimum number of individual animals (MNI) is only 22. A lack of fauna is common at Hohokam sites, although in the historic period, Papago villages obtained between 12 and 15 deer annually, in addition to numerous rabbits and smaller animals. Masse discusses several possible explanations for the limited amount of archaeological animal bone, including scavenging by dogs and coyotes, poor preservation, and the possibility that hunters butchered animals in the field and returned little bone to the village. These may be important, but none can be conclusively demonstrated. The degree to which the residents of Gu Achi depended on hunting remains unknown.

The plant remains (pollen and macrobotanical samples) indicate the collection and use of mesquite pods and paloverde beans, agave, and prickly pear. Mesquite and paloverde were available within the floodplain in the immediate vicinity of Gu Achi. The agave and prickly pear had to be obtained from the foothills and mountain flanks considerably north of the village.

The evidence for agriculture at Gu Achi consists of hundreds of charred corn kernels, corn pollen, cotton pollen, and cotton seed. A morphological study of the corn suggests that it may have been grown under conditions of moisture stress. Masse considered the possibilities of two farming strategies: dry farming, dependent on rainfall, and *akchin* farming, dependent on rainfall and runoff. Irrigation from a permanent water source would have been impossible at Gu Achi. Masse notes that dry farming was practiced widely by the Hohokam; however, because of inadequacies in rainfall, dry farming relied on the use of a variety of water-conserving devices. These included check dams, contour terraces, and some bordered gardens. In two Hohokam areas, these features are absent. Hohokam settlements near Gila Bend have no indication of dry farming or water-conservation features. This is to be expected, because the area is extremely arid, with an annual mean of only about 15 cm of rainfall. The remains of water-conserving devices are also absent in the Papagueria, despite the fact that the eastern portions of the area receive about as much rainfall as those areas in which Hohokam water-conserving devices occur. Masse notes that piles of rock, about 1.5 m in diameter and 20.3 cm high, do occur in the northeastern Papagueria, and it has been suggested that these features may have augmented runoff to fields located downslope from them. The absence of other technological devices of water conservation suggest that even if the rock piles are agricultural features, dry farming was less important in the Papagueria than elsewhere in the Hohokam area.

The topographic setting at Gu Achi, especially its proximity to Gu Achi Wash, is appropriate for *akchin* farming. Brush diversion dams and ditches, low brush dikes, embankments, and small ditches may all be used to divert runoff to *akchin* fields. The technical components of *akchin* farming are similar therefore, to those used by Hohokam practicing riverine irrigation. The difference is that in *akchin* farming, the water source is not permanent. Yields from *akchin* farms can be substantial—up to 25–30 bushels of corn per ha. Masse suggests that *akchin* farming was the predominant form of subsistence production at Gu Achi and that it was productive enough to sustain a permanent residence at the site for over a century.

Finally, archaeological material from Gu Achi includes abundant evidence of the manufacturing of marine shell items. Finished marine shell objects, such as bracelets, are abundant in the Hohokam sites of the Gila and Salt drainages. Thus, close ties between sites such as Gu Achi and those of the core Hohokam area are indicated by the occurrence of shell as a trade item. A number of investigators have suggested that shell items manufactured in the Papagueria may have been exchanged for subsistence items (especially crops) from their neighbors to the north, especially those at settlements along the Gila and Salt rivers. There are presently no methods for discerning the possible role of subsistence items in this trade system. However, the technological similarities between the devices used in *akchin* farming and those used in irrigation, as well as the evidence of shell manufacture in the Papagueria, indicate that cultural similarities between Hohokam living in both areas are closer than separate cultural branch status may imply. This contention is further supported by the relatively early dates for the major settlement at Gu Achi (A.D. 850–1000). These indicate that the level of cultural development in the Papagueria is similar to that achieved in the riverine area at the same time.

The Gu Achi situation represents one in which the range of agricultural strategies possible is quite narrow. Given the lack of permanent water sources and rainfall, some form of runoff-dependent agriculture is the most reasonable alternative. *Akchin* farming does not require a very great investment of labor. It is important that despite an unfavorable natural environment, the desert Hohokam were able to establish large settlements and to specialize in production of marine shell items.

Diverting Runoff at Chaco Canyon

Within Chaco Canyon, in the San Juan Basin of northwestern New Mexico, are some of the most spectacular Anasazi ruins anywhere in the Southwest. Lt. James H. Simpson published the first description of the ruins in 1850 (Simpson 1850). Archaeological excavation in the canyon began in the 1890s and culminated in an intensive study of the archaeology, environment, and paleoenvironment begun in 1971 under the auspices of the Chaco Center of the National Park Service and the University of New Mexico. The focus of this discussion is an earlier, independent analysis of Chacoan water-control systems by Vivian (1970, 1974). Vivian's work is based on the combined use of aerial photographs, site survey, and test excavation. His study is supplemented by more recent survey data (Hayes 1981a) and paleoenvironmental reconstructions (Betancourt and Van Devender 1981; Hall 1977; Robinson 1979). The Chacoan agricultural system provides an interesting contrast to Gu Achi. In both cases the basic technology involved the use of runoff; however, the elaboration at Chaco reflects the influences of different topographic features and a larger labor pool.

The environment of Chaco Canyon is not favorable for agriculture. The average growing season is about 140–150 days, but there is considerable variation from year to year, and sometimes the season is insufficient for corn. Precipitation in the canyon is marginal for agriculture. The mean annual rainfall is a scant 2.2 cm, about 40% of which falls in summer (Betancourt and Van Devender 1981). Hayes (1981a) suggests that although winter snows may provide enough ground moisture for the germination of seed, spring and fall precipitation is low and ineffective. Variation in precipitation from year to year is also characteristic.

Where present, soils consist primarily of Quaternary silty alluvium, and sand dunes are common. Over much of the Chaco, however, there are large areas of exposed sandstone and shale, and soils are lacking. Today, Chaco Wash is an entrenched ephemeral stream, but there are indications that it was not entrenched during the entire period of prehistoric occupation of the canyon (Bryan 1954; Hall 1977).

Paleoenvironmental reconstructions available for Chaco Canyon are not entirely consistent, but they indicate that the climate during the Anasazi occupation was similar to that of the present. Tree-ring reconstructions of precipitation (Robinson 1979) show increased variability in precipitation between A.D. 950 and 999.

All investigators agree that Chaco Canyon was densely inhabited in prehistoric times, but estimating the number of prehistoric inhabitants when the major Anasazi ruins were occupied (A.D. 1025–1125) is difficult at best. Published estimates range from about 4000 people to nearly 25,000 people (Hayes 1981a; Vivian 1974), depending on assumptions about the contemporaneity of sites and the relative numbers of storage rooms and habitation rooms. A recent estimate, based on the inventory survey conducted by the National Park Service, suggests 5562 people (Hayes 1981a).

There are contour terraces and check dams in Chaco Canyon, but the most prevalent prehistoric water-control systems consist of a combination of dams, canals, ditches, headgates, and earth-bordered gardens (Vivian, 1974). These systems depended on rainfall and not on water from Chaco Wash. They were designed to capture runoff water from the intercliff zone above the canyon and to divert it to fields and bordered gardens on the canyon floor. One of these systems, the Rincon-4 North system, is illustrated in Figure 6.3.

The Rincon-4 North system is on the north side of Chaco Canyon. Above it is an intercliff zone of sandstone that slopes gently toward the canyon rim. Runoff from rainfall on the intercliff zone drains into the canyon through natural reentrants. The

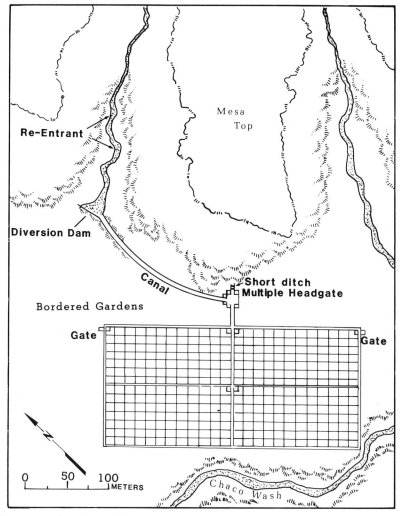

Figure 6.3   Rincon-4 North agricultural system at Chaco Canyon. Runoff from the mesa top drains into the canyon through natural reentrants. The dam and the canal funnel the water into a multiple headgate, from which a short canal brings the water to the bordered garden. Excess water could be drained into Chaco Wash. (Illustrated by Charles M. Carrillo, after Vivian [1974:104].)

Rincon-4 North system includes a dam that diverted water from the reentrant to a canal. The canal, in part lined with masonry, carried water 230 m to a multiple headgate. The headgate received water from the canal and from another short ditch that collected runoff from the cliff above. The headgate slowed the velocity of water and channeled it to the bordered garden alongside Chaco Wash.

The Rincon-4 North system depended on runoff from the intercliff zone, so it is important to know how much water could have been derived from this source. In spite of the difficulty in estimating runoff, the amount of runoff received through any one reenetrant depends on the size of the intercliff zone and the amount of precipitation. As an example, Vivian notes that a storm on July 22, 1970 produced 3.04 cm of rain in 1 hour and would have provided 540,000 gal of water for the fields at Rincon-4 North. Vivian found that the intercliff zone is narrow toward the head of the canyon, but it is relatively wide along the lower 14.5 km of the canyon. The diversion systems were located along this lower portion of the canyon. Vivian used aerial photographs of the north side of the canyon to locate reentrant drainage areas. Of the 28 areas found, diversion systems were found in 15.

Aerial photographs were also used to locate the bordered gardens. One of these, near the site of Chetro Ketl, consists of 4.8 ha divided into two canal-bordered plots. Each of the plots contains a number of individual earth-bordered gardens. Vivian suggests that each garden was irrigated through temporary openings in the earth borders. The size of the gardens and the size and number of plots associated with each diversion system would have varied depending on the amount of land available, the drainage pattern, and the size of the drainage area. In all, Vivian estimates that there were as many as 10,000 individual bordered gardens on the north side of the canyon (Vivian 1974).

Rainfall is both scant and unpredictable at Chaco Canyon; but water is the limiting factor for agricultural success. The water-control systems, of which Rincon-4 North is an example, increase the amount of water provided to fields by collecting runoff from a wide intercliff zone. The distribution and intensity of rainfall on any part of the zone are variable. Each system of dams, canals, headgates, and bordered gardens taps runoff from a different portion of the intercliff zone. Although this design reflects the natural topography of reentrants, it also has the effect of providing irrigation water for some fields despite variability in the location of rainfall.

The water-control systems at Chaco Canyon are similar to those at Gu Achi in two respects. Both depend on rainfall, and both combine features such as those used in riverine irrigation. Compared to the water-control technology at Gu Achi, though, the Chaco example required a greater investment of labor and organization. Despite the disparities among various population estimates, all indicate that the necessary labor supply was available. Vivian (1974) argues that the standardization of the water-control systems and the intensity of land use in Chaco indicate a centralized management of water and a high degree of social control. In fact, a great many archaeological observations support the conclusion that social and political institutions were well developed at Chaco and integrated a large portion of the San Juan Basin. This point is further elaborated in Chapter 8. Whether the institutions of social control developed in response to the need to control the water supply or whether they developed within another context and subsequently subsumed the functions of controlling water is an issue of continuing theoretical interest.

A number of anthropologists have followed the theoretical propositions of the German geographer Karl Wittfogel (1957; Wittfogel and Goldfrank 1943) in arguing for a causal link between water management and strong centralized leadership. Applied to the modern peoples of the Southwest, the presence of irrigation is viewed as a causal factor in the development of permanent leaders among the Rio Grande Pueblo and the absence of such leaders among the Western Pueblo (Dozier 1970; Eggan 1950). Vivian (1970) suggested that the large sites in Chaco Canyon were organized in a manner similar to those of the Rio Grande Pueblo. His inference was based in part on the elaborate nature of the Chacoan water-control systems. In fact, the data currently available suggest that the water-control systems at Chaco Canyon were slightly later than other features that indicate social complexity (Judge *et al.* 1981). Given the extreme difficulty involved in dating water-control features, their temporal placement in the Chacoan scheme remains problematic. The link between irrigation and forms of social organization proposed for the Rio Grande area is also questionable on archaeological grounds. This issue is discussed in greater detail below.

Agriculture in the Northern Rio Grande Valley

The Rio Grande Valley of New Mexico today is the home of most of the modern Pueblo Indians. Compared to the environment occupied by the modern Western Pueblo (the Hopi towns, Zuni, Acoma, and Laguna), the Rio Grande Pueblo area is generally characterized as more favorable for agriculture. Precipitation in the northern Rio Grande is greater than it is to the west. Surface water is more abundant, and the waters of the Rio Grande are available for irrigation.

Most ethnographic studies of the Pueblo (e.g., Dozier 1970; Eggan 1950; Wittfogel and Goldfrank 1943) emphasize the importance of irrigation and its presumed consequences for Eastern Pueblo social organization. The ethnologists contrast the importance of moieties, permanent or life-long officers, and curing and war societies of the Rio Grande Pueblo with the centrality of clans, diffuse leadership, and rainmaking ceremonialism among the Western Pueblo, especially the Hopi. They suggest that the labor requirements involved in constructing and maintaining irrigation features imply strong patterns of authority that are neither necessary nor suitable in the Western Pueblo area. Most discussions emphasize the suitability of the Rio Grande Valley for agriculture and suggest that prehistorically, Rio Grande agricultural technology as characterized by limited use of dry farming combined with irrigation (Dozier 1961). The link between irrigation and centralized authority among contemporary Rio Grande Pueblo has been questioned (Ford 1980). Nevertheless, the Rio Grande area is viewed as generally less restrictive and less risky for agriculture than the Western Pueblo's homeland. Resources are considered abundant, irrigation important, and potential surpluses provide the basis for social elaboration (Cordell 1979; Plog 1978). Despite this "Garden of Eden" characterization, ethnographic, ethnohistoric, historic, and archaeological studies (Cordell and Earls 1982a) indicate specific agricultural risks and problems encountered in the Rio Grande area and suggest that rainfall-dependent agriculture was much more important in the past than is usually supposed.

The Rio Grande itself and the agricultural potential of the river floodplain are most often favorably characterized. At least four factors, however, are potential constraints on farming. First, as Ford (1972) noted, there have been devastating floods in the historic period. The classic example is the destruction in 1886 of not only the fields but much of the Pueblo village of Santo Domingo. Further south, the village of San Marcial was also destroyed by flooding in the same year. San Marcial moved to higher ground but was again destroyed by floods in 1929. The importance of flooding in the prehistoric period is not known, although there are some hints that it was significant. Archaic sites along the Rio Puerco of the East, a major tributary of the Rio Grande, were found under from 1 to 3 m of alluvium (Wimberly and Eidenbach 1980:7). Overgrazing has undoubtedly contributed to the severity of floods in the historic period; however, it is important to remember that control of major flooding was beyond the technological abilities of the Anasazi.

A second problem is related to flooding and irrigation. Irrigation waters provide nutrients that replenish the soils and are beneficial for agriculture. Conditions of poor drainage and high evaporation, however, can lead to deposits of salts and other minerals that are inimical to crops. A study in the vicinity of Cochiti Pueblo (Fosberg 1979; Fosberg and Husler 1979) examined the possibility that prehistoric agricultural production was diminished through the effects of mineralization. The study demonstrated that during the fourteenth and fifteenth centuries the locations of agricultural fieldhouses expanded to areas of inferior soils, and it documented heavy salt concentrations in the soil at a fieldhouse locality. These studies suggest that agricultural land was removed from the system on a short-term basis through floods, or for much longer periods of time through salinization.

Third, historical studies (Simmons 1969; Swadesh 1974) discussing the discontinuous distribution of early Hispanic settlements along the Rio Grande cite the difficulty involved in clearing bench lands of dense stands of vegetation. The studies suggest that land along the river that could be cleared without metal tools was severely limited by the eighteenth century. By that time the Pueblo seem to have occupied most of the land that could have been cleared relatively easily. There is reason to suspect that good bottomland was in short supply prehistorically, before Pueblo populations were decimated by European diseases.

Finally, when crops are planted along the river and irrigated, both fields and individual plants are quite close together, thus increasing the risk of crop loss due to crop disease and to insect pests (Ford 1972). In sum, despite the abundance of water from the river, the Rio Grande Valley is not without risk for agricultualists. The problems encountered by prehistoric agriculturalists—flooding, salinization, dense vegetation, insect pests, and crop disease—are not ameliorated by the labor intensification or technological solutions that were available to the Anasazi. Rather, the "solutions" include expanding agriculture to settings where rainfall agriculture could be practiced and buffering agricultural shortfalls through gathering and hunting.

The expansion of agriculture to areas dependent on rainfall faces the same risks as it does elsewhere in the Southwest. Modern climatological data spanning the past 50 years show that rainfall is insufficient for successful corn cultivation in several portions of the Rio Grande drainage. Elsewhere, especially in the northern Rio Grande Valley and in the adjacent mountains, the growing season is often too short for corn and other crops. In addition, the modern data record extreme deviations from average conditions. Recent paleoenvironmental reconstructions (Rose *et al.* 1981) based on

Table 6.2

Agricultural Features, Rio Grande Area

Location	Site	Feature type	Area (m²)	Landform
Chama Valley	Abiquiu	Grid borders with gravel; mulch-border fields	not given	Mesa tops, benches
	LA 300	Grid borders with gravel mulch	35,916	Mesa edges
	Sapawe 1	Grid borders	2,164	
	Sapawe 2	11 terraces	534	Slope
	Tributary, washes of Rio Gallina	Check dams, 21 alignments	not given	Bench
	LA 11830	Cobble alignments, grid borders, pebble mulch	1,755	Mesa edge
	LA 11831	7 clusters of stone alignments, gravel-filled rectangles	27,560	Mesa edge
	LA 11832	Grids, some gravel-filled	1,812.5	Terrace remnant
Rio Grande de Ranchos		4 sites of grid borders	not given	Upper valley
		2 contoured terrace systems	not given	Terrace
		Gridded and raised fields, small borders	not given	
Cochiti Reservoir	LA 13292	Provenience 1: 10 terraces	315	Bench
		Provenience 2: 12 terraces and grid	600	Bench
	LA 13292	2 rectangular stone alignments	30	Slope

tree rings show that very severe moisture deficiencies occurred in the A.D. 1090s, 1130–1160s, 1250s, and 1360s. At these times it is unlikely that crops depending on rainfall received adequate moisture.

Although the presence of a large river and areas of relatively high precipitation might indicate that little labor investment would be made in technological features appropriate for conserving moisture, a review of survey records pertaining to the Rio Grande Pueblo area (Table 6.2) shows that water-conservation systems predominate and cover very extensive areas of land. The kinds of systems recorded include contour terraces, bordered gardens, series of check dams, and bordered gardens with gravel mulch. All of these devices, with the exception of gravel-mulch gardens, have been discussed previously. Gravel mulch is a covering of pea- or fist-sized rock within a bordered field area. Some investigators (Ellis 1970; Vivian 1974) relate the presence of gravel mulch to moisture retention, but this may be only one of its functions. Mulch of any sort does inhibit evaporation and is therefore important in conserving moisture. An examination of the distribution of gravel-mulch gardens in the Rio Grande Valley (Figure 6.4) shows that the most extensive of these gardens are along the Chama, a Rio Grande tributary. The amount of precipitation in the Chama Valley is generally adequate for corn, but the growing season there is only 109 days, with reported variation over the last 50 years of between 86 and 134 days. It is therefore important to note that mulches also stabilize soil temperature. They reduce air movement near the ground and affect the temperature of the upper few centimeters of soil. Where mulches consist of materials that are also good conductors of solar radiation (e.g., gravel), the effect is an increase in ground temperature as well as a decrease in soil temperature variation. It is possible that the system of gravel-mulch gardens along the Chama served to slightly extend the length of the growing season.

In all, as Table 6.2 indicates, the agricultural features recorded in the Rio Grande Pueblo homeland cover large areas of land and occur on a variety of appropriate landforms, including steep and gentle slopes, flat areas, ridges, and benches. The areal

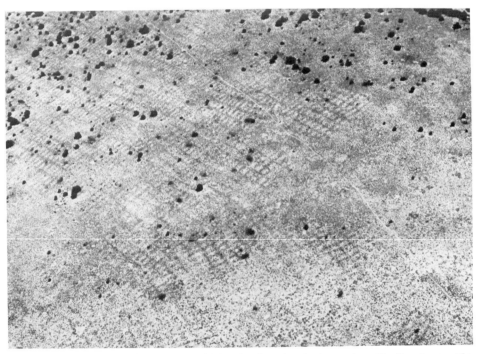

Figure 6.4 Aerial photograph of gravel-mulch bordered gardens in the northern Rio Grande area. This system, on Abiquiu Mesa, indicates the extensive nature of upland agricultural systems in the Rio Grande area. Photograph was taken at an altitude of about 188 m. (Courtesy of Stewart Peckham.)

extent of the systems suggests that rainfall farming was far more important to the Rio Grande Pueblo than is generally acknowledged.

The kinds of agricultural features found in the Rio Grande Valley do not suggest great labor investment; they seem to be similar to those reported for Point of Pines. Although it is difficult to date the features, most were probably built fairly late in the prehistoric period (after .A.D 1200). Locally, this was a time of generally increased population.

Masters of the Desert: Hohokam Canal Irrigation

The Hohokam heartland, along the lower Salt and middle Gila rivers of central Arizona, provides an excellent example of intensive agriculture on a major scale. Early Spanish explorers, military observers, and Anglo-American settlers were impressed by the remains of extensive systems of irrigation canals. At one time or another at least 579 km of prehistoric canals have been mapped in the Phoenix area alone (Nicholas 1981). Early archaeological tests indicated that some canals had been dug to a depth of over 2 m and were 3 m wide (Haury 1937; Hodge 1983; Woodbury 1961).

Most archaeologists have been pessimistic about obtaining details of Hohokam agriculture practices and subsistence because modern agriculture and more recently urban growth have obliterated Hohokam living sites and canals. As early as 1903, H. R. Patrick lamented the loss of most of Hohokam canals in the vicinity of Phoenix. Although it is true that much information is forever lost, archaeologists have learned a great deal about Hohokam irrigation and subsistence, and the application of new techniques of data recovery may permit the acquisition of additional information in the future.

One of the major goals of Haury's 1964–1965 excavations at Snaketown was to obtain a clearer understanding of the history of Hohokam irrigation agriculture. Toward that end, intensive and extensive excavations of canals at Snaketown were undertaken (Haury 1976:39). Archaeological testing and excavation in conjunction with urban development projects have augmented our knowledge of Hohokam sub-sistence techniques (Gasser 1981; Masse 1981) (Figure 6.5). A detailed study of aerial photographs enabled Nicholas (1981) to map the growth of Hohokam canals in the vicinity of Phoenix. Finally, a study of Skylab and Landsat satellite imagery suggested that some traces of Hohokam canals are still detectable within urban areas (Ebert and Lyons 1980). Research conducted at Snaketown and Gasser's detailed analyses of botanical remains from Hohokam sites form the basis of the discussion here.

In the Hohokam heartland, water is the limiting factor for agricultural success. The growing-season length of about 260 days is adequate for all crops grown in the Southwest, and it permitted the Pima to obtain two crops a year of selected domesti-cates. Rainfall, however, is only between about 19 and 25 cm annually. About half of this falls in high-intensity summer thunderstorms; the rest in milder winter rains. Corn is the most common plant species recovered at Hohokam sites and was present from the beginning of the Pioneer period. Other domesticates of the Hohokam include beans, squash, bottle gourds, cotton, possibly barley (*Hordeum pusillum,* little barley

Figure 6.5 Hohokam canals. Upper (left) and lower (right) channels of south canal, no. 3, Park of the Four Waters, Phoenix, Arizona. The canals were exposed during excavation for a freeway by the Arizona State Museum. B. Bruce Masse is standing next to the lower channel. The 3-meter stick is placed next to the upper channel. (Helga Teiwes, photographer. Courtesy of the Arizona State Museum.)

grass), and amaranth. Despite the impressive array of crops, the Hohokam depended to a seemingly great extent on wild plant foods. Mesquite is abundant at Hohokam sites and may have been a staple food. Macrobotanical and pollen remains indicate that goosefoot seeds, saguaro seeds and fruit, carpetweed seeds, various grass seeds, hedgehog cactus seeds and fruit, mustard seeds, wild primrose roots, four-o'clock roots, cholla buds, and cattail roots and catkins were also eaten.

Hohokam irrigation engineering is impressive by any standard. Haury suggests that the Pioneer period canal at Snaketown headed at Gila Butte, some 5 km east of the site. From there, water could have been diverted to the upper terrace above the Gila River floodplain and to Snaketown, which is on that terrace. If enough water was available, it could then have been used for fields on both the upper and lower terraces and on the floodplain. The remains of a Pioneer period canal were located on the edge of the upper terrace on the southwestern side of the site. This canal, in contrast to later ones at Snaketown, was relatively broad, shallow and unlined. Later canals at

Snaketown were U- or V-shaped in cross section and lined with mixtures of clay and loam. Several dipping pools along the excavated portion of the Pioneer period canal suggest that it did not hold water throughout the year. (Dipping pools are locations where water was held, to be used for domestic needs.)

The initial excavation of the canals was only the beginning of the labor investment for the Hohokam. Silt, and apparently refuse, clogged the waterways and necessitated the periodic cleaning of them. As Haury notes, piles of silt removed from the canals may substantially modify local topography. In addition, canal walls were breached as water sought the quickest path to the river. Haury's excavations revealed several areas in which breaches had been repaired during the period in which the canals were in use.

Along with the canals themselves, the Hohokam irrigation systems included vast networks of lateral ditches and diversion areas. The excavated diversion areas reveal lines of postholes, indicating headgate structures made of a series of posts that probably served as upright frames for horizontally laid branches and brush. Diversion dams of this type were constructed by the Pima during the historic period, but they did not last more than about a year and were therefore regularly rebuilt.

Archaeologists confront several interpretive problems in their discussions of Hohokam irrigation and subsistence. First, the data available are clear in showing highly developed technological skill in the construction and maintenance of irrigation systems, but the data also indicate that a diversity of wild plants were used for food. If the Hohokam were sophisticated hydrological engineers, then why did they rely heavily on wild food sources? Second, did the construction and maintenance of the irrigation systems entail elaborate mechanisms of social control? These issues have not been resolved, but consideration of the hydrological regimes of the rivers is important to clarifying the first question, and Nicholas' (1981) research suggests directions that might be pursued in order to answer the second.

The Gila and Salt rivers originate in the mountains of east-central Arizona, and both are fed by winter precipitation and summer thunderstorms. Water levels are therefore high twice during the year, in late spring and again in late summer. The biannual floods enabled the Pima to obtain two crops a year in historic times (Bohrer 1970; Castetter and Bell 1942). Variability, however, is characteristic of the precipitation pattern and in any given year one or both periods of high water might fail to occur. In a discussion of the Pima ecosystem, Bohrer (1970) showed that there were no conflicts between the schedules of activities involved in agriculture and in wild plant gathering. The Gila River Pima could harvest their first crop in late June, but if that crop failed they could harvest saguaro seeds in July.

A second crop could be planted at the end of July and the beginning of August. If there was a lack of summer rains, and the second crop failed, mesquite pods could be gathered in September. In any one year, then, subsistence activities could have involved both agriculture and gathering. Castetter and Bell (1942) noted that during the historic period the water level of the Gila was also highly unreliable from year to year, and there were crop failures as often as 2 years out of 5. The Pima compensated by gathering wild plant foods. Castetter and Bell estimated that perhaps 60% of the Pima diet was based on wild plant gathering. The variety of wild plant remains in Hohokam sites could reflect years in which agricultural production failed completely.

The accounts of historic Pima agriculture are probably best viewed as being suggestive rather than as direct analogs for the Hohokam, because Pima populations were undoubtedly much reduced as a result of European contact. The amount of archaeology in the Hohokam heartland is insufficient for determining how many settlements were contemporary, how many canals were in use at the same time, and whether prehistoric population densities were such that competition for irrigation water or for wild plant resources were additional problems requiring social solutions.

The difficulty in precisely dating the construction of Hohokam canals and determining the sizes of the settlements they served also inhibits interpretations of the degree of social coordination required to construct and maintain them. In most instances, quite small segments of canals have been exposed in excavations, and these are dated on the basis of the ceramic assemblages recovered from them. If canals have been dug through trash deposits that predate them, they will contain ceramics reflecting an age earlier than that of their use. If canals are dated simply on the basis of their proximity to sites, very precise age determinations are not possible. Based on his work at Snaketown, Haury interprets the development of Hohokam irrigation as a rather gradual process in which irrigation systems were slowly expanded and elaborated. His view is that construction of the Pioneer period canal at Snaketown did not require a greatly coordinated labor force and the work could have been accomplished by the informal cooperation of as few as 50 men. Further, Haury estimates that the founding population of Snaketown was relatively small, based on the number of Pioneer period houses excavated. Unfortunately, the dispersed nature of Hohokam settlements makes it difficult to estimate their size at any one time in the absence of complete excavation. Nevertheless, Nicholas' work supports Haury's interpretation of the modest scale of Pioneer period canals, though not of a gradual expansion of the system.

Nicholas was concerned with interpreting the extent of Hohokam irrigation systems along the Salt River south of Phoenix, and as noted, she relied on examination of a series of aerial photographs. Recognizing all the problems inherent in dating agricultural features by their proximity to dated sites, she cautiously used the method to infer the relative scale of Hohokam irrigation during the major Hohokam developmental periods. Like Haury, she found that the Pioneer period canals were relatively simple and suggests that their construction did not require highly structured coordination of a vast labor force. Her discussion indicates a persistence of this condition until the Hohokam Classic. At that time, however, she finds that the canal systems south of Phoenix had numerous branches. And it is important that the three canal systems in her area were interconnected in Classic times. She tentatively suggests that this major expansion in the irrigation systems depended on the prior development of complex sociopolitical institutions.

On the other hand, with data from the lower Agua Fria River area northwest of Phoenix, and careful consideration of Hohokam agricultural technology, and the climatic and edaphic requirements of Hohokam crops, Dove (1982) suggests that there was a favorable shift in precipitation that began sometime during the Sedentary

Period. If Dove's analysis is correct, the dramatic expansion of Hohokam irrigation canals along the Salt River may reflect Hohokam opportunism rather than or in addition to a change in the social system. Dove's study also considered Hohokam use of woody species (for fuel and house construction and as critical habitat for game). He argues that a growing population, perhaps attracted by the more favorable precipitation, would have exhausted wood resources within only a few years, necessitating technological modifications and resettlement.

Discussion

The preceding case studies touch on several matters of interest to Southwestern prehistory and on more general issues of anthropological concern. The data suggest that a level of regional population density or restricted mobility must be reached before an investment in agricultural features is made. The particular features selected primarily reflect local topography and rainfall conditions and demonstrate the abundant technological skill of all prehistoric Southwestern farmers.

The amount of labor invested in the construction of agricultural features was quite variable, with Black Mesa, Point of Pines, the Rio Grande Valley, and Gu Achi representing the lower end of the scale, and Chaco Canyon and the Hohokam heartland the upper end. The examples suggest that construction of features is not undertaken until local population densities are high enough to require it, and only some kinds of systems are effective for agricultural intensification. The amount of water in Gu Achi Wash would not increase, no matter what labor investment was made. The floods and short growing seasons of the Rio Grande Valley could only be controlled to a limited extent. Where intensification could benefit the people dramatically, it apparently sustained further growth, which seems to have been the case in Chaco Canyon and in the Hohokam heartland. The data are far from conclusive, but in these two areas it appears that certain mechanisms of social control and a degree of sociopolitical complexity were required for the further expansion of the agricultural systems. When this level of social sophistication was achieved, the growth of both systems was again great. Finally, however, growth could not be sustained, possibly because the climate deteriorated or nonagricultural resources were depleted.

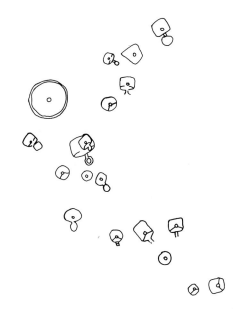

7

Early Southwestern Villages to
A.D. 900

The appearance of villages marks a change to a sedentary way of life. The change involved the use of new kinds of tools and facilities, such as ceramic containers and houses. The functional aspects of these tools and facilities are discussed in this chapter, as are the inferences about social organization that may be made on the basis of characteristics of domestic architecture and settlement layout.

Introduction

There is little evidence of sedentary villages in the Southwest before about A.D. 200. In a review of the data, Berry (1982) argues that only seven structures in the Southwest are securely dated to the period between 185 B.C. and A.D. 1. These structures are from a location on northern Black Mesa, Arizona, a site north of St. Johns, Arizona, and sites in the Hay Hollow Valley of northeastern Arizona.

Between about A.D. 200 and 900, villages were established from the Grand Canyon to central New Mexico and from Cedar Mesa in southern Utah and the Dolores River area of Colorado to Sonora and Chihuahua, Mexico. Although the earliest villages vary in size and the length of time over which they were occupied, they are composed of separate, noncontiguous houses that are generally oval to circular in shape, and many have special community structures. The inventory of material culture items associated with the early villages includes grinding stones, projectile points, scapers, knives, baskets, nets, and other items that were part of Archaic assemblages. Ceramics were an important early addition to the basic material culture inventory, and shortly after their appearance, the quantity of trade items in the villages increased. At about the same time (A.D. 500), bows and arrows replaced spears and darts.

The appearance of villages, of course, is not unique to the Southwest but is a general characteristic of all New World societies at what has been termed the Formative stage or level of development (Flannery 1968; Martin and Rinaldo 1951; Willey and Phillips 1958). This stage requires a secure resource base and social mechanisms that can integrate and sustain village economies. As Willey and Phillips (1958:144–46) indicate, in certain resource-rich settings it is possible to support sedentary communities without agriculture; however, in the relatively food-poor and marginal environments of the Southwest, the production of crops is essential for the survival of even seasonally sedentary communities.

Due in part to the variable environments of the Southwest and the possibilities these offer for various techniques of reliable agricultural production, as well as to the kinds and abundance of important wild resources, the character of sedentary villages varies considerably. In some areas, very small dispersed hamlets are the predominant settlement type; in others, fairly large communities replace the hamlets early in the period. Some locations did not permit sustained occupation by horticulturalists, and these were soon abandoned.

In many parts of the world, the appearance of villages of the Formative stage is a brief episode that gives way to complex, socially stratified societies. In the Near East and in Mesoamerica, towns, large ceremonial centers, craft specialization, and cities rapidly succeed the first villages. In these parts of the world, it is often difficult to study the early villages archaeologically, because they are frequently located under later, much larger settlements. In contrast to this development pattern, villages remained the characteristic form of settlement throughout the prehistory of the Southwest. The frequent abandonment and the lack of substantial reoccupation of many village sites in the Southwest allows relatively easy archaeological access to them. An examination of Southwestern villages therefore permits considerable insight into a form of settlement that is often obscured elsewhere. But it must be remembered that Southwestern villages are not necessarily appropriate models for early village life in those areas where complex societies developed. The temporal stability of the village model in the Southwest suggests that the opportunities and pressures that led to urbanization in other settings did not exist, and the Southwestern villages must reflect a different set of social and economic adaptations.

The Formative stage is defined in terms of both an adequate subsistence base and the social organization needed to sustain village life. Within the Southwest, the importance of agriculture is inferred from macrobotanical remains and the tools and facilities used in food preparation and storage. Considerations of economic and social organization have relied on analyses of the formal characteristics of villages and their spatial distributions, generally compared to ethnographic information. This chapter first examines the formal characteristics of early Southwestern villages, the features and artifacts of the archaeological record. As noted above, the early village period witnessed the construction of houses and the use of ceramics. In Chapter 3, variations in methods of house construction and ceramic manufacture and design were seen to be basic to the culture-historical reconstructions prevalent in Southwestern prehistory. In this chapter, a more general and functional view is offered. The distribution of village settlements and interpretations of village social organization are also discussed.

Early Village Subsistence and Tools

Archaeologists have interpreted the subsistence economies of the early villages from botanical and faunal remains and from the kinds of tools and containers found. As noted in the preceding chapter, corn, beans and squash were cultivated throughout the Southwest. Cotton was an additional cultigen in the lower Sonoran Desert and in those areas of the Plateaus where the growing season was sufficiently long for the crop. No further discussion of these crops is necessary here, but two general observations are in order. First, nowhere in the Southwest were villages sustained entirely on agricultural produce. Second, the wild resources that continued to be significant varied from one region to another.

Manos and metates were used throughout the Southwest to grind plant seeds. Initially, the basin metate and the small, one-hand mano are most common, but slab and trough metates and larger, two-hand manos increase in frequency through time. The changes in grinding tools are generally thought to indicate an increasing reliance on corn at the expense of wild plant seeds and increasingly more efficient grinding.

The generally fairly large and corner-notched projectile points associated with the earliest villages are similar to those of the late Archaic. They were most likely used with spears and spear throwers, or atl-atls. Other flaked stone tools include large choppers, knives, scapers, and drills. Later in the Archaic, small side-notched or stemmed points replace the larger forms, and this is generally interpreted as indicative of a change to the use of the bow and arrow.

Glassow (1972) suggests that the change from dart points and spears to bows and arrows may be related to the increasing importance of agriculture and an associated restructuring of other subsistence activities. He argues that as people invest more time in agriculture, hunting, which would still be necessary to supply high-quality protein, should become more efficient. He suggests that "the bow-and-arrow would have provided this efficiency by providing the advantages of ambush, by expanding the hunt to more thickly wooded lands, and perhaps by increasing the variety of smaller animals which could be effectively hunted" (Glassow 1972:298–299).

Perishable items are known from the excavations of caves and rockshelters in the northern and mountainous portions of the Southwest (Guernsey and Kidder 1921; Martin *et al.* 1952; Morris and Burgh 1954). From these locations, a variety of baskets have been recovered, as were blankets of cordage wrapped with fur and feathers, cradle boards, and sandals made of yucca, tule, and other plant fibers. Other perishable materials consisted of plain-weave cotton cloth, braided sashed, string aprons, cordage, and knotted netting. Some of the netting, consisting of yards of plant fiber cordage and human hair, was used to net rabbits. Bone awls and needles, used to make baskets and textile materials, are commonly found in early village sites.

The earliest ceramics in the Southwest date to about A.D. 200 (cf. Berry 1982; LeBlanc 1982; Schroeder 1982). Although there are numerous problems in evaluating the earliest occurrences, by A.D. 500 the use of ceramics was widespread. The early ceramics are predominantly plainwares, without texturing or paint, generally brown or buff in color, and the vessels are of a generally globular shape. Although not absolute, there are regional differences in the way that pottery was made, and later, decorated.

In the eastern and northern parts of the Southwest, the Mogollon and Anasazi areas, pottery vessels were usually built up by coiling thin ropes of clay and finished by scraping the interior and exterior surfaces smooth with a gourd or other similar object. In the lower Sonoran Desert (the Hohokam and most of the Patayan area), pottery vessels were also made by coiling, but the vessel walls were then thinned and smoothed by using a paddle and anvil. This finishing technique leaves the vessel surface slightly dimpled. In the Mogollon region, brown plainwares predominated, but polished, slipped redwares and brownwares with red painted designs were also made. In the Anasazi area, the earliest ceramics were brownwares like those of the Mogollon region. Later Anasazi ceramics were generally gray plainwares, or else the ceramics had a gray or white surface color and were decorated with black painted designs. In the Hohokam area, buff to brown plain pottery was most common. Hohokam painted pottery was buff colored with designs executed in red paint. In the Patayan area, ceramics were gray, buff, or brown. Upland Patayan painted pottery is generally black on gray. Along the lower Colorado River Valley, ceramics were rarely painted, but when paint was used it was a reddish color.

Differences in ceramic technology and decorative treatment are basic to the culture-historical reconstructions discussed previously, and ceramics are indeed very useful sources of information for the discussion and resolution of a variety of archaeological issues. Essentially, however, ceramics are containers, and their appearance in the

Southwest can be related directly to increased sedentism and indirectly to the growing importance of agriculture. Ceramic containers, because they are both heavy and fragile, are not useful items among highly mobile groups, especially those lacking pack animals. Large ceramic vessels are advantageous for storing either liquids or dry foods because they are safe from insects and rodents and may be sealed with stone or clay covers, and because they do not become fragile with age, as do baskets (Woodbury and Zubrow 1979:59). Pottery vessels are made relatively quickly, allowing their makers to devote more time to other activities (such as tending crops). Ceramic containers are also more versatile than are baskets for cooking purposes. Baskets can be made watertight, but this involves a fairly complicated process of coating them with pitch. Baskets cannot be placed directly on fires, and when it is necessary to warm their contents, heated rocks must be added to the liquid within them. Pottery vessels can be placed directly on a low fire or bed of coals and their contents allowed to simmer unattended, an important advantage among peoples with numerous activities to complete in order to survive (Glassow 1972).

The differences among the kinds of ceramics made and used in the Southwest relate to variations in production techniques. All ceramics are composed primarily of clay, and the mineral constituents of naturally occurring clays vary with the source material from which the clays are derived. Some clays have more ferrous components than do others, and these will generally take on brownish to reddish color on firing. However, the color of fired clay also depends on the amount of air permitted to circulate in firing. If air circulates freely, the clay is fired in an oxidizing atmosphere and a red or red-brown color is produced. If air is not allowed to circulate during firing, a reducing atmosphere causes the clays to become whitish to gray. Within certain limits, then, the basic color of ceramic vessels can be determined by the potter despite differences in locally available clays.

Pottery cannot be made from very pure clay, because pure clay will shrink and crack when it is dried and fired. Consequently, potters add nonplastic materials to clays. These materials, collectively referred to as *temper,* also strengthen vessel walls. In the prehistoric Southwest, sand, crushed or ground rock, and crushed potsherds were commonly used as temper. Temper particles can be seen, and often identified, under magnification. They provide valuable clues about the locations in which the pottery was produced. For example, certain kinds of temper, such as fragments of igneous rock, have a limited geographic distribution. If ceramics are found to contain temper that is unavailable in local geological formations, the vessels are likely to have been imported. Similarly, extreme geological heterogeneity in temper may indicate a variety of production locations.

Technically, vessel walls are made of a combination of clay and temper, a combination referred to as the *paste.* If the pot is to be painted, it is desirable to have a smooth surface on which to apply the design. Sometimes this surface is achieved by covering the exterior of the vessel with a thin coat of pure clay, the *slip.* Clays used for the slips were often selected because of the color they assume when fired. For example, some clays are nearly pure kaolin and will fire to a clean white color. Other clays will fire red or yellow or buff. The background color of most painted Southwestern ceramics is the color of the slip. The paste color may be quite different and can be seen only by exposing a fresh surface in cross section.

Finally, the paints used to produce designs were derived from a variety of materials. These are generally grouped in two broad categories—carbon and mineral. Carbon (organic) paints were made by boiling selected plants, such as the Rocky Mountain bee plant. Carbon paints are generally "soft"—they will seep into the slip, producing lines with faintly blurred edges. Mineral paints were produced by grinding a variety of pigment ores, such as hematite or iron oxide, and adding them to an organic base. Mineral paints are "hard,"—they do not seep or bleed into the slip, and so they produce lines with distinct edges. Late in the prehistory of the Southwest (after A.D. 1300), a particular kind of mineral paint was used very widely. This was a lead- or copper-based paint referred to as *glaze* because it vitrified on firing. The glaze was used only for decoration and never to completely cover and seal the vessel surface. Most painted vessels, and some unpainted ones, were polished before they were fired. Polishing was done with smooth hard pebbles and produced a shiny surface.

Studies of Southwestern ceramics are so numerous that they can fill entire small libraries. Archaeologists, in particular, have approached the classification of ceramics in a variety of ways. Studies of Southwestern ceramic technology were done in the early years of Southwestern archaeology, but the most systematic and detailed approach was pursued by Anna O. Shepard (1939, 1942, 1954; Kidder and Shepard 1936), whose work provides the foundation for the kinds of analytic studies that are crucial to contemporary archaeological questions regarding ceramic production, distribution, and trade.

Houses

Throughout the northern and mountainous portions of the Southwest, the early houses were pithouses, which are structures in which some portions of the walls are actually the earth sides of an excavated pit. The pithouses are generally round to oval in shape, and about 4.5–5 m in diameter. Their floors were usually dug to a depth of about 0.5 m below the surface of the ground. There is considerable variation in house floors: Some are discernable only as sterile earth compacted through use, some are of bedrock, and others are of finished mud or clay. Some houses lacked prepared floors.

Unless the pithouse burned, remains of walls and roofs are rarely preserved, so it is difficult to describe the variation in these architectural features. In the Durango, Colorado area, Morris and Burgh (1954) excavated pithouses with superstructures of cribbed logs laid horizontally in abundant mud mortar. Cribbed-log superstructures are also known from pithouses excavated in the Navajo Reservoir area of northwestern New Mexico (Eddy 1966).

More commonly, the portions of pithouse walls that extend above the surface of the ground consisted of a framework of poles set vertically around the edge of the pit, interlaced with small twigs, and then completely covered with mud on the exterior. In many pithouses, the interior earthen walls were lined with upright slabs. In cases where the pithouse interior was relatively small, the vertical poles may have been bent to form part or all of the pithouse roof. Some reconstructions indicate gabled pithouse roofs supported by a crossbeam set on posts aligned along one axis of the house. A common technique that seems to have become more widespread through time was to support the roof on four post supports arranged in a quadrilateral pattern (Bullard 1962).

Although a simple opening in a wall may have served as an entryway into some small pithouses, parallel-sided, lateral, inclined entryways are common features in the early pithouses (e.g., Haury and Sayles 1947; Lipe and Matson 1971).

Within the early pithouses, there is considerable variation in floor features. For example, in the Durango area (Morris and Burgh 1954), at the Flattop site in the Petrified Forest, Arizona (Wendorf 1953b), at the early Navajo Resevoir District sites (Eddy 1966), and at the Bluff Ruin in the Forestdale Valley, Arizona (Haury and Sayles 1947), firepits with ash and charcoal but without other evidence of burning (e.g., oxidized walls) occur in some—not all—houses. Pithouses that lack interior firepits are frequently interpreted as having been occupied only seasonally. Some archaeologists have suggested that the ephemeral hearths may have been used for occasional cooking. Other investigators have interpreted these features as "heating pits" that were used to hold rocks that had been heated at outside hearths. A variety of subfloor storage pits are commonly found in the early pithouses. These might be circular or jug shaped, basin shaped, flat bottomed, or undercut.

Through time, pithouse form underwent change and in most areas became standardized, with the regularly occurring styles and shapes varying in different areas. For example, in the Mogollon region, pithouse shape ranged from generally round or oval to rectangular with rounded corners to rectangular. After their initial appearance in the same area, pithouses also generally decreased in size. Firepits, often slab or cobble lined, became standard floor features and were set into the floor at the center axis of the room in front of the entryway. In much of the Anasazi area, pithouses were built with adobe wing walls separating the house into two main areas. Metates have been found set into the floor in the smaller, vestibular area, suggesting that this part of the house served as a kitchen and food preparation area. In both Mogollon and Anasazi areas, sipapus (small holes) are sometimes located toward the back of the house. Other features commonly found in Anasazi pithouses include ventilator openings, slab or adobe deflectors, and benches or raised platforms around most or all of the room's perimeter. The deflectors were located between the central hearth and ventilator shaft and presumably served to guide incoming air away from the open fires. As Anasazi pithouses became more standardized in form and features, they often were equipped with hatch entries through the roof, and the impressions of ladder posts are frequently found beneath these on the opposite side of the hearth from the deflector and ventilator.

In contrast to the pithouses that were the nearly universal early house form in the northern Southwest, houses in the lower Sonoran Desert areas, for example, Hohokam houses, were houses built in pits. Essentially, although house floors were excavated some 10–20 cm below the surface of the surrounding ground, the house walls were nearly always made entirely of a framework of poles covered with reeds, grass, and dirt. A four-post roof-support pattern was usual in square houses, and a two-central-post pattern with auxiliary posts along house edges was used in rectangular houses. Small, adobe-lined hearths were located in front of the entryway about half-way between the entry and the centerline of the house (Haury 1976:72). Haury indicates that most hearths do not seem to have been used for large fires but perhaps held embers brought in from outside fires. Finally, although pits and cists are features of Hohokam villages, these are outside houses rather than both outside and inside.

A Consideration of Pithouses

As noted above, there is an initial dichotomy in house form in the early South-western villages, with pithouses being the most common form over much of the northern and mountainous Southwest. Although pithouses were constructed in the late prehistoric and historic periods in some parts of the Southwest, in general this form of house gave way to multiroom surface pueblos in those areas in which it had been prevalent. Several archaeologists have attempted to explore general, processual factors involved in the transition from pithouse to pueblo (e.g., Gilman 1983; Lipe and Breternitz 1980; Plog 1974), and a few scholars have specifically examined the functional aspects of pithouses.

Farwell (1981) has considered the thermal properties of pithouses and found them to be more efficient in conserving heat than are pueblos. She cites studies indicating that heat is lost more slowly in underground structures without any additional insulation than in aboveground structures with the best modern forms of insulation. Farwell calculated the thermal efficiencies of a pithouse that was excavated in the Gallina area of New Mexico and of a four-room surface pueblo excavated near Taos. The calculations for the surface structure were made using two rooms with southern exposures and adobe walls that were 25 cm thick. Her work considered heat lost through wall openings and heat transmitted through wall surfaces. Her results indicated that while the pithouse would lose 119,614 BTUs per day over the winter months, the surface pueblo would lose 150,450 BTUs each day. As Farwell notes, "occupants of the pueblo room would have to provide 30,836 more BTUs per day (the equivalent of 30,836 kitchen matches) in auxiliary heat than the pithouse residents to achieve the desired 60 degrees F temperature on an average winter day" (1981:46).

Farwell's study considers other aspects of the thermal efficiency of pithouses, such as the lack of effect of the windchill factor on ground temperature and the effect of the ground as a heat sink. She concludes that the pithouse would require less energy to heat, either in fuel or manpower to collect fuel, than would the surface structure (Figure 7.1).

In a study of late (post-A.D. 1000) pithouses in New Mexico, Stuart and Farwell (1983) considered the influence of thermal factors by examining the high positive correlation between pithouse depth and altitude (elevation). In general, because

Figure 7.1 Artist's reconstruction of a pithouse interior. Research indicates that pithouses are thermally efficient, conserving heat in winter and generally remaining cooler than surface structures in summer. (Illustrated by Charles M. Carrillo.)

winter temperatures decrease with increasing elevation and because the temperature of the ground gradually increases with increased depth until a certain level is reached, one would expect that deeper pithouses would be found at higher elevations.

It should be noted that in her 1981 study, cited above, Farwell suggests that no single factor, such as thermal advantage, is likely to have been the most important reason for building pithouses. In another study, Gilman (1983) examines a variety of factors, including thermal efficiency, in the use of pithouses. Using ethnographic examples from a worldwide sample, Gilman found that the distribution of pithouses correlates with areas in which cold winters can be expected. But she also found that pithouses are used by groups whose settlements are of relatively small size and who are either nonagricultural or practice agriculture on a limited scale. In the ethnographic sample, groups using pithouses were semisedentary, living in pithouses only during cold months. It is possible that many of the pithouse villages in the northern Southwest and in mountainous areas were used only during the winter.

The discussion of pithouse thermal efficiency suggests one plausible reason for the distribution of pithouses in the Southwest, particularly their absence in the warm, lower Sonoran Desert. The discussion also indicates that other factors, such as settlement size, subsistence, and degree of residential permanence, are also important. Before examining these further, some of the other formal characteristics of early Southwestern villages need to be discussed.

Village Size, Layout, and Nonresidential Structures

The number of pithouses in the early villages varies considerably. For example, early villages on northern Black Mesa, Arizona, average about three to four pithouses per village (Gilman 1983). Survey data from Cedar Mesa, Utah; the middle New River and Agua Fria drainages, Arizona; Cevelon drainage, Arizona, Cibola (Zuni) area of

New Mexico, Elk Ridge, Utah; Grand Canyon, Arizona, and Long House Valley, Arizona, suggest an average of two pithouses per early village (Plog *et al.* 1978). On the other hand, some large pithouse villages, consisting of between 25 and 35 pithouses, are documented from the Petrified Forest, Forestdale Valley, and Pine Lawn Valley, New Mexico, the Hay Hollow Valley, Arizona, the Navajo Reservoir District, and elsewhere (Eddy 1966; Lightfoot and Feinman 1982; Plog 1974). At least one site in the Black River drainage, Arizona (Wheat 1954), is estimated to contain more than 100 pit-houses. This variation in size has been interpreted as reflecting social differentiation (see below); however, although some villages were undoubtedly larger than others, it is difficult to determine how many houses in a particular village were inhabited at the same time.

The problem of estimating village size is even more difficult for Hohokam settle-ments. Although Hohokam villages may have been occupied for long periods of time, individual houses probably had very short life spans. Because house walls were made of twigs, reeds, and mud, they deteriorated quickly after abandonment. Usually the only house remains left for the archaeologist are hard-packed floors. Determining how many dwellings were in use at one time, when a village consists of houses scattered over more than a square kilometer, is a task that has defied archaeologists (see Haury 1976:75–76 for a discussion of the problem). Wilcox *et al.* (1981) esti-mated that there were about 173 houses at Snaketown during the early Pioneer period.

In addition to houses, the early villages contain a number of extramural features. These are most commonly pits and cists of various kinds, which seem to have served as storage areas, and outdoor hearths and roasting ovens for cooking. In the absence of the excavation of complete site areas, it is not possible to determine how many outside firepits and storage pits or cists were commonly associated with each village. On northern Black Mesa, early villages had an average of six outside pits, of various shapes, per structure (Gilman 1983:248). Plog (1974:137) reports a range from 0.14 m^3 to 4.25 m^3 of storage space per dwelling unit in the Hay Hollow area. Wherever excavation has encompassed surfaces outside houses, both storage pits and hearths have been located.

In the early villages consisting of only two or three houses, there is no indication that the structures were used for other than residential functions. At virtually all the larger early villages that have been excavated, however, one or more community or special-function structures have been identified. Where pithouse villages occur, these special structures are similar to pithouses but are distinguished, usually, because they are larger, have unusual architectural features, and lack evidence of domestic ac-tivities. For example, LeBlanc (1983:67) describes Pithouse 8 at the Galaz site in the Mimbres Valley as an early great kiva. This structure was round, with a diameter of about 7 m and a floor area of about 37 m^2 (about two and one-half times the size of the average domestic pithouses at the site). In addition, Pithouse 8 had stylized adobe pillars adjacent to the projected rampway. These features are similar to those found in later Mogollon great kivas. Finally, although the pithouse had burned, there were no domestic artifacts (bowls, metates, etc.) on the floor. Rather, the floor contained a series of large flat stones, which LeBlanc suggests served as seats or the bases of seats for the spectators of ceremonies. In the Hohokam area, special community structures consist of platform mounds and ball courts, but these do not appear in the archaeological record until the Colonial period. During the Hohokam Pioneer period, the principal evidence cited for community-wide cooperation is the irrigation canals (see Chapter 6).

In virtually all the early villages in the Hohokam area and in the northern Southwest, houses are often described as haphazardly arranged within the village area. Early villages do not show an organized or planned use of space. There are no "courtyards" or plazas, and refuse often occurs as a thin layer of debris among the houses and around the village perimeter. In the northern Southwest, all the house entries in a village may be oriented toward the east, but the houses are not oriented with respect to each other. In the Hohokam area there is no consistent orientation of entryways.

The lack of a formal arrangement of houses and formal midden areas and the use of outdoor storage pits and cooking hearths are all characteristics of societies with low population densities. Most of the space in which daily domestic activities such as food preparation and eating takes place is public—in full view of all village residents. We do not know, from the archaeological remains, precisely what the relationships among the residents of these small villages were. Nevertheless, some of the observations anthropologists have made of small-scale societies are relevant.

Anthropologists who live for extended periods among people in small villages have to adjust to a lack of both privacy and regard for personal property that is foreign to their usual experience in large, complex societies. In a generalized sense, some of the characteristics of small, village societies have been neatly summed up by Forde and Douglas:

> Social relations are of the personal, face-to-face kind. Everyone has known everyone else from childhood, everyone is related to everyone else. The sick and unfortunate are able to depend on the kindliness of immediate neighbors. The sharing of tools and supplies to meet individual shortages are matters of moral obligation between kinsfolk and neighbors. (1956:16)

Some amount of surplus that can be stored, if only over the winter season, is required for the degree of residential permanence implied by the existence of early villages. Yet in times of food shortages, small villages are highly vulnerable. An individual's or family's rights to stored food may be respected at most times, but if times are bad, people will be expected to share what they have; and because what one has is in full view of the community, it is not possible to hoard. A number of scholars (e.g., Colson 1979; Scudder 1971; Turnbull 1978) note a regular sequence of behaviors that takes place among small-scale societies facing food shortages. At first, people consume less desirable, less nutritious "famine" foods. If the problem persists, food preparation and eating are done in private to avoid sharing. Finally, the villages disintegrate and families move away to forage or try to join kinsmen in areas that are not experiencing deprivation. Within the Southwest in general, aridity, unpredictable rainfall, short growing seasons in the northern and mountainous areas create situations of high risk for horticulturalists. It is not surprising that many small villages failed to

sustain themselves. Further, within the Southwest, those groups living at high northern elevations would face the most risk of crop failure. It might be expected that there
would be a higher rate of village abandonment in these settings than in the lower
Sonoran Desert. These factors may account for the fact that Hohokam villages appear
to have been inhabited for much longer periods of time than Anasazi or Mogollon
settlements. The differences in subsistence security may also have been important to
the topographic settings selected for the early villages.

Unfortunately, there are two few Pioneer period Hohokam sites known to generalize about their topographic settings. However, Haury's (1976:9) comments about
Snaketown seem to be relevant to other early Hohokam villages as well. He notes that
the site selected for Snaketown has three important characteristics: (1) it is located
where an underground aquifer is shallow, and wells not more than 3 m deep could
have been dug to provide domestic supplies of water. This seems to have been an
important consideration to the location of Gu Achi as well (see Chapter 5); (2) good
agricultural land was available on both the upper and lower terraces of the Gila at
Snaketown; and (3) the Gila itself could be tapped several kilometers upstream from
Snaketown to provide irrigation water for crops. The combination of arable land and
water was also essential to the location of Gu Achi, and it was provided by Gu Achi
Wash and its outwash fan (Masse 1981). Of interest is that Haury specifically comments
on the lack of defensive considerations in the positioning of Snaketown: "The flatlands
location of Snaketown and the eventual dispersal of residence units over nearly a
square kilometer of landscape, together with the absence of closeby natural refuges,
suggest that the choice of location was not influenced in the slightest by fear of hostile
people" (1976:9). This lack of defensive positioning contrasts with early Mogollon
villages, which seem commonly to be situated on high bluffs or ridges to which access
is difficult, and some investigators (Anyon *et al.* 1981) have used the hilltop setting as
one of the hallmarks of the early pithouse period. The specific topographic settings of
early Anasazi villages seem to be more diverse than those of the Mogollon, although
again the tops of benches and bluffs were commonly selected and possibly for the
same reasons.

Although a variety of explanations for this strategy, including aesthetic considerations and the need for resources available at higher elevations, have been offered, the
need for defense is a common, supportable interpretation; First, the mountainous
setting of the Mogollon region is one that is favorable for hunting (and hunting
continued to be an important aspect of Mogollon economy throughout their prehistoric sequence). It is reasonable to suggest that early Mogollon villages were
established within the same general areas as were groups of people who continued a
hunting and gathering way of life. (It is unlikely that everyone in the Southwest
adopted agriculture at the same time.) It is perhaps plausible to suggest that small
communities with enough agricultural produce to store over the winter felt threatened by potential raids from neighboring hunters and gatherers. Alternatively, it may
be suggested that given the higher risks to agriculture in mountainous Southwestern
settings, villagers would want to protect what foods were being stored from potentially hostile agriculturalists whose own crops had failed.

In both the Anasazi and Mogollon areas after about A.D. 500, pithouse villages are more consistently located away from high eminences and instead on alluvial terraces or the first benches above rivers. This shift in settlement location has been interpreted as indicating greater reliance on agriculture (Glassow 1972). It is also possible that the change involved the development of social mechanisms that served to integrate villages in effective opposition to remaining hunter–gatherer populations and to each other for effective sharing to even out local food shortages.

Social Organization

Discussions of social organization from an archaeological perspective are a relatively recent phenomena in the Southwest. The early investigators, such as Bandelier, Fewkes, and Cushing, offered numerous interpretations of social organization, but these were drawn from a variety of implicit sources, including legends, ethnographic observations, and the notions of unilineal evolution. Among the pioneering archaeological statements was that of Paul S. Martin (1950) concerning the Mogollon of the Pine Lawn Valley, New Mexico. Martin's approach followed two directions. First, he synthesized general trends in the archaeological data and made some assumptions about the meaning that might be attached to these trends. Second, he offered some interpretations based on George P. Murdock's (1949) classic ethnographic cross-cultural study of social structure.

Although Martin's discussion begins with the Archaic Chiricahua Cochise, from whom he saw direct continuity to the Pine Lawn Mogollon, this summary concerns his observations and interpretations of the Mogollon villagers from about A.D. 500 to 1000. Within this period, Martin compared the materials from the Pine Lawn phase (ca. A.D. 500) to those from the Georgetown, San Francisco, and Three Circle phases (A.D. 500–900) in order to have a comparable sample size. The trends Martin addressed in the archaeological data are as follows: House size became smaller; the number of houses in each village and the number of villages increased; the number of metates per house, and the number of tools in general per house, decreased; finally, there was a decrease in the proportions of basin metates and mortars to slab and trough metates.

Martin suggested that the change in house size reflected a shift from houses that were occupied by extended families to nuclear family households. The decline in the number of metates and other tools in each house was viewed as strengthening this interpretation. At the same time, the increase in the number of houses and villages suggested an overall population increase. Martin suggested that mortars and basin metates might be correlated with the processing of wild plant seeds, whereas slab and trough metates indicated corn processing. He therefore proposed that the change in metate shape showed an increasing reliance on agriculture that was important to the increase in population. Murdock's study suggested that matrilocal residence, matrilineal descent, matrilineal inheritance, politically independent villages, and probably monogamy are also reasonably inferred from the subsistence and settlement interpretations.

Ten years after Martin's work appeared, Bluhm (1960) published an analysis of settlement patterns in the Pine Lawn Valley that modified one of Martin's interpretations. Bluhm noted that whereas the larger villages had one or more ceremonial structures, such structures were lacking in the small pithouse villages. Rather than presuming complete village autonomy, then, she concluded that the ceremonial rooms may have served both the large villages and a number of small villages, "so there may have been multi-village communities in the valley at an early time" (Bluhm 1960:542).

Lightfoot and Feinman (1982) reevaluated social organization in Mogollon pithouse villages from a different perspective. These authors assume that there is a continuum from household-based political systems to village-level organizations wherein managerial decisions are vested in one or several village leaders. Village leaders may function full- or part-time, but they "constitute an administrative level separate from the rest of the local population" (1982:64). They cite a number of theoretical statements suggesting that with increased sedentism, population growth, agricultural intensification, and increased volume of long-distance trade, suprahousehold decision-making positions are required; and they develop a model for such leadership positions that has implications that can be explored using archaeological data.

The implications, framed as hypotheses, are that (1) households of village leaders are associated with more storage space than other village households; (2) households of village leaders are associated with agriculture; (3) households of village leaders are more active in long-distance trade than other village households; and (4) if great kivas were locations at which goods were exchanged, the houses of village leaders should be in close proximity to the kivas. Obviously, testing each of these hypotheses requires that the particular household of village leaders be identifiable in the archaeological record. Lightfoot and Feinman assume that village leaders would occupy larger pithouses than others, and they identify a number of large pithouses in excavated villages. They find that in a comparison of the group of large pithouses with other pithouses, the former are statistically significantly associated with more storage space, evidence of agriculture (macrobotanical remains of corn), and more nonlocal goods (marine shell, turquoise, or Hohokam ceramics). The larger pithouses were found to be generally closer to great kivas than other houses in the village. A problem acknowledged by the authors, and one for which they attempted some control, is that the pithouses within the villages may not have been occupied at the same time. Unfortunately, this is a very serious problem with the potential to undermine the rest of the study.

Lightfoot and Feinman also contrast a set of villages that they argue appear to have a suprahousehold decision-making structure (based on the presence of a large pithouse associated with greater than expected storage space and nonlocal goods) with a set that do not. They find that the "decision-making villages" are, as a group, not later in time than the other villages, which they interpret as indicating that the development of leadership was not a gradual, linear process. They did find that more of the "decision-making villages" were near rivers, which they suggest were prehistoric trade routes.

The authors conclude that control over interregional exchange may have been an important factor in the development of decision-making structures.

The Lightfoot and Feinman study involves a large number of untested assumptions: for example, that village leaders occupy houses that are larger than others; that spatial proximity of a house to particular outside storage areas indicates that the residents of the house controlled those storage areas; that storage pits found in a village were even in use at the relevant time; or that early great kivas were places where goods were exchanged. Also, as Schiffer (1983) points out, Lightfoot and Feinman fail to consider transformation processes when they assume that exotic goods found in large pit-houses were used by the occupants of the houses. Schiffer's evaluation of the data shows that the trade goods were in fill contexts, having been deposited after the pithouses were abandoned.

Perhaps the greatest difficulty with the Lightfoot and Feinman study, though, is their initial premise regarding decision-making structures and their presumed correlates. Decisions at the low end of their continuum are made at the household level. Yet, among highly mobile hunters and gatherers today, decisions are guided by part-time leaders, who are generally the respected, older men. The model for the development of decision-making structures from which Lightfoot and Feinman derive their hypotheses is implicit, but it relies heavily on descriptions of the "Big Man" systems of New Guinea. The major problem with this is not that New Guinea has no historical connections to the Southwest; rather, it is that all of the "Big Man" systems occur in situations of much higher population density and with far greater agricultural intensification than can be demonstrated for the prehistoric Southwestern systems that interest Lightfoot and Feinman. If, as they argue, there are positive relations among population density, argicultural intensification, long-distance trade, and managerial hierarchies, then the pithouse villages of the early Mogollon fall at the lower end of any projected continuum.

As the data cited by Lightfoot and Feinman indicate, there are indeed differences in the size of early villages, the amount of trade goods in the villages, and the sizes of houses and storage facilities within the villages. Initially, much finer control over the basic chronological positions of the villages, and their component structures, is essential. We need to know if larger villages were occupied longer than smaller villages, or if larger villages were reoccupied more frequently than smaller villages.

We also need a better understanding of productive specialization and exchange. For example, it was common for Southwestern archaeologists to assume that pottery production was almost entirely a household craft, with each woman producing the vessels used by her family. But precise identification of materials used to temper ceramics indicates that in some cases, within very small villages, large numbers of ceramic vessels were not locally made (S. Plog 1980). It is important to know whether the amount of imported ceramics at the villages that Lightfoot and Feinman regard as lacking decision-making structures is in fact less than that at those villages for which a managerial hierarchy has been suggested.

A different approach, but one that leads to some similar conclusions, has been suggested by Plog (1983). Plog is concerned with the differential spatial and temporal distributions of strongly normative patterns in architecture and ceramics in the Pueblo Southwest from about A.D. 400 to the time of the Spanish Conquest. He argues, correctly, that before the 1960s, Southwestern archaeologists generally recorded and tested or excavated those sites that promised to have abundant material culture remains (see Chapter 3). Sites selected for excavation were usually large, with surface indications of substantial architecture and quantities of identifiable ceramic types. The ceramic types were viewed as the most reliable indicators of the temporal placement of the site and its cultural affiliation. If investigators were interested in sites dating to the A.D. 800s, they would select sites with the ceramic types that were diagnostic of that time. The majority of excavated sites, then, were those that were large and had "typical" material culture inventories. The data from these sites form the frameworks on which Southwestern prehistory has been written. The sites themselves, however, are not necessarily representative.

With the advent of the major salvage archaeology projects and, later, the enormous amount of work done within the context of cultural resources management, archaeologists recorded, tested, and excavated thousands of sites that were not typical but appeared to be representative. The first statement of the way Southwestern prehistory would have to be changed was made by Jennings (1963), who drew upon his experience as director of the Glen Canyon project, one of the first intensive, large-scale, modern salvage programs. Jennings concluded that

> huge centers are rare and scattered, found only in very favorable locations. . . . Most settlements are small family settlements; they consist of one or two dwellings and a cluster of storage rooms, which can be most descriptively called little ranches or *rancherias*. The settlement pattern can be described as a scattered single family homestead type. (1963:12)

Subsequent work has confirmed Jennings' observation. Over much of the northern Southwest, from the beginning of known village settlements, most sites are small and seem to have been inhabited for rather short periods. Further, many of these sites yield ceramic inventories that are not clearly diagnostic. For example, site survey information from the San Juan Basin of New Mexico, which includes the large, distinctive sites of Chaco Canyon, lists 6759 Anasazi sites that could be assigned to a general temporal framework. Another 1440 sites, however, are listed simply as "unknown Anasazi" (Cordell 1982).

Jennings' initial observation and subsequent cultural resources management studies confirm that in some areas the diagnostic sites are representative, but elsewhere are rare. Plog (1983) contends that diagnostic sites showing strong normative patterning differed organizationally from the contemporary, nondiagnostic settlements, although the basis he suggests for the organizational disparity is not that indicated in Jennings' remarks.

According to Plog, those sites showing strong normative patterns reflect alliances characterized by some evidence of specialized production, evidence of trade and exchange, and sometimes evidence of social ranking or stratification. The earliest alliance to which Plog refers is the Adamana pattern. Dating to within the period between about A.D. 400 and 700 and found at sites in the Little Colorado area of Arizona from the vicinity of Holbrook south to Springerville, Adamana sites consist of shallow pithouses bounded by stone cobbles. Typically situated on high bluffs or mesas, several sites contain large, communal structures. The diagnostic ceramics are Adamana brownware, a paddle-and-anvil-finished, rough-surfaced, sand-tempered pottery. Sites dating to the same period, but outside the Adamana area, exemplify what Plog refers to as a *weak pattern,* in that they are small and heterogenous, contain limited quantities of trade items or evidence of agricultural intensification, and are socially egalitarian.

In discussing the general character of alliances, Plog is careful to note that none of the Southwestern societies showing strong normative patterning reached a degree of economic and political complexity characteristic of major centers in the Old World or Mexico. Specifically, craft production was not centered in workshops with full-time laborers, nor did agricultural intensification reach even the level of complexity indicated by the Hohokam irrigation systems. Plog proposes that the alliance systems developed episodically in response to population–resource imbalances which people attempted to ameliorate by increasing the extent of trade and exchange, and sometimes, by intensifying agricultural production. In contrast to Jennings' position that strong normative patterns occurred in particularly favorable environments, Plog (1983) has suggested that they occurred in locations and at times when variability in rainfall was greater than usual. The alliance structure is viewed primarily as an attempt to compensate for subsistence shortfalls through exchange.

In the immediate context of a discussion of early village social organization, Plog's treatment is somewhat vague. Inasmuch as he characterizes all strong normative patterns as examples of alliances, there is no discussion of how different alliances were structured. Some of the proposed alliances were very extensive geographically—others involved agricultural intensification; therefore, it is highly unlikely that all alliances were organized in the same way. Although Plog does not invoke an implicit or explicit model of "Big Man" systems, or any other ethnographic analog of the proposed alliances, he also has not yet elaborated any specific organizational mechanisms that may have characterized the alliances.

An appreciation of the difficulty may be gained by looking at the second of Plog's proposed alliances—the White Mound pattern. White Mound sites, named after White Mound Village in eastern Arizona (Roberts 1939), are generally fairly large and consist of a row of jacal surface-storage rooms, a pithouse, kiva, and trash mound. The sites date to about A.D. 750–850. The ceramics associated with the White Mound pattern are a group of stylistically very similar types—Kana'a, Kiatuthlanna, and White Mound Black-on-white. Compared to the distribution of Adamana villages, the White Mound pattern is much more widespread. It extends from the Rio Grande Valley to Flagstaff and north to south throughout the Anasazi area. Nowhere within this enormous area, however, are White Mound sites particularly numerous. In some drainages they occur among smaller, more heterogeneous, apparently contemporary sites.

Both the Adamana and White Mound patterns relate to pithouse villages. The patterns differ in scale and in the distinctiveness of their ceramic assemblages, yet on the basis of Plog's discussion of alliances, they both represent strong, normative patterns and are described as organizationally similar. (Plog recognizes these issues and intends to address them further.) Plog's paper also defines later alliances that appeared episodically on the Colorado Plateaus. Two of these, the Chaco pattern and the White Mountain pattern, are considered examples of regional integration in this volume and are described in subsequent chapters.

In sum, archaeological interpretations of social organization in the early pithouse villages have diverged considerably from Martin's (1950) original statements. There has been particular recognition of the likelihood that the villages were not all politically, socially, and economically independent. Bluhm's (1960) initial observations were critical in this regard. Further work has demonstrated marked heterogeneity in the forms, sizes, and assemblage inventories of these villages. Most recently, these differences have been interpreted as indicating differences in social organization. Whether or not these interpretations are substantiated by subsequent research, they are an important contribution. The culture-historical explanations of the past are not adequate to represent the variation *in* and the similarities *among* regions that the newer frameworks address.

The Pithouse-to-Pueblo Transition

Throughout the northern and mountainous parts of the Southwest, between about A.D. 700 and 1000 there was a change from villages composed of pithouses to villages comprising multiroom surface structures with adobe or masonry walls. In some areas, such as the Mesa Verde, the change is apparently gradual, with a row of jacal surface rooms being built behind a pithouse and used for storage while the pithouse continued to be used for habitation. Later, people moved into the surface rooms, and the pithouses, with modifications in architecture, were used as ceremonial rooms or kivas. In other areas, such as the Mimbres Valley, the change from pithouses to pueblos appears abrupt and without transitional forms. Whether gradual or rapid, the change in the nature of villages has been a subject of archaeological inquiry since the 1920s.

Before discussing explanations for the change, some qualifications are in order. First, although pithouse villages are "typical" prior to A.D. 1000 and pueblos after that date, pithouses continued to be constructed and used into the late prehistoric period. In New Mexico, for example, Stuart and Farwell (1983) note that some 60 pithouse sites dating to the post-A.D. 1000 period have been excavated, and many more are known from site survey. These authors estimate that there may be as many as 500 "atypically" late pithouse sites in New Mexico alone. Second, as mentioned previously, pithouses were built in the early twentieth century at the Hopi village of Bacabi (Whiteley 1982). Finally, in some parts of the northern Southwest, pithouses were in use up to the time the area was abandoned prehistorically, and no transition to pueblo architecture was made. With these primarily temporal qualifications in mind, it is clear that no single event or exogenous variable (such as a widespread climatic change or diffusion of the idea of aboveground housing) can logically be invoked to explain the transition where it occurred.

Two approaches toward an explanation of the change from pithouse to pueblo are discussed here. Gilman (1983) has examined the change by focusing on the architectural forms themselves. In an earlier study, Plog (1974) explored the change as one aspect of changes in a systematically linked complex of behaviors reflected in a variety of material remains. Although distinct, the approaches are in fact complementary.

For her analysis, Gilman defined pueblos as multiple room structures of adobe or masonry that occur in aggregated clusters. As such, pueblos are not limited to the North American Southwest, and some insights can be obtained by examining their distribution on a worldwide basis. Gilman focused on the differences between pithouse and pueblo architectural forms as they relate to different ways in which space is used. Accordingly, the change involves the placement of food-preparation and cooking facilities (grinding areas and hearths, for example) into large indoor and aboveground settings. It also involves a difference in food storage techniques: In pithouse villages, storage pits and cists are located both inside and outside dwellings. In pueblos, food storage areas are inside and above ground level in rooms adjoining habitation rooms.

Gilman links these changes to population growth, increase in agricultural activities, and increase in sedentism. She accepts the basic contention, supported empirically in the Southwest, that population growth entailed increased dependence on agriculture and argues that the increased dependence on agriculture changed both information networks among groups of people and the timing and character of food preparation and storage activities. Although her discussion involves much greater detail than can be addressed here, some of her major points follow.

When people depend on wild food resources and some agriculture, foods may be stored at various times during the year or as they become available. Furthermore, stores are used only when wild foods are not available. In the northern Southwest, this may be over a period of just a few weeks during the winter. In addition, because wild foods must be gathered over very large areas in the generally resource-poor Southwest, high mobility and extensive information networks are necessary. With increased dependence upon crops, food that is to be stored becomes available over a much shorter period, generally the few weeks of the autumn harvest. Larger quantities of food must be prepared for storage in a short period. The labor requirements of agriculture (field preparation, planting, weeding, cultivating, and watering) necessitate increased sedentism, and there must be larger quantities of stored food to last over a greater part of the year. The storage requirements of agriculturalists also include seed for the following season, and given the unpredictability of crops in many parts of the Southwest, enough corn for emergency needs, that is, enough to last for a year or more. Group mobility and extensive information networks become less important, but the time spent processing food for storage (grinding corn and cooking) greatly increases.

Gilman suggests that as the lengths of time for food preparation and cooking increase, they will occupy special locations within a structure in order not to interfere

Figure 7.2 Specialized milling room. Room 92 at Broken K Pueblo, Arizona, as excavated by crews from the Field Museum of the University of Chicago's Southwestern Archaeological Expedition, 1963. Four milling bins, each containing a metate, are located along one wall of the room. A fire hearth and adjacent ash pit are in the center of the room. The room dates to about A.D. 1250. (Courtesy of Lewis R. Binford.)

with other activities (Figure 7.2). Because these tasks must be conducted daily throughout the year, and at times of inclement weather, she argues that they will be done indoors. They might, of course, be done indoors in belowground structures, but as the use of space becomes more specialized, it would become necessary to build contiguous belowground rooms. Gilman cites a number of modern ethnographic examples in which precisely this type of dwelling is built, in areas where winters are cold and the thermal efficiency of belowground dwellings is important. They are also instances in which the special conditions of the soil and climate allow contiguous belowground rooms to be built without the danger of walls collapsing. These conditions do not exist in the Southwest.

Gilman supposes that the reasons for moving stored foods from pits and cists to aboveground structures are not the same as those involved in deciding to live above ground level. She suggests that the increased length of time over which food is stored among agriculturalists is the key factor. Where food is stored for a year or more, it must be protected from rain seepage and burrowing rodents. Aboveground store-rooms become a logical solution, and one that predominates in the ethnographic record of agricultural societies depending on grain crops.

The specialized aboveground storage and living spaces need not, of course, be contiguous, and villages need not be composed of massed blocks of storage rooms and living rooms. Gilman suggests that although the thermal properties of pithouses are superior to those of aboveground structures, when the latter are necessary for other reasons (such as the ones she describes), the arrangement of the surface rooms in the pueblo style is more thermally efficient than other plans. She cites a number of studies of the thermal properties of prehistoric Southwestern pueblos and the modern Pueblo village of Acoma that support her view. Finally, she notes that pueblo-like arrangements are distributed throughout the ethnographic record among agricultural groups in areas where winters are cold and the soils and climate do not permit contiguous underground rooms.

In Gilman's study, the pithouse-to-pueblo transition was seen as a problem accompanying a change in the use of space. The differences in space use were examined analytically, in that the requirements of space for certain activities were examined separately from the problems of different kinds of storage space. Gilman did not attempt to examine all possible alternative methods of house construction or storage techniques. She developed some reasonable expectations based on her ideas of the use of space. These involved correlations among winter temperature regimes, degree of dependence on agriculture, and the like. She then examined a worldwide sample of societies to see if her expectations were supported and considered the Southwestern situation as a particular example of more general patterns. There are likely to be important factors that Gilman did not consider. For example, despite the probable thermal efficiency of massed room blocks, there were many parts of the northern Southwest in which one- and two-room masonry or jacal structures were the standard post-pithouse structural form and a rancheria pattern of dispersed homesteads prevailed. A number of reasons might be suggested to explain the differential occurrence of aggregated pueblos and dispersed homesteads, such as differences in agricultural technologies and field systems, in regional population densities, or in the local availability of wood for winter fuel. In each case, however, it would be appropriate to specify the conditions thought to be causal and to examine these on a global basis.

In his study of the pithouse-to-pueblo transition, Plog (1974) was concerned with the broad, systemic factors in cultural change rather than in the specific architectural features. His study was of the Basketmaker-to-Pueblo transition, which he viewed as an instance of more general processes of technological change. He examined factors derived from a general model of growth describing technological changes in the developing nations of the modern world, because it provided precise statements regarding the processes of change. The relevant dimensions derived from the model of growth are *population, differentiation, integration,* and *energy.* Each of these dimensions involved a number of variables. For example, *population* refers to the number of individuals within an area, the age structure of the aggregate of these individuals at a given time, and the density of individuals at a specific time in a defined area. Further, a model of growth must identify the relations among the dimensions of interest. Of the logically possible relations among the dimensions, the literature of developing countries indicated that seven were plausibly related to growth. These provided a set of hypotheses for examining the Basketmaker-to-Pueblo transition.

In order to examine the hypotheses themselves, Plog had to develop test implications that were appropriate for the nature of archaeological data as well as the model. For example, the model indicates that a change in population should be associated with the transition. Plog uses the number of dwelling units that are inhabited at a given time as an archaeological measure of population. If the relations specified by the model are correct, the number of dwelling units should increase rapidly during the Basketmaker-to-Pueblo transition; the rate of increase should be as great or greater than at any other time in the culture history of the region being considered and should result in a population maximum for the region. If the model is accurate, there should also be changes in the density of population, which is measured by the number of sites per unit area, the mean distance between sites, and the nearest-neighbor distribution of sites.

Although all the details of Plog's model and the test implications derived from it cannot be elaborated here, it is important to explain how the seemingly rather abstract concepts of *differentiation, integration,* and *energy* were examined archaeologically. *Differentiation* refers to a diversity in activities; it might be measured archaeologically by examining changes in the number of different kinds of limited activity sites or in the diversity in the location of sites. Within sited, differentiation would be reflected in changes in the room-to-room variability in artifacts and in artifact distributions in extramural areas of sites.

Integration involves the more complex or more effective coordination of activities, an admittedly difficult aspect of change to measure archaeologically. Nevertheless, Plog considers three variables that should be relevant. First, there might be changes in the kinds of family groups within and between sites. Second, changes in social roles might be examined by observing changes in the differential treatment of individuals within burial populations. Third, integration might be reflected in the appearance of new integrative structures reflected in distinct architectural units.

Energy might be measured, most directly, through an examination of subsistence data derived from faunal remains, macrobotanical remains, and pollen. Unfortunately, these kinds of data were not available for the area in which Plog conducted his study. An indirect measure of subsistence might have been obtained by estimating the amount of storage space and storage facilities, but Plog concluded that too many assumptions about the contemporaneity of storage areas would have to be made.

Given these problems, Plog decided to leave the energy dimension out of his test of the model.

Plog relied on survey and excavation data from the upper Little Colorado River Valley. These were supplemented by information derived from the literature of Southwestern prehistory. He found that in the upper Little Colorado area, the transition from Basketmaker to Pueblo was accompanied by a population increase and an increasing differentiation of activities (Figure 7.3). New integrative structures also appeared during the transition. Specifically, kivas became specialized, nonhabitation features; they were found to be associated with rooms that could typologically be considered storerooms. Plog suggests that kivas may have been the centers of a redistribution system, which would have been a new strategy of integration. Plog also cites burial data that indicate little evidence of social differentiation during the Basketmaker period but good evidence for status differentiation at Pueblo sites.

Although the data confirmed that the Basketmaker-to-Pueblo transition was associated with changes in the dimensions predicted by the general model of growth, drawing causal inferences about the relations among the dimensions of the model required a different analytical approach. Plog used multivariate statistical analyses. These indicated that the technological changes associated with the transition "are a result of differentiation, which in turn is caused by population increase. Changes in integration associated with the transition appear to be more a result of attempts to manage increasing numbers of individuals than attempts to manage increasingly differentiated activities" (Plog 1974:156). Moreover, the statistical analyses indicated that the relations among the dimensions of the model were different during the transition than they were before or after it occurred. This observation suggested that the pro-

Figure 7.3 Artist's reconstruction of the interior of a Pueblo room. The transition from pithouse to pueblo involved increasingly specialized use of space. (Illustrated by Charles M. Carrillo.)

cesses of change are not gradual or broadly cumulative, but that the transition was set in motion by underlying events or "kickers" that disrupted conditions of equilibrium.

The data from the upper Little Colorado showed an increase in sedentism, manifested by the appearance of pithouse villages, at about A.D. 200. By about A.D. 500, the pithouse villages had become quite large, and they were gradually abandoned as population dispersed into smaller villages. The dispersal does not coincide with climate change, and Plog suggests that the dispersal was the result of a failure to develop appropriate social mechanisms of integration. He comments: "the villages were too large and social organization too simple to handle the complex environmental and interpersonal problems that must have existed" (1974:158).

The dispersal of population into smaller communities would, however, have had detrimental effects on the economy of the local group. The established networks of hunting, gathering, and sharing would have broken down, necessitating, Plog argues, a resource base that would be more productive with fewer individuals. He proposes that it was within this context that a commitment to agriculture was made. The new subsistence strategy was apparently successful and to a period of population increase, which further seems to have initiated the period of growth marked by the Basketmaker to Pueblo transition. During the transition, of course, new mechanisms of integration were developed.

Plog's discussion of the Basketmaker-to-Pueblo transition raises a number of important issues. One of his goals was to examine the change in terms of a more general model of growth. The success of the model indicates that the change is an example of broader, underlying processes rather than something to be understood in particularist, culture-historical terms. His analysis also indicates that the underlying processes are interrelated in a complex fashion, one that changes over time. For instance, population growth is not apparently linked in a positive and direct manner to the technological change involving a dependence on agriculture, but it is positively correlated with a change in integration at a later time. The study also demonstrates some of the difficulties involved in developing test implications that are appropriate for archaeological data. Not only were the data related to subsistence insufficient to examine the role of the energy dimension over time, but some of the variables Plog did include in his study are ambiguous indexes of the behaviors of interest. For example, Plog used studies of social integration at two Hay Hollow Valley sites in which the number of social groups had been inferred from the nonrandom distributions of ceramic design elements within room blocks at the sites. A number of subsequent studies have questioned these inferences on empirical and theoretical grounds. The problem is very similar to that mentioned in regard to the Lightfoot and Feinman study discussed above. It cannot be assumed that high-ranking individuals occupy larger pithouses, nor can it be assumed that clusters of design elements in a series of pueblo rooms unambiguously indicate that the rooms were inhabited by members of the same social group. Similarly, and more directly, it was assumed that an increase in the number of small pithouse villages indicates an increase in population. Although not an unreasonable assumption, the same observation can also indicate an increase in residential mobility if the pithouses were not occupied year-round.

Plog later (1979) reworked some of the results of his study in light of general discussions of the complexity of episodes of change, and he found some problems with his initial interpretations. The difficulties arise because for each of the variables of interest there was more than one episode of change, and there may not have been a sufficient number of observations for each variable to characterize accurately the course of change for that variable. The restudy suggested that population growth and the organization of work, or intensification, were more closely linked than indicated in the original analysis.

Finally, one of Plog's original (1974) conclusions was that although the model was useful in explicating the processes involved in the Basketmaker-to-Pueblo transition, it did not fully explain the change. Certainly, archaeology is very far from being able to fully explain any complex cultural transition, and Plog is not to be faulted for his admission. The direction of future enquiry may depend on the development of science in general, as well as of the science of archaeology. For example, because Plog noted that the dimensions he examined interrelated in different ways before and during the period of transition, he suggested that specific factors should be sought that could cause the initial disequilibrium. The development of catastrophe theory in mathematics (Thom 1975) and discussions of its applicability to some archaeological examples of change (Renfrew 1978) indicate that external kickers may not be required to disrupt equilibrium conditions. In archaeology, discussions of cultural and natural transformation processes (Schiffer 1972, 1976) show that our level of understanding—of interpreting—purely archaeological data may not be adequate for the level of hypothesis testing Plog attempted. For example, although Plog was careful to examine activity differentiation among rooms by looking at only those artifacts recovered from room floors, the artifacts found on floor surfaces may not represent activities that were carried out when the room was in use.

Gilman's and Plog's studies of the pithouse-to-pueblo transition are good examples of current approaches in Southwestern archaeology. In both cases, the change is explored as part of more general phenomena. Whether viewed from the perspective of the architectural change or as an example of general growth, the transition is properly portrayed as highly complex, involving the restructuring of activities and new methods of integrating communities. There is continuity in material culture from Basketmaker to Pueblo, but the differences emphasize the organizational heterogeneity within the Formative stage.

Social Organization and Ideology in Early Pueblo Villages

Throughout the northern Southwest, primarily in the Colorado Plateaus, the period between about A.D. 750 and 900 witnessed the general expansion of village settlements. Since the late nineteenth century, Southwestern archaeologists have been concerned with the social and ideological aspects of village life. It must be remembered, however, that most of the statements made about social organization and ideology generalize from the strong normative patterns in the archaeological record. Whether or not one accepts Plog's (1983) characterization of alliances discussed above, Jennings' initial observation of organizational hetereogeneity is amply demonstrated in the archaeological record. The large sites, dense site clusters, and strong normative patterns represent only a small portion of the known inventory of sites. Unfortunately, virtually all summary discussions of social organization and ideology pertaining to the early Pueblo villages have been based on diagnostic, strongly normative, rather than representative, cases.

With the appearance of villages, architectural differentiation of habitation, storage, and ceremonial rooms (Figure 7.4), ceramics, and other artifacts of sedentary life, there is an obvious continuity from the archaeological record to the historic and contemporary Eastern and Western Pueblo communities of Arizona and New Mexico. Archaeologists commonly refer to ceremonial rooms as *kivas,* using the contemporary ethnographic term. They also recognize specific features and artifact types, such as *sipapus* and seed jars, because these are in use among the modern Pueblo. Although few archaeologists would insist that village life has remained unchanged from A.D. 700 to the twentieth century (ethnographic present), the interpretative emphasis has been on continuity rather than on change. Archaeologists tend to interpret the prehistoric

Figure 7.4 Kiva room at Broken K Pueblo, Arizona. The special features of this room include the loom holes to the left of the arrow, the firepit, and the deflector and ventilator at the top of the photo. This room was in use at about A.D. 1250, and is shown as excavated by the Field Museum of the University of Chicago's Southwestern Archaeological Expedition, 1963. (Courtesy of Lewis R. Binford.)

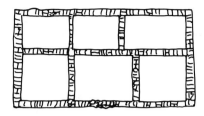

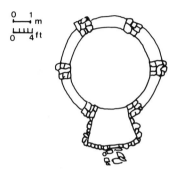

Figure 7.5 Prudden unit pueblo. Unit pueblos consist of a series of masonry surface rooms, a kiva, and a trash mound oriented along a north–south axis. (Adapted from Prudden [1918:8] by Charles M. Carrillo.)

Southwestern villages as though they were integrated by the same organizational and ideological structures as are the modern pueblos. Without denying that some Pueblo symbols are very old, subsequent chapters consider in detail the archaeological evidence pertaining to profound changes in Pueblo life over the past 1200 years. Just as interpretations based on strong normative patterns are likely to be only partially correct, those based on assumed continuity must also be reevaluated.

Among the earliest types of Pueblo villages is the *unit pueblo,* first described by T. Mitchell Prudden (1903, 1914, 1918) and sometimes named after him (Figure 7.5). Prudden unit pueblos consist of masonry surface structures—arranged in a line, arc, or L—a kiva, and a refuse midden. The three components are generally oriented along a north–south axis. Settlements of this type seem to date to between about A.D. 700 and 900 on the Colorado Plateaus. The ceramics associated with these settlements are Anasazi graywares, Lino Gray, and Kana-a neckbanded. Prudden suggested that each settlement was the residence of an extended family or clan. Plog (1983) considers the unit pueblos a strong normative pattern indicative of an alliance. He notes that the unit peublos are partially contemporary with the White Mound villages and proposes that they represent a smaller but distinctive system that developed from the White Mound pattern.

Gorman and Childs (1980–1981) have evaluated the concept of the unit type settlement. They are concerned with examining the consistency with which archaeologists have applied the designation to sites, as well as the interpretive meanings that archaeologists have assigned to them. Their review of the literature indicates that the term *unit pueblo* has been applied quite consistently by archaeologists, and that on this basis, the unit pueblos occur in the Kayenta, Mesa Verde, and Chacoan branches of the

Anasazi area (see Chapter 3). Further analysis, however, also suggests that there is more than one type of unit pueblo, but more importantly, that the variants or subtypes of unit pueblo sites are not clustered geographically or temporally. This observation indicates that the variation is not the result of culture-historical factors. One subtype consists of a single site that is different simply in that it has the smallest number of surface rooms. Gorman and Childs suggest that this reflects attenuated settlement growth, for the site was apparently abandoned shortly after it was occupied. Another subtype consists of three sites that apparently grew to larger sizes than other unit peublos, perhaps indicating greater site longevity. Two remaining subtypes are similar in size and plan. However, one has surface rooms that are divided into more spatially discrete blocks than is common among the unit pueblos in general. Gorman and Childs suggest that these two subtypes of unit sites represent social variants of the same settlement class, with the group showing spatially discrete blocks having been formed by the amalgamation of two or more previously distinct social groups. The authors admit that this interpretation requires testing. In general, considering the number of sites to which the designation *unit pueblo* has been applied, the number of different archaeologists who have used the term, and the wide geographic area in which these sites occur, there is a remarkable degree of uniformity represented.

The meanings that archaeologists have attached to the uniformity of the unit pueblo sites have emphasized either the directional spatial arrangement of the components or the sizes of the settlements. Reed, for example, considered the orientation of components highly significant, noting that "it surely must reflect something basic in personality structure, outlook, national character—something comparable to the difference between the Spanish inward-facing patio-type house on the edge of the street and our front-facing dwellings with the lawn on the outside" (1956:13). Those who have addressed settlement size and the number of surface rooms and kivas have proposed social interpretations, generally referring to the unit pueblos as clan, family, or lineage houses. Discussions of the origins of Pueblo clans have figured prominently in both the ethnology and archaeology of the Southwest. Whereas early investigators relied on Pueblo clan-origin myths or the ideas of unilineal evolution (see Chapter 3), more recent scholars are indebted to the thoughts of Julian Steward, who addressed the issue from the perspective of cultural ecology.

Steward (1955) was interested in the origins of the matrilineal western Pueblo multiclan villages. His analysis differed from those proposed earlier in that it did not rely on Pueblo migration legends, derivation from an outside source, or a late shift in the mode of lineality (from patrilineal to matrilineal). He argues that the origins of Pueblo clan organization were processual and could be understood in terms of economic and ecological factors. Steward's work also marked a departure from previous studies in that he used archaeological data in an innovative manner.

Steward noted that the late Basketmaker pithouse villages of the San Juan drainage consisted of small clusters of houses and that the clusters were quite close to one another. He believed that this was consistent with the importance of horticulture, because the vast hunting and gathering territories did not separate the small village clusters. Further he proposed that

> the small house clusters were unilateral groups living on or near their farm lands is consistent with their size and distribution. Motives for concentration of these clusters in larger villages were absent. It appears that population increased, small lineages budded off, and each set up a new house cluster at no great distance from its neighbors and former kin. (Steward 1955:162)

Steward's interpretation accorded well with the archaeological facts at his disposal. It should be noted, however, that the prevalence of the dispersed household, rancheria pattern had not yet been documented, nor had archaeologists questioned either the permanence or precise contemporaneity of small, pithouse village sites.

Steward did not see any *organizational* differences between these Basketmaker villages and the early Pueblo ones. He proposed that later, in Pueblo II, when there is evidence of the development of more aggregated Pueblo villages, "small groups were amalgamated but did not lose their social and ceremonial integrity" (Steward 1955: 163). Citing a fairly consistent ratio of five or six rooms to each kiva as evidence, Steward argued that the initial social unit in the late Basketmaker villages was a local lineage, because each cluster of houses consisted of more than one family and he could imagine no other motive than kin relationships for families living together. The later amalgamation of local groups, in which the room-to-kiva ratio was maintained, suggested a system of exogamous, nonlocalized clans. In the larger villages, clan solidarity, and the clans themselves, could have been lost (as Steward maintained they were among the Eastern Rio Grande Pueblo). Clan association with the kiva was also lost among the Western Pueblo, and Steward suggested that the loss occurred in the 1300s, when there was a dramatic increase in the number of rooms per kiva. For Steward, strong clan solidarity had to be maintained through ritual and other devices, which are most prevalent among the Hopi. The persistence of clans was not viewed as inevitable. It was a path, processual in nature, that could be taken—one logical development that might be followed.

There are two additional aspects of Steward's model that require consideration. First, although the local lineage segments were viewed as natural developments, common on a cross-cultural basis, such segments might be either patrilineal or matrilineal. Steward suggested that Western Pueblo matriliny was an outcome of the long horticultural history of Southwestern groups where the tending of crops was initially done by women as an outgrowth of gathering. Second, Steward could find no ecological reason for the amalgamation of groups into larger villages, assuming land to be abundant, and he suggested defense as a motive. Again, had Steward been aware of the prevalence of the rancheria pattern, he might have considered the possibility that population pressure was an alternative.

Archaeologists have just begun to explore the implications of the contemporaneity of rancherias and unit-type settlements, yet there are no curret statements relating to the organization of early Pueblo villages that specifically supercede Steward's. In part, the absence of new interpretations reflect a late reluctance among Southwestern archaeologists to attempt to describe prehistoric social organization. There had been, in the late 1960s and early 1970s, an exuberant enthusiasm in Southwestern archaeology to examine prehistoric social organization, particularly kinship and residence rules (e.g., Hill 1970; Longacre 1968, 1970). These studies were provocative but subject to a variety of valid criticisms (Aberle 1970; S. Plog 1980; Stanislawski 1969). Until new methods of archaeological analysis are developed, within the context of a rigorous body of theory, this level of inquiry will remain dormant. This is probably less discouraging than it might seem. Fieldwork in the Southwest is demonstrating a degree of heterogeneity among roughly contemporary sites that had not been appreciated in the past. Further, as noted, variations in site plans and assemblages do not coincide with circumscribed geographic zones or with brief periods of time; they cannot therefore be interpreted in purely culture-historical terms. Until the patterns of heterogeneity are thoroughly examined and rigorously tested, archaeologists risk developing explanations for patterns that do not exist or that represent only a small part of the archaeological record.

Summary

In the early centuries of the Christian era, village life spread throughout the Southwest. The appearance of houses, storage facilities, and ceramic containers is related to the sedentism that was made possible by an increased dependence on agriculture. Within the generally risky environments of the Southwest, agriculture was neither productive nor certain enough to provide complete subsistence security, and a number of cultural devices seem to have been used to mitigate subsistence problems.

In the northern and mountainous parts of the Southwest, the success of horticulture is more uncertain than in the Lower Sonoran Desert area. In the more risky settings, early villages seem to have been positioned defensively, perhaps in an effort to ensure that the stores were protected from hostile incursions by neighboring groups of people. In these areas too, the multiplication of storage structures and the adoption of aboveground storerooms may be in response to requirements for storing food for longer periods of time and for more regular emergency situations. The early use of pithouses in these settings may in part be a function of the thermal efficiency of these types of dwellings and to relatively low population densities. In the Sonoran Desert area, crop production seems to have been more secure, villages were not located in defensive situations, and specialized storerooms were not built. The absence of true pithouses in the Hohokam area may be related to warmer winter temperatures.

Heterogeneity in architectural forms, village layout, and ceramic assemblages does not pattern spatially or temporally in ways that are compatible with normative culture-historical interpretations. Further, it is generally acknowledged that the transition to sedentary villages implies that new organizational principles were adopted by Southwestern peoples. These seem to have involved a more specialized use of space; the construction of special ceremonial buildings, perhaps associated with redistribution of goods; and the development of exchange systems among some villages. Whether these developments were associated with marked differences in social roles and social hierarchy is a matter of continued discussion and debate.

Throughout the Southwest, and interdigitated among settlements showing strong normative patterning, are numerous small settlements with heterogenous architectural patterns and apparently less indication of trade. The possible relations among these different kinds of settlements have only begun to be explored. However, the kinds of heterogeneity reflected in the early villages becomes more marked in succeeding centuries, and some of the strong normative patterns seem to indicate short-lived attempts at regional integration. These manifestations are examined in the following chapters.

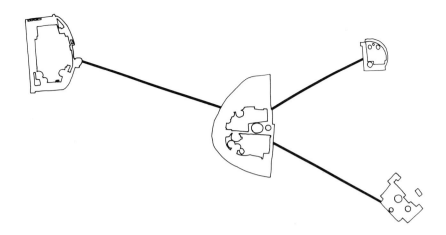

8

Systems of Regional Integration,
A.D. 900–1150

During the latter half of the eleventh century, a large part of the northern Southwest was dominated by a regional system of interaction centered at Chaco Canyon. The nature of this system, the way in which it was organized, is not well defined, but various views are discussed here. Other complex social systems that seem to have developed among the Mogollon and Casas Grandes, Chihuahua, and later among the Hohokam of the Gila and Salt basins are also discussed in this chapter. Finally, despite the presence of these systems, most of the people in the Southwest of this period lived in more simply organized communities, reflecting a considerable amount of adaptive diversity. Some examples of these "areas in between" are given.

The Chaco Phenomenon

In the tenth century a distinctive organization developed within Chaco Canyon. Although probably localized at first, the system eventually incorporated an area of about 53,107 km² of the San Juan Basin and adjacent uplands (Figure 8.1). The Chaco Phenomenon is characterized by construction of large planned towns, the presence of contemporaneous unplanned villages, roads, water-control features, luxury items such as turquoise, copper bells, macaw remains, and inlay, and construction of the Chacoan outliers. Chacoan outliers are sites that are physically outside Chaco Canyon yet exhibit "Chacoan masonry, Chacoan ceramics, Great Kivas or Tower Kivas, and connections to Chaco by means of a roadway and visual communiication system" (Judge 1979:901).

Chaco Canyon

The differences between the town and village sites characteristic of the Chaco Phenomenon are so great that it was generally believed that the village sites predated the town sites or that the two were manifestations of different cultural groups (Gladwin 1945). Hosta Butte phase was used to refer to the village sites and Bonito phase to the town sites. The contemporaneity of the two construction forms was first demonstrated by Florence Hawley Ellis (1934a, 1937a) on the basis of tree-ring dates. That the two types of sites are essentially of the same culture is manifest by the similarity of their material culture inventories. Because the two are contemporary, *phase* is an inappropriate designation. *Style* will be used instead. Hosta Butte style villages are similar to the earlier Pueblo sites in Chaco Canyon. Averaging about 16 rooms, they are single-story structures, generally oriented southeast, that appear to have grown accretionally. Their walls are often of somewhat irregular, simple compound masonry (Figure 8.2). Rooms are typically small and have low ceilings. Plazas are open, not enclosed by walls or room blocks. Kivas are small, with vertical post or pilaster roof supports. Great kivas (discussed below) are not associated with Hosta Butte villages, although a single great kiva (such as the one at the cluster of small villages referred to as Casa Rinconada) may have served several Hosta Butte villages (Figure 8.3). Burials occur in refuse or in subfloor locations. Hosta Butte villages are distributed on both the north and south sides of Chaco Canyon and throughout much of the San Juan Basin. They are apparently more numerous in the vicinity of Bonito towns and Chacoan outliers. The Hosta Butte villages lack tower kivas and luxury items such as inlay,

Figure 8.1 Sites discussed in Chapters 8 and 9. 1, Combwash, Milk Ranch Point, Utah; 2, Cedar Mesa, Utah; 3, Mesa Verde National Park, Colo.; 4, Aztec Ruins National Monument, N. Mex.; 5, Salmon Ruin, N. Mex.; 6, Gallina Area, N. Mex.; 7, Crumbled House, N. Mex.; 8, Mesa Tierra, N. Mex.; 9, Chaco Culture: National Historic Park, N. Mex.; 10, Mesa Pueblo, N. Mex.; 11, Cochiti Pueblo; White Rock Canyon, N. Mex.; 12, Canyon de Chelly National Monument, Ariz.; 13, Manuelito Plateau, N. Mex.; 14, Yellow House, Zuni, N. Mex.; 15, Hopi Buttes, Ariz.; 16, Winona, Ariz.; 17, Hay Hollow, Ariz.; 18, Point of Pines, Ariz.; 19, Los Colonias, Ariz.; 20 Gatlin Site, Ariz.; 21, Snaketown, Ariz.; 22, Escalante Group Ruins, Ariz.; 23, Casa Grande, Ariz.; 24, Mimbres Valley Sites, N. Mex.; 25, Casas Grandes, Chihuahua, Mexico.

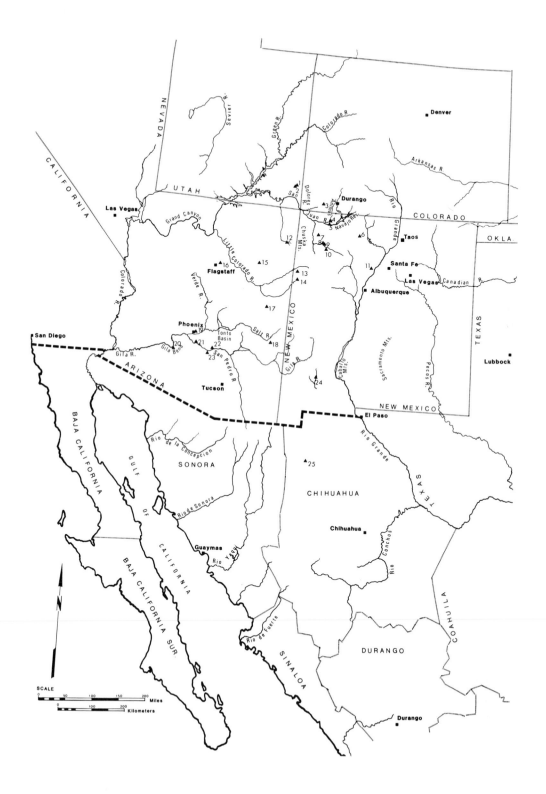

Figure 8.2 Hosta Butte style village, Chaco Canyon, New Mexico. Hosta Butte style villages are of single-story masonry construction. Small kivas are incorporated within the irregular roomblocks, and the room themselves are small. This is site BC-53 as excavated by the University of New Mexico. (Frank H. H. Roberts photographer. Courtesy of the Chaco Center, National Park Service.)

copper bells, macaws, and cylindrical vases. The room-to-kiva ratio is approximately 6.5 to 1 (Hayes 1981a:59; Vivian 1970).

The most striking aspect of the Bonito towns is that they were planned; major architectural units were built at one time by a well-organized labor force (Figure 8.4). In contrast to Hosta Butte sites, Bonito style sites are large, averaging 216 rooms, and multistoried, with up to at least four floors (Figure 8.5 and 8.6). Room size is also large and ceilings are high. The Bonito sites were constructed of cored, veneered masonry in which the load-bearing wall core was composed of rough flat stones set in ample mortar with each stone oriented to only one face of the wall and overlapping or abutting the stone on the reverse face, creating a structurally sound wall. The wall core was then covered on both sides with veneer of coursed ashlar, often in alternating bands of thick and thin stones, forming various patterns. The strikingly decorative veneers (Figure 8.7) were then covered with adobe plaster or matting. Bonito sites are oriented to the south with plaza areas almost always enclosed by a room block or a high wall. Small kivas within the towns occur in a ratio of 1 to every 29 rooms. In contrast to the Hosta Butte kivas, the Bonito kivas had cribbed roofs supported by horizontal logs, generally placed at regular intervals along low benches. The cribbed-log roofs of the Bonito style kivas (Figure 8.8) (Lister and Lister 1981:79) have been found to contain as many as 350 highly dressed pine timbers, many of which must

Figure 8.3 Great kiva at Casa Rinconada, Chaco Canyon, New Mexico. This great kiva served several Hosta Butte style villages. (Photographed by Steve Lekson, 1981. Courtesy of the Chaco Center, National Park Service.)

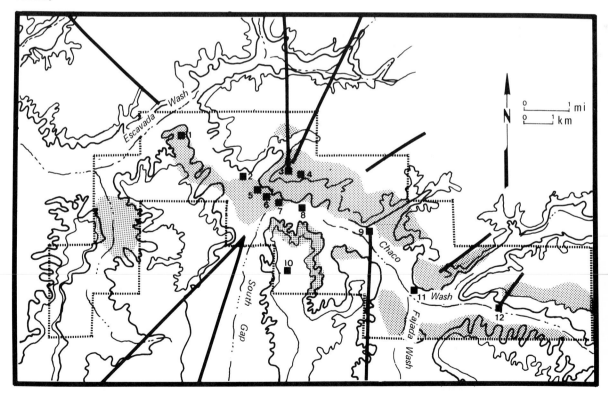

Figure 8.4 Major Bonito sites in Chaco Culture Historical Park. The shaded area shows dense concentrations of Hosta Butte sites. 1, Peñasco Blanco; 2, Casa Chiquita; 3, New Alto; 4, Pueblo Alto; 5, Kin Kletso; 6, Pueblo del Arroyo; 7, Pueblo Bonito; 8, Chetro Ketl; 9, Hungo Pavi; 10, Tsin Kletzin; 11, Una Vida; 12, Wijiji.

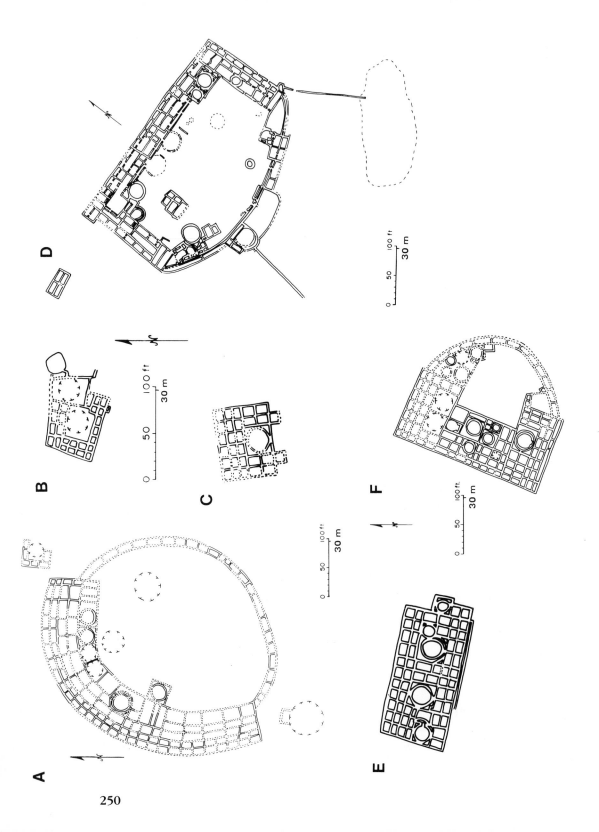

250

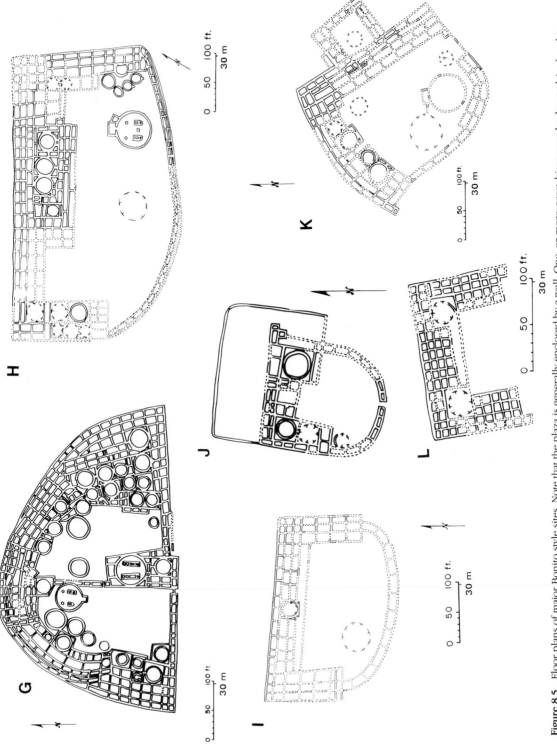

Figure 8.5 Floor plans of major Bonito style sites. Note that the plaza is generally enclosed by a wall. One or more great kivas may be located in the plaza area. Rooms are large and regular in size. These ruins are composed of structures several stories high. Currently, archaeologists interpret the Bonito style sites as public architecture and the Hosta Butte style sites as residential structures. A, Peñasco Blanco; B, Casa Chiquita; C, New Alto; D, Pueblo Alto; E, Kin Kletso; F, Pueblo del Arroyo; G, Pueblo Bonito; H, Chetro Ketl; I, Hungo Pavi; J, Tsin Kletzin; K, Una Vida; L, Wijiji.

251

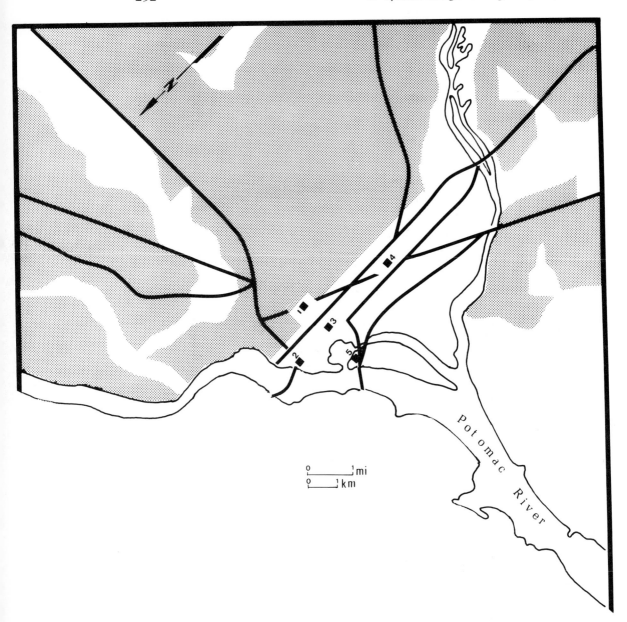

Figure 8.6   The density of public architecture in Chaco Canyon can be compared to that of Washington, D.C. (compare Figure 8.4). The shaded areas represent residential areas. 1, White House; 2, Lincoln Memorial; 3, Washington Monument; 4, U.S. Capitol; 5, Jefferson Memorial.

have been imported from considerable distances. In the wood-poor setting of Chaco Canyon, the use of these cribbed-log roofs is a "constructional extravagance" that indicates considerable ritual significance (Marshall and Doyel 1981:61).

Each of the nine Bonito towns within Chaco Canyon proper has at least one great kiva incorporated within the plaza area. Isolated great kivas, great kivas associated with Hosta Butte villages and with some of the Chacoan outliers, are also documented. Chacoan great kivas are unusual, both in terms of their size and their distinctive floor features. The great kiva at Casa Rinconada (Figure 8.3) is about 19.2 m in diameter; a great kiva at Chetro Ketl (Figure 8.9) is 16.8 m in diameter. Antechambers are com-

Figure 8.7 Decorative ashlar veneer masonry at Bonito style sites, Chaco Canyon, New Mexico. A, Type 2 masonry; B, Type 3 masonry; C, Type 4 masonry. Some scholars suggest that the masonry styles are of chronological significance. (Photographs courtesy of the Chaco Center, National Park Service.)

Figure 8.8 Cribbed-log roof in Bonito style kiva. Enormous numbers of logs were used to roof these structures. The logs were brought into Chaco Canyon from as far away as about 60 km. The roof contained 350 log timbers. (Drawing adapted from the photograph of Kiva L, Pueblo Bonito, as excavated by the National Geographic Society Expedition in 1923. Illustrated by Charles M. Carrillo.)

monly associated with great kivas, and entry to the kiva is either through recessed masonry stairways or by ladder. Floor features are oriented north–south and include square, raised fireboxes, paired masonry "vaults," and roof supports consisting either of four masonry columns or four massive timbers. Huge, shaped sandstone disks were used as seatings for the roof-support timbers (Figure 8.10). Wall niches or crypts have been commonly recorded for great kivas; those at Chetro Ketl II were sealed with masonry and contained strings of stone and shell beads and pendants (Vivian and Reiter 1965). Although it is difficult to estimate the depth of great kivas because the original wall height is not always known, Judd (1922:115–116) estimated that a great kiva at Pueblo Bonito had a wall height of 3.35 m. Considering the size of these structures and the fact that they were largely subterranean, the amount of labor necessary to construct them was enormous.

Fourteen tower kivas (Figure 8.11) are well documented at Bonito sites. These are circular kivas of two or more stories. Although some are free standing, they are most often incorporated within a room block and enclosed by rectangular walls with rubble filling the intervening spaces.

As virtually all investigators have discussed, to their chagrin, burials are scarce at Bonito towns. Hayes (1981a:62) notes that only between 50 and 60 individuals can be associated with the Bonito construction at Pueblo Bonito, a town of over 800 rooms that was occupied over a period of 150 years and, according to Judd, should have experienced between 4700 and 5400 deaths. Although the amount of luxury goods associated with Bonito towns may be exaggerated (this is especially true for the turquoise), some items so far have been found only in Bonito, as opposed to Hosta Butte, contexts. These include cylindrical vases, human effigy vessels, pottery incense burners, copper bells, *Strombus* or *Murex* shell trumpets, painted tablets and effigies of wood, macaw skeletons, and inlay of selenite, mica, or turquoise on shell, wood, or basketry.

Within the 16.1-km stretch of Chaco Canyon surveyed by Hayes (1981a), Bonito town sites are located only on the north side of the canyon. This directional association breaks down when the outliers are included. Hayes notes that the north-side placement of the towns would have put them in greater danger of being flooded by

Figure 8.9 Great kiva at Chetro Ketl. This great kiva is 16.7 m in diameter. The standard great kiva features include the wall niches and encircling bench, central square raised firebox, paired rectangular masonry "vaults," and stair entryway. The antechamber beyond the stairs is a common great kiva feature. (Photograph courtesy of the Chaco Center, National Park Service.)

Figure 8.10 Great kiva at Chetro Ketl during excavation (1936). The massive sandstone disks were supports for the equally huge roof-support timbers. (Photograph courtesy of the Chaco Center, National Park Service.)

Chaco Wash, but their southern exposures provided greater solar radiation, making winter temperatures milder and winters slightly shorter. In addition, Hayes tentatively suggests that the north-side placement of the towns within the canyon proper allows for easier direct visual communication to the signaling stations that are also part of the Chacoan system. These stations are arc-shaped stone structures on high points with direct line-of-sight visibility to the Bonito towns.

The efficacy of the signaling stations was demonstrated experimentally during a recent summer field season. Archaeologists working in Chaco Canyon equipped themselves with railroad flares and stationed themselves at these features. At 9:00 P.M. the flares were lit and visual communication was established between each signaling station and its two neighboring stations. The only locations at which the flares could not be seen were in the vicinity of the modern town of Crownpoint, where electric lights interfered. Although some may object that the use of railroad flares does not constitute a true test, the experiment lends some credence to the interpretation of the otherwise rather enigmatic features. Another Bonito feature, primarily associated with the topography of the north side of Chaco Canyon, is the system of headgates, dams, and ditches of the water-control systems (as discussed in Chapter 6).

The Chacoan roads were known to the Navajo living in Chaco Canyon, and parts of them were first described in print by Holsinger (1901). Only recently, however, has there been a systematic attempt to define them and trace their extent (Lyons and Hitchcock 1977; Obenauf 1980; Robertson 1983; Vivian 1972). Among the most consistent attributes of the Chacoan roads is their straight course: The roads are not contoured to topographic relief. Changes in direction are accomplished with a sharp angular turn rather than a curve. When roads approach a major topographic obstacle, such as a cliff or ledge, they are associated with stairways or ramps . The stairways vary in form from shallowly pecked finger- and toe-holds, to masonry steps consisting of two or three stones piled in front of a rock ledge, to well-constructed flights of wide steps with treads and risers cut out of the bedrock (Figure 8.12). Ramps are either stone or earth-filled masonry structures that may occur in conjunction with stairways or with road segments interrupted by ledges.

There is also variability in the form and preparation of the roads. In some instances they were cut into bedrock or through aeolian soil to a depth of 1.5 m, but other roads were simply created by the removal of vegetation, loose soil, and debris. Some road segments are lined with masonry borders; others are visible only as slight swales on

Figure 8.11   Salmon Ruin, Bloomfield, New Mexico. Salmon Ruin is a major Chacoan outlier. Note the similarity in ground plan to Bonito style sites in Chaco Canyon. The arrow points to the tower kiva. The great kiva can be seen in the plaza. (Photograph courtesy of the Chaco Center, National Park Service.)

the landscape. The widths of the roadways are also distinctive; for example, major roadways are about 9 m wide and secondary roads are about 4.5 m wide (Vivian 1972). The extent of the roads has been defined through the use of aerial photography, with some ground-checking and more limited excavation, but the entire road system is not completely documented. Obenauf (1980) provides the most reliable map available (Figure 8.13).

Figure 8.12 Jackson Staircase, Chaco Canyon, New Mexico. Well-constructed flights of steps cut into the bedrock are components of the Chacoan road system. (Photograph courtesy of the Chaco Center, National Park Service.)

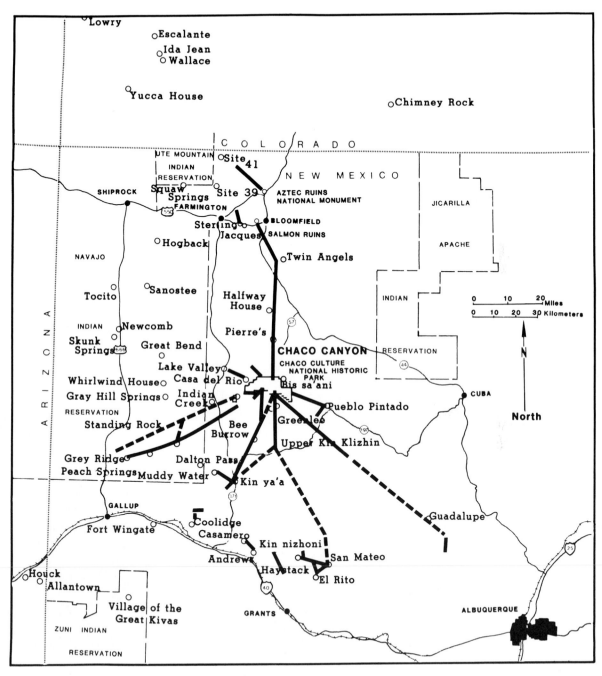

Figure 8.13   Chacoan road system and outliers. Chacoan outliers are named and indicated by open circles. The road segments shown as solid lines have been documented by ground surveys. The dashed line segments are known only from aerial photographs. (Illustrated by Charles M. Carrillo, after Obenauf [1980].)

The roads themselves are, of course, difficult to date; because they connect Bonito style sites, there seems little doubt that they are associated with the major developments of the Chaco Phenomenon. Some of the roads lead from Chaco Canyon toward outliers such as Salmon Ruin (Figure 8.11), Aztec (Figure 8.14), and Kin Bineola. Other roads seem to lead to resources areas, such as the relatively well-watered and wooded Dutton Plateau and the Yellow House area of the modern Zuni Reservation. About 402.3 km of roads have been identified. The massive engineering effort involved in their construction—their linearity and width—clearly sets them apart from the aboriginal trail systems. The function of the road system is not known; however, the roads may have been used to facilitate communication or to transport resources to and from Chaco Canyon. As the Listers state, "No other aboriginal land communica-

Figure 8.14 Aztec Ruins National Monument, Aztec, New Mexico. Aztec ruins is very similar to Salmon Ruin (Figure 8.11). Both are Chacoan outliers with later "Mesa Verde" occupations. The great kiva at Aztec has been reroofed by the National Park Service. (The photograph, taken in 1974, is used through the courtesy of Steven A. LeBlanc.)

tion system of such magnitude and purpose has been recognized north of Mexico. Certainly it was a product of group organization, controls, and a lot of human energy" (1981:147)

Chaco Outliers

The Chacoan outliers are heterogeneous in formal characteristics, but they share the following attributes. They are outside Chaco Canyon proper, yet they exhibit Chacoan core veneer masonry, Chacoan ceramic assemblages, and either great kivas or tower kivas (or both), and they are connected to Chaco Canyon by means of a roadway or a visual communication system of signaling stations. About 70 outliers have been identified, varying in distance from Chaco Canyon from about 4.83 to about 80.5 km. Two that have been the focus of recent excavation projects are discussed here.

Salmon Ruin, near Bloomfield, New Mexico, like Aztec (Morris 1915), is a dual-component site with an earlier Chacoan structure and a later "Mesa Verde" occupation. Excavation at the site has been carried out by the San Juan Valley Archaeological Project (Irwin-Williams 1980a,b). The Chacoan structure consists of about 290 rooms, a great kiva, and a tower kiva. It was built in three planned building episodes between 1088 and 1106 (Figures 8.11, 8.15). Construction is of core veneer masonry in the Chacoan style. The principal architectural grouping of the pueblo consists of room suites composed of four rooms oriented from front to back. The front room of each suite is a large, single-story square room with a T-shaped doorway facing the plaza or opening into the gallery. Front rooms contain internal features such as firepits. Behind the front room of each suite, and connected to it and to each other by doorways, are three smaller, rectangular, two-story rooms that generally lack floor features. The plaza gallery runs along the north room block and is a single-story covered walkway with entrances to the front rooms and the plaza. Two ceremonial areas are contained within the pueblo. A great kiva, 15 m in diameter, is located off center in the plaza. The second ceremonial area consists of a tower kiva, 10 m in diameter, built on top of a large circular cobble platform, and a series of rooms that are contiguous to the tower kiva.

Planning and productive specialization were important features of the Chacoan occupation at Salmon. Excavations indicate that foundations for the entire town were laid out prior to construction. The timbers used were of large trees, such as ponderosa pine, Douglas fir, and white fir, which are available in quantity only in areas as much as 80 km from the site. Productive specialization is further indicated by milling rooms, each of which contained an average of six to eight milling stones set in place. Only four milling rooms were encountered in the excavation of the Chacoan occupation of the site. Domesticates make up the bulk of the subsistence items found here, and, of these, productive varieties of flint corn are the most abundant. This hard-shelled corn, although possibly somewhat more difficult to process than flour corn, is superior to flour corn in storage qualities because it is resistant to insects and rodents. Additional evidence of productive specialization is a room that contained deep trough metates

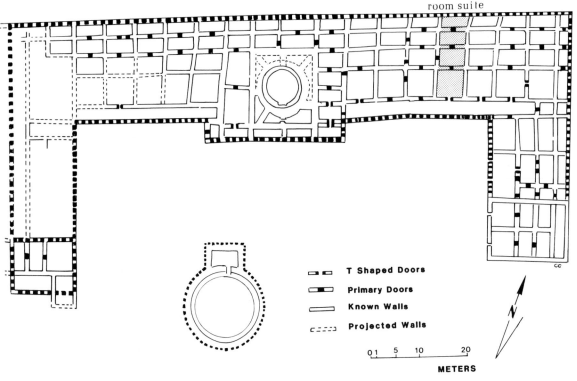

Figure 8.15 Plan of Salmon Ruin, Bloomfield, New Mexico. Plan shows the Chacoan construction phase III (A.D. 1100–1107) at Salmon. A standard room suite has been shaded. (Adapted from Irwin-Williams [1980a] by Charles M. Carrillo.)

(necessary for milling the flint corn) in all stages of manufacture, maintenance, and repair.

Studies of the distributions of ceramic forms and wares were interpreted to indicate the orderly way in which space was used in the Chacoan occupation of Salmon Ruin and are informative about specialization and the likely composition of the site's founding population. The interpretations, however, assume that the ceramics and other items were excavated from areas in which they were used rather than just discarded. The large front rooms contained high frequencies of jars of all kinds, indicating a primary storage function. Ceremonial features, such as the great kiva, had high frequencies of bowls and unusual forms such as canteens and pitchers (Figure 8.16), suggesting food consumption and ceremonial use but not food preparation or storage. The wares represented at Salmon include both locally produced San Juan types and intrusive Cibola ceramics. Studies of the distributions of these were used to examine views about the origins of the founders of the pueblo.

Irwin-Williams (1980a) proposes that if a group of colonists from Chaco Canyon founded Salmon, the residence units should contain a large proportion of imported ceramics. In fact, locally produced San Juan pottery dominates the room suites, suggesting that the potters belonged to the local population. Irwin-Wiliams also considered the notion that the founding population was purely local and borrowed ideas and traded ceramics from the Chaco. As she states, this is unlikely because

> what is present in these large outliers is not simply a group of "traits," objects, or architectural characteristics. Rather, it involves an integrated cultural phenomenon reflecting a high degree of technical knowledge and specialization and a centralized authority structure, tight social control, and membership in a complex network economically and physically linked to the Chaco. (Irwin-Williams 1980a:163)

The distribution of ceramic wares imported from the Cibola area was, in fact, neither random throughout the pueblo nor patterned in a way that would indicate general accessibility to imported goods. Rather, the Cibolan ceramics were concentrated in the residences on the west side of the pueblo and at specialized activity areas such as the milling rooms, the milling-stone production and repair room, and the tower kiva and its associated rooms. This distribution suggests that the founding population was composed of both a local San Juan group and a group of Chacoan origins, and that the specialized ceremonial and production and processing activities were controlled by the Chacoan elements. The distribution of Washington Pass chert, an imported, high-quality lithic material, essentially follows that of the imported Cibolan ceramics and lends additional support to the idea that specific activities involved personnel with access to the Chacoan system.

Figure 8.16 Chacoan pitcher. Unusual forms such as this are found at Bonito style sites but not at Hosta Butte style sites. At Salmon Ruin the unusual forms are more frequently located in association with the great kiva than at other parts of the site. (Photograph courtesy of the Museum of New Mexico.)

The research at Salmon also concerned itself with the question of social or economic ranking. Non-Cibolan imported ceramics, which might be considered status items, were found not to distribute with the Chaco-related group. Although differential mortuary treatment is a good indicator of social ranking, in the Salmon case, as with other Chacoan sites, the lack of burials precluded this kind of inquiry. In fact, only three burials could be related to the Chacoan occupation at Salmon. Finally, the standardization in both size and arrangement of the room suite units indicated no internal ranking with regard to differential use or control of space.

These observations led to the conclusion that within the Salmon community there was no evidence of social or economic ranking. On the other hand, the occurrence of Chacoan imports with the tower kiva and associated rooms, in addition to the labor investment in these structures, suggested that "ideology played a central role in systemic organization" (Irwin-Williams 1980a:172). However, if the Chacoan outliers such as Salmon represent the "elite" accomplishments of a regionally based complex system, then the lack of ranking within a single outlier is entirely expectable. As noted, there are some 70 outliers currently documented; the number of small Anasazi villages contemporaneous with the Chacoan Phenomenon currently recorded in the San Juan Basin is more than 5364 (Cordell 1982). It would be expected that these small, local villages, which greatly outnumber the Chacoan outliers in the basin, represent the lower order of the hierarchy.

The work at Salmon was primarily concentrated on that site, and only a small-scale effort was involved in local and regional surveys. In addition, the area around Salmon (along the San Juan River) has been tremendously impacted by modern land development, and the archaeological resources have suffered accordingly. Nevertheless, the San Juan Valley Archaeological Project did examine the regional expansion of the Chacoan system through surveys of settlements on the San Juan, Animas, and La Plata rivers. These surveys suggested a model of Chacoan regional expansion that is given here and evaluated at the conclusion of this section.

The survey data suggested that Chacoan penetration into new areas was conducted in two sequential phases. First, either small colonies or special-function sites (such as great kivas) were located in a new area without impacting the local population or integrating that population into the Chacoan trade network. Subsequently, presuming the first stage was successful, the new region was fully incorporated within the Chacoan distribution system and the region was connected to Chaco by the construction of a roadway. The survey suggested that the San Juan drainage in the vicinity of Salmon was so incorporated, but that the Animas Valley was not, although Chacoan outliers are known from the latter area.

A different variety of Chacoan outlier is discussed in the preliminary reports of the excavation of Bi sa' ani on Escavada Wash (Figure 8.17) about 4.82 km northwest of Fajada Butte in Chaco Canyon (Marshall and Doyel 1981). (Only suggestions from the first season of excavation and analysis are considered here.) Bi sa' ani is situated on an eroded badland ridge some 15–20 m above the surrounding desert plain. The ruin consists of five separate structures: An eastern complex comprising four distinct buildings is separated by 110 m of eroded badland ridge from the western complex, which

Figure 8.17 Bi sa' ani Ruin. Artist's reconstruction of the unusual Chacoan outlier of Bi sa' ani. The complex pictured overlooks residential sites. Bi sa' ani was constructed late in the history of the Chacoan system. (Illustrated by Charles M. Carrillo.)

consists of one major ruin. All of the construction material used, an estimated 1250 m³ of rock and earth, was imported to the ridgetop from below, and most of the rock was obtained from a source about 1 km away. As the excavators note, "this type of elevated structural mass attests to the communal energies of the Bi sa' ani Anasazi and truly qualifies for the title of monumental architecture" (Marshall and Doyel 1981:6).

The oldest structure at Bi sa' ani is a 20-room pueblo built of puddled coursed adobe, a form of construction so far unique to Chacoan contexts in the San Juan Basin. (The use of adobe "turtle backs" and jacal occurs in the basin, but coursed adobe construction had not been documented previously.) The outside of the structure was apparently decorated with a bright band of red plaster at the base and white plaster above this. Room interiors also show the use of white plaster. Although most of the artifacts found within the structure are typically early twelfth-century Bonito style, some of the ceramics are Socorro Black-on-white, a type prevalent in the central Rio Grande Valley. The three other structures on the eastern side of the ridge consist of massive Chacoan masonry buildings, including four kivas. The ruin on the western portion of the ridge is a single, enclosed, masonry kiva backed by an elevated block of 10 masonry rooms. Although it is much closer to Chaco Canyon than is Salmon, tree-ring dates indicate that Bi sa' ani was built somewhat later, in about 1125. The excavators believe it was inhabited for no more than 30–50 years. Among the artifacts from the Bi sa' ani assemblage are a cache of cult objects found in the adobe structure, five shell beads, a copper bell, and a few stone ornaments including a turquoise pendant and a highly polished jet ring. With the exception of the Socorro Black-on-white ceramics and a few brownware sherds, most of the Bi sa' ani ceramics are not unusual, that is, exotic forms (effigies, cylinder vases) were not encountered. Utility vessels occur in relatively high frequency, and nearly two-thirds of these exhibit carbonization, indicating that they were used for cooking rather than for storage. Corn and squash remains were recovered from the site, as were various wild plant taxa. The latter did not contain species maturing in spring or early summer, suggesting that Bi sa' ani was only fully occupied in the late summer and fall.

The major architectural features at Bi sa' ani are the kivas. The artifact assemblage does not indicate that food storage or craft-related activities (manufacture of stone tools, ceramics, etc.) were important activities at the site. Food preparation is indicated by the carbonized utility vessels. The investigators note that "food processing and preparation do not necessarily mean that these areas had strictly domestic functions. Food processing and preparation activities are often associated with public functions as well" (Marshall and Doyel 1981:51–52).

One the desert plain below the badland ridge where the Bi sa' ani structures were built, 37 Anasazi sites roughly contemporaneous with Bi sa' ani were located. These "community" sites have been only partially investigated; however, they are unusual in some respects within the Chacoan complex. First, they show a high percentage of Socorro Black-on-white and Mogollon brownware ceramics. Second, at least three of the small sites are of puddled coursed adobe construction. Some of the sites have unusual architectural features, such as subterranean storage rooms, and one site consists of a masonry kiva constructed with typical Chacoan kiva features but completely above ground (Breternitz and Doyel 1983).

Models of Development

In discussing the character of Bi sa' ani with respect to the entire Chacoan system, Marshall and Doyel refer to Bi sa' ani and similar communities (Pierre's site, Grey Hill Springs, Whirlwind Lake) as *scion,* meaning descendant, communities. Scion communities are characterized by having been established late in the Chacoan period in areas that appear to have marginal agricultural potential. The researchers suggest that they developed (1) as a result of increased population in order to increase regional carrying capacity, (2) as a response to factional splits in ancestral communities, (3) as a result of an organized effort to develop logistical nodes along roadways, (4) or as satellite colonies for the exploitation of regional resources. Whatever the strict function of the various types of Chacoan outlying structures, Marshall and Doyel provide poetic insight:

> Bonito-style architecture is, however, more than the construction of a building having a certain characteristic form. It is also an architectural tradition which utilizes masonry to produce monumental structures. . . . Bonito-style architecture, particularly in outlying regions, makes considerable use of the dramatic character of the landscape. The buildings often appear as extensions of pinnacle spires, mesa cliffs, and canyon walls. They may also appear in great topographic isolation, a human monument in the void of the desert plain. A sense of place is clearly a very important aspect of Bonito-style architecture, especially in the outlying districts. It is as if the environment were personified with attributes of mythological character, and the placement of the structures were dictated by Chacoan cosmography and sacred geography, balanced by certain economic considerations. (1981:61)

Irwin-Williams' (1980b) discussion of Chacoan colonization of the middle San Juan and La Plata areas and Marshall and Doyel's (1981) treatment of scion communities reflect attempts, from different perspectives, to account for the development of the Bonito style and the Chaco Phenomenon. The spectacular nature and high density of Bonito style sites within the Chaco Canyon proper had, of course, provoked a long history of discussions among archaeologists regarding the origins of these developments. (Lister and Lister 1981 is a good source for these.) What has changed as the result of definition of the road systems and Chacoan outliers is that archaeologists are now attempting to explain the nature and development of a regional system—the Chaco Phenomenon. Not surprisingly, there are several alternative models. Some of these are discussed here.

W. James Judge, director of the National Park Service's Chaco Project, views the Bonito developments as the result of two factors: the history of developments within Chaco Canyon prior to the appearance of the Bonito style, and specific geological and geographic characteristics of the area (Judge *et al.* 1981). Survey data (Hayes 1981a) indicate that between A.D. 500 and 900 population increased within Chaco Canyon. A settlement shift away from the elevated mesas above the canyon had occurred by 700, suggesting an increase in the importance of agriculture. Judge believes that by A.D. 900 subsistence probably consisted of a primary reliance on crops supplemented by game and wild plant foods, but without major labor investments in permanent water- and soil-control facilities. At the same time, variability in both the quantity and spatial distribution of summer rainfall would have created a situation of subsistence stress involving both cultigens and wild resources. Increased populations throughout the basin would have largely precluded the option of compensating for resource stress through increased mobility. More intensive hunting and gathering would likewise be limited by competition. Judge suggests that the solution adopted in the late ninth and early tenth centuries was to increase the amount of acreage under cultivation by expanding into nearby areas of relatively high risk.

Dendroclimatological data indicate an increase in summer rainfall at about A.D. 910, which would have somewhat lowered the amount of risk involved in cultivating more marginal areas. Nevertheless, the results of this strategy would have been variable locally, seasonally, and yearly. Judge suggests that an appropriate mechanism for equalizing these risks would have been resource "pooling" or redistribution. "[Pooling] requires a central repository to which goods can be brought for immediate distribution, or stored for redistribution at a later time. Further, even on an elemental level, the process requires some kind of administration or management, be it by an individual or group" (Judge *et al.* 1981:80).

Whether or not the managerial requirements involved in resource pooling entailed differential status positions, pooling itself necessitates some kind of center or repository to serve as a locus for collection, communal storage, and redistribution. Judge suggests that in the tenth century three sites were constructed in Chaco Canyon that served this function. These are Una Vida, situated at the confluence of the Chaco, Gallo, and Fajada washes; Pueblo Bonito, located on Chaco Wash across the canyon from the South Gap drainages; and Peñasco Blanco, built near the confluence of

Chaco, Escavada, and Padilla washes. The locations of these sites are important because the drainage areas of the various washes differ, and while one wash may be dry another may be running. The sites are therefore in positions that maximize the opportunity to receive moisture despite high local variability in rainfall patterns. Although each of the three sites eventually became classic Bonito style towns, their configurations in the early 900s were of an arc-shaped room block of three "modular" units consisting of a front room backed by two smaller rooms. Despite their basic similarity to other sites of the period, three characteristics are cited that set them apart. First, they were multistoried. Second, they were larger than most contemporary sites, being composed of more "modular units." Finally, the masonry at each site was distinctive evidence of a higher degree of craftsmanship than that at other sites.

The architectural similarities among the three sites and their nearly contemporaneous construction suggests to Judge that a canyon-wide organization existed at Chaco in the tenth century. Expansion of the spatial extent of the redistributive network may have occurred during periods of increased subsistence stress from a variety of causes, such as decreased summer rainfall or increased population–resource imbalances. "As more redistributive networks and alliance groups were brought into the system, Chaco Canyon itself could emerge as a central place of a different magnitude within the San Juan Basin as a whole" (Judge et al. 1981:88).

Judge considers it possible that the later Chacoan outliers initially served as redistributive centers for their own local and subregional systems, and that they were later incorporated into the Chacoan network. On the other hand, he considers it equally likely that Chaco Canyon itself had primacy in this development, the system expanding outward from this initial core. Elsewhere, Judge (1979) argues that a regionally-based system was essential to the stability and resource security of Chaco. In essence, this expansion of agricultural production would have entailed local risks that could be offset by a regionally based redistributive system. The system, in turn, would require full-time specialists, but these could not have been supported by a single community. Consequently, a region-wide system is envisioned, and Judge suggested that turquoise, which was processed at Chaco, may have functioned as a medium of exchange within the system.

A somewhat different opinion on the matter of Chacoan primacy is expressed by Marshall and Doyel. These investigators note that "the pattern of centralized community organization, involving the constellation of various habitation and special-function sites about a great kiva or Bonito-style building" (Marshall and Doyel 1981:71), is a common feature of the eastern Anasazi area as a whole, but it is lacking among the western Anasazi of the Kayenta and Virgin areas. Viewed as an Eastern Anasazi characteristic, with origins in the great kivas of the Basketmaker III period, it cannot be considered Chaco-specific. In fact, Marshall and Doyel suggest that:

> Chaco Canyon as a central place evolved as a product of interaction with the peripheral area of developments. Chaco Canyon may be envisioned as a central node developed by the outlying communities to create an intercommunity regional organization. From this perspective, it is possible that the great pueblos of Chaco Canyon are regional affiliates representative of certain community aggregates in the outlying provinces. (1981:72)

They acknowledge, of course, that their notion must be viewed as a hypothesis and tested.

In commenting on the view expressed by Marshall and Doyel, four issues may be raised. First, the tremendous diversity of kiva styles present in some of the Bonito style structures in Chaco Canyon does make one wonder if the populations contributing to this manifestation of public architecture represented many local traditions. On the other hand, the suggestion that Chaco served as a central node for regional affiliates is similar to the contention of Blanton (1978) that the founding of Monte Albán in Oaxaca, Mexico, is an example of a *disembedded capital.* Blanton's argument, that Monte Albán was founded by political fiat involving the agreement of autonomous regional governments, has been severely criticised, from the perspective of both Mesoamerican (Sanders and Santley 1978) and worldwide (Willey 1979) studies. Many of the same criticisms would be appropriate to the Chaco case. More important however, is the difficulty of imagining several local polities in the eastern Anasazi area having enough political centralization in the early tenth century to found a regional center by governmental agreement. Another objection that may be raised is empirical and regards the lack of early dates for highly centralized communities outside of Chaco Canyon itself. If new early dates for such communities are obtained, the argument will be strengthened. Finally, Marshall and Doyel apparently assume the structural equality of all aggregated communities in the eastern Anasazi area.

Irwin-Williams (1980a) provides conceptual and empirical support for a different interpretation. She argues that, over time, Pueblo adaptive systems have involved three systemic states—dispersed, aggregated, and nucleated—and that each of these three results from different processes. The dispersed state is not of direct concern here. The aggregated state is understood as the result of the process of increasing concentration of previously dispersed populations. The aggregation of population into larger settlements requires new integrative mechanisms, such as community-wide sodalities, community leadership, and internal regulating mechanisms. Nevertheless, these are quite different, in her view, from the organizational properties of nucleated communities, which she avers are uniquely represented by the Chaco Phenomenon. The nucleated pattern would involve

> an abrupt increase in the internal integrated centralization or nucleation of all elements around a dominant socio-economic core of institutions and unique personnel, and the development of a suprasystem with numerous characteristics not found in the component subsystems. It is characterized by an elaboration at all levels of internal self-regulating mechanisms, beyond those required for simple homeostatic adjustments. (Irwin-Williams 1980a:5–6)

In order to explore further the differences between aggregated and nucleated community structure, a comparison between the Chacoan and "Mesa Verdean" occupations at Salmon Ruin is informative. As noted above, the secondary occupation at Salmon showed changes in architecture and in ceramics that are generally interpreted as more closely affiliated with the Mesa Verde Anasazi than with the Chaco. A similar pattern is documented at Aztec and in Chaco Canyon itself. The nature of the "Mesa Verde" influence within Chaco Canyon is discussed in somewhat more detail below;

here, the emphasis is on Salmon, in part because the secondary occupation used the same site (i.e., the same space) but radically reorganized the community pattern.

In about A.D. 1130 a number of architectural modifications were made at Salmon. The entryways to the room suites and internal connecting doorways were sealed. Access to these spaces then would have been by hatchways in the roofs. The rear interior rooms were abandoned, and the total amount of storage space within the site was reduced. The gallery exits were closed off and the interior gallery space was subdivided. The masonry used to subdivide the gallery and to close off the entryways was of consistently inferior quality. It is important that the gallery rooms are not aligned architecturally with the domestic divisions of the Chacoan component. In contrast to the imported, large tree species used in the Chacoan component, structural wood of the secondary occupation was largely locally available juniper.

Changes are also noted in food-preparation space. Again in contrast to the Chacoan component, the secondary-occupation milling rooms contained only an average of 1.5 milling stones per room, and a total of nine milling rooms were excavated. Cooking areas were placed in some of the gallery rooms and in the plaza of the secondary component, but a large, presumably communal area of maize-parching pits was also located outside, behind the main structure. In contrast to the Chacoan occupation, the later occupation showed an increase in the use of wild plant species for food and a change to the use of the various flour varieties of maize. Although the great kiva and tower kiva continued to be in use during the secondary occupation, more than 20 small kivas were set into existing room block structures and plaza areas, indicating far less integration and centralization of the ideological aspects of the community. Both bone tools and projectile points of the secondary occupation showed more stylistic variation than those of the preceding occupation. Finally, in contrast to the Chacoan occupation, 90% of the secondary-occupation ceramics consisted of locally produced ceramics.

Irwin-Williams (1980a) argues that the secondary occupation at Salmon is representative of the more usual Anasazi pattern of aggregation, lacking the tight social control and specialization reflected in the nucleated Chacoan communities. Furthermore, she maintains that the path of development over much of the Anasazi area was from dispersed to aggregated communities of this type, whereas the nucleated pattern reflected very different constraints imposed by the Chacoan developments. This is an important distinction. By grouping all large aggregated communities together as examples of a single Eastern Anasazi pattern, the crucial differences in community organization are obscured. What becomes abundantly clear when aggregated and nucleated community types are distinguished is that the nucleated structure of the Chaco Phenomenon was a very short-lived and apparently fragile mechanism of regional interaction. The aggregated pattern, on the other hand, appears to have been far more resilient and flexible, persisting in some areas into the late prehistoric and historic periods.

With the disruption of the Chacoan system, the period of regional integration within the San Juan Basin came to an end; however, there was no immediate complete abandonment. Rather, between A.D. 1120 and 1220, changes occurred in Chaco Canyon that have been interpreted as evidence of the intrusion of Mesa Verde migrants into the area (Lister and Lister 1981; Vivian and Mathews 1965). Within Chaco Canyon these late developments are sometimes referred to as the McElmo phase and include the pueblos referred to as Casa Chiquita, Kin Kletso, New Alto, and Tsin Kletzin in addition to various modifications of and increments to existing Chacoan sites such as Pueblo del Arroyo and Pueblo Alto. The changes in Chaco consist of the construction of Mesa Verde keyhole-shaped kivas, the use of double-coursed masonry (but not core veneer masonry), of which the exterior facings were shaped by pecking, a change in burial practices (in that burials are present), and the use of carbon-painted Mesa Verde style ceramics (such as Chaco McElmo, McElmo, and Mesa Verde Black-on-white types).

Toll *et al.* (1980) have reexamined the character of the McElmo phase. Their work, which includes a great many archaeomagnetic dates, indicates that the late twelfth- and early thirteenth-century occupation of Chaco Canyon was much more extensive than previously known. There is thus occupational continuity between the Bonito and McElmo styles. Additionally, detailed analyses of ceramics, including petrographic and microscopic discriminations of tempers, refiring experiments, and stylistic studies, demonstrate that there is also continuity in the ceramic tradition that would not be expected if the McElmo style pottery were the result of an intrusion of Mesa Verde immigrants. Some ceramics from the late assemblages were imported from the San Juan area; ceramics were still imported from the Chuskas were found, as well as those of local manufacture. "Since the attributes of the latest ceramics show affinities to those of the preceding times, it is likely that the 'old' system was still in part operative, and the most parsimonious explanation for its continuation is that Chaco residents remained" (Toll *et al.* 1980:114).

One current interpretation of the McElmo phase in Chaco Canyon and elsewhere is that it represents a change in economic affiliation toward the Mesa Verde area that was the major remaining population center after the disruption of the Chaco Phenomenon. With respect to the changes in burial practices noted, Toll and others comment: "if, as seems nearly undeniable, the San Juan area succeeded Chaco as a regional center, it is not at all unreasonable to suggest that its influence was much more than merely economic in the sense of purely goods exchange" (Toll *et al.* 1980:115); or, more bluntly: "It is well to remember than an economic shift will inevitably have effects on the rest of the cultural system" (Toll *et al.* 1980:115).

The regional interpretations of the Chaco Phenomenon have emphasized both ideology (ceremonial control) and economy (resource acquisition and trade). Although the general aspects of planning and stylistic uniformity within the regional aspects of the Chacoan system imply a strong ideological basis of the system, in the absence of written records the ideological component of culture is one of the most difficult for archaeologists to address. Two directions of archaeological inquiry into the nature of ideological systems are presented here: archaeoastronomy and symmetry analysis.

Agricultural peoples throughout the world are concerned with calendrical observations. These are crucial to the timing of planting and harvesting outside the equatorial regions and to water management where supplemental watering is necessary to ensure the success of crops. In Chaco Canyon, and in the San Juan Basin as a whole, both short growing seasons and inadequate rainfall are problems for agriculturalists, so it is likely that accurate astronomical observations were important to the Chaco Anasazi. Furthermore, the contemporary Pueblo make such observations for the timing of ritual and secular activities. With these considerations in mind, a number of investigators have examined alignments of architectural features and rock art for their relevance to astronomical observation. None of these studies is conclusive; however, there have been some suggestive results. For example, two third-story, exterior, corner windows at Pueblo Bonito may have been used to record the sunrise at the winter solstice (Figure 8.18) (Reyman 1976). Similarly, wall niches in the great kiva at Casa Rinconada have been related to observations of the sunrise at solstices and equinoxes (Morgan 1977; Williamson *et al.* 1977). Finally, Sofar *et al.* (1979) describe a solar marking construct consisting of boulders and a spiral petroglyph at Fajada Butte;

Figure 8.18 Solstice window at Pueblo Bonito. The window may have been positioned to permit the observance of the sunrise at winter solstice. (Photograph courtesy of he Chaco Center, National Park Service.)

Reyman (1980), although agreeing that the formation functions as a solar calendar is not convinced that it is associated with the Anasazi occupation at Chaco. In general, although there is considerable interest in documenting astronomical features in Chaco, some of the difficulties encountered include stabilization and renovation of buildings that may have altered the original appearance of doors, walls, and other features (Lister and Lister 1981:177), the deterioration of architecture and bowing of walls and windows (Reyman 1976), and the ambiguity of the effects of roofing on observations made at great kivas.

Archaeoastronomical studies involve replication experiments, including observations of the position of the sun with respect to features at solstices and at other times. It is far more difficult to infer the content of other ideological components of the Chacoan system. In one attempt along these lines, Fritz (1978) discusses the Chacoan architectural design as a symbolic representation of a Chacoan world view. He examines the symmetrical and asymmetrical aspects of Chacoan architectural design at the level of individual spaces (the partitioning of a single "feature" like the great kiva at Casa Rinconada), aggregated spaces (divisions of space within Pueblo Bonito), and spaces within the Chacoan core area (the distribution of sites within the canyon). Fritz finds a quite consistent relation between the equivalency of spaces east and west of a north–south dividing line and asymmetry of structures and spaces north and south of the east–west lines. Whether these patterns represent metaphors for natural, social, and ideological relations, as suggested, they are nevertheless quite consistent.

In sum, analyses of the Chaco Phenomenon view it as a highly organized, centralized, hierarchical, regional sociopolitical system. The views discussed vary to the extent that some see the expression as originating within the Chaco Canyon core area and expanding outward, whereas others suggest that it is one aspect of a pan-eastern Anasazi development. These views recognize the importance of the ideological component of the systemic integration, but they consider the Chaco Phenomenon as a short-lived indigenously Anasazi response to the basically economic constraints of population–resource imbalances within the agriculturally risky San Juan Basin. Another group of scholars (Di Peso 1974; Hayes 1981a; Kelley and Kelley 1975; Lister and Lister 1981) attribute the development of the Chaco Phenomenon to the influence of Mesoamerican cultures effected through the actions of long-distance traders. This view is generally referred to as the *pochteca* (or *puchteca*) model.

The *pochteca* were a class of long-distance traders, middlemen (and sometimes spies) who occupied this special status within Aztec society, as documented by various historic and ethnohistoric accounts (e.g., Sahagún 1959: Vol. 2). The Aztec period in Mesoamerica was a post-Classic development that occurred several hundred years after the Chaco Phenomenon, and no one attributes Chacoan developments to the Aztecs. Rather, the *pochteca* model is an analogy that suggests that a group of long-distance traders similar to the Aztec *pochteca* operated out of earlier states in Mesoamerica, and in their activities "created" the Chaco Phenomenon, as well as other regionally based systems (such as Casas Grandes).

Support for the *pochteca* model minimally depends on clear evidence of Mesoamerican traits in the Southwest, trade items from the Southwest in Mexico, and an abrupt change in technology or settlement configurations in the Southwest that is attributable to Mesoamerican interference. The *pochteca* model has been invoked to account for core veneer masonry, column-fronted galleries, possibly a platform mound with an inset stairway at Talus Unit I behind Chetro Ketl, and towers. To this list, proposed nearly 30 years ago (Ferdon 1955), other possible features have been added including seating disks for roof support posts, T-shaped doorways (see Love 1975 for the distribution of these features), effigy vessels, ceremonial wooden canes, roadways and signaling stations, rock-cut stairways, and irrigation devices (Lister and Lister 1981).

Even the most ardent devotees of indigenous development of the Chaco Phenomenon do not deny that there was trade with areas far to the south. The presence of macaw skeletons indicates trade, as do copper bells and possibly shell inlay. Documenting trade from north to south is far more difficult. Most supporters of the *pochteca* model assume that the Mesoamerican incentive for trading with Chaco was the desire to acquire turquoise (Kelley and Kelley 1975; Lister and Lister 1981). Yet Hayes (1981a), who advocates a Mesoamerican connection, sums up the situation succinctly:

> There is no native turquoise within many miles of Chaco, although it is not impossible that the district served as an exchange point into which the gemstones were drawn. A quantity—exaggerated though it is—of turquoise was found at Pueblo Bonito, but there is no evidence that it was stored or worked up locally in any appreciable quantity. (Hayes 1981a:63)

Of importance here is the observation that, although Chacoan outliers are found in resource areas, there are no known Chacoan outliers at those turquoise mines that are suggested sources for the turquoise found at Chaco Canyon (McGuire 1980).

Although many writers suggest that the *pochteca* model should be viewed as a hypothesis (Kelley and Kelley 1975) that requires testing, as it is generally presented it is not amenable to refutation. For example, although one might conclude from the model that a particular single source or home area for the *pochteca* in Mesoamerica might be necessary, it has been argued that the *pochteca* operated independently and from several loci. This discounts the necessity of finding a single Mesoamerican source for the introduced traits. Also, there is no indication of precisely how the *pochteca* presence is to be recognized. The *pochtecas* are viewed as coming in small numbers, possibly altering some sites, but using native architecture elsewhere. Finally, refutation is further complicated by the ideas that the *pochteca* may have influenced people living in intervening areas, and that only small amounts of trade items may have been involved (Kelley and Kelley 1975:184–185). Hypotheses must have test implications that can be refuted with empirical information. Until the *pochteca* model is framed in such a way as to make refutation possible, it is not a testable hypothesis.

At present, it seems most reasonable to consider the few items of Mesoamerican origin in Chaco as evidence of some long-distance trade, principally in luxury goods. But there are enough specific differences between the other items mentioned and their supposed Mesoamerican counterparts to question that derivation (e.g., Obenauf 1980; Weaver 1981), and some of the traits themselves seem to be logical developments within the Anasazi system (e.g., irrigation devices).

Casas Grandes

A stronger case for a regional system based on trade has been made for the Casas Grandes area of Chihuahua (Di Peso *et al.* 1974). Throughout most of its prehistory, the Casas Grandes region generally resembles other Southwestern culture areas in terms of artifact inventory and settlement form. Specific items most closely resemble those of the Mogollon. The Casas Grandes area lies in the relatively high Basin and Range country of northern Chihuahua. The Casas Grandes Valley itself is wide, fertile, and relatively well watered, and the indigenous, Mogollon-like population experienced a general population growth. Perhaps as early as A.D. 1060 and lasting until about 1340, a time span referred to as the Medio period, a number of radical changes occurred in the Casas Grandes area, and these have been attributed to the influence of *pochteca*-like mercenaries.

During the first part of the Medio period, termed the Buena Fe phase to which Di Peso assigns the dates of 1060 and 1205, population was organized into what he refers to as the City of Paquimé (1974: Vol. 2). At this time, Paquimé apparently consisted of a series of 20 independent but associated house clusters, each with an open plaza area surrounded by an enclosing wall. The houses were single-story adobe structures, and the configuration of settlement is described as resembling that of the site of Los Muertos on the Gila River. Although the house compounds were separate, a single water system served the entire site. A single Buena Fe phase compound enclosed an area of nearly four-fifths of an acre. Architectural features included massive cast "mud concrete" bearing walls, T-shaped doorways, raised fire hearths, square-column fronted galleries, and stairways. Among the ceramic containers, some of the Buena Fe phase storage jars had a capacity of nearly 18 gallons. A variety of painted ceramic types were produced locally and some, especially Ramos Polychrome, were widely traded. Within the excavated Buena Fe compound, referred to as the House of the Serpent, rows of rectangular macaw breeding boxes were found. Palynological data provided evidence of the original nesting material, and eggshell fragments, skeletons, and holes for wooden perches made it possible to interpret the use of these features. If, as is suggested, the macaws were traded, Paquimé would be the likely source of these birds found among the Anasazi.

In about 1205, the beginning of the Paquimé phase, the entire city of Paquimé was reorganized and rebuilt. At its height, the Casas Grandes system, centered at Paquimé, was much larger than that of Chaco. It encompassed an area of about 87,000 km², and Paquimé itself is estimated to have housed about 2240 people (Figure 8.19). After remodeling, multistoried adobe apartment complexes were built, and a great deal of space, estimated at about one-half the site, was allocated for public and ceremonial use. Unlike the Chacoan area, the domestic units formed the central core of the city, and the public and ceremonial areas were distributed outside of this core. Among the public and ceremonial features were double T-shaped ball courts, a small T-shaped ball court with subfloor burial groups that included some individuals who appear to have been ceremonially dismembered, stone-faced platform and effigy mounds, an elaborate subterranean walk-in well, a reservoir, a system of stone slab-covered drains, and a market area. The domestic space was provided by massive multistoried

Figure 8.19 Paquimé, Casas Grandes, Chihuahua, Mexico. A small part of the vast adobe ruins of Paquimé. In contrast to the Chacoan sites, plaza areas and public space at Paquimé are located outside of and surround the room blocks. (Photograph courtesy of Steven A. LeBlanc.)

dwellings, the walls of which are well described by Bandelier as "not of adobe but a kind of marly concrete, mixed with pebbles and small stones" (quoted in Di Peso 1974: Vol. 5. p. 440). The ends of the vigas (roof beams) were generally square. A little over half the domestic rooms at Paquimé had evidence of bed platforms raised about a meter off the floor.

In addition to the architecture, smaller items at Paquimé provide abundant evidence of craft specialization. The lost-wax casting method was used to produce both the elaborate copper bells and the ceremonial copper axe heads. Other copper objects include sheet-copper armlets, disk beads, rings, and pendants. One of the most important industries at Paquimé appears to have been the production of shell items, involving "tons of marine mollusks" (Di Peso 1974:501). Engraved *Strombus* shell, *Strombus* shell trumpets, and turquoise-inlayed shell were produced.

Although Di Peso interprets Paquimé as a Mesoamerican *pochteca* frontier outpost (incorporating the local population), he also suggests a number of similarities or parallels with the Chacoan system (Di Peso *et al.* 1974:208–211). These include a regional system based on a capital (or core area) and satellite communities; however, as noted, the Paquimé system was much larger than that of Chaco. Another difference is that Paquimé is a single, very large site, whereas the Chacoan core area consists of several separate communities within Chaco Canyon. The Paquimé system, like Chaco, was linked through a system of roads and signaling devices. The Paquimé roads are not as wide or as consistently engineered as those of Chaco. Both systems had elaborate water-control features. Those at Casas Grandes included stone check dams and terraces, ditches, and the reservoirs mentioned above. Certain structural details are also similar, including aligned T-shaped doorways, the use of shaped sandstone disks as timber seatings, square columns, and the incorporation of stairways in buildings. In addition, although less convincing, Di Peso suggests that the two masonry-enclosed refuse mounds at Pueblo Bonito may be similar to some of the stone-faced mounds at Paquimé. Another similarity of interest is that the Medio period at Paquimé shares with the Bonito sites an extreme underrepresentation of burials. Finally, and obviously, both Paquimé and Bonito structures indicate a considerable amount of planning and social control.

The Diablo phase, dated from A.D. 1261 to 1340, followed the Paquimé phase and is described as a time

> when two and one-half generations sat idly by and watched the magnificent city of Paquimé fall into disrepair. The artisan-citizens continued to produce an abundance of marketable goods, but civil construction and public maintenance all but ceased. The populace took over various public and ceremonial areas and with crude alterations made living quarters of them (Di Peso 1974: Vol. 2: p. 319).

During the Diablo phase the population within Paquimé apparently increased. Domestic living space was increased by subdividing some rooms and, particularly, by altering and subdividing open space. The square-columned galleries were walled off and subdivided into rooms in a way that is very similar to that described for Salmon Ruin above. Burials of the Diablo phase were sometimes placed in the former plaza drains, and the wells were no longer used. As with the "Mesa Verde" occupation of Chaco, Salmon, and other outliers, the population of Paquimé remained in residence long after public construction had ceased, and abandonment finally occurred in about A.D. 1340.

Hohokam

There is a considerable amount of data and some interpretive agreement indicating that a form of very broad regional integration developed in the Hohokam area during the Colonial and Sedentary periods (Doyel 1980; Fish *et al.* 1980; Wilcox 1980; Wood and McAllister 1980). The lack of an adequate Hohokam chronology (see Chapter 3) and varying interpretations of the Hohokam manifestations outside the core area of the Gila and Salt river basins preclude describing the character of the Hohokam regional system or the trajectory of its development. Nevertheless, sometime between about A.D. 900 and 1150 the Hohokam system shows a number of features indicating considerable social complexity.

A recent reevaluation of the core-area site of Snaketown (Figure 8.20) (Wilcox 1980) suggest that during this period (Sacaton phase) the population of the site grew exponentially and the population at any one time within the period consisted of between about 630 and 1000 individuals. The layout of the site at this time indicates an inner habitation zone around a central plaza, surrounded by a series of mounds and two ball courts, and an outer habitation zone. Possible prehistoric trails lead to the north and northeast. All the houses are pithouses; there are more large houses in the central area than in the peripheral area. In addition, house clusters consisting of houses the

Figure 8.20 Snaketown, Arizona. Part of the core area of Snaketown as excavated in 1965. In this aerial view, more than 60 house floors, representing various periods in Snaketown's history, are shown. (Photograph by Helga Teiwes. Courtesy of the Museum of Arizona.)

doorways of which may have a common focus are much more extensive in the central than in the peripheral areas of the site. In addition to this bimodal distribution of houses, there appears to have been differential treatment of the dead. Doyel (1980) notes that some cremations are associated with quantities of mortuary offerings, such as figurines, projectile points, and copper bells, whereas other cremations have only a few sherds or lack grave goods.

Craft specialization at Snaketown is reflected by the organization of labor necessary to the construction of the caliche-capped platform mound and by the inventory of shell and ceramic items. The shell inventory of the Sedentary period includes an abundance of beads, heavy bracelets, carved ornaments, and *Strombus* trumpets. In addition, during the Sedentary period etched and painted shell ornaments were produced. At Snaketown an unusually high 40% of the Sedentary ceramics are painted. Very large storage jars, some holding up to 30 gallons, are also found in Sedentary contexts. It has also been suggested that the distinctive serrated projectile points (Figure 8.21) may have been produced by craft specialists (Crabtree 1975; Doyel 1980).

Within the core area, Doyel (1980) notes a settlement hierarchy. "Each canal network, representing an irrigation community, possessed at least one large village site as well as smaller villages or *rancherias*" (Doyel 1980:31). The distributions of various elaborate items, such as copper bells, shell jewelry, serrated projectile points, and figurines, suggest that these occur predominantly at the larger sites.

The geographic extent of Hohokam communities is greater during the Sedentary period than at any other time. Sites are found not only in the core area but in the Papagueria, the lower Gila, Santa Cruz, San Pedro, middle Gila, Pinal, and Tonto drainages, and in many drainages north of Phoenix (Doyel 1980). Among the most elaborate Sedentary Hohokam sites is the Gatlin site near Gila Bench (Wasley 1960; Wasley and Johnson 1965). The site consisted of an elaborate, artificially constructed platform mound that was modified and repaired through six stages of construction. Caliche plaster was used to cap the platform during each stage of construction. Eventually the platform mound consisted of a flat-topped rectangular structure with sloping sides measuring about 29 m in length, 21 m in width, and about 3.7 m in height. In addition to the platform mound, the Gatlin site contained 22 trash mounds, two oval (Casa Grande type) ball courts, two crematoria, and an irrigation canal. Despite extensive testing throughout the site, only two pithouses were located, indicating that the Gatlin site may have been a specialized ceremonial site. The site yielded evidence of the manufacture of shell jewelry, finished shell objects, copper bells, and a macaw skeleton. Data from site survey and from excavation indicate that the prehistoric population of the Gila Bend area reached its greatest density during the Sedentary period.

The evidence throughout the Papagueria indicates increased and more intensive occupation and more abundant production of shell items (McGuire and Schiffer 1982:191). In the Papagueria, where irrigation agriculture is not possible, various farming techniques were practiced, such as those described for Gu Achi (Chapter 6), as were combinations of farming and wild plant gathering (Goodyear 1975; Raab 1977). The evidence for production of shell items is not uniform throughout the Papagueria, however. Statistical analyses undertaken by McGuire and Schiffer (1982:245–259) show that sites with the most unfinished shell items, indicating manufacture, occur in the western Papagueria. Western Papagueria sites also have the lowest number of finished shell items. Sites in the eastern Papagueria, on the other hand, have significantly less shell, but most of this shell consists of finished items. Sites in the Gila Bend and the Salt areas have about the same amount of unfinished shell when compared to each other, although they have less unfinished shell than the western Papagueria and more than the eastern Papagueria. The Gila Bend and Salt

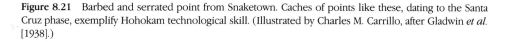

Figure 8.21   Barbed and serrated point from Snaketown. Caches of points like these, dating to the Santa Cruz phase, exemplify Hohokam technological skill. (Illustrated by Charles M. Carrillo, after Gladwin *et al.* [1938].)

River sites are also similar to each other, and different from either group of Papagueria sites, in that they have an intermediate amount of shell. These results, which are suggestive rather than conclusive due to variations in sample size among other things, indicate that the western Papagueria served as specialized centers for the procurement and manufacture of shell for exchange to the Gila Bend and Gila–Salt regions. Within this trade network, the eastern Papagueria appears to have been marginal. Of particular interest is the observation that the relative roles of the western and eastern Papagueria appear to have been socially defined, inasmuch as the eastern Papagueria is closer to the shell sources of the Gulf of California than either the Gila Bend or the Gila and Salt basin (McGuire and Schiffer 1982:249). Masse (1980) has suggested that the western Papagueria may have been trading shell to the Gila Bend and Gila and Salt areas for agricultural produce, an idea that merits further investigation. What is apparent is that a complex set of social and perhaps political relations existed among the Sedentary Hohokam communities in the Gila Bend, Gila and Salt basins, and the western and eastern Papagueria.

An equally if not more complex set of relations appears to have existed between the Gila and Salt basins and the Verde Valley and Flagstaff areas (Fish *et al.* 1980). The Verde Valley sites, perhaps in part because they are closer to the Gila and Salt basins, exhibit more Hohokam items than do the Flagstaff-area sites. Some specific items, such as copper bells, are lacking in the Verde Valley sites but are present in the Flagstaff area. Furthermore, although full-scale migrations of Hohokam colonists have been postulated to account for the appearance of Hohokam traits in both areas, in neither case is this supported by the finding of a complete complex of the more mundane domestic Hohokam items. Rather, the distributions of Hohokam traits have been interpreted as representing changing patterns of interregional trade. Fish and others (1980) suggest that interregional trade may develop along a trajectory of increased interaction. In the first stages, down-the-line trade or village-to-village trade, which can produce geographically broad chain-like networks, is expected. These authors suggest that the character of early (pre-900) trade between the Hohokam core area and the Flagstaff region was of this sort, as indicated by the presence of Pioneer and early Colonial Hohokam sherds on Flagstaff-area sites known from survey. In this context, too, the Hohokam may have provided the Flagstaff area with a few items of Mexican origin, such as copper bells, macaws, and onyx ornaments. Actually, very few early sites in the Flagstaff area have been excavated, but there appears to have been "a dribble of limited trade items" from early on (Fish *et al.* 1980:167). The authors caution that this interpretation may reflect excavation bias, in that only small sites of the early period have been excavated in the Flagstaff area.

A more intensive trade mechanism is expeditionary trade, in which one party travels to the source of the desired goods. Expeditionary trade may result in the establishment of more permanent contacts. In this way the traders may develop relations with local people who procure resources for exchange, or they may extract the resources themselves. A site in the Verde Valley, dating from 800 to 1000, seems to be an example of the former. Pithouses at this site consist of both northern and Hohokam styles. At one of the northern (local) style pithouses, finished and unfinished argillite items in Hohokam styles were recovered, and large numbers of shell bracelets of Hohokam origin were found throughout the site. Sites dating to between 700 and 1000 in the Verde Valley consist of both very large villages and dispersed rancheria-type settlements. Both ball courts and mounds occur at sites of this period, but only at the larger sites. This pattern suggests that the establishment of expeditionary trade may depend on the nature and status of the resident population. After A.D. 1000 the settlement pattern in the Verde changed, and large villages no longer occurred in the upper Verde. Between A.D. 1000 and 1125, large settlements were present in the middle Verde and continued to feature public architecture, including adobe-capped mounds.

With increased and more intensive trade relations, formalized trade routes are expected to develop. Fish and others tentatively identify two of these between the Verde and Flagstaff regions (Figure 8.22). The authors further suggest that trade fairs or periodic markets would occur during periods of most active trade, and that these activities might be associated with ceremonial activities and formalized trading centers. They note that in the Flagstaff area the presence of a ball court and a Hohokam-style pithouse seem to be the major indications of trading centers. Eight large sites postdating A.D. 1000 contain such structures and might have been centers of this sort. Finally, it is possible that, with regular predictable trade, professional full- or part-time traders may be present in the resource area. Pilles (1979) suggests that this situation may account for the presence of a "typical" Sacaton phase pithouse at Winona Village. It is also possible that the famous "magician" burial from Ridge Ruin (McGregor 1943), near Winona Village, was of an individual involved in the interregional trade.

Fish and others (1980) note that the relatively formal trade network, probably imbedded in ceremonial organization, also reflects a situation in which the Verde and Flagstaff groups shared, with the Hohokam, elements of a common belief system. Others (Doyel 1980; Wilcox 1981) agree with this interpretation, viewing the great geographic dispersal of some Hohokam traits as evidence of a widespread socioreligious system based largely on trade. During the Sedentary, the system extended far beyond the Hohokam area, incorporating locations at which resources such as red argillite, serpentine, turquoise, obsidian, and jet were obtained. If Hohokam ball courts are considered simply as indications of a certain level of social integration, the trade network extended from Gila Bend on the west to the Point of Pines area on the east, and from Tucson to Flagstaff. Given the enormity of this area, it is not surprising that considerable variability would characterize the "Hohokam" presence. It would appear from the data presented that some of the variability can be related to the character of local populations involved in Hohokam interactions and the nature and degree of intensity of the Hohokam presence. The data do not indicate the establishment of pure Hohokam colonies in most areas; however, whether Hohokam traders stimulated the development of local social complexity or simply operated within a sphere of already highly organized groups is not known. The excavation of sites of different periods and of different sizes within those periods is necessary to clarify this issue.

By the end of the Sedentary, at about A.D. 1150, the nature of Hohokam settlement

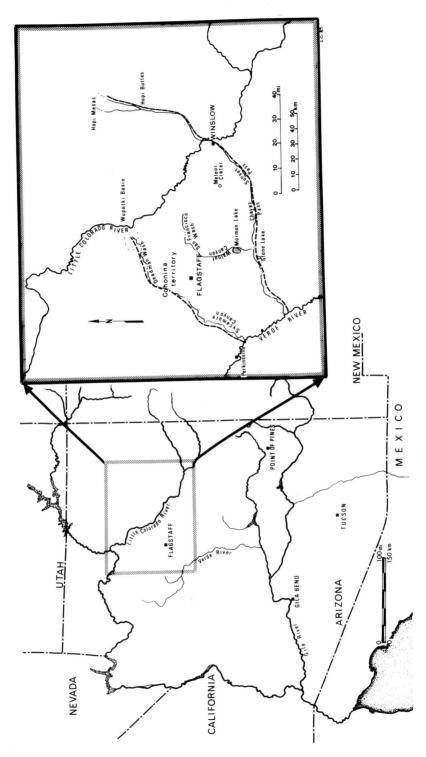

Figure 8.22 Hohokam trade routes in the Flagstaff area. Fish *et al.* (1980) identify these two formal trade routes between the Verde and Flagstaff regions. They suggest that these developed after A.D. 1000.

changed, and this appears to represent an organizational shift that again had variable effects on the areas of Hohokam contact. In the Flagstaff region, ball courts continued to be constructed after they had diminished in the Hohokam heartland (Fish *et al.* 1980). Between about 1130 and 1200, many large sites are known in the Flagstaff area, and diversity and social distinctions within the population are evident. After about 1200 there was an aggregation of population into fewer but larger sites and participation in another system of regional integration and exchange. In the Verde area after about 1150, local populations seem to have shifted their alliances to the western Anasazi. In the Papagueria, a change toward a different exploitation pattern is manifest in the Sells phase (Masse 1980), which also is part of the regional integration of a later period. Thus, it appears that the effects of changing organization within the Hohokam core area on its peripheries was not abandonment but a variety of local changes, some of which also had regional implications.

Areas in Between: Aggregated Systems

Between about 900 and 1150, most of the Southwest was *not* incorporated into any of the ongoing regional systems in a direct way, nor were most areas the centers of their own regionally based systems. Rather, the prevailing pattern seems to have been of continued local development. This statement does not indicate that either cultural elaboration or "stylistic" boundaries were lacking outside the regional systems. On the contrary, population density increased in many areas, soil- and water-control features were constructed, some villages became quite large, structures reflecting village-level organization were built, and recognizable traditions of ceramic styles developed. The differences between the regional systems and the "areas in between" are apparent in the presence of regionally based hierarchies in the Chaco, Paquimé, and Sedentary Hohokam systems, and in the absence of such hierarchies elsewhere. The contrast thus parallels Irwin-Williams' (1980a) distinction between aggregated and nucleated organizations discussed earlier. The contrasts are here elaborated by examining examples of "areas in between."

Mesa Verde

The Mesa Verde area provides a good contrast to Chaco Canyon for several reasons: The two are representative of the San Juan Anasazi tradition and therefore share a number of general cultural features; they are in fairly close proximity to each other; some survey data from the two areas may be compared because the techniques of survey were identical; and finally, the Mesa Verde type of organization survived that of Chaco, and came to influence the Chaco region.

The Mesa Verde area covers a broad area north and northwest of the San Juan Basin. Compared to Chaco Canyon, the environment of the Mesa Verde is relatively lush. Because of its altitude and latitude, it is not as dry as other areas of the Southwest. The climax vegetation consists of piñon and Utah juniper, with fairly dense understory shrubs. Although the water sources are neither very numerous nor completely reliable, there are many seeps and springs. Hayes (1964) surveyed Wetherill Mesa, a portion of Mesa Verde National Park, as part of the Wetherill Mesa Archeological Project. He (1981a) also surveyed Chaco Canyon for the National Park Service. "A comparison of the results of the two surveys is interesting, because they were as nearly comparable as two surveys could be. They were conducted by the same man—using the same techniques, recording the same kinds of data, and applying the same prejudices" (Hayes 1981a:20).

Hayes found that site density in Chaco Canyon was somewhat more than half that on Wetherill Mesa. Chaco Canyon had a greater number of Navajo sites than the Navajo, Ute, or Euro-American sites at Mesa Verde. If only the Anasazi sites are considered, site density at Chaco Canyon is 49/km² and at Wetherill Mesa 129/km². The difference is even more outstanding when the dense vegetation of Mesa Verde is considered, because small and unobtrusive sites are more likely to have been missed in that setting. The difficulty in observing limited-activity sites at Mesa Verde is suggested by the fact that only 38% of the sites recorded in the Wetherill Mesa Survey were of this type, whereas 68% of the sites in Chaco Canyon were unobtrusive, limited-activity sites. Hayes emphasizes that, because sites were more likely to have been missed due to the topographic and vegetative conditions at Mesa Verde, the magnitude of the difference in prehistoric Anasazi settlement between Chaco Canyon and Mesa Verde is impressive.

The full sequence of Anasazi development from Basketmaker through Pueblo III is present at Mesa Verde. The Anasazi occupation ended at about A.D. 1300. Rohn (1977) views the demographic trajectory from A.D. 600 to 1300 as one of population growth. His observation is based on the survey he completed of Chapin Mesa. Hayes, using the Wetherill data, suggests a general population increase over time, with a possible decrease in numbers locally between about A.D. 900 and 1050. Without comparable data from the Mesa Verde area as a whole, it is difficult to decide between these two views. Nevertheless, it is likely that, despite a considerable amount of local movement, population in the whole region probably grew within the Pueblo portion of the Anasazi continuum.

There has been some difference of opinion regarding interpretations of the material culture differences between the Mesa Verde and Chacoan manifestations of the San Juan Anasazi. Reed (1946) emphasized the general continuities between the two areas, with Chacoan influence being stronger until about A.D. 1150 and Mesa Verde influence predominating thereafter. Vivian (1959), while acknowledging the similarities between Chaco and Mesa Verde when compared to other Anasazi branches such as the Virgin-Kayenta, emphasizes distinctions that can be made between the two San Juan groups. For instance, he notes that from the beginning there were differences in ceramics and architecture. The beginnings of the sequence are not of concern here. It is important to note that Vivian stresses "that from perhaps A.D. 950 or earlier the branches (Chaco and Mesa Verde) had separate identities when compared to each other" (Vivian 1959:3). The kinds of differences with which Vivian is concerned are those in kiva style, domestic architecture, burial practices, and possibly ceramics. The differences Vivian notes are (1) the presence in Chacoan kivas of low, wide benches and subfloor vents, (2) the general absence of these features, but the use of pilasters, above-floor vents, and masonry deflectors in Mesa Verde kivas, and (3) the general absence of burials in Chacoan sites and their more frequent occurrence at Mesa Verde sites. On a less salient level, Chacoan ceramics are decorated with iron- or mineral-based paints, and Mesa Verde ceramics use organic-based paints. Not specifically mentioned by Vivian, but of importance, are the differences in construction type: the use of core-veneer masonry at Chaco and the use of single- or double-coursed masonry at Mesa Verde. Probably most important from the perspective of regional development, however, are the differences between village and community organization at Mesa Verde sites and at Chaco (previously discussed).

This discussion of Mesa Verde villages and communities follows that developed by Rohn (1977). Rohn (1977) quite rightly discriminates between sites (each notable building—in some cases, each distinguishable artifact locus, such as a ceramic scatter) and communities (local groups) "determined not by kinship but by spatial proximity that brings its individual members into face-to-face contact" (Rohn 1977:266). This distinction is one that is commonly made by ethnologists. What is of interest here is that Rohn finds that "village settlements can be identified during all phases of the prehistoric Pueblo occupation of Chapin Mesa" (Rohn 1977:266). Because our concern here is the period between about A.D. 950 and 1150, a brief description of a Chapin Mesa community of that time is given. The description should serve two purposes. First, it offers a comparison to the Chacoan settlement described above. Second, it demonstrates the relative ease with which Chapin Mesa (and, in general, Mesa Verde) *communities* can be distinguished in comparison to *communities* within the regional centers or villages constituting parts of a regional system.

As noted, the timing of events at Mesa Verde lags behind that of Chaco Canyon: The population peak at Mesa Verde appears to have been about A.D. 1200, perhaps some 150–200 years after that in Chaco Canyon. Additionally, as Rohn notes for Chapin Mesa, from about A.D. 950 until 1300, one large settlement at a time dominated the entire mesa. The first of these settlements is Mummy Lake II, which consisted of some 36 separate sites with an estimated population of about 200–400 people. One of these sites (Pipe Shrine House, Site 809) was excavated by Fewkes (1923). The floor plan of the site is shown in Figure 8.23. According to Rohn, rooms numbered 1–9, consisting of single-coursed masonry with chipped-edge stones, were constructed first. Later, the occupants added the east, south, and west wings in pecked faced masonry, some single- and some double-coursed walls. The kiva also showed remodeling, finally having the narrow bench, six pilasters, and a subfloor ventilator typical of the kivas in Chaco Canyon. The additions and remodeling, of different masonry styles, are a departure from the planned Bonito style structures of the Chacoan system. The size of the Mummy Lake settlement is attributable to the construction of the artificial water supply at Mummy Lake, which can probably be dated to about A.D. 950–1000.

Mummy Lake itself is an impressively engineered reservoir with associated features, indicating considerable technological skill and labor organization. Mummy Lake is a stone-lined depression about 27 m in diameter, with high artificial banks on its south and east sides. The lake was fed by diverting water from a 10 ha catchment area

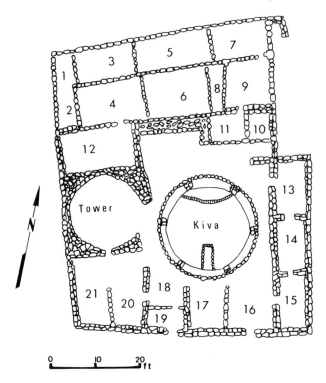

Figure 8.23 Pipe Shrine House, Mesa Verde National Park, Colorado. The north room block (Rooms 1–9) was constructed first. Later, the east, south, and west room blocks were added, and the kiva was remodeled. (Adapted from Rohn [1977: Figure 13] by Charles M. Carrillo.)

through a series of ditches that converged into a shallow, natural drainage head modified by a stone bank built across its low end. This ditch then fed water into a main feeder ditch that ran 804 m to Mummy Lake (Figure 8.24). Although water could be channeled to another distributor ditch before its entry into Mummy Lake, it did not run out of Mummy Lake once impounded there. The lake probably served primarily as a domestic water supply for the quite large community of sites around it. The Mummy Lake system is the largest and most impressive water-control system on Chapin Mesa. The most abundant soil–water control features at Chapin Mesa, and elsewhere on Mesa Verde, are the series of check dams across arroyos. The Chapin Mesa survey documented over 900 stone check dams, but these provided only 18–20 ha of prime agricultural land.

Between about 1200 and 1300, the population focus on Chapin Mesa shifted from the area around Mummy Lake to Cliff and Fewkes canyons, a move south along the mesa. The late Pueblo III settlement in the latter area consisted of 33 habitation sites with an estimated total of between 530 and 545 rooms, 60 kivas, and between 600 and 800 people. Site size within this group ranges from a one-room site to Cliff Palace, the largest ruin on Chapin Mesa, with an estimated 220 rooms and 23 kivas. Rohn suggests that about half of the thirteenth-century population of Chapin Mesa inhabited this site group. Despite the dense concentration of population, there is very little in the

Fewkes Canyon group that indicates any form of social hierarchy. It does appear as though the largest settlement, Cliff Palace, was central to the community. The other Chapin Mesa site groups of this period also have one large, more or less central site. Except for its size, however, the Cliff Palace structure is not unusual.

There are two special-purpose, probably ceremonial sites associated with the Fewkes Canyon group: Fire Temple and Sun Temple. Fire Temple, well described as a modified great kiva (Cassidy 1965), is a rectangular structure with adjoining rooms on each side that may have served as antechambers. Wall construction is of double-coursed block masonry with a narrow interior core. Except for its shape, the ruin has features that are similar to the great kivas of Chaco Canyon (Figure 8.25): paired vaults, bench, and raised firebox. Sun Temple (Figure 8.26) is a **D**-shaped structure with two massive (1.22 m thick) stone walls enclosing two kiva-like features. The kivas had Chacoan subfloor ventilators. Rohn suggests that these features, which are also present at Pipe Shrine House (discussed above), link the population of the Far View group to the Fewkes Canyon community. The notion here is that these people moved from Far View to the Fewkes Canyon area. The two ceremonial structures and the large scale of

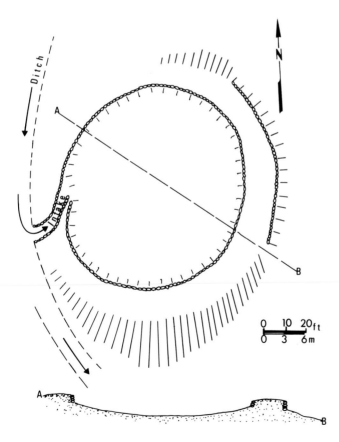

Figure 8.24 Mummy Lake Reservoir, Mesa Verde National Park, Colorado. This shallow, stone-lined reservoir provided water for domestic use. (Adapted from Rohn [1977: Figure 38] by Charles M. Carrillo.)

Figure 8.25   Fire Temple, Mesa Verde National Park, Colorado. The floor features of this site are similar to those of the great kivas of Chaco Canyon (cf. Figure 8.9), including the paired vaults, bench, and raised firebox. (Photograph courtesy of the Chaco Center, National Park Service.)

construction at the cliff dwellings in Fewkes Canyon certainly indicate village integration and ceremonial organization. Neither these nor other structures on Chapin Mesa are suggestive of hierarchies of community settlement. The only other class of functionally different habitation sites found appears to be that of fieldhouses.

The major Chapin Mesa cliff ruins were excavated by Fewkes in the early part of this century. It is interesting to quote from his summary of his work at Spruce Tree House (Figure 8.27):

> It is evident that the people who once inhabited Spruce Tree House were not highly developed in culture, although the buildings show an advanced order of architecture. . . . The pottery is not inferior to that of the other parts of the Southwest but has fewer symbols and is not as fine or varied in colors as that from Sikyatki or from Casas Grandes in Sonora. . . . The remaining minor antiquities, such as cloth, basketry, wood, and bone, are of the same general character as found elsewhere in the Southwest. Shell work is practically lacking; no objects made from marine shells have been found. (Fewkes 1909:53)

Elsewhere in the same report, Fewkes comments on the lack of jewelry at Spruce Tree House and other Mesa Verde cliff dwellings (1909:27). He acknowledges that Spruce Tree House itself had been thoroughly ransacked by treasure seekers prior to his investigations and notes that turquoise was rumored to have been found in the

Mesa Verde ruins, although he himself had found none. "The absence of bracelets, armlets, and finger rings of sea shells, objects so numerous in the ruins along the Little Colorado and the Gila, may be explained by a lack of trade, due to culture isolation" (Fewkes 1909:27).

Fewkes' work on Chapin Mesa antedated the routine use of refined field techniques, so it is not possible to use his descriptions as a basis for interpreting the social components of the sites at which he worked. Fortunately, Rohn (1971) provides a study of Mug House, a 94-room cliff dwelling that although it is on Wetherill rather than Chapin Mesa, provides a great deal of information regarding the social configuration of a thirteenth-century settlement at Mesa Verde. Rohn identified four levels of organization at Mug House: room suites (corresponding to households), courtyard units (clusters of households sharing a common courtyard), moieties, and the community as a whole. The lowest level, the room suites, should be compared to those described for Salmon and for the "modular units" at Chaco Canyon. Unlike the Chacoan examples, Rohn's work indicates that the Mug House room suites were not constructed at once in a planned fashion.

> The primary criteria used in delimiting suites center around mutual accessibility of their component spaces and relative isolation of these same spaces from other room blocks. Throughout the ruin, doorways tend to connect clusters of rooms and outdoor areas around one large nuclear space. Wall abutments generally indicate separate building stages between suites as well as sequential construction within a single unit. (Rohn 1977:31)

Figure 8.26 Sun Temple, Mesa Verde National Park, Colorado. Two massive stone walls enclose two kiva-like features that had Chacoan subfloor ventilators. (Illustrated by Charles M. Carrillo.)

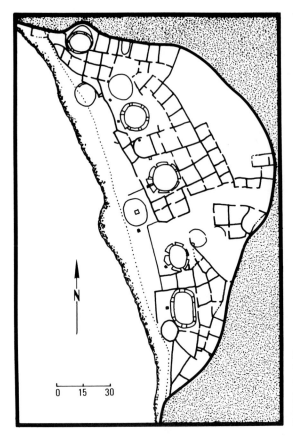

Figure 8.27 Spruce Tree House, Mesa Verde National Park, Colorado. This cliff dwelling was excavated by Fewkes and reported in 1909. (Ground plan adapted from Fewkes [1909: Plate I] by Charles M. Carrillo.)

0   15   30

Three examples of room clusters are given in Figure 8.28. In describing Suite 12/1, Rohn (1977:33) comments that it consists of two storerooms, two dwelling rooms, and most of the enclosed space in the back of the cave in which Mug House is located. Rooms 12/1 and 11/1 were apparently constructed first, with Rooms 57 and 14 added later to increase the amount of storage space. The courtyard units (of which Figure 8.28 is an example) also show additions and modifications over time. The earliest courtyard units at Mug House resemble earlier habitation units found on the mesa top, generally consisting of a series of contiguous rooms with an associated kiva and a refuse heap. The units are referred to as courtyard units because the kiva roof served as a ground-level courtyard for the adjoining house clusters. Rohn has been able to trace the building sequence for the courtyard units at Mug House. His reconstruction indicates that initially there was but one courtyard unit. Later there were four units, two within Mug House Cave itself, one in nearby Adobe Cave, and one at a site in the immediate vicinity. During the latest period, these four merged into one pueblo. The suggested dual division is less convincing. Rohn infers that it came into being only during the latest period of occupation and was marked by a 6-room suite with en-

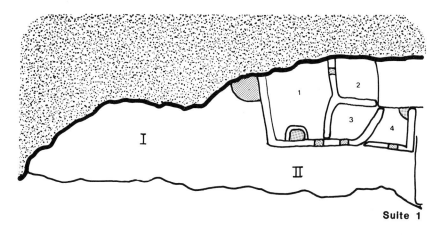

Suite 1

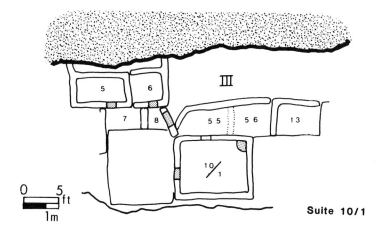

Suite 10/1

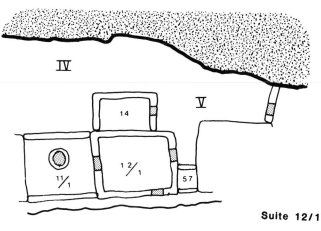

Suite 12/1

Figure 8.28 Domestic room suites at Mug House, Mesa Verde National Park, Colorado. The rooms within each suite are accessible to each other but are not easily entered from other room suites. In Suite 12/1, Rooms 11/1 and 12/1 were built first and Rooms 14 and 57 were added later. (Adapted from Rohn [1971:32–33]. Illustrated by Charles M. Carrillo.)

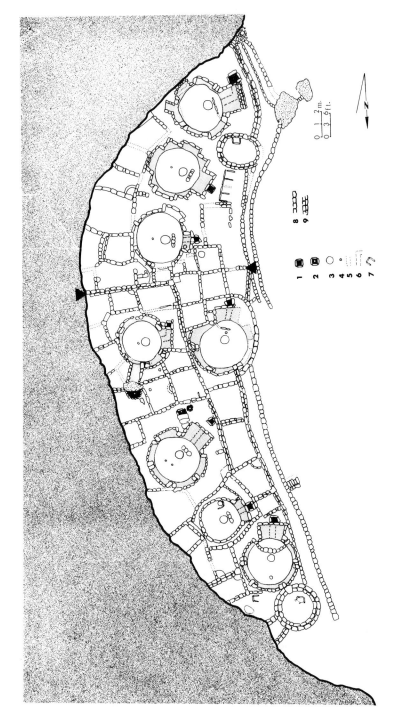

Figure 8.29 Ground plan of Mug House, Mesa Verde National Park, Colorado. Domestic room suites are grouped around kivas, the roofs of which would have served as courtyards. Triangles indicate the wall that separates the site into two divisions. (Adapted from Rohn [1977] by Charles M. Carrillo.)

tryways from three of the rooms to the north and three to the south but no direct access between north and south portions of the pueblo (Figure 8.29). In addition, the five kivas in the northern sector are architecturally very similar to each other, whereas the three kivas in the southern sector do not resemble each other. Finally, studies of wall abutments indicate that construction in the southern segment did not begin until the northern segment had attained a large size.

The community level distinguished by Rohn consists of the inhabitants of Mug House and the residents of several smaller contemporary sites in the immediate vicinity. As Rohn points out, in social terms the community would have included those people who are frequently in day-to-day interaction, and the sites involved are all in very close proximity and apparently contemporary.

In essence, despite the constraints imposed by the shapes of caves and rock over-hangs in which they were built, the communities at Mesa Verde did attain consider-able size. The multiple kivas and specialized structures, such as Fire Temple, indicate considerable ceremonial activity. Further, the reservoirs and check dams suggest technological skill and cooperative labor investment. Nevertheless, the planning and stylization of building so evident in the Bonito structures is not apparent at Mesa Verde, and there is little indication that the communities were centralized or nucle-ated as opposed to aggregated. Even large structures such as Mug House show a development from a smaller community, with additions and modifications of struc-tures being common.

Mimbres

The Mimbres area during the Mimbres Classic of around A.D. 1000 to 1130 is also considered an "area in between," because it did not develop a nucleated regional system. The Mimbres Classic is best known for its aesthetically appealing, finely craft-ed, pictorial (Figure 8.30) and geometric ceramics (Figure 8.31). Mimbres bowls are most often recovered in burial contexts, individuals having been interred with one or more Classic bowls inverted over their heads. In addition, the bowls were cere-monially "killed" at the grave site by having a small hole punched out of them. (Archaeologists romantically suggest that the Mimbrenos thus let the spirit of the bowl free.) The artistic appeal of Mimbres ceramics, to contemporary Westerners at any rate, the undoubtedly religious or ceremonial themes represented on some bowls, and their mortuary association may lead modern observers to expect that the Classic Mimbres witnessed a form of regional integration similar to that at Chaco, Casas Grandes, or the Sedentary Hohokam sites. Examinations of Classic Membres site configurations, ceremonial rooms, and burial populations, however, fail to support such a view.

Among the best-known Classic Mimbres sites are the Mattocks, Cameron Creek, and the Swarts ruins (Figure 8.32). Two others, the Galaz site and the NAN Ranch pueblo (Anyon *et al.* 1981; Shafer 1982) are discussed here. Both of these sites do, in fact, conform to the "Classic Mimbres type." Classic Mimbres architecture is far from impressive, and, in fact, a great deal of it appears not to have been structurally sound.

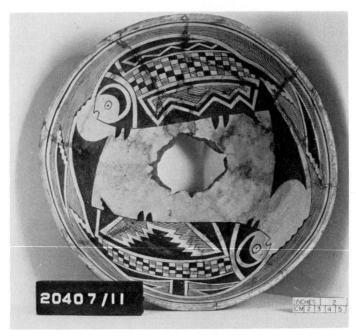

Figure 8.30 Classic Mimbres bowl with pictorial fish design. Classic bowls are often recovered in burial contexts. Generally a small hole was punched in the center of the bowl before it was buried at the grave site. (Photograph courtesy of the Museum of New Mexico Collections.)

The common building form in the Classic was a series of contiguous, single-story rectangular rooms with walls made of unshaped river cobbles set in abundant adobe or mud mortar (Figure 8.33). Roofs were supported by the walls and from one to three or four roof-support posts. Studies of the composition of Mimbres sites are hampered by the generally poor state of preservation of structures and by the overt destruction of many Mimbres sites by treasure hunters. Nevertheless, information from the NAN Ranch site and the Galaz site shows that Classic Mimbres pueblos grew accretionally. The Galaz site appears to have evolved from a small number of core surface rooms into a number of larger separate room clusters. Although there was no apparent village-level planning, the room clusters were loosely organized around an open plaza area. At the NAN Ranch site, Shafer (1982) examined wall junctures to determine the horizontal sequence of room construction. He then defined room clusters as those rooms that were linked by common doorways and built during a single construction episode. His data therefore are comparable to those obtained by Rohn at Mug House and by Irwin-Williams at Salmon. The room clusters at NAN Ranch pueblo are more comparable to those at Mug House than to the formal room suites characteristic of the Bonito construction at Salmon. Entry to each room cluster appears to have been through a roof hatchway. The number of rooms in each room cluster varies somewhat, room clusters were added to, and rooms within them were

sometimes divided. Shafer suggests that the number of rooms in a cluster was probably a function of the space needs of the residential groups. Rooms that can be interpreted as primarily habitation rooms were somewhat larger than other rooms in
the cluster and generally had interior features such as hearths. Smaller rooms at both
the NAN Ranch pueblo and the Galaz site generally had well-prepared floors but
lacked interior features, often had only unpainted ceramics, and seem to be reasonably interpreted as storage rooms. Although Mimbres Classic pueblos grew to be quite
large, 150 or so rooms, they appear to typify aggregated, as opposed to nucleated,
settlements (Figure 8.34).

Ceremonial or communal architecture does, of course, occur at Classic Mimbres
sites. Anyon and LeBlanc (1980; LeBlanc 1983) indicate that during the Classic there
are two classes of ceremonial structures: those used by segments of the village and
those used by the village population as a whole. Early in the Classic, communal
structures were very large, rectangular, semisubterranean kivas, showing considerable
continuity to Mogollon kivas of preceding periods. The floor area of one such struc-

Figure 8.31 Classic Mimbres bowl with geometric design. Note the kill hole in the center of the vessel.
(Photograph courtesy of the Museum of New Mexico.)

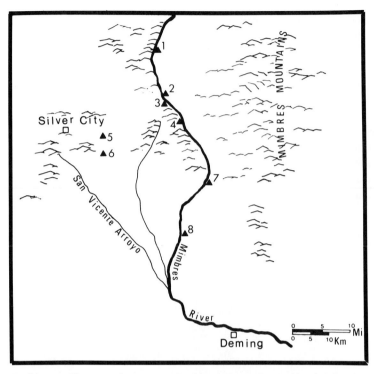

Figure 8.32   Well-known Classic Mimbres sites. 1, Bradsby; 2, Harris; 3, Mattocks; 4, Galaz; 5, Treasure Hill; 6, Cameron Creek; 7, Swarts; 8, Old Town. (Illustrated by Charles M. Carrillo.)

ture at the Galaz site was 146.8 m². This structure and others had rampways oriented to the east. Ceremonial offerings or caches were sometimes located below the floor. For example, in this large structure objects found below the floor included a carved shell effigy, a painted tuff frog, beads, crystals, a *glycymeris* shell bracelet, and turquoise, shell, and stone beads and pendants. In another ceremonial structure at the Galaz site, which was apparently used slightly later than the one just discussed, a subfloor offering consisted of a military macaw skeleton with a string of 67 turquoise and 11 shell beads wrapped around its skull and wings and additional strings of shell beads wrapped around its legs. In addition to these large kiva structures, it is possible that open plaza areas served for village-wide ceremonial activities as well as for other social functions, as they do among contemporary Pueblo people.

Some ceremonial rooms located in Classic Mimbres pueblos were too small to have served the village as a whole and may have been used by village segments (sodalities of one kind or another—i.e., either kin or non-kin based). One kind of small ceremonial structure was the semisubterranean kiva, a remodeled pithouse. These small kivas lacked rampways, entry being through the roof. They were of quadrilateral shape and had floor features like those of Classic habitation rooms. In addition, some extra large (floor area greater than 28 m^2 surface rooms and walled plaza areas may have been used for ceremonial purposes by segments of the Classic Mimbres communities.

Despite the common association of Mimbres Black-on-white bowls with burials, researchers have not been able to discern differential mortuary offerings, which would be an indication of social hierarchies. Further, Mimbres bowls are found in habitation contexts as well as with burials; in some cases, where they have been found with burials, the bowls' interiors show light scrape marks that would have resulted from using a gourd dipper on the inside of the bowl. Thus, the bowls seem to have been used for general serving functions before they were interred as burial offerings.

The number of trade items and the distances over which trade items were transported in the Classic Mimbres vary, but the items do not seem to reflect large quantities of exotic goods. Shell is present, mostly in finished items, as it is in the preceding Mogollon phases. Turquoise does appear in jewelry, but it probably originated in the Hueco Mountains or other copper-bearing deposits in the general vicinity of the Mimbres Valley. Finally, although there is petrographic support for the idea that not every Classic Mimbres village produced its own ceramics, very little exotic ceramic tradeware was being imported into the Mimbres area. Of equal importance in this regard is that Mimbres Classic ceramics had limited distributions outside the Mimbres area proper. In fact, the only area in which they appear in quantity is the Jornada Mogollon region. There, during the local Late Pithouse period, the only identifiable

Figure 8.33   Classic Mimbres room. Classic Mimbres wall consists of unshaped river cobbles in abundant mud mortar. (Photograph courtesy of Steven A. LeBlanc.)

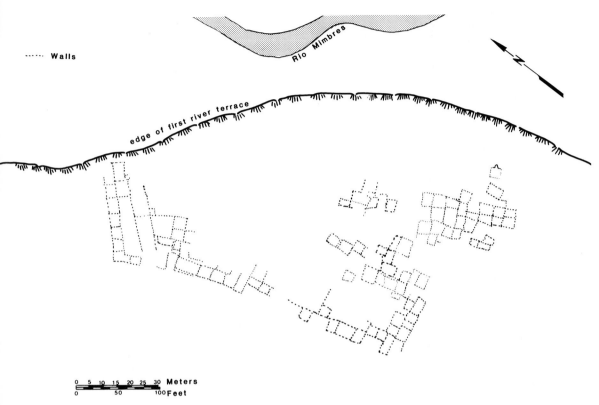

Figure 8.34 Galaz site ground plan. This site and other Classic Mimbres pueblos are not planned construc-
tions. The configuration of rooms and room blocks indicates an aggregated pattern. (Illustrated by Charles
M. Carrillo.)

nonlocal ceramics are Mimbres Black-on-white (Whalen 1981); however, even in the
Jornada, Mimbres ceramics do not make up a great amount of the ceramic assemblage.

In general, then, the lack of planned structures in the Classic Mimbres, the absence
of evidence of a widespread trade organization, and the lack of a defined hierarchical
treatment of burials indicate a relatively egalitarian social situation among the people
of the Classic Mimbres. Despite the obvious excellence of the ceramic craft items and
the appeal of these items in our own culture, there is nothing that suggests specialized
production or regional integration of a broad scope. The organization of ceremonial
activities must have been important at the village and perhaps the local level, and the
esoteric nature of Mimbres art suggests a rich ceremonial life; but this is not a
nucleated system.

The examples of aggregated systems discussed, such as that of the Mesa Verde and
Mimbres areas, are of interest, in part, because the size of the settlements might lead
to the conclusion that they were nucleated. These systems are also of interest because
they are recognizable stylistically; that is, they manifest particular forms of architecture

and ceramics that are quite homogeneous throughout their local areas. Nevertheless, the aggregated systems are not necessarily representative of the kinds of settlements in which most Southwestern peoples were living between about A.D. 900 and 1150. Rather, in many areas a far more dispersed system of community organization seems to have characterized much of the Southwest. In order to give a better understanding of the range of community types, a brief description of examples of dispersed systems is given.

Areas in Between: Dispersed Systems

The Rio Grande Valley

The central and northern Rio Grande Valley, from about Albuquerque north, appears to have been only relatively sparsely inhabited from A.D. 900 to 1150, a period that falls within the Rio Grande Developmental period as described by Wendorf and Reed (1955; also see Chapter 3). Excavated habitations most often consist of pithouses, some with associated jacal structures and outside work areas. For the most part, pithouse architecture is relatively simple in that these houses are either round or rectangular with an interior hearth and roof-support posts being the most consistent internal features. Wing walls, benches, pilasters, and other features known from pithouse architecture in the San Juan drainages are not present. The simplicity of Rio Grande pithouses is not a reflection of a lack of labor investment in housing. In mountainous areas, pithouses were excavated to a considerable depth, which involved relatively great expenditures of energy. In the Taos area, for example, pithouses in excess of 3 m in depth and 5 m in diameter are reported (Woosley 1980). Pithouses at lower elevations and latitudes, such as those on the Rio Grande terraces in the vicinity of Albuquerque, are generally considerably shallower. Quantitative data allowing an assessment of the degree of agricultural dependence reflected by these small pithouse communities are lacking; and it is not known if the sites were occupied on a year-round basis. Some investigators (Blevins and Joiner 1977) suggest that many sites were used only seasonally.

In the Rio Grande area, most ceramics were probably locally produced, although this has not been substantiated by petrographic studies. Of interest, however, is that many of the local ceramic types are considered *cognates*, or local imitations of types that were produced in the San Juan area. For example, in the Taos, Santa Fe, and Albuquerque areas, mineral-painted types such as a local variety of Red Mesa Black-on-white, Taos Black-on-white, and Kwahe'e Black-on-white are viewed as copies of Chacoan types. In the immediate vicinity of Albuquerque and somewhat south, ceramic assemblages are more diverse and include various Mogollon types or imitations thereof, such as Corrales Red (Frisbie 1967), and types, such as San Marcial Black-on-white, that are common in the Rio Grande area south of Albuquerque.

Although little systematic information is available and pithouse communities are often difficult to locate because they are buried under more recent aeolian deposits, it appears that settlements in the middle and northern Rio Grande area were relatively small, perhaps consisting of two to four pithouses, sometimes with associated jacal structures. Pithouses are found in a variety of topographic situations and elevations, with those in higher settings being deeper (see Chapter 7). The relative permanence of pithouse settlements is not known. Many were probably used seasonally, and some may have been used year-round for only a very few years. The sparse population indicated does not appear to have interacted frequently or with great intensity with the people of the San Juan area, which would have been the closest regionally organized system. No known Chacoan outliers exist in the Rio Grande Valley. As noted above, the resources of the Rio Grande Valley might have been attractive to the Chacoans, especially the turquoise of the Cerrillos Hills and perhaps the obsidian and cherts of the Jemez Mountains. Nevertheless, direct evidence of exploitation of these resources is lacking for this period. The various cognate ceramics produced certainly indicate general knowledge of the San Juan Basin area and, perhaps, some cognitive attempt to affiliate with this larger system, but the overall view is one of a dispersed population living in relative isolation.

The Jornada Mogollon

Perhaps an even more dramatic case of a dispersed settlement system is that of the southern Jornada Mogollon on the southeastern edge of the Southwest. The southern Jornada Mogollon "tradition" extends from the northern end of the Caballo Mountains to the junction of the Rio Grande and Conchos rivers on the south, and from the Sacramento Mountains to the El Paso area (Figure 8.1). It is of interest here that the southern Jornada area is in close proximity to both the Casas Grandes and Mimbres areas. As described by Lehmer (1948), the period between A.D. 900 and 1100, referred to as the Mesilla phase, is characterized by the use of pithouses, growing reliance on agriculture, and social and economic ties with the Mimbres Valley represented by the occurrence of Mimbres Boldface and Classic Mimbres Black-on-white in the Jornada area, in addition to locally produced Jornada brownwares. In a reexamination of the applicability of this description, Upham (in press) synthesized survey data that indicate that less than 5% of the recorded Jornada Mogollon sites are classified as habitation sites. Rather, the sites are typically sherd and lithic scatters, which indicates a highly mobile population.

Discussion

Between about A.D. 900 and 1150, village life had spread throughout much of the Southwest. In the past, archaeologists emphasized the differences among the remains in each of the major culture areas (Anasazi, Mogollon, and Hohokam) and within each of these areas (e.g., Desert branch vs. River branch Hohokam) by reference to distinct cultural or ethnic traditions (Chapter 3). Lately, archaeological interpretation has been concentrated on the organizational heterogeneity within each of the culture areas.

From this perspective, the similarities in organization among the Chaco Anasazi, the Colonial and Sedentary period Hohokam, and the Mogollon residents of Paquimé are highlighted. Each of these systems shows evidence of standardization in architectural construction, some public architecture, craft specialization, and substantial trade networks. As yet, there is little agreement about the organization of these systems or the impetus for their development. The integration of ceremonial systems seems to have been important in each case, but it is not clear how trade was organized, labor groups recruited, or craft specialists supported. These are important issues for future archaeological research. Finally, it is not likely that each of the major systems was organized in the same way, and it will be important to fully characterize and explain the differences among them.

Despite the fact that each of the major regional systems seems to have incorporated a large area, most of the people living in the Southwest at the time of these systems seem to have been participating in more simply organized systems. Two patterns of systems that lack hierarchical development were presented. An aggregated system was exemplified in the discussions of the Mesa Verde and Mimbres areas; a dispersed pattern by the Rio Grande and Jornada areas. Aggregated systems contain very large sites, but in these cases sites are predominantly residential and appear to be aggregates of formerly dispersed local communities. There were undoubtedly social mechanisms serving to integrate these villages, but relatively egalitarian relationships among household residential groups are reflected in the architecture of these settlements. This architectural observation suggests that the aggregated communities were organized in ways more nearly approximating the modern Pueblo than were the nucleated systems. Future research needs to address this issue.

In both the Rio Grande and Jornada areas, and probably much of the Patayan area as well, populations seem to have remained relatively more mobile throughout the period. It is likely that villages, when they existed, were small and perhaps somewhat temporary. They may have housed only a few related families and been sustained as much by gathering and hunting as by agriculture.

After about A.D. 1150, the nucleated systems seem to have failed in the northern Southwest (see Chapter 9). When these systems collapsed, however, the organizational strategies reflected in both the aggregated and dispersed systems continued. This situation indicates the regional importance of organizational heterogeneity and adaptive flexibility. The presence of aggregated and dispersed systems might provide models of successful forms of integration.

9

Abandonments

*Large areas of the Southwest were abandoned in
prehistoric times, providing archaeologists with a puzzle.
This chapter reviews the traditional explanations offered.
New chronological studies and reevaluation of the
existing data suggest that abandonment is a more
complex issue than had been previously described. In fact,
the term* abandonment *has been used to refer to several
different kinds of change and population movement that
should be kept conceptually distinct. This chapter
examines processes influencing the abandonment of
single sites, small geographic areas, and regions.*

Introduction

At the time of their discovery by Euro-Americans, the more spectacular ruins of the Colorado Plateaus—the cliff dwellings of the Mesa Verde, the multistoried stone ruins of Chaco—had long been deserted by their builders. The general similarities in architecture and other material culture remains between the plateau ruins and the modern pueblos left little doubt as to the ultimate fate of the descendants of the people who occupied the ruined villages. Explaining the abandonment of the northern portion of the Pueblo heartland became the subject of popular speculation and scientific interest, and abandonment remains an important issue in the literature of Southwestern prehistory. Most notions that were initially advanced to explain the plateau abandonment have been neither confirmed nor entirely discarded, and each has its strong advocates. This chapter first reviews the major reasons for abandonment offered by various scholars and the currently available data that either tends to support or contradict these explanations.

At present, some researchers have come to view the formulation of the abandonment issue as inappropriate. In essence, the notion of abandonment has been applied to phenomena that are more productively viewed as distinct kinds of events. For example, the term *abandonment* has been applied to situations of depopulation and to instances of a cessation of building without depopulation. *Abandonment* has also been used to refer to instances in which large regions were apparently depopulated and to cases in which local areas or single sites were depopulated. Treating this diversity as though it represents one kind of event or process can lead to considerable confusion and weaken the explanatory power of any suggested causal argument. A reexamination of the data in light of conceptually more precise statements of the kind of behavior reflected in the archaeological record is therefore presented at the conclusion of this chapter.

Traditional Explanations for Abandonment

One can divide the proposed explanations for abandonment in a variety of ways: catastrophic or processual, cultural or environmental, or single or multiple cause, for example. None of these is entirely satisfactory, for there are always some explanations that have aspects pertaining to more than one mode. Nevertheless, in part for convenience and in part to emphasize the distinctiveness of the proposed reasons, they are here treated as primarily cultural or primarily related to the natural environment. The cultural explanations discussed are warfare, factionalism, disease, and disruption of trade contacts with Mesoamerica. Those explanations relating to the natural environment are drought, environmental degradation other than drought, changes in seasonality and periodicity of rainfall, and resource depletion.

Cultural Explanations

Warfare models are usually differentiated into those that invoke fighting with non-Pueblo, particularly Ute or Athapaskan, peoples, and those that cite internecine warfare among Pueblo peoples themselves. Harold Gladwin was one of the more articulate proponents of the idea that the Pueblo were driven from their homes by hostile nomads. Gladwin wrote, "in every village in the Southwest at A.D. 1200, the same questions are being asked: Where to go? What to do? to obtain relief from the ceaseless persecution of the marauding Athabascans." (Gladwin 1957:269).

The notion of warfare with nomads, either Athapaskan or Ute, seemed plausible because within the historic period there have been times of considerable hostility between Pueblo and non-Pueblo groups. Pueblo legends and stories describe the Navajo as traditional enemies, and folk sayings caution that Navajo and Apache could be fearful adversaries. Despite this, there are two oft-stated objections to invoking the "Athapaskan menace" as a reason for abandonment. As Linton (1944) pointed out, the Utes and Athapaskans were strong enemies of the Pueblo only after the former had acquired horses from the Europeans. Far less numerous than the Pueblo, and lacking the ability to carry out swift surprise attacks that the horse made possible, the "nomads" would have been at an extreme tactical disadvantage.

Second and rather more devastating to the notion of combat with the Athapaskans is the fact that despite years of research there is no convincing evidence that there were any Athapaskan people in the Southwest much before the arrival of the Spaniards. The Navajo and Apache have displayed considerable adaptive flexibility over time, and this is reflected in their settlement patterns and items of material culture available for study by archaeologists. There is no accepted constellation of material remains predating the arrival of the Spaniards that is recognizably Athapaskan. Glottochronological studies (Hoijer 1956) suggest that the separation of southern and northern Athapaskan speakers may have occurred between 1000 and 600 years ago, but neither the particular route by which the southern Athapaskans entered the Southwest nor the length of time this migration took is known with certainty. As yet, the oldest archaeological materials that may be identified as Athapaskan date no earlier than the seventeenth century (Schaafsma 1976).

Another problem with the notion of warfare with the Athapaskans as a reason for the abandonments is that, in historically and ethnographically documented situations, Pueblo and Athapaskans were often involved in close and rather friendly interactions. During the time of the great external threat posed by the Europeans, between the Pueblo Revolt of 1680 and Don Diego de Vargas' reconquest of 1692–1696, Pueblo and Navajo lived together in refugee communities. These consisted of masonry "pueblitos" in the Largo–Gobernador area and in the Jemez Mountains (Brugge 1983), as well as large fortified settlements in the Jemez area. After the reconquest (1696), the Pueblo again revolted against the Spaniards and some fled from their villages; for example, the Picuris fled and remained for about 10 years with Apache groups on the Plains (Brown 1979).

In times of peace, there was considerable trade between Pueblo and Athapaskan peoples. For example, Brown (1979) notes that relations between the Picuris and the Apache were generally friendly, and Jicarilla families visited the pueblos and participated in feast days during the summer. The apparent paradox of the historic period Pueblo–Athapaskan relations is that, although the Athapaskans are viewed as traditional enemies, much of the interaction among these groups involved friendly social relations and trade. Kelley (1952) discusses relations between the La Junta villagers of northern Mexico and southwest Texas and bands of Apache. La Junta women did not go great distances from their pueblos when gathering wild plant foods and explained the circumscribed foraging radius as a response to potential attack from the Apache. In fact, observations indicated a considerable amount of trade between the two groups, no instances of overt hostility, and only one situation in which a hostile incident was recalled by villagers. Kelley suggests that under "normal" conditions the villagers had sufficient agricultural produce to trade with the Apache, and the Apache had surpluses of meat to offer in exchange. He suggests that during times of drought neither group had much surplus. The Apache might depend on the Pueblo groups at a time when the Pueblo had no surpluses to trade. With decreased crop yields, Pueblo women would have to forage more widely, going further from the village than usual. This activity could coincide with a time when the Apache were most likely to be turned away and, therefore, be expected to have ill feelings toward the Pueblo. Kelley's argument considers a condition of the natural environment as a key variable underlying the character of Pueblo–Apache interactions. In the case of the prehistoric period, however, given the lack of evidence for the presence of Athapaskan groups in the Southwest, hostility from Athapaskan speakers is not supported.

Some scholars (e.g., Davis 1965; Ellis 1951) suggest that inter-Pueblo warfare is a more likely explanation for the thirteenth-century abandonments. These writers rightfully point out that the characterization of Pueblo groups as essentially peaceful is inaccurate and that, prior to their subjugation by Europeans, internecine conflict and warfare may have been prevalent. The evidence for this position consists of the ethnographically documented importance of warrior sodalities (and scalp societies) among the Pueblo, the military success of the Pueblo Revolt of 1680, and historically recorded inter-Pueblo combat at the time of the reconquest. Although it is undeniable that no entire group is "inherently" peaceful, and fighting probably was of considerable importance among the Pueblo, whether such warfare accounts for the abandonment of large areas is questionable. Generally, the results of warfare are that victorious groups may either subjugate their enemies and extract tribute or labor from them or drive them away and occupy their land and villages. If casualties are very great there would, of course, be an initial regional reduction in population; however, demographic studies indicate that the population recovery following such catastrophies is generally quite rapid. Additionally, the lack of both burials and sufficient numbers of skeletons showing evidence of violent death provide no support for the argument of abandonment as a result of severe fighting. The large late sites of the Colorado Plateaus do not yield much evidence of conflict; they were neither burned nor destroyed prehistorically.

Although not necessarily invoking warfare of any kind (Pueblo–Athapaskan or Pueblo–Pueblo) as an explanation for abandonment, some writers have nevertheless assumed that the late movement of some local populations into sites located in caves or rock overhangs reflects a concern for defense (Rohn 1977). While many late prehistoric southwestern sites are in defensive settings, the role of the cave locations, particularly at Mesa Verde (Figure 9.1), is difficult to assess. Remote from fields and, at

Figure 9.1 Cliff Palace, Mesa Verde National Park, Colorado. Access to cliff dwellings such as these is difficult, and the dwellings are commonly thought of as defensive. (Photograph from the collection of Fay-Cooper Cole. Courtesy of Lewis R. Binford.)

least from the western European point of view, relatively uncomfortable places to live, it is argued that the only reason people would move into cave sites would be for protection.

An examination of the admittedly limited information on Pueblo warfare, combined with cross-cultural data, does not support this interpretation. In most situations (excluding the capturing of satellite villages for tribute), the motives for intergroup aggression are capturing goods or capturing or killing individuals or sometimes destroying a village. Raiding for goods generally involves taking food, and in such situations, the raiders are anxious not to be caught. At Mesa Verde and elsewhere, most of the crops and many of the storage structures are located on the mesa tops in places that cannot successfully be guarded from caves located some 6–12 m below. Capturing and killing some individuals—as acts of vengeance—is known among the Pueblo. Cross-culturally, ambush is the most effective and most frequently used method of taking one or a few individuals. Cliff dwellings offer virtually no defense against this. In daily tasks of going to and from fields and to and from water sources, the cliff dweller is in complete view on narrow paths and on toe holds or stairways cut into the rock. An ambush party need only lie in wait. The defensive nature of the cliff dwellings is probably most convincing if one considers an attack directed toward the destruction of an entire village. It is difficult to imagine large numbers of enemy warriors sneaking up the talus slopes or jumping silently down 6.5-m cliffs to sack a village. On the other hand, if the few reports of attacks on entire villages are credible, Pueblo warriors had developed methods of gaining access to villages primarily through intrigue. Ellis reports of the Jemez:

> In what seems to have been a favorite method of retaliation, members of an aggrieved group posed as guests or watched until all the men of an offending village had left on a hunting trip. Then little packets containing pine tar and fragments of pine needles or dried juniper leaves were tucked around kiva- and house-beams where they would not be noticed. Later, a light touched to one packet caused it to burst into flame, much as if the material had been soaked in gasoline. The fire spread quickly from packet to packet through the kiva rafters so quickly that the men inside the kiva suffocated before they could escape. (Ellis 1951:187)

Certainly, if such tactics were employed by the prehistoric Pueblo the least desirable location for a village would be inside a rockshelter limited both in space and escape routes. It might be suggested that some alternative motives for living in cave or rockshelter sites include expansion of agricultural activities and the concomitant removal of villages from potentially cultivable land, or the extra protection from the elements afforded by natural shelters. The latter might become important if groups invested more time in subsistence pursuits than in village construction and repair.

Another frequently cited cultural cause of abandonment is factionalism and internal strife within villages. The ethnographic case most frequently cited is the twentieth-century example of the Hopi village of Old Oraibi (Bradfield 1971; Titiev 1944). The net result of the long-term factional dispute at Old Oraibi was the almost complete abandonment of that village and the founding of several others (New Oraibi, Bacabi, and Hotevilla). Critics of factionalism as an explanation for abandonment have argued that the conflict at Old Oraibi was largely the result of U. S. Government intervention in the Hopi way of life; it therefore is not an appropriate example of abandonment in the prehistoric period. However, the possibly inappropriate use of this example as an analog may not be the key issue. Factional disputes are unfortunately common in villages throughout the world; they could indeed account for the depopulation of a village, as well as for the founding of a new one. They do not account for either regional or local depopulation involving more than one site.

Colton (1960) discussed the possibility of relating abandonments to the effects of epidemic diseases. He emphasized that, prior to the major depopulation of the Colorado Plateaus, Pueblo communities had become quite large, aggregated settlements. Within these settlements, trash was sometimes deposited in unoccupied rooms, and burials were placed both in abandoned rooms and in refuse mounds in the immediate vicinity of living areas. Colton suggested that crowded conditions, the proximity of trash to living areas, and possibly contaminated water supplies would have been ideal for the spread of potentially devastating epidemic diseases. There is little information that might substantiate or refute Colton's idea. Very large burial populations are certainly lacking, and this would tend to counter the notion of a period of increased mortality. The skeletal remains from the Colorado Plateaus sometimes show osteoporosis, a pitting of the bone that is interpreted as evidence of poor nutrition. On the other hand, infectious diseases that are generally involved in epidemics generally do not leave observable marks on skeletons.

Finally, those scholars who favor some form of *pochteca* model to account for the rise of the regional systems of the Southwest generally attribute the ultimate failure of these systems to the disruption of intellectual and trade contacts with the advanced civilizations of Mesoamerica. As noted in Chapter 8, substantial evidence for a Mesoamerican presence in the northern Southwest is lacking, although this is not strictly required by the *pochteca* model. Whether the Southwestern centers were ever in any way dependent on Mesoamerica is an open question. Another aspect of the idea is that a disruption of contact with Mesoamerica requires that events in the two areas be understood in their appropriate chronological sequences. The first major civilization of the Valley of Mexico, centered at Teotihuacán, declined about A.D. 700, far too early to have had any relation to the abandonments in the Southwest. Tula, the Toltec capital, seems to have come to ascendancy in about A.D. 950 and to have fallen in about A.D. 1150 or 1200. Although the Toltecs are often cited as the group from which *pochteca* may have originated, the scale and extent of the Toltec system was more limited than that of Teotihuacán, and the fall of Tula appears to have predated some of the Colorado Plateau abandonments by about 100 to 150 years. The following major civilization of Mesoamerica, the Aztec, did not become a major force until about A.D. 1425 and thus after the Southwestern abandonments. Finally, Di Peso's (1974: Vol. 2) dating of the culture history of the Paquimé would indicate that the regional abandonments in the northern Southwest occurred during the Diablo phase. As discussed in Chapter 8, this was to have been a time during which construction and maintenance ceased but marketable goods continued to be produced. If any of these goods involved raw materials, such as turquoise from the Anasazi area, the *pochteca* influence should have continued until about A.D. 1340.

In sum, the cultural reasons cited to explain the late thirteenth-century abandonments of the Colorado Plateaus may account for some of the features observed archaeologically. Although there is no evidence of an Athapaskan intrusion at the time, warfare among Pueblo groups may have caused local population declines and the abandonments of some villages. Evidence of hostilities in the form of burned or sacked villages is, however, lacking. Factionalism also would be expected to have affected only single villages at a time and should also have been accompanied by evidence of the founding of new communities rather than regional depopulation. Epidemic diseases may have had deleterious effects on both local and regional populations, but evidence of increased mortality is not available, given the paucity of skeletal remains from the Plateaus. A disruption of trade connections with Mesoamerica might have affected the scale of regional organization, but it is difficult to see the role of this factor in depopulation.

Environmental Explanations

Various natural environmental causes of abandonment have been proposed in the literature and are somewhat more in favor than the cultural reasons discussed. Some environmental causes are linked to behavioral practices (i.e., agricultural technology). One of the most simplistic natural environmental explanations, and one that is not linked to particular behavior patterns, is the "great drought" notion. Ideas of the potentially devastating effects of droughts were among the earliest suggested reasons given for abandonments (i.e., Hewett *et al.* 1913); however, it was not until 1929, as a result of Douglass' work in dendroclimatology and dendrochronology, that a specific incident of drought was linked to depopulation of the Plateaus. Douglass calculated that there had been a great drought in the northern San Juan area between 1276 and 1299, and he argued that the people, being heavily dependent on agriculture, could not survive this episode and so abandoned their homes. Although Douglass' interpretation of the tree-ring sequence from the northern San Juan was accurate, the explanatory power of the "great drought" idea has been disputed.

First, the tree-ring chronology that Douglass himself made available showed that some sites, such as Betatakin and Kiet Siel, had been built in the 1270s and 1280s—at a time when they should have been abandoned if the great drought were of regional importance. Second, it was argued that because some of the Hopi towns were founded prior to the drought and were not abandoned, there was little reason to believe that the northern San Juan, which is generally much wetter than the Hopi mesas, should have been abandoned. If drought had been the major problem, one would have expected a population influx into the areas of highest rainfall in the Southwest—the Mogollon Rim, White Mountain, and upper Gila drainage. But the archaeological evidence indicates that these regions also suffered a population decline during the period. Finally, the "great drought" notion was to have been best applied to the Mesa Verde, but tree-ring data from that location showed that there had been a series of severe droughts prior to the one between 1276 and 1299, and in spite of these, the Mesa Verde had not been abandoned. (See Figure 8.1 for sites and areas mentioned in this chapter.)

Among the Western Pueblo, supplemental water is usually obtained by diverting floodwater from arroyos. Both Hack (1942) and Bryan (1929, 1941) proposed that during periods of deficient rainfall (though not necessarily times of severe drought) the water tables would be lowered and arroyos would cut deeper channels and erode headward. Entrenchment and the headward cutting of arroyos would greatly reduce the amount of field area over which floodwater could be diverted. The progression of these events would cause fields to be abandoned and would lead eventually to the population movement from the Colorado Plateaus. In fact, Bradfield (1971) was able to show that headward cutting of arroyos greatly decreased the amount of land the Hopi of Oraibi could cultivate in the vicinity of their village; the tension engendered by the land shortage was an important element in the factional dispute that eventually split the village. Although lowering water tables and arroyo cutting are severe problems for Southwestern agriculture and should not be underestimated, there are difficulties in attributing some aspects of regional abandonments to these factors. Some of the objections to the "great drought" notion can also be applied to the arroyo-cutting hypothesis. A lowering of the water table regionally would probably have more severe effects on the Hopi mesas, which were not abandoned, than on the Mesa Verde, which was abandoned. Also, the tree-ring data do not support the idea of generally diminished rainfall for the latter part of the thirteenth century.

Of equal importance are a number of issues raised by paleoclimatologists about the conditions that lead to arroyo cutting. According to Bryan (1941), erosion would have occurred during dry periods when vegetation is reduced and runoff is not slowed or dispersed by plant roots. Arroyo cutting would occur because during a dry period, although rains are infrequent, the intensity of individual storms is not diminished. Conversely, a wet period would encourage vegetation and periods of alluvial deposition or channel filling. Martin (1963:64) and others have argued, on the contrary, that arroyo cutting and headward erosion occur more rapidly in wet than in dry conditions because the amount of runoff is generally increased. The climatic conditions responsible for arroyo cutting are not fully resolved (see Chapter 2), but it appears likely that erosional and depositional events over the Colorado Plateaus were conditioned by variations in stream size, drainage basin size and form, and other local geological conditions. This criticism applies as well to the notion that a change in the seasonal distribution of rainfall, as interpreted from some pollen studies, caused regimal abandonments (e.g., Schoenwetter and Dittert 1968).

Finally, there are cultural practices that can have major deleterious effects on arroyo cutting. The most important of these in the prehistoric period included clearing land for agricultural fields and cutting firewood (Betancourt and Van Devender 1981; Lister 1966). In general, it is likely that lowered water tables and arroyo cutting diminished the amount of agricultural land available to some groups. In order for the importance of this factor in the various explanations for abandonment to be evaluated, more information is required. It is necessary to know the degree to which specific local groups relied on floodwater farming and the other subsistence options that might have been available to them. It is also important that the several possible causes of arroyo cutting be fully evaluated on local and regional bases.

Finally, two studies (Jorde 1977; Slatter 1973) have reexamined the tree-ring data from the Colorado Plateaus. This work has shown that, whereas the evidence for major droughts accompanying abandonments is not supported, there does seem to have been a change in the periodicity of the episodes of drought, indicating that after about A.D. 1150, droughts may have been more frequent, though of shorter duration, than they had been previously. This work, and criticisms of simplistic climatic models, stimulated a conference (fall 1981) to develop a more precise view of paleoclimatic change for the Colorado Plateaus area. The conference participants concluded that prior to A.D. 900, rainfall patterns were characterized by low-amplitude, high-frequency variation. Between about 900 and 1150, the patterns changed to high-amplitude, low-frequency events. After 1150, the original pattern of high frequency and low amplitude was reestablished (Figure 9.2) A positive correlation between these shifts and changes in the hydrological curve, indicating an increase in water tables, and

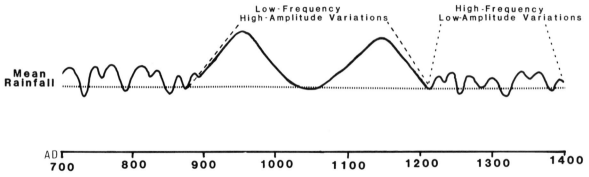

Figure 9.2 Schematic representation of changes in the pattern of rainfall. Low-frequency, high-amplitude variations would occur during long periods of very wet or very dry conditions. High-frequency, low-amplitude variations would accompany a rapid change from wet to dry. (Illustrated by Charles M. Carrillo.)

hydrological competence between 900 and 1150 was also apparent. The effects of these changes for agriculturalists would have been that strategies that were appropriate for compensating for crop failures during the period between 900 and 1150 would not be adequate either before or after that interval. For example, years of good rainfall conditions before and after 900 to 1150 may not have been good enough to obtain sufficient storable surpluses to sustain communities during the frequent years of poor rainfall and poor harvests. Similarly, wild plant and animal resources would have a greater chance of recovery between 900 and 1150, when there were longer periods of very good conditions. These resources, if collected and stored, might have been available for use by human populations during the intervals of poor agricultural yields. The particular mix of subsistence strategies any local group selected must in part have been conditioned by the local population, the quantity and quality of available agricultural land and the quantity and quality of wild food resources. The new climatological data promises to provide considerable insight into the problems faced by various groups in the Colorado Plateaus area, but it does not explain apparent regional depopulation.

In sum, none of the entirely cultural or environmental models available provides a sufficient explanation for the abandonment phenomenon. Most writers would probably agree that the causes were complex, entailing both environmental and cultural aspects. As stated at the beginning of this chapter, however, abandonment itself is a rather more complex process than is sometimes imagined. If explanatory models are to be developed and evaluated, they must apply to accurate descriptions of the events to be explained. For this reason, we now turn to a review of the various processes that have been categorized as *abandonment*.

Abandonment: Reevaluation of the Concept

The numerous ruins of the Southwest attest to site abandonment as a phenomenon common among Pueblo peoples. Parsons (1939:14) characterized the Pueblo as semi-nomadic, and Kidder (1962:149) commented that the Pueblo were "ready to abandon their dwellings on what seems to us as the slightest pretext." Hantman (1983:158–163) demonstrates that the mean length of occupation for all dated sites on the Colorado Plateaus is 80 years. This mean is biased by the inclusion of many very large pueblos. If only small sites (10 rooms or less) are examined, the mean occupation is 34 years. The pattern of frequent movement and short-term residential stability contrasts markedly with occupation patterns among some Old World (Near Eastern) agriculturalists, where *tells* representing the accumulated settlement debris of millennia are salient features of the landscape. At one level of analysis, then, Southwestern archaeologists must determine the factors that are important to residential mobility.

In addition to the abandonment of single sites, many local areas were inhabited for only brief periods or were inhabited intermittently over longer periods. For example, the Gallina area of New Mexico was occupied between about A.D. 1200 and 1300. Matson and Lipe (1978) describe the Anasazi occupation of the Cedar Mesa, Utah, area as one of boom and bust, with Anasazi occupation dating from A.D. 200 to 400 followed by a hiatus, reoccupation briefly in the late 600s followed by another gap, and a period of occupation between about 1100 and 1270. The Grand Canyon appears to have been used only sporadically by various groups. It would be expected that the explanations offered for short-term or periodic use of localities would not necessarily be the same as those given for short-term use of single sites.

Finally, very large regions were abandoned by villagers during the prehistoric and historic periods. Most of the central San Juan Basin appears to have been abandoned in the late 1200s, the San Juan and Mesa Verde areas by 1300, the upper Little Colorado and White Mountain areas by 1450, and most of the southern Rio Grande Valley by the 1680s. These rather large-scale abandonments have been the subjects of most of the abandonment models discussed in the preceding section of this chapter. It should be clear from that discussion that the level of explanation offered for the regional abandonments must be different from those used for either site or local abandonments.

In the preceding section, mention was made of distinguishing abandonment from the cessation of building or the disruption of highly distinctive archaeological patterns. For example, an abundance of tree-ring dates indicates that the major Bonito style sites in Chaco Canyon were constructed between A.D. 950 and 1150, and it had long been thought that the canyon was abandoned by the Bonito population in the late twelfth century. However, Toll *et al.* (1980) have demonstrated that, although Bonito style construction did cease, neither abandonment nor the complete disruption of the trade network ensued immediately. Similarly, Di Peso's description of the Diablo phase at Paquimé shows population growth and continuation of trade, but an absence of major building, for a period of about 80 years. The disruption of a highly distinctive pattern, rather than an absence of building, characterizes the change from the Classic Mimbres phase to the Animas phase of the Mimbres area. A change in pattern is also the major feature of the transition from the Sedentary to the Classic Hohokam.

In much of the Southwestern literature, changes in pattern have been interpreted as evidence of the migration of a new cultural group into an area: A Mesa Verde incursion was to have occurred in Chaco Canyon (and outliers such as Salmon and Aztec), and a Salado migration was postulated for the Mimbres and the Hohokam areas. These interpretations have been questioned and have been found wanting, as is discussed in detail below. It should also be noted that changes in pattern may involve a change in the intensity of use of a particular area. For example, an area that supported agricultural production may become an area in which gathering and hunting are pursued. Even if the change in activities involved the same group of people, the nature of the archaeological record will be one in which there is an apparent discontinuity—one that might be interpreted as abandonment. An examination of changes in pattern, particularly involving large geographic areas, must distinguish periods during which there was a lack of major construction from periods, during which there were changes in land use. Explanations for each of these will differ considerably from explanations that are appropriate for abandonments of single sites or small local areas. Each of these diverse phenomena, which sometimes and inappropriately have been grouped together as examples of abandonment, are examined separately below.

Abandonment of Single Sites

Explanations for the abandonment of single sites must reflect the nature of the occupation represented by the site; some sites were temporary fieldhouses that show little labor investment, whereas other sites not only provided year-round shelter for groups of people but contained ceremonial facilities (kivas) that were important to community integration. Fieldhouses and similar temporary structures might have been abandoned for any number of reasons, including their structural decay during seasons when they were not maintained or the disuse of the field with which they were associated. Fields themselves might be abandoned for a number of reasons. For example, Hack's (1942) data from the modern Hopi villages documents an upstream movement of fields with progressive arroyo cutting. In a study of prehistoric fields and fieldhouses in the White Rock Canyon–Cochiti area of New Mexico, Fosberg (1979) and Fosberg and Husler (1979) noted an expansion of fieldhouses to locations of inferior soils during the fourteenth and fifteenth centuries and documented heavy salt concentrations in the soils at a fieldhouse locality. This work suggests that the fields and fieldhouses were abandoned because of irreversible damage to the soils.

More permanent sites, including villages, also often had only brief periods of occupation despite considerable labor investment in their construction and the presence of kivas (usually indicative of long-term occupancy). Some studies indicate that apparently for as long as there was sufficient land for cultivation, villagers moved frequently, possibly in response to the local effects of minor climatic changes or to the depletion of resources. For example, in a study of changes in settlement location on Mesa Verde, it was possible to quite accurately predict the abandonment of some sites and the continued occupation of others from the tree-ring record of rainfall fluctuations and the effects these would have had on potentially arable land (Cordell 1975, 1981). This study found that during intervals of less than adequate rainfall, sites that were exposed to the south or west (thus receiving the most solar radiation), sites that were more than 0.40 km from a water source, and sites that were located near eroding arroyos were abandoned. During times of greatly increased rainfall, and probably cooler temperatures, mesa sites at high elevations, those with northern exposures, and those in the immediate proximity to water sources that could inflict flood damage were abandoned. Depletion of resources essential to the Pueblo economy may also have been an important influence on the length of residence in an area. Relying on palynological data, Stiger (1979) suggested that swidden agriculture was important to the Mesa Verde Anasazi and that site abandonment could have been related to the local reduction of trees. Site abandonments could also have occurred as the result of the depletion of the supply of firewood in the area.

Local Abandonments

A commonly occurring Southwestern pattern seems to have been the abandonment of sites within relatively limited areas during part of the prehistoric sequence. In some cases, small areas were inhabited repeatedly, but in others, evidence of any occupation seems to cover only a relatively brief period. Although this sort of abandonment pattern seems to have been common, it has not received the major attention that regional abandonments have, primarily because there has been little mystery regarding the probable relocations of the groups involved. In most cases, continuities in material culture have been found in adjacent areas that could have absorbed a population increase. In some cases the population movements are accompanied by changes in settlement form, such as a shift from dispersed to aggregated villages. Nevertheless, explanations offered for the local shifting of populations have virtually all been based on changes in the degree of dependence on agriculture or on postulated changes in climate and the effects they might have had on agriculture. A few examples are given below.

As noted, the Anasazi occupation of Cedar Mesa in southeastern Utah was not continuous. Matson and Lipe (1978) note an apparent hiatus in occupation between Basketmaker II, locally dated from about A.D. 200 to 400, and late Basketmaker III, dated to the late A.D. 600s. They view the transition between Basketmaker II and Basketmaker III as an expansion of the agricultural component of the subsistence base that was occasioned by the acceptance of improved cultigens or improved techniques of farming dependent on rainfall. When this change occurred, there was also an apparent local abandonment of Cedar Mesa, suggesting that the economic shift occurred in areas better suited to rainfall farming. These areas would have been at somewhat higher and better-watered locations to the northeast and east. Survey data from Comb Wash east of Cedar Mesa and from Milk Ranch Point northeast of Cedar Mesa both indicate little Basketmaker II occupation, but these areas do show evidence of habitation during the Basketmaker III period. The data suggest that the transition from Basketmaker II to Basketmaker III was accompanied by a movement to areas receiving relatively abundant rainfall, and the population of Cedar Mesa could have moved to any such locality—for example, either Comb Wash or Milk Ranch Point.

An argument based on agricultural technology and changes in precipitation patterning was also advanced to explain site abandonments in the Hay Hollow Valley of southeastern Arizona (Zubrow 1972, 1974). Zubrow argues that population growth is a function of the carrying capacity of the environment and that a population will first fill optimal areas and then expand into less productive zones. If there is no change in the abundance of resources, it is expected that populations will fill the optimal zones first, the next most optimal zones next, and so on. If there is a change in carrying capacity involving a decrease in resources, however, the expectation is that less optimal zones will be depopulated first. Zubrow examined this model using data from the Hay Hollow Valley and found that up to A.D. 1150 the population of marginal zones did increase after the best zones were "full." After 1150, however, there was a drop in the population curves, and the less-optimal zones were abandoned. The change was interpreted as reflecting a shift in the seasonality of rainfall (from summer to winter dominant), which would have adversely affected agriculture. The change in rainfall seasonality was inferred from palynological studies. It is important to note here that Zubrow considers the abandonment of less optimal zones, suggesting that although these zones could have yielded enough resources to support some people, the numbers that might have been supported were probably too low to permit the continued functioning of a community. In order to sustain continued community activities involving subsistence and ceremonial pursuits, the inhabitants of the marginal zones would have joined ongoing communities in the optimal zones.

The Hay Hollow Valley is not unique in this respect. One of the consistent patterns in the late prehistoric occupation of many areas of the Southwest is the aggregation of population in a few large settlements. Population agregation would, of course, entail abandonments of numerous small sites. Zubrow's discussion attempts to elucidate the aggregation process by reference to both a change in the relative abundance of resources and the necessities of maintaining community activities.

Two studies have attempted to correlate population movements and regional changes in climate. One involves compilation of a large amount of interdisciplinary data for the Colorado Plateaus (Euler *et al.* 1979); the other examines the elevational changes in sites in New Mexico (Stuart and Gauthier 1981). The study by Euler and his colleagues indicates generally moist conditions from about A.D. 450 to 850, dry conditions from about 850 to 950, and a long, relatively wet period from 950 to 1425 within which are short intervals of drought at about 1150 and 1300. Finally, there appears to have been a trend to generally increasing moisture after 1500. The authors argue that "major population trends are both parallel and reciprocal to the long-term hydrologic fluctuations" (Euler *et al.* 1979:1098). They view population as expanding within the drier areas of the Colorado Plateaus (Hay Hollow Valley, Grand Canyon, Hopi Buttes, Cedar Mesa, Black Mesa, and Canyon de Chelly) during wet intervals and as either abandoning these areas or diminishing in growth during dry periods. On the other hand, the Mesa Verde and Navajo Reservoir districts, which are generally wetter and higher, are seen to support population growth during periods of decreased moisture and to lose population during wet intervals. In this view, local abandonments are at least partially correlated with population growth and expansion into other areas.

In Stuart and Gauthier's (1981) study of New Mexico, several changes in the elevation of sites are noted. Basketmaker sites dating to about A.D. 350–600 tend to be in upland settings between about 1220 and 1520 m. Late Basketmaker and early Pueblo I sites, dating to about 600–700, are located at lower elevations. There is an upland shift in site location at about A.D. 750. Their data suggest that between 850 and 1140 there is a general pattern of both upstream and downhill site movement followed by a change to downhill locations between 1200 and 1300. The period from 1300 on is one in which the bulk of the population seems to have been located along rivers, thus primarily at low elevations. These elevation changes were determined by examining survey information derived for all of New Mexico by a variety of institutions, and the consistency of the documented patterns is quite striking. Stuart and Gauthier suggest that the shifts may reflect adaptations to regional changes in weather patterns, particularly the seasonal distribution of rainfall. The implication that pertains to local abandonments is that in these cases groups may have moved only short distances but to areas of more favorable moisture conditions.

The short-term occupation of the Gallina area of New Mexico also has been interpreted as the result of climatic change. In a series of papers, Mackey and Holbrook (1978; Holbrook 1975; Holbrook and Mackey 1976) use analyses of microtine rodents, corn, pollen, and arroyo cutting to document increasingly dry conditions from A.D. 1250 until the area was abandoned sometime after 1300. Despite the diversity of information sources cited in these studies, questions regarding the archaeological contexts of the data can be raised. Nevertheless, it may be that the Gallina area was only suitable for occupation by Anasazi farmers under a narrow range of climatic conditions that were of short duration in that region.

An alternative view of local abandonments has been presented by Hunter-Anderson (1979) in a study of land-use patterns in the Cochiti area of New Mexico. The Rio Grande in general, and the Cochiti area in particular, saw an increase in population after 1300. Hunter-Anderson interprets population aggregation as a result of demographic influx and competition for the home range. A clustering of the population should occur at the expense of dispersed upland settlements, which are abandoned to leave buffer areas between population aggregates. The abandoned uplands are then used for hunting, gathering, and limited farming. Evidence of these activities would be an ephemeral and essentially nondiagnostic archaeological record that would have the appearance of abandonment.

In general, the abandonments of local areas seem to have recurred frequently in the Southwest. Explanations for these occurrences invoke changes in subsistence practices and movement to areas where new or different subsistence strategies may be best used, changes in the amounts and seasonal timing of rainfall and population movements to well-watered areas, and abandonment of marginal or wooded buffer areas as a concomitant of processes of population aggregation. These explanatory frameworks are each amenable to testing with the techniques available to archaeology today. For example, local and regional paleoclimatic reconstruction can be refined with sufficient tree-ring and subsidiary studies. If abandonment of upland areas left buffer zones among aggregated settlements, then there should be no decrease in game or wild plant foods at aggregated communities. As yet, none of the proposed explanations for local abandonments has been adequately tested, but archaeologists are examining these questions in the context of ongoing research.

Regional Abandonments

In contrast to the rather frequent movements in and out of limited areas, regional abandonments were uncommon in the prehistoric Southwest. When they did occur, they seem to have followed periods during which there was a change in the archae-ological pattern. The change in pattern had traditionally been viewed as evidence of migration and population displacements, interpretations that are no longer accept-able. New interpretations of the pattern changes, once they have been adequately tested, promise to shed considerable light on the areal abandonments that succeeded them. This section, therefore, examines two examples of pattern changes and subse-quent regional abandonment: the Chaco–Mesa Verde transition in the San Juan Basin and the Sedentary–Classic changes in the Hohokam area. A comparison suggests lines of inquiry that may lead to a better understanding of the background for the later abandonments.

Aspects of the changes in pattern within Chaco Canyon and at Salmon have been described in the context of the discussion of regional organizations. To recapitulate, within Chaco Canyon proper the change has been described in terms of differences between the Bonito and McElmo phases (Figure 9.3), or early and late Pueblo III. According to Hayes (1981a) there was a decrease in population within the canyon. A total of 221 sites contained evidence of a late Pueblo III occupation, compared to 400 early Pueblo III sites. Some of the sites in each period were limited-use sites, but there was also a decrease in the number of pueblos recorded: 172 for late Pueblo III and 282 for early Pueblo III. In addition to building some new pueblos in Chaco Canyon during late Pueblo III (New Alto, Kin Kletso, and Casa Chiquita), much of the popula-

Figure 9.3 McElmo style masonry at Chaco Canyon, New Mexico. The use of large, pecked blocks of sandstone in walls occurs late in the Anasazi occupation of Chaco Canyon. Contrast this method of wall construction with the veneers shown in Figure 8.7. The late McElmo style masonry resembles the wall construction at Mesa Verde. (Photograph courtesy of the Chaco Center, National Park Service.)

tion lived in parts of older, largely abandoned early Pueblo III structures (e.g., Pueblo del Arroyo) of both Bonito and Hosta Butte styles. Changes in village layout include construction of more compact villages that lack plazas but incorporate kivas within the house blocks. Wall construction is of large shaped blocks rather than ashlar veneer. Ceramic types include McElmo and Mesa Verde Black-on-white and a carbon-painted pottery that is referred to as Chaco–San Juan. In addition, St. Johns Polychrome is found on late Pueblo III sites.

Outside the canyon proper, but within the Chacoan sphere of the San Juan Basin Mesa Verdean construction is evident at some of the Chacoan outliers. Salmon Ruin and Aztec are the best-known examples, but Mesa Tierra, Mesa Pueblo, and Crumbled House, among others, also are of Mesa Verde-type construction. Marshall *et al.* (1979) note that in contrast to the Chaco-Bonito style outliers, those in use during late Pueblo III are not associated with roads or with a high density of domiciliary sites. They are generally on productive agricultural land and have soil- and water-control features, though these lack the complexity of similar agricultural features associated with Chaco-Bonito style sites. As at Salmon, the Mesa Verdean occupation at the outliers is characterized by smaller rooms, generally lacking great kivas and core veneer masonry. Survey data from large areas of the San Juan Basin (Cordell 1982) seem to indicate a population decline, but this is most obvious in the central portion of the basin, particularly in proximity to Chaco Canyon.

The change from Chaco–Bonito style to Mesa Verdean style was traditionally interpreted as a migration of peoples from the Mesa Verde into the San Juan Basin. According to this formulation, the Bonito occupants were viewed as having completely abandoned Chaco Canyon itself, and probably much of the basin, leaving the area essentially vacant for a brief period of time. Peoples from the Mesa Verde region were then seen as reinhabiting parts of the Bonito territory for about 75 or 100 years prior to the eventual Anasazi abandonment of the San Juan area. The reexamination of materials from the Chaco Canyon area proper (Toll *et al.* 1980) makes this interpretation untenable. Rather, new data from excavation have shown that the late Pueblo III occupation of Chaco Canyon was more extensive than had previously been imagined, and studies of the ceramics from the late components indicate that much of the previous network involving importation of whole vessels was still intact. Further, as the discussion of the differences between the Chacoan and Mesa Verdean occupations at Salmon indicate, the use of that outlier continued to be intensive, although the pattern of use changed from one of a centralized, nucleated community to one better described as aggregated. Given the kinds of data available for both periods, it is not possible to determine if the two occupations at Salmon, in Chaco Canyon, or elsewhere in the basin involved the same biological populations. Such determinations would require a great number of skeletons from both occupations, and although burials are more frequently found in the late Pueblo III sites, they are lacking for the early Pueblo III components. Nevertheless, the continuation of the trade pattern discerned in the Chaco ceramic studies suggests continuity, and this is certainly the most parsimonious solution.

The nature of the differences between the Chacoan and Mesa Verdean occupations in the San Juan Basin allows insight into the traditional interpretation of abandonment and replacement and also into the scale and complexity of the Chacoan system itself. As noted, the Chaco-Bonito manifestation is characterized by highly organized construction involving a relatively large labor force. The evidence of this effort in the archaeological record is in the durable and *distinctive* structures, be they great kivas, the walls of buildings, irrigation systems, or roads. The shift in pattern involved more emphasis on subdividing apparently domestic or household space and less centralized agricultural and ceremonial organization. The pattern change from high and organized to lower and less well-organized labor investment will give the appearance of a decrease in population, whether or not such a decrease actually occurred, because the modifications are less obtrusive and less recognizable in the archaeological remains. It is likely, too, that some areas, especially Chaco Canyon itself, were in such environmentally impoverished settings that only through the coordinated regional efforts (indicated by the road system and complex irrigation features) could a large resident population have been sustained. With the sociopolitical collapse of the Chacoan system, outward migration would have been a necessity. These two factors, a lack of specialized, distinctive labor investment and some movement out of the area, give the appearance of abandonment and short-term reoccupation.

It is enlightening in view of the reinterpretation of the Chaco–Mesa Verde transition in the San Juan Basin to examine an area on the periphery of the basin that was not incorporated into the Chacoan system, for example, the southwestern corner of the San Juan Basin on a portion of the Manuelito Plateau between the Rio Puerco and the Chuska Mountains. The discussion is based on results of excavations and analysis of Anasazi sites dating from about A.D. 925 to 1220 (Nelson and Cordell 1982) and interpretations of alliance networks expressed in ceramic wares found at these sites (Acklen 1982). The area is of interest for two reasons. First, like much of the San Juan Basin, agricultural land is available but of low potential. Rainfall is deficient, there are no permanent streams, and highland areas that generate runoff are not abundant. Second, the area is between two important population centers. Chaco Canyon itself is to the northeast; Manuelito Canyon, which sustained a very high density of Anasazi occupation and continued to flourish as a population center after the collapse of the Chacoan system, is to the southwest. Sites within the area have been grouped in three temporal periods: an early period dates between 925 and 1050, a middle period between 1050 and 1150, and a late period between 1150 and 1220.

All of the Anasazi sites in the area are proximally located with respect to arable land. However, the population density seems never to have been very great, and not all of the sites are year-round settlements. During the early period most of the sites were used seasonally or for limited activities, probably involving agriculture. The middle period is characterized by a great increase in population, probably involving immigration, and most of the sites seem to have been occupied year-round. During each of these periods most of the ceramics and stone tools were produced locally, but the types of ceramics represented are stylistically similar to those found within Chaco Canyon and at Chacoan outliers. There are, in fact, a number of Chacoan outliers in the vicinity of the study area, although the Anasazi occupation cannot be linked to any of them. During the late period of occupation there is again a great increase in the number of sites, but most of these are seasonal or limited-activity sites. During this period, ceramics include some tradewares from the White Mountain area and types that are stylistically similar to those found in Manuelito Canyon. There was no gradual abandonment of the area. The Anasazi occupation ceases abruptly, shortly after 1220.

The study of Anasazi sites on a portion of the Manuelito Plateau illustrates the complexity of the Anasazi "adaptation." A single locality was used variably over a relatively short period. In general, the area did not offer sufficient agricultural or resource potential to encourage the establishment of a Chacoan outlier. Nevertheless, the local population, whatever its original homeland, identified with the Chacoan "style." Given the probably low numbers of people who were present, it is possible that participation in the larger networks would have been necessary at least for the exchange of marriage partners. After the collapse of the Chacoan system, when Chaco Canyon was under the influence of the Mesa Verde region, the people of the Manuelito Plateau shifted their stylistic alliance to the southwest, to the Manuelito Canyon area. Throughout the period of occupation, Manuelito Canyon sustained a much higher population density than the Manuelito Plateau, but while Chaco was at its height, its influence transcended a local population center. After the collapse of the Chacoan system, the San Juan Basin witnessed a fragmentation of alliance structures. The northern basin affiliated with the Mesa Verde area, which was still populated, but the western and southern portions affiliated with closer population centers such as Manuelito Canyon. The abrupt abandonment of the Manuelito Plateau coincided with a period of major population agregation in Manuelito Canyon, and it is most likely that the residents of the plateau were incorporated into that area. The local abandonment was not associated with any evidence of subsistence risk, major droughts, or apparent food shortages. Rather, it appears to have been conditioned by organizational changes taking place nearby.

While construction of town sites, roads, and irrigation features continued at Chaco Canyon and the outliers, they must have depleted the human and natural resources from an enormous area, if only seasonally. The regional integration lasted for about 200 years. During this time the redistribution of population, foodstuffs, and other resources, as well as the networks through which marriage partners were obtained and ceremonial activities were organzied, transcended local populations over an enormous area. Communities such as those on the Manuelito Plateau that were not directly incorporated into the system nevertheless were influenced by it. It is most likely that the efficiency of the Chacoan system in producing and distributing food enabled support of a greater number of people than the basin could otherwise support. Economic historians (e.g., North and Thomas 1973) generally point out that the gains obtained through increasing the efficiency with which a system operates are not as great as those achieved through an increase in production. Given the variable and unstable environment of the San Juan Basin and the Southwest as a whole, the production technology practiced by the Chacoans could not be improved. It is worth considering in this regard that the central San Juan Basin today supports fewer people than it did during the eleventh century. With the social and political collapse of the

Chacoan system, even the marginal gains of an efficient system were lost. Some decline in the basin population was inevitable. Those people remaining apparently continued to pursue diverse subsistence options, ranging from greater to less intensive agriculture, depending on the opportunity afforded by local settings. After a relatively brief interval of about 80 years, population aggregation along the basin margins absorbed some of these groups. The stage was being set for the next phase of regional integration—a very different period of regional organization (see Chapter 10) that crystalized about 1350 and lasted until the disruptions caused by the Spanish Conquest.

Similar pattern changes have been noted for the Sedentary–Classic transition of the Hohokam area, and, as had been the case in the San Juan Basin, the traditional interpretation has involved migration and population displacement, although inferred migrations are no longer acceptable to most scholars. The Hohokam Classic has been divided into two phases: the Soho, dating from about 1150 to 1350, and the Civano, dating from about 1350 to 1425. During the Soho phase, "new traits" that have been cited as evidence of an intrusion of outsiders consist of smudged pottery and polished redware, extended inhumations in addition to cremations, platform mounds, construction of aboveground post-reinforced adobe structures, and compounds. It is important too, that the Soho phase witnessed the abandonment of sites in the Gila Bend and lower Verde Valley, although it has been suggested that population density in the Salt Basin may have increased, as it did in the Papagueria. Snaketown was abandoned at this time. During the Soho, irrigation systems seem to have been consolidated. Finally, there is less evidence of interregional trade; particularly notable is the absence of macaws, tripod vessels, figurines, and other items either of Mesoamerican origin or inspiration. Nevertheless, manufacture of shell items continued to be important throughout the Classic.

The change in pattern during the Soho phase has been interpreted as the peaceful invasion of the Hohokam area by the Salado branch of the Anasazi, presumably from the Tonto Basin (Gladwin and Gladwin 1935; Haury 1958). Alternatively, the intruders have been interpreted as Sinagua from the Flagstaff area (Schroeder 1953a, b). Currently, most investigators have argued that the changes were indigeneous to the Hohokam area (Doyel 1980; Wasley and Doyel 1980). The smudged and redware ceramics have been found in Sedentary contexts at Snaketown. Extended inhumations are characteristic of the Papagueria and, as Morris' (1969) excavations at Red Mountain demonstrated, are known from the Pioneer period in the Salt Basin. Platform mounds at both Snaketown and at the Gatlin site predate the Classic, and post-reinforced adobe was used at Snaketown during the Sedentary. Given these observations, the Sedentary–Classic transition, although marked, does not require a migration of outsiders.

The changes from the Soho to the Civano phase have received somewhat less attention. Gila and Tonto polychrome ceramics first appear in the central Hohokam area during the Civano, as do surface structures with solid adobe walls multistoried great houses (such as the famous great house at Casa Grande), and walled compounds. Doyel (1980; Wasley and Doyel 1980) notes that the distribution of the polychrome types is variable; that is, they were very rare at Casa Grande but abundant at Los Colinas and Escalante Ruin. More information is needed on the distribution of these types in the Hohokam area in order to determine if there is any patterned association between the distribution and sites of various types, settings, or periods. Wasley (in Wasley and Doyel 1980) suggests that the experimentation with adobe construction at Snaketown during the Sedentary is sufficient to explain the eventual development of the multistoried great houses and compound walls of the Civano. Alternatively, he also notes the similarity in construction to Casas Grandes (Paquimé) and sites in western Mexico, and argues against invoking migrants from either the Anasazi or Sinagua areas to account for the Civano manifestations.

The pattern changes in the Hohokam area between the Sedentary and Classic periods in some ways resemble those discussed for the Chaco–San Juan. There was some population decline and certainly population movement: The Gila Bend, lower Verde, and Gila basins were partially abandoned, but sites in the Papagueria increased in numbers. There was also a change in ceramic styles, although, as in Chaco, the ceramics demonstrate considerable continuity. This is clearest for the Hohokam area; in addition to the redwares and eventually the polychromes, the majority of ceramics continued in the Hohokam buff tradition. An additional parallel is the change in communal architecture. As noted for the Chaco–San Juan, great kivas were no longer built, nor are open plazas characteristic of large post-1150 sites. In the Hohokam area, ball courts are not a Classic feature, but platform mounds are. Hohokam development has been traced through the sequence present at Snaketown, and because Snaketown was largely abandoned during the Classic, interpretations of the Sedentary–Classic transition have emphasized the discontinuities and regional entrenchment of the Hohokam. A similar view of the Anasazi would undoubtedly derive if virtually all interpretations were based on Pueblo Bonito rather than on the San Juan area as a whole. The situation for the Hohokam should be remedied in the course of research. Excavations in the Gila and Salt basins and surveys and excavation in the Papagueria have contributed to some understanding of the complexity of the Sedentary–Classic transition and have led to a number of reinterpretations of the phenomena observed.

Several researchers (e.g., Doyel 1980; Grebinger 1976; Weaver 1972) suggest that some form of environmental instability that was not readily compensated for through the traditional Hohokam irrigation systems taxed the subsistence base in the 1100s. Subsistence insecurity, in turn, led to a political reorganization among the Hohokam. Doyel (1980) argues that the change in focus from ball courts to platform mounds reflects an organizational change from religious and ceremonial control to su-pravillage political organization. He observes that during the Soho phase, platform mounds typically seem to have had a single structure built on their summits, and that these structures may have been residences of persons of special status. The suggestion is that the Hohokam expansion of the Colonial and Sedentary period took place within the framework of a complex ceremonial organization in which sacred power formed the basis of control. During the Classic, the power base is thought to have become secular and to have involved a high-status personage within each irrigation communi-ty. The secular leaders might have been involved in settling disputes over land and water rights, coordinating exchange, resolving conflicts, allying communities, and possibly reallocating resources, as well as serving as loci of socioreligious power. Doyel agrees that the specific features of the organization that are observable in the archaeological remains (i.e., platform mounds) derived from Mesoamerican counterparts but were incorporated within the needs of the Hohokam structure.

There is not sufficient evidence of environmental change in the Hohokam area during the twelfth century. The models discussed above rely on environmental data from the Colorado Plateaus, which may not be applicable to the lower Sonoran Desert. On the other hand, two observations may be related to increased subsistence insecurity during the transition. First, surveys in the Papagueria (Goodyear 1975) indicate increased use of the eroded slopes and uplands during the Sells phase, which is contemporary with the Classic in the Gila and Salt basins. Many of the upland sites seem to have been loci of wild plant procurement and processing. Second, Gasser (1981) has identified an abundance of barley seeds from Sedentary contexts at the Salt River site of La Ciudad. The barley has formal characteristics that are suggestive of deliberate cultivation. If the barley was salt tolerant, as it is in the Old World, then it is possible that the Hohokam experienced the effects of salinization of irrigated fields shortly before the Sedentary–Classic transition. In the absence of climate change, a salinization problem would increase the subsistence insecurity of irrigation and make procurement of wild plant foods important.

By the Civano phase (circa A.D. 1300) and lasting until about 1425, the Hohokam reorganization seems to have been complete. The presence of Gila, Pinto, and Tonto polychromes at some Civano phase sites indicates that the Hohokam were participating to some extent in the pan-Southwestern interaction system that is discussed in the next chapter. Two observations are relevant to the current discussion of abandonment, however. First, the change in pattern that involved a cessation of the building of certain typical Hohokam structures, such as ball courts, and the decrease of items such as macaws, turquoise, and figurines, is not evidence of abandonment. Second, some of the pattern changes may or may not have involved population displacements, although typically Hohokam sites are not found in the Verde Valley after the Sedentary, sites of the Kayenta Anasazi tradition are found in that area, similarly, although Hohokam sites do not persist in the Gila Bend region, sites with Patayan ceramics occur there for the first time. As was the case with the discussion of Mesa Verde "traits" in the San Juan Basin, it is not known if there was biological discontinuity between the Sedentary Hohokam and the Verde Valley Kayenta or the Patayan of the Gila Bend Area. Such discontinuity has generally been assumed by archaeologists, but the more important point is that, rather than depopulation, there was a change in the strategy of use of the areas concerned. In both cases, too, the later strategy (Kayenta Anasazi or Patayan) involved less coordinated labor investment than had the previous Hohokam adaptation, giving the appearance of population decline.

Discussion

The prehistoric abandonment of Southwestern villages has long been considered a great mystery by laymen and archaeologists. The traditional literature offers many suggested reasons for abandonment, none of which is entirely acceptable. In this chapter, it has been argued that a major impediment to understanding abandonment derives from a conceptual failure to distinguish different orders of abandonment and changes in behavior that falsely give the appearance of abandonment.

First, single sites throughout the Southwest were rarely occupied for more than one or two human generations. Discussions of abandonment must consider that this level of residential mobility was the rule and not an exception. Second, small areas (such as single stream valleys) were frequently abandoned with the population moving only short distances. These local abandonments are often attributable to changes in agricultural practices or adjustments to minor climate change. In these instances, movement over short distances was probably an option that was preferable to warfare or major technological investments that would have involved high risk (such as building elaborate water conservation features that would still depend on variable rainfall).

The large-scale regional abandonments of the A.D. 1200s and 1300s are more complex and reflect the scale of the social systems that preceded them. The highly organized systems of the Chacoan San Juan, Paquimé, and the Sedentary Hohokam seem not to have been able to maintain themselves structurally or energetically. Initially, there is the *appearance* of population decline, but the situation may have been one of decentralization, reduced coordination of labor, and changes in village layout. Some trade networks, albeit fragmented, were maintained.

Abandonment of the central San Juan Basin, Paquimé, and sites in the Hohokam core area coincide with population increases in surrounding and upland regions. These movements coincide with a temporary shift from intensive agricultural production to more hunting and gathering and less-intensive agriculture. Within only a short period of time, however, much of the Southwest was once again incorporated within regionally organized systems. The later systems were different from those of the A.D. 1100s and 1200s. They are the subject of the next chapter.

10

The Late Prehistoric Aggregated Villages

The period between about A.D. 1300 and 1540 witnessed geographic shifts in human settlement, the formation of very large aggregates, and the development of distinctive regional art styles in ceramic decoration and kiva wall paintings. This chapter describes these changes and explores contrasting interpretations of Pueblo social and economic organization at aggregated settlements.

Introduction

Following the disintegration of the first systems of regional integration and the end of major residential use of large areas of the Southwest, several new patterns emerged (between about A.D. 1275 and initial contact with Europeans in 1540). The new features included the redistribution of aggregated populations in parts of the Southwest that seem formerly to have been only thinly populated, the formation of very large communities in some areas, and the production and wide distribution of new and colorful types of ceramics. In addition, the archaeological recovery of highly distinctive representational art from this period affords a rich view of some aspects of Southwestern culture.

Many of the larger sites occupied between 1300 and the historic period were intensively tested or excavated during the first half of the 1900s. The work was done, in part, because using the direct historical approach, these sites could provide a relative chronology from historic times to the prehistoric period. For example, early, chronologically oriented studies were conducted in New Mexico at San Cristobal, Pueblo Largo, Pueblo Blanco, and San Lazaro in the Galisteo Basin, (Nelson 1914); at Pecos Pueblo, (Kidder 1924, 1958); at Tyounyi and other sites on the Pajarito Plateau, (Hewett 1909); at the ancestral Zuni site of Hawikuh, (Smith *et al.* 1966); and at the ancestral Jemez Pueblo sites of Unshagi and Giusewa (Reiter 1938). (See Figure 10.1 for these and other sites mentioned in this chapter.) In Arizona, similar kinds of investigations were carried out at large sites in the vicinity of Hopi, such as Kawaika-a and Awatovi on Antelope Mesa (Montgomery *et al.* 1949; Smith 1952, 1971) and Chavez Pass Pueblo (Nuvaqueotaka), and the Homolovi Ruins near Winslow (Fewkes 1896b, 1904). In addition to chronology, these investigations and others continuing into more recent times have been concerned with the origins of specific Pueblo and non-Pueblo groups (Ellis 1967; Ford *et al.* 1972; Hall 1944).

More recently, work involving sites of this late prehistoric period has been directed toward elucidating the nature and degree of social integration reflected within the large aggregated communities and among these sites and their sustaining areas (e.g., Clark 1969; Longacre *et al.* 1982; Upham 1982). Some investigators argue for the presence of social ranking within communities and economic interaction among individuals occupying elite status. Others find the evidence for social ranking unconvincing. In both cases, the focus of inquiry involves examination of burial populations

Figure 10.1 Sites discussed in Chapter 10. 1, Taos area (Old Corn Field Taos, Pot Creek Pueblo, Picuris Pueblo); 2, Chama area (Tsping, Howiri, Tsama, Sawapi); 3, She; 4, Tsankawi and Otowi; 5, Tyuoyi, in Bandelier National Monument; 6, Jemez area (Guisewa, Unshagi); 7, Santa Fe area (Arroyo Hondo, Cienega, Pindi); 8, Pecos area (Pecos, Rowe, Arrowhead, Dick's Ruin); 9, Galisteo Basin (San Cristobal, Pueblo Largo); 10, Albuquerque area (Kuana, Alameda); 11, Tijeras area (Tijeras, San Antonio, Pa-ako); 12, Acoma; 13, Pottery Mound; 14, Salinas District (Chilili, Abo, Quarai, Gran Quivira); 15, Capitan; 16, Tsegi Canyon; 17, Black Mesa; 18, Antelope Mesa (Kwaika-a, Awatovi); 19, Winslow and Homolavi; 20, Anderson Mesa area Middle Little Colorado, (Chavez Pass); 21, Zuni–Hawikuh; 22, Grasshopper and Canyon Creek; 23, Kinishba; 24, Point of Pines; 25, Globe–Miami District (Gila, Togetzoge, Beshbagowa, Tonto Ruin); 26, Virgin River; 27, Pueblo de los Muertos; 28, Escalante group ruins; 29, Casa Grande; 30, Casa Grandes.

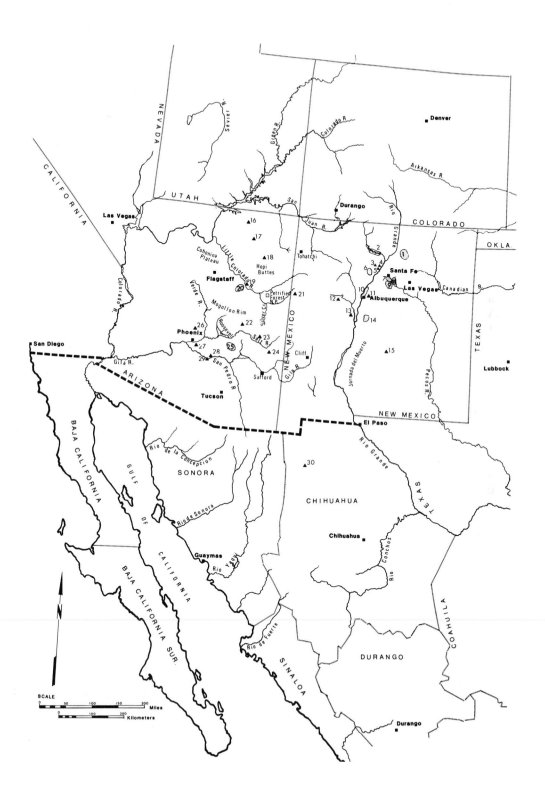

and artifactual evidence of craft specialization and trade. Because the period under consideration terminates with the presence of Europeans in the Southwest and the first written eyewitness accounts of Southwestern peoples, there is considerable concern with evaluating the chronicles of the Spanish explorers and determining the effects of the initial contact on native peoples (e.g., Upham 1982; Wilcox and Masse 1981).

This chapter first examines the distributions of settlements that were founded in the late 1200s and early 1300s. The more common spatial organizations within these communities are also discussed. The chapter then describes the characteristics and distributions of the ceramic diagnostics of the period, particularly those that seem to reflect widespread networks of social interaction and trade. The form, content, and interpretations of the art styles of this period are discussed, specifically in regard to how they inform us about Pueblo ritual systems and to the continuing debate about the possibility of their Mesoamerican origins. The chapter develops the interpretative arguments about the nature of some Southwestern societies at the time of contact through extended discussion of two research projects in the western Pueblo area: the University of Arizona's investigations at Grasshopper Pueblo and Arizona State University's work at Chavez Pass Pueblo, (also known by its Hopi name, Nuvaqueotaka). Finally, this chapter provides a brief introduction to the beginnings of the historic period in the Southwest and to some of the issues relating to Spanish disruption of the native traditions and to southern Athapaskan archaeology.

Distributions and Patterns of Settlements

Most of the Rio Grande Valley and immediately adjacent portions of eastern New Mexico seem not to have been densely inhabited by sedentary peoples before 1300. There were quite large villages of pithouses and associated surface structures in the mountains near Taos and in the Gallina country northwest of Santa Fe (Cordell 1979; Green 1976; Hibben 1948; Woosley 1980) and numerous small pueblos of contiguous aboveground rooms scattered throughout the valleys of the Rio Grande and its tributaries (Cordell 1979; Dickson 1979; Wendorf and Reed 1955); nevertheless, these do not compare in number or size to the later prehistoric sites in the area.

Some of the better known, very large sites of the Chama River valley, the Pajarito Plateau, and the Taos area include the 600 room Te'ewi (Wendorf 1953b), Tsiping, Howiri, Tsama, the Sapawe (a vast adobe ruin that has multiple room block and plaza areas covering an estimated 29 ha), Tsankawi, Tshirege, Puyé (the ancestral Santa Clara pueblo [Figure 10.2]), Otowi, Tyounyi (Figure 10.3), Pot Creek Pueblo, Old Picuris, and "Cornfield Taos" (the ancestral Taos village) (Cordell 1979; Dick 1965b; Ellis and Brody 1964; Hewett 1906; Steen 1977; Wetherington 1964). Further south, near Santa Fe, large, late prehistoric pueblos include Arroyo Hondo (Schwartz and Lang 1972), Cieneguilla Pueblo, Pindi Pueblo (Stubbs and Stallings 1953), and the Galisteo Basin pueblos—Pueblo Largo, San Cristobal, San Marcos, Las Madres, and Pueblo Lumbre (Lang 1977a). There is a series of large sites of this period along the upper Pecos, for

Figure 10.2 Caveate Ruins at Puyé, New Mexico. Rooms are cut out of the soft Bandelier tuff formation below the mesa top at the ancestral Santa Clara Pueblo. (Photograph courtesy of the Museum of New Mexico.)

example, the early portions of Pecos Pueblo, Rowe Ruin, Arrowhead, and Dick's Ruin (Cordell 1979; Holden 1955; Kidder 1958). Near Albuquerque, aggregated pueblos include Kuaua, Alameda, Paako, Tijeras, and San Antonio. Some of these sites contain historic period components (Cordell 1979; Lambert 1954; Tichy 1938). South of Albuquerque, the large and unusual site of Pottery Mound (Hibben 1975) dates to this period, as do the Piro pueblos described by the early Spanish explorers (Cordell and Earls 1982b; Marshall and Walt 1984).

There was an expansion of settlement to the east in New Mexico. Quite large settlements were founded on the margins of the Estancia Basin and the Llano Estacado: for example, the pueblos of the Salinas District (the salt lakes of the Estancia Basin), such as Chilili, Abo, Quarai, and the impressive stone pueblo of Gran Quivira (Hayes 1981b). The latter three sites became locations of seventeenth-century Spanish missions, as did some of the Piro pueblos. Finally, on the southeastern edge of the Southwest, the Lincoln phase sites of the Capitan and Jornada del Muerto areas (Jane Kelley 1966) are manifestations of the eastward expansion of Southwestern peoples.

The sites of the Rio Grande area and eastern New Mexico exhibit considerable variation in construction materials and techniques. Some, like Sapawe, Kuaua, Arroyo Hondo, Tijeras Pueblo, Pottery Mound, and the Lincoln phase sites, were built of

Figure 10.3 Tyounyi, Bandelier National Monument, New Mexico. The ruins of Tyounyi in the Rito de los Frijoles are among the late Anasazi sites that are visited by thousands of visitors each year. (Photograph taken in 1910 by Jesse Nusbaum and reproduced courtesy of the Museum of New Mexico.)

coursed, puddled adobe. The larger sites had multiple plaza areas surrounded by room blocks, one very large kiva or great kiva, and frequently smaller kivas as well. Other large sites, such as Tsiping, Tsankawi, Pecos (Figure 10.4), and Rowe Pueblo, are multistory, multiplaza masonry pueblos. The Piro pueblos are somewhat smaller than those farther north. One excavated example was constructed of coursed adobe with an interior core of unshaped river cobbles. Again, small round kivas and sometimes a very large kiva are typical, but kivas are neither uniformly present nor always round. For example, there does not appear to be a kiva at Rowe Pueblo, and Tijeras Pueblo has a very large round kiva (20 m in diameter) as well as rectangular kivas that were incorporated within room blocks (Cordell 1979). In none of the excavated examples of kivas, however, were the elaborate floor features known from Chacoan great kivas (benches, niches, paired vaults, etc.) present. The lack of these features has been problematic for some archaeologists, who would view the major, aggregated Rio Grande pueblos as the result of population influx from the San Juan Basin. It must be recalled, however, that the Chacoan system failed at least 50–100 years prior to the construction of these Rio Grande sites, and if the Chacoan great kivas were somehow emblematic of their cultural contexts, that context has disappeared. In much the same way, archaeologists have also been concerned about the absence of kivas and other architectural features that are closely similar to those of the Mesa Verde, which is also viewed as a population source for the Rio Grande pueblos. At the same time, some types of Rio Grande ceramics, particularly Santa Fe Black-on-white and Galisteo Black-on-white, resemble Chacoan and Mesa Verde types, respectively (Ford *et al.* 1972).

The major issue is that whereas the large, aggregated sites of the Rio Grande area do suggest a population influx, and the archaeological record of the San Juan Basin and Mesa Verde indicate that they are likely sources of population, there are no sites that are so closely similar to those of the population source areas that they can be considered evidence of a migrant community. In fact, the kind of migration pattern that might produce a "site unit intrusion" (Rouse 1958:64) is relatively rare ethnographi-

Figure 10.4   Pecos National Monument, New Mexico. The view is to the south, toward the church and the National Park Service buildings. The kiva in the foreground has been reconstructed for visitors. (Photograph taken in 1967 by Fred Mang and reproduced courtesy of the National Park Service.)

cally. More commonly, individuals and family groups follow separate migration paths, integrating themselves into ongoing communities where they have kinship or friendship ties (e.g., Colson, 1979; Scudder 1979). Archaeologically, this form of migration would be visible primarily as a regional increase in population. The accompanying shift from relatively small, dispersed settlements to large, aggregated villages is a different, but related, aspect of the problem. Because large villages are also a feature of the late prehistoric period of other parts of the Southwest, aggregation is treated separately in more detail below.

Changes in population distribution and some population increase also occurred in the Acoma and Zuni areas (Anyon and Ferguson 1983; Kintigh 1980; Ruppé 1966). On the western flanks of Cebolleta Mesa, west of Acoma Pueblo, the period between 1200 and 1400 witnessed a change in settlement distribution and site plans. The southwestern portion of Cebolleta Mesa was abandoned, but very large, planned, defensive sites were built further to the north. Among these are sites consisting of between 200 and 367 rooms, one of which is associated with a sandstone masonry defensive wall that still stood to a height of more than 3 m in the twentieth century. Ruppé (1966:330) notes that the population of the areas around Acoma that he surveyed was greater than it had been previously, suggesting migration into the area. Although he anticipated that supporting evidence of migration would be found in the recovery of greater amounts of "foreign" ceramics, this was not the case. The amounts of imported ceramics appear to have remained about the same as they had been.

In the Zuni area, there were also marked changes in settlements. Between 1175 and 1275, there was an increase in site size from previous periods, and also closer spacing of sites. Most sites at this time were located at fairly high elevations in settings where runoff from large watersheds could be tapped for agriculture. Between 1275 and 1400, the high valley sites were completely abandoned and population aggregated within fewer exceptionally large (over 1000 rooms), multistoried pueblos with room blocks arranged around internal plazas and walls encircling the sites. These very large sites seem not to have been occupied for long periods, and there was a relocation of sites toward downstream settings at this time. Between 1400 and 1700, the Zuni district continued to be dominated by large sites, six or seven of which were inhabited at the time of the first contact with Europeans in 1540. In contrast to the previous period, the later sites seem to have had longer periods of uninterrupted occupation (Smith *et al.* 1966), and it was not until about 1700 that the population of Zuni was restricted to a single permanently occupied village at Halona:wa, or present-day Zuni Pueblo (Ferguson 1983). A long period of residential stability also characterizes Acoma Pueblo, which may have been continuously inhabited from about 1200.

The distribution of settlements in the Anasazi area west of Zuni parallels that to the east. Prior to 1200 the inhabitants withdrew from the northern portions of Black Mesa, the Virgin River area, the Cohonina Plateau west of Flagstaff, and much of the Kayenta region with the exception of the Tsegi Canyon area (Dean 1970). Large aggregated pueblos, consisting of from 50 to several hundred rooms, were located at Anderson Mesa, the middle Little Colorado, Silver Creek, Hopi Buttes, and Tsegi Canyon. Dean's (1970) analysis of tree-ring dates from the Tsegi Canyon area sites, including Betatakin

Figure 10.5   Granary at Kiet Siel, Navajo National Monument, Arizona. Kiet Siel, a well-known Tsegi phase site, was inhabited for only about 50 years, from A.D. 1250 to 1300. (Photograph from Dean [1969: Figure 86]. Courtesy of the Arizona State Museum.)

and Kiet Siel (Figure 10.5), indicates that the Tsegi phase, which consisted of large cliff dwellings, lasted only 50 years, from 1250 to 1300. Other sites, such as Chavez Pass Pueblo, Awatovi, and Kawika-a, were occupied for much longer periods. Sites on the Hopi mesas that were apparently small villages in the 1100s became sites of 200 or more rooms by the 1300s and 1400s (Adams 1983). Typically, the large western sites are of multistory masonry construction, with plazas surrounded by room blocks. Kivas are of both circular and rectangular form.

Large aggregated sites and apparently some population influx are also noted for the mountainous portions of eastern Arizona near the Mogollon Rim, and within the Gila,

Salt, and San Pedro drainages. Some of the better known of these sites are Kinishba (Cummings, 1937, 1940), Canyon Creek, and other sites in the Sierra Ancha (Haury 1934), Point of Pines (Haury 1958, and see Chapter 6), and Grasshopper Ruin (Graves and Longacre 1982). Specifically within the Tonto Basin and Globe–Miami areas of central Arizona, the aggregated villages of the fourteenth century include Gila Pueblo (Gladwin 1957), Togetzoge (Schmidt 1928), Besh-ba-gowah (Vickery 1939), and Tonto Ruin (Steen *et al.* 1962). The Tonto Basin sites have been termed Salado (Gladwin and Gladwin 1930) because they reflect a constellation of traits that the Gladwins believed originated within the Salado branch of the Mogollon and intruded into the Tonto area. These traits include compound pueblos with multistory contiguous rooms, post-reinforced adobe walls, extended inhumations, and Pinto, Tonto, and Gila poly-chrome ceramics (Figure 10.6). There is considerable debate about the utility of defining the Salado as a cultural entity and viewing the appearance of these traits as evidence of an invasion of foreign elements (Doyel and Haury 1976). The issue is discussed in greater detail below. Nevertheless, there is an apparent population in-crease and the restructuring of settlements in the Tonto Basin, the San Pedro Valley, the Safford area of Arizona, and the Cliff region of New Mexico.

The Hohokam heartland also witnessed settlement restructuring, and possibly pop-ulation increase, as is indicated by "Salado" features at sites such as Los Muertos, Casa Grande, and the Escalante Ruin group (Doyel 1975, 1976; Weaver 1972). The popula-tion aggregates of the Arizona desert and mountain regions were not as stable as those of northern New Mexico in that the large villages were not inhabited into the sixteenth century. There is little agreement among prehistorians of the area about the manifesta-tions that can be regarded as ancestral to the Pima and Papago, but there is no indication that the "Salado" compounds were inhabited much later than about 1450.

Finally, but important, the imposing multistory adobe compounds of Paquimé

Figure 10.6   Gila Polychrome jars. Gila Polychrome is a diagnostic Salado type. A, photograph courtesy of the Museum of New Mexico; B, illustration by Charles M. Carrillo.)

(Casas Grandes) in Chihuahua were certainly occupied, if not expanded, throughout the fourteenth and fifteenth centuries. The regional influence of Paquimé as a center of population, craft specilization, and exchange should not be underestimated in discussions of the period.

Although the emphasis in the preceding discussions has been on the large sites of the post-1300 era, it is somewhat misleading to consider these sites as altogether typical. It is probably true that most people maintained residences in or affiliated with the large pueblos; however, throughout the inhabited areas there are numerous very small sites, fieldhouses, and limited-activity loci. In many of the areas that remained occupied after 1300 or witnessed a population increase in the fourteenth century, the first evidence of soil- and water-control features dates to this time. Agricultural field systems are frequently associated with small sites that may have been occupied only seasonally. The soil- and water-control features at Point of Pines and in the northern Rio Grande that were described in Chapter 6 date to this period.

Ceramic Production and Distribution

Throughout much of Southwestern prehistory, there is an apparent continuity of ceramic styles within local areas. At the same time, some styles of decoration were used over very broad areas within which there were many centers of production, as seen, for example, in the relatively early Kana-a design styles of the Anasazi area. At other times, some specific types of ceramics were produced in one or a few locations and very widely traded. This situation seems to be true of the eleventh-century Chacoan types discussed in previous chapters. The relatively new development of the late thirteenth and fourteenth centuries is that a few ceramic types were produced and traded over enormous distances and a few decorative styles were widely copied on locally produced types. Although the social processes underlying these distributions are not completely understood, the result is great homogeneity among some classes of ceramics across most of the Southwest. Finally, particularly in cases where trade types are involved, locally produced types continued to be manufactured and were often more numerous than trade pieces.

The three most important and well documented of the late prehistoric ceramic wares contributing to the patterns described above are the White Mountain redwares, the Salado polychromes, and the Rio Grande glazes. Some of the more important characteristics of each of these are described in detail below.

The White Mountain redwares (Carlson 1970) consist of 15 related types that were produced between about A.D. 1000 and 1500 in east-central Arizona and western New Mexico. The types consist of bichromes (black-on-red, such as Puerco, Wingate, St. Johns, and Pinedale) and related polychromes (black-and-white-on-red, such as St. Johns, Springerville, Pinedale, and Fourmile). Carlson (1970) notes that there are three regions in which White Mountain redware variants are found: the Cibola area, extending from Tohatchi, New Mexico, on the north to Carizzo Wash on the south and from the Petrified Forest on the west to the Continental Divide on the East; the

Mogollon Rim area from Roosevelt Lake to the White River and from Silver Creek to the Salt River; and the Rio Grande Valley.

Carlson (1970) defines six temporally significant though partially overlapping design styles for the time span during which the White Mountain redwares were produced. These are distinguished primarily on the basis of the treatment of motifs and layout or focus rather than on design content. Each of the design styles is similar or related to those produced on black-on-white ceramic types.

One type of White Mountain redware—St. Johns Polychrome—and one design style—Pinedale—are of particular interest in the context of the present discussion. St. Johns Polychrome was made between about A.D. 1175 and 1300. The type is represented almost entirely in the form of bowls with a red or orange-red slip on both the interior and exterior. Painted designs are executed in black matte or glaze paint on the interiors and in chalky, kaolin white on the exteriors. Most of the vessels discussed by Carlson are decorated in the Tularosa style, which consists of a wide band of decoration on the bowl wall with the center of the bowl unadorned (Figure 10.7). Design elements on bowl interiors most commonly consist of massed, joined, interlocked solid and hatched units. The white designs on the bowl exteriors generally consist of frets, keys, meanders, opposed half terraces, and scrolls in continuous patterns and medium line widths.

St. Johns Polychrome, and probably its associated type, St. Johns Black-on-red, were among the most widely distributed and technological variable types known in the Southwest. The spatial distribution of St. Johns extends from Mesa Verde on the north to Casas Grandes on the south. It has been found as far east as Pecos, New Mexico, and as far west as the Chino Valley in Arizona. Carlson notes that the type is most frequent to the south and west of the center of this enormous area. He suggests that the types were made in the Cibola area, perhaps in more than one locality. The temporal and spatial distribution of St. Johns Polychrome is interesting. It was produced very late in the Chacoan period and continued to be made and traded through the collapse of the

Figure 10.7 Tularosa style bowl decoration. The Tularosa style with both solid and hatched elements occurs on pottery of different types. (Illustrated by Charles M. Carrillo.)

Chacoan system. Although the kinds of petrographic analyses that would help determine the specific loci at which it was made have not been done, the abundance of the
type at sites near Zuni, at Manuelito Canyon, and along the Tularosa and San Francisco
rivers suggests that these areas began to become population centers before the final
dispersal of populations out of the Mesa Verde and San Juan Basin areas (see Chapter
9).

The Pinedale style (Figure 10.8) appears on some late St. Johns vessels but becomes
common between about A.D. 1300 and 1375 (Carlson 1970). Carlson (1982) suggests
that the style came out of the Kayenta tradition of Arizona and spread very widely
throughout the Southwest. In contrast to St. Johns, the types included within the
Pinedale style are decorated with designs executed in both black and white on the
exterior of the bowls. The style is similar to the preceding Tularosa style but is bolder
in execution, contains more squiggled line fillers and less repetition of motifs, and
focuses decoration on the entire field of the bowl interior. Pinedale Black-on-red,
Pinedale Polychrome, and Cedar Creek Polychrome are types decorated in Pinedale
style. Although these types center in the Mogollon Rim country between Silver Creek
and Roosevelt Lake, most are distributed over a broader area. Of particular interest
here is that some types in the Pinedale style are considered ancestral to Hopi ceramics
(e.g., Kintiel and Klagetoh Polychrome) and some are ancestral to Zuni pottery
(Heshotauthla Polychrome). The Hopi and Zuni types, in turn, inspired the Rio
Grande glazes produced by the Pueblo of the Rio Grande Valley. Carlson (1982:223)
also includes the earliest Salado polychrome type within the Pinedale style.

The Salado polychromes are of three types—Pinto, Gila, and Tonto—originally
defined on the basis of the Gladwin's work in the middle Gila area of Arizona (Gladwin and Gladwin 1930). There is considerable debate about the dating and origins of
the Salado types and whether the distributions of the types represent the migrations of
groups of people or a similarity in production styles over a broad area. Carlson (1982)
suggests that Pinto Polychrome was produced between about A.D. 1275 and 1400 and

Figure 10.8 Pinedale style decoration. The Pinedale
style, bolder than Tularosa style, occurs on some late
St. Johns vessels; it continued to be used on later
types. (Illustrated by Charles M. Carrillo.)

considers its decoration to be similar to the Pinedale and later Fourmile style of design in the White Mountain redwares. In Pinto Polychrome the bowl exterior is slipped with light orange and is not painted. The interior is generally slipped white and decorated with black carbon-paint designs. The distribution of Pinto Polychrome alone, in the absence of Gila and Tonto polychromes, is limited (Doyel and Haury 1976). Gila Polychrome was produced from 1300 to perhaps as late as 1600 and is the most widely distributed of the Salado polychromes. The color scheme is that of Pinto Polychrome, but the black painted designs cover the bottom of bowl interiors. Tonto Polychrome may have begun slightly later than Gila Polychrome (ca. 1350), but it too may have been produced until 1600. Tonto Polychrome has black-and-white designs painted on the red slipped exterior of bowls but is otherwise similar to Gila Polychrome. Gila and Tonto polychromes are, once again, distributed over an enormous area extending from Casas Grandes, in Chihuahua, to the Agua Fria drainage north of Phoenix and from the Gila–Salt area in the west to the Mimbres Valley in the East. In some locations, such as Casas Grandes, the Gila Polychrome was locally produced (Di Peso 1976), whereas in other areas, such as the Lower San Pedro River Valley, it seems to have been imported (Franklin and Masse 1976).

Carlson comments that in the 1300s Gila Polychrome replaced St. Johns Polychrome of the previous century "in the sense that both were the most widespread common polychromes of their respective centuries, and both were luxury items, fancy containers painted in specific styles and color patterns and probably necessary to the maintenance of some cultural sub-system" (1982:224).

The Rio Grande glazes were produced between about A.D. 1300 and 1700, initially probably in imitation of the St. Johns and Heshotauthla polychromes of the Cibola area that had been traded into the Rio Grande Valley. The use of glaze black paint for decoration occurred in some White Mountain and Zuni ceramics until the mid-1400s; however, after that time the use of this kind of paint was continued only in the Rio Grande Valley area. The glaze itself was achieved by using copper and manganese or copper and lead as pigments.

Petrographic work by Warren (1977) suggests that the earliest Rio Grande glazes were made at a number of different centers in the vicinity of Albuquerque and were widely traded not only in the Rio Grande area itself but also to the adjacent Plains. After about 1450, sites in the Galisteo Basin became production locations for glazes with cream or yellow colored interior slips. Although glazes originating in the Galisteo Basin were traded to other localities within the Rio Grande Valley, especially to sites on the Pajarito Plateau and the Santa Fe plain, they seem not to have been distributed as widely south of Albuquerque or east of the Sandia Mountains.

Finally, during the 1600s, glaze pottery was produced at only a few locations: the Salinas area, the Galisteo Basin, and at Pecos Pueblo and Zia Pueblo (Snow 1982). During the early Spanish Colonial Period, some glaze pottery was made that incorporated European forms such as soup plates and pitchers, and Pueblo pottery was widely used by the Spanish colonists. Following the Pueblo Revolt of 1680 and the Spanish Reconquest of 1692, both Pueblo and Spanish colonial economies underwent considerable reorganization. By the mid-1700s, Spanish land grants and mineral claims precluded Indian access to their previous sources of lead, and the native production of glaze-painted ceramics ended (Snow 1982).

In sum, a tradition of polychrome ceramic manufacturing began in the Cibola area in the twelfth century with the White Mountain redwares. Not only were these types widely traded, but the styles used in their decoration became the bases for two other polychrome traditions. These were the Salado polychromes and the Rio Grande glazes, each of which was widely traded as well. Although ceramic types and styles of decoration are certainly distinguishable, the color schemes and design layouts of ceramics produced from the late twelfth century into the historic period show a considerable homogeneity throughout much of the Southwest. In some places, local production of types that continued pre-twelfth-century traditions persisted. For example, in the Jemez, Taos, and Chama country of the northern Rio Grande Valley, a black-on-white and black-on-gray tradition continued despite the neighboring contemporary manufacture of glaze polychromes. In the Hohokam area, buff wares and Salado polychromes were used within the same villages. The latter instance is one aspect of the invasion interpretation of the Salado.

Interpretations of Salado Cultural Identity

A brief recapitulation of the controversy surrounding the Salado is given here, because it exemplifies a larger problem in the archaeological interpretation of cultural identity. As noted above, the Gladwins (e.g., 1934, 1935) suggested the name *Salado* be applied to a "people who colonized the upper Salt River drainage" from the Tonto–Globe area. The evidence for a Salado intrusion into the Hohokam heartland was the apparently abrupt appearance of Salado polychrome pottery, coursed adobe multistory great houses (at Casa Grande, especially), and extended inhumations under room floors and accompanied by Salado pottery at the great houses. Within the Hohokam heartland and in fact at Casa Grande and Los Muertos, paddle-and-anvil finished Hohokam buffware ceramics, cremations, and single-story adobe compounds continued as part of the archaeological record of the Hohokam Classic period. Further, the Hohokam canal system was maintained, if not expanded, during the Classic; Hohokam ball courts and platform mounds apparently continued as well. The existence of two ceramic traditions, architectural styles, and burial modes at the same sites leads to the conclusion that "Salado people" had peacefully colonized the Hohokam area, and that "the two societies, with their distinctive brands of Southwestern culture, lived side by side in apparent peace for more than a century" (Willey 1966:228).

In the past, most of the debate regarding the Salado has focused on who they were and from where they came. The Salado have been viewed as Mogollon, as Anasazi, as a "blend" of Mogollon and Anasazi, and as a "blend" of Anasazi and Hohokam. They have been described as originating within the Tonto–Globe area, the Flagstaff area, the upper Little Colorado, and the Casas Grandes area of Chihuahua (for reviews see Doyel 1976; Lindsay and Jennings 1968; Whittlesley and Reid 1982).

Continuing discussion on the Salado (e.g., Doyel and Haury 1976) has concentrated primarily on describing local and regional manifestations that have been termed

Salado and on examining the locations at which the Salado traits are demonstrably early. No consensual view has prevailed in these discussions. Rather, investigators have pointed out that in several areas, including the Hohokam heartland, Salado ceramics occur at a small percentage of Classic period sites and, in fact, make up a very small percentage of the ceramics at most sites where they do occur (Weaver 1976); that inhumations occur in pre-Classic Hohokam contexts and in Classic Hohokam sites associated with non-Salado ceramics; and that adobe walled compounds in the Hohokam area are not exclusively associated with Salado ceramics (Pailes 1963). Multistory adobe great houses are exceptionally rare in the Hohokam area; however, multistory construction is, of course, common in the Southwest and, on temporal grounds alone, might have been introduced from a number of different locations (Schroeder 1953b; Weaver 1976).

In a thoughtful discussion of the Salado issue, based on data from the Tonto–Roosevelt region (one of the posited Salado homelands), Whittlesley and Reid (1982) argue that insufficient attention has been given to describing assemblage variability among contemporary sites in the Hohokam core area and its peripheries. For example, their analyses indicate that the method of vessel thinning (paddle and anvil vs. coil and scrape), which has been used as a cultural or ethnic marker for distinguishing Hohokam from Salado ceramics, varies with vessel form. They suggest that the Tonto Basin was used over time by a diversity of groups, some more closely allied to the Hohokam and some to the Mogollon. By A.D. 1200, after the Hohokam system contracted spatially, the Tonto Basin became more similar to the mountain Mogollon. Whittlesley and Reid, however, eschew cultural labels. They state that "it is abundantly clear that traditional conceptions of monothetic cultural types (Hohokam, Mogollon, Anasazi) and their cultural varieties (Salado, Sinagua, and others) cannot cope with the polythetic phenomena that we see throughout the Southwest after A.D. 1150" (Whittlesley and Reid 1982:80).

Given the difficulties in locating a Salado homeland and in consistently defining the Salado manifestation, it seems preferable to relinquish the notion that the Salado were a people with a cultural identity. It appears more productive to relate the changes in the Hohokam area to a structural reorganization of Hohokam society and Hohokam participation within a pan-Southwestern system of economic interaction (Doyel 1976; Gumerman and Weed 1976; Weaver 1976). Without specifying the kind of structural reorganization or economic interaction, this says very little, and most authors have eschewed elaboration. Nevertheless, Doyel (1976) and Grebinger (1971, 1976) view the late 1200s as a time when Hohokam populations began to contract spatially, possibly as a response to deteriorating climatic conditions. Grebinger suggests that the contraction and aggregation of population led to participation within a vast trading network organized through the activities of families of long-distance traders and regularized interaction among communities in adjacent valleys. Although there is no particular objection to either of these notions, they are far from explanatory.

If Casas Grandes, during the Medio period, functioned as a regional trade center, which seems likely, we must have a better understanding of how that trade was organized and pursued. If Salado ceramics were social markers of participation within an interaction sphere, we must have a better understanding of their cultural and archaeological contexts. It is difficult to envision diffusion of a mode of architecture, such as the compound, unless such architecture also served real functional requirements within the societies accepting them. We need to know more precisely what these were. In sum, the diversity of remains that have been referred to as Salado do not seem to represent a socially bounded group of people. The Salado manifestation does seem to be part of a general Southwestern trend toward village aggregation and formal mechanisms of exchange among aggregated villages, but it remains to carefully document the actual exchange of materials and the contexts in which they are found, and to explain these within a more specific model of social interaction.

Kiva Murals

Four archaeological sites dating to the period of the fourteenth to the sixteenth centuries provide evidence of a strong tradition of religious art. The locations of the sites and the general similarities in the content and execution of the art also indicate a widely shared religious tradition among the late prehistoric pueblos. Two of the sites, and the first to be excavated, are Kawaika-a and Awatovi, ancestral Hopi sites in the Jeddito area of Arizona (Montgomery *et al.* 1949; Smith 1952). The other two sites are Kuaua, on the banks of the Rio Grande just north of Albuquerque (Dutton 1963), and Pottery Mound, located on the Rio Puerco of the East, near the town of Los Lunas south of Albuquerque (Hibben 1975).

At each of these sites, multiple layers of murals were preserved on the interior walls of rectangular kivas. The kiva walls had been plastered, many times, with a mixture of clay and sand, and some of the plaster layers had been painted. Although the details of the paintings differ among the sites, there are also many similarities. For example, figures are commonly shown wearing flaring kilts with sashes and holding similar ritual objects such as staffs, gourd water containers, and quivers. In each case, too, the ritual nature of the paintings is reflected not only in their subject matter but also by the practice of deliberately plastering over the painting, presumably once its purpose had been fulfilled.

The colors used in the kiva paintings include yellow, red, blue, pink, green, orange, black, and white. Most of the colors were obtained from mineral pigments such as limonite, hematite, or copper carbonate. Some of the kiva paintings are of geometric designs that are very similar to those painted on the contemporary Hopi Sikyatki polychrome ceramics (an elaborated descendant of the late White Mountain redwares). Other designs, however, are naturalistic.

The naturalistic designs in the kiva murals show a variety of costumed figures, masked figures, emblems, plants, some animals, insects, mythical creatures, feathers, and birds—flatly painted. Although several of the figures are done as isolated elements, some of the paintings show figures interacting in scenes along one or more walls. The murals incorporate symbolic elements that are recognizable among Pueblo people today and many of which are still used in ritual context, such as lightning motifs, terraced clouds, and moisture representations. The detail in costumed figures provides an extraordinary view of textiles, headdresses, and other adornment that is rarely preserved archaeologically (Figure 10.9).

The practice of painting on kiva walls is documented as early as Pueblo II among the Anasazi (Brew 1946; Smith 1952). Prior to the fourteenth century, however, paintings were either simple lines and dots or small, stylized figures. The early stylized figures were not shown interacting with each other in recognizable scenes as they are in the later murals discussed here. The realistic detail of the late prehistoric kiva murals as well as their ritual significance is well documented in Dutton's (1963) study of the Kuaua murals—in which many of the specific activities depicted were interpreted by a Zuni informant.

Controversial aspects of the kiva murals involve their particular origin and mode of introduction into the Southwest and the degree to which their content represents a pan-Pueblo symbolic structure. Some investigators (e.g., Brody 1979; Di Peso *et al.* 1974:301–308; Hibben 1975) attribute the murals and their symbols to Mesoamerican sources. Examples of Mesoamerican elements include the *awanyu* or plumed serpent, sometimes associated with a star, and depictions of various parrots. Kelley and Kelley (1975) have argued that the *awanyu* representations indicate the introduction,

Figure 10.9 Kiva mural figures. Despite minor differences, the figures represented in late prehistoric Pueblo kiva paintings are similar in execution. Kiva murals are invaluable sources of information regarding prehistoric costume and adornment. Many of the rituals and symbols represented are recognizable to modern Pueblo peoples. A, adaptation of a figure found on a kiva mural at Pottery Mound, south of Albuquerque, New Mexico. (Courtesy of the Maxwell Museum of Anthropology, University of New Mexico.) B, adaptation of a figure found on a kiva mural at Kuaua, in Bernalillo, New Mexico (Dutton 1963: Figure 113). C, adaptation of a figure found on a kiva mural found at Awatovi, on Antelope Mesa, Arizona. (Adapted from *Kiva Mural Decorations at Awatovi and Kawaika-a* [Smith 1952, Peabody Museum Papers, vol. 37, fig. 81b] with the permission of the Peabody Museum of Archaeology and Ethnology, Harvard University.

Figure 10.10 Figure from Mesoamerican codex. The costume and figurative treatment do not resemble the Pueblo kiva mural figures illustrated in Figure 10.9. (Adapted from *Indian Clothing Before Cortes: Mesoamerican Costumes from the Codices,* by Patricia Rieff Anawalt. Copyright 1981 by the University of Oklahoma Press. Illustration adapted by Charles M. Carrillo.)

presumably by *pochteca,* of the Toltec cult of Quetzalcoatl into the Southwest. In a critique of various discussions of Mesoamerican–Southwestern connections, McGuire (1980) points out that snake symbolism, in general, seems to be of great antiquity in the Southwest. He also notes that whereas Quetzalcoatl is associated with sky symbolism among the Toltecs and Aztecs, the *awanyu* of Pueblo religion is related to water and may be thought to be responsible for floods, earthquakes, and landslides. McGuire suggests that the Pueblo *awanyu* does not represent the introduction of a Toltec cult but rather that it defines the northern extent of "a basic set of beliefs and symbols that were variously combined in different cults" (McGuire 1980:25) both in Mesoamerica and in the Southwest. In addition, although certain elements shown in the kiva murals may be of Mesoamerican origin, the manner of representation as well as specific elements, designs, and motifs are entirely Puebloan (Figure 10.9; cf. Figure 10.10). Kiva murals are unlike Mesoamerican art in their flat, rather simple quality and in their inclusion of pottery and blanket designs, butterflies, dragonflies, frogs, and animal tracks.

In an analysis of rock art, Schaafsma and Schaafsma (1974:539) define a "Rio Grande Style" that in many ways parallels the fourteenth-century kiva art. The Schaafsmas suggest that the "Rio Grande Style" derives from the Jornada Mogollon area and represents the introduction of kachina ceremonialism in the Southwest. They argue that the kachina cult entered the Pueblo world between 1325 and 1350 and spread from the Rio Grande Valley west to Zuni and Hopi within the fourteenth century. Although it is very difficult to interpret rock art and date it with any accuracy, the Schaafsmas' discussion emphasizes the pan-Pueblo nature of the art forms described. The kachina cult itself, as known among the Pueblo in historic times, has been considered to be possibly of Mesoamerican origin (Brew 1943; Kelley and Kelley 1975), but most investigators do not find the evidence of direct connection convincing. Again, some basic elements seem to be part of a very ancient, shared tradition of symbols, perhaps augmented by occasional contacts.

Late Prehistoric Organization

Arguments about the origins of Pueblo symbols and cults are less important than an understanding of the ways in which the societies participating in the tradition were organized. McGuire (1980) rightly states that trade cannot be treated either as a prime mover explaining cultural developments or as a factor independent of production and demand that is imbedded in other aspects of culture. He suggests examination of the dynamic patterns of interaction among societies in the Southwest and those in northern and northwestern Mexico (Durango, Sonora, and Sinaloa), noting that at times, "trade within the Southwest and with northwest Mexico may have reinforced and accelerated this increase in social complexity through the establishment of emissary or middleman trade between elites" (1980:27).

McGuire's paper raises the issue of determining the level of complexity achieved in some parts of the Southwest in the centuries immediately preceding contact with European culture. As the examples discussed below indicate, this issue is far from resolved. Some investigators maintain that a tribal level of society like that ethnographically documented among the Pueblo is an appropriate analog for the prehistoric era as well, but other prehistorians have developed the idea that contact with Europeans, the decimation of native Southwestern populations by introduced diseases, and changes in social organization resulting from European political and religious administrative regulations disrupted and altered a situation that differed fundamentally from that of the ethnographically known Pueblo. The precontact situation, they aver, was one characterized by social hierarchies and by supravillage integration coordinated through individuals of elite status.

These alternative interpretations have been presented in discussions of sites that are roughly contemporary and not more than about 96.5 km apart: Grasshopper Pueblo (Graves, *et al.* 1982; Longacre and Reid 1974) and Chavez Pass Pueblo (Upham 1982). Each of these is discussed here.

Grasshopper Pueblo: A Tribal Model

Grasshopper Pueblo is located on an old channel of the Salt River Draw, below the Mogollon Rim in east-central Arizona. Between about A.D. 1200 and 1300, prior to the founding of Grasshopper Pueblo itself, small settlements of from 1 to 20 rooms were dispersed within the Grasshopper region. Although the specific location at which Grasshopper Pueblo was built was occupied before 1300, the initial construction of the pueblo room blocks took place in about 1300. At that time, two small construction units of 5 and 10 rooms and a larger unit of 21 rooms were built on each side of the creek channel. It has been suggested that the founding population was attracted to the area by the presence of arable land of good quality, and that the large unit of rooms may have been constructed by migrants from the nearby village of Chodistas, which was apparently burned just before 1300. The major building activity at Grasshopper was completed just after A.D. 1330. By then, the pueblo consisted of about 500 rooms, a corridor connecting two of the room blocks had been roofed, and an open plaza had been roofed and converted into a great kiva.

The very rapid growth of Grasshopper Pueblo could not have resulted solely from a population increase; the community at Grasshopper must have been augmented by people moving to the site from smaller sites in the Grasshopper area. In addition to the attraction of arable land, Graves *et al.* (1982) suggest that the network of alliances that had operated among the small communities, especially those ensuring marriage partners, would have been disrupted by the presence of an aggregated village at Grasshopper. These small communities could no longer sustain themselves and grow, so they were abandoned and their population moved to Grasshopper and perhaps some of the other larger pueblos in the region. Finally, it is suggested that people were attracted to Grasshopper Pueblo because it was a center of intercommunity exchange. Items traded into Grasshopper included White Mountain Redware from the north, shell, perhaps from the Hohokam area to the south, at least 20 macaws, probably from Casas Grandes, and white-fronted parrots, possibly from southern Sonora, Mexico. In return for these imported items, Grasshopper may have provided agricultural products initially, but manufactured items such as chipped and ground stone, iron-based pigments, bone tools, and ornaments became increasingly important items of exchange through time. Studies of the agricultural features associated with Grasshopper Pueblo as well as an examination of the faunal remains from the site indicate that there was little investment in agricultural intensification. Graves *et al.* state that "trade could have buffered the Grasshopper population from subsistence stress and at the same time sustained continued population growth by ensuring that resources matched or exceeded the needs of the community" (1982:200).

By A.D. 1375, population began to decline in the Grasshopper region, and by 1400, Grasshopper Pueblo and the other aggregated communities in the region were largely abandoned. There is no evidence of climatic deterioration or other environmental change associated with the population decrease; rather, it has been maintained that the instability and failure of the aggregated communities occurred because "the political organization of these communities did not undergo significant development in the direction of increased complexity and differentiation" (Graves *et al.* 1982:210).

The data from Grasshopper suggest that some changes in social organization and economy accompanied the period of aggregation; for example, there was a change from the use of small kivas dispersed throughout the community to the use of the single great kiva, and the manufacture of items for trade became increasingly important. Nevertheless, Graves and his colleagues maintain that although the population at Grasshopper probably exceeded 500 persons, it failed to develop the social and political institutions that would have been necessary to ensure stability of a community of this size. They argue that factional disputes may have divided the community and precipitated its decline. In addition to factionalism, and perhaps underlying it, they note that agricultural productivity had probably reached the limits of the traditional technology and no further attempts at intensification were made, so there may have been periods of agricultural shortfalls. In addition, the trade relations that had previously operated to even out these lean times failed. Again, the failure of the trade networks is attributed to social factors.

Graves and others view the relations among the aggregated villages of the region as inherently unstable.

> Through time, as populations grew and agricultural productivity leveled off, exchange was employed to subsidize energy flow into the sytem in place of agricultural intensification, and thus buffered the population of these communities. This process was successful in the short run; population growth and aggregation were maintained and traditional forms of socio-cultural organization were continued as well. There were no local elites who controlled and administered exchange relationships between communities. (Graves *et al.* 1982:205)

In risky and fluctuating environments, they state, economic interdependency among relatively egalitarian groups may not be a viable strategy. They conclude that the "lack of a political structure that could have countered divisive trends within and among communities, intensified agricultural production, or controlled the exchange of goods led to regional depopulation" (Graves *et al.* 1982:206).

This interpretation of the Grasshopper region relies heavily on three factors. First, the process of aggregation is viewed as involving most of the settlements in the area. The existence of one or more aggregated communities disrupts the alliance and marriage ties among small villages, so the continued existence of small, dispersed communities does not occur. With aggregation, there is no formation of settlement hierarchies. Second, political organizations that might have served to intensify agricultural production within the aggregated settlements failed to develop, and these villages relied increasingly on trade and exchange to buffer short-term agricultural failures. Finally, the establishment of a degree of interdependence among the villages was not an appropriate solution to the unreliable environment, and depopulation of the region is seen as an inevitable result. The historically and ethnographically documented organization of the Western Pueblo communities, which involves far less economic interdependence among villages and a more intensive agricultural base, is viewed as a more successful, temporally stable adjustment.

Another interpretation of archaeological data and very different conclusions regarding the nature of the late prehistoric period north of the Mogollon Rim are provided in the evaluations of Chavez Pass Pueblo, a site considered ancestral by the Hopi.

Chavez Pass Pueblo: Regional Integration and Hierarchies

Chavez Pass Pueblo is a large site consisting of more than 1000 rooms in three primary room blocks and many smaller room blocks and features on Anderson Mesa, above the Mogollon Rim near Winslow, Arizona. Work at the site, involving limited excavation, was done by Arizona State University (Upham 1982). Like Grasshopper Pueblo, Chavez Pass Pueblo was occupied before 1300; however, the most intense period of occupation was early in the fourteenth century. At that time, the major site components consisted of two pueblos separated by an open ridge of about 150 m in length (Upham 1982:170). Most of the construction of the two room blocks was done with basalt boulder cobble masonry for ground floor rooms and tabular sandstone or limestone for second and third stories. Abundant mortar and plaster were used. The larger of the two room blocks comprises an estimated 434 single-story, 217 two-story, and 30 three-story rooms, two large plaza areas, a great kiva outside the room blocks, and a multistory perimeter wall. The smaller of the two room blocks comprises an estimated 179 single-story, 90 two-story, and 45 three-story rooms, a massive retaining wall, and plaza and kiva areas. It is associated with an extramural stairway leading down a steep slope to a plaza and a spring. Although the spring is the only naturally occurring permanent water source at the site, five or six reservoirs were built to catch and conserve rainfall and runoff water.

In contrast to Grasshopper, the area in the immediate vicinity of Chavez Pass Pueblo has abundant agricultural features. These are primarily large terrace systems constructed perpendicular to small drainages and fieldhouses. Nevertheless, Upham (1982) estimates that the amount of arable land in the vicinity of Chavez Pass Pueblo was sufficient to support only about half the fourteenth-century population. Four additional differences between Chavez Pass Pueblo and Grasshopper are critical to Upham's interpretation. (1) The larger of the two room blocks appears to contain about twice as many storage rooms as is usual in sites of this period (an estimated 70% compared to the more usual 40%. (2) Although the two room blocks at Chavez Pass Pueblo clearly represent population aggregates, the area around these is seen as continuing to be densely inhabited by groups living at much smaller sites. (3) At Chavez Pass Pueblo burial data tend to support the notion of social ranking, and furthermore, high status burials are often marked by the use of polychrome ceramics as burial furniture. (4) Certain kinds of items occur differentially at Chavez Pass Pueblo and the smaller sites in its vicinity. In comparison to the smaller sites, Chavez Pass Pueblo contained more types of ceramics, painted ceramics, black-on-red and polychrome ceramics, and imported turquoise, obsidian, marine shell, pigments, minerals, figurines, and copper bells.

Upham (1982) interprets the role of Chavez Pass Pueblo and other sites, from a broad regional perspective and a reconsideration of fourteenth-century Western Pueblo sites, historic documents, and ethnographic accounts of Western Pueblo social organization. He finds that ethnographic data on the Western Pueblo indicate that status is reflected in differential access to and possession of ritual and ceremonial information and that certain key leadership positions tend to be hereditary within specific clan and clan segments. Further, he argues that the effects of European contact on the population structure of the Western Pueblo were far more devastating than is generally acknowledged. During the fourteenth century, the Western Pueblo area comprised nine settlement clusters, each consisting of several large (more than 50 rooms) sites. The settlement clusters he identifies (using nearest-neighbor and connectivity analyses based on graph theory) are in the Verde Valley, Anderson Mesa, middle Little Colorado, Hopi, Rio Puerco, Silver Creek, upper Little Colorado, Zuni, and Acoma areas. Chavez Pass Pueblo is just one site in the Anderson Mesa cluster; others in this cluster are the Grapevine, Kinnickinick, and Pollock sites.

Upham examines some of the possible relations among the nine settlement clusters by looking at the distributions of four ceramic wares (technologically related types) among them. The distributions deviate from those that would be expected if either there were a uniform exchange of ceramics among the settlement clusters or the flow of ceramics were proportional to the distance from the area of manufacture to each settlement cluster. He finds that some locations, far from the source of manufacture of a particular ware, have more of that ware than do intervening areas. Following Renfrew (1977), he suggests that such distributions "would suggest organizational ties between sets of settlement clusters" (Upham 1982:139). Further consideration of one of these wares, Jeddito Yellow from the Hopi area, indicates that although it was the most widely traded fourteenth-century ware, it is generally scarce at sites at which it occurs and is distributed differentially within some sites. Upham suggests that Jeddito Yellow had a higher value than other wares and that its distribution represents an exchange network among elite individuals. Pursuing this line of inquiry, Upham argues that elite relations united some of the settlement clusters. The Jeddito Alliance links the Hopi, middle Little Colorado, Anderson Mesa, Puerco, and Verde settlement clusters. Upham suggests that a similar Salado Alliance operated below the Mogollon Rim. The Silver Creek and upper Little Colorado settlement clusters seem to have participated in both alliances.

In characterizing the nature of the alliances, Upham suggests that

> close bonds, both practical and symbolic, connected the decision-making structures of widely separated polities. . . . The Jeddito Alliance can thus be viewed as an alliance of the decision-making elite and may have involved the establishment of affinal kins ties, the transmission of esoteric knowledge, and the exchange of exotic nonlocal materials. (1982:157)

Although Upham's view of the fourteenth-century developments in the Western Pueblo area contrast markedly with those advanced for the Grasshopper region, there is some similarity in the discussions of regional collapse and the abandonment of large, aggregated sites.

> Postulating a series of economic and political dependencies between participants in this system, . . . the collapse of the fourteenth-century regional system can be understood as a series of failures, either in agricultural production or in political management, that had a domino effect on the remaining polities in the system. This effect would prove most costly to population centers that were proximate to one another and that may have established dependency relationships with their neighbors. (Upham 1982:201)

In this view, the modern Western Pueblo survived because they were peripheral to and less economically dependent on the remainder of the system.

The discussions of Grasshopper and Chavez Pass Pueblo emphasize the importance of trade and exchange during the fourteenth century, and both view a high degree of village interdependence as somewhat unstable. Aside from these areas of agreement, the interpretations depart on theoretical, methodological, and empirical issues. Although not overtly espousing a theoretical basis, the interpretations of Grasshopper seem to be ecologically oriented, and the emphasis on the absence of water-control devices as an indicator of a lack of agricultural intensification suggests that the authors are persuaded by the arguments of Wittfogel (1957; Wittfogel and Goldfrank 1943).

Their method of inquiry has been to study a small area intensively and suggest generalizations based on limited comparison. As noted, the empirical data they cite that differ from those in Upham's discussion are an absence of small sites that are year-round communities contemporary with Grasshopper and a lack of evidence of both status differentiation in the Grasshopper mortuary population and agricultural intensification. In his discussion of Chavez Pass Pueblo and other fourteenth-century centers, Upham draws on the economic theory of Wallerstein (1974, 1979) and on locational models derived from Central Place Theory (Christaller 1966; Lösch 1954). Upham's method of analysis is both broadly regional and quantitative. Many archaeologists would dispute the applicability of either Wallerstein's formulations or central place models to the prehistoric Southwest, because these models were developed for relations within the context of market based, state level economies. Nevertheless, the distributional analyses presented by Upham require an explanation, although perhaps one separate from the theories from which the analyses were derived. We need a better understanding of the kinds of nonmarket exchanges occurring in societies organized at varying levels, and most important we need studies that address the properties of different kinds of exchange that will be visible to the archaeologist, who must view the composite results of long-term and varying patterns of human behavior. Given the potential magnitude of these tasks, it might seem more efficient to work toward resolution of the empirical issues, although this effort will be far from simple.

The Southwest at the Beginning of History

The year 1540 marks the beginning of the historic period in the Southwest, because it was then that the Francisco Vasquez de Coronado expedition made its way from Compostela to the Zuni Pueblo of Hawikuh. Members of Coronado's forces explored as far west as the Grand Canyon. Pedro de Tovar's group encountered the Hopi villages and Hernando de Alvarado visited Acoma and the Rio Grande Pueblo from modern Bernalillo to Taos and journeyed east to Pecos and the Great Plains. The Coronado expedition wintered in Bernalillo and in the spring of 1541 returned to Pecos. Some members of the expedition were sent to Taos to obtain supplies. Others were led far onto the Plains, where they became mistrustful of their Indian guide, killed him, and returned to the central Rio Grande Valley. As the general situation deteriorated and the troops threatened mutiny, Coronado retreated to Mexico in the spring of 1542. Juan de Padilla, a Franciscan, and two lay brothers who had been left behind were killed by the Indians. Not until 1581 did another European expedition enter the Southwest, that of Fray Agustin Rodriguez and Captain Francisco Chumascado. From 1581 on, expeditions of soldiers and friars, and soon colonists, forever changed the relations of groups to each other and to the land.

Historic Documents

The historic period provides European eyewitness accounts of Southwestern peoples. The wealth of descriptive materials constitute an invaluable resource, but great care must be taken in using these data. Some of the problems involved are mentioned here. First, the Southwest was explored, conquered, and colonized under the Spanish Empire. The cultural values and historic forces affecting the Spanish explorers and colonists are generally poorly understood by people of the Anglo-American tradition.

Sixteenth-century Spain had been united only recently (1492) under a single strong monarchy, which had expelled its Moorish overlords from Spanish territory. The important arena for Spanish accomplishment was in Europe, where the strongest competition for power lay with the newly developed mercantile states of the north (principally Holland and England). Spanish exploration and conquest was fueled by a strong nationalism in which Catholicism was a major component. Colonies were sought in order to provide mineral wealth for the monarchy and human souls for the Church. In the Americas, Spain had been remarkably successful in these endeavors. The Aztec Empire had been conquered in 1521 and the Inca Empire in 1535. The rich Mexican mining areas were supplying quantities of silver for the Spanish crown. When Coronado's expedition reached New Mexico in 1540, lured by tales of the wonderous Seven Cities of Cibola, the disappointment must have been acute. Not only was there a lack of obvious mineral wealth, but the scale of the local societies was far simpler than either the Aztec Empire or the Spanish monarchy.

It is often difficult to interpret Pueblo social, economic, and political organization from the firsthand accounts of the Spanish chroniclers. The Spanish explorers were keen observers, but they were not social scientists interested in comparative political organization. As Upham (1982), Wilcox (1981), and others point out, the early chronicle accounts of Southwestern people are sometimes conflicting and vague. For example, the Zuni are described as having "no rulers as in New Spain" but as having influential "priests," who told the people what to do (Hammond and Rey 1940:174). Chronicle accounts of the Hopi (Bolton 1930:185–186), the Rio Grande Tiguex (Winship 1904:47–48), and the Pecos (Kessell 1979) refer to "chiefs" who seem to have had considerable authority among their people. Some scholars (e.g., Upham 1982; Wilcox 1981) argue that the egalitarian character of Pueblo society has been overemphasized, in part, because the early Spanish accounts have been misunderstood. These authors contend that Pueblo society was characterized as having weak leadership positions (no "rulers"), because the Spanish chroniclers were comparing the Pueblo to the Aztec, Tarascan, and other state-level societies of New Spain.

Although neither Upham nor Wilcox contends that Pueblo organization was as complex as that in Mesoamerican states, they suggest that Pueblo leadership may have been more formal than is usually credited. Wilcox (1981), for example, interprets some documents as indicating the presence of hierarchies composed of three levels of decision makers among the Pueblo. He also finds some statements in the documents that suggest that some Pueblos may have owed tribute to others.

Another problem involved in the interpretation of the Spanish documents relates to evaluating the effects of European diseases that the Spaniards introduced to the Southwest. In general, Spanish explorers' accounts provide population estimates that many historians and anthropologists consider greatly exaggerated. A common refutation of these estimates is made by pointing out that the official reports were designed to impress the authorities with the need to continue to finance and support expeditions of conquest. It is argued that the chroniclers deliberately overestimated the numbers of Indians who needed to be subdued or who could be converted to Catholicism in order to request support from the Crown. Although it is undoubtedly true that some reports were exaggerated for these and other purposes, it is as likely that the Spaniards introduced European diseases to the Pueblo, who, having no immunities to these illnesses, suffered very high mortality levels. For example, as late as 1853, a severe smallpox epidemic struck the Hopi First Mesa villages. The First Mesa population of 1200 persons was reduced to 650 by 1862 (Adams 1981:327). Using various lines of evidence, Upham (1982:39) estimates that within 100 years of their first contact with Europeans, the Western Pueblo of Hopi, Zuni, and Acoma lost 75–80% of their populations.

In his review of various archival records, Schroeder (1979b:239) lists 61 pueblos known to have been abandoned since 1540. Although reasons other than epidemic disease are given for some of these abandonments, disease is an all too common factor in most cases. Heavy population losses must have had profound effects on Pueblo economy and political organization. For example, some villages may not have been able to perform traditional ceremonies because there were not enough people to carry out important roles, or the leadership positions of various societies could not be filled. It is also possible that there were not enough able-bodied people to plant, tend, and harvest crops. Villages that could not continue to survive socially may have joined other villages, such as the inhabitants of Pecos did when they went to Jemez in the nineteenth century.

It is also important for students to remember that Southwestern societies, particularly the Pueblo, were greatly influenced by Spanish Colonial policies. For example, conversion of the Indians to Roman Catholicism, supported by a complex body of law and procedures, was a primary aim of the colonial effort. Before the codification of the *Law of the Indies* in 1680, it was legal to pursue Indian conversions by force if necessary. Not only were Indian religious practices prohibited, and religious paraphernalia confiscated and burned, but Indian religious leaders were tortured and killed. One effect of the Spanish policy was that "the native priesthood became implacable foes of the Spaniards" and native religious practices were continued in secret (Simmons 1979:181).

Also prior to 1680, Indians were required to pay tribute and labor to Spanish colonists under the *encomienda* and *repartimiento* systems. The *encomienda* was a grant of tribute from either a particular Pueblo or a group of Indians to the person holding the grant (the *encomendero*). The *repartimiento* was a system of conscripting Indian labor for Spanish farms, haciendas, or mines. Although the Indians were supposed to be paid a wage for their labor, abuses were common (Simmons 1979:182). The Pueblo Revolt of 1680, which lead to the withdrawal of the Spaniards from New Mexico for 12 years, was a logical outcome of the injustices of the Spanish system.

According to Spanish law, land that was tilled by the Indians could not be confiscated by colonists. Further, the law required colonists to establish their communities on land not already occupied by the Indians. These regulations provided for physical separation of Indian and Hispanic communities. Although it is probably true that the absence of Spanish colonists within Indian villages enabled the Indians to preserve many of their cultural traditions, the rules would have served to disrupt at least some aspects of the native system. For example, Spanish settlements were established around and among Pueblo villages. European domestic livestock grazed on land that had provided wild plant and animal foods for the Pueblo. It is difficult to know precisely how much daily or seasonal interaction characterized the relations among Pueblo villages in the late prehistoric period, but the presence of the Spanish Colonial settlements probably disrupted and diminished these interactions.

The early historic period provides the first written observations of the Southwest; yet the accounts were written by men whose roots were in a political and intellectual tradition that was completely alien to the societies they encountered. The experiences of the Spanish explorers and colonists were also markedly different from those of the British settlers of the eastern United States, whose traditions are at the core of American society; therefore, the Spanish accounts are sometimes difficult for modern Americans to appreciate. The native peoples of the Southwest were vassals of the Spanish Empire until 1821, when Mexico achieved independence from Spain. In order to understand the impact of nearly 300 years of Spanish Colonial rule on the native peoples of the Southwest, it is necessary to be familiar with the cultural traditions of Colonial Spain as well as those of the Indians of the Southwest. Despite these problems, historic period archaeology in the Southwest can be of inestimable value, providing insights into specific events and models for general interpretations of cultural interactions and change. Three examples are explored, briefly, here.

History, Legend, and Archaeology at Awatovi

In the seventeenth century, the village of Awatovi, on Antelope Mesa, was the easternmost Hopi village and the site of the Franciscan mission of San Bernardo de Aguatubi. The Mission period at Hopi lasted from 1629 to 1680, the year of the Pueblo Revolt. The mission of San Bernardo de Aguatobi was destroyed in conjunction with the revolt. The mission has been excavated by the Peabody Museum of Harvard University (Montgomery *et al.* 1949). Following the reconquest of 1693, missions were again established among the Pueblo except among the Hopi, who successfully resisted.

According to an account written in 1732 (cited in Montgomery *et al.* 1949:222), in 1700 two Franciscan friars traveled to the Hopi, and at Awatovi they successfully converted the Indians and baptized many of them. During their stay they were threatened by Indians from the other Hopi villages, whom they tried, unsuccessfully, to convert. Intending to return with soldiers to protect the Christian Indians of Awatovi and the mission, the friars left. Upon their departure, Hopi warriors from several other villages raided Awatovi. According to the historic accounts, archaeology, and Hopi legend, Awatovi was burned, many of its men were killed, and captives, primarily women and children, were taken to the other villages. According to a Hopi legend recorded by Fewkes (1893), on the way back to the other villages, several of the captives were killed, dismembered, and cruelly mutilated. Excavations at Awatovi provided data that make the Hopi destruction of Awatovi comprehensible, and subsequent archaeological work and osteological research lends support to the Hopi legendary account.

The friars who came to Awatovi in 1700 were apparently not content with obtaining only the reconversion of the residents of Awatovi. Rather, they planned to use Awatovi as a staging area for the reconversion of the other Hopi villages to the west. Therefore, before their departure, the friars directed the construction of the foundations of a large military barrack and stable complex. The foundations were excavated by the Harvard Peabody archaeologists (Montgomery *et al.* 1949:231). The destruction of Awatovi may be viewed as a reaction to a very real threat to all the Hopi. The mutilation of some of the Awatovi captives was verified through osteological analysis of human skeletal remains excavated in 1964 at a site on Polacca Wash (Olson 1966). At least 30 individuals, of both sexes and all age groups, were found in a mass burial about 6.5 km from the Hopi villages. Analysis of the bones (Turner and Morris 1970) revealed the individuals to be of Western Pueblo physical type, and all had been "intentionally and violently mutilated at the grave site. Skulls, jaws, and long bones were broken with multiple crushing, splintering, and fracturing blows while the bone was still vital" (Turner and Morris 1970:330). The osteologists also note that some of the bones indicate cannibalism. A radiocarbon date of 1580 ± 95 years places the mass grave within the historic period, and Turner and Morris (1970) conclude that the evidence best fits the Hopi account of the incident as related to Fewkes. Additional information about the cultural background for this event is provided by archaeological work at the Hopi village of Walpi.

Cultural Context at Walpi

Walpi, a First Mesa Hopi village, was established shortly after 1690 and continues to be inhabited today. Archaeological work was undertaken between 1975 and 1977 in conjunction with a program of village restoration (Adams 1981, 1983). During the project, archaeologists partially excavated 97 rooms and mapped 103 rooms. A great deal of information about room function, room ownership, and chronology was obtained from the current residents of Walpi. Chronological information, especially important to the findings discussed here, was obtained from the Hopi and from tree rings.

During the Hopi Mission period (1629–1680), the Spaniards introduced many useful items, such as domestic animals, the use of wool in textiles, and European crops such as wheat. Hopi ceramics of the Mission period included vessels of European form, such as flaring-rimmed stew or bread bowls, and bowls with ring bases that copy the form of wheel-made ceramics. In addition, various design motifs on ceramics incorporated European motifs.

The village of Walpi was established in its current mesa-top location during the turbulent period in Hopi history of the Pueblo Revolt and the destruction of Awatovi. At that time, defensive positions were selected for villages in fear of Spanish reprisals.

Many Pueblo refugees from the Rio Grande area fled to Hopi in fear of the return of the Spaniards. From 1690 until the 1730s, there was a swelling of population among the Hopi villages, but there was considerable solidarity among the Hopi and between Hopi and Rio Grande refugees. There was also, as expected, a great deal of anti-Spanish feeling. The situation is reflected in an interesting way in the Hopi ceramics produced from 1690 to the 1730s. Adams (1981:325–326) notes that all Spanish vessel forms and design motifs disappear from the Hopi ceramics, which he states is "best explained as a symbolic rejection of Spanish culture." In fact, the forms of bowls and jars, and the designs used, are similar to Rio Grande pottery of the period, which seems to reflect the importance of the refugee elements within the Hopi communities.

During the 1730s a series of dry years diminished the available food supply, and general solidarity among the villages weakened. In 1742 the Rio Grande refugees began to return to their former territories, except for the residents of Hano, who remain at Hopi today (see Chapter 1). Adams notes that along with these events, the anti-Spanish feeling among the Hopis began to decline, and after 1750 "Spanish elements reappear on Hopi pottery, though the form and overall design motifs remained a mixture of Tewa and Tewa and Hopi" (Adams 1981:326).

Between 1777 and 1780, a major drought struck the Hopi country, followed by a smallpox epidemic in 1781. In response to these disasters, many Hopi families left their villages and moved to Zuni, Acoma, Zia, and other pueblos where they had friends or relatives. When the rains returned, the Hopi went back to their villages; the pottery subsequently produced showed striking changes. The unslipped tan or orange pottery that had been made during the previous period was replaced by ceramics with white slips, which resemble Zuni and Acoma pottery. Further, Spanish forms, such as stew bowls, and Spanish design elements again became popular. Adams suggests that "these intrusions of Spanish culture into Hopi were assimilated indirectly through their acculturated Pueblo relatives and friends" (Adams 1981:326).

The Walpi study demonstrates that material culture, especially ceramic form and design, can be a remarkably sensitive indicator of cultural events. It also shows the ways in which knowing the "facts of history" can help elucidate changes in the material culture record. In the absence of historic documentation, it would be difficult to ascertain whether the reintroduction of Spanish influence in ceramics had been a result of direct or of indirect contact with the Europeans.

A related though far more complex problem involves identifying the remains of the early Athapascan speaking Indians and dating the time of their arrival in the Southwest.

Southern Athapaskans: Apache and Navajo

Today, the closest neighbors of many of the traditional peoples of the Southwest are Athapaskan-speaking Indians whose original homelands are in interior Alaska and Canada. One Athapaskan-speaking tribe, the Navajo, has the fastest rate of population growth of any North American Indian tribe. Despite their prominence in the twentieth century, there is little agreement among scholars regarding when these peoples entered the Southwest or by which routes they came. Unfortunately, most archae-ological data are ambiguous on these issues; there are problems interpreting the early historic documents and linguistic data as well.

During the historic period, most southern Athapaskan groups pursued a way of life that included limited agriculture and stock raising. The "typical" residence pattern was generally dispersed, and most groups moved several times throughout the year in order to obtain grazing land for their livestock. Agricultural techniques were identical to those of other Southwestern peoples. Much of the material culture that is recogniz-able as southern Athapaskan relates to their adaptations as stockmen, for example, single family shelters (either wickiups or hogans), corrals, sheep pens, and saddles. Because livestock was introduced into the Southwest by the Spaniards, the herding adaptation and associated material culture are not useful in identifying southern Athapaskan remains that date prior to the sixteenth or seventeenth centuries.

It is also well known that the southern Athapaskans have displayed considerable adaptive flexibility over time, a fact reflected in the settlement patterns and items of material culture available for archaeological study. For example, during the Refugee period following the Pueblo Revolt and de Vargas' reconquest, Pueblo and Navajo refugees lived together in the Largo–Gobernador area. The refugee sites consist of stone masonry *pueblitos,* which are defensively located and impressive in their extent (Brugge 1983). At that time, one of considerable Pueblo–Athapaskan interaction, the Navajo produced a distinctive polychrome pottery that was similar to contemporary Pueblo styles. Although the pottery is distinctively Navajo, the pueblito house form is not. In other cases, the ceramics are ambiguous indicators of Athapaskan cultural affiliation. For example, Brugge (1963:19) suggests that seventeenth-century Navajo ceramics were of a generalized Woodland type produced by a paddle-and-anvil tech-nique. Pointed bottom pottery, often thought to be an Athapaskan hallmark, is known from prehistoric Pueblo sites in the Gallina area of New Mexico. Finally, although some archaeologists (Gunnerson 1969; Gunnerson and Gunnerson 1971) regard a particular type of micaceous pottery as Apachean, others (Schaasfma 1976) find it difficult to distinguish from similar types produced at Taos, Picuris, and Nambe pueblos in the seventeenth and eighteenth centuries. These examples indicate that it is often very difficult to identify an archaeological site as unambiguously that of an Athapaskan-speaking group.

Identifying the remains of the first Athapaskan speakers to enter the Southwest is a far more difficult task. This is so because prior to the introduction of livestock by the Europeans and of agriculture by the Pueblo or other agricultural groups, the Athapas-kan speakers are generally thought to have been hunters and gatherers, as are their linguistic relatives to the north. Their campsites would be ephemeral and their mate-rial culture composed largely of nondiagnostic stone tools. If there are any distinctive early southern Athapaskan stone tool technologies or types, these have not been identified by archaeologists. Although the Southern Athapaskans may have entered the Southwest in the late prehistoric period, no remains of this antiquity have been unambiguously ascribed to them.

The possible routes by which the southern Athapaskans may have entered the

Southwest are also in dispute. Some scholars (e.g., Hester 1962) argue that these people followed a route east of the Rocky Mountains to the southwest. Others (e.g., Huscher and Huscher 1942) contend that their route was through the Rocky Mountains. If an eastern route were demonstrable, it is possible that the southern Athapaskan speakers learned agriculture and ceramic manufacture from Plains groups, an idea that some scholars (e.g., Gunnerson and Gunnerson 1971; Hester 1962) support. On the other hand, Opler (1983) discusses linguistic data that may favor the more western route. Without very convincing archaeological evidence either view is difficult to support.

The kinds of linguistic analyses that are generally useful to questions of prehistory are glottochronolgical and other lexicostatistical studies that indicate the temporal frame for language divergence. Opler (1983) summarizes these studies for the southern Athapaskan-speaking groups. The work suggests that until about 1300, the Apache were a single group or a series of very closely related groups. However, as Opler (1983:381) notes, this information does not tell us where they were at this time or their subsequent patterns of migration and dispersal. Nevertheless, recent lexicostatistical data indicate that the southern Athapaskans entered the Southwest at about A.D. 1400 (Opler 1983:382). There are, as yet, no archaeological data that can confirm this date, primarily because the remains would not necessarily be distinguishable from the hunting and gathering camps of other peoples.

Finally, the early Spanish documents are also ambiguous regarding the identification of southern Athapaskans. The Spaniards at first used the term *Querecho* to refer to any nomadic group of people they encountered. Some scholars (e.g., Forbes 1966; Gunnerson and Gunnerson 1971; Schroeder 1979b) routinely translate *Querecho* as "Apache" and suggest that the Spanish descriptions might be valuable clues to the distribution of these people in the sixteenth century. Opler, however, argues that *Querecho* was a generic term, noting specifically that "whenever the traits described are more specific, they do not seem to be particularly Apachean" (1983:383). Upham (1982:47–51), in fact, suggests that some of the peoples that the early accounts refer to as *Querecho* may have been indigenous Pueblo peoples who were not living within compact villages, but pursuing a more mobile way of life, perhaps living in rancherias. The concern here, however, is that none of the usual sorts of information—material culture, historical linguistics, or Spanish documents—is an unambiguous guide to the identification of early historic or protohistoric southern Athapaskan remains.

Although this situation is discouraging for those interested in documenting the time of the arrival of southern Athapaskans in the Southwest, there are many other questions that can be addressed using a combination of historic documents and the archaeology of southern Athapaskan sites. For example, Boyer (1982) examined the history of Navajo settlement in a portion of the San Juan Basin for general implications regarding archaeological interpretations of settlement patterns. As he notes, archaeologists commonly use economic-maximization models, which consider the proximity of archaeological sites to natural resources in interpretations of settlement distributions. In such studies, high densities of sites in specific resource zones or close to particular resources (such as arable land) may be interpreted as indicating that the zones or resources were the most favored or highly valued. Using this assumption, one might predict that, in general, the density of Navajo sites would be greater in areas with good grazing land than in areas where grazing land is poor. Boyer suggested that the overall economic context within which a society functions is a more important determinant of settlement behavior and tested his idea using the historic Navajo economy.

Boyer divided Navajo history in the San Juan Basin into three economically distinct periods that also can be differentiated at many Navajo sites. The first period, 1882–1930, is characterized by the emergence of wool production as the major source of income for the basin Navajo. Within the general context of the U.S. economy, Navajo were encouraged to expand herds and produce wool for market. Given a maximization model, one might expect the number of Navajo sites in good grazing areas to have increased greatly and perhaps for there to have been fewer sites in poor grazing areas. During the second period, 1930–1950, the federal government instituted a program of forced stock reduction because overgrazing had become a severe problem on Navajo lands. With reduced herds it might be anticipated that the more marginal grazing areas would have been abandoned and that site density would either increase or remain the same in the better grazing areas. The third period, 1950–1979, saw the general decline of herding in the Navajo economy of the basin as more Navajo engaged in wage work. It would be expected that the density of Navajo sites in good grazing areas would decline.

In fact, Boyer suggested that the expectations of the maximization assumption should not always hold, because the changing external economic system creates differential opportunities for Navajo families and individuals. It is important that during the first period, Navajo individuals had the opportunity to greatly increase their wealth if they could amass very large herds and effectively monopolize the best grazing land. If they did so, however, the site densities in the best grazing areas would be the opposite of that predicted in the maximization model, because a few individuals would be using the land for very large herds. Boyer tested his ideas using several study areas in the San Juan Basin. He found that for the period between 1892 and 1930, there were low site densities in the best grazing areas and higher site densities in marginal grazing areas. Where there was sufficient historical information on land use and herd size, the low-density situations could be related to developing wealth stratification among the Navajo. The high density of sites in poor grazing areas was a function of the monopolization of the best lands by a few individuals and not by an abundance of resources. During the second period there was an overall decrease in sites associated with grazing areas, but the decline was more pronounced in the poorer grazing zones because families with small herds suffered the greatest loss in the stock-reduction program. During the final period, sites tended to cluster near access routes to wage labor, as expected.

Boyer's study, although obviously specific to the Navajo economy, demonstrates the importance of considering the entire economic system when evaluating and interpreting settlement distributions. Clearly too, the study depended on adequate documentation of Navajo economy in the area in question. Because Navajo and Apache today occupy many areas that were inhabited by Pueblo peoples prehistorically, archae-ologists sometimes find it useful to develop models of prehistoric behavior based on Navajo and Apache ethnoarchaeological studies. The seasonal use of Anasazi sites on Black Mesa, Arizona (Chapter 6), is a good example of this work.

Finally, archaeological study of Refugee period sites that were inhabited by both Pueblo and Navajo people during the late eighteenth and early nineteenth centuries provide insights into the development of modern Navajo culture (Brugge 1983:493; Carlson 1965). During this period, much of what is modern Navajo culture crystalized as a unique amalgam of Athapaskan and Pueblo elements. It is possible that future studies of this acculturative period in Navajo history may provide insights into the character of earlier Navajo material culture that might help to resolve the problem of recognizing protohistoric and early historic southern Athapaskan remains.

Discussion

Following the abandonment of large areas of the Southwest in the late thirteenth and early fourteenth centuries, large aggregated communities were founded in pre-viously sparsely inhabited areas. Some of these sites are recognized as ancestral villages by modern Pueblo people. At some of these sites too, rock art and kiva mural representations depict figures that are recognizably aspects of kachina ritual, which is an important component of modern Pueblo religion.

Other aspects of the archaeological record of the fourteenth century depart from modern Pueblo culture. For example, the stylistic homogeneity in ceramic design, an abundance of traded ceramics at some sites, and the detailed similarities among the kiva mural depictions from widely separated areas suggest a higher level of inter-village interaction than is characteristic of the modern period. The nature of relations among aggregated villages is the subject of research and scholarly disagreement. The extended discussions of Grasshopper Pueblo and Chavez Pass Pueblo highlight the problems involved and indicate areas of future research.

The year 1540 marks the end of the prehistoric period in the Southwest. The imposition of Spanish colonial policies and the introduction of European diseases, new crops, and domestic animals forever disrupted traditional patterns of adaptation. The written accounts of the Spanish chroniclers, however, provide the first views of Southwestern societies from a European perspective. The documentary data are a rich source of information that can greatly elucidate the archaeological record. There are, of course, ambiguities in the documentary history, but comparisons of the historic, legendary, and archaeological records, as demonstrated by the work at Awatovi and Walpi, are leading to a clearer understanding of the ways in which events are reflected in the archaeological record. It is hoped that innovative use of these materials will eventually provide a better basis for understanding both the prehistoric period and the historic integration of traditional Southwestern cultures and their southern Athapaskan neighbors.

Conclusion

The prehistoric Southwest provides an extraordinary record of human behavior over a period of 11,000 years. The archaeological remains have been of interest to scholars for more than 100 years. Archaeology in the Southwest, as elsewhere, has become increasingly specialized and technical, and it is probably impossible to present a synthesis of Southwestern prehistory that adequately represents all the complexities of the "current state of the art." Nevertheless, my intent has been to provide the interested student with a means of access to the vast literature of Southwestern prehistory and a sense of both the current understanding of the past and the areas of disagreement requiring new and innovative research. One of my hopes is that some interested students will be inspired to conduct the research that needs to be done and that others will develop an enhanced appreciation for the record of human adaptations to the Southwest.

The prehistoric Southwest is of interest for many reasons, which have been examined in the preceding chapters. From my perspective, one of the most intriguing is the record it provides of flexible and heterogeneous responses to environmental diversity and extremes. The arid Southwestern climate, with cold winters and hot summers, establishes a difficult baseline for human adaptation. The long prehistoric record indicates that successful adaptation was accomplished, in part, by maintaining a diversity of subsistence and organizational options. At any one time, the people of the Southwest engaged in a mosaic of behavorial strategies ensuring the success of at least some of them.

References

Aberle, David F.
    1970   Comments. In *Reconstructing prehistoric Pueblo societies,* edited by William A. Longacre, pp. 214–224. University of New Mexico Press, Albuquerque, and School of American Research, Santa Fe.

Acklen, John C.
    1982   Ceramic analysis. In *Anasazi and Navajo land use in the McKinley mine area near Gallup, New Mexico* (Vol. I, Part II), edited by Christina G. Allen and Ben A. Nelson, pp. 578–596. Office of Contract Archeology, University of New Mexico, Albuquerque.

Adams, E. Charles
    1981   The view from the Hopi mesas. In The protohistoric period in the North American Southwest, A.D. 1450–1700, edited by David R. Wilcox and W. Bruce Masse, pp. 321–335. *Arizona State University Anthropological Research Papers* 24.
    1983   The architectural analogue to Hopi social organization and room use, and implications for prehistoric Southwestern culture. *American Antiquity* 48(1):44–61.

Adovasio, James M., J. D. Gunn, J. Donahue, and R. Stuckenrath
    1978   Meadowcroft rockshelter, 1977: an overview. *American Antiquity* 43(4):632–651.

Agenbroad, L. D.
    1980   Quaternary mastodon, mammoth and men in the New World. *Canadian Journal of Anthropology* 1(1):99–101.

Agogino, George A., and James J. Hester
    1953   The Santa Ana pre-ceramic sites. *El Palacio* 60(4):131–140.

Aikens, C. Melvin
    1966   Virgin–Kayenta cultural relationships. *Anthropological Papers of the University of Utah* 79. (*Glen Canyon Series* 29). Salt Lake City.
    1976   Cultural hiatus in the eastern Great Basin? *American Antiquity* 41(4):543–550.

1978   The far west. In *Ancient Native Americans,* edited by J. D. Jennings, pp. 131–182. W. H. Freeman, San Francisco.

Alexander, H. C., and P. Reiter
1935   The excavation of Jemez Cave, New Mexico. *Monograph of the School of American Research* 4. Santa Fe.

Allan, William C., A. Osborn, W. J. Chasko, and David E. Stuart
1975   An archeological survey: road construction right-of-ways, Block II, Navajo Indian Irrigation Project, edited by F. J. Broilo and D. E. Stuart, pp. 91–143. *Working Draft Series* 1. Office of Contract Archeology, University of New Mexico, Albuquerque.

Anderson, Edgar, and Hugh C. Cutler
1942   Races of *Zea mays:* Their recognition and classification. *Annals of the Missouri Botanical Garden* 29.

Antevs, E.
1955   Geologic–climatic dating in the West. *American Antiquity* 20(4):317–335.
1959   Geologic age of the Lehner mammoth site. *American Antiquity* 25(1):31–34.
1962   Late Quaternary climates in Arizona. *American Antiquity* 28(2):193–198.

Anwalt, Patricia Reff
1981   *Indian clothing before Cortes: Mesoamerican costumes from the Codices.* University of Oklahoma Press, Norman.

Anyon, Roger, and T. J. Ferguson
1983   *Settlement patterns and changing adaptations in the Zuni Area after* A.D. *1000.* Paper presented for the Anasazi Symposium, San Juan Archaeological Research Center and Library, Bloomfield, New Mexico.

Anyon, Roger, Patricia A. Gilman, and Steven A. LeBlanc
1981   A re-evaluation of the Mimbres–Mogollon sequence. *The Kiva* 46(4):209–225.

Anyon, Roger, and Steven A. LeBlanc
1980   The architectural evolution of Mogollon–Mimbres ceremonial structures. *The Kiva* 45(4):253–277.

Axlerod, D. I.
1967   Quaternary extinctions of large mammals. *University of California Publications in Geological Science* 4:1–25.

Bachuber, Frederick W.
1971   *Paleoclimatology of Lake Estancia, New Mexico.* Unpublished Ph.D. dissertation, Department of Biology, University of New Mexico.

Bailey, R. G. (compiler)
1980   Description of the ecoregions of the United States *Miscellaneous Publication 1391.* U.S.D.A. Forest Service. U.S. Government Printing Office, Washington, D.C.

Baker, Craig, and Joseph C. Winter (editors)
1981   *High altitude adaptations along Redondo Creek: the Baca Geothermal Project.* Office of Contract Archeology, University of New Mexico, Albuquerque.

Bandelier, Adolph F.
1890   Final report of investigations among the Indians of the southwestern United States (Part 1). *Papers of the Archaeological Institute of America, American Series* 3.
1892   Final report of investigations among the Indians of the southwestern United States (Part 2). *Papers of the Archaeological Institute of America, American Series* 4.

Beadle, G. W.
1981   Origin of corn: pollen evidence. *Science* 213:890–892.

Beckett, P. H.
1980   *The Ake site: collection and excavation of LA 13423, Catron County, New Mexico.* Cultural Resources Management Division, Department of Sociology and Anthropology, New Mexico State University, Las Cruces.

Bennett, C. L.
1979   Radiocarbon dating with accelerators. *American Scientist* 67(4):450–457.

Berman, Mary Jane

1979 *Cultural resources overview of Socorro, New Mexico.* U.S. Government Printing Office, Washington, D.C.

Berry, Michael S.

1982 *Time, space and transition in Anasazi prehistory.* University of Utah Press, Salt Lake City.

Betancourt, J. L., and T. R. Van Devender

1981 Holocene vegetation in Chaco Canyon, New Mexico. *Science* 214:656–658.

Binford, Lewis R.

1968 Post-Pleistocene adaptations, In *New perspectives in archaeology,* edited by S. R. Binford and L. R. Binford, pp. 313–342. Aldine, Chicago.

1980 Willow smoke and dogs' tails: hunter–gatherer settlement systems and archaeological site formation. *American Antiquity* 45(1):4–20.

Binford, L. R., and W. J. Chasko, Jr.

1976 Nunamiut demographic history: a provocative case. In *Demographic anthropology: quantitative approaches,* edited by E. B. W. Zubrow, pp. 63–144. University of New Mexico Press, Albuquerque.

Blanton, R. E.

1978 *Monte Alban, patterns at the ancient Zapotec capital.* Academic Press, New York.

Blevins, Byron B., and Carol Joiner

1977 The archeological survey of Tijeras Canyon. In *The 1976 excavation of Tijeras Pueblo, Cibola National Forest, New Mexico, Archeological Report 18.* Edited by Linda S. Cordell, pp. 126–152. U.S.D.A. Forest Service, Southwestern Region, Albuquerque.

Bluhm, Elaine A.

1960 Mogollon settlement patterns in Pine Lawn Valley, New Mexico. *American Antiquity* 25(4):538–546.

Bohrer, Vorsila L.

1962 Ethnobotanical materials from Tonto National Monument, Arizona. In Archeological studies at Tonto National Monument, Arizona, by Charlie R. Steen, Floyd M. Pierson, Vorsila L. Bohrer, and Kate Peck Kent, edited by Louis R. Caywood, pp. 75–114. *Southwestern Monuments Association, Technical Series* 2. Globe, Arizona.

1970 Ethnobotanical aspects of Snaketown, a Hohokam village in southern Arizona. *American Antiquity* 35(4):413–430.

Bolton, Herber E. (editor)

1930 *Spanish explorations in the Southwest, 1542–1706.* Scribner's Sons, New York.

Boserup, Ester

1965 *The conditions of agricultural growth.* Aldine, Chicago.

Boyer, Jeffrey

1982 An economic model for Navajo habitation site locations. In *The San Juan tomorrow: planning for the conservation of cultural resources in the San Juan Basin,* edited by Fred Plog and Walter Wait, pp. 107–126. National Park Service, Southwest Region, Santa Fe, and the School of American Research, Santa Fe.

Bradfield, Maitland

1971 Changing patterns of Hopi agriculture. *Journal of the Royal Anthropological Institute* 30.

Bradfield, Wesley

1931 Cameron Creek village: a site in the Mimbres area in Grant County, New Mexico. *School of American Research Monograph* 1. Santa Fe.

Breternitz, Cory Dale, and David E. Doyel

1983 *Methodological issues for the identification of Chacoan community structure: lessons from the Bi sa' ani community study.* Paper presented at the 48th Annual Meetings of the Society for American Archaeology, Pittsburgh.

Breternitz, David A.

1966 An appraisal of tree-ring dated pottery in the Southwest. *Anthropological Papers of the University of Arizona* 10. Tucson.

Brew, John O.

  1943   On the Pueblo IV and on the katchina–tlaloc relations. In *El Norte de Mexico y el sur de Estados Unidos: tercera reunion de mesa redonda sobre problemas antropologicos de Mexico y Centro America,* pp. 241–245. Sociedad Mexicana de Antropologia, Mexico, D.F.

  1946   Archaeology of Alkali Ridge, southeastern Utah. *Papers of the Peabody Museum of American Archaeology and Ethnology* 21. Harvard University, Cambridge.

Briuer, F. L.

  1975   *Cultural and noncultural deposition processes in Chevelon Canyon.* Unpublished Ph.D. dissertation, University of California at Los Angeles.

Brody, J. J.

  1979   Pueblo fine arts. In *Southwest,* edited by Alfonso Ortiz, pp. 603–608. *Handbook of North American Indians* (Vol. 9). Smithsonian Institution, Washington, D.C.

Broilo, Frank J.

  1971   *An investigation of surface-collected Clovis, Folsom, and Midland projectile points from Blackwater Draw and adjacent localities.* Unpublished M.A. thesis, Department of Anthropology, Eastern New Mexico University, Portales.

Brown, Donald N.

  1979   Picuris Pueblo. In *Southwest,* edited by Alfonso Ortiz, pp. 268–277. *Handbook of North American Indians* (Vol. 9). Smithsonian Institution, Washington, D.C.

Brugge, David M.

  1963   Navajo pottery and ethnohistory. *Navajoland Publications Series* 2. Navajo Tribal Museum, Window Rock, Arizona.

  1983   Navajo prehistory and history to 1850. In *Southwest,* edited by Alfonso Ortiz, pp. 489–501. *Handbook of North American Indians* (Vol 10). Smithsonian Institution, Washington, D.C.

Bryan, Alan L.

  1965   Paleo-American prehistory. *Occasional Papers of the Idaho State University Museum* 16. Pocatello.

Bryan, Kirk

  1925   Date of channel trenching (arroyo cutting) in the arid southwest. *Science* 62:338–344.

  1929   Flood-water farming. *Geographical Review* 19:444–456.

  1941   Precolumbian agriculture in the Southwest as conditioned by periods of alluviation. *Annals of the American Association of Geography* 31(4):219–242.

  1954   The geology of Chaco Canyon, New Mexico, in relation to the life and remains of the prehistoric peoples of Pueblo Bonito. *Smithsonian Miscellaneous Collections* 122(7).

Bryan, Kirk, and J. H. Toulouse, Jr.

  1943   The San Jose non-ceramic culture and its relation to Puebloan culture in New Mexico. *American Antiquity* 8(3):269–290.

Bryson, R. A., D. A. Baerreis, and W. M. Wendland

  1970   The character of late-glacial and post-glacial climatic change. In Pleistocene and recent environments of the central Great Plains, edited by W. Dort, Jr., and J. K. Jones, pp. 53–74. *Department of Geology, University of Kansas, Special Publication* 3. Lawrence.

Bullard, William R., Jr.

  1962   The Cerro Colorado site and pithouse architecture in the southwestern United States prior to A.D. 900. *Papers of the Peabody Museum of American Archaeology and Ethnology* 44(2). Harvard University, Cambridge.

Campbell, John Martin, and Florence Hawley Ellis

  1952   The Atrisco sites: Cochise manifestations in the middle Rio Grande Valley. *American Antiquity* 17(3):211–221.

Carlson, Roy L.

  1965   Eighteenth century Navaho fortresses of the Gobernador District. *University of Colorado Studies, Series in Anthropology* (The Earl Morris Papers 2). University of Colorado Studies, Series in Anthropology 10. Boulder.

  1970   White Mountain redware. *Anthropological Papers of the University of Arizona* 19.

1982 The polychrome complexes. In Southwestern Ceramics: a comparative review, edited by Albert H. Schroeder, pp. 201–234. *The American Archaeologist* 15. Phoenix.

Cartledge, Thomas R.
1979 Cohonina adaptation to the Coconino Plateau: a re-evaluation. *The Kiva* 44(4):297–317.

Cassidy, Francis
1965 Fire Temple, Mesa Verde National Park. In The Great Kivas of Chaco Canyon and their relationships, by Gordon Vivian and Paul Reiter, pp. 73–81. *School of American Research Monographs* 22. Santa Fe.

Castetter, Edward F.
1935 Uncultivated native plants used as sources of food. *Ethnobiological Studies in the American Southwest* 1. *University of New Mexico Bulletin, Biological Series* 4(1). Albuquerque.

Castetter, Edward F., and Willis M. Bell
1942 *Pima and Papago Indian agriculture.* University of New Mexico Press, Albuquerque.

Christaller, W.
1966 *Central places in southern Germany,* translated by C. W. Tsaskin. Prentice-Hall, Englewood Cliffs, New Jersey.

Clark, D. L.
1961 The obsidian dating method. *Current Anthropology* 2(2):111–114.

Clark, Jeoffrey A.
1969 A preliminary analysis of burial clusters at the Grasshopper site, east-central Arizona. *The Kiva* 35(2):57–86.

Classen, M. M., and R. H. Shaw
1970 Water deficit effects on corn (Part II: Grain component). *Agronomy Journal* 62:652–655.

Coe, M. D., and K. V. Flannery
1964 Microenvironments and Mesoamerican prehistory. *Science* 143:605–654.

Cohen, Mark Nathan
1977 *The food crisis in prehistory: overpopulation and the origins of agriculture.* Yale University Press, New Haven.

Colbert, E. W.
1973 Further evidence concerning the presence of horse at Ventana Cave. *The Kiva* 39(1):25–33.

Collins, G. N.
1914 Pueblo Indian maize breeding. *Journal of Heredity* 5:255–267.

Colson, E.
1979 In good years and in bad: food strategies of self-reliant societies. *Journal of Anthropological Research* 35(1):18–29.

Colton, Harold S.
1939 Prehistoric culture units and their relationships in northern Arizona. *Museum of Northern Arizona Bulletin* 17.
1945 The Patayan problem in the Colorado River valley. *Southwestern Journal of Anthropology* 1(1):114–121.
1946 The Sinagua: a summary of the archaeology of the region of Flagstaff, Arizona, *Museum of Northern Arizona Bulletin* 22. Flagstaff.
1956 Pottery types of the Southwest. *Museum of Northern Arizona Ceramic Series* 3C. Flagstaff.
1958 Pottery types of the Southwest: wares 14, 15, 16, 17, 18. *Museum of Northern Arizona Ceramic Series* 3D. Flagstaff.
1960 *Black Sand: prehistory of northern Arizona.* University of New Mexico Press, Albuquerque.

Comeaux, M. L.
1981 *Arizona geography.* Westview Press, Boulder.

Cooke, R. U., and R. W. Reeves
1976 *Arroyos and environmental changes.* Clarendon, Oxford.

Cordell, Linda S.
1975 Predicting site abandonment at Wetherill Mesa. *The Kiva* 40(3):189–202.

1979   *Cultural resources overview of the middle Rio Grande Valley, New Mexico.* U.S. Government Printing Office, Washington, D.C.

1980   *Tijeras Canyon: analyses of the past.* University of New Mexico Press, Albuquerque.

1981   The Wetherill Mesa simulation: a retrospective. In *Simulations in archaeology,* edited by Jeremy A. Sabloff, pp. 119–141. University of New Mexico Press, Albuquerque.

1982   The Pueblo period in the San Juan Basin: an overview and some research problems. In *The San Juan tomorrow,* edited by Fred Plog and Walter Wait, pp. 59–83. National Park Service, Southwest Region, Santa Fe, and School of American Research, Santa Fe.

Cordell, Linda S., and Amy C. Earls

1982a   *Mountains and rivers: resource use at three sites.* Paper presented at the Second Mogollon Conference, Las Cruces, New Mexico.

1982b   *The Rio Grande glaze "sequence" and the Mogollon.* Paper presented at the Second Mogollon Conference, Las Cruces, New Mexico.

Cordell, Linda S., and Fred Plog

1979   Escaping the confines of normative thought: a reevaluation of Puebloan prehistory. *American Antiquity* 44(3):405–429.

Cosgrove, H. S., and C. B. Cosgrove

1932   The Swarts ruin: a typical Mimbres site in southwestern New Mexico. *Papers of the Peabody Museum of American Archaeology and Ethnology* 15(1). Harvard University, Cambridge.

Cowgill, G. L.

1975   Population pressure as a non-explanation. In Population studies in archaeology and biological anthropology, edited by A. C. Swedlund, pp. 127–131. *American Antiquity* 40(2) and *Society for American Archaeology Memoirs* 30.

Crabtree, D. E.

1975   Experiments in replicating Hohokam points. *TEBIWA* 16(1):10–45.

Crane, H. R.

1955   Antiquity of the Sandia culture: carbon 14 measurements. *Science* 122:689–690.

1956   University of Michigan radiocarbon dates (Part 1). *Science* 124:66–672.

Culbert, T. P.

1978   Mesoamerica. In *Ancient Native Americans,* edited by J. D. Jennings, pp. 403–454. Freeman, San Francisco.

Cully, Anne C.

1979   Some aspects of pollen analysis in relation to archaeology. *The Kiva* 44(2-3):95–100.

Cummings, Byron

1915   Kivas of the San Juan drainage. *American Anthropologist* 17(2):272–282.

1937   Excavations at Kinishba pueblo. *The Kiva* 3(1):1–4.

1940   *Kinishba, a prehistoric pueblo of the Great Pueblo period.* Hohokam Museum Association and the University of Arizona, Tucson.

Cushing, Frank H.

1890   Preliminary notes on the origin, working hypothesis, and primary researches of the Hemmingway Southwestern Archaeological Expedition. *Compte-rendu de la septieme session, Congres International des Americanistes, Berlin,* 1888, pp. 152–194.

Dall, W. H.

1912   On the geological aspects of the possible human immigration between Asia and America. *American Anthropologist* 14:14–17.

Davis, Emma Lou

1965   Small pressures and cultural drift as explanations for abandonment of the San Juan area, New Mexico. *American Antiquity* 30(3):353–355.

Dawson, Jerry, and W. James Judge

1969   Paleo-Indian sites and topography in the middle Rio Grande Valley of New Mexico. *Plains Anthropologist* 14–44(1):149–163.

Dean, Jeffrey S.

1969   Chronological analysis of Tsegi phase sites in northeastern Arizona. *Papers of the Laboratory of Tree-Ring Research* 3. Tucson.

1970 Aspects of Tsegi phase social organization: a trial reconstruction. In *Reconstructing prehistoric Pueblo societies,* edited by William A. Longacre, pp. 140–174. School of American Research, Santa Fe, and University of New Mexico Press, Albuquerque.

1983 Environmental aspects of modeling. In *Theory and Model Building: Refining Survey Strategies for Locating Prehistoric Resources, Trial Formulations for Southwestern Forests,* edited by Linda S. Cordell and Dee F. Green, Cultural Resources Document 3, USDA Forest Service, Southwestern Region, Albuquerque.

Deetz, James F.

1972 Archaeology as a social science. In *Contemporary archaeology,* edited by Mark P. Leone, pp. 108–117. Southern Illinois University Press, Carbondale.

Dick, Herbert W.

1965a Bat cave. *School of American Research Monograph* 27. University of New Mexico Press, Albuquerque.

1965b *Picuris Pueblo excavations.* Clearinghouse for Federal Scientific and Technical Information No. PB-177047. Springfield, Virginia.

Dickson, Bruce D.

1979 Prehistoric pueblo settlement patterns: the Arroyo Hondo, New Mexico, site survey. *Arroyo Hondo Archaeological Series* (Vol. 2). School of American Research Press, Santa Fe.

Di Peso, Charles C.

1956 The upper Pima of San Cayetano del Tumacacori: an archeohistorical reconstruction of the O'otam of Primeria Alta. *Amerind Foundation Publication* 8. Dragoon, Arizona.

1974 Casas Grandes: a fallen trading center of the Gran Chichimeca, Vols. 1–3. *Amerind Foundation Series* 9. Dragoon, Arizona.

1976 Gila Polychrome in the Casas Grandes region. *The Kiva* 42(1):57–63.

1979 Prehistory: southern periphery. In *Southwest,* edited by Alfonso A. Ortiz, pp. 152–161. *Handbook of North American Indians* (Vol. 9). Smithsonian Institution, Washington D.C.

Di Peso, Charles C., John B. Rinaldo, and G. Fenner

1974 *Casas Grandes: a fallen trading center of the Gran Chichimeca* (Vols. 4–13). Amerind Foundation, Dragoon, and Northland Press, Flagstaff.

Dove, Donald E.

1982 *Prehistoric subsistence and population change along the lower Agua Fria River, Arizona: A model simulation.* Unpublished M. A. Thesis, Department of Anthropology, Arizona State University, Tempe.

Doyel, David E.

1975 Excavations in the Escalante Ruin Group, southern Arizona. *Archaeological Series* 37. Arizona State Museum, University of Arizona, Tucson.

1976 Salado cultural development in the Tonto Basin and Globe–Miami areas, central Arizona. *The Kiva* 42(1):5–16.

1980 Hohokam social organization and the Sedentary to Classic transition. In Current issues in Hohokam prehistory: proceedings of a symposium, edited by David E. Doyel and Fred T. Plog, pp. 23–40. *Anthropological Research Papers* 23. Arizona State University, Tempe.

Doyel, David E., and Emil H. Haury (editors)

1976 The 1976 Salado Conference. *The Kiva* 42(1).

Doyel, David E., and Fred T. Plog (editors)

1980 Current issues in Hohokam prehistory: proceedings of a symposium. *Arizona State University Anthropological Research Papers* 23. Tempe.

Dozier, Edward P.

1961 The Rio Grande Pueblos. In *Perspectives in American Indian culture change,* edited by E. H. Spicer, pp. 94–186. University of Chicago Press, Chicago.

1970 *The Pueblo Indians of North America.* Holt, Rinehart, and Winston, New York.

Duncan, Rosalind

1971 *The "Cochise culture": analysis and explanation of archeological remains.* Unpublished M.A. thesis, Department of Anthropology, University of California at Los Angeles.

Dutton, Bertha P.
   1963   *Sun Father's Way.* University of New Mexico Press, Albuquerque.
Ebert, James I., and Thomas R. Lyons
   1980   Prehistoric irrigation canals identified from Skylab III and Landsat imagery in Phoenix, Arizona. In *Cultural resources remote sensing,* edited by Thomas R. Lyons and Frances Joan Mathien, pp. 209–228. National Park Service and University of New Mexico, Albuquerque.
Eddy, Frank W.
   1966   Prehistory in the Navajo Reservoir district, 2 parts. *Museum of New Mexico Papers in Anthropology* 15. Santa Fe.
Eggan, Fred
   1950   *Social organization of the Western Pueblos.* Aldine, Chicago.
El-Najjar, M. Y.
   1974   *People of Canyon de Chelly: a study of their biology and culture.* Unpublished Ph.D. dissertation, Department of Anthropology, Arizona State University, Tempe.
El-Najjar, M. Y., D. J. Ryan, C. G. Turner II, and B. Lozoff
   1976   The etiology of porotic hyperostosis among the prehistoric and historic Anasazi Indians of the southwestern United States. *American Journal of Physical Anthropology* 44:477–488.
Ellis, Florence Hawley
   1951   Patterns of aggression and the war cult in Southwestern Pueblos. *Southwestern Journal of Anthropology* 7(2):177–201.
   1967   Where did the People come from? *El Palacio* 74(3):35–43.
   1970   *Irrigation and water works in the Rio Grande Valley.* Paper presented at the 1970 Pecos Conference, Symposium on Water Control, Santa Fe, New Mexico.
   1974a Anthropology of Laguna Pueblo land claims. In *American Indian Ethnohistory. Indians of the Southwest: Pueblo Indians,* (Vol. III), compiled and edited by David Agee Horr, pp. 9–120. Garland, New York.
   1974b Anthropological data pertaining to the Taos land claim. In *American Indian Ethnohistory* (Vol. I). *Indians of the Southwest,* compiled and edited by David Agee Horr, pp. 29–150. Garland, New York.
Ellis, Florence Hawley, and J. J. Brody
   1964   Ceramic stratigraphy and tribal history of Taos Pueblo. *American Antiquity* 29(3):316–327.
Emory, W. H.
   1848   Notes of a military reconnaissance from Fort Leavenworth in Missouri to San Diego in California, etc. U.S. Senate Document 7, 30th Congress, 1st Session. Washington, D.C.
Emslie, Steven D.
   1981   Prehistoric agricultural ecosystems: avifauna from Pottery Mound, New Mexico. *American Antiquity* 46(4):853–860.
Euler, Robert C.
   1954   Environmental adaptation at Sia Pueblo. *Human Organization* 12:27–30.
   1964   Southern Paiute archaeology. *American Antiquity* 29(3):379–381.
   1975   The Pai: Cultural conservation in environmental diversity. In *Collected Papers in Honor of Florence Hawley Ellis,* edited by Theodore R. Frisbie, pp. 80–88. Papers of the Archaeological Society of New Mexico, No. 2, Albuquerque.
Euler, Robert C., and H. F. Dobyns
   1962   Excavations west of Prescott, Arizona. *Plateau* 34(3):69–84.
Euler, Robert C., and Dee F. Green
   1978   An archeological reconnaissance of middle Havasu Canyon, Arizona. *Cultural Resources Report* 22. U.S.D.A. Forest Service, Southwestern Region, Albuguerque.
Euler, Robert C., George J. Gumerman, Thor N. V. Karlstrom, Jeffrey S. Dean, and Richard H. Hevly
   1979   Colorado Plateaus: cultural dynamics and paleoenvironment. *Science* 205:1089–1101.
Farwell, Robin E.
   1981   Pit houses: prehistoric energy conservation? *El Palacio* 87(3):43–47.

Ferdon, E. N., Jr.

1955 A trial survey of Mexican–Southwestern architectural parallels. *School of American Research Monograph* 21. Santa Fe.

Ferguson, T. J.

1983 Towards understanding the role and function of aggregated communities in the North American Southwest: a proposal for investigation of the changing structure of regional settlement in the Zuni area after A.D. 900. Unpublished paper, Department of Anthropology, University of New Mexico, Albuquerque.

Fewkes, Jesse W.

1893 A-Wa'-tobi: an archaeological verification of a Tusayan legend. *American Anthropologist* 6:363–375.

1896 The prehistoric culture of Tusayan. *American Anthropologist* 9:151–174.

1904 Two summers' work in Pueblo ruins. *Smithsonian Institution, Bureau of American Ethnology, 22nd Annual Report, 1900–1901.* Washington, D.C.

1909 Antiquities of the Mesa Verde National Park—Spruce Tree House. *Bureau of American Ethnology Bulletin* 41. Smithsonian Institution, Washington, D.C.

1911a Preliminary report on a visit to the Navaho National Monument, Arizona. *Bureau of American Ethnology Bulletin* 50. Smithsonian Institution, Washington, D.C.

1923 Archaeological field-work on the Mesa Verde National Park, Colorado. Explorations and field-work of the Smithsonian Institution in 1922. *Smithsonian Miscellaneous Collections* 74(5):89–115. Washington, D.C.

Fish, P., P. Pilles, and S. Fish

1980 Colonies, traders, and traits: the Hohokam in the north. In *Current issues in Hohokam prehistory: proceedings of a symposium,* edited by David Doyel and Fred Plog, pp. 151–175. *Arizona State Museum Anthropological Research Papers* 23. Tempe.

Fladmarck, M. R.

1979 Routes: alternate migration corridors for early man in North America. *American Antiquity* 44(1):55–69.

Flannery, Kent V.

1968 Archeological systems theory and early Mesoamerica. In *Anthropological archeology in the Americas,* edited by B. J. Meggers, pp. 67–87. Anthropological Society of Washington, Washington, D.C.

Forbes, Jack D.

1966 The early western Apache, 1300–1700. *Journal of the West* 5(3):366–374.

Ford, Richard I.

1972 An ecological perspective on the Eastern Pueblos. In *New perspectives on the Pueblos,* edited by Alfonso A. Ortiz, pp. 1–18. University of New Mexico Press, Albuquerque.

1975 Re-excavation of Jemez Cave, New Mexico. *Awanyu* 3(3):13–27.

1980 *Gardening and farming before A.D. 1000: patterns of prehistoric cultivation north of Mexico.* Paper presented at the Advanced Seminar on the Origins of Plant Husbandry in North America, School of American Research, Santa Fe.

1981 Gardening and farming before A.D. 1000: patterns of prehistoric cultivation north of Mexico. *Journal of Ethnobiology* 1(1):6–27.

Ford, Richard I., Albert H. Schroeder, and Stewart L. Peckham

1972 Three perspectives on Puebloan prehistory. In *New perspectives on the Pueblos,* edited by Alfonso A. Ortiz, pp. 22–40. School of American Research, Santa Fe, and University of New Mexico Press, Albuquerque.

Forde, Daryll, and Mary Douglas

1956 Primitive economies. In *Man, culture, and society,* edited by Harry L. Shapiro, pp. 330–344. Oxford University Press, Oxford.

Fosberg, S.

1979 Geologic controls of Anasazi settlement patterns. In *Archeological investigations in Cochiti*

Reservoir, New Mexico (Vol. 4), edited by J. V. Biella and R. C. Chapman, pp. 145–168. Office of Contract Archeology, University of New Mexico, Albuquerque.

Fosberg, S., and J. Husler

1979 Pedology in the service of archeology: soil testing at LA 13086. In *Archeological investigations in Cochiti Reservoir, New Mexico* (Vol. 4), edited by J. V. Biella and R. C. Chapman, pp. 307–318. Office of Contract Archeology, University of New Mexico, Albuquerque.

Franklin, Hayward H., and W. Bruce Masse

1976 The San Pedro Salado: a case of prehistoric migration. *The Kiva* 42(1):47–55.

Friedman, I., and Robert L. Smith

1960 A new dating method using obsidian: the development of the method (part 1). *American Antiquity* 25(4):476–522.

Frisbie, T. R.

1967 The excavation and interpretation of the Artificial Leg Basketmaker III–Pueblo I sites near Corrales, New Mexico. Unpublished M. A. thesis, Department of Anthropology, University of New Mexico, Albuquerque.

Frisch, R. E.

1977 Population, food intake, and fertility. *Science* 199:22–30.

Frison, George C.

1974 (editor)*The Casper site: a Hell Gap bison kill on the High Plains.* Academic Press, New York.

1978 *Prehistoric hunters of the High Plains.* Academic Press, New York.

1980 Man and bison relationships in North America. *Canadian Journal of Anthropology* 1(1):75–76.

Frison, George C., and B. A. Bradley

1980 *Folsom tools and technology at the Hanson site, Wyoming.* University of New Mexico Press, Albuquerque.

Fritts, Harold C.

1976 *Tree rings and climate.* Academic Press, New York.

Fritts, Harold C., David G. Smith, and Marvin A. Stokes

1965 The biological model for paleoclimatic interpretation of Mesa Verde tree-ring series. In Contributions of the Wetherill Mesa Archeological Project, edited by D. Osborne, pp. 101–121. *Memoirs of the Society for American Archaeology* 19.

Fritz, John M.

1978 Paleopsychology today: ideational systems and human adaptation in prehistory. In *Social archaeology: beyond subsistence and dating,* edited by Charles L. Redman, Mary J. Berman, E. V. Curtin, W. T. Longhorne, Jr., N. M. Versaggi, and J. C. Wanser, pp. 37–60. Academic Press, New York.

Galinat, W. C., and James H. Gunnerson

1963 Spread of eight-rowed maize from the prehistoric Southwest. *Harvard University Botanical Museum Leaflets* 20(5):117–160.

Gasser, Robert E.

1976 Hohokam subsistence: a 2,000 year continuum in the indigenous exploitation of the lower Sonoran Desert. *Archeological Report* 11 USDA Forest Service, Southwestern Region, Albuquerque.

1980 Gu Achi: seeds, seasons, and ecosystems. In *Excavations at Gu Achi, a reappraisal of Hohokam subsistence in the Arizona Papagueria,* edited by W. Bruce Masse, pp. 314–342. Western Archeological Center, Tucson.

1981 Appendix IV: Hohokam plant use at La Ciudad and other riverine sites: the flotation evidence. In *Final report for archaeological testing at La Ciudad (group III), West Papago Inner Loop (I-10), Maricopa County, Arizona,* prepared by Ronald K. Yablon. Department of Anthropology, Museum of Northern Arizona, Flagstaff.

Gasser, Robert E., and E. C. Adams

1981 Aspects of deterioration of plant remains in archaeological sites: the Walpi Archaeological Project. *Journal of Ethnobiology* 1(1):182–192.

Gilman, Patricia Ann

1983 *Changing architectural forms in the prehistoric Southwest.* Unpublished Ph.D. dissertation, Department of Anthropology, University of New Mexico, Albuquerque.

Gladwin, Harold S.

1928 Excavations at Casa Grande, Arizona, February 12–May 1, 1927. *Southwest Museum Paper* 2:7–30. Los Angeles.

1945 The Chaco Branch, excavations at White Mound and in the Red Mesa Valley. *Medallion Papers* 33. Gila Pueblo, Globe, Arizona.

1957 *A history of the ancient Southwest.* The Bond Wheelwright Company, Portland, Maine.

Gladwin, Harold S., Emil W. Haury, Edwin B. Sayles, and Nora Gladwin

1938 Excavations at Snaketown I: material culture. *Medallion Papers* 25. Gila Pueblo, Globe, Arizona.

Gladwin, Winifred, and Harold S. Gladwin

1930 Some Southwestern pottery types, Series I. *Medallion Papers* 8. Gila Pueblo, Globe, Arizona.

1933 Some Southwestern pottery types, Series III. *Medallion Papers* 13. Gila Pueblo, Globe, Arizona.

1934 A method for designation of cultures and their variations. *Medallion Papers* 15. Gila Pueblo, Globe, Arizona.

1935 The eastern range of the Red-on-Buff culture. *Medallion Papers* 16. Gila Pueblo, Globe, Arizona.

Glassow, Michael A.

1972 Changes in the adaptations of Southwestern Basketmakers: a systems perspective. In *Contemporary archaeology,* edited by Mark P. Leone, pp. 289–302. Southern Illinois University Press, Carbondale.

1980 Prehistoric agricultural development in the northern Southwest: a study in changing patterns of land use. *Ballena Press Anthropological Papers* 16. Socorro, New Mexico.

Goodyear, A. C., III

1975 Hecla II and III: an interpretive study of archaeological remains for the Lakeshore Project, Papago Reservation, south-central Arizona. *Arizona State University Anthropological Research Papers* 9. Tempe.

Gorman, Frederick J. E., and S. Terry Childs

1980– Is Prudden's unit type of Anasazi settlement valid and reliable? *North American Archaeologist*
1981 2(3):153–192.

Goss, J. A.

1965 Ute linguistics and Anasazi abandonment of the Four Corners Area. In Contributions of the Wetherill Mesa Archaeological Project, edited by D. Osborne, pp. 73–81. *Memoirs of the Society for American Archaeology* 19. Salt Lake City.

Graves, Michael W., Sally J. Holbrook, and William A. Longacre

1982 Aggregation and abandonment at Grasshopper Pueblo: evolutionary trends in the late prehistory of east-central Arizona. In Multidisciplinary research at Grasshopper Pueblo, Arizona, edited by William A. Longacre, Sally J. Holbrook, and Michael W. Graves, pp. 110–121. *Anthropological Papers of the University of Arizona* 40.

Graves, Michael W., and William A. Longacre

1982 Aggregation and abandonment at Grasshopper Pueblo, Arizona. *Journal of Field Archaeology* 9(1):193–206.

Graybill, Donald D.

1973 *Prehistoric settlement pattern analysis in the Mimbres region, New Mexico.* Ph.D. dissertation, Department of Anthropology, University of Arizona, Tucson. University Microfilms, Ann Arbor.

Grebinger, Paul

1971 *Hohokam cultural development in the middle Santa Cruz River valley, Arizona.* Unpublished Ph.D. dissertation, Department of Anthropology, University of Arizona, Tucson.

1976 Salado—perspective from the middle Santa Cruz valley. *The Kiva* 42(1):39–46.

Green, Ernestine L.

1976 Valdez phase occupation near Taos, New Mexico. *Fort Burgwin Research Center* 10. Southern Methodist University, Dallas.

Greenleaf, J. C.
  1975   Excavations at Punto de Agua in the Santa Cruz River basin, southeastern Arizona. *Anthropological Papers of the University of Arizona* 26. Tucson.
Guernsey, S. J., and A. V. Kidder
  1921   Basketmaker caves of northeastern Arizona. *Peabody Museum Papers in American Archaeology and Ethnology* 8(2). Harvard University, Cambridge.
Guilday, J. E.
  1967   Differential extinction during late Pleistocene and recent times. In *Pleistocene extinctions, the search for a cause,* edited by P. S. Martin and H. E. Wright, pp. 121–140. Yale University Press, New Haven.
Gumerman, George J., and Robert C. Euler
  1976   Black Mesa: retrospect. In *Papers on the archaeology of Black Mesa, Arizona,* edited by George J. Gumerman and Robert C. Euler, pp. 162–170. Southern Illinois University Press, Carbondale.
Gumerman, George J., and Emil W. Haury
  1979   Prehistory: Hohokam. In *Southwest,* edited by Alfonso Ortiz, pp. 75–90. *Handbook of North American Indians* (Vol. 9). Smithsonian Institution, Washington, D.C.
Gumerman, George J., and Carol S. Weed
  1976   The question of Salado in the Agua Fria and New River drainages of central Arizona. *The Kiva* 42(1):105–112.
Gunnerson, James H.
  1969   Apache archaeology in northeastern New Mexico. *American Antiquity* 34(1):23–39.
Gunnerson, James H., and D. A. Gunnerson
  1971   Apachean culture: a study in unity and diversity. In Apachean culture history and ethnology, edited by Keith Basso and Morris E. Opler, pp. 7–27. *Anthropological Papers of the University of Arizona* 21. Tucson.
Guthrie, R. D.
  1980   Bison and man in North America. *Canadian Journal of Anthropology* 1(1):55–74.
Hack, John T.
  1942   The changing physical environment of the Hopi Indians of Arizona. *Papers of the Peabody Museum of American Archaeology and Ethnology* 35(1). Harvard University, Cambridge.
Hackenberg, Robert A.
  1964   Aboriginal land use and occupancy of the Papago Indians. Ms. on file, Arizona State Museum, Tucson.
Hafsten, U.
  1961   Pleistocene development of vegetation and climate in the southern High Plains as evidenced by pollen analysis. In Paleoecology of the Llano Estacado, edited by Fred Wendorf, pp. 55–91. *Fort Burgwin Research Center Publications* 1. Southern Methodist University, Dallas.
Hall, Edward T., Jr.
  1944   Recent clues to Athabascan prehistory in the Southwest. *American Anthropologist* 46:98–105.
Hall, Stephen A.
  1977   Late Quaternary sedimentation and paleoecologic history of Chaco Canyon, New Mexico. *Geological Society of American Bulletin* 88:1593–1618.
Hammond, George P., and Agapito Rey (translators)
  1940   *Narratives of the Coronado Expedition, 1540–1542.* University of New Mexico Press, Albuquerque.
Hantman, Jeffrey L.
  1983   *Social networks and stylistic distributions in the prehistoric plateau Southwest.* Unpublished Ph.D. dissertation, Department of Anthropology, Arizona State University, Tempe.
Harlan, Jack
  1967   A wild wheat harvest in Turkey. *Archaeology* 20(2):197–201.
Harrington, H. D.
  1967   *Edible native plants of the Rocky Mountains.* University of New Mexico Press, Albuquerque.

Harrington, M. R.
  1957   A Pinto site at Little Lake, California. *Southwest Museum Paper* 17. Los Angeles.
Hassan, F. A.
  1981   *Demographic archaeology.* Academic Press, New York.
Haury, Emil W.
  1934   The Canyon Creek ruin and cliff dwellings of the Sierra Ancha. *Medallion Papers* 14. Gila
         Pueblo, Globe, Arizona.
  1936   The Mogollon culture of southwestern New Mexico. *Medallion Papers* 20. Gila Pueblo, Globe,
         Arizona.
  1937   A pre-Spanish rubber ball from Arizona. *American Antiquity* 2(4):282–288.
  1950   *The stratigraphy and archaeology of Ventana Cave.* University of Arizona Press, Tucson.
  1957   An alluvial site on the San Carlos Indian Reservation, Arizona. *American Antiquity* 23(1):2–27.
  1958   Evidence at Point of Pines for a prehistoric migration from northern Arizona. In *Migrations in
         New World culture history,* edited by R. H. Thompson, pp. 1–7. University of Arizona Press,
         Tucson.
  1960   Association of fossil fauna and artifacts at the Sulpher Springs stage, Cochise culture. *American
         Antiquity* 25(4):609–610.
  1976   *The Hohokam, desert farmers and craftsmen: excavations at Snaketown, 1964–1965.* Univer-
         sity of Arizona Press, Tucson.
Haury, Emil W., and J. D. Hayden
  1975   Preface 1975. In *The stratigraphy and archaeology of Ventana Cave,* by Emil W. Haury, pp. v–vi.
         University of Arizona Press, Tucson.
Haury, Emil W., and E. B. Sayles
  1947   An early pit house village of the Mogollon culture, Forestdale Valley, Arizona. *University of
         Arizona Social Science Bulletin* 16. Tucson.
Haury, Emil W., E. B. Sayles, and W. W. Wasley
  1959   The Lehner mammoth site, southeastern Arizona. *American Antiquity* 25(1):2–30.
Hawley, Florence M.
  1934   The significance of dated prehistory of Chetro Ketl, Chaco Canyon, New Mexico. *University of
         New Mexico Bulletin, Monograph Series* 1(1). Albuquerque.
  1936   Field manual of prehistoric Southwestern pottery types. *University of New Mexico Bulletin* 291.
         Albuquerque.
Hayden, Julian D.
  1970   Of Hohokam origins and other matter. *American Antiquity* 35:87–93.
Hayes, Alden C.
  1964   The archeological survey of Wetherill Mesa. *Archaeological Research Series* 7A. National Park
         Service, Washington, D.C.
  1981a A survey of Chaco Canyon. In Archeological Surveys of Chaco Canyon, New Mexico, by Alden C.
         Hayes, David M. Brugge, and W. James Judge, pp. 1–68. *Publications in Archeology* 18A. *Chaco
         Canyon Studies.* National Park Service, Washington, D.C.
  1981b *Contributions to Gran Quivira archaeology.* National Park Service, Washington, D.C.
Hayes, Alden C., D. Brugge, and W. J. Judge
  1981   Archeological surveys of Chaco Canyon, New Mexico. *National Park Service Publications in
         Archeology* 18A. Washington, D.C.
Haynes, C. Vance, Jr.
  1969   The earliest Americans. *Science* 166:709–715.
  1970   Geochronology of man–mammoth sites and their bearing on the origin of the Llano complex.
         In Pleistocene and recent environments of the Central Plains, edited by Wakefield Dort, Jr., and
         J. Knox Jones, Jr., pp. 78–92. *Department of Geology, University of Kansas, Special Publication* 3.
         Lawrence.
  1975   Pleistocene and recent stratigraphy. In Pleistocene and recent environments of the southern
         High Plains, edited by Fred Wendorf and James J. Hester, pp. 57–96. *Fort Burgwin Research
         Center Publications* 9. Southern Methodist University, Dallas.

1980   The Clovis culture. *Canadian Journal of Anthropology* 1(1):115–121.
Haynes, C. Vance, Jr., and E. T. Hemmings
1968   Mammoth bone shaft wrench from Murray Springs, Arizona. *Science* 159:186–187.
Haynes, C. Vance, Jr., and Austin Long
1976   Radiocarbon dating at Snaketown. In *The Hohokam, desert farmers and craftsmen: excavations at Snaketown, 1964–1965,* by Emil W. Haury, pp. 333–338. University of Arizona Press, Tucson.
Heller, M. M.
1976   *Zoo-archaeology of Tularosa Cave, Catron County, New Mexico.* M.A. thesis, Department of Biology, University of Texas, El Paso.
Hester, James J.
1962   Navajo migrations and acculturation in the Southwest. *Museum of New Mexico Papers in Anthropology* 6. Santa Fe.
1972   *Blackwater Locality No. 1.* Fort Burgwin Research Center, Southern Methodist University.
1975   Paleoarchaeology of the Llano Estacado. In Late Pleistocene environments of the southern High Plains, edited by Fred Wendorf and James J. Hester, pp. 247–256. *Fort Burgwin Research Center Publications* 9. Southern Methodist University, Dallas.
Hevly, Richard H.
1964   *Pollen analysis of Quaternary archaeological and lacustrine sediments from the Colorado Plateau.* Unpublished Ph.D. dissertation, Department of Geology, University of Arizona, Tucson.
Hewett, Edgar L.
1906   Antiquities of the Jemez Plateau, New Mexico. *Bureau of American Ethnology Bulletin* 32. Smithsonian Institution, Washington, D.C.
1909   The excavations at Tyounyi, New Mexico, in 1908. *American Anthropologist* 11:434–455.
Hewett, Edgar L., Junius Henderson, and Wilfred William Robbins
1913   The physiography of the Rio Grande Valley, New Mexico, in relation to Pueblo culture. *Bureau of American Ethnology Bulletin* 54. Washington, D.C.
Hibben, Frank C.
1941   Evidences of early occupation in Sandia Cave, New Mexico, and other sites in the Sandia–Manzano region. *Smithsonian Institution Miscellaneous Collections* 99(3):1–44.
1946   The first thirty-eight Sandia points. *American Antiquity* 11(2):257–258.
1948   The Gallina architectural forms. *American Antiquity* 14(1):32–36.
1955   Specimens from Sandia Cave and their possible significance. *Science* 122:688–689.
1975   *Kiva art of the Anasazi at Pottery Mound.* K. C. Publications, Las Vegas, Nevada.
Hill, James N.
1970   Broken K Pueblo: prehistoric social organization in the American Southwest. *Anthropological Papers of the University of Arizona* 18. Tucson.
Hill, W. W.
1938   Navaho agricultural and hunting methods. *Yale University Publications in Anthropology* 18. New Haven.
Hillerud, J. M.
1980   Bison as indicators of geologic age. *Canadian Journal of Anthropology* 1(1):77–80.
Hitchcock, R. K., and James I. Ebert
in press   Foraging and food production among Kalahari hunter–gatherers. In *The causes and consequences of food production in Africa,* edited by J. D. Clark and S. A. Brandt. University of California Press, Berkeley and Los Angeles.
Hodge, F. W.
1893   Prehistoric irrigation in Arizona. *American Anthropologist* 6:323–330.
Hoijer, Harry
1956   The chronology of the Athapaskan languages. *International Journal of American Linguistics* 22(4):219–232.
Holbrook, Sally J.
1975   *Prehistoric paleoecology of northwestern New Mexico.* Unpublished Ph.D. dissertation, Department of Biology, University of California, Berkeley.

Holbrook, Sally J., and James C. Mackey
    1976   Prehistoric environmental change in northern New Mexico: evidence from a Gallina phase archaeological site. *The Kiva* 41(4):309–317.

Holden, Jane
    1955   A preliminary report on Arrowhead Ruin. *El Palacio* 62(4):102–119.

Holsinger, S. J.
    1901   Report on prehistoric ruins of Chaco Canyon National Monument. General Land Office. Ms. on file, Division of Cultural Research, National Park Service, Albuquerque.

Honea, Kenneth
    1969   The Rio Grande complex and the northern Plains. *Plains Anthropologist* 14(43):57–70.

Hopkins, D. M.
    1967   Quaternary marine transgressions in Alaska. In *The Bering land bridge,* edited by D. M. Hopkins, pp. 47–90. Stanford University Press, Stanford.

Hough, Walter
    1914   Culture of the ancient Pueblos of the Upper Gila. *Smithsonian Institution Bulletin* 87. Washington, D.C.
    1920   Explorations of a pit house village at Luna, New Mexico. *Proceedings of the U.S. National Museum* 35:409–431. Washington, D.C.

Houghton, Frank E.
    1959   *Climate of New Mexico.* U.S. Department of Commerce, National Oceanic and Atmospheric Administration, Environmental Data Service. Silver Spring, Maryland.

Hrdlicka, A.
    1926   The race and antiquity of the American Indian. *Scientific American* 135:7–10.

Hunt, Charles B.
    1967   *Physiography of the United States.* W. H. Freeman, San Francisco.

Hunter-Anderson, Rosalind
    1979   Explaining residential aggregation in the northern Rio Grande: a competition reduction model. In Adaptive change in the northern Rio Grande, edited by Jan V. Biella and Richard C. Chapman, pp. 169–175. *Archeological investigations in Cochiti Reservoir* (Vol. 4). Office of Contract Archeology, University of New Mexico, Albuquerque.

Huscher, B. H., and H. A. Huscher
    1942   Athapaskan migration via the intermontane region. *American Antiquity* 8:80–88.

Irwin, Henry T.
    1971   Developments in early man studies in western North America, 1960–1970. *Arctic Anthropology* 8(2):42–67.

Irwin, Henry T., and C. C. Irwin
    1959   Excavations at the LoDaiska site in the Denver, Colorado area. *Proceedings of the Denver Museum of Natural History* 8.

Irwin, Henry T., and H. M. Wormington
    1970   Paleo-Indian tool types in the Great Plains. *American Antiquity* 35(1):24–34.

Irwin-Williams, Cynthia
    n.d.   Paleo-Indian and Archaic cultural systems in the southwestern United States. Ms. prepared for the Handbook of North American Indians, Smithsonian Institution, Washington, D.C.
    1967   Picosa: the elementary Southwestern culture. *American Antiquity* 32(4):441–456.
    1973   *The Oshara tradition: origins of Anasazi culture.* Eastern New Mexico University Contributions in Anthropology 5(1). Portales.
    1979   Post-Pleistocene archeology, 7000–2000 B.C. In *Southwest,* edited by Alfonso Ortiz, pp. 31–42. *Handbook of North American Indians* (Vol. 9). Smithsonian Institution, Washington, D.C.
    1980a Investigations at Salmon Ruin: methodology and overview. In *Investigations at the Salmon site: the structure of Chacoan society in the northern Southwest,* edited by Cynthia Irwin-Williams and Phillip H. Shelley, pp. 107–170. Eastern New Mexico University, Portales.
    1980b San Juan Valley Archaeological Project: synthesis, 1980, Part 12. In *Investigations at the Salmon site: the structure of Chacoan society in the northern Southwest,* edited by Cynthia Irwin-Williams and Phillip H. Shelley, pp. 135–211. Eastern New Mexico University, Portales.

Irwin-Williams, Cynthia, and P. Beckett
  1973 Excavations at the Moquino site: a Cochise culture locality in northern New Mexico. Ms. on file, Department of Anthropology, Eastern New Mexico University.

Irwin-Williams, Cynthia, and C. Vance Haynes, Jr.
  1970 Climatic change and early population dynamics in the southwestern United States. *Quaternary Research* 1:59–71.

Irwin-Williams, Cynthia, and Henry T. Irwin
  1966 Excavations at Magic Mountain: a diachronic study of Plains–Southwest relations. *Denver Museum of Natural History Proceedings* 12.

Irwin-Williams, Cynthia, Henry T. Irwin, George Agogino, and C. Vance Haynes, Jr.
  1973 Hell Gap: a Paleo-Indian occupation on the High Plains. *Plains Anthropologist* 18(59):40–53.

Irwin-Williams, Cynthia, and S. Tompkins
  1968 Excavations at En Medio shelter, New Mexico. Interim report of the Anasazi Origins project of Eastern New Mexico University. *Eastern New Mexico University Contributions in Anthropology* 1(2). Portales.

Jennings, Calvin H.
  1971 *Early prehistory of the Coconino Plateau, northwestern Arizona.* Ph.D. dissertation, Department of Anthropology, University of Colorado, Boulder.

Jennings, Jesse D.
  1963 Anthropology and the world of science. *Bulletin of the University of Utah* 54(18). Salt Lake City.
  1964 The desert West. In *Prehistoric man in the New World,* edited by J. D. Jennings and E. Norbeck, pp. 149–174. University of Chicago Press, Chicago.
  1966 Glen Canyon: a summary. *Anthropological Papers of the University of Utah* 81. *Glen Canyon Series* 31. Salt Lake City.
  1978 Prehistory of Utah and the eastern Great Basin. *Anthropological Papers of the University of Utah* 98. Salt Lake City.

Johnson, A. E.
  1966 Archaeology of Sonora, Mexico. In Archaeological frontiers and external connections, edited by Gordon F. Ekholm and Gordon R. Willey, pp. 26–37. *Handbook of Middle American Indians* (Vol. 4). University of Texas Press, Austin.

Johnson, E., and V. T. Holliday
  1980 A Plainview kill/butchering locale on the Llano Estacado—the Lubbock Lake site. *Plains Anthropologist* 25(88):89–111 (Part 1).

Jorde, Lynn B.
  1977 Precipitation cycles and cultural buffering in the prehistoric Southwest. In *For theory building in archaeology: essays on faunal remains, aquatic resources, and systemic modeling.* edited by Lewis R. Binford, pp. 385–396. Academic Press, New York.

Judd, Neil M.
  1922 Archaeological investigations at Pueblo Bonito. *Smithsonian Miscellaneous Collections* 72(15):106–117. Washington, D.C.

Judge, W. James
  n.d. Early man: Plains and Southwest. An interpretive summary of the PaleoIndian occupation of the Plains and Southwest. Ms. prepared for the Handbook of North American Indians (Vol. 3), Smithsonian Institution, Washington, D.C.
  1970 Systems analysis and the Folsom–Midland question. *Southwestern Journal of Anthropology* 26(1):40–51.
  1973 *The Paleo-Indian occupation of the central Rio Grande Valley, New Mexico.* University of New Mexico Press, Albuquerque.
  1979 The development of a complex cultural ecosystem in the Chaco Basin, New Mexico. In *Proceedings of the First Conference on Scientific Research in the National Parks,* edited by Robert M. Linn, pp. 901–905. U.S. Government Printing Office, Washington, D.C.
  1982 The Paleo-Indian and Basketmaker periods: an overview and some research problems. In *The*

San Juan Tomorrow, edited by Fred Plog and Walter Wait, pp. 5–57. National Park Service, Southwest Region, Santa Fe.

Judge, W. James, and J. Dawson

1972   PaleoIndian settlement technology in New Mexico. *Science* 176:1210–1216.

Judge, W. James, W. B. Gillespie, Stephen H. Lekson, and H. W. Toll

1981   Tenth century developments in Chaco Canyon. *Archaeological Society of New Mexico Anthropological Papers* 6.

Kaplan, Lawrence

1963   The archaeoethnobotany of Cordova Cave. *Economic Botany* 18(4):350–356.

1965   Beans of the Wetherill Mesa. In Contributions of the Wetherill Mesa Archaeological Project, edited by D. Osborne, pp. 153–155. *Memoirs of the Society of American Archaeology* 19. Salt Lake City.

Kelley, Jane H.

1966   *The archaeology of the Sierra Blanca region of southwestern New Mexico.* Unpublished Ph.D. dissertation, Department of Anthropology, Harvard University, Cambridge.

Kelley, J. Charles

1952   Factors involved in the abandonment of certain peripheral southwestern settlements. *American Anthropologist* 54:356–387.

1971   Archaeology of the northern frontier: Zacatecas and Durango. *Handbook of Middle American Indians* (Vol. 11, Part 2), edited by Robert Wauchope, pp. 768–801. University of Texas Press, Austin.

Kelley, J. Charles, and Ellen Abbott Kelley

1975   An alternative hypothesis for the explanation of Anasazi culture history. In Collected Papers in honor of Florence Hawley Ellis, edited by Theodore R. Frisbie, pp. 178–223. *Papers of the Archaeological Society of New Mexico* 2. Santa Fe.

Kessell, John L.

1979   *Kiva, cross, and crown: the Pecos Indians of New Mexico, 1540–1840.* National Park Service, U.S. Government Printing Office, Washington, D.C.

Kidder, Alfred Vincent

1917   The old north pueblo of Pecos: the condition of the main Pecos ruin. *Archaeological Institute of America, Papers of the School of American Research* 38. Santa Fe.

1924   An introduction to the study of Southwestern archaeology, with a preliminary account of the excavations at Pecos. *Papers of the Southwest Expedition* 1. (Reprinted in 1962 by Yale University Press, New Haven.)

1927   Southwestern archaeological conference. *Science* 68:489–491.

1931   The pottery of Pecos (Vol 1). The dull-paint wares, with a section on the black-on-white wares by Charles A. Amsden. *Papers of the Southwestern Expedition* 5. Yale University Press, New Haven.

1936a   Discussion. In *The pottery of Pecos* (Vol. 2), edited by Alfred Vincent Kidder and Anna O. Shepard, pp. 589–628. Yale University Press, New Haven.

1936b   Speculations on New World prehistory. In *Essays in anthropology presented to A. L. Kroeber,* edited by Robert H. Lowie, pp. 143–152. University of California Press, Berkeley.

1958   Pecos, New Mexico: archaeological notes. *Papers of the Robert S. Peabody Foundation for Archaeology* 5. Andover, Mass.

1962   *An introduction to the study of Southwestern archaeology with a preliminary account of the excavations at Pecos, and a summary of Southwestern archaeology today,* by Irving Rouse. Yale University Press, New Haven.

Kidder, Alfred Vincent, and S. J. Guernsey

1919   Archaeological exploration in northeastern Arizona. *Bureau of American Ethnology* 65. Smithsonian Institution, Washington, D.C.

Kidder, Alfred Vincent, and Anna O. Shepard

1936   The pottery of Pecos (Vol. 2). The glaze-paint, culinary, and other wares. *Papers of the Southwest Expedition* 7. Phillips Academy, Andover, and Yale University Press, New Haven.

Kintigh, Keith
  1980 An archaeological clearance survey of Miller Canyon and the southwest boundary fenceline, Zuni Indian Reservation, McKinley County, New Mexico. Ms. on file, Zuni Archaeology Program, Pueblo of Zuni.

Knight, Paul J.
  1978 *The role of seed morphology in identification of archeological remains.* Unpublished M.S. thesis, Department of Biology, University of New Mexico, Albuquerque.

Knudson, Ruthann
  1973 *Organizational variability in late PaleoIndian assemblages.* Ph.D. dissertation, Department of Anthropology, Washington State University, Pullman.

Kroeber, Alfred L.
  1916 Zuni potsherds. *Anthropological Papers of the American Museum of Natural History* 18(Part 1).

Lambert, Marjorie F.
  1954 Paa-ko: archaeological chronicle of an Indian village in north central New Mexico. *School of American Research Monograph* 19. University of New Mexico Press, Albuquerque.

Lance, J. F.
  1959 Faunal remains from the Lehner mammoth site. *American Antiquity* 25(1):35–59.

Lang, Richard W.
  1977a *An archaeological survey of certain state lands within the drainages of Arroyo de la Vega de los Tanos and Arroyo Tonque de los Tanos and Arroyo Tonque, Sandoval County, New Mexico.* School of American Research Archaeology Contract Program, Santa Fe.
  1977b *Archeological survey of the upper San Cristobal Arroyo drainage, Galisteo Basin, Santa Fe County, New Mexico.* School of American Research Contract Program, Santa Fe.

LeBlanc, Steven A.
  1982 The advent of pottery in the Southwest. In Southwestern ceramics: a comparative review, edited by Albert H. Schroeder, pp. 27–51. *The Arizona Archaeologist* 15. Phoenix.
  1983 *The Mimbres people: ancient pueblo potters of the American Southwest.* Thames and Hudson, London.

Lee, Richard B.
  1968 What hunters do for a living, or how to make out on scarce resources. In *Man the hunter,* edited by Richard B. Lee and I. DeVore, pp. 30–48. Aldine, Chicago.

Lee, Richard B., and I. DeVore (editors)
  1968 *Man the hunter.* Aldine, Chicago.

Lehmer, D. J.
  1948 The Jornada branch of the Mogollon. *Social Science Bulletin* 17. *University of Arizona Bulletin* 19(2). Tucson.

Lenihan, Daniel J., Toni L. Correll, Thomas S. Hopkins, A. Wayne Prokopetz, Sandra L. Rayl, and Cathryn S. Tarasovic
  1977 The preliminary report of the National Reservoir Inundation Study. National Park Service, Santa Fe.

Lightfoot, Kent G., and Gary M. Feinman
  1982 Social differentiation and leadership development in early pithouse villages in the Mogollon region of the American Southwest. *American Antiquity* 47(1):64–86.

Lindsay, Alexander J., and Calvin H. Jennings
  1968 Salado Red Ware Conference: Ninth Southwestern Ceramic Seminar. *Museum of Northern Arizona Ceramic Series* 4. Flagstaff.

Linton, Ralph
  1944 Nomadic raids and fortified pueblos. *American Antiquity* 10(1):28–32.

Lipe, William D.
  1978 The Southwest. In *Ancient Native Americans,* edited by Jesse D. Jennings, pp. 403–454. Freeman, San Francisco.

Lipe, William D., and Cory D. Breternitz
  1980 Approaches to analyzing variability among Dolores structures, A.D. 600–950. *Contract Abstracts and CRM Archeology* 1(2):21–28.

Lipe, William D., and R. G. Matson

1971　Human settlement and resources in the Cedar Mesa area, southeast Utah. In The distribution of population aggregates, edited by George J. Gumerman, pp. 116–151. *Prescott College Anthropological Reports* 1. Prescott, Arizona.

Lister, Robert H.

1966　Contributions to Mesa Verde archaeology III: site 866 and the cultural sequence at four villages in the Far View group, Mesa Verde National Park, Colorado. *University of Colorado Studies, Series in Anthropology* 12. Boulder.

Lister, Robert H., and Florence C. Lister

1981　*Chaco Canyon: archaeology and archaeologists.* University of New Mexico Press, Albuquerque.

Long, A., and Bruce Rippeteau

1974　Testing contemporaneity and averaging radiocarbon dates. *American Antiquity* 39(2):205–215.

Longacre, William A.

1964　A synthesis of upper Little Colorado prehistory, eastern Arizona. In Chapters in the prehistory of eastern Arizona (Vol. II), edited by P. S. Martin, John B. Rinaldo, William A. Longacre, C. Cronin, L. G. Freeman, and James Schoenwetter, pp. 201–215. *Fieldiana, Anthropology* 55.

1968　Some aspects of prehistoric society in east-central Arizona. In *New perspectives in archaeology,* edited by S. R. Binford and L. R. Binford, pp. 89–102. Aldine, Chicago.

1970　Archaeology as anthropology: a case study. *Anthropological Papers of the University of Arizona* 17. Tucson.

Longacre, William A., and M. W. Graves

1976　Probability sampling applied to an early multi-component surface site in east-central Arizona. *The Kiva* 41(3–4):277–288.

Longacre, William A., Sally J. Holbrook, and Michael W. Graves

1982　Multidisciplinary research at Grasshopper Pueblo, Arizona. *Anthropological Papers of the University of Arizona* 40. Tucson.

Longacre, William A., and J. Jefferson Reid

1974　The University of Arizona archaeological field school at Grasshopper: 11 years of multidisciplinary research and teaching. *The Kiva* 40:3–38.

Lösch, A.

1954　*The economics of location.* Yale University Press, New Haven.

Love, David W.

1980　*Quaternary geology of Chaco Canyon, northwestern New Mexico.* Unpublished Ph.D. dissertation, Department of Geology, University of New Mexico.

Love, Marian F.

1975　A survey of the distribution of T-shaped doorways in the Greater Southwest. In Collected papers in honor of Florence Hawley Ellis, edited by Theodore R. Frisbie, pp. 296–311. *Papers of the Archaeological Society of New Mexico* 2. Santa Fe.

Lyons, Thomas R., and Robert K. Hitchcock

1977　Remote sensing interpretation of Anasazi land route system. In Aerial remote sensing techniques in archeology, edited by Thomas R. Lyons and Robert K. Hitchcock, pp. 111–134. *Reports of the Chaco Center* 2. Southwest Cultural Resource Center, National Park Service, and University of New Mexico, Albuquerque.

McGregor, John C.

1936　Dating the eruption of Sunset Crater, Arizona. *American Antiquity* 2(1):15–26.

1937　Winona Village. *Bulletin* 12. Museum of Northern Arizona, Flagstaff.

1941　Winona and Ridge Ruin, part 1: architecture and material culture. *Bulletin* 18. Museum of Northern Arizona, Flagstaff.

1943　Burial of an early American magician. *Proceedings of the American Philosophical Society* 86(2):270–298. Philadelphia.

1951　*The Cohonina culture of northwestern Arizona.* University of Illinois Press, Urbana.

1965　*Southwestern archaeology.* University of Illinois Press, Urbana.

McGuire, Randall H.

1980　The Mesoamerican connection in the Southwest. *The Kiva* 46(1–2):3–38.

1982   Problems in culture history. In *Hohokam and Patayan, prehistory of southwestern Arizona,* edited by Randall H. McGuire and Michael B. Schiffer, pp. 153–222. Academic Press, New York.

McGuire, Randall H., and Michael B. schiffer (editors)
1982   *Hohokam and Patayan, prehistory of southwestern Arizona.* Academic Press, New York.

McKern, William C.
1939   The Midwestern Taxonomic Method as an aid to archaeological study. *American Antiquity* 4(3):301–313.

Mackey, James C., and Sally J. Holbrook
1978   Environmental reconstruction and the abandonment of the Largo–Gallina area. *Journal of Field Archaeology* 5(1):29–49.

MacNeish, Richard S.
1958   Preliminary archaeological investigations in the Sierra de Tamaulipos, Mexico. *Transactions of the American Philosophical Society* Vol. 48, Pt. 6. Philadelphia.
1964   Ancient Mesoamerican civilization. *Science* 143:531–537.
1967   A summary of the subsistence. In *Environment and subsistence: the prehistory of the Tehuacan Valley* (Vol. 1), edited by Douglas S. Byers, pp. 290–309. University of Texas Press, Austin.
1971   Speculation about how and why food production and village life developed in the Tehuacan Valley, Mexico, *Archaeology* 24(4):307–315.

Madsen, David B., and Michael S. Berry
1975   A reassessment of northeastern Great Basin prehistory. *American Antiquity* 40(1):82–86.

Mangelsdorf, Paul C.
1954   New evidence on the origin and ancestry of maize. *American Antiquity* 19(4):409–410.
1974   *Corn, its origin, evolution, and improvement.* Harvard University Press, Cambridge.

Mangelsdorf, Paul C., H. W. Dick, and J. Camera-Hernandez
1967   Bat Cave revisited. *Harvard University Botanical Museum Leaflets* 22:213–260.

Mangelsdorf, Paul C., and Robert H. Lister
1956   Archaeological evidence on the diffusion and evolution of maize in northern Mexico. *Harvard University Botanical Museum Leaflets* 17:151–178.

Marshall, Michael P., and David E. Doyel
1981   An interim report on Bi sa' ani Pueblo, with notes on the Chacoan regional system. Ms. on file, Navajo Nation Cultural Resource Management Program, Window Rock, Arizona.

Marshall, Michael P., and Henry Walt
1984   *Rio Abajo: the prehistory and history of a Rio Grande province.* New Mexico Historic Preservation Division, Santa Fe.

Marshall, Michael P., John R. Stein, Richard W. Loose, and Judith E. Novotny
1979   *Anasazi communities of the San Juan Basin.* Public Service Company of New Mexico, Albuquerque, and New Mexico Historic Preservation Bureau, Santa Fe.

Martin, Paul Schultz
1963   *The last 10,000 years.* University of Arizona Press, Tucson.

Martin, Paul Schultz, and William Byers
1965   Pollen and archaeology at Wetherill Mesa. In Contributions of the Wetherill Mesa Archaeological Project, edited by D. Osborne, pp. 5–13. *Memoirs of the Society for American Archaeology* 10:5–13. Salt Lake City.

Martin, Paul Schultz, and James Schoenwetter
1960   Arizona's oldest cornfield. *Science* 132:33–34.

Martin, Paul Schultz, and H. E. Wright (editors)
1967   *Pleistocene extinctions: the search for cause.* Yale University Press, New Haven.

Martin, Paul Sidney
1950   Conjectures concerning the social organization of the Mogollon Indians. In Sites of the Reserve phase, Pine Lawn Valley, western New Mexico, by Paul S. Martin and John B. Rinaldo. *Fieldiana, Anthropology* 38(3):556–569. Chicago.

1973   The Desert Culture: a hunting and gathering adaptation. In *The archaeology of Arizona, a study of the Southwest region,* by P. S. Martin and F. Plog, pp. 69–80. Doubleday/Natural History Press, Garden City, New York.

1979   Prehistory: Mogollon. In *Southwest,* edited by Alfonso Ortiz, pp. 61–74. *Handbook of North American Indians* (Vol. 9). Smithsonian Institution, Washington, D.C.

Martin, Paul Sidney, and Fred Plog
1973   *The archaeology of Arizona.* Doubleday/Natural History Press, Garden City, New York.

Martin, Paul Sidney, and John B. Rinaldo
1939   Modified Basketmaker sites, Ackman–Lowry area, southwestern Colorado, 1938. *Anthropological Series, Field Museum of Natural History* 23(3). Chicago.
1951   The Southwestern co-tradition. *Southwestern Journal of Anthropology* 7:215–229.
1960   Table Rock Pueblo, Arizona. *Fieldiana, Anthropology* 51(2).

Martin, Paul Sidney, John B. Rinaldo, and Ernst Antevs
1949   Cochise and Mogollon sites in Pine Lawn Valley, western New Mexico. *Fieldiana, Anthropology* 38(1).

Martin, Paul Sidney, John B. Rinaldo, and Elaine A. Bluhm
1954   Caves of the Reserve area. *Fieldiana, Anthropology* 42.

Martin, Paul Sidney, John B. Rinaldo, Elaine A. Bluhm, Hugh C. Cutler, and R. Grange, Jr.
1952   Mogollon cultural continuity and change: the stratigraphic analysis of Tularosa and Cordova caves. *Fieldiana, Anthropology* 40.

Martin, Paul Sidney, John B. Rinaldo, and William A. Longacre
1961   Mineral Creek site and Hooper Ranch pueblo. *Fieldiana, Anthropology* 52.

Masse, W. Bruce
1980   Excavations at Gu Achi: a reappraisal of Hohokam settlement and subsistence in the Arizona Papagueria. *Western Archaeological Center Publications in Anthropology* 12. Tucson.
1981   Prehistoric irrigation systems in the Salt River Valley, Arizona. *Science* 214:408–415.

Matson, R. G., and William D. Lipe
1978   Settlement patterns on Cedar Mesa: boom and bust on the northern periphery. In *Investigations of the Southwestern Anthropological Research Group: the proceedings of the 1976 conference,* edited by Robert C. Euler and George J. Gumerman, pp. 1–12. Museum of Northern Arizona, Flagstaff.

Mehringer, P. J., Jr.
1967   Pollen analysis and alluvial chronology. *The Kiva* 32(3):96–101.

Mehringer, P. J., Jr., and C. Vance Haynes, Jr.
1965   The pollen evidence for the environment of early man and extinct mammals at the Lehner mammoth site, southeastern Arizona. *American Antiquity* 31(1):17–23.

Michels, Joseph W., and Carl A. Bebrich
1971   Obsidian hydration dating. In *Dating techniques for the archaeologist,* edited by H. N. Michael and Elizabeth K. Ralph, pp. 164–223. MIT Press, Cambridge.

Michels, Joseph W., and Ignatius S. T. Tsong
1980   Obsidian hydration dating: coming of age. In *Advances in Archaeological Method and Theory.* Vol. 3, edited by Michael B. Schiffer, pp. 405–439. New York, Academic Press.

Mindeleff, Cosmos
1896   Aboriginal remains in Verde Valley, Arizona. *13th Annual Report of the Bureau of American Ethnology,* pp. 176–261. Smithsonian Institution, Washington, D.C.

Minnis, Paul E.
1980   *Domesticating plants and people in the greater Southwest.* Paper presented at the Advanced Seminar on the Origins of Plant Husbandry in North America, School of American Research, Santa Fe.
1981   *Economic and organizational responses to food stress by non-stratified societies: an example from prehistoric New Mexico.* Unpublished Ph.D. dissertation, Department of Anthropology, University of Michigan, Ann Arbor.

Montgomery, R. G., W. Smith, and John O. Brew
  1949   Franciscan Awatovi: the excavation and conjectural reconstruction of a 17th century Spanish
          mission establishment at a Hopi Indian town in northeastern Arizona. *Papers of the Peabody
          Museum of American Archaeology and Ethnology.* Harvard University, Cambridge.
Morgan, J. R.
  1977   Were Chaco's great kivas ancient computers of astronomy? *El Palacio* 83(1):28–41.
Morris, Donald H.
  1969   Red Mountain: an early Pioneer period Hohokam site in the Salt River Valley of central Arizona.
          American Antiquity 34(1):40–53.
Morris, Earl H.
  1915   The excavation of a ruin near Aztec, San Juan County, New Mexico. *American Anthropologist*
          17:656–684.
Morris, Earl H., and Robert F. Burgh
  1954   Basket Maker sites near Durango, Colorado. *Carnegie Institution of Washington Publication*
          604. Washington, D.C.
Morss, Noel
  1931   The ancient culture of the Fremont River in Utah. *Peabody Museum Papers* 12(3). Peabody
          Museum of Archaeology and Ethnology, Harvard University, Cambridge.
Munson, Patrick J., Paul H. Parmalee, and Richard A. Yarnell
  1971   Subsistence ecology of Scovill, a terminal Middle Woodland village. *American Antiquity*
          36(4):410–431.
Murdock, George Peter
  1949   *Social structure.* Macmillan, New York.
Nabhan, Gary Paul
  1977   Viable seeds from prehistoric caches? Archaeobotanical remains in Southwestern folklore. *The
          Kiva* 43(3):143–159.
Nagata, Shuichi
  1970   Modern transformations of Moenkopi Pueblo. *Illinois Studies in Anthropology* 6. University of
          Illinois Press, Urbana.
Neller, E.
  1976   Botanical analysis in Atlatl Cave. Ms. on file, Southwest Cultural Resources Center, National Park
          Service, Albuquerque.
Nelson, Ben A., and Linda S. Cordell
  1982   Dynamics of the Anasazi adaptation. In *Anasazi and Navajo land use in the McKinley Mine area
          near Gallup, New Mexico* (Vol. 1, Part 1), edited by Christina G. Allen and Ben A. Nelson, pp.
          867–893. Office of Contract Archeology, University of New Mexico, Albuquerque.
Nelson, Nels C.
  1914   Pueblo ruins of the Galisteo Basin, New Mexico. *Anthropological Papers of the American
          Museum of Natural History* 15(Part 1).
  1916   Chronology of the Tano ruins, New Mexico. *American Anthropologist* 18(2):159–180.
Nicholas, Linda M.
  1981   *Irrigation and sociopolitical development—the Salt River Valley, Arizona: an examination of
          three prehistoric canal systems.* M.A. Department of Anthropology, Arizona State University,
          Tempe.
North, Douglass C., and Robert Paul Thomas
  1973   *The rise of the Western World: a new economic history.* Cambridge University Press, Cambridge.
Noy-Meir, I.
  1973   Desert ecosystems: environment and producers. *Annual Review of Ecology and Systematics*
          4:25–51.
  1974   Desert ecosystems: higher trophic levels. *Annual Review of Ecology and Systematics* 5:195–214.
Obenauf, Margaret
  1980   *The Chacoan roadway system.* Unpublished M.A. thesis, Department of Anthropology, Univer-
          sity of New Mexico, Albuquerque.

O'Bryan, Deric
    1950   Excavations in Mesa Verde National Park, 1947–1948. *Medallion Papers* 39. Gila Pueblo, Globe, Arizona.
O'Laughlin, Thomas C.
    1980   *The Keystone Dam site and other Archaic and Formative sites in northwest El Paso, Texas. Publication No 8, El Paso Centennial Museum, University of Texas at El Paso.*
Oldfield, F., and James Schoenwetter
    1975   Discussion of the pollen analytical evidence. In *Late Pleistocene environments of the southern High Plains,* edited by Fred Wendorf and James J. Hester, pp. 149–171. *Fort Burgwin Research Center Publication* 9. Southern Methodist University.
Olson, A. P.
    1966   A mass secondary burial from northern Arizona. *American Antiquity* 31(4):822–826.
Opler, Morris E.
    1983   The Apachean culture pattern and its origins. In *Southwest,* edited by Alfonso Ortiz, pp. 368–392. *Handbook of North American Indians* (Vol. 10) Smithsonian Institution, Washington, D.C.
Ortiz, Alfonso A. (editor)
    1979   *Southwest. Handbook of North American Indians* (Vol. 9) Smithsonian Institution, Washington, D.C.
Pailes, Richard A.
    1963   *An analysis of the Fitch Site and its relationship to the Hohokam Classic period.* M.A. thesis, Department of Anthropology, Arizona State University, Tempe.
Parsons, Elsie C.
    1939   *Pueblo Indian religion.* University of Chicago Press, Chicago.
Pilles, Peter J., Jr.
    1979   Sunset Crater and the Sinagua: a new interpretation. In *Volcanic activity and human ecology,* edited by Payson D. Sheets and Donald K. Grayson, pp. 459–485. Academic Press, New York.
Plog, Fred T.
    1974   *The study of prehistoric change.* Academic Press, New York.
    1978   The Keresan bridge: an ecological and archaeological analysis. In *Social archaeology: beyond subsistence and dating,* edited by Charles L. Redman, E. B. Curtin, N. M. Versaggi, and J. L. Wagner, pp. 349–372. Academic Press, New York.
    1979   Alternative models of prehistoric change. In *Transformations, mathematical approaches to culture change,* edited by Colin Renfrew and Kenneth L. Cooke, pp. 221–236. Academic Press, New York.
    1980   Explaining culture change in the Hohokam Preclassic. In Current issues in Hohokam prehistory: proceedings of a symposium, edited by David E. Doyel and Fred T. Plog, pp. 4–22. *Arizona State University Anthropological Research Papers* 23. Tempe.
    1980a   *The Sinagua and their relations.* Paper presented at the School of American Research Advanced Seminar on Dynamics of Southwest Prehistory, October 1983, Santa Fe.
    1983   Political and economic alliances on the Colorado Plateaus, A.D. 400–1450. In *Advances in world archaeology* (Vol. 2), edited by Fred Wendorf and A. Close, pp. 289–330. Academic Press, New York.
Plog, Fred T., Richard Effland, and Dee F. Green
    1978   Inferences using the SARG data bank. In *Investigations of the Southwestern Anthropological Research Group: an experiment in cooperation,* edited by Robert C. Euler and George J. Gumerman, pp. 139–148. Museum of Northern Arizona, Flagstaff.
Plog, Fred T., and Cheryl K. Garrett
    1972   Explaining variability in prehistoric Southwestern water systems. In *Contemporary archaeology: a guide to theory and contributions,* edited by Mark P. Leone, pp. 280–288. Southern Illinois University Press, Carbondale.
Plog, Stephen E.
    1980   *Stylistic variation in prehistoric ceramics: design analysis in the American Southwest.* Cambridge University Press, New York.

Powell, Shirley
    1983   *Mobility and adaptation: the Anasazi of Black Mesa, Arizona.* Southern Illinois University Press, Carbondale.

Powers, W. E.
    1939   Basin and shore features of the extinct Lake San Agustin, New Mexico. *Journal of Geomorphology* 2(2):345–356.

Prudden, T. Mitchell
    1903   The Prehistoric ruins of the San Juan watershed of Utah, Arizona, Colorado, and New Mexico. *American Anthropologist* 5:224–228.
    1914   The circular kivas of small ruins in the San Juan watershed. *American Anthropologist* 16:33–58.
    1918   A further study of prehistoric small house ruins in the San Juan watershed. *Memoirs of the American Anthropological Association* 5(1).

Raab, M. L.
    1977   The Santa Rosa Wash Project: notes on archaeological research design under contract. In *Conservation archaeology,* edited by Michael B. Schiffer and George J. Gumerman, pp. 167–182. Academic Press, New York.

Ralph, Elizabeth K.
    1971   Carbon-14 dating. In *Dating techniques for the archaeologist,* edited by H. N. Michael and Elizabeth K. Ralph, pp. 1–48. MIT Press, Cambridge.

Reed, Erik K.
    1946   The distinctive features of the San Juan Anasazi culture. *Southwestern Journal of Anthropology* 2(3):295–305.
    1948   The western Pueblo archaeological complex. *El Palacio* 55(1):9–15.
    1949   Sources of upper Rio Grande Pueblo culture and population. *El Palacio* 56:163–184.
    1956   Types of village-plan layouts in the Southwest. In Prehistoric settlement patterns in the New World, edited by Gordon R. Willey, pp. 11–17. *Viking Fund Publications in Anthropology* 23.

Reher, Charles A.
    1977b *Settlement and subsistence along the lower Chaco River: the CGP Survey.* University of New Mexico Press, Albuquerque.

Reher, Charles A., and D. C. Witter
    1977   Archaic settlement and vegetative diversity. In *Settlement and subsistence along the lower Chaco River: the CGP Survey,* edited by Charles A. Reher, pp. 113–126. University of New Mexico Press, Albuquerque.

Reiter, Paul
    1938   The Jemez Pueblo of Unshagi, New Mexico, with notes on the earlier excavations at "Amoxiumqua" and Giusewa. *University of New Mexico Bulletin* 326, *Monograph Series* 1(4). Albuquerque.

Renfrew, Colin
    1977   Alternative models for exchange and spatial distribution. In *Exchange systems in prehistory,* edited by T. K. Earle and J. E. Erickson, pp. 71–90. Academic Press, New York.
    1978   Trajectory discontinuity and morphogenesis: The implications of catastrophe theory for archaeology. *American Antiquity* 43(2):203–244.

Reyman, Jonathan E.
    1976   Astronomy, architecture, and adaptation at Pueblo Bonito. *Science* 193:957–962.
    1978   Pochteca burial at Anasazi sites. In *Across the Chichimec Sea: papers in honor of J. Charles Kelley,* edited by Carroll L. Riley and Basil C. Hedrick, pp. 242–259. Southern Illinois University Press, Carbondale.
    1980   An Anasazi solar marker? *Science* 209:858–859.

Rice, Glen E.
    1980   An analytical overview of the Mogollon tradition. In Studies in the prehistory of the Forestdale region, Arizona, edited by C. R. Stafford and Glen E. Rice, pp. 9–40. *Anthropological Field Studies* 1. Office of Cultural Resource Management, Department of Anthropology, Arizona State University, Tempe.

Rinaldo, John B.
1974 Projectile points. In *Casas Grandes: a fallen trading center of the Gran Chichimeca* (Vol. 7), by Charles DiPeso, John B. Rinaldo, and G. J. Fenner, pp. 389–398. The Amerind Foundation, Dragoon, Arizona, and Northland Press, Flagstaff, Arizona.

Roberts, Frank H. H., Jr.
1935a A Folsom complex: preliminary report on investigations at the Lindenmeier site in northern Colorado. *Smithsonian Institution Miscellaneous Collections* 49.
1935b A survey of Southwestern archaeology. *American Anthropologist* 37:1–33.
1936 Additional information on the Folsom complex: report on the second season's investigations at the Lindenmeier site in northern Colorado. *Smithsonian Institution Miscellaneous Collections* 95(10).
1938 The Folsom problem in American archaeology. *Annual Report of the Smithsonian Institution,* pp. 531–546. U.S. Government Printing Office, Washington, D.C.
1939 Archaeological remains in the Whitewater district, eastern Arizona, Part I—house types. *Bureau of American Ethnology Bulletin* 121. Washington, D.C.

Robertson, Benjamin P.
1983 Other New World roads and trails. In *Chaco roads project, phase 1: A reappraisal of prehistoric roads in the San Juan Basin,* edited by Chris Kincaid, pp. 2.1–2.7. U.S.D.I., Bureau of Land Management, State Office, Albuquerque Distinct Office, Albuquerque.

Robinson, David G.
1980 *Ceramic technology and later Pine Lawn/Reserve branch exchange systems.* Paper presented at the 45th Annual Meeting of the Society for American Archaeology, Philadelphia.

Robinson, William J.
1979 Preliminary report to the Chaco Center. Ms. on file, Southwest Cultural Resource Center, National Park Service, Albuquerque.

Rogers, Malcolm J.
1939 Early lithic industries of the lower basin of the Colorado River and adjacent desert areas. *San Diego Museum Papers* 3. San Diego.
1945 An outline of Yuman prehistory. *Southwestern Journal of Anthropology* 1:167–198.

Rohn, Arthur H.
1971 *Mug House, Mesa Verde National Park, Colorado.* Archaeological Research Series 7D. National Park Service, Washington, D.C.
1977 *Cultural change and continuity on Chapin Mesa.* The Regents Press of Kansas, Lawrence.

Roosa, William B.
1956a Preliminary report on the Lucy site. *El Palacio* 63(2):36–49.
1956b The Lucy site in central New Mexico. *American Antiquity* 21:(3)310.

Rose, Martin R., Jeffrey S. Dean, and William J. Robinson
1981 The past climate of Arroyo Hondo, New Mexico, reconstructed from tree rings. *Arroyo Hondo Archaeological Series* 4. School of American Research, Santa Fe.

Rosenthal, E. J., D. R. Brown, M. Severson, and J. B. Clonts
1978 *The Quijota Valley Project.* National Park Service, Western Archeological Center, Tucson.

Rouse, I.
1958 The inference of migration from anthropological evidence. In Migrations in New World cultural history, edited by R. H. Thompson, pp. 63–68. *Social Science Bulletin* 27. University of Arizona, Tucson.

Ruppé, Reynold J., Jr.
1953 *The Acoma culture province: an archaeological concept.* Unpublished Ph.D. dissertation, Department of Anthropology, Harvard University, Cambridge.
1966 The archaeological survey: a defense. *American Antiquity* 31(3):313–333.

Russell, G. S.
1981 Preliminary results of the Redondo Valley obsidian study. In *High altitude adaptations along Redondo Creek: the Baca geothermal project,* edited by Craig Baker and Joseph C. Winter, pp. 363–370. Office of Contract Archeology, University of New Mexico.

Rutter, N. W.
>   1980   Late Pleistocene history of the western Canadian ice-free corridor. *Canadian Journal of Anthropology* 1(1):1–8.

Sahagún, Fray Bernardino de
>   1959   *Florentine Codex: general history of the things of New Spain. Book 9: the merchants,* edited and translated by A. J. O. Anderson and C. E. Dibble. School of American Research, Santa Fe, and University of Utah, Salt Lake City.

Sanders, William T., Jeffrey R. Parsons, and Robert S. Santley
>   1979   *The Basin of Mexico: ecological processes in the evolution of a civilization.* Academic Press, New York.

Sanders, William T., and Robert S. Santley
>   1978   Review of *Monte Alban, settlement patterns at the ancient Zapotec capital* by R. E. Blanton. *Science* 202:303–304.

Sanders, William T., and D. Webster
>   1978   Unilinealism, multilinealism, and the evolution of complex societies. In *Social archaeology: beyond subsistence and dating.* edited by Charles L. Redman, Mary J. Berman, E. B. Curtin, N. M. Versaggi, and J. L. Wagner, pp. 249–302. Academic Press, New York.

Saunders, J. J.
>   1980   A model for man–mammoth relationships in late Pleistocene North America. *Canadian Journal of Anthropology* 1(1):87–98.

Sayles, E. B.
>   1945   The San Simon branch, excavations at Cave Creek and in the San Simon Valley, I. Material culture. *Medallion Papers* 34. Gila Pueblo, Globe, Arizona.

Sayles, E. B., and A. Antevs
>   1941   The Cochise culture. *Medallion Papers* 29. Gila Pueblo, Globe, Arizona.

Schaafsma, Curtis F.
>   1976   *Archaeological survey of maximum pool and Navajo excavations at Abiquiu Reservoir, Rio Arriba County, New Mexico.* School of American Research, Santa Fe.

Schaafsma, Polly
>   1971   The rock art of Utah from the Donald Scott Collection. *Papers of the Peabody Museum of Archaeology and Ethnology* 65. Harvard University, Cambridge.

Schaafsma, Polly, and Curtis F. Schaafsma
>   1974   Evidence for the origins of Pueblo katchina cult as suggested by Southwestern rock art. *American Antiquity* 39(4):535–545.

Schiffer, Michael B.
>   1972   Cultural laws and reconstruction of past lifeways. *The Kiva* 37(3):148–157.
>   1976   *Behavioral archaeology.* Academic Press, New York.
>   1982   Hohokam chronology: an essay on history and method. In *Hohokam and Patayan: prehistory of southwestern Arizona,* edited by Randall H. McGuire and Michael B. Schiffer, pp. 299–344. Academic Press, New York.
>   1983   Toward the identification of formation processes, *American Antiquity* 48(4):675–706.

Schmidt, E. F.
>   1926   The Mrs. William Boyce Thompson expedition. *Natural History* (Nov.–Dec.)1926:635–644.
>   1928   Time-relations of prehistory pottery in southern Arizona. *Anthropological Papers of the American Museum of Natural History* 30:245–302.

Schoenwetter, James
>   1966   A re-evaluation of the Navajo Reservoir pollen chronology. *El Palacio* 73(1):19–26.

Schoenwetter, James, and Alfred E. Dittert, Jr.
>   1968   An ecological interpretation of Anasazi settlement patterns. In *Anthropological archaeology in the Americas,* edited by Betty J. Meggers, pp. 41–66. Anthropological Society of Washington, Washington, D.C.

Schroeder, Albert H.
>   1952   *The excavations at Willow Beach, Arizona, 1950.* National Park Service, Santa Fe.

1953a   Brief history of the Chama Basin. In Salvage archaeology in the Chama Valley, New Mexico, edited by Fred Wendorf, pp. 5–8. *Monographs of the School of American Research* 17. Santa Fe.

1953b   The problem of Hohokam, Sinagua, and Salado relations in southern Arizona. *Plateau* 26(2):75–83.

1957   The Hakataya cultural tradition. *American Antiquity* 23(2):176–178.

1958   Lower Colorado buffware. In *Pottery types of the Southwest,* edited by Harold S. Colton, Ware 16. *Museum of Northern Arizona Ceramic Series* 3D. Flagstaff.

1960   The Hohokam, Sinagua, and Hakataya. *Society for American Archaeology, Archives of Archaeology* 5.

1965   Unregulated diffusion from Mexico into the Southwest prior to A.D. 700. *American Antiquity* 30(3):297–309.

1979a   Prehistory: Hakataya. In *Southwest,* edited by Alfonso Ortiz, pp. 100–107. *Handbook of North American Indians* (Vol. 9). Smithsonian Institution, Washington, D.C.

1979b   Pueblos abandoned in historic times. In *Southwest,* edited by Alfonso Ortiz, pp. 236–254. *Handbook of North American Indians* (Vol. 9). Smithsonian Institution, Washington, D.C.

1982   (editor) Southwestern ceramics: a comparative review. *The Arizona Archaeologist* 15. Phoenix.

Schulman, Edmund

1956   *Dendroclimatic changes in semiarid America.* University of Tucson Press, Tucson.

Schwartz, Douglas W.

1956   The Havasupai, 600 A.D.–1955 A.D.: a short culture history. *Plateau* 28(4):77–85.

1959   Culture area and time depth: the four worlds of the Havasupai. *American Anthropologist* 61:1060–1070.

Schwartz, Douglas W., and Richard W. Lang

1972   Archaeological investigations at the Arroyo Hondo site. *School of American Research, Third Field Report, 1972.* Santa Fe.

Scudder, Thayer

1971   *Gathering among African woodland savannah cultivators. A case study: the Gwembe Tonga.* Manchester University Press, Manchester, England.

Sellards, E. H.

1940   Early man in America: index to localities, and selected bibliography. *Bulletin of the Geological Society of America* 51:373–432.

1952   *Early man in America: a study in prehistory.* University of Texas Press, Austin.

Sellards, E. H., G. L. Evans, and G. E. Meade

1947   Fossil bison and associated artifacts from Plainview, Texas. *Bulletin of the Geological Society of America* 58:927–954.

Shafer, Harry J.

1982   Classic Mimbres phase households and room use patterns. *The Kiva* 48(1–2):17–38.

Shepard, Anna O.

1939   Technology of La Plata pottery. In Archaeological studies in the La Plata district, by Earl H. Morris, pp. 249–287. *Carnegie Institute of Washington Publication* 519. Washington, D.C.

1942   Rio Grande glaze paint ware. *Contributions to American Anthropology and History* 39. *Carnegie Institute of Washington Publication* 528. Washington, D.C.

1954   Ceramics for the archaeologist. *Carnegie Institute of Washington Publications* 609. Washington, D.C.

Simmons, Marc

1969   Settlement patterns and village plans in Colonial New Mexico. *Journal of the West* 8:7–21.

1979   History of Pueblo–Spanish relations to 1821. In *Southwest* edited by Alfonso Ortiz, pp. 170–177. *Handbook of North American Indians* (Vol. 9). Smithsonian Institution, Washington, D.C.

Simpson, James H.

1850   Journal of a military reconnaissance from Santa Fe, New Mexico, to the Navaho country. Report of the Secretary of War to the 31st Congress, 1st Session, Senate. Executive Document 64. Washington, D.C.

Slatter, Edwin D.

1973   *Climate in Pueblo abandonment of the Chevelon drainage, Arizona.* Paper presented at the 38th Annual Meeting of the American Anthropological Association, New Orleans.

Slaughter, B. H.

1967   Animal range as a clue to late Pleistocene extinction. In *Pleistocene extinctions, the search for a cause,* edited by Paul S. Martin and H. E. Wright, Jr., pp. 98–120. Yale University Press, New Haven.

Smith, C. E., Jr.

1950   Prehistoric plant remains from Bat Cave. *Harvard University Botanical Museum Leaflets* 14:157–180.

Smith, Watson

1952   Kiva mural decorations at Awatovi and Kawaika-a. *Peabody Museum Papers* 37. Peabody Museum of Archaeology and Ethnology, Harvard University, Cambridge.

1971   Painted ceramics of the western mount at Awatovi. *Papers of the Peabody Museum of Archaeology and Ethnology* 38. Harvard University, Cambridge.

Smith, Watson, R. B. Woodbury, and N. F. S. Woodbury (editors)

1966   *The excavation of Hawikuh by Frederick Webb Hodge.* Museum of the American Indian, Heye Foundation, Contributions. New York.

Snow, David H.

1982   The Rio Grande glaze, matte-paint, and plainware tradition. In Southwestern ceramics: a comparative review, edited by Albert H. Schroeder, pp. 235–278. *The Arizona Archaeologist* 15. Phoenix.

Sofar, A., V. Zinser, and R. M. Sinclair

1979   A unique solar marking construct. *Science* 206:283–291.

Spaulding, Albert C.

1953   Statistical techniques for the discovery of artifact types. *American Antiquity* 18(4):305–313.

1960   The dimensions of archaeology. In *Essays in the science of culture,* edited by G. E. Dole and Robert L. Carneiro, pp. 437–456. Crowell, New York.

Spicer, Edward H.

1962   *Cycles of conquest.* University of Arizona Press, Tucson.

1969   The Yaqui and Mayo. In *Handbook of Middle American Indians* (Vol. 8, Part 2), edited by Evon Z. Vogt, pp. 830–845. University of Texas Press, Austin.

Spier, Leslie

1917   An outline for a chronology of Zuni ruins. *Anthropological Papers of the American Museum of Natural History* 18 (Part 4). New York.

Spooner, Brian (editor)

1972   *Population growth: anthropological implications.* MIT Press, Cambridge.

Stafford, C. R., and G. E. Rice (editors)

1980   Studies in the prehistory of the Forestdale Region, Arizona. *Anthropological Field Studies* 1. Office of Cultural Resource Management, Department of Anthropology, Arizona State University, Tempe.

Stalker, A. MacS.

1980   The Geology of the ice-free corridor: the southern half. *Canadian Journal of Anthropology* 1(1):11–14.

Stanislawski, Michael B.

1969   The ethnoarchaeology of Hopi pottery making. *Plateau* 42(1):27–33.

Steen, Charles R.

1977   *Pajarito Plateau archaeological survey and excavation.* Los Alamos Scientific Laboratories, Los Alamos, New Mexico.

Steen, Charles R., Lloyd M. Pierson, Vorsila L. Bohrer, and Kate Peck Kent

1962   Archaeological studies at Tonto National Monument, Arizona. *Southwestern Monuments Association Technical Series* 2. Globe, Arizona.

Stevens, Dominique E., and George Agogino
  1975   Sandia Cave: a study in controversy. *Eastern New Mexico Contributions in Anthropology* 7(1). Portales.
Steward, Julian H.
  1955   *Theory of culture change.* University of Illinois Press, Urbana.
Stiger, Mark A.
  1979   Mesa Verde subsistence patterns from Basketmaker to Pueblo III. *The Kiva* 44(2):133–145.
Struever, Mollie
  1979   Evidence of ancient and modern human behavior in flotation remains from Howiri pueblo. Unpublished ms. on file, Museum of New Mexico, Santa Fe.
Stuart, David E., and Robin E. Farwell
  1983   Out of phase: late pithouse occupations in the highlands of New Mexico. In High altitude adaptations in the Southwest, edited by Joseph C. Winter, pp. 115–158. *Cultural Resources Management Report* 2. U.S.D.A. Forest Service, Southwestern Region, Albuquerque.
Stuart, David E., and Rory P. Gauthier
  1981   *Prehistoric New Mexico: background for survey.* New Mexico Historic Preservation Bureau, Santa Fe.
Stubbs, S. A., and W. S. Stallings, Jr.
  1953   The excavation of Pindi Pueblo, New Mexico. *Monographs of the School of American Research* 18. Santa Fe.
Swadesh, Frances Leon
  1974   *Los primeros pobladores: Hispanic Americans of the Ute frontier.* University of Notre Dame Press, Notre Dame, Indiana.
Tainter, Joseph A., and David "A" Gillio
  1980   *Cultural resources overview, Mount Taylor area, New Mexico.* U.S. Government Printing Office, Washington, D.C.
Tanner, Clara Lee
  1976   *Prehistoric Southwestern craft arts.* The University of Arizona Press, Tucson.
Taylor, Walter W.
  1966   Archaic cultures adjacent to the northeastern frontiers of Mesoamerica. In Archaeological frontiers and external connections, edited by Gordon F. Ekholm and Gordon R. Willey, pp. 59–94. *Handbook of Middle American Indians* (Vol. 4). University of Texas Press, Austin.
Thom, R.
  1975   *Structural stability and morphogenesis.* Benjamin, Reading, Pennsylvania.
Thomas, David Hurst
  1971   On distinguishing natural from cultural bone in archaeological sites. *American Antiquity* 36(3):366–371.
Tichy, Marjorie F.
  1938   The archaeology of Puaray. *El Palacio* 46(7):145–162.
Titiev, Mischa
  1944   Old Oraibi: a study of the Hopi Indians of Third Mesa. *Papers of the Peabody Museum of American Archaeology and Ethnology* 22(1). Harvard University, Cambridge.
Toll, H. Wolcott, Thomas C. Windes, and Peter J. McKenna
  1980   Late ceramic patterns in Chaco Canyon: the pragmatics of modeling ceramic exchange. In *Models and methods in regional exchange,* edited by Robert E. Fry, pp. 95–118. Society for American Archaeology Papers 1.
Traylor, Diane, Nancy Wood, Lyndi Hubbell, Robert Scaife, and Sue Waber
  1977   Bandelier: excavations in the flood pool of Cochiti Lake, New Mexico. Ms. on file, Southwest Cultural Resource Center, National Park Service, Santa Fe.
Trewartha, G. T.
  1966   *The earth's problem climates.* Methuen, London, and University of Wisconsin Press, Madison.

Tuan, Yi-Fu, Cyril E. Everard, Jerold G. Widdison, and Iven Bennett
    1973   *The climate of New Mexico.* New Mexico State Planning Office, Santa Fe.

Turnbull, Colin M.
    1978   Rethinking the Ik: a functional non-social system. In *Extinction and survival in human populations,* edited by Charles D. Loughlin, Jr., and Ivan A. Brady, pp. 49–75. Columbia University Press, New York.

Turner, Chris G., II., and N. T. Morris
    1970   A massacre at Hopi. *American Antiquity* 35(3):320–331.

Upham, Steadman
    1982   *Polities and power: an economic and political history of the Western Pueblo.* Academic Press, New York.
    1984   Adaptive diversity and Southwestern abandonment. *Journal of Anthropological Research,* 40(2).

Van Devender, T. R., and W. G. Spaulding
    1979   Development of vegetation and climate in the southwestern United States. *Science* 204:701–710.

Van Devender, T. R., D. E. Wiseman, and J. G. Gallagher
    1978   Holocene environments and archeology in Rocky Arroyo and Last Chance Canyon, Eddy County, New Mexico. Ms. on file, Office of Contract Archeology, University of New Mexico, Albuquerque.

Vickery, Irene
    1939   Besh-ba-gowah. *The Kiva* 4(5):19–21.

Vivian, Gordon
    1959   The Hubbard site and other tri-wall structures in New Mexico and Colorado. *National Park Service Archaeological Research Series* 5. Washington, D.C.

Vivian, Gordon, and Tom W. Mathews
    1965   Kin Kletso, a Pueblo III community in Chaco Canyon, New Mexico. *Southwestern Monuments Association, Technical Series* 6. Globe, Arizona.

Vivian, Gordon, and Paul Reiter
    1965   The great kivas of Chaco Canyon and their relationships. *Monographs of the School of American Research* 22. Santa Fe.

Vivian, R. Gwinn
    1970   *Aspects of prehistoric society in Chaco Canyon, New Mexico.* Unpublished Ph.D. dissertation, Department of Anthropology, University of Arizona, Tucson.
    1972   Prehistoric water conservation in Chaco Canyon: final technical letter report. On file, Division of Cultural Resources, National Park Service, Albuquerque.
    1974   Conservation and diversion: water-control systems in the Anasazi Southwest. In Irrigation's impact on society, edited by Theodore Downing and McGuire Gibson, pp. 95–112. *University of Arizona Anthropological Papers* 25. Tucson.

Vogt, Evon Z.
    1969   Introduction. In *Handbook of Middle American Indians* (Vol 7, Part 1), pp. 3–17. University of Texas Press, Austin.

Wait, Walter K.
    1976   *An archaeological survey of Star Lake: a report on the prehistoric, historic, and current cultural resources of the Star Lake area, northwestern New Mexico.* Southern Illinois University Press, Carbondale.
    1981   *Some old problems and a new model for the Paleo/Archaic transition in the San Juan Basin, New Mexico.* Paper presented at the 54th Pecos Conference, Fort Burgwin Research Center, Taos, New Mexico.

Wallace, W. J.
    1978   Post-Pleistocene archaeology, 9000 to 2000 B.C. In California, edited by Robert F. Heizer, pp. 25–36. *Handbook of North American Indians* (Vol. 8). Smithsonian Institution, Washington, D.C.

Wallerstein, I.
    1974   *The modern world system.* Academic Press, New York.
    1979   *The capitalist world economy.* Cambridge University Press, New York.

Warren, A. Helene
1977 Prehistoric and historic ceramic analysis. In Excavation and analysis, 1975 season, edited by Richard C. Chapman and Jan V. Biella, pp. 97–101. *Archeological investigations in Cochiti Reservoir* (Vol. 2). Office of Contract Archeology, University of New Mexico, Albuquerque.

Warren, C. N.
1967 The San Dieguito complex: a review and hypothesis. *American Antiquity* 32:168–185.

Wasley, William W.
1960 A Hokokam platform mound at the Gatlin site, Gila Bend, Arizona. *American Antiquity* 26(2):244–262.

Wasley, William W., and David E. Doyel
1980 Classic period Hohokam. *The Kiva* 45(4):337–352.

Wasley, William W., and A. Johnson
1965 Salvage archaeology in Painted Rocks Reservoir, western Arizona. *Anthropological Papers* 9. University of Arizona, Tucson.

Waters, Michael R.
1982 The lowland Patayan tradition. In *Hohokam and Patayan: prehistory of southwestern Arizona*, edited by Randall H. McGuire and Michael B. Schiffer, pp. 275–297. Academic Press, New York.

Watson, Patty Jo
1976 In pursuit of prehistoric subsistence: a comparative account of some contemporary flotation techniques. *Mid-Continental Journal of Archaeology* 1(1):77–100.

Weaver, David S.
1981 An osteological test of changes in subsistence and settlement patterns at Casas Grandes, Chihuahua, Mexico. *American Antiquity* 46(2):361–363.

Weaver, Donald E., Jr.
1972 A cultural ecological model for the Classic Hohokam period in the lower Salt River Valley, Arizona. *The Kiva* 38(1):43–52.
1976 Salado influences in the lower Salt River Valley. *The Kiva* 42(1):17–26.

Weaver, Kenneth F.
1967 Magnetic clues help date the past. *National Geographic* 131:696–701.

Weber, Robert H., and George A. Agogino
1968 *Mockingbird Gap Paleo-Indian site: excavations in 1967.* Paper presented at the 33rd Annual Meeting of the Society for American Archaeology, Santa Fe.

Weissner, Polly
1983 Style and social information in Kalhari San projectile points. *American Antiquity* 48(2):253–276.

Wendorf, Fred
1953a Archaeological sites in the Petrified Forest National Monument. *Museum of Northern Arizona Bulletin* 27. Flagstaff.
1953b Excavations at Te'ewi. In Salvage archaeology in the Chama Valley, New Mexico, assembled by Fred Wendorf, pp. 34–100. *Monographs of the School of American Research* 17. Santa Fe.
1961 (editor) Paleoecology of the Llano Estacado. *Fort Burgwin Research Paper* 1. Museum of New Mexico Press, Santa Fe.
1970 The Lubbock subpluvial. In Pleistocene and recent environment of the Central Plains, edited by W. Dort, Jr., and J. K. Jones, Jr., pp. 23–35. *Department of Geology, University of Kansas, Special Publication* 3. Regents Press of Kansas, Lawrence.
1975 The modern environment. In Late Pleistocene environments of the southern High Plains, edited by Fred Wendorf and James J. Hester, pp. 1–12. *Fort Burgwin Research Center Publication* 9. Southern Methodist University.

Wendorf, Fred, and James J. Hester (editors)
1975 Late Pleistocene environments on the southern High Plains. *Fort Burgwin Research Center Publication* 9. Southern Methodist University.

Wendorf, Fred, and John P. Miller
1959 Artifacts from high mountain sites in the Sangre de Cristo range, New Mexico. *El Palacio* 66(2):37–52.

Wendorf, Fred, and Erik Reed
  1955   An alternative reconstruction of northern Rio Grande prehistory. *El Palacio* 62(5–6):131–173.
Wetherington, Ronald Knox
  1964   *Early occupation in the Taos district in the context of northern Rio Grande culture history.* Unpublished Ph.D. dissertation, Department of Anthropology, University of Michigan, Ann Arbor.
  1968   Excavations at Pot Creek Pueblo. *Fort Burgwin Research Center Report* 6. Rancho de Taos, New Mexico.
Whalen, Michael E.
  1981   Cultural–ecological aspects of the pithouse-to-pueblo transition in a portion of the Southwest. *American Antiquity* 46(1):75–92
Whalen, Norman M.
  1971   *Cochise culture sites in the central San Pedro drainage, Arizona.* Unpublished Ph.D. dissertation, Department of Anthropology, Arizona State University, Tempe.
  1975   Cochise site distribution in the San Pedro River valley. *The Kiva* 40(3):203–211.
Wheat, Joe Ben
  1954   Crooked Ridge Valley (Arizona W:10:15). *University of Arizona Social Science Bulletin* 24. Tucson.
  1955   Mogollon culture prior to A.D. 1000. *Memoirs of the Society for American Archaeology* 10. *Memoirs of the American Anthropological Association* 82.
  1972   The Olsen–Chubbock site: a PaleoIndian bison kill. *Society for American Archaeology Memoir* 26:1–179.
Whiteley, Peter Michael
  1982   *Third Mesa Hopi social structural dynamics and sociocultural change: the view from Bacavi.* Unpublished Ph.D. dissertation, Department of Anthropology, University of New Mexico, Albuquerque.
Whiting, Alfred J.
  1937   Hopi Indian agriculture II. *Museum Notes* 10:11–16. Museum of Northern Arizona, Flagstaff.
Wilcox, David R.
  1978   The theoretical significance of fieldhouses. In Limited activity and occupation sites: a collection of conference papers, edited by Albert E. Ward, pp. 25–32. *Contributions to Anthropological Studies* 1. Center for Anthropological Studies, Albuquerque.
  1980   The current status of the Hohokam concept. In Current issues in Hohokam prehistory: proceedings of a symposium, edited by David E. Doyel and Fred T. Plog, pp. 236–242. *Arizona State University Anthropological Research Papers* 23. Tempe.
  1981   Changing perspectives on the protohistoric Pueblos, A.D. 1450–1700. In The protohistoric periods in the North American Southwest, A.D. 1450–1700, edited by David R. Wilcox and W. Bruce Masse, pp. 378–409. *Arizona State University Anthropological Research Papers* 24. Tempe.
Wilcox, David R., Thomas R. McGuire, and Charles Sternberg
  1981   Snaketown revisited: a partial cultural resource survey, analysis of site structure, and an ethnohistoric study of the proposed Hohokam–Pima National Monument. *Arizona State Museum Archaeological Series* 155.
Wilcox, David R., and W. Bruce Masse (editors)
  1981   The protohistoric period in the North American Southwest, A.D. 1450–1700. *Anthropological Research Papers,* 24. Arizona State University, Tempe.
Willey, Gordon R.
  1966   North and Middle America. *An introduction to American archaeology* (Vol. 1). Prentice-Hall, Englewood Cliffs.
  1979   The concept of the "disembedded capital" in comparative perspective. *Journal of Anthropological Research* 35(2):123–137.
Willey, Gordon R., and Philip Phillips
  1958   *Method and theory in American archaeology.* University of Chicago Press, Chicago.

Williamsen, R. A., J. Fisher, and D. O'Flynn
  1977 Anasazi solar observatories. In *Native American astronomy,* edited by A. Aveni, pp. 204–217. University of Texas Press, Austin.
Wilmsen, Edwin N.
  1965 An outline of early man studies in the United States. *American Antiquity* 31(1):172–192.
  1974 *Lindenmeier: a Pleistocene hunting society.* Harper and Row, New York.
Wilson, M.
  1980 Morphological dating of the late Quaternary bison on the northern Plains. *Canadian Journal of Anthropology* 1(1):81–86.
Wimberly, Mark
  1972 Training bulletin for the Tularosa Valley Project. Ms. on file, Human Systems Research, Tularosa, New Mexico.
Wimberly, Mark, and Peter Eidenbach
  1980 *Reconnaissance study of the archaeological and related resources of the lower Puerco and Salado drainages, central New Mexico.* Human Systems Research, Inc., Tularosa, New Mexico.
Windes, Thomas C.
  1980 *Archeomagnetic dating: lessons from Chaco Canyon, New Mexico.* Paper presented at the 45th Annual Meeting of the Society for American Archaeology, Philadelphia.
Wing, E. S., and A. B. Brown
  1979 *Paleonutrition, method and theory in prehistoric foodways.* Academic Press, New York.
Winship, G. P. (editor)
  1904 *The journey of Coronado: 1540–1542.* Aberton, New York. (University Microfilms, Ann Arbor, 1966)
Winter, Joseph C.
  1976 The process of farming diffusion in the Southwest and Great Basin. *American Antiquity* 41(4):421–429.
Wittfogel, K.
  1957 *Oriental depotism.* Yale University Press, New Haven.
Wittfogel, K., and E. Goldfrank
  1943 Some aspects of Pueblo mythology and society. *Journal of American Folklore* 56:17–30.
Wood, S., and M. McAllister
  1980 Foundation and empire: the colonization of the northeastern Hohokam preipher. In Current issues in Hohokam prehistory: proceedings of a symposium, edited by David E. Doyel and Fred T. Plog, pp. 180–200. *Arizona State University Anthropological Research Papers* 23. Tempe.
Woodbury, Richard B.
  1961 Prehistoric agriculture at Point of Pines, Arizona. *Memoirs of the Society for American Archaeology* 17. *American Antiquity* 26(3, Part 2).
Woodbury, Richard B., and Ezra B. W. Zubrow
  1979 Agricultural beginnings, 2000 b.c.–a.d. 500. In *Southwest,* edited by Alfonso Ortiz, pp. 43–60. *Handbook of North American Indians* (Vol. 9). Smithsonian Institution, Washington, D.C.
Woosley, Anne I.
  1980 *Taos archaeology.* Fort Burgwin Research Center, Southern Methodist University, Dallas.
Wormington, H. M.
  1957 Ancient man in North America. *Denver Museum of Natural History Popular Series* 4.
  1961 Prehistoric Indians of the Southwest. *Denver Museum of Natural History Popular Series* 7.
Zubrow, Ezra B. W.
  1972 Carrying capacity and dynamic equilibrium in the prehistoric Southwest. In *Contemporary archaeology,* edited by Mark P. Leone, pp. 268–279. Southern Illinois University Press, Carbondale.
  1974 Population, contact, and climate in New Mexican Pueblos. *Anthropological Papers of the University of Arizona* 24. Tucson.

Index